BUDGETING AND BUDGETARY INSTITUTIONS

Introduction to the Public Sector Governance and Accountability Series

Anwar Shah, Series Editor

A well-functioning public sector that delivers quality public services consistent with citizen preferences and that fosters private market-led growth while managing fiscal resources prudently is considered critical to the World Bank's mission of poverty alleviation and the achievement of the Millennium Development Goals. This important new series aims to advance those objectives by disseminating conceptual guidance and lessons from practices and by facilitating learning from each others' experiences on ideas and practices that promote *responsive* (by matching public services with citizens' preferences), *responsible* (through efficiency and equity in service provision without undue fiscal and social risk), and *accountable* (to citizens for all actions) public governance in developing countries.

This series represents a response to several independent evaluations in recent years that have argued that development practitioners and policy makers dealing with public sector reforms in developing countries and, indeed, anyone with a concern for effective public governance could benefit from a synthesis of newer perspectives on public sector reforms. This series distills current wisdom and presents tools of analysis for improving the efficiency, equity, and efficacy of the public sector. Leading public policy experts and practitioners have contributed to this series.

The first 14 volumes in this series, listed below, are concerned with public sector accountability for prudent fiscal management; efficiency, equity, and integrity in public service provision; safeguards for the protection of the poor, women, minorities, and other disadvantaged groups; ways of strengthening institutional arrangements for voice, choice, and exit; means of ensuring public financial accountability for integrity and results; methods of evaluating public sector programs, fiscal federalism, and local finances; international practices in local governance; and a framework for responsive and accountable governance.

Fiscal Management

Public Services Delivery

Public Expenditure Analysis

Local Governance in Industrial Countries

Local Governance in Developing Countries

Intergovernmental Fiscal Transfers: Principles and Practice

Participatory Budgeting

Budgeting and Budgetary Institutions

Local Budgeting

Local Public Financial Management

Performance Accountability and Combating Corruption

Tools for Public Sector Evaluations

Macrofederalism and Local Finances

Citizen-Centered Governance

PUBLIC SECTOR
GOVERNANCE AND
ACCOUNTABILITY SERIES

BUDGETING AND BUDGETARY INSTITUTIONS

Edited by ANWAR SHAH

THE WORLD BANK
Washington, D.C.

©2007 The International Bank for Reconstruction and Development / The World Bank
1818 H Street, NW
Washington, DC 20433
Telephone: 202-473-1000
Internet: www.worldbank.org
E-mail: feedback@worldbank.org

This volume is a product of the staff of the International Bank for Reconstruction and Development / The World Bank. The findings, interpretations, and conclusions expressed in this volume do not necessarily reflect the views of the Executive Directors of The World Bank or the governments they represent.

The World Bank does not guarantee the accuracy of the data included in this work. The boundaries, colors, denominations, and other information shown on any map in this work do not imply any judgement on the part of The World Bank concerning the legal status of any territory or the endorsement or acceptance of such boundaries.

ISBN-10: 0-8213-6939-3
ISBN-13: 978-0-8213-6939-5
eISBN-10: 0-8213-6940-7
eISBN-13: 978-0-8213-6940-1
DOI: 10.1596/978-0-8213-6939-5

Library of Congress Cataloging-in-Publication Data
Budgeting and budgetary institutions / edited by Anwar Shah.
    p. cm.
  Includes bibliographical references and index.
  ISBN-13: 978-0-8213-6939-5
  ISBN-10: 0-8213-6939-3
  ISBN-10: 0-8213-6940-7 (electronic)
    1. Budget—Developing countries. 2. Finance, Public—Developing countries.
I. Shah, Anwar.

HJ2216.B86 2007
336.09172'4—dc22

2006102152

Contents

Part I A Primer on Budgeting and Budgetary Institutions

CHAPTER

8

Budget Preparation and Approval   235
Salvatore Schiavo-Campo

9

Budget Execution   279
Daniel Tommasi

Part II Reforming Public Expenditure Management in Developing Countries: The African Case

13

Budgeting in Postconflict Countries   435

Salvatore Schiavo-Campo

14

Country Case Study: Kenya   461

Alta Fölscher

15

Country Case Study: South Africa   501

Alta Fölscher

Index   535

BOXES

FIGURES

TABLES

Foreword

In Western democracies, systems of checks and balances built into government structures have formed the core of good governance and have helped empower citizens for more than two hundred years. The incentives that motivate public servants and policy makers— the rewards and sanctions linked to results that help shape public sector performance—are rooted in a country's accountability frameworks. Sound public sector management and government spending help determine the course of economic development and social equity, especially for the poor and other disadvantaged groups, such as women and the elderly.

Many developing countries, however, continue to suffer from unsatisfactory and often dysfunctional governance systems that include rent seeking and malfeasance, inappropriate allocation of resources, inefficient revenue systems, and weak delivery of vital public services. Such poor governance leads to unwelcome outcomes for access to public services by the poor and other disadvantaged members of society, such as women, children, and minorities. In dealing with these concerns, the development assistance community in general and the World Bank in particular are continuously striving to learn lessons from practices around the world to achieve a better understanding of what works and what does not work in improving public sector governance, especially with respect to combating corruption and making services work for poor people.

The Public Sector Governance and Accountability Series advances our knowledge by providing tools and lessons from practices in improving efficiency and equity of public services provision and strengthening institutions of accountability in governance. The series highlights frameworks to create incentive environments and pressures for good governance from within and beyond governments. It outlines institutional mechanisms to empower citizens to demand accountability for results from their governments. It provides practical guidance on managing for results and prudent fiscal management. It outlines approaches to dealing with corruption and malfeasance. It provides conceptual and practical guidance on alternative service delivery frameworks for extending the reach and access of public services. The series also covers safeguards for the protection of the poor, women, minorities, and other disadvantaged groups; ways of strengthening institutional arrangements for voice and exit; methods of evaluating public sector programs; frameworks for responsive and accountable governance; and fiscal federalism and local governance.

This series will be of interest to public officials, development practitioners, students of development, and those interested in public governance in developing countries.

Frannie A. Léautier
Vice President
World Bank Institute

Preface

Budgetary institutions and the budgetary process fulfill several important functions. These include setting priorities in the allocation of public resources; planning to achieve policy goals; establishing financial control over inputs to ensure compliance with rules; managing operations with fiscal prudence, efficiency, and integrity; and ensuring accountability to taxpayers. The effectiveness of budgetary institutions has been recognized in the economics and political science literature as contributing to improved fiscal and economic outcomes. In developing countries, especially in Africa, budgetary processes and institutions are not yet well enough developed to perform the above-mentioned functions adequately; instead, they provide work as means of legalistic controls. The reform of these institutions is critical to improving government performance in service delivery and to strengthening parliamentary and citizens' oversight on government operations.

This volume provides a comprehensive guide to reforming budgeting and budgetary institutions. The book is divided into two parts. The first part provides a primer on budgeting and budgetary institutions. It covers budget processes, methods, and associated tools and practices. Both the traditional and modern concepts of budgeting and accounting are elaborated. In addition, implementation issues in introducing integrated financial information management systems and assessment methods for public expenditure management and financial accountability are discussed. The second part of this volume presents an overview of issues involved in prioritizing and sequencing public expenditure management in Africa and in postconflict countries. In addition, two case studies on budgeting are presented that cover Kenya and South Africa.

This volume represents an example of a collaborative effort by the Swedish International Development Agency and the World Bank Institute to further the exchange of knowledge on better practices in public expenditure management reform to improve access to public services by the poor in African and other developing countries. I hope that policy makers in developing countries will find this volume useful in their future endeavors to improve their budgetary processes and institutions.

Roumeen Islam
Manager, Poverty Reduction and Economic Management
World Bank Institute

Acknowledgments

This book brings together learning modules on budgeting and budgetary institutions prepared for the World Bank Institute learning programs directed by the editor over the past three years. These learning modules and their publication in the current volume were primarily financed by the government of Sweden through its Public Expenditure and Financial Accountability (PEFA) partnership program, sponsored jointly with the World Bank Institute and directed by the editor. The government of Japan provided additional financial support for the editing of this volume. The editor is grateful to Hallgerd Dryssen of the Swedish International Development Agency (SIDA) in Stockholm, for overall guidance and support of the PEFA program. In addition, Bengt Anderson, Goran Anderson, Gunilla Bruun, Alan Gustafsson, and other members of the external advisory group for PEFA contributed to the design and development of the program. Thanks are also due to Cecilia Nordin Van Gansberghe for her contributions as a SIDA secondee to the PEFA program at the World Bank Institute.

The book has benefited from contributions to World Bank Institute learning events by senior policy makers and scholars from Africa and elsewhere. In particular, thanks are due to Ismail Momoniat, deputy director-general (acting) of the National Treasury of South Africa; Neil Cole, National Treasury of South Africa; Paul Boothe, former associate deputy minister of the Ministry of · Finance of Canada; Tania Ajam, director of AFReC (the Applied Fiscal Research Centre of South Africa); Christina Nomdo of IDASA (the Institute for Democracy in South Africa); Anders Haglund, PricewaterhouseCoopers, Stockholm; and Florence Kuteesa, public finance consultant, Ministry of Finance, Uganda.

The editor is grateful to the leading scholars who contributed chapters and to the distinguished reviewers who provided comments. Alta Fölscher, Adrian Shall, and Chunli Shen helped during various stages of the preparation of this book and provided comments and editorial revisions of individual chapters. Kaitlin Tierney provided excellent administrative support for this project.

I am grateful to Stephen McGroarty for ensuring a fast-track process for publication of this book. The quality of the book was enhanced by excellent editorial inputs provided by a team of exceptionally qualified editors under the direction of Janet Sasser. Denise Bergeron is to be thanked for the excellent print quality of the book.

Contributors

MATTHEW ANDREWS is assistant professor of public policy at the John F. Kennedy School of Government, Harvard University. He has worked in development for more than a decade, focusing particularly on public financial management issues. The chapter included here reflects work he conducted in Armenia as part of an integrated assessment of Armenia's public financial management processes.

PAUL BOOTHE is professor and fellow of the Institute for Public Economics at the University of Alberta. He served as deputy minister of finance and secretary to the Treasury Board for the province of Saskatchewan from 1999 to 2001. He was associate deputy minister of finance and the Group of Seven deputy for Canada from 2004 to 2005. He has also worked in the International Department of the Bank of Canada. He has held visiting positions at Queen's University, the University of Tasmania, and the Alberta Treasury and has served as an adviser or consultant to federal and provincial government departments and international agencies.

GARY COKINS is a manager in performance management solutions with SAS Institute Inc. He is an internationally recognized expert, speaker, and author in advanced cost management and performance improvement systems. Cokins has been a strategic planner at Ford Motor Company's Link Belt Division and then served as financial controller and operations manager. He has been a management consultant for Deloitte & Touche and for KPMG. Cokins also headed the National Cost Management Consulting Services for Electronic Data Systems. His publications include *An ABC Manager's Primer, Activity-Based Cost Management: Making It*

Work, Activity-Based Cost Management: An Executive's Guide, Activity-Based Cost Management in Government, and *Performance Management: Finding the Missing Pieces to Close the Intelligence Gap.*

ALTA FÖLSCHER is an independent researcher and consultant. She has worked in Africa; Southeast, South, and Central Asia; the Balkan states and Eastern Europe; the Middle East; and the Caribbean on public finance and public policy. Her areas of work include governance, public accountability, and fiscal transparency; public expenditure and financial management; pro-poor expenditure analysis, forecasting, and costing; and education financing. She has published several papers and edited three books on public finance management in Africa. In recent years, she has coedited books on economic transformation in South Africa. She has a master's degree in public policy and management from the University of London.

STEPHEN B. PETERSON is a lecturer in public policy and directs the executive program in public financial management at the John F. Kennedy School of Government, Harvard University. For more than 20 years, he has advised governments in transitional and developing countries in public finance. For the past 10 years, he has directed an integrated financial management reform program in Ethiopia. He is the author and coauthor of several books and numerous articles on public financial management, public management, and fiscal decentralization. He holds a doctorate from the University of California at Berkeley and an MBA in finance from the University of California at Los Angeles.

A. PREMCHAND is a former assistant director at the International Monetary Fund. Since retirement, he has worked as a consultant with the Asian Development Bank, the World Bank, the United Nations, the John F. Kennedy School of Government at Harvard University, the Andrew Young Center for Public Policy at Georgia State University, and the National Institute of Public Finance and Policy in New Delhi. He has published 12 books, 30 book chapters, and 70 papers. Many of his books and papers have been translated into Arabic, Chinese, Russian, and Spanish.

SALVATORE SCHIAVO-CAMPO has held senior positions at the World Bank, Asian Development Bank, International Monetary Fund, and U.S. Agency for International Development. He now works as an independent international consultant. He has also been a professor and chairman of the Department of Economics at the University of Massachusetts, Boston. He has taught at the University of the South Pacific and the University of Puerto Rico. He has published 31 articles and 12 books on public sector management, economic development, international trade and finance, and monitoring and evaluation—including the classic *Perspectives of Economic Development* (with Hans W. Singer). He has also authored several treatises on government expenditure management and public administration.

ANWAR SHAH is lead economist and program and team leader for public sector governance at the World Bank Institute, Washington, D.C. He is a member of the Executive Board of the International Institute of Public Finance, Munich, Germany, and a fellow of the Institute for Public Economics, Alberta, Canada. He has previously served in the Canadian Ministry of Finance in Ottawa and in the government of the province of Alberta and held responsibilities for federal-provincial and provincial-local fiscal relations, respectively. He has written extensively on public and environmental economics and has published books and articles dealing with governance, the global environment, fiscal federalism, and fiscal management. He has lectured at leading educational institutions, including Harvard University, the Massachusetts Institute of Technology, Duke University, Peking University, and Wuhan University.

CHUNLI SHEN is a World Bank consultant on budgeting, public financial management, and fiscal decentralization issues. She has a master's degree in public management and is pursuing a doctorate from the School of Public Policy, University of Maryland. She has worked in the government of Montgomery County, Maryland; the Center for Public Policy and Private Enterprise; and the National Association of Housing and Redevelopment Officials. She has written on budgeting and fiscal decentralization and coedited with Anwar Shah several Chinese-language books: *Fiscal Federalism and Fiscal Management* (2005), *Local Public Finance and Governance* (2005), and *Regional Disparities in China* (2006).

DANIEL TOMMASI is an international consultant in the areas of fiscal policy, public expenditure management, and macroeconomic management. He is an adviser to governments and a consultant for international organizations, including the World Bank, the International Monetary Fund, the European Commission, and the Asian Development Bank. He has worked for more than 30 years in some 40 countries in Africa, Asia, the Caribbean, Central and Eastern Europe, and the Pacific Islands. He is the coauthor of two manuals on public expenditure management: *Managing Government Expenditure*, published by the Asian Development Bank, and *Managing Public Expenditure: A Reference Book for Transition Countries*, published by the Organisation for Economic Co-operation and Development.

JÜRGEN VON HAGEN is professor of economics and director of the Center for European Integration Studies at the University of Bonn, Germany. He is a research fellow of the Centre for Economic Policy Research, a member of the Council of the German Economic Association and the Academic Advisory Council of the German Federal Ministry of Economics, a former member of the Council of the European Economic Association and the French National Economic Committee, and the first recipient of the Gossen Prize of the German Economics Association. He has been a consultant to the International Monetary Fund, the European Commission, the Federal Reserve Board, the Inter-American Development Bank, the World Bank, and numerous governments.

Abbreviations and Acronyms

ABC	activity-based costing
ABC/M	activity-based cost management
ACCA	Association of Chartered Certified Accountants (United Kingdom)
AIDS	acquired immune deficiency syndrome
AMA	aid management agency
BCEAO	Banque Centrale des États de l'Afrique de l'Ouest (Central Bank of West African States)
BDA	Budget Disbursement and Accounts
BIS	Budget Information System
BOB	Bureau of the Budget (Thailand)
BOPA	Budget Outlook Paper
BSP	Budget Strategy Paper
CCS	commitment control system
CNED	Caisse Nationale pour l'Équipement et le Développement (National Center for Infrastructure for Development) (Algeria)
COBOL	common business-oriented language
COFOG	Classification of the Functions of Government
CPM	Critical Path Method
CREAM	clear, relevant, economical, adequate, and monitorable
DFID	Department for International Development (United Kingdom)
DORA	Division of Revenue Act (South Africa)
DSA	Decentralization Support Activity (Project) (Ethiopia)
EBF	extrabudgetary fund

EU	European Union
G8	Group of Eight
GAAP	generally accepted accounting principles
GDP	gross domestic product
GPRA	Government Performance and Results Act of 1993 (United States)
HIPC	Heavily Indebted Poor Countries (Initiative)
HIV	human immunodeficiency virus
IBEX	Integrated Budget and Expenditure (system)
ICT	information and communication technology
IFAC	International Federation of Accountants
IFM	institutional fund mechanism
IFMIS	integrated financial management information system
IMF	International Monetary Fund
INTOSAI	International Organization of Supreme Audit Institutions
IP-ERS	Investment Programme for the Economic Recovery Strategy for Wealth and Employment Creation (Kenya)
IT	information technology
JAM	joint assessment mission
KISS	Keep it simple, sir.
LAN	local area network
M&E	monitoring and evaluation
MBO	management by objectives
MBS	Modified Budgeting System
MDTF	multidonor trust fund
MEWG	Macroeconomic Working Group (Kenya)
MIP	Management Improvement Program (Chile)
MPER	ministerial public expenditure review
MSP	more strategic practices
MTBPS	Medium-Term Budget Policy Statement
MTEC	medium-term expenditure committee
MTEF	medium-term expenditure framework
NES	National Expenditure Survey (South Africa)
NGO	nongovernmental organization
NPM	new public management
NRA	National Road Authority (Malawi)
O&M	operations and maintenance
OECD	Organisation for Economic Co-operation and Development
OED	Operations Evaluation Department

OMB	Office of Management and Budget (United States)
OTS	off-the-shelf
PART	Program Assessment Rating Tool
PAYGO	pay-as-you-go
PBB	performance-based budgeting
PDB	performance-determined budgeting
PEFA	Public Expenditure and Financial Accountability (indicators)
PEM	public expenditure management
PER	public expenditure review
PERT	Project Evaluation and Review Technique
PETS	public expenditure tracking survey
PFA	Public Finance Act 1989 (New Zealand)
PFM	public finance management
PFMA	Public Finance Management Act of 1999 (South Africa)
PIB	performance-informed budgeting
PIP	public investment program
PMORALG	Prime Minister's Office for Regional Administration and Local Government (Tanzania)
PPB	planning-programming-budgeting
PPBS	Planning, Programming, and Budgeting System (United States)
PRB	performance-reported budgeting
PSI	preshipment import inspection
PSIP	Public Sector Investment Programme (Malawi)
SWG	sector working group
TA	technical assistance
TANROADS	Tanzania National Roads Agency
TSA	Treasury single account
UN	United Nations
VFM	virtual fund mechanism
VSAT	very small aperture terminal
WAEMU	West African Economic and Monetary Union
WAN	wide area network
XBRL	extensible business reporting language
ZBB	zero-based budgeting

Overview

ANWAR SHAH

Budgetary institutions have historically played a critical role in a gradual movement toward responsive, responsible, and accountable public governance in industrial countries. Yet the electorate in those countries is not satisfied with this progress because significant problems of political opportunism and fiscal mismanagement remain. A comprehensive budget that includes all government operations, a results-based chain demonstrating their performance, transparency of the budget process, and use of the budget as an instrument for strategic management and citizen empowerment are seen as important elements of a reform to overcome perceived limitations of budgetary institutions. These reforms of budgetary institutions are expected to strengthen the government's accountability to the electorate and ensure improved fiscal outcomes. In developing countries, budgetary institutions are in their infancy and are mainly used as tools for legalistic controls and micromanagement. A reform of these institutions therefore becomes paramount in improving public sector performance. This volume provides a comprehensive review of budgetary institutions and practices, and it draws lessons for reform in developing countries. The volume provides detailed practical guidance in designing budgetary institutions for accountable governance. The topics covered include budgetary institutions; budget methods and practices, including performance budgeting; budget preparation and execution; accrual accounting; activity-based costing; information and communication technology in budgeting; frameworks for assessing country public

1

finance management systems; public expenditure management (PEM) reforms; and budgeting in postconflict countries. The volume also provides two case studies of budgeting reforms: Kenya and South Africa. The following discussion highlights the contributions of individual chapters.

The core of public finances is that some people spend other people's money. In democracies, voters delegate the power over public spending and taxes to elected politicians. In chapter 1, Jürgen von Hagen argues that two aspects of this delegation arrangement are particularly important for the conduct of fiscal policy. The first is the principal-agent relationship between voters (the *principals*) and politicians (the *agents*): elected politicians can extract rents from being in office and spend public moneys on projects other than those that the voters desire. The second is the common pool problem of public finances: governments spend money drawn from a general tax fund on public policies targeted at individual groups in society. As a result, the net benefits for the targeted groups typically exceed the net benefits for society as a whole, and this situation leads to excessive levels of public spending and deficits. The adverse consequences of the principal-agent problem and the common pool problem can be mitigated by appropriately designing the institutions governing the budgeting process.

Budgeting institutions can strengthen the accountability of political agents and the competitiveness of the political system and thus contribute to controlling the principal-agent problem of public finances. Comprehensiveness of the budget, transparency of the budgeting process, and use of the budget as a tool for strategic management rather than for purely legalistic control are therefore important.

The common pool problem of public finances can be reduced through institutional mechanisms that force the actors in the process to take a comprehensive view of the costs and benefits of all public policies. This shift can be achieved if strong agenda-setting powers in the budgeting process are delegated to the minister of finance (the *delegation approach*) or if the process is focused on a set of numerical fiscal targets negotiated at the outset (the *contracts approach*). Both these approaches require strong monitoring and control capacities of the finance ministry during the implementation of the budget; the reaction to unforeseen events will rely more on that ministry's discretion under the delegation approach and more on conditional rules under the contracts approach. The choice between the approaches depends on a country's political system: delegation is appropriate for countries with single-party governments, whereas contracts are suitable for multiparty coalition governments. Institutional design of the budgeting process is, therefore, an important part of a reform project aiming at better fiscal outcomes.

Chapter 2 by Salvatore Schiavo-Campo is concerned with the budget document and its coverage. The fundamental requirement of fiscal management is that the executive branch of government can take no moneys from the public, nor make any expenditure, except with explicit approval of the legislature as the representative organ of the citizens. Consequently, the budget should be the financial mirror of society's economic and social choices, and should reflect all components of good governance—accountability, transparency, participation, and predictability.

The unity of the budget is therefore a basic principle. It is impossible for the budget to reflect the choices of society if it does not include the bulk of revenues and expenditures. Otherwise programs cannot be compared and there is no assurance that scarce resources will be allocated to the priorities. Also, expenditure not included in the budget is uncertain and opaque, making macroeconomic programming difficult and increasing the risk of corruption and waste.

Extrabudgetary funds (EBFs) are government operations set up outside the annual budget process and thus not subject to the same legislative approval procedure as the budget. The reasons for setting up EBFs include:

- Bypassing budgetary procedures when they are too rigid
- Protecting and insulating high-priority expenditure programs
- Purchasing goods for future delivery, payment of which occurs after the fiscal year
- Financing autonomous entities such as universities or research institutes
- Avoiding scrutiny and accountability for the use of public funds.

In industrial countries, the largest EBFs are for social security and public health. In Africa, the major types of funds are as follows:

- Aid-financed expenditures, per requirements of different donors
- Road funds, the design and management of which have improved in recent years
- "Black boxes" and parallel budgets, fueled from revenue from natural resources or commodity boards.

Although there may be a rationale for setting up an EBF, there is never a good reason for secrecy on revenues and rarely a good reason for secrecy on expenditures.

Whatever the reason for setting up an EBF, the fundamental requirement of fiscal management must be met, by legislative approval of its establishment, with clear delegation of revenue and spending authority, satisfactory EBF governance arrangements, and transparent financial information. The bottom line is that management autonomy must not lead to loss of expenditure control or erosion of integrity. Thus, four rules apply to every program financed in whole or in part by public resources, whether within the budget or managed separately in an EBF:

1. Estimates of revenue and expenditures should be shown in gross terms, not netted out.
2. Expenditures and revenues should be classified on the same basis as the overall budget so that comparisons of relative efficiency can be made and for reasons of accountability.
3. All accounts must be subject to regular external audit.
4. Financial reports of government activities should consolidate the operations of autonomous funds and agencies with regular budget operations.

Revenue earmarking and the treatment of contingent liabilities are two other major issues central to budget coverage. As a general rule, earmarking revenue for specific expenditures is acceptable only when there is a direct link between the two, such as road taxes to finance road maintenance. On contingent liabilities—and particularly government loan guarantees—the minimum requirement is full disclosure in the budget documentation.

Many African countries incorporate the basic principles of budget coverage and classification, among others, in an organic budget law that contains the basic rules for managing public finances, allocating powers and accountabilities, providing financial oversight, and so on. Subsidiary legislation regulates the implementation of the organic budget law and defines the operational parameters.

A. Premchand, in chapter 3, presents principles and practices of capital budgeting. Capital budgets in governments have multiple objectives: as instruments of compensatory fiscal policy; as windows on the net worth of public bodies; and as vehicles of development, particularly in the area of economic infrastructure, through greater reliance on debt than on the conventional sources of financing. Governments in the past have introduced one or more of these practices, depending on the context. Notwithstanding the seeming virtues of capital budgets, opinion has been divided, during the past seven decades, about their utility in governments. Now, as several industrial countries have budgetary surpluses and are using them to reduce levels of public debt, there is little incentive to revive the debate about the need for capital budgets. Elsewhere, in the developing world, however, where many governments still are on the edge of financial instability, debate continues about capital budgets and their equivalents.

The practices of countries vary considerably and reveal several categories. The first category includes those countries that have moved or are moving to accrual accounting and budgeting and therefore observe the distinction between operational and investment budgets. Australia, Chile, and New Zealand are in this group; the United Kingdom has had what it calls *resource accounting and budgeting* since fiscal year 2000/01. The second category of countries includes those that show current and capital transactions in their accounts, which are now based on an accrual system. The budget itself, however, makes no such distinction, although, for analytical purposes, extensive data are presented on capital formation. The United States belongs to this category. The third category includes some countries that have introduced accrual accounting but with a modification: they record expenditures on a commitment basis but do not show depreciation allowances because, in their view, such a practice is more appropriate for the corporate than the government sector. This approach, for want of a better description, has acquired the label *modified accrual system*. The fourth category comprises most industrial countries (including some of the former centrally planned economies, which have in recent years adopted an improved economic classification system). Countries in this category show expenditures in terms of those incurred on physical and financial assets and those transfer payments that are of a capital nature. This classification is also used, either as a part of the budget or as a part of the international reporting system, by most developing countries. These approaches do not include depreciation allowances, and capital receipts may not be shown or recorded separately. Countries in the fifth group had capital budgets, but they have moved to an investment budget. Denmark is one such country; it now maintains an investment budget that can be spent beyond the fiscal year. The sixth group includes those countries that have equivalents of capital budgets. Japan, the Republic of Korea, and Southeast Asian countries have special accounts (in Japan, the Fiscal Investment and Loan Program is the most important one, and it acquired even more importance during recent years as the primary instrument for the revival of the economy) that have selected features of capital budgets. In many developing countries, governments have developmental budgets of a hybrid character. Some capital outlays are included in these budgets; the receipts include loans received for their financing but are not restricted to capital items only. The last category includes countries, such as India, that have a capital budget but do not maintain depreciation allowances. China announced in the early 1990s its intention to introduce a capital budget and to refine it over a period. Initially, following Chinese tradition, the capital budget was limited to construction outlays.

Premchand suggests that in most central governments the bulk of the capital budgets would be in the form of transfers to autonomous agencies and other levels of government; asset formation therefore takes place at the receiving end. It may be more useful to have capital budgets at local rather than central levels of government. The main problem with the capital budget has been that its implementation was never in line with the conceptual framework; the extensive prevalence of equivalents and distorted variations has also changed the debate during recent years. In essence, therefore, capital budgets, with all the possibilities and the discipline that they bring to the process, are in need of a fresh focus.

Alta Fölscher, in chapter 4, provides guidance on methods and practices. Budgeting in the public sector is a complex exercise, and fragmentation is inevitable. Ubiquitous problems arise in the public sector context, including the tendency of spending agencies to consider their own spending increases to be too small to affect the total significantly, information asymmetry, and dysfunctional political processes. Over time, budgeting systems, methods, and practices have evolved to address these problems.

Traditionally, budgeting systems have coped with the complexity of budgetary decision making and its inherent problems by using a strategy that can be called *satisficing*. Incremental line-item budgeting practices offer well-established methods for satisficing within a time-delimited budget process. In such a traditional system, particularly when it is combined with a line-item input classification system, the base of spending is taken almost as a given for each agency, and the focus of the budget process is on marginal changes to this base. Once programs are judged to be satisfactory, they become part of the budgeting base (that is, all programs and activities approved in previous years at the same level) and are rarely challenged. Line-item incremental budget systems include an array of institutionalized behaviors that detract from good budget outcomes. These behaviors are particularly severe in developing countries. Spending agencies pad budgets, and finance ministries respond by effecting deep and often arbitrary expenditure cuts. Agencies also use underestimating to their benefit; the finance ministry will accept new programs, only to be faced with their true cost once government is committed to their implementation. Typically in developing countries, the budget is never examined comprehensively but made and approved in fragments. A significant form of fragmentation is found in many developing countries in the split between development budgets and recurrent budgets. Much of the budget process focuses on relatively small spending on investment projects, whereas the bulk of spending is planned in the incremental system.

Since the 1970s, the cost of leaving budgeting to an incremental line-item approach has become clear in the form of unsustainable deficits and fiscal crises. This realization has resulted in several efforts to make more rational and strategic budget methods and practices. The development of principal-agent theory and theoretical frameworks around public policy decision making has underpinned the shift in practice. Three early attempts to bring better information and greater rationality to the budgeting table were initiated in the United States at the federal level. Of these, one—namely, program budgeting systems—was exported through the United Nations to developing countries. None of these three attempts—program budgeting systems, planning-programming-budgeting systems, and zero-based budgeting— was successfully implemented, but they did set the stage for later systems that follow the same tenets. Criticisms of these early systems include that they produced huge amounts of paper to no effect and were implemented too ambitiously without the necessary capacity. In addition, these comprehensive, pure, rational methods ran into the cognitive limits of decision makers' ability to consider all possible options and all relevant information. Further innovations in budget practices located themselves on a spectrum between incrementalism and pure, comprehensive rationality. To a large extent, modern budgeting techniques do not operate on their own. Where they are successful, they are linked to an overall approach to managing the public sector, with the budget and its associated methods as a central process to operationalize the approach. In this way, they are often linked to New Public Management approaches. The shift from old public administration to New Public Management has had fundamental implications. Traditional budgeting practices focus on economy of inputs, financial regularity, and adherence to procedure. New Public Management systems permit greater flexibility of inputs and processes in return for greater emphasis on outputs and performance. Countries focus their efforts on making clearer the links between objectives, inputs, outputs, and outcomes; on developing mechanisms to make the goal definition clearer; and on developing appropriate policy management structures.

A parallel development in budget practice has been the widespread shift from annual planning for one year ahead to budgeting for an extended time horizon. A functional medium-term expenditure framework (MTEF) offers opportunities to make budgeting practices compatible with incentives, thus reducing the burden on the center of analysis and calculation. MTEFs are often complemented by innovations in budget methods and practices. These innovations are either process oriented mechanisms (for example, running adversarial bidding processes) or cooperative mechanisms of analysis, review, and forward planning. Recent years have also seen the development of information-based mechanisms to shift budgeting systems from incremental to better-informed, rational decision making. These mechanisms include the use of public expenditure reviews, as well as activity-based costing and programming techniques. In the final analysis, however, the effectiveness of changing budget rules (and introducing new methods and techniques) depends on their credibility, which, in turn, depends on political support for their implementation coupled with the availability of capacity and information systems.

The past two decades have witnessed a renewed interest in tools that would empower citizens to hold their governments accountable for service delivery performance. Performance budgeting holds promise of such empowerment by letting the sunshine in on government operations. Governments in several industrial countries and a handful of developing countries have initiated public budgeting reforms to incorporate government performance information in budgeting. These reforms are intended to transform public budgeting systems from control of inputs to focus on output and outcome focus in the interest of improving operational efficiency and promoting results-oriented accountability. The emphasis on performance in the budget process reflects a compelling need to grapple with the disappointing public sector performance, and in some countries, such as Malaysia and New Zealand, it has been closely associated with a broader set of reforms that are changing the way in which the public sector is managed. Anwar Shah and Chunli Shen (chapter 5) provide a primer on performance budgeting, in which they document performance budgeting practices, as well as lessons from these experiences, for countries contemplating similar reform efforts in the future.

Shah and Shen conclude that performance budgeting is a useful tool for performance accountability and budget transparency in line (sectoral) ministries but of limited relevance for ministries performing central policy functions such as the ministry of finance or the ministry of foreign affairs. Furthermore, in the absence of an incentive environment for better performance or results-based accountability, the introduction of performance budgeting may not lead to improved performance. Managerial accountability must be on outputs and not on outcomes, because the latter are influenced by external factors. Outcomes, however, should be monitored. Performance budgeting cannot be expected to be a mechanistic, rational system that replaces the political process of making resource choices in a complex environment of competing demands. Instead, it has the potential of facilitating informed political choices. Transparency of the budget and citizens' evaluation of outputs, if these are embodied in performance budgeting, can be helpful in improving budgetary outcomes. Performance budgeting is a costly exercise, but it has the potential to yield positive net benefits if accompanied by a performance management culture and results-accountability to citizens.

In chapter 6, Paul Boothe revisits the debate over the adoption of accrual accounting in the public sector with a particular focus on providing guidance to policy makers in developing countries. After a brief review of the workings of cash- and accrual-based accounting systems in the public sector, the chapter examines the arguments for and against adoption of accrual accounting in industrial countries. It further explores the interaction between fiscal rules and accounting regimes, as well as the incentives that are created for policy makers. The chapter concludes with a review of the arguments for and against the adoption of accrual accounting in developing countries and lessons for policy makers.

Despite strong encouragement from a number of international agencies and accounting organizations, the adoption of accrual accounting for the public sector in industrial countries is still an issue of considerable controversy. At the most fundamental level, there is ongoing disagreement about whether the accounting needs of the public sector, which center around democratic accountability, are well served by a private sector–based accounts system that focuses primarily on financial performance and profitability. Concerns are also expressed regarding the difficulties encountered in valuing assets (such as museums, hospitals, and military hardware) that produce no income stream and for which no market exists. A final area of disagreement is related to whether the benefits of moving to accrual accounting in the public sector outweigh the substantial costs of transition from cash accounting.

The analysis in chapter 6 of the interaction of accounting regimes and fiscal rules shows that seemingly simple fiscal rules, such as committing to budget balance, have substantially different implications under cash and accrual accounting. Indeed, the initial fiscal environment and the nature of the fiscal rule could lead authorities to prefer one accounting regime over another. Only one of the simple fiscal rules—a net debt rule—was seen to be neutral with respect to accounting regime. Thus, careful attention should be paid to the implications for fiscal rules when changes in accounting regimes are being considered.

In conclusion, Boothe recommends that in deciding whether to set accrual accounting as a goal of public sector reform, policy makers in developing countries need to make a hard-headed assessment of their institutional environment and capacities, as well as of the benefits and costs of such a reform.

Chapter 7, by Gary Cokins, introduces activity-based costing. In their pioneering book *Relevance Lost: The Rise and Fall of Management Accounting*, H. Thomas Johnson and Robert S. Kaplan (1987) said that managerial cost accounting fell out of favor as industry paid more attention to financial accounting and reporting for external compliance rather than to managerial information for internal planning and control. One might say that financial accounting came to loom so large in the minds of business executives and stockholders that they lost sight of the meat-and-potatoes cost accounting that helps managers make daily decisions. When the top executives no longer cared about cost accounting, its value diminished in the eyes of managers.

The situation is no different in federal, state, and municipal governments, where fund accounting has long eclipsed any other method of determining how taxpayer money will be spent. As with financial accounting, fund accounting is difficult; it is often impossible to understand what something costs (and why) or to estimate future costs accurately. However, fund accounting is what most legislators, political appointees, and career civil service executives are familiar and comfortable with. Only in the past few years have government leaders started to require the use of managerial cost accounting, but as yet not many at the very top know how to use it. If they do, they are not sufficiently skilled to use it effectively.

Public sector organizations at all levels and of all types are facing intense pressure to do more with less. Federal, national, state, county, municipal, and local governments in almost all countries in the world are feeling some sort of fiscal squeeze. This constraint extends to departments, administrations, branches, foundations, and agencies.

Activity-based cost management (ABC/M) is a widely accepted cost-accounting method in the commercial sector. The public sector does adopt managerial methodologies applied in business, and the adoption of ABC/M is accelerating. New uses for ABC/M, such as performance-based budgeting, have also increased demand for this accounting approach. This trend bodes well for a future government that is more cost conscious and capable of delivering cost-effective services to citizens.

Why are government organizations interested in ABC/M? Organizations increasingly desire to understand their costs and the behavior of factors that drive their costs. ABC/M uses cost modeling, which traces an organization's expenses, both direct and indirect expenses, to the products, services, channels, citizens, and users (that is, customers) that cause those expenses to be incurred.

ABC/M provides fact-based data. Many senior managers have become used to making decisions without good information, so they think they do not need it. But the pressure to make better decisions and use resources more intelligently has increased. ABC/M provides valuable information that can be used to make a broad range of decisions, from outsourcing to operational planning and budgeting.

Activity-based concepts are very powerful techniques for creating valid economic cost models of organizations. By using the lens of ABC/M, organizations of all sizes and types can develop the valid economic models required for their executives and managers to make value-creating decisions and take actions to improve their productivity and resource usage—and ultimately to better serve their constituencies.

The pressure on the public sector is undeniable. People want government to work better and cost less. To meet this pressure, public sector managers will have to change their way of thinking about the true costs—and value— of the services they provide.

In chapter 8, Salvatore Schiavo-Campo reviews budget preparation and approval practices. He lists three prerequisites that permit the budget to serve to control expenditure, allocate it in conformity with government policy, and provide the conditions for operational efficiency: (a) a medium-term perspective, (b) early decisions on hard choices and tradeoffs, and (c) a hard expenditure ceiling at the start of the process. Failure to meet any of those conditions results in a number of inefficient practices, including incremental budgeting, dual budgeting, and excessive bargaining. In particular, postponing until budget execution the hard choices between competing claims for resources makes them even harder and complicates program management.

The starting point of the process should be the preparation of a consistent and public medium-term macroeconomic framework, showing the fiscal targets (deficit, total expenditures, revenues, and so forth) and including the medium-term fiscal perspective to frame the preparation of the annual budget. The fiscal perspective covers three to five years and is updated yearly. (It is important to prevent the estimates of various expenditures over the medium term from being seen as entitlements, which would straitjacket annual budgeting in the future.) The medium-term perspective, as well as the sector expenditure ceilings, must be approved by the top political leadership.

The next steps are (a) preparation by the ministry of finance of a budget circular, giving guidelines for the preparation of ministry budgets and the expenditure ceilings for each ministry; (b) preparation of ministries' budgets on the basis of these guidelines; (c) budgetary discussions between the line ministries and the ministry of finance; and (d) finalization of the draft budget.

Three broad stages of budgeting can be identified: (a) a top-down stage that defines and communicates to each ministry the financial resources available; (b) a bottom-up stage in which the ministries formulate their spending program proposals, within the spending limits; and (c) a stage of iteration, negotiations, and reconciliation to produce a draft budget that is internally consistent and within the aggregate resources available.

A special issue is that of fiscal responsibility laws—that is, laws setting rigid fiscal rules to restrict fiscal policy, such as the so-called golden rule by which public borrowing must not exceed public investment. The difficulty is that such laws are in effect a government contract with itself and are thus easy to violate or disregard. Fiscal responsibility laws may, however, limit wasteful bargaining in fragile coalition governments, and they can serve to improve fiscal discipline in subnational governments if the central government can provide effective enforcement.

When completed in the manner described above, the draft budget is then presented to the legislature for debate and approval. Powers of the legislature to amend the budget vary: (a) unrestricted power to change both expenditure and revenue, (b) restricted power to amend expenditure or revenue within set limits, and (c) balanced power to change revenues or expenditures but with an accompanying measure to maintain the budget deficit targets.

Finally, any major amendment of the budget during the fiscal year should receive legislative approval through the same process by which the budget is originally approved. Too many amendments during the year weaken the credibility of the budget. However, in the fluid conditions of most African developing countries, in-year amendments are necessary. As a general rule, budget amendments should be limited to one or two a year and should be brought to the legislature in a package of proposed changes instead of in a series of individual requests.

Daniel Tommasi, in chapter 9, reviews budget execution practices. Budget execution is the phase when resources are used to implement policies incorporated in the budget. Budget execution procedures must ensure compliance with the initial programming, but they must also adapt to intervening changes and promote operational efficiency.

Effective expenditure control requires that transactions be tracked and controlled at each stage of the expenditure cycle (commitment, verification, issuance of payment order, and payment). Clear definitions of tasks and responsibilities are required. For efficient budget implementation, internal controls and audit systems, set up within line ministries, should be generally preferred to ex ante controls performed by a central agency. In any case, excessive interference from the ministry of finance in line ministries' budget management should be avoided.

For efficient implementation of programs, managers should have a certain degree of flexibility in determining which inputs are needed to produce the services. Nevertheless, to keep expenditure under control, rules for limiting transfers between personnel and nonpersonnel items must often be established. Transfers between programs should not alter the priorities stated in the budget.

A comprehensive midterm review of the implementation of the budget, which may include a budget revision, is needed to ensure that programs are being implemented effectively and to consider changes in the economic environment and other unforeseen developments that have budgetary implications. Amended budgets should be submitted to the legislature, and their number should be limited to no more than one or two per year.

Fiscal control of personnel expenditures is one of the most crucial issues in budget management. The ministry of finance must be involved in the budgetary control of personnel expenditures, which includes (a) decisions on changes in staffing levels in line ministries; (b) short- and longer-term financial implications of staff reduction and retrenchment policies, including pension liabilities; and (c) financial components of the pay structure for the civil service as a whole. Special attention should be paid to ensuring a proper link between the personnel and payroll databases.

A properly functioning public procurement system that promotes fair and transparent competition for contracts awarded by public and private bodies is essential both to encouraging market development and to promoting good governance.

Control of cash is a key element in budget and macroeconomic management. Cash management should be aimed at implementing the budget efficiently, reducing the cost of government borrowing, and maximizing return on excess operating balances. To this end, a centralization of cash balances through a treasury single account (TSA) is required. A TSA is an account or a set of linked accounts through which all government payment transactions are made. In any case, whatever the organization of the payment system, the ministry of finance should be responsible for supervising all central government bank accounts.

Efficient cash management is having the right amount of money in the right place and time to meet the government's obligations in the most cost-effective way. Therefore, for smooth implementation of the budget, in-year financial planning is essential. If delays in payment and arrears generation are to be avoided, commitments must be planned and monitored. An annual budget implementation plan, which will be rolled over quarterly, as well as monthly cash and borrowing plans, should be prepared. Cash planning must be done in advance and communicated to spending agencies so that they can implement their budgets efficiently. Except under special circumstances, in-year financial plans must be in line with budget forecasts.

Generally, in African countries, it is particularly important to get the basics right. To ensure efficient program implementation and to keep expenditure under control, the most pressing needs are to strengthen the arrangements for reporting, accounting, and internal control systems. Cash management and in-year financial planning should be strengthened in most countries. Reliance on arbitrarily determined cash control systems—notably on cash budgeting systems—should be reduced through preparation of a more realistic budget and transparent control of commitments.

Strong political willingness to ensure that the budget is implemented according to the policies adopted by the legislature and to ensure that the existing rules are enforced with rigor will be required to bring about lasting improvements in the PEM system in Africa.

Stephen B. Peterson, in chapter 10, reviews the experience with automated public financial management systems. The principal recommendation to developing countries for automating their financial systems is to adopt off-the-shelf integrated financial management information systems (IFMISs). Experience shows that these systems usually fail or underperform, yet research to date has not adequately explained their poor performance.

Peterson presents two frameworks and a case study from Ethiopia that illustrates an approach to automation that has worked. The first framework distinguishes between business process innovation (reengineering) and process change. *Process innovation* is a comprehensive change of procedures and organization, driven by information technology. *Process change* is an incremental strategy, driven by procedural reform and supported by information technology. Process change is far less risky than process innovation. The conventional off-the-shelf IFMIS reform is principally process innovation, and it exceeds the capacity of most public bureaucracies in developing countries. Process innovation is appropriate because the financial systems in most developing countries are relatively sound and thus provide a basis for improvement.

The second framework concerns the three factors of risk to an automation project: scope, schedule, and budget. The availability of concessionary aid to many developing countries means there is not a hard budget constraint; consequently, schedule and scope slip. The virtual absence of a financial and social cost-benefit analysis of these large and questionable investments is a serious failing in the use of development assistance and loans.

Finally, the custom IFMIS developed to support the Ethiopian reform is presented as an example of a successful low-risk strategy of automation in a difficult environment. The case illustrates the two frameworks; the reform focused on process change, and the automation component was delivered on budget, ahead of schedule, and beyond specification. The Ethiopian case demonstrates several lessons about automation in developing countries: the benefit of process change, automation as a support and not a driver of reform, the "optimal obscurity" of automation projects given that high-level commitment cannot be assumed, and the value of an incremental development strategy of frequent operational upgrades.

Matthew Andrews, in chapter 11, provides a framework for assessing a country's public finance management (PFM) system. What does a strong, functioning PFM system look like? This is a great question and arguably one that lies behind the Group of Eight's finance ministers' recent call for elaboration of a PFM code. The donor community can certainly claim to have preempted this call, having already created a tool to standardize thinking about PFM process quality—the Public Expenditure and Financial Accountability (PEFA) indicators. The PEFA model could provide an excellent basis for identifying a common and standardized PFM code. However, complexities inherent in all PFM systems suggest limits in using any single indicator set like PEFA. It is important to go beyond PEFA and consider the systemic nature of the PFM system. Systems derive their strength from the quality of individual process areas *and* links between processes. PEFA indicators cover most process areas, but some are not covered at all (including policy development), and there is no real treatment of the dynamic links between processes. PFM's multiplicity of role players is another complexity that calls for treatment beyond PEFA. PFM outcomes result from the engagement of many role players across the system—from central ministries of finance to line ministries and agencies, procurement departments, and even civil society entities at various levels of government (central, regional, and local). PEFA's treatment of this issue is limited, as indeed is the stove-piped approach many governments take to PFM (which seems to hold that individual process areas stand alone). Finally, the appropriate look of a PFM system is contingent on the kind of goal the system is addressing—another complication in the effort to standardize thinking about PFM systems. There is a strong argument that systems focused on achieving fiscal discipline require different process elements than systems intended to foster efficient resource allocation—with the different process elements reflecting different levels of development and stimulating different kinds of accountability. Single indicator sets like PEFA are arguably too static to reflect on the ideal PFM look at different levels. PEFA indicators do not extend beyond critical basics, for instance, thus limiting the indicator set to assessments of only the foundational levels of PFM development.

The challenge of strengthening public expenditure management in Africa is addressed in chapter 12 by Salvatore Schiavo-Campo. Many New Public Management practices were introduced into African countries from the early 1990s, supported by development organizations and encouraged by the international consulting industry, but these efforts were oblivious to the pitfalls of transplanting institutional models. Some innovations proved useful. Others did not take root in the different institutional and administrative climate. The key lesson of this experience is to be wary of fashionable and ideological approaches to reform and to rely instead on careful consideration of the costs and benefits of each administrative practice in light of local realities. In the future, it will be critical to sift from among proposed innovations those that are most likely to be suitable (with adaptation) to African developing countries.

The first obvious requirement of reform is to protect the resources mobilized from society or provided by donors to assist in the achievement of society's goals. Preventing public resources from being misappropriated is the paramount fiduciary duty of public financial managers. Corruption is the greatest single impediment to effective management of public financial resources and, conversely, improvements in public expenditure management are at the center of the struggle against corruption. It is a hopeful sign that public integrity appears to have improved over the past decade in most African countries that do not suffer from severe internal security problems. But much remains to be done.

Schiavo-Campo then discusses the main reform priorities in the various aspects of expenditure management, from legal and organizational issues to expenditure programming and budget preparation, budget execution, accounting, reporting, and audit. The common theme is the importance of not introducing advanced expenditure management systems until and unless the basic building blocks of financial management are in place, but then introducing them rapidly and in a sustained manner when circumstances permit.

The key consideration in these strategic reform choices is the country's implementation capacity, without which the best reform programs and carefully designed measures are not worth the paper they are written on. Yet budget reform programs have too often been designed and pushed onto African governments with no attention to implementation capacity, no consideration of the commitments the civil servants concerned have to meet, and no appreciation of the red tape and transaction costs imposed on the country's public administration.

When considering implementation capacity, one must first recognize that capacity is inherently relative to the complexity of the tasks the system is asked to perform. Too often, technical assistance and international consultants have pushed complex budgeting practices onto a reasonably well-functioning system and thus created capacity constraints where none may have existed. In turn, these capacity limitations are then used to justify the need for continuing external assistance. The perverse outcome is that the creation of local African capacity is preempted by the expatriate assistance rather than facilitated by it.

The components of an entity's capacity go well beyond employee skills; they include the institutions—that is, the rules and incentives governing the behavior of individuals in that entity; the organization that enforces or implements those rules; the information needed; and, finally, the stock and quality of resources in the organization, including, of course, human capital. With reference to information, experience demonstrates how the implementation of integrated financial management systems is a costly, complex, and lengthy process that has been successfully accomplished in only a few countries and has failed in most. With reference to human capital formation, generic training in budgeting is useful, but training should normally focus on the specific skills required for better employee performance in a current or prospective job. Thus, training programs should be designed as a corollary of the institutional, organizational, and information changes and should be initiated only after these changes have been put in place—or at least concurrently with them.

An important priority in every African country is gradually to impart to public expenditure management a stronger orientation to actual results. The pitfalls of performance measurement are legion; results indicators must be introduced only when appropriate, and then through a careful and consultative process; and reform must be mindful of diminishing returns, never pushing a good new practice past the point at which the marginal costs outweigh the marginal benefit. Nevertheless, a more robust dialogue on actual achievements of the previous fiscal year should systematically become part of the preparation of the new budget.

Finally, the need for appropriate sequencing and time period of a reform is generally recognized, particularly to make sure that the reform will fit the absorptive capacity of the system and not cause reform fatigue. Moreover, just as ex post evaluation is necessary for good budgeting, periodic reassessments of actual costs and benefits and midcourse adjustments are typically necessary for sustainable reform. Occasional digestion and consolidation periods are therefore advisable—to make sure that the people in the system have understood and internalized the changes and to give them a temporary respite from uncertainty. Accordingly, it appears wise to call from time to time a reform timeout that, without halting the reform momentum, will permit adjustments to the course or speed of specific reforms and will allow reality checks. Starting budget reforms in African countries has never been difficult; the difficulty has been in achieving permanent improvements in expenditure control, strategic resource allocation, operational effectiveness, and public financial integrity.

Chapter 13, by Salvatore Schiavo-Campo, adapts the principles of good budgeting to the special problems and realities of postconflict situations. Experience in Africa and elsewhere shows that the two core requirements of budgeting in postconflict situations are (a) simplicity and (b) adaptation to the very limited capacity of the new transitional government. At the same time, a reasonably comprehensive budget is critical to successful reconstruction—to reflect an agreed and coherent program of reconstruction; to allow interaction between donors and the government; to incorporate basic economic policies; to make the allocation of resources clear to all concerned parties; and, most important, to foster through the budget preparation process the practice of public consultation, open debate, and habits of compromise that have been disabled by the conflict.

A recapitulation of the conceptual background of the issue of investment strategy for development concludes that the otherwise weak notion of strategic project acquires new meaning in a postconflict setting. The prerequisites are a simple but robust process of investment programming and the basic mechanisms of financial management and control. In addition, a medium-term expenditure perspective—even if very simple and aggregated—helps resolve the typical postconflict financing dilemma: most aid is offered right after the conflict, when it cannot be used because capacity is at a minimum, and is no longer available when capacity improvements would permit it to be used effectively. Such a perspective facilitates firm donor pledges of aid over the medium term that can be disbursed as and when the absorptive and implementation capacity permits.

Although aid for postconflict reconstruction can come from a variety of sources, the bulk of the aid for the agreed program of reconstruction has often been channeled through an umbrella multidonor trust fund, generally administered by the World Bank. Substantial experience has been gained with these financing mechanisms during the past 15 years, the lessons of which are briefly summarized in chapter 13. Also relevant to budgeting in postconflict settings is the special role of an aid management agency. In contrast to a steady-state situation, in which aid management is entrusted to a small facilitation unit (normally in the ministry of finance), the depleted government capacity makes it necessary in most postconflict transitions to set up a special aid management agency that can also advise on the reconstruction program as well as guide project and program implementation. It is essential to set a clear sunset clause for such an agency that will preclude an adverse impact on the growth of regular organs of government, to define a path for the transfer of responsibilities to regular government organs, and to implement concomitantly a substantial capacity-building program for those organs.

After a number of suggestions on how to screen requests for the various categories of current and investment expenditure in assembling the first postconflict budgets, the chapter underlines that transparency, consultation, and participation are even more important to budgeting in a postconflict environment than in stable situations. They are essential to dispel the climate of suspicion and help re-create the social capital that was destroyed by the conflict (along with destruction of physical infrastructure and, of course, the loss of human life). In conclusion, although budgeting must be adapted to the urgent needs of the postconflict transition, the objective of immediate achievements must not be allowed to short-circuit long-term institutional development. Thus, though the starting point of budgeting in a postconflict situation is necessarily to meet the immediate needs and fit the transitional limitations, the principles and practices of good budgeting described in the previous chapters provide a vision of the end point toward which all interventions ought to move.

In chapters 14 and 15, Alta Fölscher presents case studies of public finance management reforms in Kenya and South Africa, respectively. Reforming systems of public finance management has long been a Kenyan government priority. Improvements in planning, budgeting, budget execution, and oversight were recognized to be fundamental to achieving key development objectives. The first reforms were introduced as early as the 1970s. The latest wave of reforms commenced at the beginning of the 21st century, as deteriorating budget outcomes exacted a toll on macroeconomic growth, fiscal management, and service delivery. The case study reviews earlier reforms but focuses its discussion on the current system of budget management. It highlights the challenges of reforming complex systems when human resource capacity is limited, accountability is insufficient, and the reforms do not quickly address the nuts and bolts of underlying budgeting systems.

By the end of the 1990s, despite three major reform initiatives, the credibility of the budget process and the budget itself was extremely low. The introduction of an MTEF in 2000/01 spearheaded a series of reforms that recognized that poor links between policy and planning are a result not only of problems in budget preparation but also of deficiencies in budget execution, monitoring, and audit. As a result, Kenya strengthened its macrofiscal framework preparation by building its macroeconomic modeling capacity, establishing the Macroeconomic Working Group, and involving its cabinet and legislature. Prebudget statements—namely, the Budget Outlook Paper (containing the macrofiscal framework) and the Budget Strategy Paper (containing ministry ceilings and key policy commitments)—were introduced. These statements proved key innovations to improve fiscal transparency and firm up government commitment to budgetary decisions.

The budget process now includes ministry- and sector-level expenditure reviews. First, as in Tanzania, Kenya has institutionalized the preparation of ministerial public expenditure reviews. The reviews are undertaken at the start of the expenditure planning process and feed into sector work groups. The nine sector working groups review component sector ministries' spending proposals against national and sector priorities and allocate funds to component institutions within the indicated sector expenditure ceiling. Open sector hearings are held at which stakeholders comment on sector policies and allocations. The final sector working group reports take the hearings into account.

The Budget Strategy Paper is subsequently developed, allocating funds to ministries in line with the sector working groups' recommendations and a revised macroeconomic forecast and fiscal framework. Once the Budget Strategy Paper is published, detailed budget planning commences. It is at this point that a lot of the good analytical work done during the MTEF phase of the process is undone, and planning and budgeting become fragmented. The detailed budget classification system does not allow for an easy translation from priorities to budget lines and, in effect, budgeting is still largely incremental. Spending ministries and political officeholders have limited roles in this phase, with the result that there is very little ownership of the tradeoffs made. Despite compliance with the International Monetary Fund's *Government Finance Statistics Manual* economic classification reforms (IMF 2001), the budget structure is still almost exclusively administrative and offers little help in adjusting spending along programmatic lines. A virtual program grouping was introduced in 2000/01 that identifies spending that is directly targeted at poverty alleviation against a set of criteria. Since the introduction of this grouping, the core poverty expenditures have constituted a significant and increasing share of ministerial expenditure. Although the core poverty programs are supposed to be ring-fenced from expenditure cuts, ring-fencing does not always occur.

Despite progress achieved, effective allocation of resources is still hindered by persistent shortcomings, such as poor links between policy and budget allocations, low budget credibility, pending bills, and stalled projects. Although there is a need to streamline and sequence the allocation process, significant gaps and deficiencies remain. The archaic underlying budget classification and structure are problematic; the development of thorough planning and budgeting processes in line with MTEF principles at ministerial levels is behind the central process; costing or baselines and new proposals are not robust; the division of roles and responsibilities between the ministries of finance and planning does not support good outcomes, and coordination is sometimes lacking; and the divide between the recurrent and development budgets remains. Moreover, the sector working groups' composition and scope do not support their effectiveness, and large portions of spending remain outside of the scrutiny of the budget preparation process.

Budget implementation in Kenya comes with a long history of deviation from the planned budget. In a departure from the pre-MTEF years, the public finance reform program in Kenya extended its scope to include budget execution issues. Key reforms have been the introduction of a cash management and zero-balance accounts system that attempts to provide ministries with greater predictability regarding cash releases, while reducing liquidity in the system. Other budget execution rules exist, such as that new spending proposals submitted in-year for cabinet approval and bailouts of parastatals occur from within existing allocations to ministries. A major reform has been the introduction of an IFMIS in 2003, a reform critical to improved expenditure control and better financial information. Implementation has, however, been slow, and so far not a single ministry uses the system to its full capacity.

The government and its development partners have designed a long-term reform process that systematically and in sequence aims to address remaining weaknesses. Ultimately, the success of this initiative will be contingent on the political will in Kenya to make it happen.

The South Africa case study is presented in chapter 15. Since the democratic transition in 1994, management of the public finances in South Africa has undergone complete reform to reorient spending toward new priorities and to overcome fiscal imbalances. The reforms have been underpinned by the key themes of comprehensiveness and integration; political oversight and a focus on policy priorities; the strategic use of information; changes to incentives and behavior; and minimizing of incrementalism and maximizing of strategic reallocation of funds. Key aspects of budget reform follow:

■ *Integrating the intergovernmental system into a sequenced budget process.* An integrated national and provincial annual budget process provides the vehicle for operationalizing the intergovernmental finance system. The size of the subnational share is a result of the intergovernmental process and political decision making, weighing the macroeconomic outlook, fiscal policy, and priorities against the competencies of the various spheres. The distribution between provinces is based on a proportionate formula.

■ *Creating a credible budget process.* The budget process allows government to involve various role players who provide political and technical advice when faced with tradeoffs between competing spending priorities.

■ *Reforming the budgeting institutions.* The MTEF operates at the center of the South African budget reforms, and frames, in the final instance, all policy discussions in the country. The MTEF system is as much about the structures, institutions, and rules of the budget process as it is about the sets of three-year plans that result. Fiscal policy targets are generally determined in the absence of any detailed expenditure bids. The budget framework presents a comprehensive and transparent picture of all revenue and expenditure in general government. All bids competing for the same envelope of available funds are considered together within an overall hard budget constraint. The macroeconomic assumptions are credible and are published in the prebudget statement and debated in public forums. The system makes no differentiation between an MTEF and the annual budget process, and the MTEF is also the only avenue to funding for spending ministries. Spending departments start their budget preparation from their existing funding baseline. A contingency reserve plays an important function in providing flexibility and protecting stability in the MTEF (and thereby its credibility) against uncertainty. The budget submission format encourages departments to focus on maximizing the alignment of policy and budgets over time by making changes at the margin. Treasury-led medium-term expenditure committees assess whether there is a clear link between budget proposals, broad policy priorities, and key sector challenges; whether new funding is required; whether the department is able to implement the plan over the MTEF period; and whether the expected outputs are clearly defined. The cabinet makes the final decisions. The MTEF system uses key sets of budget preparation and reporting documentation to extract strategic information for decision making, to ensure commitment to decisions made, and to encourage accountability. Changing the format of budget documentation has been an important aspect of the budget reform process.

■ *Implementing a new framework for public financial management and reporting.* The new legal framework for public financial management shifts the onus of managing the use of resources from central control to the managers of spending departments and agencies. The legislation specifies who is responsible for putting in place such procedures, what the procedures should achieve, what the information and reporting requirements are, how the procedures are to be overseen, and how compliance is to be assured. It sets clear sanctions.

- *Improving the classification system.* Since 1997, the underlying budget and classification structure has been modernized and the chart of accounts revised. The new system is tailored to South African needs but is compliant with the *Government Finance Statistics Manual* (IMF 2001) for easy international reporting.
- *Improving budget management for service delivery.* South Africa has made slow progress toward more output-focused budgeting through improved budget documentation, but it has not succeeded in putting in place a comprehensive, functional system. Budgeting is still largely focused on inputs.

The reforms set out above have brought huge benefits, but the reform process is far from complete. Some areas that were targeted for reform in the initial vision of a results-oriented, accountable budgeting environment, such as a fully fledged performance budgeting system, have just not yet been reached. Other issues, such as performance management and the planning, budgeting, and reporting links, have been tackled, but progress has been slow. A key remaining shortcoming of the South African process is that better processes are still being conducted, but mostly at the center of government. Penetration to spending ministries and agencies at all levels is less robust, compromising the benefits from the new system. The question is whether institutional overload and misalignment of incentives are fundamental underlying problems preventing progress.

References

IMF (International Monetary Fund). 2001. *Government Finance Statistics Manual.* Washington, DC: IMF Statistics Department. http://www.imf.org/external/pubs/ft/gfs/manual/pdf/all.pdf.

Johnson, H. Thomas, and Robert S. Kaplan. 1987. *Relevance Lost: The Rise and Fall of Management Accounting.* Boston: Harvard Business School Press.

One

A Primer on Budgeting and Budgetary Institutions

1

Budgeting Institutions for Better Fiscal Performance

JÜRGEN VON HAGEN

The core of public finances is that some people spend other people's money. In democracies, voters delegate the power over public spending and taxes to elected politicians. Two aspects of this delegation arrangement are particularly important for the conduct of fiscal policy. The first is the principal-agent relationship between voters (the principals) and politicians (the agents). The second is the common pool problem of public finances (von Hagen and Harden 1995).

The delegation of power to elected politicians implies that politicians can extract rents from being in office and spend public moneys on projects other than those the voters desire. Voters might wish to limit these opportunities by subjecting politicians to strict and detailed rules that prescribe what they can and cannot do under specific circumstances. However, the uncertainty and complexity of the economic and political environment render the writing of such complete contracts impossible. Therefore, the principal-agent relationship resembles an "incomplete contract" (Persson, Roland, and Tabellini 1997; Seabright 1996), leaving politicians with considerable residual powers. The greater these residual powers are, the greater will be the divergence between voter preferences and actual policies.

The common pool problem of public finances arises from the fact that, in all modern democracies, politicians spend money drawn from a *general* tax fund on public policies targeted at *individual* groups in society. As a result, the group of those who pay for specific policies (the general taxpayers) is typically larger than the group of those who benefit from these policies. The net benefits of such policies accruing to the targeted groups, therefore, typically exceed the net benefits for society as a whole, and the targeted groups and their political representatives usually demand more spending on such policies than what is optimal for society at large. Thus, the common pool problem leads to excessive levels of public spending. Putting the argument into a dynamic context, one can show that it also leads to excessive deficits and government debts (see, for example, Milesi-Ferretti 2004; Velasco 2000; von Hagen and Harden 1995).

This tendency toward excessive spending, deficits, and debt increases with the number of politicians who have access to the same general tax fund, a point empirically confirmed by Kontopoulos and Perotti (1999). In societies divided along ideological, ethnic, language, and religious lines, there can be an increased tendency of people in one group to neglect or ignore the tax burden falling on other groups, making the common pool problem more severe. Empirical studies showing that such schisms result in higher spending levels, deficits, and debt confirm the importance of the common pool problem (Alesina, Baqir, and Easterly 1997; Alesina and Perotti 1996; Annett 2000; Roubini and Sachs 1989).

The adverse consequences of the principal-agent problem and the common pool problem can be mitigated by appropriately designing the institutions that govern the decisions over public finances. This chapter focuses on the role of budgeting institutions and the scope for institutional design to achieve better fiscal outcomes. The analysis rests on the fundamental claim that institutions shape the outcome of the decision-making processes they govern. One may, of course, object that people always do what they want regardless of the rules under which they operate, or that institutions are themselves endogenous and are created to facilitate the outcomes the relevant actors wish to achieve. However, there is now a large amount of empirical evidence supporting our basic claim that institutions matter.[1]

The next section begins with a characterization of budgeting institutions. It then focuses on the principal-agent problem and how budgeting institutions can promote accountability of and competition among the political agents. The section that follows shows how budgeting institutions can address the common pool problem. The final section concludes.

Budgeting Institutions

The government budget is a record of the revenues and expenditures of a government during a given period of time. Ex ante, it shows what the government intends to do during that period and how it intends to finance these activities. Ex post, it shows what the government actually did and who had to pay for it and in what form.

The budget itself is the result of the budgeting process, the way in which decisions about the use and funding of public resources are made, from the drafting of a budget law to its implementation. We define budgeting institutions generally as the collection of the formal and informal rules and principles governing the budgeting process within the executive and the legislature. Budgeting institutions divide the budgeting process into different steps, determine who does what and when in each step, and regulate the flow of information among the various actors. In doing so, such institutions distribute strategic influence and create or destroy opportunities for collusion and for holding individual agents accountable for their actions. The constitutional role of the budgeting process is to provide a framework in which all competing claims on public funds are manifested and reconciled with each other.

Budgeting processes can be proximately divided into four stages, each involving different actors with different roles. The *executive planning stage* involves the drafting of the budget by the executive. The *legislative approval stage* involves the passage of the budget law through the legislative process, including the process of parliamentary amendments to the budget proposal, which may involve more than one house of parliament. The *executive implementation stage* covers the fiscal year to which the budget law applies. The *ex post accountability stage* involves a review of the final budget documents by a court of auditors or a similar institution, checking the consistency of such documents with the legal authorization.

We distinguish three types of budgeting institutions:

1. Institutions shaping the environment of the budgeting process
2. Output-oriented rules
3. Procedural rules.

Institutions Shaping the Environment of the Budgeting Process

Unless it is comprehensive, the budgeting process cannot fulfill its constitutional role as the framework within which all claims on public finances compete with each other. That is, no claims on public funds must be allowed to be made outside the framework of the budgeting process or the budgeting process will not be able to control the principal-agent and the common pool problems of public finance. Comprehensiveness is, therefore, an important requirement of the budgeting process. There are four important deviations from comprehensiveness.

The first deviation is the use of off-budget funds to finance government activities. Off-budget funds allow policy makers to circumvent the constraints of the budgeting process and to shield their decisions against the challenges of conflicting distributional interests.

The second deviation is the spreading of nondecisions; these occur when expenditures included in the budget are determined by developments exogenous to the budgeting process. Prime examples are the indexation of spending programs to macroeconomic variables such as the price level or aggregate nominal income, and open-ended spending appropriations, such as the government wage bill and welfare payments based on entitlements with legally fixed parameters. Nondecisions conveniently allow policy makers to avoid tough decisions (Weaver 1986), but they degrade the budgeting process to a mere forecast of exogenous developments.

The third deviation is the lack of sufficient distinction between (a) nonfinancial laws that create the legal basis for the public policies pursued by the government and (b) financial laws—the budget—that authorize annual government expenditures for these policies. In most modern democracies, legislative processes differ for financial and nonfinancial laws. Where this is not the case, mandatory spending laws—nonfinancial laws that make certain government expenditures compulsory during the fiscal year—may exist. The budget then becomes a mere summary of existing spending mandates created by simple legislation. Even where legislative rules distinguish between financial and nonfinancial laws, politicians may be allowed to attach riders to nonfinancial laws that require the government to spend funds on certain projects. The use of such riders, which was pervasive in the U.S. Congress until the 1980s, facilitates logrolls constructed to ensure that there is "something for everyone" in a legislative proposal. An effective budgeting process requires that riders with financial implications be prohibited.

The fourth deviation occurs when the government enters into contingent liabilities such as guarantees for the liabilities of other public or nonpublic entities. Promises, implicit or explicit, to bail out subnational governments (as in Germany in the late 1980s), regional development banks (as frequently in the past in Brazil), financial institutions (as in the savings and loans debacle of the 1980s in the United States), or large corporations (as in the fiscal crisis in the Republic of Korea in the late 1990s) can suddenly turn into large government expenditures outside the ordinary budget. In practice, contingent liabilities cannot be fully avoided, because government by its very nature provides a social insurance function, and a proper accounting of such liabilities is a difficult task. Still, the existence of such liabilities and their importance for the government's financial stance can be brought to the attention of decision makers in the budgeting process by requiring the government, as part of the budget documentation, to submit a report on the financial guarantees it has entered into.

A second, important requirement of the environment of the budgeting process is transparency. According to Kopits and Craig (1998: 1), transparency of the budgeting process "involves ready access to reliable, comprehensive, timely, understandable, and internationally comparable information on government activities . . . so that the electorate and financial markets can accurately assess the government's financial position and the true costs and benefits of government activities." Poterba and von Hagen (1999) argue that the inclusion of special accounts and the failure to consolidate all fiscal activity into a bottom-line measure reduce transparency. Alesina and Perotti (1996) include the use of optimistic forecasts on economic developments and the effects of new policies and creative accounting among the factors reducing transparency. The availability of links between the budgetary figures and national accounts is another prerequisite of transparency. The budget should not allow policy makers to hide expenditures or to use them for purposes other than those stated in the executive's budget proposal and authorized by the legislature.

Aiming at the control of political agents, transparency requires that the budget be organized according to administrative functions and responsibilities. Program-oriented budgeting, which aims at identifying a government's policies across administrative functions, is useful, but it should not replace budgeting according to administrative functions, because program-oriented budgeting tends to obscure political responsibilities. Procedural transparency is also required. Budgeting processes should be transparent in the sense that all actors know what they and others are expected to do, and when and how. Opaque processes for bargaining and conflict resolution promote logrolling and reciprocity and obscure the responsibilities of the actors involved. Alt and Dreyer-Lassen (2006) point out four dimensions of procedural transparency. The first is the number of separate documents in which a given amount of information is processed; the larger this number, the lower the degree of transparency. The second is the possibility for outsiders independently to verify the data and assumptions given in the budget. The third is a commitment to avoid use of opaque and arbitrary language and to apply generally accepted accounting standards. The fourth is the provision of explicit justifications of the data and explanations of the assumptions underlying the budget.[2]

A third, important requirement of the budgeting process is the achievement of an appropriate balance between the legal function of the budget and its function as a management instrument. The legal function emphasizes the conformity of all expenditures with formal rules and legal criteria. Pursued to the extreme, it leads to perfect legalistic control of government spending, yet without asking whether the implementation of the budget meets the political and economic goals of government policy. Where this occurs, as, for example, in Italy until the 1990s or in Poland today, the ministry executing the legal control, which is usually the treasury, typically regards itself as very powerful in budgetary matters, but this power is limited to purely formal aspects of the budget.

As a management instrument, the budget can be regarded as a plan stating how the government intends to meet its policy goals given the expected economic developments during the relevant fiscal year. As new information arises during the fiscal year, meeting these goals efficiently may require reactions and some flexibility in the execution of the budget. A budgeting process overemphasizing the legality of government spending fails to account for this need. During the planning stage, overly legalistic budgeting processes tend not to ask whether the expenditures demanded by the spending branches of the executive are adequate to fulfill the policy goals. During the implementation stage, such budgeting processes tend not to ask whether the expenditures authorized by the budget act are still adequate and make little room for adjustments.

At the same time, ex post accountability must be preserved; therefore, the legal role of the budget must not be neglected entirely. One way to strike a balance between the two functions is to put less emphasis on the legality of each expenditure and more on the legality of the decision-making processes under which these expenditures are made—that is, on ensuring that budgeting decisions are made by the proper actors following the proper procedures. Such a shift in emphasis allows for more flexibility in the execution of the budget while ensuring that this flexibility is used in conformity with the government's policy goals.

Output-Oriented Rules

Output-oriented rules are ex ante numerical rules focusing on certain parameters of the budget. The most prominent ones are balanced-budget constraints of the kind prevailing today in almost all U.S. states and many provinces of Argentina and Canada.[3] There is a fair degree of variation in these rules. Balancing the budget typically applies to the current expenditure budget; that is, borrowing for capital expenditures is not forbidden. Some rules oblige the executive branch of the government to present a balanced-budget proposal to the legislature, and perhaps the legislature to pass a balanced budget, but allow government borrowing ex post. Others require the government to cover any deficits occurring ex post with surpluses during the following year. In some states, special referenda are required to authorize government borrowing. In the European Union (EU), member states must keep their annual government budget deficits below 3 percent of gross domestic product (GDP) and their government debt below 60 percent of GDP. Germany, Italy, Japan, and the Netherlands introduced rules requiring balanced current budgets after World War II to enhance the credibility of their macroeconomic stabilization programs. Since the late 1990s, the U.K. government must achieve balance on its current budget on average over the business cycle. The U.S. Congress adopted a fiscal rule in the Balanced Budget and Emergency Deficit Control Act (Gramm-Rudman-Hollings Act I) of 1985, which established numerical targets for the federal budget deficit for every fiscal year through 1991. In Switzerland, a constitutional amendment was passed in 1998 requiring the federal government to balance the budget by 2001 and to set annual ceilings for federal government expenditures afterward. The Convergence, Stability, Growth, and Solidarity Pact adopted by the member countries of the West African Economic and Monetary Union also contains numerical limits for certain fiscal aggregates.[4]

The advantage of output-oriented rules is that they are very specific: they spell out exactly what a government can do. But this specificity is also a drawback, because it implies a lack of flexibility in the reaction of fiscal policy to unforeseen events. The question of whether balanced-budget rules keep U.S. states from responding efficiently to revenue and expenditure shocks has been the subject of considerable debate (see, for example, Canova and Pappa 2005; Fatás and Mihov 2003). Similarly, the political debate over the fiscal rules in the European Monetary Union focused largely on the question to what extent these rules keep governments from smoothing taxes and expenditures over the business cycle. Output-oriented rules forcing governments to refrain from macroeconomic stabilization and tax smoothing may thus have a cost in terms of the efficiency of fiscal policies. The experience of the European Monetary Union suggests that governments will tend to ignore or circumvent the rules if they perceive this cost to be very large. Thus, very stringent output-oriented rules may lack credibility precisely because they are so strict. Credibility requires some flexibility for reacting to unexpected developments. Too much flexibility obviously implies that the rules no longer control the political agents' performance effectively. Thus, output-oriented rules imply a tradeoff between effectiveness and credibility.

One way to address this tradeoff is to condition output-oriented rules on the state of the business cycle. For example, the need to balance the budget might be stated in terms of the cyclically adjusted budget deficit rather than the actual deficit, or a deficit or spending limit might be stated as a ratio of potential GDP rather than actual GDP. Both of these measures would require smaller deficits and spending during cyclical upswings but would allow larger deficits and spending during cyclical downswings; they would work as automatic stabilizers built into the tax and transfer system. In practice, however, this approach is difficult because the cyclical component of GDP and government spending and revenues is not easily determined in real time, when fiscal policy decisions have to be made.[5]

The attractiveness of output-oriented rules as a means to control the behavior of political agents stems from the apparent simplicity of a rules-based framework. Once the rule is in place, it seems straightforward to measure the government's performance against it. Historically, in fact, voters often imposed such rules in response to episodes of fiscal crisis and rising taxes that they believed were the result of the profligacy of their political representatives (see, for example, Eichengreen and von Hagen 1996). Empirical evidence, however, suggests that the effectiveness of output-oriented rules is rather questionable. For example, U.S. state governments subject to stringent numerical debt limits tend to borrow using debt instruments not covered by the legal rule, with no significant effect on total debt (Strauch 1998; von Hagen 1991). Kiewiet and Szakaly (1996) find that state governments subject to more restrictive borrowing constraints tend to substitute municipal debts for state debt. Fatás and others (2003) find that the deficit limits of the European Monetary Union did not constrain deficits effectively in the large member states. Also, von Hagen and Wolff (2006) show that member states of the European Monetary Union use creative accounting to circumvent the deficit limits. In U.S. states, constitutional expenditure limits tend to induce a shift from the (constrained) current budget to the (unconstrained) investment budget (Strauch 1998). Rueben (1997) and Shadbegian (1996) find in cross-section studies of U.S. states that tax and expenditure limits have no significant effect on the level of spending. The key insight from this research is that the effectiveness of output-oriented rules is limited at best, because the rules can be circumvented.

Procedural Rules

Procedural rules define the processes under which budgeting decisions are made. In practice, there are two types: rules that focus on decision makers and rules that focus on content. Rules focusing on decision makers define the authorities of the actors involved in the budgeting process. At the executive planning stage, such rules determine the role and power of the finance minister and the spending ministers and set forth the rules of conflict resolution among them. At the legislative stage, procedural rules determine the agenda-setting power of the executive vis-à-vis the legislature, the scope for parliamentary amendments, and the legislature's information rights. At the implementation stage, they determine the finance minister's power to manage the execution of the budget and to enforce the budget law, and they define the limits for deviations from the original budget law.

Procedural rules focusing on content determine the calendar of the budgeting process and emphasize the role of numerical targets. As discussed below, numerical targets for budgetary aggregates such as the annual deficit, total spending, and overall allocations for the individual spending ministries can be a commitment device for fiscal discipline. For example, since the mid-1980s, the Danish budgeting process begins with an agreement on the total allocations for all spending ministries negotiated among the members of the executive. Such rules may also require the government to embed the budget for any given fiscal year in multiannual fiscal programs highlighting the consistency of government policies over time. A prime example is the Stability and Growth Program that each member state of the European Monetary Union is required to submit annually to the European Commission. These programs state the budget for the following year together with the budgetary plans for the following three years.

At the implementation stage, content-related procedural rules are often backed up by precise prescriptions for dealing with unexpected revenue and expenditure shocks. An example is Belgium's "Golden Hamster," the rule that any unexpected surpluses in the budget arising from unexpected revenues or unexpectedly low expenditures must be spent to pay down the national debt.

Budgeting Institutions and the Principal-Agent Problem

In this section, we show how the principal-agent problem of public finances can be addressed by political institutions.

Controlling Agents through Accountability and Competition

In a democracy, the main instrument for dealing with the principal-agent relationship between voters and elected politicians is the election. According to the retrospective-voting paradigm, voters use elections to hold politicians accountable for past performance (Persson and Tabellini, 2000). They reappoint incumbents if they find their behavior satisfactory; otherwise, they vote for competing candidates. This paradigm suggests that rents can be limited by strict accountability and fierce competition. Research in this area has examined the effect of electoral institutions on public finances and shown that they affect both the size and the structure of public spending as well as the size of the deficit and the level of public debt.[6]

Electoral institutions are characterized by district magnitude, electoral formula, and ballot structure. *District magnitude* relates to the number of representatives elected from each electoral district. *Electoral formula* translates votes into seats. *Ballot structure* determines how citizens vote, such as whether they cast votes for individual candidates or whether they vote for entire party lists. Small district magnitude, plurality rule, and votes cast for individual candidates focus elections on the personal performance of the candidates and allow voters to hold them personally accountable. Large district magnitude, proportional representation, and votes cast for fixed party lists focus elections on the average performance of all candidates on the party list and weaken personal accountability. The smaller districts, pluralities, and districts with individual candidates more effectively limit the scope for extracting political rents from being in office.

We now turn to the other aspect of control, competition. The need to gain a large share of votes in a district under plurality rule is an important barrier to entry for small parties. Political newcomers find it difficult to challenge incumbent politicians, because they need a majority to succeed from the start. In contrast, newcomers can win at least a small number of seats in parliament under proportional representation. Political competition is, therefore, more intense under the latter system, particularly when minimum vote thresholds are low. If contestants use the election campaign to identify waste and point to instances of rent extraction, one can expect more intense competition to lead to less waste and smaller rents and, therefore, smaller levels of public spending and public deficits.

Furthermore, Skilling and Zeckhauser (2002) argue that voters inherently favor smaller over larger levels of public debt, and the more so, the larger the level of debt to begin with. The more competitive an electoral system, the better the voters can discipline governments by voting them out of office if they run undesirably large deficits. Skilling and Zeckhauser's empirical work confirms that the competitiveness of electoral systems reduces deficits and public spending.

Budgeting Institutions, Accountability, and Competition

Budgeting institutions can strengthen the accountability of political agents and the competitiveness of the political system and thus contribute to controlling the principal-agent problem of public finances. Comprehensiveness of the budget is important in this regard. If government expenditures can be hidden in off-budget funds and shielded from democratic control, voters are unable to hold the government accountable for its performance.

Political accountability can also be weakened by nondecisions, as described above. The more automatic adjustments a budget contains and the more appropriations are driven ex post by private sector demands for entitlements, the less a government can be made responsible for budgetary outcomes. A similar point relates to the tension between the use of the budget as a legal instrument and its use as a management tool. Emphasizing the use of the budget for making decisions on and implementing political strategies and developing medium-term economic plans creates opportunities for voters to compare the government's performance with its past intentions. The result is greater political accountability. In contrast, if budgeting is perceived as a mere legal exercise, it may facilitate accountability in a legal sense, but not in a political sense.

Transparency of the budgeting process is another important element of political accountability. Transparency enables voters to understand a government's fiscal plans. The ability to compare the actual performance of the government against its past plans and intentions is an essential condition of the retrospective voting paradigm. Focusing budgets and budget negotiations on numerical targets for the main budgetary parameters creates natural yardsticks by which voters can assess the actual performance of a government. Similarly, the ability to understand the political bargaining process around the budget and to check whether individual policy makers kept the commitments they entered into during this process is an important condition for holding policy makers personally accountable in elections.

Thus, the institutions shaping the environment of the budgeting process can be designed to promote fiscal discipline by strengthening the accountability of political agents to their political principals, the voters.

Budgeting institutions can also be designed to increase the competitiveness of the political system. Incumbent governments naturally have a competitive advantage resulting from the fact that they have more data available to develop their electoral platforms. At the same time, parties challenging the incumbent government can make lots of promises that are based on incomplete information about the actual state of the government's finances. In both cases, it is consequently difficult for voters to judge between the incumbent and the challengers. Here, the Netherlands offers an interesting example of institutional design. The Dutch Central Planning Bureau is an independent economic research institute that is charged with presenting an assessment of the government's annual budget proposal. In Dutch elections, opposition parties present their economic and fiscal programs to the Central Planning Bureau, which publishes an evaluation of the economic and fiscal consequences of the programs. This puts the incumbent and the challengers on more equal grounds in the electoral competition.

Other countries in Europe use similar arrangements to improve and guarantee the objectivity of the economic forecasts and assumptions underlying the budget (Hallerberg, Strauch, and von Hagen 2001). Generally, transparency of the budget and publicly available fiscal data will reduce incumbent advantages and increase political competition.

Budgeting Institutions and the Common Pool Problem

At the heart of the common pool problem of public finances is an externality that results from using general tax funds to finance targeted public policies. Individual politicians perceive that an increase in spending on targeted policies will provide their constituencies with more public services at only a fraction of the total cost. The resulting spending and deficit biases can be reduced by inducing politicians to take a comprehensive view of the costs and benefits of their decisions. A *centralized* budgeting process contains elements that induce decision makers to internalize the common pool externality by taking a comprehensive view of their decisions. A *fragmented* budgeting process fails to do so.[7]

At the executive planning stage of the budgeting process, the purpose of institutional rules of centralization is to promote agreement on budget guidelines (spending and deficit targets) among all actors involved, thereby ensuring fiscal discipline. The rules of centralization at this stage must foster consistent setting of such guidelines and ensure that they constrain executive decisions effectively. A key issue concerns the way conflicts are resolved. Uncoordinated and ad hoc conflict resolution involving many actors simultaneously promotes logrolling and reciprocity and, hence, fragmentation.

At the legislative approval stage, rules of centralization should control the debate and voting procedures in the legislature. Because of the much greater number of decision makers involved, the common pool problem is even larger in the legislature than in the executive. Fragmentation spreads when there are no limits to the changes that parliament can make to the executive's budget proposal, when spending decisions are made in legislative committees with narrow and dispersed authorities (the "Balkanization of committees"— see Crain and Miller 1990), and when there is little guidance of the parliamentary process either by the executive or by the speaker of the legislature. Centralization comes with strengthening the executive's agenda-setting power by placing limits on the scope of amendments, controlling the voting procedure, and raising the political stakes of a rejection of the executive's budget, such as by making it equivalent to a vote of no confidence. Centralization can also come with strengthening the roles of the speaker and the financial committee in the legislature.

At the implementation stage, rules of centralization ensure that the budget law effectively constrains the spending decisions of the executive. One important element is the finance minister's ability to monitor and control spending flows during the fiscal year. Another important element is the limitation of changes to the budget law during the year.

Delegation and Contracts

Empirical studies of the budgeting process in member countries of the Organisation for Economic Co-operation and Development and developing countries show that there are two basic approaches to centralization of the budgeting process: delegation and contracts. Delegation vests special authority in a "fiscal entrepreneur," whose functions are to set the broad parameters of the budget and to ensure that all other participants in the process observe these constraints. To be effective, this entrepreneur must have the ability to monitor the other members of the executive and to use selective punishments against possible defectors. Among the cabinet members, the entrepreneur is usually the finance minister, who is typically perceived as being less bound by individual spending interests. Under the contracts approach, the budgeting process starts with an agreement among the main actors on a set of binding fiscal targets—that is, a fiscal contract. For this approach to be effective, there must be a significant punishment for breaching the contract at the later stages of the process.

Delegation

In practice, delegation can take a variety of forms. In the French model, the finance minister and the prime minister together determine the overall allocations of the spending departments. These limits are considered binding for the rest of the process. Here, the finance minister has a strong role as agenda setter in the budgeting process. The U.K. model, in contrast, evolves as a series of bilateral negotiations between the spending departments and the finance minister, who derives bargaining power from superior information, seniority, and political backup from the prime minister. In the German model, the finance minister has weak agenda-setting power but strong veto power in the cabinet, as his objection against the budget bids of a spending ministry can be overruled only by a cabinet majority including the chancellor.

Under the delegation approach, drafting the budget proposal is mainly the responsibility of the finance ministry, which monitors the individual bids, negotiates directly with the spending departments, and approves the bids submitted to the final cabinet meeting. Unresolved conflicts between spending ministers and the finance minister are typically arbitrated by the prime minister or a senior cabinet committee.

At the legislative stage, the delegation approach gives large agenda-setting powers to the executive over parliament. One important instrument here is a limit on the scope of amendments parliamentarians can make to the executive's budget proposal. In France, for example, amendments cannot be proposed unless they reduce expenditures or create a new source of public revenues. In the United Kingdom, amendments that propose new charges on public revenues require the consent of the executive. Such restraints result in the budget constraint being felt more powerfully.

Another form of delegation operates through the voting procedure. The French government, for example, can force the legislature to vote in a block on large parts of or the entire budget, with only those amendments considered that the executive is willing to accept. In the United Kingdom, the executive can make the vote on the budget a vote of confidence, considerably raising the stakes for a rejection. A final element concerns the budgetary authority of the upper house. Where both houses have equal budgetary authority, as in Italy or Belgium, finding a compromise is a necessary part of the budgeting process. The effect tends to weaken the position of the executive because it now faces two opponent bodies. The executive may be strengthened by limiting the budgetary authority of the upper house, as in France and Germany, where the lower house prevails if an agreement between the two chambers cannot be reached. In the United Kingdom, the upper house has no budgetary authority at all, leaving the executive with only one chamber to deal with. The position of the executive can also be strengthened by giving the finance minister veto power over the budget passed by the legislature, as in Germany and Spain.

A popular argument holds that low transparency can improve the executive's agenda-setting power over an otherwise strong legislature. In a number of African countries, for example, finance ministers systematically withhold information about government revenues and the cost of public policies from the members of parliament in an effort to prevent parliament from enacting budget bills with excessive spending and deficits. Such a practice would suggest that there is a tradeoff between centralization and transparency of the budgeting process. This argument is a fallacy because it fails to recognize where the bias for excessive spending and deficits comes from. Hiding important information from the legislature shifts the relevant decisions outside the budgeting process. The result is that spending and deficits are still excessive. The better solution is to strengthen the agenda-setting powers of the executive, perhaps in a trade against more monitoring and ex post control powers of the legislature. Where such a trade is politically difficult, the budgeting process can be improved by forcing the legislature to vote on a bill setting the main parameters of the budget at a very early stage of the budgeting process, as, for example, in Italy today.

At the implementation stage, centralization requires that the finance minister be able to monitor and control the flow of expenditures during the year. At this stage, in particular, the budgeting process should emphasize the role of the finance ministry as a manager of the government's financial resources rather than as a mere controller of the legality of public spending. A necessary condition is the existence of a unified system of government accounts through which the finance minister can manage cash flows during the year. Spending departments should be required to obtain the finance minister's authorization to disburse funds. The finance minister's authority to impose cash limits during the year is another control mechanism. Effective monitoring and control are also important to prevent spending departments from behaving strategically—that is, from spending their appropriations early in the year and demanding additional funds later under the threat of closing down important public services.

Furthermore, centralization requires tight limits on any changes in the original budget law through the modification of appropriations once the fiscal year has begun. One example is the requirement that transfers of funds between different chapters of the budget be authorized by the finance minister or parliament. The same applies to transfers of funds between different fiscal years. "Rainy day funds"—unspecified appropriations under the control of the finance ministry that can be used to cover unexpected revenue shortfalls or spending increases—can be used to give the finance minister more flexibility for managing the budget during the implementation stage. An example is the contingency reserve included annually in the U.K. budget. The purpose of the reserve, which amounts to 2 to 4 percent of the budget total, is to deal with unanticipated expenditures without overrunning the aggregate targets imposed on the spending departments. According to a rule introduced in 1976, a refusal by the finance minister to charge expenditures against the reserve can be overruled only by the entire cabinet.

An allocation made from the reserve does not increase a spending department's baseline allocation for the subsequent budget planning processes.

Finally, the use of supplementary budgets should be very restrictive. Where supplementary budgets during the fiscal year become the norm, as in Belgium and Italy in the 1980s and Germany and Japan in the 1990s, one cannot expect that policy makers will take the constraints embedded in the original budget law seriously.

Contracts

Under the contracts approach, the budgeting process starts with an agreement on a set of binding fiscal targets negotiated among the members of the executive. Emphasis here is on the bargaining process as a mechanism to reveal the externalities involved in budget decisions and on the binding nature of the targets. In contrast to the hierarchical structure created by delegation, the contracts approach relies on a more equal distribution of strategic powers in the executive. A prime example is the Danish budgeting process, which, since 1982, has started with negotiations among the cabinet members to fix spending limits for each spending department. Often, these spending limits are derived from medium-term fiscal programs or the coalition agreement among the ruling parties. For example, Irish coalition agreements since 1989 have regularly included medium-term fiscal strategies to reduce the public debt, and these strategies have provided the background to the annual negotiations over budget targets. Furthermore, the negotiations leading to the fiscal targets often include the leaders of the parties supporting the government in the legislature, in addition to the members of the executive.

The finance ministry's role under this approach is to evaluate the consistency of the individual departments' spending plans with these targets. As in the Netherlands, for example, the finance minister usually has an information advantage over the spending ministers in the budget negotiations but no extra strategic powers. Conflict resolution involves senior cabinet committees and often the leaders of the coalition parties in the legislature.

At the legislative stage, the contracts approach places less weight on the executive's role as an agenda setter and more weight on the role of the legislature as a monitor of the faithful implementation of the fiscal targets. Institutionally, this means that the contracts approach relies less on the executive branch of government controlling parliamentary amendments and more on the legislature's ability to monitor the fiscal performance of the executive. This ability depends on the legislature's right to request information from the executive. It can be strengthened by setting up committees with the same authorities as the spending departments, with the formal right to request information from the executive and to call witnesses from the executive to testify. The Danish parliament, for example, has all three of these rights, whereas the German parliament has only the first, and the U.K. parliament has none of the three.

At the implementation stage, the contracts approach resembles the delegation approach in emphasizing the monitoring and control powers of the finance minister. However, the contracts approach achieves flexibility to react to unforeseen budgetary developments less by giving the finance minister managerial discretion and more by setting up contingent rules for dealing with such events. For example, the Swedish government adopted a budgeting process in the early 1990s that allows spending departments to charge expenditures against future budgets or to transfer unused appropriations to the next year. Transfers are possible, however, for only a limited number of years. Because the charges and transfers must be budgeted in the following year, the provision combines flexibility with transparency and gives both the legislature and the finance minister the ability to control the flow of expenditures.

Esfahani (2000) reports that finance ministries in developing countries often have the authority to slash expenditures during the implementation stage in order to keep spending in line with revenues. Such authority is regarded as an effective way of dealing with revenue shortfalls and expenditure shocks. Such a strong position of the finance minister could be consistent with both the delegation and the contracts approach. Importantly, however, a strong position of the finance minister in the implementation stage must not be seen as a way to correct institutional weaknesses—and the resulting bias toward excessive spending and deficits—at the earlier stages of the budgeting process. The spending ministries and the members of parliament would anticipate the finance ministry's behavior at the implementation stage and use overly optimistic revenue forecasts and unrealistically high cost estimates to increase their spending allocations ex ante. The result would be low transparency and effectiveness of the budgeting process. Furthermore, the finance ministry would not necessarily set the priorities in slashing expenditures in line with the government's political and economic goals. An effective budgeting process requires strong centralization based on either delegation or contracts at all stages.

A rich body of empirical research exists today showing that centralization of the budget process promotes fiscal discipline. This research has analyzed the link between budgeting institutions and fiscal performance in EU countries, European transition economies, Japan and other Asian countries, and Latin American countries, as well as subnational governments in Argentina and the United States.[8]

Delegation, Contracts, and Electoral Systems

The delegation approach relies on hierarchical structures within the executive and between the executive and the legislature. In contrast, the contracts approach builds on a more even distribution of authorities in government. In democratic settings, hierarchical structures typically prevail within political parties, while relations between parties are more even. This difference suggests that the key to the institutional choice between the two approaches lies in the number of parties in government.

Parliamentary systems

In parliamentary systems, delegation is the proper approach to centralization for single-party governments, whereas contracts are the proper approach for multiparty coalition governments (Hallerberg and von Hagen 1998, 1999). There are two reasons for this statement.

First, members of the same political party are more likely to have similar political views regarding the basic spending priorities than are members of different political parties. Spending ministers in a one-party government can, therefore, be fairly sure that the finance minister holds more or less the same spending preferences they do. Disagreement will be mainly a result of the common pool problem—that is, the perceived cost of distributive policies. In a coalition government, in contrast, cabinet members are likely to have more diverging views regarding the distribution of government spending over different groups of recipients. Agreement on a budget, therefore, involves a compromise between the coalition partners. For a coalition government, delegation of strategic powers to the finance minister would create a new principal-agent problem. A strong finance minister might abuse his or her powers and unduly promote the political interests of his or her own party. The same principal-agent problem does not arise in the contracts approach, because the contracts are negotiated by all cabinet members. Thus, governments formed by two or more parties are more likely to opt for the contracts approach.

Second, delegation and contracts rely on different enforcement mechanisms for the budget agreement. In one-party governments, the ultimate punishment for a spending minister reneging on the budget agreement is dismissal from office. Such punishment is heavy for the individual minister who overspends but generally light for the government as a whole. It can be used because the prime minister is typically the strongest cabinet member in one-party governments and has the authority to select and replace cabinet members. In coalition governments, in contrast, punishments cannot be applied easily to defecting ministers. The coalition agreement sets the distribution of portfolios. Therefore, the prime minister cannot easily dismiss intransigent spending ministers from parties other than his or her own, because that would be regarded as an intrusion into the internal party affairs of coalition partners.

The most important punishment mechanism in coalition governments is the threat of breaking up the coalition if a spending minister reneges on the budget agreement. This punishment is heavy for the entire coalition, because it leads potentially to the death of the government rather than the dismissal of a single individual. The point is illustrated by the fact that fiscal targets are often part of the coalition agreement. The credibility of this enforcement mechanism hinges on two important factors. The first is the existence of alternative coalition partners. If other potential partners exist with whom the aggrieved party can form a coalition, the threat to leave the coalition is clearly more credible than if no alternative coalition partner is available. The second factor is the expected response of the voters, because a coalition may be broken up with the anticipation of new elections.

The different enforcement mechanisms also explain the different relations between the executive and the legislature in the legislative phase of the budgeting process. Single-party governments typically arise in two-party settings such as pre-1994 New Zealand, the United Kingdom, or the United States, where each party is large and party discipline is low. Although the ruling party enjoys a majority, the main concern in the legislative stage of the budgeting process is to limit the scope of defections from the budget proposals by individual members who wish to divert government funds to their electoral districts. Multiparty coalitions, in contrast, typically arise in settings where parties are small and relatively homogeneous and party discipline is strong. In that situation, defections from the budget agreement are a weaker concern, but each party involved in the coalition will want to watch carefully to be sure that the executive sticks to the coalition agreement. The delegation approach, therefore, typically makes the executive a much stronger agenda setter in parliament than the contracts approach, whereas the contracts approach gives more monitoring powers to the legislature.

Finally, the commitment to fiscal targets embedded in the contracts approach is not credible for one-party governments. Consider a single-party government with a weak prime minister and a weak finance minister. Assume that this government announced a set of fiscal targets at the outset of the budgeting process and that some spending ministers renege on the agreement during the implementation phase. Other cabinet members cannot credibly threaten the defectors with dissolving the government because they would punish themselves. Absent a credible threat, the entire cabinet would just walk away from the initial agreement.

In summary, the contracts approach is more likely to be found in countries where coalition governments are the norm, and the delegation approach is more likely to be found in countries where the government is typically formed by a single party.

Presidential systems

Presidential systems of government differ from parliamentary systems in that presidents do not rely directly on the legislature for their position as leader of the executive. Voters can—and often do—support a president from one party while denying that party a majority in the legislature. In Latin American and Caribbean countries from 1990 to 1995, half of the 20 countries with presidential systems had presidents facing opposition-controlled lower houses (Stein, Grisanti, and Talvi 1999). Coordination of budgetary decisions between the executive and legislative branches becomes obviously more difficult when the president and the majority come from two different parties.

The role of the executive in the budgeting process is not much different in presidential systems than in parliamentary ones. The president typically appoints the members of the administration, with confirmation by the legislature where applicable. The structure of the administration thus lends itself more to a delegation approach than to a contracts approach in centralizing the budgeting process. The relationship between the executive and the legislature, however, is often more difficult, because the two are conceived to be more equal than in parliamentary governments.

Centralization in presidential systems then must emphasize two institutional dimensions. One is the internal organization of the legislature. Here, centralization can be achieved by creating strong leadership, through an elevated position of the speaker and through a hierarchical committee structure. For example, the Budget Enforcement Act, passed in the United States under the first Bush administration in the early 1990s, reformed congressional procedures to protect decisions about budgetary parameters reached at the budget summit between the president and the legislature against later modifications. The other dimension regards the relation between the executive and the legislature. The more the constitution puts the two institutions on an equal footing, the more budget agreements between the two must rely on the contracts approach.

Outside enforcement of fiscal discipline

As in other principal-agent relationships, it is possible to pursue enforcement of good fiscal performance with the help of agents who are not directly part of this relationship. In the context of budgetary policies, a number of practices and proposals exist. First, International Monetary Fund (IMF) assistance to countries in financial crises usually comes with the obligation to meet certain fiscal constraints to consolidate the budget. The IMF's enforcement power rests on the threat that the financial assistance will not be disbursed if the fiscal constraints are violated. But this approach has severe limitations. Assistance programs are based on agreements between the IMF and the executive, and the legislature may not feel bound by the agreement. It is, therefore, doubtful that outside enforcement works in political settings where the executive has weak control over the legislature. Furthermore, the approach works only in times of crisis, when public finances are already in disarray. In more normal times, the IMF has little enforcement power, because it has no penalties to impose.

A second approach has been adopted by the European Union. Member states of the European Monetary Union are subject to the Excessive Deficit Procedure and the rules of the Stability and Growth Pact. These two measures define a process under which the European Commission and the European Council of Ministers monitor the fiscal performance of the member states. The process revolves around numerical targets for the annual budget deficit. According to the Maastricht Treaty, member states with excessive deficits can be subject to penalties ranging from public reprimands to financial fines.

So far, the experience with this arrangement has been mixed. Importantly, there is a strong correlation between the institutional design of the budgeting process and the extent to which countries comply with the EU rules and procedures (von Hagen 2006a). Countries that have adopted the contracts approach typically comply very strongly, while countries that have adopted the delegation approach typically do not. The external enforcement agent can strengthen the effectiveness of a fiscal contract in countries where the political environment calls for the contracts approach to deal with the common pool problem. In countries where the delegation approach is the appropriate one, the fiscal targets an external agent seeks to enforce are unlikely to become effective, because they do not fit the design of the domestic budgeting process.

In developing countries, it may be possible to involve the main donor agencies and institutions in the budgeting process as a mechanism of external enforcement. Specifically, the donors could be asked to approve the set of fiscal targets negotiated among the members of the executive at the outset of the annual budgeting process. These targets could in turn be anchored in multiannual fiscal programs subject to the donors' scrutiny. An official approval of these targets by the donors would give these targets additional political weight and protect them against later efforts by domestic interest groups and politicians to unravel the fiscal contract. Compared with outside enforcement by the IMF, this form of involvement would have the advantage of working not only in times of fiscal crises. As in the European case, however, involving the donors as outside enforcement agents can be expected to work only in countries where the contracts approach is appropriate.

Conclusions

Good institutional design of the budgeting process is an important prerequisite of good fiscal performance. This chapter has discussed the main institutional approaches that can be followed to mitigate the principal-agent problem and the common pool problem of public finances.

Budgetary institutions can be designed to reduce the adverse effects of the principal-agent relationship between voters and politicians. The environment in which the budgeting process evolves strongly affects accountability and competitiveness, which are strengthened by ensuring that the budget is comprehensive, that the budgeting process is transparent, and that budgeting is understood as a management exercise and not just a legal one.

The common pool problem of public finances can be reduced by centralizing the budgeting process—that is, by introducing institutional mechanisms that force the actors in the process to take a comprehensive view of the costs and benefits of all public policies. Depending on a country's political system, this goal can be achieved by means of the delegation approach or the contracts approach.

Institutional reform of the budgeting process is, therefore, an important part of a policy aiming at achieving better fiscal outcomes. This does not mean that a change in legal and procedural rules mechanically produces better results. Nevertheless, a large body of research and practical experience now shows that the outcomes of political decision-making processes are systematically shaped by the institutional environments within which these processes evolve and that reforms of the budgeting process have contributed significantly to achieving better fiscal outcomes. In practice, institutional reforms are often the result of acute fiscal crises, of times when there is widespread awareness of the principal-agent and the common pool problems of public finances and a general recognition of the need for change. Better institutions help to make this awareness a durable one and thus serve as a commitment device for good fiscal performance.

Notes

1. For a review of this literature as it relates to fiscal policy, see von Hagen (2006b).
2. Alt and Dreyer-Lassen (2006) operationalize their approach and calculate indexes of transparency that facilitate international comparisons.
3. For a discussion of balanced-budget constraints in the United States and other countries and their effects on fiscal performance, see Canova and Pappa (2005), Fatás and Mihov (2003), Kennedy and Robbins (2001), Kopits (2001), and von Hagen (1991).
4. See Dore and Masson (2002), Emmerson, Frayne, and Love (2002), and Kennedy and Robbins (2001). Daban and others (2001) provide a description of fiscal rules in a variety of countries.
5. For example, Mills and Quinet (2002) report estimates from the Organisation for Economic Co-operation and Development of the output gap in France for 1995. The 1995 estimate was below −3.0 percent, whereas the 1999 estimate was −0.5 percent.
6. For a review of the literature, see von Hagen (2006b).
7. Note that in the current context, centralization refers to the internal organization, not the geographic structure of budgetary decisions.
8. See von Hagen (2006b) for a review of this literature.

References

Alesina, Alberto, Reza Baqir, and William Easterly. 1997. "Public Goods and Ethnic Divisions." NBER Working Paper 6009, National Bureau for Economic Research, Cambridge, MA.

Alesina, Alberto, and Roberto Perotti. 1996. "Fiscal Discipline and the Budget Process." *American Economic Review* 86 (2): 401–7.

Alt, James E., and David Dreyer-Lassen. 2006. "Fiscal Transparency, Political Parties, and Debt in OECD Countries." *European Economic Review* 50 (6): 1403–39.

Annett, Anthony. 2000. "Social Fractionalization, Political Instability, and the Size of Government." IMF Working Paper 00/82, International Monetary Fund, Washington, DC.

Canova, Fabio, and Evi Pappa. 2005. "Does It Cost to Be Virtuous? The Macroeconomic Effects of Fiscal Constraints." NBER Working Paper 11065, National Bureau for Economic Research, Cambridge, MA.

Crain, W. Mark, and James C. Miller. 1990. "Budget Process and Spending Growth." *William and Mary Law Review* 31 (4): 1021–46.

Daban, Teresa, Enrica Detragiache, Gabriel di Belli, Gian Maria Milesi-Ferretti, and Steven Symansky. 2001. "Rules-Based Fiscal Policy and the Fiscal Framework in France, Germany, Italy, and Spain." IMF Occasional Paper 225, International Monetary Fund, Washington, DC.

Dore, Ousmane, and Paul R. Masson. 2002. "Experience with Budgetary Convergence in the WAEMU." IMF Working Paper 02/108, International Monetary Fund, Washington, DC.

Eichengreen, Barry, and Jürgen von Hagen. 1996. "Fiscal Policy and Monetary Union: Federalism, Fiscal Restrictions, and the No-Bailout Rule." In *Monetary Policy in an Integrated World Economy*, ed. Horst Siebert, 211–31. Tübingen, Germany: JCB Mohr.

Emmerson, Carl, Chris Frayne, and Sarah Love. 2002. "The Government's Fiscal Rules." Briefing Note 16, Institute for Fiscal Studies, London.

Esfahani, Hadi Salehi. 2000. "What Can We Learn from Budget Institutions Details?" Department of Economics, University of Illinois, Urbana-Champaign, IL.

Fatás, Antonio, Andrew Hughes Hallett, Anne Sibert, Rolf R. Strauch, and Jürgen von Hagen. 2003. *Stability and Growth in Europe: Towards a Better Pact*. Monitoring European Integration Vol. 13. London: Centre for Economic Policy Research.

Fatás, Antonio, and Ilian Mihov. 2003. "The Case for Restricting Fiscal Policy Discretion." *Quarterly Journal of Economics* 118 (4): 1419–48.

Hallerberg, Mark, Rolf R. Strauch, and Jürgen von Hagen. 2001. "The Use and Effectiveness of Budgetary Rules and Norms in EU Member States." Report prepared for the Dutch Ministry of Finance, Zentrum für Europäische Integrationsforschung, Bonn.

Hallerberg, Mark, and Jürgen von Hagen. 1998. "Electoral Institutions and the Budget Process." In *Democracy, Decentralization, and Deficits in Latin America*, ed. Kiichiro Fukasaku and Ricardo Hausmann, 65–94. Paris: Organisation for Economic Cooperation and Development.

———. 1999. "Electoral Institutions, Cabinet Negotiations, and Budget Deficits in the EU." In *Fiscal Institutions and Fiscal Performance*, ed. James Poterba and Jürgen von Hagen, 209–32. Chicago: University of Chicago Press.

Kennedy, Suzanne, and Janine Robbins. 2001. "The Role of Fiscal Rules in Determining Fiscal Performance." Working Paper 2001-16, Department of Finance, Ottawa.

Kiewiet, D. Roderick, and Kristin Szakaly. 1996. "Constitutional Limitations on Borrowing: An Analysis of State Bonded Indebtedness." *Journal of Law, Economics, and Organization* 12 (1): 62–97.

Kontopoulos, Yianos, and Roberto Perotti. 1999. "Government Fragmentation and Fiscal Policy Outcomes: Evidence from OECD Countries." In *Fiscal Institutions and Fiscal Performance*, ed. James Poterba and Jürgen von Hagen, 81–102. Chicago: University of Chicago Press.

Kopits, George. 2001. "Fiscal Rules: Useful Policy Framework or Unnecessary Ornament?" IMF Working Paper 01/145, International Monetary Fund. Washington, DC.

Kopits, George, and Jon Craig. 1998. "Transparency in Government Operations." IMF Occasional Paper 158, International Monetary Fund, Washington, DC.

Milesi-Ferretti, Gian Maria. 2004. "Good, Bad, or Ugly? On the Effects of Fiscal Rules with Creative Accounting." *Journal of Public Economics* 88 (1–2): 377–94.

Mills, Philippe, and Alain Quinet. 2002. "How to Allow the Automatic Stabilizers to Operate Fully? A Policy-Maker's Guide for EMU Countries." In *The Behavior of Fiscal Authorities—Stabilization, Growth, and Institutions*, ed. Marco Buti, Jürgen von Hagen, and Carlos Martinez-Mongay, 115–29. Houndmills, U.K.: Palgrave.

Persson, Torsten, Gerard Roland, and Guido Tabellini. 1997. "Separation of Powers and Political Accountability." *Quarterly Journal of Economics* 112 (4): 1163–202.

Persson, Torsten, and Guido Tabellini. 2000. *Political Economics: Explaining Economic Policy*. Cambridge, MA: MIT Press.

Poterba, James, and Jürgen von Hagen. 1999. "Introduction." In *Fiscal Institutions and Fiscal Performance*, ed. James Poterba and Jürgen von Hagen, 1–12. Chicago: University of Chicago Press.

Roubini, Nouriel, and Jeffrey D. Sachs. 1989. "Political and Economic Determinants of Budget Deficits in the Industrial Democracies." *European Economic Review* 33 (5): 903–38.

Rueben, Kim. 1997 "Tax Limitations and Government Growth: The Effect of State Tax and Expenditure Limits on State and Local Government." Public Policy Institute of California, San Francisco.

Seabright, Paul. 1996. "Accountability and Decentralization in Government: An Incomplete Contracts Model." *European Economic Review* 40 (1): 61–89.

Shadbegian, Ronald J. 1996. "Do Tax and Expenditure Limitations Affect the Size and Growth of State Government?" *Contemporary Economic Policy* 14 (1): 22–35.

Skilling, David, and Richard J. Zeckhauser. 2002. "Political Competition and Debt Trajectories in Japan and the OECD." *Japan and the World Economy* 14 (2): 121–35.

Stein, Ernesto, Alejandro Grisanti, and Ernesto Talvi. 1999. "Institutional Arrangements and Fiscal Performance: The Latin American Experience." In *Fiscal Institutions and Fiscal Performance*, ed. James Poterba and Jürgen von Hagen, 103–34. Chicago: University of Chicago Press.

Strauch, Rolf R. 1998. "Budget Processes and Fiscal Discipline: Evidence from the U.S. States." Zentrum für Europäische Integrationsforschung, Bonn.

Velasco, Andrés. 2000. "Debts and Deficits with Fragmented Fiscal Policymaking." *Journal of Public Policymaking* 76 (1): 105–25.

von Hagen, Jürgen. 1991. "A Note on the Empirical Effectiveness of Formal Fiscal Restraints." *Journal of Public Economics* 44 (2): 199–210.

———. 2006a. "Fiscal Rules and Fiscal Performance in the EU and Japan." *Monetary and Economic Studies* 14: 25–60.

———.2006b. "Political Economy of Fiscal Institutions." In *The Oxford Handbook of Political Economy*, ed. Barry Weingast and Donald Wittman, 464–78. Oxford, U.K.: Oxford University Press.

von Hagen, Jürgen, and Ian J. Harden. 1995. "Budget Processes and Commitment to Fiscal Discipline." *European Economic Review* 39 (3): 771–79.

von Hagen, Jürgen, and Guntram B. Wolff. 2006. "What Do Deficits Tell Us about Debt? Empirical Evidence on Creative Accounting with Fiscal Rules in the EU." *Journal of Banking and Finance* 30 (12): 3259–79.

Weaver, R. Kent. 1986. "The Politics of Blame Avoidance." *Journal of Public Policy* 6 (4): 371–98.

The Budget and Its Coverage

SALVATORE SCHIAVO-CAMPO

The government budget is often viewed as a purely technical assemblage of words and numbers, to be left to the bureaucrats and a few politicians. In reality the government budget is at the center of public policy and the development prospects of a country. Under legitimate governance, the government is expected to fulfill the roles and respect the limitations decided by society. Those roles are articulated into policy objectives—quantitative ones, such as raising the literacy rate by a certain amount, or qualitative ones, such as correcting market imperfections. Some of these policy objectives may be met by issuing regulations or prescriptions, granting loan guarantees, or intervening in other ways that do not require direct and immediate expenditure. Most policy objectives, however, require financial resources, which can come only from the public in the form of taxes and fees—and, for most African countries, are complemented by aid from external partners.

The fundamental principle of fiscal management in countries with good governance is that the executive branch of government can neither take moneys from the public nor make any expenditure from those moneys, except by explicit approval of the legislature as the representative organ of the citizens. Consequently, properly understood, the budget should be the financial mirror of society's economic and social choices and, thus, at the very center of the country's governance structure. As such, the budget is anything but a mere technical document and should reflect all components of good governance.

Good Governance and Public Expenditure Management

Good governance rests on four pillars: accountability, transparency, predictability, and participation. *Accountability* means the capacity to call public officials to task for their actions. *Transparency* entails low-cost access to relevant information. *Predictability* results primarily from laws and regulations that are clear, known in advance, and uniformly and effectively enforced. *Participation* is needed to generate consensus, supply reliable information, and provide a reality check for government action. These concepts are universal in application but relative in nature. Accountability is a must, but it does not become operational until one defines accountability of whom, for what, and to whom. Transparency can be problematic when it infringes on necessary confidentiality or privacy. Full compliance with regulations is not a great advantage if the regulations are inefficient. And it is evidently impossible to provide for participation by everybody in everything and unwise to use participation as an excuse to avoid making tough but necessary decisions. It is also clear that none of these four components can stand by itself: each is instrumental in achieving the other three, and all four together are instrumental in achieving sound development management. For example, accountability mechanisms in the budget process are hollow if financial information is not reliable, and they are meaningless without predictable consequences.

In public expenditure management, a lack of predictability of financial resources undermines strategic prioritization and makes it hard for public officials to plan for the provision of services (and gives them an excellent alibi for nonperformance, to boot). Predictability of government expenditure in the aggregate and in the various sectors is also needed as a signpost to guide the private sector in making its own production, marketing, and investment decisions. And budgetary rules must be clear and uniformly applied to everyone.

Transparency of fiscal and financial information is a must for an informed executive, legislature, and public. Normally, it takes place through the filters of a competent legislative staff and capable and independent public media. It is essential not only that information be provided, but that it be relevant and in understandable form. Dumping immense amounts of raw budgetary material on the public does nothing to improve fiscal transparency. The IMF (International Monetary Fund) Code of Good Practices on Fiscal Transparency underlines the importance of clear fiscal roles and responsibilities; public availability of information; open processes of budget preparation, execution, and reporting; and independent reviews and assurance of the integrity of fiscal forecasts, information, and accounts (IMF 2001). (Although not all

African countries can meet all aspects of the IMF Code at this time, its principles are generally applicable, and progress toward achieving its standards should be a major objective of budget reform in Africa.)

Participation, in appropriate ways, can improve the quality of budgetary decisions and provide an essential reality check for their implementation. Predictability, transparency, and participation, in turn, are the essential ingredients of accountability, which is the key to good budgeting (and good government in general). Accountability entails both the obligation to render accounts of how the budgetary resources have been used and the possibility of significant consequences for satisfactory or unsatisfactory performance.

The Meaning of Fiduciary Risk in Public Finance

In recent years, the major international development agencies have become concerned about the fiduciary risk of development assistance, partly but not exclusively in relation to the Heavily Indebted Poor Countries (HIPC) initiative. The notion of fiduciary risk in public expenditure is grounded on the basic governance principle that no funds can be mobilized from the citizens—or spent—without the explicit approval of their elected representatives. Thus, the executive branch has a fiduciary responsibility to the country to ensure that the budget is executed as approved by the legislature, and *fiduciary risk* can be defined as the risk that government expenditures diverge from those authorized in the budget (World Bank 2003). In this sense, fiduciary risk in African countries was high until recently; it has been reduced somewhat by a variety of measures advocated by the international community, particularly in the context of HIPC debt relief.

Other, more expansive definitions of *fiduciary risk*—for example, that of the U.K. Department for International Development (DFID)—add to the risks of misappropriation and misallocation the additional risk that the budgeted resources are either wasted or spent ineffectively. By this broader definition, in most African countries public financial management has a long way to go before fiduciary risk can be brought down to acceptable levels: efficiency and effectiveness call for longer-term and sustained capacity-building measures, as discussed later.

The Unity of the Budget

It is clear that it is impossible for the government budget to reflect the preferences and choices of society and to incorporate the principles of good governance if it includes only a small proportion of revenues and expenditures.

In such cases, the legislature can review and approve only some of the activities for which the expenditures are made. The lack of information on the other expenditures may lead to abuses of executive power and provides a wide opening for corruption and a large-scale theft of public resources. Two major issues are involved here: first, if the budget excludes major expenditures, there can be no assurance that scarce resources are appropriately allocated to priority programs and that legal control and public accountability are properly enforced. Only if all proposed expenditures are on the table at the same time does it become possible to review them in relation to one another and to choose those that have higher relative benefits for the community. Second, the amount of expenditures that are not included is itself often uncertain and opaque. In turn, this uncertainty makes macroeconomic programming more difficult and increases the risk of corruption and waste. Imagine that, as the head of a household, you have large sources of income in addition to your salary but discuss with your family the allocation of only your salary. At best, even if the additional income is allocated well, family members cannot cooperate in making sure that it is spent well, nor can they feel any responsibility for mistakes in this respect. At worst, the additional income will be frittered away on frivolous expenditures, with adverse impacts on the family's future finances and well-being.

For all these reasons, the budget should in principle cover all transactions financed through public financial resources. Budget comprehensiveness does not mean that all expenditures should be managed according to the same set of procedures. In practice, as discussed later, certain categories of transactions may need to be administered separately from the overall government budget. For efficiency, specific arrangements may be established for administering some programs financed through public resources, provided that they are not allowed to lead to a fragmented approach to budgeting and expenditure policy formulation.

Coverage, Periodicity, and Definitions

The requirements of good governance, fiduciary responsibility, and budget unity are reflected in certain practical principles for the coverage of the budget, its annuality, and the guiding concepts.

The Coverage of the Budget

The coverage of the budget naturally depends on the scope of activities of the government, as decided, directly and indirectly, by the society it represents. Whatever revenues and expenditures are included in the budget, it is important to review them and present them together. Government policy objectives can be achieved through tax policy, through public expenditure policy, or through a combination of the two. Therefore, direct comparisons are needed of the costs and benefits of alternative revenue and expenditure packages. Moreover, a sound program of public expenditure requires as a starting point a realistic estimate of revenue. This is because the choices among different expenditure proposals, choices that are at the center of the budgeting process, cannot be made without a clear idea of how much money is likely to be available. An expenditure program that does not conform to a realistic limit on resources available is a wish list, not a program, and the budget that contains it is only a bulky paper document. That being said, this chapter focuses on the expenditure side.

The Annuality of the Budget

Obviously, the legislature's approval to collect revenue and spend it cannot be given on a weekly or monthly basis, or for an indefinite period of time. In almost all countries, the budget covers 12 months and both the government's revenue-collecting authority and its spending authorization expire at the end of the fiscal year. (This fiscal, or financial, year is usually but not always the calendar year.) The annuality rule is justified both by the need for legislative control of the executive and—especially in developing countries—by fluid economic circumstances, which would make budgeting for two or more years totally impractical. The annual nature of the budget is often confused with the multiyear periodicity of the medium-term expenditure frameworks (MTEFs) used in many countries to frame the annual budget process. It is important to keep in mind the distinction between the legislative authorization to spend, which covers only one fiscal year, and the multiyear forecasts and intentions of the MTEF. There is no such thing as a multiyear budget anywhere in the developing world.

Some Definitions

To understand the following discussion, it is important to understand the meanings of *budget* and *government*.

The budget

The word "budget" comes from *budjet*, a Middle English word for the king's purse. The meaning of the term has, of course, changed since the days when a country's resources were deemed to be the personal property of the king, along with the political evolution from absolute monarchies to constitutional governments. In most countries today, including a majority of African countries, approval of the budget (the "power of the purse") is the main form of legislative control over the executive, with public money spent only under the law. And public money *should* be spent only under the law. In a few African countries, however, the public perception persists that some of the country's resources are the personal property of the leader or of the ruling group. This perception should progressively be dispelled and executive accountability should be established as the system evolves toward greater legitimacy and better governance. Here again, the public expenditure management system can be seen as both cause and effect of the overall governance climate in a country.

The government

The general government includes all government authorities and their instrumentalities and comprises three categories of government:

1. *Central government* includes all governmental departments, establishments, and other bodies that are instruments of the central authority of a country, plus the extensions of central government authority that operate at the regional or local level but lack the attributes necessary for existence as separate government units.
2. *Local government* consists of governmental units that exercise independent competence in the various urban and rural jurisdictions of a country's territory, including counties, cities, towns, school districts, and the like. An entity is treated as local government only if it is entitled to own assets and raise funds, has some discretion in its spending, and is able to appoint its own officers independently of external administration. These are the key differences between decentralization, which entails devolution of policy authority and deconcentration, by which the authority of the center is exercised more effectively through local entities acting as agents of the central government.
3. *State governments* are intermediate subnational entities in federal countries (for example, Australia, India, and Nigeria). In unitary countries, the intermediate level of government is usually called a *province*.

For decentralized or autonomous agencies, the nature of their function and the source of their authority constitute the criteria for assessing the level of government at which they belong (for example, a hospital managed by the central ministry of health, wherever it is located, is part of the central government).

The basic principle of national budgeting is that each level of the government should have its own budget to cover its own sphere of activity and responsibility. Most countries, including those in Africa, generally have and enforce clear revenue and expenditure assignments. However, in a few African countries (and in several transition economies of the former Soviet Union), the division of revenue and expenditure responsibilities is either unclear or not observed in practice: parallel systems of revenue collection or of informal expenditure are superimposed on the formal systems. In these cases, the distribution of responsibilities among the different levels of the government must be clarified and stable and transparent arrangements are needed to ensure that it is respected in practice.

Sound analysis of a country's fiscal stance and prospects calls for looking at general government rather than only central government. Indeed, attention to central government generates the temptation to download fiscal difficulties onto subnational levels of government by decentralizing expenditure responsibilities without decentralizing the revenue to go with them. This downloading masks real problems for some time, until they surface in a more virulent form owing to the lack of policy attention. The risk is especially acute in African countries, where fiscal data from levels of government below the central government may not be available in a timely and reliable fashion.

The public sector

In addition to general government, the public sector includes entities that are majority owned by the government, such as state-owned enterprises or state financial institutions. In market economies, state enterprises should be commercially oriented and thus have a separate legal persona and full operational autonomy. As such, their expenditures and revenues cannot be submitted to the same scrutiny and approval mechanisms as the government budget. The budget should include the financial transactions between the state enterprises and the government but not their transactions with the rest of the economy, for which the government is not directly responsible.[1] However, a financial approach should be developed for the public sector as a whole. Thus, the budget can show the consolidated account of the public sector (sometimes called the *consolidated budget*, although it does not have the legal status of the government budget) in an analytical table, presented for information only. In any event, for accountability and transparency, the government should report regularly on the performance and the financial situation of both financial and nonfinancial state enterprises.

Principles of Expenditure Policy Choices and of Budget Coverage

Because the budget, as noted, should be the mirror of society's choices, the expenditure management mechanism should include strong links between the policies that are decided by government and the budget that is intended to implement them.

The Policy-Budget Link

For the link between resource allocation and policies to be a strong one, the policy choices themselves must first meet certain basic criteria. Decision-making authority belongs to the political leadership of the country. With that authority, however, comes the responsibility to make sound decisions. The main criteria of good decision making (loosely related to the components of good governance) are the following:

- *Discipline*. Policies should be consistent, without internal contradictions.
- *Realism*. Policies should be affordable and implementable.
- *Stability*. Frequent policy reversals should be avoided: a clear vision and sense of direction for the medium term are necessary for good policy making.
- *Openness and clarity*. Although the deliberations leading to budgetary policy decisions must usually be confidential, political accountability requires that the criteria and processes of decision making be explicit and public.
- *Selectivity*. In developing countries, the capacity to make good policy decisions is perhaps the scarcest resource of all. Because the focus ought to be on important issues, an appropriate administrative mechanism is needed to filter out minor matters and prevent wasting political leaders' time and attention.
- *Communication*. A badly understood policy cannot be implemented and is unlikely to be properly reflected in the budget.

Minimum Rules of Budget Presentation and Classification

To successfully link revenues and expenditure allocations to government policies, the budget must follow a number of practical rules that apply to every program financed in whole or in part by public resources, whether managed within the budget or separately:

- Estimates of revenue and expenditures should be shown in the budget in gross terms. Netting out these estimates would give a misleading impression of the importance of the transactions—as when a very small net surplus hides huge expenditures and slightly larger revenues and, thus, prevents appropriate scrutiny of the transactions.

- Expenditures and revenues should be classified on the same basis as the overall budget in order to permit comparisons of relative efficiency and for accountability.
- All accounts must be subject to regular external audit.
- Financial reports of government activities should consolidate the operations of autonomous funds and agencies with regular budget operations.

Extrabudgetary Funds

In many countries, a significant share of public expenditure is managed through special arrangements outside the normal budgetary management arrangements. These special arrangements, which are known as *extrabudgetary funds* (EBFs), are used, for example, when existing budgetary procedures are inappropriate for managing particular types of activity, when such procedures do not allow spending agencies to use revenues from cost recovery, or when certain priority expenditures need protection. In the clear definition provided by the IMF Code of Fiscal Transparency, EBFs are government operations that are set up outside the annual budget appropriations process. The dividing line is thus clear: if transactions involving public financial resources are not subject to the same legislative approval process as the annual budget, they are outside the budget. However, they are not outside the bounds of legislative authority and oversight: the fundamental requirement of authorization by the people's representatives is still met if the legislature approves the establishment of the EBF—provided that (a) the delegation of revenue and spending authority is made for specific purposes and under clear criteria; (b) EBF governance arrangements are satisfactory and explicit; and (c) transparent information on the financial operations of the EBF is regularly included in the annual budget documentation, although it is not subject to annual approval.

Reasons for Creating EBFs

The reasons for creating EBFs depend on the country. They may include protecting priority expenditures from budget cuts; avoiding implementation problems in budget execution; sidestepping some appropriation management rules in the interest of powerful politicians or lobbies; insulating donors' projects and programs in priority sectors at their request; and, in some cases, hiding transactions from public or legislative scrutiny, usually to permit theft and abuse. Specifically, there are four main reasons:

1. To bypass budgetary procedures when they are not suitable to certain categories of expenditures. In many African countries, traditional appropriation rules, such as virements (transfers between line items) or the cancellation of appropriations at the end of the fiscal year, are too rigid for efficient management of specific programs (see chapter 9). In these cases, introducing greater flexibility in the budgetary rules would reduce the need to set up special arrangements.
2. To purchase goods that will be delivered at some future time, for which the payment would otherwise be jeopardized by the budget annuality rule. Departmental enterprises, for example, need such revolving funds to carry out their trading activities.
3. To allow managerial flexibility and for institutional reasons, such as the special status of certain professions or activities (notably in higher education). Autonomous entities exist in many countries for those purposes. The entities are financed mainly by transfers from the budget of the central government, but they also have their own budget (called an *annexed budget* in some countries). Universities, with their own resources from tuition and other fees, fall in this category.
4. To improve service delivery by separating it from policy formulation. Thus, a few industrial countries have created autonomous agencies (sometimes called *executive agencies*) and established contractual relations with the competent line ministry. This approach generally has not proven suitable to many industrial countries, let alone to the institutional landscape and administrative capacity of developing countries. In very specific instances, however, setting up a separate agency could improve operational efficiency, provided that the arrangement is designed with great care and is monitored very closely.

The Costs and Risks of EBFs

EBFs pose a variety of problems and risks for the allocation of resources and for the integrity of the budget:

■ Transactions outside the budget are not subject to the same kind of fiscal discipline as budget operations, partly because they "carry their own money" and partly because they are not explicitly compared with other expenditures. Consequently, activities that would not normally survive the scrutiny of a regular budget process often continue because of inertia or vested interests.

- Transactions made from EBFs are often not classified according to the same system as budgetary expenditures, which hampers a sound analysis of the overall government expenditure program. This difference in classification can lead to loss of expenditure control and less efficient allocation of resources.
- The lack of transparency generates governance and efficiency risks.
- EBFs make the expenditure program dependent on specific revenues and can lead to a misallocation of resources—with excessive spending simply because the funds are available—or to shortages because the activities in question do not benefit from general tax revenues.
- Most troublesome is that earmarking makes expenditure decisions subject not to efficiency criteria but to the ability of politicians and lobbies to secure protection for their favored programs.
- Finally, EBFs tend to proliferate over time: the existence of an EBF in one ministry is often used by other ministries to justify their right to earmark revenues and set up their own special funds. This situation can reach the point where ministers' status and self-respect depend on having an EBF of their own. (This was the state of affairs in the early 1990s in Turkey, for example, before the major improvements of the past decade.) Eventually, the budgeting system becomes totally fragmented, and the government loses this essential instrument of economic policy. However, as we will discuss, earmarking can be desirable in specific cases and under some precise conditions.

The proliferation of EBFs leads directly to an important operational implication: the need to build in robust gatekeeping mechanisms, both political and technical ones, to reduce the probability that unjustified EBFs will slip under the radar and eventually weaken the integrity of the budgeting system. Once again, there is a connection between the overall quality of governance in the country and the EBF issue. In conditions of perfect governance, a plethora of EBFs may not be a major problem; in conditions of extremely weak governance, a fully unified budget would not be a solution. However, the tendency of EBFs to proliferate presents a clear risk, in time, to even a good governance system.

Approaches to Dealing with EBFs

For all these reasons, the standard advice of international organizations to developing countries has been to avoid creating EBFs and to eliminate them as quickly as possible when they do exist. In principle, when the normal budgetary arrangements are unsuitable for managing certain types of transactions, the optimal policy response is to improve the budgetary procedures, to set up specific procedures for those particular transactions, or to do both, rather than placing the transactions themselves outside the budget process. In practice, especially in developing countries, earmarking arrangements, separate funds, or autonomous management may be desirable to improve efficiency in public spending.

Nevertheless, EBFs are a common feature of budgetary systems almost everywhere. In industrial countries, nonbudgetary functions account, on average, for about one-third of total government expenditures (mostly for pensions, which account for about 90 percent of nonbudgetary expenditures). In African developing countries, the importance of pension EBFs is much lower, but other extrabudgetary expenditures are much higher, and EBFs account for between one-fifth and two-fifths of total spending (the variation between countries is much greater than in industrial countries).[2] Thus, an alternative to avoiding EBFs is to distinguish between different types of EBFs and make provisions to manage them and reduce their attendant risks. This pragmatic and sensible approach is taken in a recent study by Richard Allen and Dimitar Radev (forthcoming).

The bottom line is that budgetary management authority must not be allowed to lead to loss of expenditure control or erosion of financial integrity. Thus, the standards of scrutiny and accountability for expenditures financed from funds, autonomous agencies, or special accounts should be no lower than those applied to other expenditures. To verify that EBFs meet these standards, their gross financial transactions must be regularly included in the budget documentation even if no legislative approval is sought.

Types of Special Arrangements

EBFs come in many forms, the main types of which are discussed in turn below, beginning with the most frequent, social security funds.

Social security funds

Social security covers a variety of services classified into three broad categories:

1. Social insurance, which is generally financed with contributions from employers and employees and yields benefits linked to the contributions
2. Direct provision of a service or cash payment to a defined group of beneficiaries, such as family allowances, pensions, and maternity grants
3. Social assistance—that is, payments or services contingent on investigation of the needs and financial status of the beneficiary (assistance to the elderly, handicapped, jobless, and so on).

The compulsory nature of social insurance and its far-reaching social, economic, and financial implications call for the inclusion of social security funds in the budget. A possible exception exists for countries in which management of these funds also involves employers and employee unions. It could be difficult to integrate into the budget those social security funds that are not directly managed by government entities. Nevertheless, because social security funds may cover a significant share of government expenditures, they should at least be consolidated in a financial report, and their budget should be annexed to the budget of the central government.

Funds managed by the ministry of finance

Many treasury departments hold special accounts (for example, in India, Indonesia, Japan, and the Republic of Korea). Some of these accounts are used to manage EBFs placed under the authority of the ministry of finance or line ministries. They therefore pose the same problems as other EBFs, as regards allocation of resources. In some cases, transactions made through these special accounts concern internal financial transfers within the government, rather than true expenditures. To some extent, these accounts are comparable to a common treasury account in which internal transactions are accounted for separately. However, such arrangements are complicated and time consuming, and they provide an opportunity for opaque expenditures.

"Black boxes" and parallel budgets

In some countries, revenue from natural resources is treated more as a contribution to the purse of the president or to a political slush fund or "black box" than as a contribution to the government budget. Secrecy about revenues from oil resources and their uses is still common. In some developing countries in the 1970s, revenues from commodity boards were used to set up a parallel budget, which was not submitted to any scrutiny. Including these revenues and expenditures in the budget is a prerequisite to improving transparency and governance. Although there could be a few exceptions (for example, for security reasons), there is never a good reason for secrecy concerning revenues and rarely a good reason for secrecy concerning expenditures. Thus, although exceptions are possible, the existence of black boxes or secrecy about revenues should be interpreted as prima facie evidence of weaknesses in governance or outright corruption.

In many countries, there is also a general tendency to allocate windfall revenues and some nontax revenues to particular programs. This tendency hampers adequate prioritization of expenditure programs. From a fiscal sustainability viewpoint, the optimal (and safest) use of windfall revenues is to pay off the more expensive types of debt in the government's portfolio. Under unusual circumstances and for specified and basic human needs (such as drought relief and crash vaccination programs), it may be appropriate to assign windfall revenues to those needs. Before the actual expenditures are made, however, sound and well-designed administrative arrangements must be in place.

Aid-financed expenditures

In the 1970s and 1980s, expenditures that were financed with tied external loans or grants were routinely omitted from the budgets of aid-recipient countries. Progress has been made toward better coverage of externally financed expenditures in the budget, although in many African countries the budgetary coverage of grants, technical assistance, and expenditures financed by external loans often remains incomplete. The motivation—or rationalization—for ring-fencing project aid funds in a country is allegedly the ineffectiveness of the budget system. In practice, however, the ring-fencing itself (and the problematic project implementation units it requires) is often ineffective even at protecting the aid resources and is itself a cause of continued budgeting weaknesses.

Enclaving a large portion of aid moneys outside the budget weakens the incentive for the recipient government to improve its budgeting system. And enclaving does not motivate donors to move away from ring-fencing their project aid, when they can live under the delusion that the ring-fencing fully protects the resources and their use. In any case, project aid can and should be accounted for in the budget—as has been shown most recently in a budget system as conflict damaged as Burundi's—even if separate arrangements are made for its administration. In sum, there is bound to be a need in many countries to continue special arrangements to manage certain project aid funds. These arrangements must be considered strictly transitional, however; they must not be allowed to interfere with the clear priority to support the improvement in the budget system that will render them unnecessary. Donors have a key responsibility to facilitate the incorporation of these expenditures into the budgets of recipient countries.

Expenditures financed from counterpart funds generated by sales of commodity aid also must be managed under specific procedures, mandated by requirements of the donors. That such tying of counterpart funds is generally inefficient does not relieve the recipient country of the burden of satisfying donor requirements. (Whether the aid should be accepted in the first place, given these restrictions and the risk of an adverse impact on local production of close substitutes for the imported commodities, is a different issue.)

Expenditures financed from counterpart funds must be included in the budget, but specific rules are needed to manage them (for example, exemption from the annuality rule and a flexible spending limit linked to the amount of revenues collected from the sales of commodities).

Road funds

The fact that road users are identifiable and that they bear some taxes (such as gasoline taxes) is used to justify earmarking arrangements for road maintenance or construction. Road funds have been set up in many developing countries. Some are simple accounting arrangements, while others finance the provision of services. The main objective has been to insulate from the vagaries of the budget the maintenance and development of roads—a crucial priority, especially in Africa. Unfortunately, the generally disappointing experience with road funds in the 1970s and 1980s has led to the conclusion that, with some qualifications, they ought to be avoided (McCleary 1991). Not only did road funds reduce fiscal transparency and provide openings for misappropriation and inefficiency, when money was tight, the earmarked funds were also often diverted to other uses and were no longer available for their original purpose. Thus, the existence of road funds did not even guarantee an appropriate mix of maintenance, rehabilitation, and new investment in roads. Box 2.1 describes the experience of Ghana.

Taking that experience into account, the World Bank developed the concept of second-generation road funds in the mid-1990s, again with a special focus on Africa (Heggie 1995; Pennant-Rae and Heggie 1995; and, more recently, Potter 2005).This concept was inspired by the "agency model" developed in some Organisation for Economic Co-operation and Development (OECD) member countries. The main features of the approach are to involve road users in the management of roads, to define responsibilities for all parties, to set up an autonomous and independent board with private participation, to establish clear accountability rules, and to set up and devise charging instruments related to road use that are easy to separate from other taxes and simple to administer (such as tolls).

The effectiveness of this approach depends on several critical issues: whether good governance and anticorruption requirements are met; whether the board of directors represents consumer and the public interest rather than being captured by contractor and producer interests; the degree to which the funds are fully protected for roads rather than merely being a convenient parking place for money that can be diverted elsewhere; how the more demanding financial management requirements are handled; whether there is a robust independent audit of fund operations; and, of course, whether

> ### BOX 2.1   Ghana: A First-Generation Road Fund
>
> The road fund in Ghana was established in 1985, as part of a program of road maintenance and rehabilitation supported by the World Bank. Twelve years later, the country still had not been able to create the basis for sustainable road maintenance financing.
>
> Financing from the fund has been unstable, generating unpredictability in funding that has made it difficult to plan properly and issue contracts on a timely basis. In turn, some have used the lack of funding predictability as an excuse for inaction or as a way to short-circuit the procurement procedures for various vested interests. As a result, significant portions of the road network in Ghana remained in very poor condition at the end of the past century.
>
> In the mid-1990s, the government decided to increase the fuel tax sufficiently to fully finance the road fund. Overcoming the internal difficulties, including getting the treasury to agree to this graduated path of sustainable financing, was a significant accomplishment. Thus, to avoid passing all the proposed increase in the fuel levy directly and immediately on to consumers, the treasury agreed to cede some of its other excise tax revenues to the road fund, thereby keeping fuel taxes at basically the same level even though the proportion earmarked for the road fund increased.
>
> A key lesson from the Ghanaian experience—shared by many other African countries—is that setting up a fund is insufficient in itself to ensure financing for road maintenance. It is essential to create a board of directors with enough authority and independence to resist raids on the fund by other government entities. Moreover, when contrasted with experiences in some other African developing countries, Ghana's road fund experience seems even more disappointing. For example, Burkina Faso was able to finance virtually the entirety of its road maintenance requirements through the regular budget processes, without a dedicated road fund. It appears that when the budget system works reasonably well, it can meet priority expenditures without the need for EBFs to finance them.
>
> *Source:* Adapted from Mwale 1997.

the rules are observed in practice. So far, the simulation of market discipline in second-generation road funds appears to have improved the management and maintenance of African roads, albeit not uniformly in every country. Boxes 2.2 and 2.3 contrast recent experience in two African countries.

Revenue Earmarking and User Fees

Although EBFs can be funded in a variety of ways, tax earmarking and user fees are the most common sources of financing, as discussed in turn below.

BOX 2.2 Tanzania: A Promising Second-Generation Road Fund

Tanzania's road fund in its current form came into operation in 2000. Its board is composed of a chairman from the private sector; the permanent secretaries of the Ministry of Works, Ministry of Finance, and Prime Minister's Office for Regional Administration and Local Government (PMORALG); a senior civil servant; and several representatives of the private sector and of civil society associations, who were appointed by the minister of works. The road fund has its own dedicated secretariat.

More than 95 percent of the resources of the fund come from a fuel tax (about US$0.08 per liter). The fund is mandated to use at least 90 percent of its resources for maintenance and emergency repair. It allocates 63 percent of its funding to TANROADS (the Tanzania National Roads Agency) for maintenance of the national and regional roads, 7 percent to the Ministry of Works for development projects on those roads, and 30 percent for local roads. The latter funds are mostly passed through to the 100 or so local councils, according to a formula agreed with PMORALG, which takes into account population, road length, and division into equal shares. Of the local road funding, PMORALG itself controls directly only 1 percent for administration and 3 percent for development projects.

All these transfers are governed by performance agreements between the road fund board and the implementation agencies. The agreements specify the respective responsibilities of each party, policies, definitions, performance indicators with means of verification, agency action plans, reporting requirements, and budgets, giving details of works to be undertaken during the year.

Tanzania has made good progress, following the creation of a road fund board and TANROADS. The road network has improved, and funding has increased from T Sh 47.3 billion (about US$58 million) in fiscal year 2000/01 to T Sh 73.4 billion in fiscal year 2003/04 (about US$67 million). The performance agreements between the road fund board and the implementation agencies have contributed to improved accountability. Local roads now receive significant funds for maintenance, and the country's decentralization has been enhanced by disbursing the funds directly to the local councils. Because funds are still insufficient to maintain the roads, owing to a large backlog of maintenance works, legislative revisions are under way—among other things, to establish road boards at the national and regional levels to cater specifically to development and management.

Sources: Andreski 2005; Gwilliam and Kumar 2002.

Tax earmarking

Different tax earmarking arrangements can be found (McCleary 1991):

- A specific tax or fee for a specific end use, such as social security taxes and gasoline taxes for highway investments

BOX 2.3 Malawi: The Patronage Risks of Road Funds

Malawi's road fund was created in 1997 under the National Road Authority (NRA) Act as an integral part of the NRA itself. Initially, following the establishment of the fund, the management and financing of Malawi's paved road network improved. It was not long, however, before the flaws in the institutional setup of the NRA became apparent. Whereas at first the governing board was selected on the basis of technical competence, in the early 2000s many of the members were chosen on the basis of political influence, de facto eliminating the board's formal independence.

In particular, the board chairman appeared to come under the control of the chief executive, who paid him "board sitting" allowances for every day of the month. Critical decisions were made by the chief executive, board chairman, and roads minister without the participation of the other board members and with their concerns not being heard or being largely sidelined. Private sector participation and consultation with civil society were perfunctory when they took place at all.

Thus, although on the surface the Malawi road fund that was created in 1997 appears to be an illustration of a second-generation road fund, in reality it operated with much the same handicaps of politicization and patronage as did the old road funds of the 1970s and 1980s, with equally disappointing results.

It is hoped that the situation will change following the election of a new president, who has already replaced many top officials in various sectors. Additional legislation may be needed to insulate the road fund board from undue political interference and to mandate more systematic participation in and transparency of decision making.

Source: Adapted and expanded from Andreski 2005.

- A specific tax or fee for a broad end use, such as lottery proceeds that finance investments
- A general tax earmarked for a specific end use, such as a fixed-percentage revenue devoted to specific programs.

In most cases, arrangements that earmark a share of total revenues from general taxes are questionable (issues of social security are reviewed later). Concerning other specific taxes and fees, a distinction is generally made between (a) *strong earmarking,* in which the link between the payment of a user charge and the associated expenditure is close (for example, fees for attending courses of a university), and (b) *weak earmarking,* in which the link between the benefit and the fees or the taxes is less clear (for example, the use of lottery proceeds for investments) (see Hemming and Miranda 1991).

As mentioned in the earlier discussion on road funds, when there is a strong benefit-revenue link and the service is provided to well-identified users, earmarking may be desirable to induce agencies to improve performance and facilitate cost recovery. Also, in some observers' view, the use of earmarked taxes could increase taxpayers' knowledge of how the taxes they pay are used, making it more likely that they will exercise vigilance over the efficiency of the services.

User fees

The issue of user charges is very complex, especially in poor developing countries. As a general principle, the benefits need to be weighed against the additional transaction costs of defining and collecting the charges. Thus, in most African countries, it would not be cost-effective to levy user fees on essential social services such as basic health and primary education—even aside from the adverse moral and social implications of attempting to do so. In other parts of the world, governments providing quasi-private goods and services should charge, if practical, a fee commensurate with users' ability to pay and should allow the agencies that collect the revenue to retain at least a significant portion of it. Doing so would meet both revenue and technical efficiency objectives. A hospital or a university, for example, would have no incentive to improve its efficiency if it could not use freely some of the revenue from selling its services.

In any event, when user charges are both cost-effective and desirable, an estimate of the revenue and the corresponding expenditures must be provided in the budget. Also, user charges must be transparent and efficient. The following principles, drawn up by the OECD (1998), should be adopted:

- *Clear legal authority.* The legal basis to charge for services should be clearly defined but limited to the general framework, without setting the precise amount of the fees, so that they can be adjusted without further legislative authority.
- *Consultation with users.* Consultations serve both to prevent misunderstandings and to improve the design and implementation of the charging system.
- *Full costing.* The full cost of each service should be determined, regardless of whether the intention is to recover costs fully or only partly. For partial cost recovery, this information will make transparent the subsidy granted for the service.
- *Appropriate pricing.* Wherever relevant, pricing should be based on competitive market prices, or reflect full cost recovery, or take into account

studies on variations in demand to limit congestion. Prices set in this manner will allow efficient distribution of the services.

- *Competitive neutrality.* When pricing services, the costing should be accurate and should incorporate all cost items faced by the private sector entities operating in the same sector.
- *Equity considerations.* Reduced or zero fees can be applied to lower-income individuals, users located in remote areas, and the like. The criteria for reduced charges must be transparent and difficult to manipulate. Different ways of meeting these equity objectives should be considered, because providing benefits directly is generally more transparent and efficient than providing benefits through reductions in user fees.
- *Effective collection system.* The efficiency of user-fee collection can make or break the system. If the fees have been set efficiently and equitably, a failure to pay should be followed up immediately.
- *Audit.* As always, regular external audits of the organization that levies and collects the charge are required.
- *Performance.* The performance of organizations should be monitored regularly to ensure appropriate levels of efficiency and service quality. User fees cannot be allowed to serve as indirect financial support for continued inefficiency.

Several countries include in the budget only the net expenditures of agencies that exercise commercial activities or recover costs, and the budget appropriation corresponds to the difference between planned expenditures and expected revenues. As noted at the outset, revenues and expenditure must be shown in gross terms. If the gross amounts are large, netting out impedes sound analysis of the government activities, accurate estimates of economic costs, and valid comparisons between countries. Convenience cannot supersede the need of the executive to know how the services are performed nor the right of the legislature and the public to know what public agencies are doing.

Beyond Direct Expenditure

As mentioned at the start of the chapter, a number of government objectives can be achieved without direct and immediate government spending, and the corresponding activities are thus not within the scope of the government budget. Nonetheless, they have important fiscal and financial implications for the country. First is a discussion of the category that is most relevant to African developing countries, for its significant potential as a policy instrument and also as a source of substantial fiscal and governance risks: government guarantees and other contingent liabilities.

Types of Government Liabilities

In addition to legal commitments, governments have other explicit or implicit commitments that can have an immediate or future fiscal impact.[3] Fiscal risks and uncertainties are increasing. The international integration of financial markets generates more abundant, rapid, and volatile cross-border flows, and governments may become obliged to intervene to support the financial system. State guarantees and insurance schemes have become common. Privatization is often accompanied by implicit or explicit state guarantees.

Government liabilities can therefore be certain or uncertain (contingent), and explicit or implicit. In descending order of fiscal predictability, these liabilities are as follows:

- *Explicit liabilities and commitments* are legally mandatory and predictable. This category includes budgeted expenditure programs, multiyear investment contracts, civil service salaries, pensions, and debt obligations.
- *Explicit and contingent liabilities* are legal or contractual obligations triggered by a discrete event that may or may not occur. This category includes, for example, state guarantees for loans contracted by entities outside central government (subnational governments, public and private enterprises) and state insurance schemes (for banking deposits, floods, crop damage, and the like). Often the probability that the event will trigger the guarantee is high, because these guarantees are typically granted to support ailing enterprises or sectors in difficulties.
- *Implicit liabilities* represent obligations or expected burdens for the government that are not contractual or prescribed by law but arise from public expectations. For example, governments are expected to maintain public infrastructure and to support a social security scheme, even when they are not required to do so by law.
- *Implicit and contingent liabilities* are the least predictable category, representing a nonlegal obligation triggered by a discrete event that may or may not occur. For example, the government is generally expected to intervene if the banking sector risks bankruptcy or the country faces a natural catastrophe.

Table 2.1 lists some of the measures that can be taken to deal with different kinds of government liabilities and fiscal risks.

TABLE 2.1 Dealing with Liabilities and Fiscal Risks

Liabilities and risks	Possible measures
Explicit liabilities and commitments	
Budgetary outlays	Budget
Debt	Debt accounting
	Data annexed to budget
Entitlements	
Salaries	Multiyear expenditure programs
Pension liabilities	Modified accrual accounting
Explicit and contingent liabilities	
Loan guarantees	Disclosure in financial reports and the budget
	Assessment of risk of default
State insurance schemes (for floods, crop failure, and so forth)	Actuarial assessment of risk of event
Implicit liabilities	
Forward costs of ongoing programs	Multiyear expenditure programs
Recurrent costs of investment projects	Public investment program
Hidden liabilities (for example, pensions in public enterprises)	Projections and actuarial assessment
Future health and social security financing	Projections and actuarial assessment
Implicit and contingent liabilities	
Local government and public enterprise debts	Consolidated accounts and financial reports
Financial sector risks	Qualitative assessment and continuous dialogue with financial institutions
Social welfare	Qualitative assessment and continuous dialogue with main stakeholders
Environmental or natural catastrophe	Simulations of nature and possible range of damage

Source: Author's compilation.
Note: This list is illustrative, not exhaustive.

Generally, in budgeting, decision making focuses on expenditure programs and on multiyear legal commitments, such as debt servicing. In most countries, no attention is paid in the budget to other long-term obligations or to implicit or contingent liabilities. When a country faces financial difficulties or is undergoing fiscal adjustment, it often tends to overlook nonimmediate or nonexplicit fiscal risks. Sometimes, to solve immediate problems, the country develops an evasion strategy of substituting contingent liabilities for direct spending or making promises for the future to overcome immediate pressures. This tendency makes future problems worse than they would have been had the risks been confronted in the first place.

Unfunded liabilities are explained partly by the variety of sources of fiscal risk for central governments and partly by the fact that they are insufficiently taken into account when formulating the budget. Pension liabilities are demographically driven and, in most countries, are increasing steadily. Financing requirements for health care are rising in aging societies. Meanwhile, lack of funding for the recurrent costs of investment reduces the efficiency of the original investment, and government commitments and promises outside the budgetary systems reduce fiscal sustainability.

Sound budgeting and policy formulation requires a wider approach, covering the fiscal risks governments face in the short term as well as in the long term. Good methodologies are needed, especially actuarial ones. Most important, however, are political determination, leadership, and effective communication of the fiscal realities to the public. Accordingly, the obligations arising from current or new expenditure programs and policy measures must be assessed realistically, whatever their nature (implicit or explicit, direct or contingent). Explicit liabilities, both actual and contingent, should be disclosed in the budget documentation. Implicit contingent liabilities, by definition, cannot be quantified or predicted accurately; however, the reality of their existence should add to fiscal prudence efforts, and decision-making mechanisms should be in place to permit a rapid and efficient response if and when the event occurs.

Certain instruments reviewed in this book can help in this assessment and disclosure. For example, multiyear expenditure programming permits governments to assess the fiscal sustainability of ongoing policy commitments over a medium-term period, as well as some implicit liabilities (such as the recurrent costs of investment projects; see chapter 8). However, these instruments are neither necessary nor sufficient for assessing fiscal risk. The key requirements are as follows:

■ Awareness of the existence of fiscal risks
■ Some assessment
■ Full disclosure
■ Explicit consideration of fiscal risks during the budgeting process.

Transparency, candor, and good judgment can go a long way to help recognize and address fiscal risk.

Loan Guarantees

The most common explicit contingent liabilities are loan guarantees. The government can guarantee loans by agencies, enterprises, and other autonomous agencies under its broad control as well as for private sector corporations in selected situations, whether from domestic or foreign sources of financing. In general, loans to nongovernment entities by international financial institutions require a government guarantee.

Although guarantees have long been recognized as an appropriate government instrument, they can have a significant impact on fiscal deficits, sustainability, and vulnerability. This impact became evident from the experience of many countries in Latin America and Africa in the 1980s, where borrowers defaulted on most loans. The government naturally had to assume debt servicing and repayment of those loans, thereby adding a lasting burden to an already stretched budget.

In general, government guarantees are justified if the borrower lacks the required creditworthiness (or if limited creditworthiness entails high borrowing costs), as long as the purposes of such guarantees are consistent with government objectives, programs, and policies. When imperfect information gives potential lenders an inadequate picture of a borrower's creditworthiness, government guarantees remedy the market distortion and are appropriate from both an economic and a policy viewpoint. In practice, however, these guarantees are often granted without an assessment of the capacity of the beneficiary entity to reimburse the loan or are provided as favors to well-connected borrowers, and they are not systematically recorded.

The expenditure equivalent of guarantees is difficult to estimate without a long series of data on the frequency of loan default. However, the budget should at least include a list of guarantees that the government intends to grant and an aggregate monetary ceiling for those guarantees. In several countries, the government levies a fee when it guarantees loans. This procedure presents the advantage of creating a mechanism for registration and monitoring, and it also constitutes to some extent an insurance payment in case of default. If the guarantee fee is proportionate to the risk of default (and the risk is assessed correctly), it will, in the aggregate, suffice to cover the eventual cost. Of course, the implicit subsidy element will then disappear, but the purpose of guarantees is to offset a lack of creditworthiness, not to subsidize credit.

Effective budgeting calls for tight management of guarantees. Such management should, first, compel consideration of the implications of each proposed guarantee and allow the subsidy element in such guarantees to be calculated. Second, procedural safeguards should minimize the adverse impact of guarantees on the fiscal position. Third, the financial performance of the recipients of guarantees should be monitored. Finally, there should be sufficient scrutiny and accountability to prevent the misuse of this instrument.

A well-designed system to provide guarantees should recognize the important role of guarantees in the context of all other government policy instruments. As noted, direct expenditures, loans, guarantees, and tax incentives each offer some scope for pursuing a stated objective. A ceiling on guarantees could also be prescribed. Without such ceilings, liberal provision of guarantees could adversely affect the creditworthiness of the government itself and, as a consequence, could lead to higher interest costs in the medium term. Moreover, such ceilings induce a more rigorous scrutiny and thus promote competition among potential borrowers, channeling the guarantees to entities that are financially sounder. The risk element therefore needs to be computed and to be explicitly recorded and shown in the budget documents.

Finally, monitoring of guarantees, in parallel with the budget system, would require a periodic review and anticipate possible defaults and ways of financing them. An initial important step would be the publication of data on guarantees as part of the budgetary information and of the completed accounts of the government.

The Budgetary Treatment of HIPC Debt Relief

Among the actions with an effect on the budget but no immediate direct expenditure implications is a country's eligibility for debt relief under the HIPC process. A comparative study of five highly indebted poor countries in Africa that was commissioned by the European Commission identified three broad approaches to budgeting expenditures financed from the countries' savings, as described in box 2.4.

Quasi-Fiscal Activities

Quasi-fiscal activities are financial transactions undertaken by the central bank or state-owned banks to achieve government policy goals (see Mackenzie and Stella 1996; Robinson and Stella 1993). These operations include interest rate subsidies, support for ailing enterprises and financial institutions, payment of government debt, and financing of exchange rate losses incurred by the government. Accomplishing the desired goal through transparent subsidies in the budget rather than through quasi-fiscal operations is generally preferable. Also, a country's monetary authorities should concentrate on monetary policy and operations; they should not get involved in activities that in effect substitute for fiscal operations through the budget. In any case, the quasi-fiscal operations of the central bank and other banking institutions should be scrutinized, as

BOX 2.4   Alternative Approaches to the Budgetary Treatment of HIPC Debt Relief

Burkina Faso and Cameroon have set up an institutional fund mechanism (IFM) (see IMF and World Bank 2001) with strict ring-fencing of savings from the HIPC initiative. HIPC savings are lodged in special accounts at the Banque Centrale des États de l'Afrique de l'Ouest (Central Bank of West African States, or BCEAO) and managed separately from general budget expenditures. Special HIPC implementation units have been set up.

In Benin, Ghana, and Tanzania expenditures financed from the HIPC debt relief are made through the normal budget procedures and are presented in the budget in the same manner as the other expenditures. Benin and Ghana, however, have introduced a virtual fund mechanism (VFM): some budget items are tagged as HIPC expenditures, but only for reporting purposes. In Ghana, the HIPC account is a subaccount of the consolidated fund account at the central bank. In Benin, the HIPC account is kept at the treasury and used for accounting purposes only. By contrast, Tanzania has neither established an HIPC account nor implemented a tracking system for HIPC expenditures. The Tanzanian government has chosen to move toward a comprehensive expenditure tracking mechanism instead of focusing on a few budget items.

In Burkina Faso and Cameroon, donors' worries about the use of these HIPC savings led to the establishment of an IFM. By contrast, the government of Benin resisted the initial donor request to lodge the HIPC savings in a special account at the BCEAO on the grounds that doing so would contradict its ongoing budget reforms, which are aimed at better unifying the different components of the budget.

The IFM implemented in Burkina Faso and Cameroon is said to divert attention from scrutiny of overall public spending and its impact on poverty reduction; moreover, it does not ensure that additional public resources are being allocated to poverty reduction, because of the fungibility of money. The IFM may also complicate budget execution and put unnecessary strain on the already weak institutional capacity of the Ministry of Finance. In fact, Burkina Faso and Cameroon have experienced longer execution delays for expenditures financed from HIPC funds than for other expenditures.

The experiences of Benin and Ghana appear to show that the VFM may meet donor concerns without fragmenting the budget. However, the VFM should be a temporary mechanism, because it focuses attention on only a few activities, not on overall strategic resource allocation for poverty reduction. The experience of Tanzania shows that comprehensive expenditure tracking is feasible, at least in the medium term. Although further strengthening of the overall expenditure management system is still needed in Tanzania, the current quality of the system has provided donors with sufficient comfort to endorse the country's comprehensive expenditure tracking system.

Source: Adapted from De Groot, Jennes, and Cassimon 2003.

should direct government expenditure programs, and should be shown in the budget documents. At a minimum, a statement on the quasi-fiscal activities of the banking sector should be annexed to the budget. The production of transparent accounts from the central bank is also important, because estimating the cost of quasi-fiscal operations is not a simple matter.

Government Lending

Government loans are another possible means of achieving government policy goals, and they can substitute for direct spending. Therefore, loans should be decided on in a transparent manner, submitted to the same scrutiny as direct spending, and appropriately shown in the budget.

Government lending is often directed to entities that cannot afford to borrow at commercial terms, either because these entities need to be subsidized or because the creditworthiness of beneficiary entities is weak (a typical example is lending for crop production or to state-owned enterprises). Government lending can also be used to leverage commercial lending and to supplement it. This lending is frequent in developing countries because external loans that finance public sector entities are granted to the government to on-lend them to the beneficiary entity.

The fact that loans are (in principle) repayable can make government lending a more cost-effective instrument for achieving public policy than direct spending. However, lending can also be a way of avoiding budget constraints. Loans are often submitted to weaker scrutiny than direct spending and do not have to be authorized by the legislature.

Typically, government loans include an interest subsidy and present higher risks than loans granted by commercial banks. Concessional external loans granted to the government to be on-lent to public entities usually include a provision that the on-lending be at commercial terms, to avoid creating distortions in the financial market. In practice, this provision is not systematically enforced. Exchange rate losses may be incurred and borne by the government, and risks of insolvency can be high. Hence, the budgetary treatment of government lending should include the following:

- Because lending must be traded off against expenditure decisions, the lending program should be reviewed together with the expenditure programs during budget preparation.
- Loans should be included in the budget, with full explanations of their terms, and submitted to the authorization of the legislature.
- Interest subsidies must always be budgeted as expenditures. Two approaches may be considered: (a) budgeting the discounted value of the subsidies

when the loan is granted (as in the United States) or (b) budgeting the subsidy according to the interest schedule. The first approach is preferable because the subsidy is budgeted in the year the decision is made, but this approach requires adequate technical capacity in financial analysis and accounting.

■ To ensure accountability and allow review lending programs together with expenditure programs, lending must be included in gross terms in the budget.

Tax Expenditures

Tax expenditures are defined as the revenue forgone because of preferential tax provisions. Like government lending and any other instrument of fiscal policy, they should be transparent and included in the budget. Tax expenditures cover the following:

■ Exemptions, which exclude the revenues of a group of taxpayers from the tax base
■ Deductions, which reduce the tax base by some expenses or a lump sum
■ Credits, which are deducted from the tax due (as opposed to deductions, which reduce taxable income)
■ Deferrals, or postponements of the deadline to pay taxes, without interest or penalties
■ Reduced tax rates for certain categories of taxpayers or activities.

Tax expenditures are aimed at achieving certain public policy objectives by providing benefits to qualified individuals or entities or by encouraging particular activities. They may also be intended to improve tax equity or offset imperfections in other parts of the tax structure. The same set of objectives (for example, financial assistance to families) can be achieved either through direct spending or through tax waivers or exemptions. In principle, spending a given amount is exactly equivalent to reducing the tax on the beneficiary by the same amount. In practice, tax expenditures and direct expenditures are handled separately.

To determine whether a particular tax measure generates a tax expenditure, it is necessary first to identify the normal tax structure from which the measure departs. Such identification is relatively easy when the tax expenditure corresponds to specific exemptions (for example, a special income tax rate for agriculture activities), but when the whole tax structure is affected (for example, a differentiated income tax rate according to family status), the existence of a tax expenditure may be debated. There is also debate about the methodology for assessing the impact of tax expenditures, because some tax expenditures may have an impact different from that of direct spending if changes in the behavior of taxpayers are taken into account.

Tax expenditures are granted through tax laws. In several countries, these expenditures are presented together with the expenditure budget but are not submitted to the same system of internal control and legislative authorization as other expenditures. Therefore, tax expenditures are often an easy and less transparent way of granting special benefits to specific groups. In certain cases, the beneficiaries are less clearly identified than are those who would benefit from direct spending. As a result, tax offsets can often produce results that are completely different from the stated objectives. For example, high-income households can benefit more than needier households from tax credits than they can from family allowances targeted to low-income groups. Moreover, tax offsets (particularly on goods and services) create loopholes within the tax system itself.

Tax expenditures should be subject to an explicit tradeoff against new spending initiatives and should be as transparent as possible. Ideally, as for government lending, the direct impact of tax expenditures should be budgeted in gross terms. This procedure is possible for tax expenditures that are easy to measure and monitor (such as tax refunds or tax offsets granted according to the provisions of a contract). However, because measuring most tax expenditures is difficult, this approach cannot be generalized.

Even though explicit budgeting of tax expenditures can be considered only in specific cases, an assessment should be included in the regular process of budget decision making. For this purpose, a statement of tax expenditures should be produced regularly, to allow a review of tax expenditure policy during budget preparation and to make tradeoffs between tax expenditures and direct spending. Some industrial countries (for example, Belgium, France, and the United States) append such a statement to the budget document. This approach enhances legislative scrutiny of government policy.

An illustration of good reporting of tax expenditures in a developing country is provided in box 2.5.

Basic Budget Legislation

Because the budget is a fundamental legal instrument, the budgetary principles and rules must be codified in a form appropriate to the legal and administrative culture of the country concerned.

> **BOX 2.5**   Morocco: Reporting on Tax Expenditures
>
> In 2005, the government of Morocco prepared a report on tax expenditures, which was included in the budget document. The report is organized as follows:
>
> ■ Chapter 1 presents the methodology used to estimate the tax expenditures:
>   —Definition of the scope of the study
>   —Definition of the baseline for each main category of taxes: (a) corporate income tax, (b) individual income tax, (c) value added tax, (d) registration fees, (e) customs duties, and (f) excise taxes
>   —Definition of the methodology for estimating the tax expenditures.
> ■ Chapter 2 presents the tax expenditures estimates. It includes both summary and detailed presentations of tax expenditures according to
>   —The tax category
>   —The economic activity that benefits from the tax expenditures
>   —The objectives that the tax expenditures aim to achieve (for example, promoting access to housing, encouraging teaching)
>   —The beneficiary group (enterprises, households, international organizations, and so on).
>
> The 2005 report has identified 337 exceptional measures that depart from the normal structure. The total tax expenditures related to 102 of these measures that have the most significant impact accounted for 3.4 percent of gross domestic product and 15.7 percent of collected taxes in 2004.
>
> *Source:* Ministére des Finances et de la Privatisation 2005.

A Hierarchy of Laws

Depending on their importance, the budget principles and rules can be enshrined in descending order of legal hierarchy, in the constitution, a framework law, other laws and regulations, administrative instructions and circulars, and—of course—the annual budget law. These are the general criteria:

■ It should be cumbersome to modify the basic rules, because they must be underpinned by a very broad consensus, and easy to modify the detailed rules, because they are likely to require frequent modifications as circumstances change.
■ Effective legal changes require consultation with the key stakeholders, because unenforced law is no law at all and the effectiveness of enforcement depends largely on the voluntary cooperation of those affected.

Therefore, only the most fundamental principles should find their way into the country's constitution. Subject to and consistent with those fundamental principles, a framework law—often called an *organic budget law*—contains the basic rules for managing public finances, allocating powers and accountabilities, providing financial oversight, and the like. Subsidiary legislation will then regulate implementation of the organic budget law and define the operational parameters. Administrative budget instructions follow in the legal hierarchy, primarily instructions to formulate the macroeconomic and fiscal framework and the budget circular that starts the budget preparation process (see chapter 8). Finally, provisions and resource allocations for the coming fiscal year are incorporated in the annual budget law that is presented to the legislature and in supplemental allocations or other amendments during the course of the year.

Organic Budget Law

Generally, an organic budget law defines four things:

1. The objectives of public financial management—fiscal control, strategic resource allocation, operational effectiveness, service orientation
2. The principles—accountability, integrity, transparency, compliance with rules, participation
3. The process—budget preparation, execution, reporting, audit
4. The responsibilities—of whom, for what, how, and when at various stages in the process, including the division of powers between the executive and the legislature.

Specifically, an organic budget law should contain the following elements:

- An introduction stating the objectives and principles
- Definitions, including a definition of *fiscal deficit*
- General provisions, such as the basis of accounting and financial reporting
- Rules of budget coverage and presentation, including treatment of extra-budgetary funds and fiscal risks
- Stages and rules for budget preparation
- Procedures for budget debate, approval, and legislative amendment
- Stages and rules for budget execution, including commitment and payment regulations, internal control, monitoring, and evaluation
- Principles and rules of external audit
- Accountability provisions
- Relations with local government.

Division of powers in budgeting

The specific arrangements for division of responsibilities between the executive and the legislature depend on the nature of the country's political system—whether parliamentary or presidential, unitary or federal, the legal tradition and role of the judiciary, and the historical and cultural context.

In general, the executive and the legislature are jointly responsible for defining the broad directions of economic and fiscal policy. The executive is responsible for formulating the expenditure program consistent with the broad directions, within the limits of affordability; the legislature is responsible for approving the expenditure program and monitoring its execution.

The key principles

The organic budget law should have as its first section a clear statement of the fundamental principles of good governance and of public finance. These principles also recapitulate the major points made in this chapter:

- No moneys to be collected from natural or legal persons, nor any moneys expended, nor services provided, nor exemptions granted, except as duly authorized by the law and other legal instruments
- Transparency of fiscal and service information, requiring not only openness but an affirmative effort to provide to the public in usable form the basic budgetary information and government plans and programs, in accordance with international standards on fiscal transparency
- Conformity of fiscal policy with macroeconomic and social objectives, requiring, among other things, the placement of the annual budget process in a multiyear perspective
- Individual responsibility of ministers, heads of agencies, and other senior managers for the acquisition, use, accounting, and reporting of public resources and for the taking of necessary measures to prevent abuses of such resources
- Equal obligation of all government employees to comply with the rules and regulations of public financial management, and equal application of sanctions to violators of said rules
- Maximum feasible participation by government employees, members of the legislature, and other concerned persons, in the budget preparation and budget execution process, as may be appropriate and realistic
- Public financial management conducted to ensure expenditure control, efficient resource use, effective service provision, and high integrity
- Unity of the budget and the treasury, among other reasons to make possible comparisons of the relative effectiveness of different types of proposed expenditures

■ Conformity with or progress toward accepted international standards in budget preparation and execution, financial management and control, and audit.

Box 2.6 shows the detailed structure of the organic budget law in a francophone African country. (Because the law was still in draft form at the time of writing, the country's name and the actual contents are not mentioned.)

BOX 2.6 Contents of an Organic Budget Law in a Francophone African Country

Part I	**General Provisions**
Article 1	Object of the Organic Law
Article 2	Definitions
Article 3	The Scope of the Law
Article 4	General Guiding Principles
Article 5	Establishment, Coverage, and Control of the Consolidated Fund
Article 6	Withdrawals from the Consolidated Fund
Part II	**Powers for Budget Management**
Article 7	Powers of Parliament, Local Government Councils, and Other Public Bodies
Article 8	Powers and Responsibilities of the Council of Ministers
Article 9	General Responsibilities of the Minister
Article 10	Specific Powers of the Minister
Article 11	Powers of the Minister to Delegate Authority
Article 12	Powers and General Responsibilities of the Secretary General and Secretary to the Treasury
Article 13	Specific Powers of the Secretary General and Secretary to the Treasury
Article 14	Powers and Missions of Chief Budget Managers
Article 15	Delegation of Chief Budget Managers' Responsibilities
Article 16	Powers and Duties of Local Government Council Chairpersons
Part III	**Preparation, Presentation, and Approval of Budgets**
Article 17	Revenues
Article 18	Expenditures
Article 19	Unforeseen Expenditures for Emergencies
Article 20	Deficit or Surplus
Article 21	Estimation of Revenue of the Central Government and Local Governments
Article 22	Estimation of Expenditure of the Central Government and Local Governments
Article 23	Documentation for the Annual Budget
Article 24	Budget Annexes

(Box continues on the following page.)

Notes

1. In centrally planned economies, the distinction between the activities of state enterprises and those of government is fuzzy, because state enterprises are also heavily involved in the delivery of public services. The virtual disappearance from Africa of the centrally planned mode of economic management restores the need to differentiate between activities carried out by the government and those carried out by publicly owned but autonomous entities that presumably are managed on commercial principles.

2. The exact proportions are not easy to estimate, because some EBF expenditures are in fact internal financial transactions. When the accounting system does not fully preclude duplicate accounting, as in many African countries, the real size of transactions made through EBFs is lower than the recorded amount—by some margin that is probably substantial but is impossible to determine without a costly dedicated exercise. What is beyond dispute, however, is that EBF transactions in African countries add up to an amount sufficiently large to generate substantial concern and to justify policy and management attention.

3. This section is based largely on the original taxonomy by Hana Polackova, first outlined in Polackova (1998) and then elaborated in her subsequent publications.

References

Allen, Richard, and Dimitar Radev. Forthcoming. "Managing and Controlling Extrabudgetary Funds." *OECD Journal of Budgeting.*

Andreski, Adam. 2005. "Case Study of Road Funds in Ghana, Malawi, and Tanzania." I.T. Transport, Oxfordshire, U.K. http://www.ittransport.co.uk/publications.htm.

De Groot, Albert, Geert Jennes, and Danny Cassimon. 2003. "The Management of HIPC Funds in Recipient Countries: A Comparative Study of Five African Countries." Rotterdam, Netherlands: ECORYS.

Gwilliam, Kenneth M., and Ajay Kumar. 2002. "Road Funds Revisited: A Preliminary Appraisal of the Effectiveness of 'Second Generation' Road Funds." TWU 47, World Bank, Washington, DC.

Heggie, Ian. 1995. *Management and Financing of Roads: An Agenda for Reform.* World Bank Technical Paper Series, World Bank, Washington, DC.

Hemming, Richard, and Kenneth Miranda. 1991. "Pricing and Cost Recovery." In *Public Expenditure Handbook: A Guide to Public Expenditure Policy Issues in Developing Countries,* ed. Ke-young Chu and Richard Hemming, 139–45. Washington, DC: International Monetary Fund.

IMF (International Monetary Fund). 2001. *Manual on Fiscal Transparency.* Washington, DC: IMF. http://www.imf.org/external/np/fad/trans/manual/index.htm.

IMF and World Bank. 2001. *Tracking of Poverty-Reducing Spending in Heavily Indebted Poor Countries.* Washington, DC: IMF and World Bank.

Mackenzie, G. A., and Peter Stella. 1996. *Quasi-Fiscal Operations of Public Financial Institutions.* Washington, DC: International Monetary Fund.

McCleary, William. 1991. "The Earmarking of Government Revenue: A Review of Some World Bank Experiences." *World Bank Research Observer* 6 (1): 81–104.

Ministére des Finances et de la Privatisation. 2005. *Rapport Dépenses Fiscales.* Rabat: Royaume du Maroc.

Mwale, Sam M. 1997. "Road Sector Reform: A Tale of Two Countries (Part 3)—Impact and Lessons." Africa Transport Technical Note 8, World Bank, Washington, DC. http://www4.worldbank.org/afr/ssatp/Resources/SSATP-TechnicalNotes/ATTN08.pdf.

OECD (Organisation for Economic Co-operation and Development). 1998. "User Charging for Government Services." Occasional Paper 22, Paris: OECD.

Pennant-Rae, Rupert, and Ian Heggie. 1995. "Commercializing Africa's Roads." *Finance and Development* 32 (4): 30–33.

Polackova, Hana. 1998. "Government Contingent Liabilities: A Hidden Risk to Fiscal Stability." Policy Research Working Paper 1989, World Bank, Washington, DC.

Potter, Barry, ed. 2005. *Budgeting for Road Maintenance.* Washington, DC: International Monetary Fund.

Robinson, David J., and Peter Stella. 1993. "Amalgamating Central Bank and Fiscal Deficits." In *How to Measure the Fiscal Deficit,* ed. Mario I. Blejer and Adrienne Cheasty, 236–58. Washington, DC: International Monetary Fund.

World Bank. 2003. "Country Financial Accountability Assessment Guidelines to Staff." World Bank, Washington, DC. http://www1.worldbank.org/publicsector/pe/CFAA Guidelines.pdf.

3

Capital Budgets: Theory and Practice

A. PREMCHAND

Capital budgets in governments have multiple roles: as instruments of compensatory fiscal policy, as windows on the net worth of public bodies, and as vehicles for development—particularly in the area of economic infrastructure—through greater reliance on debt than on such conventional sources of financing as taxation. Governments have introduced capital budgets to serve all these objectives, singly or collectively, depending on the context. In some cases, more attention has been paid to capital budgets as a way to reduce deficits on the current account.

Notwithstanding the seeming virtues of capital budgets, opinions continue to be divided, as they have been during the past seven decades, about their utility in governments. In the present context, in which several industrial countries have budgetary surpluses and use them to reduce levels of public debt, there is little incentive to revive the debate about the need for capital budgets. In the developing world, however, where many governments operate on the edge of financial instability, the debate about capital budgets and their equivalents continues.

Experience shows that in the absence of properly organized capital budgets, borrowing avenues proliferate, governments resort to borrowing without due consideration of the sustainability aspects (or intergenerational equity), assets are inadequately maintained, and major projects suffer from overall poor management and performance. It is arguable whether these results could have been prevented by the establishment of capital budgets. Moreover, for countries that continue to depend on debt finance as a major instrument of budgetary resources, the issue arises whether capital budgets promote an improved process of decision making and an overall management culture that permits continuing attention to the government's net worth. For both these reasons, it is important to revisit the debate about capital budgets. More specifically, it is important to consider whether capital budgets provide an improved framework for allocating, using, and accounting for resources and whether they help restrain the growth of expenditure or prove too soft a constraint in the management of debt-financed outlays. To answer these issues, one must review the evolution and content of capital budgets.

This chapter is divided into two parts. The first part is devoted to a brief discussion of the evolution of capital budgets from the 1930s to date and the different considerations that influenced that evolution. This discussion is followed by a delineation of the contents of capital budgets: planning, formulation, and implementation.[1] The second part is devoted to a discussion of country practices and the ebb and flow of the debate about the need for capital budgets. It concludes with a discussion of the leading issues.

Evolution

Although the conceptual framework of a capital budget has not undergone major change over the years, there are six discernible stages in which its various aspects came to be reviewed as integral parts of the overall debate about the applicability of the system to governments. To gain a proper perspective, readers will find it instructive to consider these stages briefly. The first stage is the Great Depression years, during which efforts were devoted to designing ways to promote recovery. The prevailing public philosophy did not favor public borrowing for financing government outlays, except during national emergencies such as wars. Borrowing, it was believed, would prove too attractive an option for policy makers looking to finance ordinary outlays. To resist this temptation and with a view to creating a favorable lobby, Sweden decided to introduce a capital budget that was to be funded by public borrowing and used primarily to finance the creation of durable and self-financing assets that would also contribute to expanded net worth in an amount equivalent to the amount of borrowing. The capital budget so launched, which was also called the investment budget, found extended application in the following years in other Nordic countries. To facilitate the implementation of a capital budget, a system of extended grants that went beyond a fiscal year was established.

The second stage reflects a different background, one that provided an impetus for the application of capital budgets to government transactions. During the late 1930s the colonial government of undivided India introduced a capital budget to reduce a revenue deficit by shifting some items of expenditures from the current budget. It was believed that the burgeoning budget deficit did not reflect well on the creditworthiness of the colonial government; the introduction of a dual-budget system provided a convenient way to reduce revenue or current account deficits while providing a rationale for borrowing.

The third stage refers to the growing importance attached to capital budgets as a vehicle for development plans. The countries that had become independent since the late 1940s recognized that the budget systems they inherited did not properly serve their needs for development. Partly influenced by the Soviet model of central planning, many developing countries formulated massive five-year plans and considered capital budgets the primary vehicle of economic development. Where capital budgets did not exist, a variant known since then as the *development budget* was introduced.

The fourth stage reflects the growing influence of economists on the allocation of resources in government. With a view to ensuring more efficient and rational allocation, quantitative appraisal techniques (hitherto applied to multipurpose river valley projects) came to be applied on a wider scale during the 1960s. These techniques established a trend of more rigorous application of investment appraisal and detailed financial planning. This feature, common to all government program or project transactions, came to be a condition for the inclusion of projects in the capital or equivalent budget.

The fifth stage saw a revival of the debate about the need for a capital budget in government, particularly in the United States. Along with the growing application of quantitative techniques during the 1960s came the view that the introduction of a capital budget could be advantageous. But this view did not gain much support. A president's commission investigating budget concepts in the United States concluded that a capital budget could lead to greater outlays on bricks and mortar, and as a result, current outlays could suffer. Having rejected capital budgets, the commission advocated the introduction of accrual accounting (as distinct from accrual budgeting) in government accounts. The introduction of accrual accounting, which did not make any progress in the United States until the early 1990s, would have meant the division of accounts into ordinary accounts and investment accounts. Such accounts were intended more as a source of information than as a basis for budgeting. Meanwhile, however, a development cast more serious doubts on the need for capital budgets. Sweden, which had made pioneering efforts in the 1930s, undertook a review of its budget system in the early

1970s. It found that excessive focus on capital budgets would need to be tempered by a recognition that the overall credibility and creditworthiness of a government depend more on its macroeconomic policy stance and less on its net worth. Although the application of capital budgets for quasi-commercial transactions was necessary, it was not to be considered as a main basis for the borrowing program.

This shift in emphasis contributed to a decline in the popularity of the capital budget until the late 1980s, when it came to be revived in a different form. By then government officials recognized that the management of government finances required a radical approach, and this radical approach was the application of accrual accounting. During this sixth stage, partly because of the experiences of Australia and New Zealand, there were renewed pleas from the professional bodies and, from the late 1990s, the international financial institutions for the introduction of accrual budgeting and accounting. These pleas found an echo in the United States, where advocates held that the absence of a distinction between investment outlays and ordinary or current outlays led to unintended neglect of infrastructure or accumulated assets. Ensuring proper asset maintenance (as important as asset creation) required a division of outlays into current and capital outlays, as a part of day-to-day budget management.

Capital Budget: Conceptual Framework

Although corporate practices provided the basic inspiration, planners recognized from the start that the nature and rationale of capital budgets would be different in public bodies. Apart from the basic distinction arising from the lack of profit motive, the structure of a government and the diversity of purposes served also differ. Unlike in the corporate sector, an entity in government may not have separate assets and frequently its power to borrow may be limited. The power to borrow and the assets created belong to the whole government. In addition, the government may not engage in direct asset creation but may frequently transfer the borrowed resources to its more specialized agencies, including state-owned enterprises, so that they can create the assets.

The more important differences lie in the rationale for capital budgets in governments. From the viewpoint of financing, it was to explore the alternative to taxation and to engage in borrowing that could bring about a better distribution of government services among taxpayers and beneficiaries. Borrowing also could contribute to a better distribution between consumption and investment, although there were clearly limits on the extent of borrowing. Moreover, investments by governments tend to be lumpy in the years in which they are incurred, contributing in turn to uneven revenue mobilization measures and tax revisions to match the growth in expenditures. Capital expenditures necessarily tend to be unevenly spread, reflecting, in large part, the projects to be financed. But properly organized and financed, they had the potential to bring about a smoother tax and revenue regime. From an accounting point of view, capital budgets have depreciation provisions and capital charges that reflect the asset over its full life span rather than just the fiscal year in which expenditures are incurred for its acquisition or completion. Finally, from the point of view of overall financial credibility, capital budgets force more rigorous examination of the impact of expenditures. To the extent that they result in corresponding assets, the net worth of government is ensured, permitting it to maintain its creditworthiness in the market.

Structure of a Capital Budget

The structure of the capital budget that has evolved from the application of the preceding considerations is laid out in table 3.1. Contrary to general belief, a capital budget also has an extensive portfolio that goes beyond borrowing—although depending on the situation, borrowing may be the most important source of funds. In principle, taxes levied on property, although paid from current income, are considered levies on capital and included in capital receipts. In some countries, income from natural resources (including oil) may be earmarked for capital projects and therefore included in receipts. In countries with development plans, surpluses from the current budget (relatively less during recent years owing to the significant growth in current outlays) are yet another source of receipts. Depreciation allowances represent, in accounting parlance, a *contra* or a balancing entry, in that allowances that are charged to the current account are treated as capital receipts. Charging depreciation allowances has the short-term effect of contributing to an increased current account deficit (or reduced surplus) and to an overall higher deficit. However, this practice must be tempered by recognition that depreciation allowances are not, in many cases, maintained on a cash basis but are more in the nature of a book entry. The receipts section includes capital transfers from external sources and proceeds from the sale of property and privatization.

The determination of capital expenditure is more complex. The first question that arises is what are capital expenditures and how are they determined? Accountants and economists' approaches to answering this question have some common and some different elements. From an accounting point of view, outlays incurred in the acquisition or creation of

TABLE 3.1   An Illustration of the Structure of a Capital Budget

Receipts	Expenditures

1. Estate and death duties
   Taxes and property
   Earmarked revenues for capital projects
2. Surpluses from the current account
3. Proceeds of borrowing:
   ■ Domestic
   ■ Trust and captive accounts
      maintained by government
   ■ External
   Repayment of loans
4. Depreciation allowances
5. Sales of property[d]
   ■ Regular
   ■ Privatization proceeds
6. Capital grants
Total
	1. Acquisition of existing assets[a]
	   ■ Plant, property, and equipment
	   ■ Financial
	2. Acquisition of new assets[a]
	   ■ Plant, property, and equipment[b]
	   ■ Financial (other than capital
	      transfers)
	3. Capital transfers
	   ■ Transfers to other levels of
	      government[c]
	   ■ Transfers to state-owned
	      enterprises
	4. Repayment of loans
	Total

Source: Author's compilation.
a. Contentious categories such as outlays on social capital are not included here.
b. May include jointly financed projects.
c. May include nonremunerative projects and some loans.
d. Do not include revaluation profits.

an asset (or a transfer leading to the acquisition or creation of an asset) are included in the capital budget as long as they meet three criteria:

1. They are used in the production or supply of goods and services (produtivity criterion).
2. Their life extends beyond a fiscal year (longevity criterion).
3. They are not intended for resale in the ordinary course of operations.

Economists first distinguish between outlays on *self-financing projects* and outlays on *self-liquidating projects*. Although both are included in a capital budget because they are funded from borrowing, self-financing projects have the potential to service only future interest payments, whereas self-liquidating projects have the potential to service both interest and principal repayments.

Economists also distinguish between the acquisition of existing assets and the acquisition of those that will be created. This approach enables a bridge to be built to the national accounts. Productivity and longevity or durability considerations are common to both economists and accountants. Unlike the accountants' approach, however, the economists' approach places more emphasis on the self-liquidating nature of the activity as an additional feature of assets. Furthermore, from the economists' perspective, certain activities of a distinct nature (such as defense) are treated as consumption expenditures even if they technically contribute to assets and thus to capital formation. The accountants' approach makes no such distinctions.[2] Taking account of an asset's life span also poses problems, in that the government acquires several items of equipment for day-to-day use that have a life span longer than a year but are not treated as capital expenditures because they do not meet the productivity criterion. In practice, governments follow a form of case law to determine which items to include. It is quite likely, however, that initial expectations about the criteria may not be fulfilled. In such situations, the nonremunerative projects may be written off through the current account.

Resource Allocation

The first and major part of public financial planning, regardless of whether a capital budget exists, relates to the determination of resources to be allocated. The criteria for this purpose need to be rigorous and applied consistently. The costs and benefits associated with government policies, programs, and projects need to be identified in detail and evaluated because these costs imply real opportunities forgone. Capital budget planning was not an essential component of capital budgets during their initial stages of application, largely reflecting the relative lack of required techniques at the time. Over the years, however, these methodologies have grown, and their application has become an accepted integral part of governmental financial planning. More specifically, such planning enables the following elements:

- Public determination of the optimal level of public stock
- Allocation of public receipts between debt and taxes—and the implicit need to keep the ratio of debt to gross domestic product (GDP) at a constant level, to the extent possible
- The role of compensatory fiscal policy.

The last element requires determination of three items: in which directions amounts are to be spent, whether recession is to be addressed, and how outlays are to be reduced if persistent inflation is the problem. Financial planning is therefore essential for determining economywide policies and strategies and sector development approaches.

To arrive at such decisions, techniques ranging from straightforward discounted cash flows to sophisticated technical, economic, financial, social, institutional, and environmental analyses are applied, as discussed in other chapters. The application of these techniques has been considerably facilitated by the fact that the institutional lenders who finance capital projects insist on the completion of these detailed studies as essential first steps leading to the financing. Periodically someone suggests that the pursuit and application of capital financial planning do not require the existence or operation of a budget. Although this suggestion is indeed true, one must also recognize that although the existence of a capital budget facilitates planning, it can also make such planning an ingrained habit and part of overall discipline. Governments depend on their fiscal machinery to make financial planning possible, and capital budgets facilitate that process. Furthermore, in the context of preparing medium-term fiscal plans, rolling medium-term expenditure plans, and associated approaches, capital financial planning becomes not a remote art but a day-to-day practice. Accrual budgeting facilitates these aspects of planning through its separation of current and capital or investment budgets.

The exercise of capital financial planning also provides an opportunity to focus on other aspects, including risk assessment. Some of the routine issues that governments face in this regard are identified, in brief, in table 3.2. Of particular importance is risk assessment—an area that governments take up in the 13th hour, when the crisis is at the doorstep. Capital financial planning needs to go beyond the project level, to the sector level, and ultimately to the national level to anticipate changes in economic parameters and to internalize them in decision making.

Resource Use

This phase entails the implementation of the capital budget. The steps, as well as the issues that arise in these steps, are listed in table 3.2. From the standpoint of financial discipline, three aspects merit explicit recognition: underfunding, cost escalation, and year-end unspent amounts. Notwithstanding all the care taken in the formulation of financial plans and budgets, governments confront sudden revenue shortfalls during the fiscal year. A typical response is to underfund projects and programs. Yet underfunding is a false choice, often contributing to considerable cost escalations that later pose formidable problems for cost recovery. Many an experience also reveals that the cost of completed projects differs considerably from original estimates, owing not merely to underfunding but also to a variety of factors

TABLE 3.2 Issues in the Management of Capital Budgets

Functional area	Issues
Resource planning and allocation	
1. Project and investment appraisal	
Application of uniform and consistent guidelines	Some techniques may be qualitatively deficient, may lend themselves to manipulation, and may become "design studies" intended to support decisions already made.
2. Funding arrangements	
Centralized borrowing	Centralized borrowing, which leads to resource fungibility and the loss of project identity (except where funded by external resources), may not promote the needed sense of financial responsibility.
Decentralized and market-based borrowing	The absence of regulated and coordinated borrowing among levels of government and governmental units could contribute to competitive borrowing, crowding out, higher costs, and overheating of the economy.
3. Budget formulation	
Medium-term rolling plans	Such plans could contribute to budgetary rigidity, and the management of austerity programs, when needed, would be rendered difficult.
Annual estimates that are based on contracted costs and that allow for inflation	Full adjustment for inflation, apart from contributing to budgetary problems, does not promote financial responsibility.
Domestic currency expenditures that are fully provided for	This part of project outlays depends on the budgetary position, and often full funding may not be provided. Underfunding leads to project delays.
Contingent liability and associated risk management as an integral part of budgetary decision making	In practice, most systems are not adequately geared for this purpose. Some countries have initiated efforts to pass legislation and associated regulations in this regard.
Consideration of the scope for compensatory fiscal action	The need for compensatory fiscal action and the magnitude of adjustment are determined as part of this exercise. In some countries (such as Japan), compensatory fiscal action (stimulus packages) may be taken throughout a fiscal year and a series of supplementary budgets may be approved. In most developing countries, however,

(continued)

TABLE 3.2 *(continued)*

Functional area	Issues
	capital (or equivalent) outlays are generally severely curtailed in order to reduce the overall size of the budget deficit. When this drop is not compensated for through increases in private investment, GDP growth may be reduced.
Risk assessment	Changes in interest and exchange rates have serious implications for self-financing and self-liquidating projects. In some cases, these costs may be borne by the general budget, and the project costs may remain unchanged. These transactions need to be transparent.
Approaches to expenditure management	During this phase, the key variable that is constantly kept in view, particularly during the past two decades, is the overall size of the budget deficit. The size of this deficit remains unaffected by any ill-guided attempts to manipulate items from the current to the capital budget.

Resource use
4. Budget implementation

Release of funds	Major capital projects have their own seasonality of expenditure flows, and each project may have its own distinctive requirements. In general, therefore, funding and associated budgetary authority are released in conformity with project requirements and the implementation schedule.
Underfunding	Projects are commonly underfunded in that even the amounts estimated in the budget may not be released. This underfunding is in addition to the budget compression in allocation at the initial stage of budget preparation. In particular, domestic counterpart outlays may be reduced in the context of a resource shortfall: if projects are financed through earmarked funds, this experience may be escaped.
Payment	In a large number of cases, given the size of the projects, payments are decentralized. In

T A B L E 3 . 2 (*continued*)

Functional area	Issues
	some cases, they are centralized, with the consequence that payments are delayed. In some cases, the payee may be compensated for the delays through interest payments. In most cases, however, arrears in payment are common, revealing a failure of the expenditure management system.
Reporting	A distinction needs to be made between financial reports for internal management and reports for macroeconomic management. The latter include national income accounts and government financial statistics, both of which involve a readjustment of budgetary categories and some imputations (such as depreciation).
Cost escalation	A common feature of most projects is the substantial difference between the initial estimated cost and the completed cost. Variations are due to delays in the acquisition of sites, gaps between estimated and completed costs, major changes in the design of projects, and delays in funding. This difference in costs poses new policy issues for cost recovery. Furthermore, in some cases, projects may prove to be less remunerative than estimated.
Year-end unspent amounts	The lapsing of budgetary funds at the end of the fiscal year induces many a project authority to engage in a spending spree. To minimize this behavior, some countries appropriate budgets that last until the project is finished. Elsewhere, governments attempt to carry forward the unspent amounts.
5. Evaluation	The implementation of each project offers its own lessons of experience for the future. Evaluation is undertaken to ascertain the lessons. For the most part, this practice remains an undervalued exercise.

Source: Author's compilation.

affecting construction and operation. To minimize such variations, techniques such as the Critical Path Method (CPM) and the Project Evaluation and Review Technique (PERT) are applied. Their effects, however, may not be sufficient to overcome inherent problems in project design. Amounts unspent at year-end reflect, in a way, leaks in the financial control system. Some countries endeavor to permit carryovers to following years, an approach that illustrates a way of living with the problem rather than avoiding it. If these procedural aspects are not recognized and addressed, they can affect outcomes and contribute to major differences between budgetary intent and outcome.

Resource Use Accounting and Financial Reporting

The traditional basis of government accounting has been the cash basis, which does not permit the preparation of a balance sheet showing government assets and liabilities. As such, it does not illustrate the net worth of government—one of the principal bases of capital budgets. The alternative approach, accrual accounting, has been advocated to resolve this problem. Accrual accounting involves three features and the possibility of an additional one. The three features relate to the following:

1. The shifting of the recording basis from cash to commitment, regardless of when the payment is made
2. The separation of financial activities into current expenditures and capital ones, with full depreciation allowances that permit the allocation of costs over the life of an asset rather than recording expenses when they are incurred
3. The preparation of financial statements that are in conformity with generally accepted accounting principles (GAAP).

The statements include a balance sheet, an operating statement, a statement of cash flows, a statement of borrowings, a statement of commitments, and a statement of contingent liabilities. These statements illustrate net worth and provide the basis for the decision of the investing public.

The possible additional feature relates to the application of activity-based costing, which enables management to identify factors that contribute to cost increases and possible ways to address such increases. Experience shows that accrual accounting remains for many governments a goal that has yet to be achieved.

Evaluation

The concluding stage of financial operations is evaluation, which seeks to learn the lessons of experience. Completed projects and programs are evaluated to ascertain whether they could have been completed at lesser cost, whether more could have been obtained for the moneys spent, and—more significant—whether the intended benefits have accrued and, if not, whether different incentive structures could have yielded a different outcome. More specifically, for capital budgets, it illustrates whether the loan-funded projects have the potential to be remunerative and self-financing and whether the nonremunerative parts must be written off from the current budget, shifting the burden to the taxpayer. Experience shows that considerable progress has been made in the evaluation of completed projects, particularly when they are funded externally; however, progress remains to be made in the transfer of nonremunerative parts to the current budgets.

Current Practices

The practices of countries vary considerably, revealing several categories. The first category includes those countries that have moved or are moving to accrual accounting and budgeting and therefore observe the distinction between operational and investment budgets. Australia, Chile, and New Zealand are in this group, and the United Kingdom has used what it calls *resource accounting and budgeting* since fiscal year 2000/01. Some of these countries previously had a system of below-the-line accounting for loan transactions. The second category includes those countries that show current and capital transactions in accounts that are now based on an accrual system but whose budgets make no such distinction—although, for analytical purposes, they present extensive data on capital formation. The United States belongs to this category. The third category includes some countries that have introduced accrual accounting but with a modification. They record expenditures on a commitment basis but do not show depreciation allowances because, in their view, such a practice is more appropriate for the corporate than the government sector. For want of a better description, this approach has acquired the label of *modified accrual system*.

The fourth category comprises most industrial countries, including some of the former centrally planned economies, which have in recent years adopted an improved economic classification system. These countries show expenditures in terms of those incurred on physical and financial assets and those transfer payments that are of a capital nature. This classification is also used by most developing countries, either as part of the budget or as part of the international reporting system. These approaches do not include depreciation allowances, and capital receipts may not be shown or recorded separately. Also, for ascertaining capital formation in central and general governments, most industrial countries rely more on national income accounts and associated forecasts. A similar trend is growing in developing countries.

The fifth category comprises those countries that had capital budgets but have moved to investment budgets. Denmark is one; it now maintains an investment budget that can be spent beyond the fiscal year. The sixth category comprises those countries that have the equivalents of capital budgets. Japan, the Republic of Korea, and other Southeast Asian countries have special accounts that have selected features of capital budgets. In Japan, the Fiscal Investment and Loan Program is the most important one; it acquired even more importance during recent years as the primary instrument for the revival of the economy. In many developing countries, governments have developmental budgets of a hybrid form. Some capital outlays are included in these budgets; the receipts include loans received for their financing but are not restricted to capital items only. In several governments, all projects and programs funded by donors and international financial institutions are included in this category. Developmental budgets have become a mixed bag of transactions with flexible applications. In the former centrally planned economies, the budget chapter on construction was the nearest approximation of a capital budget. (The slogan was that construction plus energy was equal to communism.) These economies distinguished between routine government transactions and those that were quasi-commercial and expected to have depreciation accounts.

The last category includes those countries that have a capital budget but do not maintain depreciation allowances. India belongs to this category. China announced in the early 1990s its intention to introduce a capital budget and to refine it over a period. Initially, following Chinese tradition, this capital budget was limited to construction outlays.

Perspectives and Issues

Given tradition and considerable diversity in experience, another issue is the purpose that a capital budget is to serve. In considering this important issue and in seeking an answer to the most significant question (whether capital budgets provide a better framework for the allocation of resources and, specifically, for the determination of long-term investments), one must recognize that different disciplines produce analysts with different perspectives. The different perspectives of accountants, financial managers, macroeconomists, political participants, and market participants are laid out in table 3.3. All view capital budgets as instruments that offer a world of possibilities. If that view is recognized, the question arises as to why capital budgets have not become a regular weapon in the budgetary arsenal and, where they have recently reentered the budget scene, why they had to enter as a piggyback rider of accrual accounting. These aspects require reconsideration of the arguments for and against capital budgets (recapitulated in table 3.4).

Traditional approaches are very difficult to overcome. For too long, capital budgets were considered essential for the commercial sector but not for the government sector. Nearly 50 years ago, a committee looking into the form of government accounts in the United Kingdom concluded that depreciation allowances had no place in government. At the beginning of the new century, this stance had changed, and now the U.K. government holds the view that "the introduction of resource accounting and budgeting . . . is a key part of our commitment to modernising Government for the 21st Century" and that "it will put the U.K. government accounting in line *with commercial practice* [emphasis added] and developments in government accounting and budgeting being adopted in a number of countries around the world" (United Kingdom 1999: 1). Now governments are more receptive to the idea and to exploiting the possibilities and opportunities.

TABLE 3.3   Different Perspectives on Capital Budgets

Position	Perspective
Accountant	Believes capital budgets do the following: ■ Promote a balanced approach to asset creation and asset maintenance ■ Promote the allocation of costs over the useful period of the asset's life ■ Permit clearer identification of assets and thus distinguish between investments and operational budget ■ Promote greater conformity with GAAP ■ Pave the way for full introduction of accrual accounting.
Financial manager	Believes capital budgets do the following: ■ Promote a balanced approach to asset creation and asset maintenance ■ Promote the allocation of costs over the useful period of the asset's life

(continued)

TABLE 3.3 (*continued*)

Position	Perspective
	■ Permit clearer identification of assets and thus distinguish between investment and operational budget ■ Promote greater conformity with GAAP ■ Pave the way for a full introduction of accrual accounting.
Macroeconomist	Believes capital budgets do the following: ■ Permit a greater recognition of the economic significance of some government activities ■ May contribute to better distinction of the cost of government services among beneficiaries and taxpayers ■ Because of debt financing, may promote greater intergenerational equity and may lead to more smooth tax policies (by switching lumpy investments to debt financing from pay-as-you-go methods) ■ May be useful as a tool of compensatory policy but must be tempered by the recognition that most categories of capital expenditures may have the same effect as current expenditures ■ Promote workable limits on borrowing and more coordinated borrowing ■ Require sound techniques of deficit estimation that emphasize, from the viewpoint of sustainability, the overall deficit.
Political participant	Believes capital budgets do the following: ■ Provide alternatives to tax-financed activities ■ Provide more visibility for government activities ■ Provide the much-needed infrastructure that facilitates government services ■ Have the potential to promote greater accountability ■ Provide a basis for exploring partnerships with the corporate sector.
Market participant	Believes capital budgets do the following: ■ Permit a specific link between bond issues and the projects financed ■ Facilitate an assessment of the risk factors and the net worth of the government ■ Offer a better perspective than financial statements, which are too aggregative in nature.

Source: Author's compilation.

TABLE 3.4   Arguments for and against Capital Budgets

For	Against
Capital budgets are the primary instruments of compensatory fiscal action.	The effect of most categories of expenditures is identical, and there is no particular need for capital budgets. Financing through long-term debt could contain short-term budgetary flexibility.
Capital budget planning is an important part of the capital budget and leads to the institutionalization of the application of project appraisal techniques.	Capital budget planning does not necessarily require the existence of a capital budget.
Capital budgets provide a window to the net worth of governments.	Greater importance should be attached to to the proper macroeconomic management of the economy than to the maintenance of the net worth of government.
Direction of the macroeconomic management of the country may be specified in fiscal responsibility legislation, and capital budgets provide additional support of the desire to pursue prudent fiscal policy.	Fiscal responsibility stands by itself, and evidence of its pursuit is to be found in the overall budgetary stance.
Capital budgets provide a clear identification of borrowing and its costs, use, and impact.	Capital budgets could serve as a handmaiden to political approaches that may emphasize borrowing, which may in the long run raise major hurdles to economic development.
Capital budgets permit identification of capital formation in the government sector.	Data on capital formation can be gleaned from national income accounts. Although the existence of a properly organized capital budget may facilitate the transition of government accounts into national income accounts, it is not necessary to have separate budgets. Capital budgets may contribute to a shift in emphasis toward bricks-and-mortar projects. In the absence of proper arrangements for transparency and accountability, capital budgets may contribute to budgetary gimmicks and manipulation of deficit levels by arbitrary shifting of items between current and capital outlays.

(continued)

TABLE 3.4 *(continued)*

For	Against
Capital budgets facilitate the work of bond-rating agencies.	Bond-rating agencies study a wide range of data before making an assessment, and they do not insist on capital budgets.
As a technique, capital budgets facilitate links between budgets, medium-term rolling plans, public investments planning, and the estimation of recurrent costs of maintenance.	These techniques, including rolling public investment planning, do not require capital budgets.
Capital budgets provide a link with other financial statements related to assets, balance sheets, sources and uses of funds, and so on. They show depreciation allowances and, thus, the use of assets throughout their life cycle.	Although the application of accrual accounting is now more widely accepted than before, there are limits on the application of commercial accounting techniques to the government sector. A form of modified accrual may be adequate.
Capital budgets provide a sounder basis for macroeconomic management by differentiating types of outlays and their financing.	In principle, this is true, but a capital budget is not necessary to accomplish it.
Capital budgets facilitate the participation of the corporate sector in projects identified and pursued as part of public policy.	These projects are best conceived and implemented outside the budget.
Capital budgets imply more autonomy for project managers and the application of different techniques of implementation, including project scheduling and monitoring (in which projects are carried out through contractual arrangements). Where projects are funded through borrowing, capital budgets facilitate the growth of a sense of financial responsibility.	There is an inherent danger of the development of a dual culture and enclave mentalities.

Source: Author's compilation.

For too long, however, the issue was not the appropriateness of the capital budget but whether using it was inescapable. Implicit in this approach is the argument that the informational outputs from capital budgets can be obtained from other sources. But much the same can be said about the budget itself, and the argument has been made in some quarters that the government may not need to have a budget at all, because the private sector does its business without the fanfare and ritual associated with one. This argument ignores the fundamental features of a public budget, namely, its expression of a policy intent and its signal to the national economy about what the government intends to do in the next year. If the capital budget is to serve the purposes associated with it, however, more effort is required to address some of the controversial issues and to bring about greater convergence of the different perspectives.

It is argued, for example, that the scope of expenditure items included in a capital budget is somewhat narrow and that outlays on social capital, education, health, research and training, and poverty alleviation measures should be included. In this regard, it must be recognized that the scope of the capital budget conforms to the scope of capital formation included in national accounts. Capital itself is a concept that has undergone change through public discussion. In illustration of the subtle differences between physical, financial, and social capital, distinctions are made between capital formation and investment in a broader sense that brings returns for society as a whole. The existing scope of capital items facilitates a tie-in with national accounts.

In most central governments, the bulk of the capital budgets are in the form of transfers to autonomous agencies and other levels of government; therefore, asset formation takes place at the receiving end. As such, capital budgets may be more useful at the local rather than the central level of government. A capital budget at the central level of government, however, would facilitate the establishment of a more organized buyer-seller relationship and, to that extent, would contribute to a smoother financial management system.

The good, old argument that capital budgets contribute to greater emphasis on bricks-and-mortar projects raises a more philosophical issue, analogous to the chicken-first or egg-first variety. In the context of the formulation of medium-term plans and detailed scrutiny by the legislature and the public alike, it could be difficult to introduce projects except after proper scrutiny and capital budget planning. If this emphasis persists, it would illustrate the triumph of politics and logrolling, pork barrel approaches over the organized process of budget formulation. If anything, a capital budget raises the threshold for the consideration and inclusion of projects for funding, rather than reducing it.

Depreciation is another item about which controversy abounds. Should governments follow corporate practice and depreciate all assets (including defense) as some countries have done (for example, New Zealand), or should governments use separate practices that are more appropriate for the public sector? Increasingly now, the view is moving toward separate practices, and more efforts are being made, through autonomous accounting boards, to specify the relevant accounting standards for the purpose.

The main problem with the capital budget has been that it was never implemented in conformity with the conceptual framework, except in the first phase of its introduction. The extensive prevalence of equivalents and distorted variations has changed the debate in recent years. In essence, therefore, capital budgets—with all the possibilities and the discipline that they bring to the budgeting process—need a fresh impetus.

Notes

1. Most of the available, limited, literature excludes any discussion of capital budget implementation. In governments, actions speak louder than intentions, and both the financial and political markets judge aspirations by the results achieved.
2. This could lead to peculiar applications. Despite extremely short life spans, computer technology products, including software, are treated as capital expenditures.

References and Other Sources

Bland, Robert L., and Wes Clarke. 1999. "Budgeting for Capital Improvements." In *Handbook of Government Budgeting*, ed. Roy T. Mayers, 653–77. San Francisco, CA: Jossey–Bass.

Goode, Richard. 1983. *Government Finance in Developing Countries*. Washington, DC: Brookings Institution.

Goode, Richard, and Eugene A. Birnbaum. 1956. "Government Capital Budgets." *IMF Staff Papers* 5 (1): 23–46.

Mintz, Jack M., and Ross S. Preston. 1993. *Capital Budgeting in the Public Sector*. Kingston, Canada: John Deutsch Institute for the Study of Economic Policy.

Premchand, A. 1983. *Government Budgeting and Expenditure Controls: Theory and Practice*. Washington, DC: International Monetary Fund.

———. 1995. *Effective Government Accounting*. Washington, DC: International Monetary Fund.

———. 2000. *Control of Public Money*. New Delhi: Oxford University Press.

United Kingdom. 1999. Financial Reporting Advisory Board. London: Her Majesty's Treasury.

4

Budget Methods and
Practices

ALTA FÖLSCHER

Budgeting in the public sector is a complex exercise. It involves the combination of information from multiple sources, bringing together different perspectives and dealing with diverse interest groups, all influencing complex decisions. Fragmentation is inevitable between the center and the line, between planners and financial managers, between budgeting and implementation, and between different types of spending. Over time, methods to deal with difficult choices, complexity, and fragmentation have developed within budgeting systems. This chapter provides a perspective on the problems of budgeting that different methods and practices are designed to address and then discusses a number of approaches that have developed over the past 30 years to address these problems. The chapter is written from the perspective of a developing country, but it does provide information about the experience of industrial countries with these approaches.

The Nature of the Problem

Budgeting in the public sector is fundamentally different from budgeting in the private sector. At the heart of the difference are the absence of a bottom line and the presence of a shared and limited source of funding. The dynamics that surround public budgeting play out in a financing context in which the aim is not to make money by spending money, but to reach a wide range of public objectives, some of them intangible. In a public budget, the goals of spending are complex and difficult to measure, and they may relate only indirectly to the activities that are being funded. Public budgeting, therefore, occurs in a politically fraught environment where different public objectives compete for a share of limited available funding in the absence of a relatively objective yardstick, such as contribution to profit, by which to choose among them; where the incentive to keep costs low in order to maximize profit is not present; where performance is difficult to measure; and where sanction and reward systems operate in the context of longstanding public service practices. This context of public budgeting gives rise to ubiquitous problems.

The first revolves around the incentive of individual claimants to maximize their claim on budgetary resources. Whenever many spending units depend on one source of income, each dependent unit will consider its own expenditure increases to be too small to affect the total significantly and will feel free to pursue its own interests without considering the effect of its actions on the source. In public finance, the tax burden of a spending program is spread across many groups and individuals, and claimants to resources are therefore likely to perceive a much lower cost to their proposed spending programs than the actual social cost. Consequently, claimants— for example, spending ministries or external interest groups—will therefore almost always demand a higher level of spending than is socially optimal. This phenomenon is known as the *tragedy of the commons*. It prevails between central ministries of finance and spending agencies, as much as it occurs at the level of the spending agency between different subunits and the agency itself.

It is for this reason that constraints on the aggregate level of spending are critical. Without such constraints, just adding together the total claims of ministries to produce a budget would result in unsustainable deficits or tax burdens.

Choosing among the different claimants, however, introduces a whole separate set of budgeting problems. There is not a single objective measure or reliable objective methodology by which tradeoffs can be made. Ultimately the choice between funding roads or schools, between funding region A or region B, or between funding services to poorer beneficiary groups rather than middle-income and rich groups is a political choice. And politicians often (although not exclusively) make funding choices on the basis of what they believe will keep them in office. In mature political systems, where the connection between public policy, budgetary performance, and political survival is stronger, politicians make choices that are based on their constituencies' preferences. In countries where this connection is weak, the budget shares for which politicians fight may have more to do with power, political deal making, and access to resources than with optimal policy outcomes related to stated country priorities. In these, budgeting and spending outturns remain misaligned with stated priorities.

Campos and Pradhan (1996: 7) view this problem in terms of the transaction costs associated with budgeting. Mapping expenditures to perceived preferences and getting feedback from civil society on whether the mapping is true carry high transaction costs. Parliament is an important institution in this regard, but recent practice in many developing countries includes feedback mechanisms that operate directly between the citizenship and the executive. The costs of mapping, however, are not the only transaction costs associated with negotiating tradeoffs. Decisions about budgets are rarely made in a single office by a single individual. Budget processes involve complex institutional arrangements for sequenced and often collective decision making. Invariably the tragedy of the commons will create demands by individual claimants in excess of the constraints. The result is that the cost of collective decision making increases as individuals and groups strive to structure and restructure coalitions to enlarge their share of limited funds. In a functioning budget system, this tendency to increase costs is countered by institutional arrangements that help build consensus among the competing groups on the relative expenditure allocations.

This consensus is not always easy to achieve. For one, it requires good information on what tradeoffs are being made, including what everyone has to give and will gain in relation to their expenditure mandates. These losses and gains are not always apparent to budget decision makers. An important feature of budgeting in the public domain is that those who hold the best information on spending programs are not those who decide whether one program or another should be funded. Spending agencies have better information on how best to allocate resources within their sectors to achieve given objectives, but it is often not in their interest to divulge this information in a competitive budgeting environment because doing so means that they may get penalized. Many sector-based budget reforms have failed in the long run because the savings that the reforms introduced are not available for use in the sector but are immediately usurped at the center for deployment elsewhere. This information asymmetry is at the root of many policy failures in government.

Traditionally, budgeting systems have coped with these problems by what Wildavsky and Caiden (1997: 48, quoting Herbert Simon) called "satisficing." Instead of evolving budgeting practices that meet these problems head on to produce the best possible outcomes, budget decision makers satisfice—that is, they satisfy and suffice. Instead of maximizing, the strategy is to behave in ways that allow the system to get by, come out all right, and avoid the worst. Incremental line-item budgeting practices offer well-established methods for satisficing within a time-delimited budget process.

Incremental Line-Item Budgeting

In the third edition of their seminal work, *The New Politics of the Budgetary Process*, Wildavsky and Caiden (1997) describe a traditional system of budgeting, which they dub *classical budgeting*. The main identifying characteristic of this system is incrementalism.

Wildavsky and Caiden argue that budgeting systems revert to incrementalism because budgeting is complex, with many interrelated items, and because technical difficulties arise when choosing between competing options. As Wildavsky and Caiden (1997: 45) put it, "Endless time and unlimited ability to calculate may help. But time is in short supply, the human mind can only encompass just so much, and the number of budgetary items may be huge." The programs to which funds are allocated and their associated outputs in the real world—for example, roads, teaching hours, serviced hospital beds—have different values for different people. There is no objective method of judging priorities among different programs.

The limited period of time within which budget decision makers prepare and examine a subsequent year's budget does not allow them to examine whether each stream of recurrent spending is justified or to consider all alternative uses for the funds. Besides, such a process would need to include in the calculations future funds already spoken for on account of contractual or quasi-contractual commitments that were made in previous years and that span years. The base of spending is therefore taken almost as a given, and the focus of the budget process is on making marginal changes to this base, albeit on making new spending proposals, bidding for new funds, or decreasing spending in various ways. Working with a given base enables management of the calculations and resolution of conflicts within the budget preparation time frame.

The most significant determining factors of a new year's budget are all previous budgets. Many items are rolled over from year to year as a standard. Once programs are judged to be satisfactory, they become part of the budgeting base and are rarely challenged. Because programs are usually associated with internal and external interest groups—for example, officials employed to run a program and the program's beneficiaries—discontinuing a program involves a difficult internal and external political process in which there are losers. The focus of the budget process thus becomes a narrow range of increases and decreases.

When a project or a program is included in the base, it is not only for the budget year, but for all future years until it is challenged. In other words, in classical budget practice, spending agencies have a fair expectation that the base they have established incrementally over years will be funded in the next budget year. In addition, there is also an expectation that they will receive what Wildavsky and Caiden (1997: 46) term a *fair share* of some proportion of funds that are available for distribution, whether because of an increase in total expenditure or because of decreases to some agency's funding.

How budgeting systems define the base in practice depends on whether inflation is a significant factor and whether there are significant fluctuations in the demand for spending, particularly in programs that result from separate legislation, such as the social security program or free primary education. When inflation and significant fluctuations in the demand for spending are absent, an agency's current spending is taken to be its base. However, when the cost of providing goods or services at existing levels in future years is likely to increase on account of price increases or because the number of beneficiaries will increase, the base is usually defined as the future cost of providing a program at current levels of service.

Traditionally, budgets were arranged by line item. Many countries still have budgets that are classified in accordance with specific line items. When budgets were first brought to legislatures, every separate piece of spending got approved in all its particular details. In other words, a legislature would consider an agency request to build a bridge, relevant input by input: the number of labor hours required, the number of logs for the supports, and so forth. However, as the number of agencies and their activities grew, a limited number of standardized items were selected under which activities needed to be described. Over time, previously approved programs were reflected in bulk by agency against the standardized line items, effectively for reapproval. Only new spending proposals were considered separately as a project or program, to be absorbed in subsequent years in the funding base. In recent years, many countries—including developing countries—have moved away from the line-item system to compliance with the International Monetary Fund's Government Finance Statistics system of economic classification (IMF 2001). However, this move has not necessarily brought a fundamental change to how budgeting is done: budget decision makers use the new economic classifications, instead of line items, to control inputs. It is only when allocations are first made to a classification of programs and subprograms that substantial shifts in how budgets are decided can be engineered.

This delinking of base spending from the coherent sets of activities they fund underpins typical input-based incremental line-item budgeting practices. Instead of looking at the activities that were being funded—and that were in line with the budget control requirements of budget classification—spending and central control agencies looked at classes of inputs when spending cuts were required. Instead of discontinuing lower-priority activities, these agencies applied spending cuts to inputs across all activities, whether of low or high priority.

In an incremental line-item budgeting system, decision making about the bulk of spending is thus reduced to concentrating on changes in various input items—personnel, equipment, maintenance, utilities, or transportation—that make up programs rather than to looking at programs (or subprograms) as wholes. Hence, though all programs are affected negatively by spending cuts, no single program needs to be shut down, and the difficult process of negotiating the discontinuation with stakeholders can be avoided. As Wildavsky and Caiden (1997) note, the line-item form enables decision makers to concentrate on the less divisive issue of how much for each item, rather than how much for one set of beneficiaries over another.

Budgeting Practices in Incremental Systems of Developing Countries

Line-item incremental budget systems include an array of institutionalized behaviors that detract from good budget outcomes. In their work on budgeting in developing countries, Wildavsky and Caiden (1980: 137) relate a number of departmental strategies common to budget practices in these countries. Although they undertook the research in the 1970s, practitioners will recognize some, if not all, of the strategies as still part and parcel of practice today.

First is the practice at line ministry level whereby budgeting means requesting resources equal to what spending ministries perceive their real needs to be—and then some. Instead of budgeting being the practice of planning for available resources, agencies perceive that there is always more money available and that the initial budget ceiling they receive is merely a device to limit the number of requests with which the ministry of finance has to contend. Their behavior is also motivated by a desire to protect themselves against the budgetary effect of macroeconomic uncertainty: when revenues fluctuate, agencies compete to avoid spending cuts. Overstating needs and highlighting the unavoidability of expenses are well-known strategies to guard against uncertainty.

In countries where the finance ministry is powerful, has good capacity, and is well organized, ceilings are more rigid. In countries where this is not the case, ceilings are not taken seriously at all. In both cases, however, the ceilings are perceived as merely the starting point for the annual budget struggle. In an incremental system, the informal rules of the game concern agencies' strategies to maximize their share in the budget pie, countered by the ministry of finance's strategies to bring requests down to manageable numbers and size.

A classical strategy of agencies is to pad their requests on the assumption that the ministry of finance is likely to effect cuts as a matter of course. Estimates are rarely prepared well, with the result that the ministry of finance, lacking sufficient information and, often, sufficient capacity to cut in a refined manner, resorts to percentage decreases across spending agency budgets. Budgets then are effectively made at the center, with little spending agency input.

Wildavsky and Caiden (1980: 141) note that in an incremental system with ritualistic cycles of padding and cutting, spending agencies that do not leave room for cuts disconcert their examiners. The larger the request and the number of proposals, the more the ministry of finance can cut while still giving a department additions to its previous total. A department that submits a high number of projects is at an advantage, because it is likely to receive more.

Agencies with superior information also routinely underbudget for high-priority expenditure or for expenditure driven by legislative requirements. During the spending year, ministries of finance have little choice but to provide provisional funding to cover shortfalls. Another version of asking for less than what is required occurs when spending agencies in an annual budget system provide low first-year estimates of project costs. Once the project is approved, future-year expenses are much higher, with the government committed to finish what it has started.

The difference between industrial and developing countries, however, does not lie in the existence of practices such as these, but rather in how frequently they occur and how extreme they are (Wildavsky and Caiden 1980: 142). The stable environment of industrial countries means that it is less necessary for spending agencies to inflate their requests over the previous year's totals to ensure that they hold on to funds. Finance ministries in industrial countries usually also have more accurate information on what is being spent and what is required to fulfill policy commitments, thereby putting them in a better position to penalize with confidence when spending agencies inflate bids.

In developing countries, relegating budgeting for the bulk of spending to incremental increases and reductions is also related to the presence of resources from external development partners. Typically, a lot of attention would be paid to the detail of relatively small items of expenditure, often connected to development partners that bring in external resources, while large expenditure issues remain unexamined. In practice, priority setting in developing countries can be determined by the availability of donor funds, rather than by overarching domestic priorities.

Typically, in developing countries, the budget is never examined comprehensively but is made and approved in fragments. A significant form of fragmentation is found in many developing countries, where public investment or project-type spending and spending on routine government activities are budgeted for separately in the investment (or development or capital) and operational (or recurrent) budget, respectively. Although there is some logic behind such a division—for one thing, it means that the risk of one-off project funding becoming a permanent part of the base is reduced—over time the criteria for funding activities under the development budget or recurrent budget become blurred. The development budget in many countries now includes both investment and operational funding; the determining factor is not the type of spending, but rather the source of funds. Earmarked donor funding is reflected in the development budget, together with counterpart domestic funding and domestically funded investment projects. Thus, agencies rarely budget comprehensively against priorities for all available resources, and finance ministries are even less likely to be able to consider spending bids systematically and rationally against available resources.

Research by Tohamy, Dezhbakhsh, and Aranson (2006) shows that higher inflation rates cause budgeting to be more incremental. In contrast, higher future discount rates and persistent high deficits cause departures from incremental budgeting. Of course, incrementalism is also an organizational strategy by budget holders: if the base of spending is taken for granted and new money is simply added, the result is a growing budget.

Since the 1970s, the cost of budgeting by an incremental line-item approach has become clear. In industrial countries, the upward bias it caused in spending, together with the underlying growth in government that it fostered, resulted in unsustainably high deficits when macroeconomic conditions became tight after the oil crises. In developing countries, the scarcity of resources against high development needs puts in sharp profile the need for spending to be closely aligned with priorities. In short, during the past three decades, budgets have ceased to be a complementary tool whose primary functions are to deliver on government's financial objectives and to ensure fiduciary accountability. Today there is a much better realization that they are at the heart of policy making and the only real avenue to translate a country's developmental goals into results. This realization has resulted in several efforts to change budget methods and practices. Although the approaches differ, they have in common an effort to move budgets out of the realm of satisficing and into a framework of making an effort to seek optimum outcomes. Muddling through is no longer sufficient.

One consideration behind efforts to improve budgeting methods and practices is the argument that a chain of principal-agent relationships includes the potential for agency problems (Leruth and Paul, 2006: 4). The relationship between finance ministries and spending agencies is a typical agency problem, subject to hidden information and hidden actions. The agreement to fund agencies also is contractual in nature: the spending agency is required to produce a specific level and quality of output in return for receiving funding. Other principal-agent relationships in the budget process are between parliament and the executive, between political heads of spending ministries and officials, between the center of a spending ministry and programs or institutions, and between the central government and subnational governments in decentralized systems.

The prospect of using agents' or spending ministries' own self-interest to overcome information asymmetry has generated new thinking about how to approach the budget process. A combination of incentive alignment and the traditional hierarchical coercive mechanisms of monitoring and sanctioning has become the staple of many budget reform programs.

Another influential factor in efforts to address the institutionalized incremental nature of budgeting arose out of the consensus in the 1960s that although a rational model was preferable as a model for making policy and budget decisions, the incremental model best described the actual practice of decision making in governments (Howlett and Ramesh 1995: 137). An idealized, rational policy-making process consists of rational individuals and institutions following sequential steps of establishing goals for solving problems, exploring alternative strategies for reaching those goals, setting out the significant consequences of each goal, and, finally, selecting the option that best solves the problem or solves it at least cost. Doubts about the practicality of the rational model resulted in the development of Yale University political scientist Charles Lindblom's incremental model, which portrayed public policy decision making as a political process characterized by bargaining and compromise among self-interested decision makers (Howlett and Ramesh 1995: 141). The model centers on a set of simplifying and focusing stratagems that public managers use to deal with complexity:

- Analysis is limited to a few somewhat familiar policy alternatives, which differ only marginally from the status quo.
- Analysis of policy goals is intertwined with empirical aspects of the issue at hand and with other implicit values.
- A higher focus is placed on ills to be remedied than on positive goals.
- A sequence of trials, errors, and revised trials takes place over several budget years.
- Analysis of consequences is limited.
- The analytical world is fragmented among many partisan public policy participants.

In practice, decisions never vary significantly from the status quo, because decisions are made through a process of political bargaining and because it is easier to continue the existing pattern of distribution rather than to try radically new proposals. Budget participants avoid reopening old issues or considering radically different choices, because doing so would make agreement difficult. Although further analytical models were developed subsequently to describe the way in which policy decisions are made, in practice the debate that the models sparked on how public policy choices should be made resulted in a number of experiments to change policy-making and budgeting methods, notably the introduction of a planning-programming-budgeting (PPB) system and of zero-based budgeting into federal-level budgeting in the United States.

Elsewhere, however, the idea that incentives and better information can improve purely incremental budgeting practices produced a series of innovative approaches to budgeting that focused on better information and alignment of incentives. Modern budgeting systems (and reform programs to shift more traditional systems) often include various elements of these approaches.

Beyond Incrementalism: Rationality and Incentives in Budget Methods

Three early attempts to bring better information and greater rationality to the budgeting table were initiated in the United States at the federal level. These efforts built on earlier moves to program budgeting systems, which were exported from the United States to developing countries through the United Nations (UN).

Program Budgeting Systems

Since the middle of the 20th century, the pressure to spend more effectively and develop better budgeting techniques produced an almost universal acceptance that budgeting is not only about planning for inputs, but also, perhaps primarily, about planning for the results that governments want to achieve. In developments that can be traced back to the introduction of program budgeting in the United States in the 1940s, more results-oriented budgeting techniques were developed in iterative processes that benefited from the country's own and other countries' mistakes. Although a lot of the early development occurred in industrial countries—the transfer of programming budgeting to the United Kingdom in the 1970s, New Zealand's output focus in the 1980s, Sweden's system of management by objectives—the use of results-oriented budgeting by the United Nations as a precondition for aid assistance triggered its quick spread to the developing world. There are several variants of introducing a focus on the results of spending into budgeting practices, and they are often grouped together as a movement under the term *program budgeting*. Exactly how program budgeting terms are used varies enormously in practice. Box 4.1 provides a reference to key terms and where they first came into use.

In 1965, the United Nations published *A Manual for Programme and Performance Budgeting*. This book advocated performance budgeting comprising program structures, a system of accounts and financial management, and a measurement of efficiency. Dean (1989, as quoted in Rose 2003: 7) defines *program budgeting* as follows:

■ Programming, or the subdivision of the government budget for information purposes into programs and activities representing identifiable units with similar aims or operations

■ Identifying the operational aims of each program and activity for the budget year

■ Budgeting and accounting so that the separate costs and revenues of each program are shown

■ Measuring the outputs and performance of activities so that these can be related to the activities' costs and to operational aims

■ Using the relevant data to establish standards and norms so that costs and performance can be evaluated and government resources can be used more efficiently.

BOX 4.1 A Confusion of Terms

Budgeting practices have been moving away from a focus on inputs toward outputs, and from incremental budgeting to rational approaches to decision making, over several decades. In the process, a small set of keywords has been used to describe different initiatives. In some cases, similar systems are described by different words, whereas the same words are used to name systems that differ in some, or many, significant respects. This often causes confusion and, in developing countries, the perception by practitioners lower down in the system that they have already implemented proposed reforms several decades ago. The table below, partly drawn from Rose (2003: 17–18), sets out key definitions and indicates where terms were first used.

Approach	Definition
Program budgeting	Early approach that involved the identification of programs with operational aims with costs and revenues attached. Used in the United States in the 1940s.
Output budgeting	Term used to describe the budgetary approach in the United Kingdom's central government around 1970. Broadly similar to performance budgeting.
Performance budgeting	Refers to the linking of expected results to budgets. Like program budgeting except that it adds an emphasis on targeting and measuring outputs and performance, with data analyzed against aims and standards. Usually used as a term across countries to cover a range of specific processes.
Planning-programming-budgeting system	Developed for the United States defense budget and applied by President Johnson to all federal agencies.
Management by objectives	Successor to the planning-programming-budgeting system. Linked agencies' objectives to budget requests. Introduced management responsibility for achieving outputs and outcomes. Used by the Nixon administration.
Output-purchase budgeting	The New Zealand form of performance budgeting. Ministers purchase outputs from executive agencies with their available funds.

Source: Based on Rose 2003.

Despite evaluations of the system in the United States that raised concerns about information overload, and despite problems with performance measurement in the early 1960s, the U.S. methodology was adopted almost wholesale by the United Nations and exported to developing countries. Implementation did not proceed smoothly. Typically, countries lacked trained staff members with the necessary experience and skills to undertake the reclassification of budgeting and accounting systems or to develop performance indicators. Coupled with institutional factors such as bureaucratic resistance, entrenched practices of rent-seeking that fed off traditional budgeting systems and uninterested legislatures, performance budgets were prepared in an additional layer of futile activity. Underneath, agencies and finance ministries continued to budget as previously, incrementally and by line item.

Planning-Programming-Budgeting System

A narrow application of program budgeting emerged in the 1970s in the United States. The PPB approach to budgeting was applied by Robert S. McNamara, U.S. secretary of defense and former president of the Ford Motor Company, to budgeting in the U.S. Department of Defense. Presented with a budget that specified the proposed allocations to the department by administrative unit and line items, McNamara insisted that it be reorganized in line with what the money would be used for. Spending that applied to a defense objective had to be grouped in one program, whether funds were to be spent by the Navy, the Air Force, or the land forces. Although part of the purpose of this exercise was to get the spending plans to make sense, the process also increased the leverage of the secretary in relation to the individual armed services (Nathan 2000).

In 1965, President Lyndon Johnson directed all federal agencies to apply the PPB approach to the entire budgetary process. Agencies were asked to identify their objectives and different methods of achieving the objectives. The different methods were then costed and submitted to systematic comparison of their efficiency and effectiveness. Three kinds of reports were to be submitted to the Bureau of the Budget:

1. Program memoranda describing the agency's strategy and comparing the cost and effectiveness of major alternative programs
2. Special analytic studies that looked at selected current and long-term issues
3. Program and financial plans that summarized program choices in terms of their outputs and costs over a five-year period.

Three years later, however, President Johnson revoked the order. Agencies used various strategies to continue budgeting as they used to. Some did not submit the planning memoranda and analysis; others submitted mountains of paper that the agency's senior staff members had not even read. The staff at the Bureau of the Budget was not equipped to undertake the analysis required, and it continued to operate as previously. The simple fact is that specifying the objectives of every possible policy alternative, comparing those alternatives systematically, and then reviewing all agencies' work at the center constitute an impossible task. Experience in the United Kingdom with implementing PPB approaches in defense and education shows that they require an unbroken line between strategic planning and day-to-day operations. In many policy areas, a direct line has never existed (Rose 2003: 12).

One positive aspect of program budgeting approaches, including PPB, is the recognition that public sector organizations are interdependent. PPB attempts to bring clarity about the goals of government and seeks cost-effectiveness by assessing various courses of action. Premchand (1983, quoted in Rose 2003: 13) noted, though, that a number of problems, including lack of training, shortage of skills, inadequate phasing and too ambitious an application, disillusionment with paperwork, and nonuse of the information (or its use for strengthened central control) contributed to the failures of these early forms of program budgeting.

Zero-Based Budgeting

Another effort to make government budgeting more rational was undertaken in the late 1970s under the Carter administration. Zero-based budgeting required every agency to make all its budgeting decisions as if they were completely new decisions, in other words, as if the agency were starting each year with a clean slate and an amount of money. In complete contrast to incremental budgets, zero-based budget systems assume a zero base at the beginning of each budget cycle. All spending agencies are therefore required to develop a fresh request for funding every year, which is based on a total cost analysis for each program. Continuation of programs is not guaranteed.

In a classical zero-based budgeting system, the imperative to consider all spending afresh is combined with prescriptions regarding how agencies should go about implementing the system. First, a spending agency is broken down into decision units: programs, subprograms, or institutions. Each decision unit then develops goals and associated decision packages, which include a description of funding levels and increments, activity, resource requirements, the short-term objective, and the objective's contribution to the goal. The packages are then ranked in order of priority, and an operating budget prepared. The final stage involves selection of decision packages at the decision unit and finally at the agencywide level (Mengistu 1997: 9–13).

Although such an approach would, in principle, facilitate the discontinuation of programs that are no longer required, in practice it is close to impossible to implement. First, like the PPB approach, it generates masses of paperwork for which there is neither the time nor the human capacity in budgeting systems. Second, it is not necessarily true that lower-priority programs will receive less funding or be discontinued: the approach fails to take into account the realities of institutional and public politics that drive budgets. Third, some public policy areas—for example, those that are driven by legislation—do not lend themselves to dismantling and reevaluation. In reality, most state programs are not amenable to annual evaluation, because even if they are not required by legislation, they involve multiyear contractual relationships with service providers, not to mention public officials. And fourth, it is not self-evident what is maximized if zero-based budgeting is adopted in its classical form. In this form, it is an inwardly focused process that puts emphasis on the priorities of managers. Insufficient attention is paid to mapping decisions to the preferences and priorities of beneficiaries. Zero-based budgeting, however, remains popular as the ideal budgeting technique for public institutions, particularly those with external stakeholders who are concerned with the efficacy of public budgeting methods.

Both PPB and zero-based budgeting were attempts to make public budgeting a pure, comprehensive, rational undertaking, although the first put emphasis on cost-benefit analyses while the second was more concerned with workload measurements. Both failed because, as Nobel Prize winner Herbert A. Simon has argued since the early 1950s, there are cognitive limits to decision makers' ability to consider all possible options. These limits force them to consider alternatives selectively, and even then they choose on ideological or political grounds. Like the PPB system, zero-based budgeting was also abandoned as a budgeting technique.

Making Results Orientation Work in Budgeting

Despite problems with early application in the United States and the failure of the PPB experiment, some form of program budgeting approach has persisted in the methods and practices of several developing and industrial countries. It is perhaps noteworthy that many of the modern approaches to budgeting are located on a spectrum between incrementalism and pure comprehensive rationality. These approaches involve attention to the following key issues:

- Developing budgeting institutions that respond to incentives so that more of the traditional review, assessment, and allocation work of central budget offices is done at the spending ministry level, where there is better information, because it is in the spending ministry's own interest to have it done well
- Improving but demarcating and sequencing the information that is brought to bear on budgeting decisions
- Making budget decision-making processes more transparent, including the ex ante setting of rational allocation criteria
- Introducing a focus on outputs and ultimately on results as the driver of discussions in the budget process.

To a large degree, modern budgeting techniques do not operate on their own. Where they are successful, they are linked to an overall approach to managing the public sector, with the budget and its associated methods as a central process to make the approach operational.

Modern budgeting practices now include New Public Management (NPM) approaches. NPM approaches involve the targeting of organizational incentives to leverage changes in how individual agencies budget and spend. Most notably, they involve the decentralization of responsibilities to lower organizational levels, including the discretion to decide how funds will be spent and to account for what was achieved with funds received. By bringing the responsibility to budget closer to better information about spending efficiency and effectiveness and by holding managers accountable for results, NPM approaches try to use the alignment of incentives to improve the quality of spending decisions. An NPM approach to budgeting, therefore, works only if it also includes reorganizing the budget into an output- or product-based format or narrowly linking a traditional input-based format to measurable targets.

Larbi (1999) identifies circumstances in both developing and industrial countries that lead to the proliferation of NPM-type reforms in budgeting practices (table 4.1).

NPM is a set of broadly similar structural, organizational, and managerial changes in public sectors. It shifts the emphasis from traditional public administration to public management. Table 4.2 sets out typical characteristics of an NPM approach and notes how the principles have been applied in the budgeting environment.

TABLE 4.1 Drivers of Change: Factors in Developing and Industrial Countries Underpinning Public Management Reforms

Industrial market economies	Developing economies
Economic and fiscal crises in the 1970s and 1980s	Economic and fiscal crises and increasing debt burden in the 1970s and 1980s
Quest for efficiency and effectiveness in public services	Structural adjustment lending conditions, including efforts to reduce public deficits
Ascendancy of neoliberal ideas in policy making in the 1970s and 1980s, including a belief in markets and competition and the minimal role of the state	Efforts to reduce the size and role of government under economic liberalization policies
Coming into power of conservative governments	Political and policy instability
Development of information technology to facilitate and support change	Failure of public administration institutions and the need to reform them and build their capacity
Growth and role of a network of international management consultants who believe in New Public Management	Good governance requirements and their link to public administration, management and budget reform
	Demonstration effects of reforms in the industrial world
	Technical assistance and the influence of international management consultants as advisers on reforms

Source: Based on Larbi 1999: 11.

The shift from old public administration to New Public Management has had fundamental implications for budgeting (Rose 2003: 21). Traditional budgeting practices focus on economy of inputs, financial regularity, and adherence to procedure. NPM systems permit greater flexibility of inputs and processes in return for greater emphasis on outputs and performance.

The budgeting practices of only a few countries, such as New Zealand and Singapore, however, follow a strong managerialist or NPM approach, where the public sector is divided into purchasers and providers with explicit contractual arrangements and the purchasing of outputs. More often, countries focus on a range of common issues that push their budget methodologies closer to decentralized management and a performance orientation and away from an exclusive focus on inputs, centralized decision making, and controls. Such issues include efforts to do the following:

- Make clearer links between inputs, outputs, and outcomes.
- Develop statements of goals that become the focus of attention to establish ex ante accountability when departmental requests are reviewed in relation to those goals.

TABLE 4.2 A New Public Management Approach

New Public Management characteristic	Application to budgeting practices
Decentralization of management authority within public services	Spending agencies and program managers have discretion over the allocation and use of funds within ceilings.
Shift to disaggregation of units into quasi-contractual or quasi-market forms and the introduction of competition and mixed provision contracting relationships in the public sector	Budgeting practices evolve around purchaser-provider splits, with quasi-independent agencies providing services to minimum standards within a set budget and outsourcing.
Creation of synergy between the public and private sectors	Public-private partnerships provide public infrastructure and services.
Greater emphasis on output controls and on quality and responsiveness to customers	Public opinion surveys are used to determine the effectiveness and quality of spending.
Explicit standards and measures of performance, use of performance contracts to manage human resources, and changes in employment relations	Outputs, not inputs, are funded, performance indicators are used, transparency of performance is important, future funding is linked to past performance, and personal responsibility for use of funds is emphasized.
Stress on greater discipline and parsimony in resource use	Budgeting techniques are remodeled to improve efficiency and effectiveness, budgets for certain functions are capped, and greater transparency in budgets through classification and budget documentation reforms is emphasized.

Source: Based on Larbi 1999: 14.

- Develop performance management capacity and appropriate policy management structures, including enhanced roles for legislatures and audit institutions.
- Develop ex post accountability mechanisms that focus on performance (Rose 2003: 4).

Box 4.2 provides information on how different member countries of the Organisation for Economic Co-operation and Development have applied a performance orientation to budgeting.

BOX 4.2 Selected Performance Budgeting Practices of
Organisation for Economic Co-operation and Development Members

Australia
In Australia, ministers approve outcomes and outputs that are developed by
agencies in conjunction with the relevant minister and then endorsed by the
finance ministry. The outcomes are identified in the appropriation bills and
annual portfolio budget statements, binding spending agencies to use the
appropriated resources for the identified outcomes. Annual reports provide
ex post accountability. They state the extent to which planned performance
has been achieved using indicators of efficiency and effectiveness.

Canada
Departments submit annual reports on plans and priorities, containing key
results commitments for a three-year period, to the legislature. After the spending year, departmental performance reports are tabled in the legislature.

New Zealand
The system focuses on controllable outputs rather than uncontrollable
outcomes. Outcome targets are set out in key government goals. These goals
are treated as a political responsibility of ministers. The outcome targets are
translated into departmental output-focused key priorities for which chief
executives (or spending agency heads) are held accountable. Chief executives
are contracted to deliver on the targets. Ministers (as the purchaser) review
agency performance.

United Kingdom
Departments enter into public service agreements with the treasury. These
agreements cover the aims, aspirations, and outcome targets of the department. Departments publish service delivery agreements, which include
output and process targets that are based on outcomes set out in the public
service agreements. The treasury takes a key role in oversight of the system
and of target setting. The treasury monitors outcomes quarterly with scrutiny
by the relevant cabinet committee. Progress is also monitored by the Office of
the Prime Minister.

Source: Based on Rose 2003: 3–4.

Using a Medium-Term Approach

A parallel development in budget practice has been the widespread shift from
annual planning for one year ahead to budgeting for a longer period.[1] A first
application of a coherent system of forward budgeting occurred in Australia,
where a medium-term expenditure framework (MTEF) was introduced in

the 1980s, when the incoming government had to demonstrate to interest groups that the existing policy mix would become unaffordable and result in higher taxes over the medium term.

In their seminal work on budgeting institutions and expenditure outcomes, Campos and Pradhan (1996) identified MTEFs as critical institutions to operationalize incentive compatibility in budgeting systems. First, by providing a resource-constrained expenditure framework, MTEFs enable the ministry of finance to engineer a budget process that sequences resource allocation decisions such that spending agencies are more likely to be aware of the real resource constraint, thus reducing tragedy of the commons problems. Second, by providing ex ante clear ceilings and resource allocation criteria to spending agencies, MTEFs shift the burden of calculation to where there is better information. Because the budget process happens within a predetermined medium-term indicative resource framework (linked to macroeconomic policy considerations), the burden on spending agencies to cushion themselves against uncertainty is reduced while there is transparency about the level of likely additional resources. Third, an MTEF approach to budgeting provides a medium-term planning horizon and should include a system for comparing the medium-term costs of competing policies. When the expenditure framework is comprehensive—in other words, when it includes all claims on public funds—it facilitates a more comprehensive approach to budgeting.

Narrowly defined, an MTEF is a comprehensive, governmentwide spending plan that links policy priorities to expenditure allocations within a fiscal framework—linked to macroeconomic and revenue forecasts—usually over a three-year forward planning horizon. Successful MTEFs denote more than just a set of multiyear spending plans: they should be the outcome of an approach to budgeting that requires early policy prioritization, a better evaluation of competing policies and programs, and a deliberate matching of current and medium-term plans with available resources through a disciplined process. MTEFs have been proposed as an essential element of modern budgeting practice. In reality, they have often not delivered.

Reasons for their failure include insufficient attention to the preconditions and the complementary reforms necessary for their successful introduction. Reforms are often too narrowly focused on financial planning and technical tools, such as detailed, activity-based costing. Although the technical MTEF toolkit provides important building blocks of functional systems, their effect is likely to be limited if not backed by a proper process that is based on an assessment of macroeconomic performance and creates buy-in to tradeoffs, including political buy-in. An effective MTEF system is as much about the structures, institutions, and rules of the budget process as it is about the multiyear plans that result.

An MTEF becomes unglued quickly if fiscal discipline is lacking, if there is macroeconomic instability, or if forecasts for key macroeconomic variables and revenue collection targets are unrealistic, thereby preventing the formulation of an accurate resource envelope within which to operate. Part of the failure can also be explained by the inadequacy of supporting institutions and by the technical demands placed on staff members. If MTEFs are to result in better spending and service delivery, they need to be well integrated with, and complemented by, improvements in other public policy and management processes. A critical reform is that of the budget classification system: it must provide a program view of spending for planning that is linked to an administrative and line-item view for implementation purposes. MTEFs operate best when budgets are developed using a program budgeting methodology.

However, the rules of the MTEF system itself determine the contribution it can make, particularly regarding the link between planning and budgeting. The MTEF system can ensure over time that a higher proportion of public funds is spent on priority programs if (a) within the resource-constrained framework approach marginal changes in resource availability are maximized and used to force tradeoffs between and within spending areas and (b) the medium-term perspective is used to phase out the least important spending programs and activities and overcome spending rigidities. In this context, the MTEF approach provides a feasible alternative to incremental line-item budgeting.

If this shift in approach is to be effective, fiscal policy targets and the fiscal framework must be determined first, in order to provide a transparent framework for planning. This framework disciplines the formulation of subsequent spending options and makes tradeoffs explicit. A further determinant of the success of an MTEF rests on the cooperation and buy-in from spending ministries. When there are few incentives for ministries to coordinate activities or assist in the planning exercise, or if ownership from the political level is not strong, the potential benefits of an MTEF are compromised.

The introduction of an MTEF raises the demand for technical competence not only for the ministry of finance but also for the staffs of line ministries.

Budgeting Methods to Expose Choices on the Ground

In recent years, different countries have applied different mechanisms within MTEFs to improve the quality of information used to make resource allocations. An important aspect of this trend is the introduction of program classification and a performance orientation, often combined in parallel program performance budgeting systems.

An important additional task of the budget process is to expose the choices faced by government, thus empowering political officeholders to choose among the options. Confidence in and consensus about the choices that are made require that the choices be comprehensively identified and analyzed. The discussion in this chapter makes clear how daunting this task is, given limited time and capacity. In recent years, countries have developed several budgeting methods and practices that assist with this task. These methods can be broadly categorized into process-based mechanisms and mechanisms that determine what information is brought to the budget decision-making table.

Process-based mechanisms

Some countries take advantage of the different incentives faced by players in the budget process to create an adversarial bidding (or hearing) process within government. As with courts of law in many jurisdictions, the process aims to establish the truth by requiring the parties to argue their case. The finance ministry seeks to point out the scope in ministerial budgets for improvements in efficiency and effectiveness, while the spending agencies seek to demonstrate that they are underfunded, given the level of services that are demanded. Finance ministries often depend on reputational effects to make this system work: spending agencies may choose to cooperate when they will benefit over time from building a reputation for approaching budgeting in a constructive way. For example, spending agencies may find that if they cooperate in years when more savings are required, they will benefit in years when more money is available. Finance ministries also often depend on shame-and-blame effects: if a spending ministry and its political head are made to look bad in an early bidding meeting, other ministries may want to avoid such treatment by preparing themselves better. An adversarial budget process will work only if the finance ministry (as well as its minister) is powerful, is well organized, and has good skills.

A thorough bidding process facilitates appraisal of all spending programs over time because ministries are required not only to defend their new spending proposals but also to explain why they could not generate more savings from within their own budgets to fund the spending proposals. Adversarial budgeting can also have negative consequences, as it is not necessarily the case that the truth will out. Much depends on the skills of the officials and political officers involved and the relative political strength of ministries. It is also difficult to take a long-term view under such a system: too much attention is given to scoring points rather than cooperating to develop quality policies and spending programs. Ultimately, the debate under such a system reverts to a discussion about inputs, rather than outputs or outcomes. Meanwhile, both parties continue to hoard, rather than share, information.

Several countries in Africa have evolved cooperative mechanisms to build a common understanding between finance and spending agencies of the policy choices and expenditure issues in each sector. A common variant is the institutionalization of sector working groups that bring together finance and spending agency officials, together with external stakeholders, to review past spending effectiveness and forward objectives, spending programs, tradeoffs, allocations, and expected achievements. These working groups have the benefit of sharing the burdens of (a) developing an analytical framework that can be used to identify and quantify choices between finance and spending agencies and (b) calculating and creating cooperative forums within which information asymmetry can be addressed and consensus built. Experience with sector working groups in Kenya and Uganda points to the need to make the decisions of these groups count. In both countries, sector working groups form part of a strategic MTEF process that stands separately from the annual budget process. Ministries soon learn that the budgeting that results from appropriations (and which therefore really counts) still occurs, as always, in a subsequent detailed estimates process. Participants therefore quickly lose interest in the process and instead focus their attention on the preparation of the annual budget.

Information-based mechanisms

Mechanisms under this category include using public expenditure reviews (PERs) to frame budget requests, activity-based costing, and programming techniques and using the budget submission to disentangle the components of ministerial requests.

PUBLIC EXPENDITURE REVIEWS.   Several developing countries have institutionalized PERs in the budget process. PERs involve examining ministerial programs and activities in line with the core functions of the ministry and identifying problems of effectiveness and efficiency in expenditure management. PERs that are conducted jointly by the finance ministry and line ministries (for example, as part of a sector working group process) encourage honesty in the budget process and build consensus on expenditure issues that need to be addressed and on the impact of such issues on forward budgets. PERs also have an internal function in helping ministries to link budgets and operational performance to their policies and priorities. PERs are often reviewed in a public process, thereby further improving the quality of the information they contain. Typically, they provide financial and nonfinancial outturn data for the ministry, analyzing expenditure trends and relating financial performance to policy performance. An analysis of the effectiveness and efficiency of agencies' spending forms the core of a good PER. PERs present an opportunity for joint systematic review of spending agencies' performance and for consensus on the issues that frame agencies' forward budgets. In essence, they improve the quality of information.

ACTIVITY-BASED COSTING AND PROGRAMMING TECH-NIQUES. A functional MTEF requires that resource allocations be set on the basis of a comprehensive top-down expenditure framework and costed bottom-up expenditure options. The introduction of activity-based budgeting at the sector level has therefore formed part of the implementation of MTEFs in a number of countries, including Ghana, Malawi, and Zambia. Although the specifics of systems differ across countries, they follow a similar logical framework approach to planning and budgeting at the level of ministries.

Spending agencies are first required to identify their objectives (or the changes they seek to effect in the real world) for the medium term and to set outputs (or deliverables) for each objective. *Outputs* are usually defined as the expected means for achieving the objectives, and ministries are required to set targets over the medium term. These targets are expected to be specific, measurable, achievable, realistic, and time bound. The next step is simply to identify what activities will deliver each output and its associated inputs. Inputs are required to be broken down into quantities and frequency. Common activities and inputs have unit costs that are applied across the government. The product of the unit cost, the quantity, and the frequency of the input equals the total input cost. The sum of all total input costs equals the activity cost. The activity costs are added up to arrive at the output cost, the objective cost, and eventually the spending agency's budget. Objectives are commonly associated with longstanding programs. Cost centers are also usually identified, so that the implementation of activities and the use of funds can be traced back to specific institutions and subinstitutional structures.

Experience with activity-based budgets in developing countries is mixed. First, like other pure, comprehensive, rationality-based instruments, these budgets require a luxury of information, capacity, and time that are simply not available. Significant efforts went into the development of activity-based budgets with high hopes by spending agencies that the fundamentals of a country's budget management systems would change. However, if the development of these budgets is not preceded in the MTEF development process by solid macrofiscal analytical work and policy development, budget implementation too easily reverts to historical practices that pay scant attention to the agreed prior activity-based budgets. Again, negative experiences with activity-based budgeting in developing countries are not the fault of the system itself, but rather of its implementation without robust complementary reforms.

SPENDING BASELINES, NEW POLICY PROPOSALS, AND SAVINGS BUDGETING. These mechanisms operate by guiding how ministries budget and make tradeoffs through the budget submission format. Agencies are requested to first indicate their spending baseline in their submission—namely, the cost estimate of existing programs, including cost escalations such as inflation and improved conditions of services for public sector employees. They are then requested to detail proposed new spending initiatives, such as new programs or changes in the coverage or level of existing services. This is the new policy proposal base. The savings base is the sum of proposed spending reductions achieved by introducing efficiency savings, reducing service levels in lower priority programs, or discontinuing obsolete activities. This system accepts that budgeting will always distinguish between existing programs and options for change. However, by requesting that departments detail how they will fund their new spending priorities from within their existing budgets before granting requests for additional funding, the system permits the government to reprioritize spending over time and to focus on the decisions that must be made to fund priorities within the limit of what can be afforded. The system also requires spending agencies to properly cost the forward cost of their existing policies (the base), thereby highlighting the need for policy change.

This system depends on a large degree of cooperation in the budget process to ensure that the three categories are properly identified and analyzed. For example, there is scope for disagreement between a spending agency and the ministry of finance about the meaning of "no change" in policies and the likely cost of existing policies. The task of reaching a shared analysis of the costs and benefits of new proposals remains. And there will continue to be problems of information asymmetry and incentive incompatibility that may hinder the identification of possible savings and make it difficult to reach agreement about the scope of possible savings and the implications for service delivery.

Conclusion

The introduction of new rules for budget processes and methods does not automatically mean that they will be applied in a meaningful way. Experience has shown that overcoming deeply entrenched incremental institutions and their associated patterns of behavior is an arduous task. Budget systems of developing countries are littered with the remnants of earlier efforts to introduce new techniques into the system. The debris of earlier failed attempts often impedes new reform initiatives, because target audiences are already familiar both with the terminology used and with the likelihood that no real change either is required or will result. This is no wonder. The effectiveness of budgeting rules depends on their credibility. Their credibility depends on several preconditions, including a capable and committed ministry of finance, political support, and the presence of complementary reforms (or at least the absence of competing nonbudget public administrative reform initiatives).

It is therefore important to understand that budgetary reforms do not by themselves change the fundamentally political nature of budgeting; they will not turn the budget process into a controlled, sequenced, and rational process. Budget processes are inevitably messy: the hope in the introduction of new techniques is not to completely sanitize these processes, but rather to minimize dysfunction and maximize the extent to which rational links are made between past performance, future objectives, policies, allocation of resources, and future required performance. Budgeting practice, as it has evolved over the past few decades, has sought a balance between the costs of incremental budgets and the improbability of achieving comprehensive, pure rationality.

Note

1. This section draws on Fölscher and Schoch (2005).

References

Campos, Ed, and Sanjay Pradhan. 1996. "Budgetary Institutions and Expenditure Outcomes: Binding Governments to Fiscal Performance." Policy Research Working Paper 1646, World Bank, Washington, DC.

Dean, Peter N. 1989. *Government Budgeting in Developing Countries*. London: Routledge.

Fölscher, Alta, and Michelle Schoch. 2005. "Multi-Year Budgeting." In *CABRI 2004 Budget Reform Seminar: Overview and Summary of Discussions*. Pretoria: Collaborative Africa Budget Reform Initiative.

Howlett, Michael, and M. Ramesh. 1995. "Public Policy Decision-Making—Beyond Rationalism, Incrementalism, and Irrationalism." In *Studying Public Policy: Policy Cycles and Policy Subsystems*, 137–52. Oxford, U.K.: Oxford University Press.

IMF (International Monetary Fund). 2001. *Government Finance Statistics Manual.* Washington, DC: IMF Statistics Department. http://www.imf.org/external/pubs/ ft/gfs/manual/pdf/all.pdf.

Larbi, George A. 1999. "The New Public Management Approach and Crisis States." UNRISD Discussion Paper 112, United Nations Research Institute for Social Development, Geneva.

Leruth, Luc, and Elisabeth Paul. 2006. "A Principal-Agent Theory Approach to Public Expenditure Management Systems in Developing Countries." IMF Working Paper 06/204, International Monetary Fund, Washington, DC.

Mengistu, Berhanu. 1997. "Budget Methods and Policy Priorities: The Essential Fit between Method and the Nature of the Policy Problem." Occasional Paper 6, School of Government, University of the Western Cape, Cape Town.

Nathan, Richard P. 2000. "Making Policy." In *Handbook for Appointed Officials in America's Governments.* Ithaca, NY: Rockefeller Institute.

Premchand, A. 1983. *Government Budgeting and Expenditure Controls: Theory and Practice.* Washington, DC: International Monetary Fund.

Rose, Aidan. 2003. "Results-Orientated Budget Practice in OECD Countries." ODI Working Paper 209, Overseas Development Institute, London.

Tohamy, Soumaya, Hashem Dezhbakhsh, and Peter Aranson. 2006. "A New Theory of the Budgetary Process." *Economics and Politics* 18 (1): 47–70.

UN (United Nations). 1965. *A Manual for Programme and Performance Budgeting.* New York: United Nations.

Wildavsky, Aaron, and Naomi Caiden. 1980. *Planning and Budgeting in Poor Countries.* New Brunswick, NJ: Transaction Books.

———. 1997. *The New Politics of the Budgetary Process*, 3rd ed. Washington, DC: Longman.

5

A Primer on Performance Budgeting

ANWAR SHAH AND CHUNLI SHEN

The past two decades have witnessed a growing interest in performance management and budgeting reforms, in response to louder public demands for government accountability in industrial countries. These reforms are intended to transform public budgeting systems from control of inputs to a focus on outputs or outcomes, in the interest of improving operational efficiency and promoting results-oriented accountability. These experiences have significant relevance for public sector reforms in developing countries. This chapter is intended to guide policy makers and budget practitioners who are contemplating reforms of their budgeting systems to bring them into conformity with the needs of the 21st century.

The chapter first reviews the main motivations for reform of budgeting systems and highlights the limitations of the traditional budgeting system in coping with demands for accountable governance. The second section introduces performance budgeting systems. Third is a discussion of considerations for performance budgeting reforms. The fourth section highlights the potential of performance budgeting systems as tools for improving government performance and accountability. The fifth section covers performance budgeting practices in selected industrial and developing countries. The sixth section lays out some lessons for countries that are contemplating the performance approach in budgeting. The last section highlights the main conclusions.

137

Public Budgeting: Motivations for Reform

Public budgeting systems are intended to fulfill several important functions. These functions include setting budget priorities that are consistent with the mandate of the government, planning expenditures to pursue a long-term vision for development, exercising financial control over inputs to ensure fiscal discipline, managing operations to ensure efficiency of government operations, and providing tools for making government performance accountable to citizens.

The most fundamental function of a budget is to control public expenditure, which is commonly carried out by exercising financial control over inputs. Input controls have been more concerned with how much money is spent and how it is spent than with what it is spent on. Input controls often put ceilings or caps on each category of expenditure, or even each item of expenditure.

The budget also functions as a very significant statement of government policies, one in which policy objectives are reconciled and implemented in concrete terms. The budget sets forth policy priorities and levels of spending, ways of financing the spending, and a plan for managing the funds. As Aaron Wildavsky (1986: 9) puts it, "Little can be done without money, and what will be tried is embedded in the budget." Because funds are scarcer than desires, a budget also serves as a mechanism for allocating resources. A budget is not only a tool of macroeconomic policy but also a management mechanism. It provides a key source of constraints on and incentives for public servants demanding better public services at lower costs. Last but not least, the budget document can be a major tool of accountability, whether to the legislative body or to the press and the public. It can help hold administrators accountable not only for the funds they receive but also for a given level of performance with those resources. It can either give citizens a sense of ownership and control and respond to their interests, or it can alienate them by making it difficult to participate in the budgeting process or making budgetary information inaccessible.

Each of these functions is a potential use of a public budget. Typically, a budgeting system cannot execute these functions equally well at the same time. The relative strength of each function depends on budgeting tools and techniques, but most critically on political decisions about which issues matter to the government. The government budget, therefore, is oriented around those issues.

The traditional line-item budget presents expenditures by inputs and resources purchased. The budget is classified by disaggregated objects of expenditure and by operating and capital expenditures. Operating expenses include cost objects for day-to-day operations such as salaries, pensions, and health insurance costs; office supplies and printing costs; and utility costs. Capital outlays include purchases of long-lived assets such as buildings, machinery, office equipment, furniture, and vehicles. A prominent feature of a line-item budget system is that it specifies the line-item ceiling in the budget allocation process to ensure that agencies do not spend in excess of their caps. Thus, the budget facilitates a tight fiscal grip over government operations. The strengths of such a system rest on its relative simplicity and its potential control of public spending through the detailed specification of inputs. Throughout much of the 20th century, central budget offices and finance ministries have been aggressive proponents of controlling public resources, which explains why line-item budgeting has endured despite relentless budgeting reform efforts.

The line-item approach embodies several impediments to promoting efficient and effective public planning and management as well as to fostering results-oriented accountability in public sector institutions. A line-item budget emphasizes inputs; it provides information on how much money is spent and how it is spent rather than on what it is spent. It does not link inputs with outputs and therefore says nothing about how efficiently resources are used. The line-item budget tends to focus decision making on details—whether the general office expenses (pencils used, printing paper consumed) are appropriate and how much they have gone up or down compared with the past year's budget—rather than on efficiency and effectiveness. The focus on detailed line-item control leads to micromanagement of agency operations by central budget offices and finance ministries and to hierarchical controls within the agency. Public managers thus exercise very limited managerial discretion and cannot be held accountable for the performance of government activities.

Budget reforms have sought to remedy these deficiencies (see table 5.1), first in the 1950s by linking planning with budgeting through program budgeting, and then in the 1960s by focusing on aggregate sectoral allocations through block-vote budgeting, in which line agencies were given larger blocks of appropriations so that they had the discretion to move funds across spending categories without seeking central approval. Concerns over entrenchment of historical spending patterns led to experimentation in the 1970s with zero-based budgeting, in which every item of expenditure had to be justified again every year, so that funds were allocated only to meet current policy priorities. Zero-based budgeting experiments were quickly abandoned when the technique proved impractical and politically unpalatable. More recently, renewed emphasis on public sector performance accountability has garnered significant interest in performance budgeting

TABLE 5.1 Features of Alternative Budget Formats

Feature	Line item	Program	Performance
Content	Expenditures by objects (inputs and resources)	Expenditures for a cluster of activities supporting a common objective	Presentation of a results-based chain to achieve a specific objective
Format	Operating and capital inputs purchased	Expenditures by program	Data on inputs, outputs, effects, and reach by each objective
Orientation	Input controls	Input controls	A focus on results
Associated management paradigm	Hierarchical controls with little managerial discretion	Hierarchical controls with managerial flexibility over allocation to activities within the program	Managerial flexibility over inputs and program design, but accountability for service delivery and output performance

Source: Authors' compilation.

TABLE 5.2 An Illustration of a Typical Line-Item Budget: Department of Education

(currency units, thousands)

Expenditure items	2004 actual	2005 estimated	2006 budgeted
Personnel	1,000	1,150	1,310
Salaries	600	700	760
Bonuses	400	450	550
Office expenses	750	960	1,060
Administrative	150	200	200
Printing	160	200	200
Utilities	150	180	210
Mailing	110	180	200
Travel	180	200	250
Vehicle purchase	0	0	500
Maintenance	40	50	50
Others	30	35	35
Total	1,820	2,195	2,955

Source: Authors' representation.

systems, to strengthen the performance orientation in resource allocation and management. The prominent concern of performance budgeting is to achieve operational efficiency and to improve accountability for results. Examples of a line-item budget, a program budget, and a performance budget are demonstrated in tables 5.2 and 5.3 and in box 5.1, respectively.

TABLE 5.3 An Example of the Program Budget Format: U.S. Department of Education

(US$ millions)

	Actual	Estimate	
Spending by Discretionary Budget Authority	2006	2006	2007
Elementary and secondary education			
Title I grants to local educational agencies	12,740	12,713	12,913
School improvement grants	n.a.	n.a.	200
Reading First and Early Reading First programs	1,146	1,132	1,132
State assessments	412	408	408
Teacher Incentive Fund	n.a.	99	99
Teacher quality state grants	2,917	2,887	2,887
Charter schools programs	254	251	251
America's Opportunity Scholarships for Kids	n.a.	n.a.	100
Impact aid	1,244	1,228	1,228
Safe and drug-free schools programs	672	569	216
21st-Century Community Learning Centers	991	981	981
English-language acquisition	676	669	669
Individuals with Disabilities Education Improvement Act Part B state grants	10,590	10,583	10,683
High school programs			
High school reform	n.a.	n.a.	1,475
Striving Readers Program	25	30	100
Vocational education	1,206	1,192	n.a.
TRIO Upward Bound Program	310	311	n.a.
TRIO Talent Search Program	145	145	n.a.
Gaining Early Awareness and Readiness for Undergraduate Programs	306	303	n.a.
American Competitiveness Initiative			
Math Now for Elementary School Students	n.a.	n.a.	125
Math Now for Secondary School Students	n.a.	n.a.	125
Advanced placement	30	32	122
National Mathematics Panel	n.a.	n.a.	10
Evaluation of mathematics and science education programs	n.a.	n.a.	5
Adjunct Teacher Corps	n.a.	n.a.	25

(continued)

TABLE 5.3 (continued)

Spending by Discretionary Budget Authority	Actual	Estimate	
	2006	2006	2007
Adult education	579	573	573
Higher education			
Poll grants	12,365	17,345	12,739
Perkins loans institutional recall	n.a.	n.a.	−664
Perkins loans cancellations	66	65	n.a.
National Security Language Initiative activities	n.a.	n.a.	35
Historically Black Colleges and Graduate Institutions Program	297	296	296
Hispanic Serving Institutions Program	95	95	95
Research and statistics	523	517	554
All other	9,590	4,128	7,229
Total Discretionary Budget Authority	57,179	56,541	54,411

Source: OMB 2006.
n.a. = not applicable.

BOX 5.1 An Illustration of Performance Budgeting: Australia's Child Care Support Program

Program: Child Care Support Program
Performance objectives:

■ Promote, support, and enhance quality child care
■ Improve access to child care for children and families with special or additional needs
■ Support equitable access to child care for children and families in areas or circumstances where services would not otherwise be available.

Australia's Child Care Support Program includes the following subprograms:

1. Child Care Benefit
2. Jobs Education and Training Child Care Fee Assistance
3. Stronger Families and Communities Strategy—Choice and Flexibility in Child Care
4. Support for Child Care.

    The fourth subprogram, Support for Child Care, is funded as payments are made directly to providers and to the states and territories. This program was introduced in 1997 to encompass all of the ongoing and new programs the department funds to support child care.

More information about Support for Child Care is shown in the table below:

Support for Child Care

Measure	Number or percent
Effectiveness: targeting	
Number of children with additional needs using Australian government–approved child care services	126,000
Children with disabilities	16,700
Aboriginal, Torres Strait, and Australian South Seas Islander children	15,000
Children from non-English-speaking background	95,000
Quality: access and choice	
Number of children with disabilities assisted into mainstream services	16,700
Quality assurance	
Percentage of centers satisfactorily participating in the Quality Improvement and Accreditation System	90
Percentage of family day care services satisfactorily participating in Family Day Care Quality Assurance	90
Percentage of outside school hours care services satisfactorily participating in Outside School Hours Care Quality Assurance	90
Quantity	
Number of indigenous-specific services	270
Number of services specifically targeted to rural and remote areas	1,200
Price	$A 18.4 million

Source: Department of Family and Community Services and Indigenous Affairs 2006.

Performance Budgeting: Basic Concepts

Performance budgeting is a system of budgeting that presents the purpose and objectives for which funds are required, the costs of programs and associated activities proposed for achieving those objectives, and the outputs to be produced or services to be rendered under each program. A comprehensive performance budgeting system quantifies the entire results-based chain as follows (see figure 5.1 for an illustration):

- *Inputs and intermediate inputs*—resources to produce outputs
- *Outputs*—quantity and quality of goods and services produced

■ *Outcome*—progress in achieving program objectives
■ *Impact*—program goals
■ *Reach*—people who benefit or are hurt by a program.

As a by-product of the information provided by the results-based chain, performance budgeting can also yield useful indicators of the efficiency and quality of government operations. Here are a few examples of such indicators:

■ *Quality*—measures of service such as timeliness, accessibility, courtesy, and accuracy
■ *Client satisfaction*—rating of services by users
■ *Productivity*—output by work hour
■ *Efficiency*—cost per unit of output.

In comparison with traditional line-item budgeting, performance budgeting allows for more flexible use of fiscal resources and shifts the focus from inputs to results (see an example of a performance budget in box 5.1). A performance budget focuses on the results to be achieved. With its program structure, the performance budget changes the focus of discussion from detailed line items to the broader objectives and performance of public

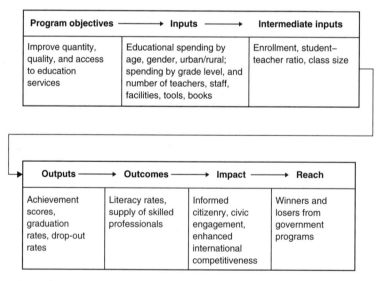

Source: Shah 2005.

FIGURE 5.1 Performance Budgeting Results Chain: An Application in Education

programs and, therefore, facilitates more informed budgetary decision making. A performance budget offers greater managerial flexibility by providing the program or department manager a fixed lump-sum allocation that may be used for various needs in order to achieve the agreed-on results in service delivery. Public managers enjoy increased managerial discretion but are held accountable for what they achieve in service delivery performance.

Considerations in Performance Budgeting Reforms

For performance budgeting reforms to achieve their objectives, a number of considerations must be kept in mind while implementing such reforms.

Budget Classification

Performance budgeting shifts the focus on resource allocation from the objects of expenditure to the public programs that are designed to serve strategic objectives of the government. Funds are allocated to various objectives (results), and spending agencies manage the lump-sum allocation in seeking more cost-effective and innovative ways of achieving results. Central budget control focuses on the achievement of program goals by each agency, rather than by the detailed line itemization of the agency's budget.

Performance Measurement and Reporting

An effective performance budgeting system depends on reliable performance measurement and reporting. Because performance measurement and reporting do not directly affect budgetary allocations, the initiative does not immediately incur financial risks for public managers and therefore serves as a good entry point for reform. The construction of a performance measurement and reporting system provides a channel for public officials to reach agreement on program goals and objectives, to discuss and compromise on the selection of performance measures, to address their questions and concerns, and to overcome misgivings about performance budgeting.

A performance budgeting system requires a basket of measures that assess public programs through a variety of filters (McGill 2001; Wang 1999), such as inputs; outputs (quantity and quality of goods and services produced); efficiency (unit cost to produce outputs); service quality (measures of service such as timeliness, accessibility, courtesy, accuracy, and satisfaction); and outcomes (progress in achieving program objectives). Different measures assess different aspects of budgeting practice. The use of a basket of indicators rather than a single measure derives from the uncertain and blurred relationship between inputs, process, and results—an inherent feature of public programs. In other words, the outcomes or service quality associated with a government program cannot be inferred just by reporting its outputs. Therefore, one must monitor the entire results-based chain in order to understand and effectively manage government programs.

Output-Focused Performance Management Paradigm

Performance management is a prerequisite for the success of performance budgeting. Governments that do not manage for results do not budget for results. Performance budgeting cannot thrive unless it is built into an overall managerial strategy for performance. Donald Kettl (2000) distinguishes two sets of performance management strategies, one relying on market-like arrangements and the other relying on managerial norms and competence (table 5.4). The first, "making managers manage," is used by New Zealand to specify contracts with budgetary allocations and competitive pressures. The second, "letting managers manage," is practiced in Australia and Sweden. Both strategies provide the flexibility that public managers need to improve performance. The critical differences are the reliance on incentives and competitive spirit in the first strategy and on goodwill and trust in the second strategy. The two approaches take different perspectives on how to

T A B L E   5 . 4 Comparison of Two Performance Management Approaches

Theoretical models	Make the managers manage	Let the managers manage
Strategy	Market-like arrangements	Managerial norms and competence
Mechanism	Contracts	Empowerment
Commonality	Gives public managers the flexibility they need to improve performance	
Difference	Uses specific, tightly written performance contracts that leave little room for trust	Implicitly trusts public managers to exercise their judgment intelligently
	Motivates improvements with extrinsic rewards	Motivates primarily by the intrinsic rewards of public service
Example	New Zealand	Australia and Sweden

Source: Adapted from Kettl 2000.

reward public servants. The contract-based approach rewards the chief executive financially if the organization achieves its performance targets. The empowerment approach holds that public servants are more motivated by the intrinsic rewards of public service than by material benefits. The contract-based approach relies on incentives and competitive market mechanisms to hold public managers accountable. The empowerment approach simply hopes that managers will be ethically and professionally motivated to perform.

It is important to stress that managerial accountability must be based on outputs rather than outcomes, because outcomes are beyond managers' direct control, difficult to define and quantify, and impossible to use as a costing basis. There are three major justifications for including output-based accountability. First, it is difficult or implausible to link outcomes directly with managerial actions and decisions because outcomes are remote in time and space from program activities and outcomes interact with other factors. The extent of a manager's direct control over outputs is usually much more substantial than his or her control over outcomes. Second, outcomes are immensely difficult to identify and certainly difficult to quantify. The time scale for measuring outcomes normally spans some time after the program intervention, a period not generally in sync with the budgeting cycle. Third, calculating the cost of the effort to achieve outcomes can be more difficult than costing outputs (Kristensen, Groszyk, and Bühler 2002). Outcomes typically are achieved not as the result of a single intervention by one program in isolation but through the interaction of a number of different planned and unplanned factors and interventions. Hence, it is inappropriate and unrealistic to hold public managers accountable for outcomes. The focus on outputs, as practiced in Malaysia and New Zealand, offers greater potential for accountability for results. Outcomes, however, should be monitored; an exclusive emphasis on quantitative output measures without a focus of at least some form on outcomes can distort attention in delivery agencies. It raises the risk that such agencies will lose sight of the bigger picture: the impact of programs on citizens and society.

On the way to fostering outputs-based accountability, it is essential to provide more managerial flexibility by relaxing central input controls. Relaxing central input controls occurs at two levels. First is the consolidation of various budget lines into a single appropriation for all operating costs (salaries, travel, supplies, and so on). Second is the relaxation of a variety of central management rules that inhibit managerial flexibility—particularly in personnel management, where most central rules focus. Because personnel cost is generally the largest component of operating expenditures, consolidating budget lines will make little difference if central rules prevent any flexibility in personnel management. Sweden's experience in dismantling central control over personnel management offers some interesting insights (Blöndal 2003).

Most industrial countries have established various forms of performance management systems. The experiences of Denmark, New Zealand, and Sweden are briefly discussed in box 5.2.

BOX 5.2 Performance Management Reforms in Denmark, New Zealand, and Sweden

Denmark: Danish Performance Management Model

Performance management arrangements are in place in all ministries and agencies in Denmark. They consist of three main instruments: (a) a performance contract between a ministry (permanent secretary) and an agency (director general) for the production of the agency's outcomes or outputs; (b) an annual report showing the results achieved relative to those specified in the performance contract, audited by the National Audit Office; and (c) a performance pay system linking the salary of the director general of an agency with achievement of the results specified in the performance contract.

Performance contracts were introduced in the late 1980s on a pilot basis, but they have now become an established feature of the management of the Danish public sector. The overall quality of the performance contracts has improved over time, but the quality of the outcome and output descriptions still leaves room for improvement. The agency annual report shows the results achieved relative to targets for all specified outcomes and outputs; it is published three months following the end of each fiscal year. The performance pay system for directors general was introduced in the mid-1990s. The criteria for performance pay are based on achieving the targets specified in the agencies' performance contracts. In addition, one-fourth of the performance pay is based on the director general's management and leadership skills, which are assessed by the permanent secretary of the respective ministry. The performance pay can take up to 25 percent of the annual salary.

The Danish performance management system, rather than being regarded as a contractual arrangement, serves more as a formal structure under which ministries and agencies discuss the results to be achieved and the ministries highlight areas they view as especially important and urgent. The performance management system has developed a more results-oriented culture in the Danish public sector (Blöndal and Ruffner 2004).

New Zealand: Performance Management Paradigm in the Form of Contractualism

New Zealand is at the forefront in transforming the public sector by using a private sector management and measurement approach to core government functions. New Zealand revamped its tenured civil service and made all public positions contractual, on the basis of an agreed set of results. Agency heads are required to negotiate purchase agreements with their ministers and are held responsible for the delivery and reporting of expected outputs relative to targets and budget. Statements of intent commit ministers to achieving progress toward outcomes. Employees negotiate individual contracts with agencies. Program management was decentralized at delivery points, and managers were given flexibility and autonomy in budgetary allocations and program implementation within the policy framework and the defined budget. The accrual-based budgeting and accounting system can provide a complete picture of the resource cost of each public sector activity (Treasury Board of Canada 2003). The contractualism version of outputs accountability in the public sector introduced by New Zealand led to significant improvement in the machinery of government and in the fiscal performance of the state sector. Departments have a clearer idea than they used to of what is expected of them, their output is specified and fully costed, chief executives have broad discretion to manage resources and operations, ministers have choice in obtaining outputs, and the overall public sector is leaner and more efficient.

Sweden: Deregulated Human Resource Management

In Sweden, directors general of agencies are responsible for recruiting, grading, and dismissing their staff members. There is no civil service in the government as a whole. Vacancies are generally advertised in the press, and all qualified applicants are treated equally. Staff members are not tenured. There is no difference between the labor legislation governing the public sector and that governing the private sector. Personnel cost is one of many items of expenditure that agency directors general must manage within the limit of their single operating appropriation. The Ministry of Finance and Parliament do not have any direct say in pay arrangements and other conditions of employment for government employees. The experience with this new framework has been predominantly positive. The increased responsibility for wage formation and employer policies in general has been well received by agencies. Significant variations in the pay agreement between agencies are evident, and it is estimated that more than 90 percent of government employees in Sweden now receive individualized salaries—that is, salaries based on their personal performance. Public sector unions have been constructive partners in this area (Blöndal 2003).

Source: Authors' compilation.

Informed Budgetary Decision Making

Performance budgeting cannot be expected to be a mechanistic, rational system that replaces the political process of making resource choices in a complex environment of competing demands. Instead, it brings more economic values into budgetary decision making and fosters an information-based deliberation process that assigns significant weight to performance information and rewards good performance with managerial flexibility and other incentives. Unrealistic expectations for performance budgeting, by creating a direct and explicit link between resource allocation and budget results (Broom 1995; Martin 1997), explain why many scholars are pessimistic about performance budgeting practices (Kelly 2003; Lu 1998; Pitsvada and LoStracco 2002): there is almost never any link between performance and resource allocation in real life. Indeed, a one-to-one direct link between performance and budget allocation is neither possible nor desirable.

Rational analysis and quantitative data are insufficient to drive out political concerns and value judgments in making budgetary decisions. The bid for rationality ignores the political nature of public budgeting. Budgeting is an ever-evolving flow and mix of programs and solutions considered by a variety of actors annually or biennially. The final budget represents the culmination of the interrelationships of actors and information (Rubin 2000). The politics of budgeting makes it infeasible for decision makers to use only rational data to allocate resources. To some extent, it is irrational to seek rational and comprehensive approaches to budgeting (Wildavsky 1979). Kelly (2003: 310) reviews public budgeting reforms in the 20th century and concludes that "for all their promise to take politics out of public budgeting, they amounted to tinkering."

It is also not desirable to pursue direct links between performance and resource allocation, because performance information does not constitute a sufficient basis for making budgetary decisions. First, performance data are about what happened in the past, whereas budgetary decisions refer to what should be done in the future. Thus, past performance at best serves as only one factor to guide future directions. Also, budgetary decisions involve value judgments. Past performance information provides some basis for considering what future priorities should be, so policy makers need to take into account the divergent views of a range of stakeholders about what future actions are most appropriate (Perrin 2002). Furthermore, a number of other factors come into play. For instance, certain government programs, even when they are poorly performed, cannot simply be done away with, owing to the legal or political imperatives that created the programs in the first place. No one would seriously suggest shutting down an inefficient health care system unless better alternatives were available.

In this regard, the Chilean system of performance budgeting offers a sensible way of using performance information in budgetary decision making. It does not seek to establish a direct association of budget allocations with performance measures. Rather, performance information is used in the budget cycle along with financial and other information as a starting point for discussions with agencies. From these discussions, performance data have been used to confirm existing allocations or—when results were poor—various actions have been taken to push agencies to improve performance (Blöndal and Curristine 2004).

Why Pursue Performance Budgeting?

Would performance budgeting reform induce some revolutionary changes in the rigid budgeting business? The extensive literature on performance budgeting reforms in the past two decades, as explained in the following paragraphs, suggests that performance budgeting reform can enhance communication between budget actors, improve public management in terms of efficiency and effectiveness, facilitate more informed budgetary decision making, and achieve high transparency of and accountability for government activities. Current performance budgeting initiatives have been less successful in terms of changing appropriation levels (Flowers, Kundin, and Brower 1999; Kristensen, Groszyk, and Bühler 2002; OECD 2004; Rivenbark and Kelly 2000; Wang 2000). Four important advantages of performance budgeting have been gleaned from recent experiences:

■ *Enhanced communication between budget actors and with citizens.* Performance budgeting clarifies program goals and objectives and identifies performance targets, thereby giving agencies and employees a better sense of the expectations for their performance. It helps public managers communicate more effectively about their activities to the executive, the legislature, and the public. The public's demand for a government that does more with less will persist, so an important thrust of current budget reform efforts is to develop budget presentations that improve communication between government and citizens. In contrast to the traditional line-item budget, a performance budget—with a description of each government program, performance measures, and budget information—is accessible to ordinary citizens and therefore makes it easier for public managers to disseminate information about their programs to the public and to obtain public understanding of and support for their activities.

■ *Improved management in government agencies.* Performance budgeting reform can help program managers specify organizational goals, monitor program performance, maintain better knowledge of problems with program structure and operation, plan for the future, improve internal control, and communicate program results. Wang (2000) analyzed survey responses from 205 U.S. local governments and found that 70.6 percent agree that performance measurement has increased their ability to determine service efficiency, 65.1 percent believe that performance measurement has increased their ability to determine service effectiveness, and 65.4 percent agree that performance measurement has improved the accountability of program performance. In Australia, a survey in 2001 by the National Institute of Labour Studies showed that 93 percent of agencies consider that the agency's performance orientation in management budgeting has contributed to improved individual and organizational performance (Scheers, Sterck, and Bouckaert 2005).

■ *More informed budgetary decision making.* Performance budgeting may not rationalize and transform the political budgeting process, but it certainly adds value to deliberations because performance information is taken into account when the level of funding is decided. With appropriate information, politicians are able to exert pressure for improvements and can better understand the issues involved. Performance information may play an active role in resource allocation in the following instances: justifying the reallocation of resources, changing the focus of discussion from line items to broader objectives and performance of agencies and programs, influencing decisions about proposed new programs and funding increases or decreases, and providing benchmarks useful to legislators in making decisions.

■ *Higher transparency and accountability.* The budget document can serve as a major tool of transparency and accountability for the legislative body and the public. Traditional budgets, typically organized according to line-item inputs, fail to deliver meaningful information regarding what and how well the government is doing. In comparison, performance budgeting classifies resources by programs and presents performance indicators. The budget makes it much easier for the public to get a sense of major government activities and their achievements. Government performance is under public scrutiny in the annual or semiannual performance reports. Accountability in the public sector has traditionally been based on compliance with rules and procedures. Basically, it has not mattered what a public servant does as long as he or she observes the rules. The performance budgeting system seeks results-based accountability—holding managers accountable for what they achieve, not how they do it.

How to Do Performance Budgeting: International Experiences

The past two decades have witnessed a wave of enthusiasm for performance management and budgeting reforms in industrial nations and in Malaysia, spreading eventually to other developing countries. The experimentation with and experience of performance budgeting are wide ranging. Because performance budgeting develops at various stages in terms of how performance information is used in the budgeting process, this chapter distinguishes performance budgeting in four categories:

1. *Performance-reported budgeting* (PRB) presents performance information as part of the budget documentation, but budgetary actors do not use it for resource allocation.
2. *Performance-informed budgeting* (PIB) refers to a budgeting process that takes program performance into account but uses the information only as a minor factor in making decisions.
3. *Performance-based budgeting* (PBB) implies that performance information plays an important role for resource allocation, along with many other factors, but does not necessarily determine the amount of resources allocated.
4. *Performance-determined budgeting* (PDB) means that allocation of resources is directly and explicitly linked to units of performance.

Table 5.5 provides a snapshot of performance budgeting reform progress in selected countries according to these categories. Overall, these reforms are still in experimental stages; there are no truly mature examples of an integrated performance budgeting system. In light of the political nature of the budgeting process and the insufficiency of information, this chapter argues that PBB, which takes performance as one of the key factors in resource allocation, stands out as the best format for bringing about the spirit of rationalism in decision making. Armed with performance data—as well as value judgments, negotiations, and compromises—policy makers are also able to make more informed budgetary decisions. Even when performance information is imperfect, making available at least some information on performance may add some greater degree of confidence to budgetary decision making and gain greater buy-in on government policies by the electorate.

TABLE 5.5 Implementation of Performance Budgeting in Selected Industrial and Developing Countries, Highlights

Government	Reform progress	Budgeting reforms
Industrial countries		
Australia	Performance-informed budgeting (strong)	An accrual-based outputs and outcomes budgeting and reporting framework was initially implemented in the budget of 1999/2000.
New Zealand	Performance-based budgeting	An outputs-based budgeting reform was implemented.
United States	Performance-reported budgeting	The Government Performance and Results Act was passed in 1993. See detailed description in the text.
Developing countries		
Bolivia	Line-item budgeting (weak)	A series of formal legislation enacted since the late 1980s had little impact on actual practices in public management and budgeting. Performance reforms were prone to fail in the environment of pervasive political patronage and weak administrative capacity in key financial management areas.
Chile	Performance-informed budgeting	Chile began experimenting with performance indicators in the budget process in 1994. Since 1997, performance evaluations have been used by the Budget Office and all agencies have been obliged to produce comprehensive management reports each year for presentation to Congress. The mechanism of the bidding fund was devised to distribute unallocated funds on the basis of program performance starting in 2001. The system did not attempt to link performance directly to appropriations. The performance indicators were reported to Congress in budget documentation as annexes.

China	Line-item budgeting	Line-item budgeting has been strengthened governmentwide since 1999. The government decided not to pursue a comprehensive reform in 2002. The Ministry of Finance circulated the Framework of Public Expenditure Performance Evaluation in Central Government in 2005, initiating performance measurement and evaluation for the first time at the central level.
Malaysia	Performance-informed budgeting	The Modified Budgeting System was set up in 1989.
South Africa	Line-item budgeting; performance-reported budgeting (weak)	Line-item controls exist. Weak performance information is included in the budget appendix. Few departments are monitored for performance. The use of performance information is limited.
Tanzania	Line-item budgeting; performance-informed budgeting (proportional; weak)	Performance budgeting has been gradually introduced since 1998. The Public Finance Act of 2001 made performance budgeting a legal requirement. A *Performance Budgeting Operations Manual* was prepared subsequently from training conducted in 1998 and 1999. Performance budgeting is still in its infancy. Only a limited proportion of the budget (about 20 percent) is effectively subject to performance budgeting; this seriously reduces the value of the approach. Performance monitoring and reporting is very weak.
Thailand	Line-item budgeting; performance-reported budgeting (weak)	The hurdle approach, implemented during 1997 to 2000, failed. Strategic performance budgeting was introduced in 2001. The budget preparation moved to an output basis in 2004. The budget was presented in both a performance and results format and a line-item format. The Bureau of the Budget was reluctant to relax inputs controls.

Sources: Andrews 2006; Blöndal and Curristine 2004; Blöndal and Kim 2006; Dixon 2005; Gilmour and Lewis 2006; Marcel and Tokman 2002; McGill 2006; Montes and Andrews 2005; New Zealand Treasury 2005; OMB 2002; Panzardi 2005; Pitsvada and LoStracco 2002; Rønsholt and others 2003; Scheers, Sterck, and Bouckaert 2005; Siddiquee 2005; Xavier 1996.

Note: Details of several of the reforms in several countries are included in the text.

Performance Budgeting in Industrial Countries

The past two decades have seen a clear trend among industrial countries toward bringing about a stronger performance orientation in public expenditure management. New Zealand and Australia were forerunners in initiating the present round of performance management and budgeting in the late 1980s, followed in the early to mid-1990s by Canada, Denmark, Finland, France, the Netherlands, Sweden, the United Kingdom, and the United States. In the late 1990s to early 2000s, Austria, Germany, and Switzerland joined the team and introduced various versions of these reforms (OECD 2004). In most countries, efforts have been limited to generating more performance data and better program evaluations. A few countries have adopted systemwide reforms, including aligning performance information with budgetary decision making. The 2003 data from the Organisation for Economic Co-operation and Development (OECD) and the World Bank's Budget Practices and Procedures Database support this observation (see table 5.6).

The priority of performance budgeting reform in most countries has been to provide information about results together with financial information in budget documents or annual reports. Of the selected industrial countries, line-item budgets are still prepared in Canada, France, and the United States (aside from other expenditure classifications). Nonfinancial performance data are integrated in the budget documentation for all programs in Australia, the Netherlands, New Zealand, Norway, Sweden, and the United States, whereas in Canada and Germany less than 25 percent of programs are covered. However, the integration of performance information into the budget documentation does not guarantee that such information will be used in decision making. That integration is a necessary rather than sufficient condition. In some OECD member countries, this information has simply been ignored when it comes to making decision about allocations (Blöndal and Curristine 2004). It is not a common practice for politicians (ministers, heads of government, cabinet, or legislators) in Australia, Canada, Finland, or the United States to use performance information in making decisions.

New Zealand: outputs budgeting

New Zealand's budgeting reforms have attracted considerable international attention over the past two decades. In 1989, the Public Finance Act (PFA) redefined the appropriation process, shifting the budget emphasis from inputs to outputs. Under the PFA, departments received appropriations for the purchase of classes of outputs. Appropriations on a full accrual basis for all agencies were achieved with the 1994 amendments to the PFA. The Fiscal Responsibility Act 1994 required governments to state their fiscal objectives

TABLE 5.6 Performance Budgeting Reforms in Selected Industrial Countries

A. How are expenditures classified in the budget system?

Country	Function (defense, health, education)	Economic classification (employee compensation, interest, grants, social benefits)	Line-item (or object) classification for procurement of goods and services (salaries, travel, printing, renting property, supplies) within programs	Administrative classification, or by organization (hierarchical levels and administrative units in line ministries)	Program classification (reflecting the government's policy objectives and individual program budgets)
Australia	✓	✓			
Canada	✓	✓	✓		✓
Denmark	✓	✓		✓	✓
Finland	✓	✓		✓	✓
France	✓	✓	✓		
Germany	✓	✓			
Netherlands	✓	✓		✓	
New Zealand	✓	✓		✓	
Norway	✓	✓		✓	
Sweden	✓			✓	✓
United Kingdom	✓			✓	✓
United States	✓	✓	✓	✓	✓

(continued)

TABLE 5.6 (*continued*)

B. Are nonfinancial performance data routinely included in budget documentation (in the process)?

Country	Yes, for all programs	Yes, for more than 75% of programs	Yes for more than 50% of programs	Yes, for more than 25% of programs	Yes, for less than 25% of programs	No
Australia	✓					
Canada					✓	
Denmark		✓				
Finland		✓				
France			✓			
Germany					✓	
Netherlands	✓					
New Zealand	✓					
Norway	✓					
Sweden	✓					
United States	✓					

C. Is it common that politicians use performance measures in decision making?

Country	Yes, the minister with responsibility for the ministry or entity that is supposed to deliver on the performance target	Yes, the head of government	Yes, the cabinet	Yes, politicians in the budget committee in the legislature	Yes, politicians in the committee overseeing the ministry or entity that is supposed to deliver on the performance target	No
Australia						✓
Canada	✓					✓
Denmark	✓					
Finland						✓
Germany	✓					
Netherlands	✓		✓			
New Zealand	✓		✓			
Norway	✓	✓				✓
Sweden	✓			✓	✓	
United Kingdom	✓				✓	
United States						✓

Source: OECD and World Bank's Budget Practices and Procedures Database.
Note: Data are from 2003.

and report progress toward achieving those outputs. Output appropriations encourage the government and Parliament to focus on the goods and services to be delivered by the entity receiving the appropriations. Thus, as much attention is directed to the value obtained from government expenditure as to how that expenditure was made. Output appropriations also provide departments with autonomy in determining the appropriate input mix and, where necessary, in altering that input mix during the period (New Zealand Treasury 2005). Resources are linked to results in three dimensions: (a) resources are linked to and appropriated against expected outputs in the budget; (b) resources are linked to and reported against actual output performance; and (c) actual outputs (and, in some cases, outcomes) are tracked and reported against targeted performance. It is widely held that budgeting reforms have contributed considerably to New Zealand's improved fiscal position.

Australia: outcome budgeting

Since the early 1980s, the Australian government has developed initiatives to make the budget and management system more results oriented (as, for example, with the introduction of program budgeting in 1983). In 1996, the introduction of an outcome budgeting and reporting framework in the Australian public sector was discussed. The framework was implemented for the first time in the budget of 1999/2000. Under the Australian outcome budgeting framework, "appropriations are structured around outcomes, whilst Portfolio Budget Statements specify the price, quality, and quantity of outputs agencies will deliver and the criteria they will use for demonstrating the contribution of agency outputs and administered items to outcomes" (Scheers, Sterck, and Bouckaert 2005: 136). Figure 5.2 illustrates how outcomes are linked to outputs and budget using the portfolio budget statements of the Department of Families, Community Services, and Indigenous Affairs. Because appropriations are made for outcomes, executive management has more freedom in spending the resources, and Parliament has less control. The key components in the framework are listed in box 5.3.

Despite the comprehensive performance budgeting framework, members of the Australian Parliament have criticized the output information in the portfolio budget statements and annual reports as too aggregated. They have complained that it is difficult to get a clear view of the agencies' contributions to the outputs. Moreover, in general, there is little evidence that the output and outcome information is actively used in political decision making, although the Department of Finance and Administration states that when savings had

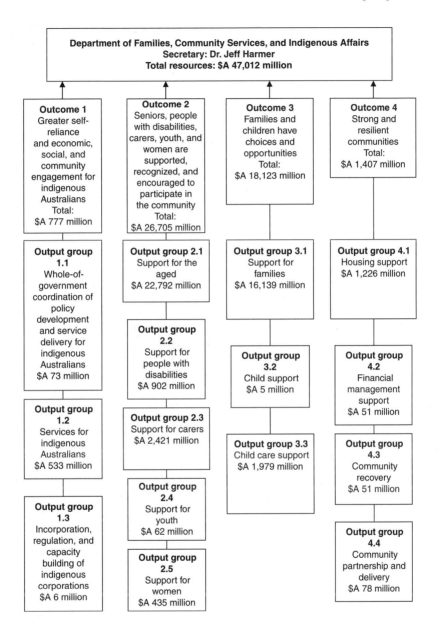

Source: Department of Families, Community Services, and Indigenous Affairs 2006.

FIGURE 5.2 Australia Portfolio Budget Statement: Department of Families, Community Services, and Indigenous Affairs, 2006 Budget

BOX 5.3 Australia: A Governmentwide Outcome Budgeting Framework

Key components of the Australian outcome budgeting framework are as follows:

■ Outcomes are the basis for appropriations and the legal authority for expenditure and, therefore, must be reported.
■ Portfolio budget statements provide information on the proposed allocation of resources to outcomes (for the budget year plus three).
■ The Mid-Year Economic and Fiscal Outlook compares estimates with actual figures.
■ The annual reports to Parliament provide financial and other information on actual performance relative to outputs and outcomes. Deviations must be explained in the reports.
■ Effectiveness, quality, and quantity indicators must appear in the portfolio budget statement; outcomes are reported against them in the annual reports.
■ Ownership agreements commit ministers to deliver outputs that will be measured against outcome expectations. Performance agreements allow ministers to hold agency heads accountable for delivering outputs for an agreed budget. Agency personnel have individual performance agreements.

Source: Adapted from Treasury Board of Canada 2003.

to be made the government did not slash funding in an arbitrary and linear way but took the new results-oriented information into account (Scheers, Sterck, and Bouckaert 2005).

U.S. federal government: performance budgeting quandary

The U.S. government has been pursuing performance-oriented resource allocation for decades. Past efforts with the Planning, Programming, and Budgeting System (PPBS), management by objectives (MBO), and zero-based budgeting (ZBB) in the 1960s and 1970s all failed to have a substantial effect on the budget process. In the 1990s, two events—the Government Performance and Results Act of 1993 (GPRA) and the issuance of the National Performance Review later that year—placed performance budgeting at the forefront of budget reform. The GPRA was intended to improve the federal government's efficiency and effectiveness and to provide greater accountability for results by transforming the federal budgetary process from an input-oriented system to a results-oriented system. Performance budgeting would also give managers significant flexibility in overseeing their resources while holding them accountable for program results.

Recently, performance budgeting was given a statutory foot in the door that it previously could not get (Pitsvada and LoStracco 2002). In an effort to fulfill the ideals of the GPRA system, President George W. Bush, on entering office, proposed a five-part presidential management agenda for fiscal year 2002. Budget and performance integration was positioned as one of the five priorities in the agenda: "Government should be results-oriented— guided not by process but guided by performance. There comes a time when every program must be judged either a success or a failure . . . . Government action that fails in its purposes must be reformed or ended" (OMB 2002: 25). The Bush administration mandated that agencies use performance-based budgeting on selected programs in the fiscal 2003 budget cycle. Starting with the fiscal year 2004 budget, the Office of Management and Budget (OMB) began to include performance and management assessments of federal programs in the budget and to use that performance information in allocating budget resources. This initiative is called PART, short for the Program Assessment Rating Tool, which was designed to help identify a program's strengths and weaknesses to inform funding and management decisions. The assessment is conducted in four weighted sections that focus on program purpose, strategic planning, management, and results. A program can receive five ratings: effective, moderately effective, adequate, ineffective, and results not demonstrated (if adequate measures of program effectiveness or other program data are not available). The plan is to complete assessments for all federal programs by the end of 2006. To date, about 80 percent of all federal programs have been evaluated (793 programs). The distribution of program ratings is summarized in box 5.4.

The OMB claims a significant relationship between PART scores and budget allocations. The Performance Institute, a nongovernmental organization working closely with the OMB in this endeavor, states that "the President's proposal rewards programs deemed effective with a 6 percent funding increase, while those not showing results were held to less than a 1 percent increase" (Performance Institute 2003: 2). In contrast, when Gilmour and Lewis (2006) examined the role of merit and political considerations in formulating recommendations for 234 programs in the president's fiscal year 2004 budget, they found that PART scores were positively related with proposed budgets, but their impact was very limited—particularly when political factors were taken into account. On the legislative side, Congress has not changed its perspective on how funds are to be appropriated. All the line-item details that have been requested over the years are still required, coupled with voluminous GPRA-related materials. With the steep rise in omnibus legislation, performance budgeting appears not to matter much (Pitsvada and LoStracco 2002). Most

---

BOX 5.4 The U.S. Office of Management and Budget's Program Assessment Rating Tool

The Office of Management and Budget's Program Assessment Rating Tool (PART) has four criteria:

- *Program purpose and design* (weight 20 percent)—Assesses whether a program's purpose is clear and whether it is well designed to achieve its objectives
- *Strategic planning* (weight 10 percent)—Weighs whether the agency establishes valid annual and long-term goals for its programs
- *Program management* (weight 20 percent)—Rates the management of an agency's program, including financial oversight and program improvement efforts
- *Program results* (weight 50 percent)—Focuses on results that programs can report with accuracy and consistency.

The distribution of program ratings under PART can be summarized as follows:

- Number of programs assessed: 793
- Percentage rated effective: 15 percent
- Percentage rated moderately effective: 29 percent
- Percentage rated adequate: 28 percent
- Percentage rated ineffective: 4 percent
- Percentage for which results were not demonstrated: 24 percent.

Source: OMB Web site: http://www.whitehouse.gov/omb/expectmore/about.html.

---

observers agree that the GPRA failed to make performance a significant factor in budget decision making. An indication of this failure is Congress's limited use of the performance information it receives.

In conclusion, what has been achieved in the U.S. federal government is a key element of a performance budgeting system—definition and quantification of outputs and outcomes for each program or agency. However, the process of creating a performance management system is still in its infancy (Blöndal, Kraan, and Ruffner 2003). Performance information is added to the budget documentation, but it is not actually used by budgetary actors in deliberating and in making decisions. Thus, the current budgeting practice in the U.S. federal government is more accurately called a PRB system.

The U.S. experience provides lessons for countries that are attempting to reform their budgeting systems. First, reforms take time, and administration initiatives (such as PPBS and maybe PART) need legislative buy-in so that they outlast current political climates. Second, simply telling people to think of performance in their provision of services is unlikely to change behavior. Performance budgeting and performance management must be linked—and the link is missing in U.S. reforms. In addition, greater attention needs to be given to details of performance measurement and budgeting: obtaining the true cost of delivering services, selecting and adhering to appropriate measures, creating confidence in the measures, using performance as an aid for decision making, and using performance in the regular administrative process. This process is difficult and long. A governmentwide approach may not work, because performance of some central ministries, such as departments of state, cannot be easily quantified. Instead, the focus should be on sectoral agencies delivering services directly to people.

Performance Budgeting Experiences in Selected Developing Countries

Malaysia: output budgeting system

Malaysia, along with New Zealand, pioneered the output-oriented approach to performance budgeting with the introduction of the Modified Budgeting System (MBS) in 1989 (Xavier 1996). It also introduced complementary reforms to strengthen performance-based accountability, such as the 1993 Client's Charter and the initiation of accrual accounting. The Client's Charter requires all agencies to identify their customers and establish their needs. Agencies are further required to notify clients about standards of services available. Public agencies are expected to report annually both on service improvements and on compliance failures. The MBS is essentially an output-based budgeting system because managers receive lump-sum appropriations and have the flexibility to use them in return for agreed-on results or outputs. Performance indicators for government agencies and other public service providers are maintained and acted upon (Siddiquee 2005).

Chilean performance budgeting system (1994 to present)

Chile has a well-developed budget system that produces a realistic and comprehensive budget, which is developed and implemented according to a well-defined timetable and processes. Since the early 1990s, Chile has made extensive efforts to integrate performance information into the budget process and has successfully pursued realistic use of this information in making budgetary decisions.

The Ministry of Finance began experimenting with performance indicators in the budget process in 1994. To facilitate the initiative, the ministry set up the Management Control Division within its Budget Office. The Management

Control Division was to assist in designing and implementing performance systems and in subsequently monitoring line ministries' results. The number of agencies taking part in this program has gradually increased. By the 2004 budget, 132 of 190 agencies were participating, and they produced 1,684 performance indicators (averaging 12.8 per agency).

Since 1997, the Budget Office has used performance evaluations as an important tool for stimulating performance and assisting in resource allocation. The annual public expenditure of the programs that have been evaluated is approximately 27 percent of total government spending. The national Budget Office is accountable for the execution of all evaluations. All final evaluation reports are sent to Congress, publicized on a Web site, and made available in the Budget Office.

The 1997 budget law requires all central government agencies to present information on their objectives, management targets, and results. This information is provided through the comprehensive management reports, which all agencies are obligated to produce at the end of each year for presentation to the Congress. Agencies' progress in implementing evaluation recommendations is reported twice a year: in the year-end comprehensive management report and in July. Also, the information databases and systems within the ministries are audited by the Government General Internal Audit Committee.

In 1998, the Management Improvement Program (MIP) established a reward system for central government employees, in which bonuses were determined by organizational performance. In 2001, when performance indicators were removed from the MIP and reintroduced into the budget, the MIP changed to focus on assessing progress in managerial systems. By 2004, the MIP functioned in 88 centralized agencies and 89 decentralized agencies.

In an effort to align resource allocation with performance, Chile has experimented since 2001 with the mechanism of the bidding fund, which was designed to provide incentives for agencies to introduce formal performance indicators and targets. The bidding fund is a pool of unallocated resources to which ministries can submit bids either for new programs or to substantially extend or reformulate existing programs. Ministries submit bids in a standard format that incorporates information on the program's objective, main components, performance indicators, targets, target population, expected results, spending request, and contribution to the relevant agency's overall strategic goals and outputs. These bids are sent to the Ministry of Planning, where they are reviewed and graded. They are then included in the relevant ministry's formal budget proposal. The president makes the final decisions about which programs will receive funding. In the 2003 budget, 116 programs received funding of US$130.4 million; more than 50 percent of resources were allocated to social functions (Panzardi 2005).

The Chilean system of performance budgeting does not attempt to directly link performance to appropriations, because it is often not possible to routinely reward good performance through the budget allocation process. Rather, performance information is used in the budget cycle, along with financial and other information, as a starting point for discussions with agencies. Following these discussions, performance data have been used to confirm existing allocations or—when results were poor—to push agencies to improve performance; in a few instances programs have been eliminated. The performance information is included in the annexes of the budget documentation to Congress. It is also reported in the comprehensive management report (Blöndal and Curristine 2004). An example of the output budgeting for compulsory education is presented in box 5.5.

BOX 5.5 Chile: Output-Focused Budgeting and Decentralized Service Delivery for Compulsory Education

The provision of public primary and secondary education in Chile is outsourced to municipal and private schools. Outsourcing payments, called *subsidies to education establishments,* are funded on the output basis. The primary and secondary education subsidy represents a large share in the budget: more than 60 percent of the education budget and more than 10 percent of the national budget in 2004.

Specifically, budget formulation for the subsidy allocation is determined in part by the laws, which stipulate the entitlement to a fixed rate per student days of attendance. The rate was set in the 1980s and is tied to increases in civil servant salaries. This rate is applied to the estimated student population and attendance, calculated on the basis of demographic statistics from the National Statistics Institute and classroom statistics from the Ministry of Education (numbers of students in each grade who will be advancing to the next level or graduating).

Meanwhile, the volume reported by the providers and compliance with the standards of quality of the service are closely and effectively monitored. The provincial department of education is responsible for organizing inspections, which provide an independent evaluation of compliance with the agreed terms of the service and the accuracy of the attendance reported. These reviews are supervised and consolidated at the regional level; at the undersecretary level, the reports are used to evaluate whether the program is being implemented in line with the program targets.

Source: Panzardi 2005.

Overall, the Chilean performance budgeting system is well developed, especially in terms of the attention and priority given to performance information in the budget process and the realistic use of this information in decision making. The weakness in the Chilean system is that the performance system is heavily centralized. It would be desirable to build up agencies' capacity so that they have more say in decisions about indicators and measures. Nevertheless, Chile remains a good example of how performance budgeting reforms have promoted efficient allocation of resources, enhanced public management, and improved transparent and accountable governance. It is important to note that Chile has pursued a top-down reform approach because of the unchallenged power of its executive in the budget process. In a country where legislatures play a more powerful role, such a centrally directed process would not be plausible (Panzardi 2005).

Thailand: strategic performance budgeting (1997–present)

Thailand's drive for performance budgeting presents an interesting case for examining the transition from a highly centralized line-item budgeting system focused predominantly on input controls to a performance-oriented budgeting system emphasizing outputs and managerial flexibility. Thailand had a centralized budgeting process based on line-item input budgeting, which contributed to strong aggregate fiscal discipline. Decisions about the details of spending were made centrally, with little or no reference to the results of the spending. The Bureau of the Budget (BOB), a very powerful budgeting entity, controls each agency's spending in detail through numerous separate budget allocations (that is, detailed line itemizing) (Dixon 2005).

Government managers recognized that strong central inputs control was being achieved at the expense of allocative and operational efficiencies. In 1997, the royal Thai government was forced by the Asian financial crisis to reorient the budget process to focus more on performance and results. The crisis mandated sharp spending cuts in response to falling revenues and shifted the normal budget surplus into a string of deficits. The reform trajectory of the Thai government can be divided into two phases, separated by the formation of the new government of Prime Minister Thaksin Shinawatra in February 2001.

PHASE 1 (1997 TO 2000): THE HURDLE APPROACH (CONDITIONAL DEVOLUTION). Thailand embarked on performance budgeting reforms cautiously. Rather than overhaul the overall budgeting process, BOB offered to reduce line itemization for spending agencies, provided that they met core financial management standards in seven areas: budget planning by the agency, output costing, financial and performance reporting, budget and funds control, procurement management, asset management, and internal audit. These seven "hurdle" standards set the criteria for a line agency to transform itself from an administrator of hundreds of BOB-determined budget lines to a manager of a few blocks of budget resources for results.

These hurdles were set at such a height that hardly any agency cleared them. Indeed, most industrial countries would have found it difficult to do so. In addition, the conditional devolution approach did not provide any time frame for agencies to upgrade their management standards. No technical assistance was offered. As a result, progress almost stalled, and when the Thaksin government came into office in 2001, the centralized, control-oriented budgeting system still dominated the process.

PHASE 2 (2001 TO PRESENT): STRATEGIC PERFORMANCE BUDGETING (INTRODUCTION OF OUTPUT BUDGETING IN 2004). The new government restored momentum to Thai budget reform, with its keen interest in upgrading the management of the public sector. Unsatisfied with the slow pace of the hurdle approach, the government decided to enact a comprehensive solution, requiring all ministries and agencies to move toward the new Strategic Performance Budgeting System. This system became effective with the budget for fiscal year 2002/03. The budget moved to an output basis in 2004. When it comes to relaxing central input controls, the government is experimenting with merging appropriations for operating expenditures into two categories: one for salaries and one for other operating expenditures.

Thailand's universal move raised some important concerns: first, that the reform was too ambitious and that some ministries and agencies were not up to the task; second, that the strict expenditure control through detailed line itemizing of line agencies' budget allocations remains largely intact, given that the Thaksin initiative focuses primarily on budget preparation. The budget is therefore presented in two formats: (a) performance and results and (b) input based. It appears that ministries and departments often formulate budgets on the basis of inputs alone, which they then translate into outcomes and outputs.

In conclusion, Thailand's budgeting practice features a combination of output budgeting and centralized input controls. The reluctance of BOB to relax input controls is clearly a response to the weak financial management capacity in line agencies (the seven hurdles). Compared with other developing countries, Thailand has a highly developed performance orientation in its budgeting system. The definition and measurement of outcomes and outputs are quite advanced. To reinforce the performance and results focus, the Thai government could consider modernizing the format of the budget and not presenting input information, where possible. Further, because output budgeting is experimented on in the current environment of highly centralized input controls, the reform also depends on line agencies' efforts to improve their financial management, particularly in the key areas of internal financial control, performance reporting, and internal audit (Blöndal and Kim 2006; Dixon 2005).

Bolivia: results orientation faltering in a pervasive patronage environment with weak public management capacity

Bolivia's performance management and budgeting reform agenda has been expansive and ambitious. The effort started with the introduction of the Integrated Financial Management Project in 1987. Three years later, the Law of Financial Management and Control was passed, with the intent of focusing managers on results, transparency, and accountability. The law required all ministries to prepare annual operating plans that were complemented by performance indicators and targets, which provided the basis for budgeting decisions and performance evaluation. Education sector reform in 1994 and health sector reform in 1999 continued the performance orientation in the central government. However, the reform agenda suffered from very limited implementation at the close of the 1990s. In 1998/99, the Institutional Reform Project was introduced to curb corruption and also to restore the momentum of reform. It affected public budgeting and financial management in two areas: (a) developing an integrated financial management system and (b) boosting results-oriented strategic budgeting and management processes (Montes and Andrews 2005).

Despite the aggressive reform agenda, progress is still very limited and uneven across ministries. Because theft and corruption are still paramount concerns, the country is unlikely to give up financial controls (the major function of line-item budgeting) for managerial discretion and accountability for results (the features of performance budgeting) in the near future. Resource allocation is often arbitrary and strongly influenced by party political factors. The budget aspires to strict control of line-item inputs but achieves only aggregate control. Indeed, the budget is not binding but allows reallocations without proper authorization. There is no systematic monitoring of budget execution. The government is increasingly using the language of performance measurement, but most public sector entities have not been able to put it into practice. Some positive progress in the Ministry of Health and Ministry of Education has been observed. The Ministry of Health has formulated targets for the entire service and has strengthened its planning. The Ministry of Education has integrated performance targets into the Poverty Reduction Strategy Paper, and strategies focused on target achievement are detailed in the annual operating plans of different units in the ministry.

In view of Bolivia's experience, performance-oriented reforms are unlikely to be successfully implemented in an environment of pervasive political patronage and weak administrative capacity in key financial management areas. In Bolivia, political parties capture the public administration and distribute rents and public jobs. Consequently, formal rules are rarely respected and easily avoided. The government tends to accept reforms to the public sector's formal rules because they do not lead to changes in actual practice or threaten business as usual. The performance-oriented reforms in Bolivia failed to account for the patronage system and to boost political consensus for reforms. Aside from the institutional problems embedded in reform design, the reforms did not take into account Bolivia's weak administrative capacity in key financial management areas, especially in budgeting and personnel management. Budgeting in Bolivia does not really function because the budget is unreliable and the remaking of budgets and constant reallocation of funds are evident. Regarding personnel management, recruitment is informal and based, not on merit, but on political loyalty; job evaluations and promotions are politicized; and salary scales are informal and not transparent. Performance-based management and budgeting reforms require strong political consensus in countries where the government is managed on the basis of informal relational mechanisms and political agreement, and they require at least a minimally effective bureaucracy in some key areas of financial management.

Critical Conditions for Successful Implementation of Performance Budgeting

What are the critical factors affecting whether performance budgeting penetrates the routines and procedures of budgeting? The basic conditions necessary to sustain the momentum of performance budgeting reform are summarized here.

Motivation to Make a Change

Consensus among participants on the need for reform is critical to successful implementation. Public officials need to identify their motives for using performance measurement and performance budgeting. Their motives may come from external demands for service quality and accountability, as well as from internal demands for efficiency and effectiveness (Wang 1999). It is also essential to identify the producers and consumers of information and to provide an appropriate incentive strategy for the use of performance-based information. Furthermore, decision makers must understand that ultimately performance-based information may be most helpful for management improvement, rather than for budgetary matters. Political will is critical to the implementation of results-based accountability. Even a less sophisticated system can achieve a great deal in the presence of political will, whereas a more sophisticated system will achieve very little if the political will to use it is not present.

Importance of Legislative Support

Strong and consistent political support from the legislature is critical for performance budgeting initiatives. To pursue internal rationality and efficiency criteria without regard to the political environment jeopardizes the prospects of the endeavor. Legislative understanding and involvement are critical but were often neglected in previous initiatives (such as PPBS, MBO, and ZBB), partly because those reforms were seen mainly as administrations' internal management initiatives (GAO 1997). Lack of legislative support is an important reason for the failure of those reforms (Melkers and Willoughby 1998).

Budgeting reform inevitably affects all branches of government. It cannot operate on a path toward technical refinement or analytical sophistication independently of the political environment (Kelly 2003). The use of performance measurement in budgeting entails changes in governments' operations, personnel, structures, and even cultures—changes that always lead to a power struggle and power transfer and, thus, result in resistance from those who are adversely affected. The role of legislators in budgeting often focuses on balancing budgets and controlling public spending. Hence, they show interest in control-oriented budget formats, such as line-item budgeting, in which they can manipulate and monitor budget revenues and expenses item by item. Legislators may resist performance measurement, fearing a shift of power to the executive branch (Carroll 1995; Jones and McCaffery 1997). Individual service agencies may also gain budgeting, personnel, and purchasing power through delegation from the legislature and central management offices. The political effect of performance budgeting reform demonstrates that implementation of this initiative needs the support of political stakeholders (Wang 2000).

As part of the effort to promote enthusiasm and acceptance from the legislature, a government needs to involve legislators in establishing performance goals, developing performance indicators, monitoring the performance process, and evaluating performance results. The reform is unlikely to succeed if the executive and legislative branches have conflicting objectives and conflicting understandings of why the reform is necessary. Clearly, development of such an open system is costly; however, without it, performance budgeting reform risks losing momentum and being abandoned.

Support and Engagement from Citizens

Aside from legislative participation on a limited scale, support from outside the administration is also necessary. Performance reforms should provide direct benefits to government stakeholders in exchange for their support (Wang 2000). Without at least some degree of public involvement, performance budgeting risks becoming an internal bureaucratic exercise detached from what the citizenry views as important. Citizens' involvement also ensures credibility and improves the meaningfulness of the data that are collected, assessed, and reported.

Minimum Administrative Capacity and Bottom-Up Approach

The history of managerial and budgeting reforms tells us that the fate of a new initiative often does not rely on logical concepts, good intentions, and sound values, but on operational issues of how well people solve practical problems and whether they can solicit continued support to sustain the momentum of a reform. Mandating the implementation of performance measurement and budgeting across the board, while politically popular, may not be administratively feasible. It is important that political leaders and policy entrepreneurs who advocate implementation of the reform allow time for agencies to learn and to build their capacities.

Rather than imposing a system for all programs to follow, the reform should respect institutional differences among agencies and help them to develop approaches suitable for their own situations and contexts, approaches that can provide them with useful information for reviewing the effect of what they are doing and identifying how this information can aid them in their planning and budgeting (Perrin 2002). Institutional capacity building in personnel, information systems, accounting standards, and—most important—funding potential are highly associated with the use of performance measurement in budgeting (Wang 2000).

Staff training

Political enforcement and managerial commitment alone will not make any change if civil servants lack the capacity to implement performance budgeting. Most of the work of developing and maintaining a performance budgeting system is done by the budget staffs in the executive and legislative branches. In the absence of adequate training, managers and staff members are unlikely to be able to understand the potential value of a results-oriented approach or be able to provide for effective implementation and use (Perrin 2002). When a performance budgeting system is attempted, a series of important questions follows: How can valid and reliable performance information be obtained? How can performance be tracked over time while still keeping data collection costs under control? What is the correct interpretation of performance results? It is not feasible to plan an evaluation of a program's effect without sufficient resources and appropriately trained personnel. Personnel training can make a difference, not only by changing attitudes but also by preparing competent staff members. Transforming an organizational culture by building performance consciousness into daily functions is a difficult undertaking. The experience of many different jurisdictions (Denmark, Norway, and the United States, among others) is that training, guidance, and availability of technical assistance are required over a period of time.

Information technology

Government agencies frequently do not have data systems that can readily generate the performance information needed. Many state agencies have collected program data in mainframe systems that cannot easily respond to information needs. Coupled with data quality needs, certain electronic systems must be in place for maintaining and tracking performance.

Accounting system

The absence of an appropriate accounting system may undermine performance budgeting reforms. The foundation for performance measurement is activity-based costing of all direct and indirect costs to a program to provide a more accurate picture of the expense of achieving a specific objective.

Accurate cost data are critical to analysis that seeks to determine the return on investment in government programs.

Financial cost of the reform

Sufficient financial resources for data collection, initial training, and ongoing system maintenance are critical for the implementation of performance budgeting. Performance budgeting information systems, which entail data collection and validation, analysis, and reporting, may be costly to develop and maintain.

Apart from these four prerequisites—the need for incentives to reform, legislative commitment, citizen support, and the necessary capacity-building measures—a preparation stage of careful practice in performance reporting and management is critical. A valid, reliable, and uniform financial and performance reporting system provides the database for performance budgeting. A performance monitoring system helps public managers understand how inputs are converted into outputs and outcomes. Given that many governments do not have any practice in performance reporting and management, a long preparation time is needed before any performance budgeting practice becomes apparent (Wang 1999).

Concluding Remarks

Performance budgeting is a useful tool for performance accountability and budget transparency in line ministries but of limited relevance for ministries that perform central policy functions, such as the ministry of finance or ministry of foreign affairs. Furthermore, in the absence of an incentive environment for better performance or results-based accountability, the introduction of performance budgeting may not lead to improved performance. Managerial accountability must be on outputs, not outcomes, because outcomes are influenced by external factors. However, outcomes should be monitored. Performance budgeting cannot be expected to be a mechanistic, rational system that replaces the political process of making resource choices in a complex environment of competing demands. Instead, it has the potential to facilitate informed political choices. A transparent budget and citizen evaluation of outputs, if embodied in performance budgeting, can be helpful in improving budgetary outcomes. Performance budgeting is a costly exercise, but it yields positive net benefits if performed in a performance management culture and with accountability to citizens for results.

References

Andrews, Matthew. 2006. "Beyond 'Best Practice' and 'Basics First' in Adopting Performance Budgeting Reform." *Public Administration and Development* 26 (2): 147–61.

Blöndal, Jón R. 2003. "Budget Reform in OECD Member Countries: Common Trends." *OECD Journal of Budgeting* 2 (4): 7–26.

Blöndal, Jón R., and Teresa Curristine. 2004. "Budgeting in Chile." *OECD Journal of Budgeting* 4 (2): 7–45.

Blöndal, Jón R., and Sang-In Kim. 2006. "Budgeting in Thailand." *OECD Journal of Budgeting* 5 (3): 7–36.

Blöndal, Jón R., and Michael Ruffner. 2004. "Budgeting in Denmark." *OECD Journal of Budgeting* 4 (1): 53–85.

Blöndal, Jón R., Dirk-Jan Kraan, and Michael Ruffner. 2003. "Budgeting in the United States." *OECD Journal of Budgeting* 3 (2): 7–53.

Broom, Cheryle A. 1995. "Performance-Based Government Models: Building a Track Record." *Public Budgeting and Finance* 15 (1): 3–17.

Carroll, James. 1995. "The Rhetoric of Reform and Political Reality in the National Performance Review." *Public Administration Review* 55 (3): 302–11.

Department of Families, Community Services, and Indigenous Affairs, Government of Australia. 2006. "Portfolio Budget Statement 2006–07." Government of Australia, Canberra.

Dixon, Geoff. 2005. "Thailand's Quest for Results-Focused Budgeting." *International Journal of Public Administration* 28 (3–4): 355–70.

Flowers, Geraldo, Delia Kundin, and Ralph S. Brower. 1999. "How Agency Conditions Facilitate and Constrain Performance-Based Program Systems: A Qualitative Inquiry." *Journal of Public Budgeting, Accounting & Financial Management* 11 (4): 618–48.

GAO (General Accounting Office). 1997. "Performance Budgeting: Past Initiatives Offer Insights for GPRA Implementation." General Accounting Office, Washington, DC.

Gilmour, John B., and David E. Lewis. 2006. "Does Performance Budgeting Work? An Examination of the Office of Management and Budget's PART Scores." *Public Administration Review* 66 (5): 742–52.

Jones, Lawrence R., and Jerry McCaffery. 1997. "Implementing the Chief Financial Officers Act and the Government Performance and Results Act in the Federal Government." *Public Budgeting and Finance* 17 (1): 35–55.

Kelly, Janet M. 2003. "The Long View: Lasting (and Fleeting) Reforms in Public Budgeting in the Twentieth Century." *Journal of Public Budgeting, Accounting, and Financial Management* 15 (2): 309–26.

Kettl, Donald. 2000. *The Global Public Management Revolution: A Report on the Transformation of Governance.* Washington, DC: Brookings Institution Press.

Kristensen, Jens Kromann, Walter S. Groszyk, and Bernd Bühler. 2002. "Outcome-Focused Management and Budgeting." *OECD Journal of Budgeting* 1 (4): 7–34.

Lu, Haoran. 1998. "Performance Budgeting Resuscitated: Why Is It Still Inviable?" *Journal of Public Budgeting, Accounting, and Financial Management* 10 (2): 151–72.

Marcel, Mario, and Marcelo Tokman. 2002. "Building a Consensus for Fiscal Reform: The Chilean Case." *OECD Journal of Budgeting* 2 (3): 35–55.

Martin, Lawrence L. 1997. "Outcome Budgeting: A New Entrepreneurial Approach to Budgeting." *Journal of Public Budgeting, Accounting, and Financial Management* 9 (1): 108–26.

McGill, Ronald. 2001. "Performance Budgeting." *International Journal of Public Sector Management* 14 (5): 376–90.

———. 2006. *Achieving Results: Performance Budgeting in the Least Developed Countries.* New York: United Nations Capital Development Fund.

Melkers, Julia E., and Katherine G. Willoughby. 1998. "The State of the States: Performance-Based Budgeting Requirements in 47 out of 50." *Public Administration Review* 58 (1): 66–73.

Montes, Carlos, and Mathew Andrews. 2005. "Implementing Reforms in Bolivia: Too Much to Handle?" *International Journal of Public Administration* 28 (3–4): 273–90.

New Zealand Treasury. 2005. *A Guide to the Public Finance Act.* Wellington: New Zealand Treasury.

OECD (Organisation for Economic Co-operation and Development). 2004. "Public Sector Modernisation: Governing for Performance." Policy Brief, OECD, Paris.

OMB (Office of Management and Budget). 2002. "President's Management Agenda for Fiscal Year 2002." OMB, Washington, DC.

———. 2006. "Fiscal Year 2007 Budget." OMB, Washington, DC.

Panzardi, Roberto O. 2005. "Chile: Towards Results-Oriented Budgeting." *En breve* 81, World Bank, Washington, DC.

Performance Institute. 2003. "Bush's '04 Budget Puts Premium on Transparency and Performance." News release, Performance Institute, Arlington, VA, February 3.

Perrin, Burt. 2002. "Implementing the Vision: Addressing Challenges to Results-Focused Management and Budgeting." OECD, Paris.

Pitsvada, Bernard, and Felix LoStracco. 2002. "Performance Budgeting—The Next Budgetary Answer: But What Is the Question?" *Journal of Public Budgeting, Accounting, and Financial Management* 14 (1): 53–72.

Rivenbark, William C., and Janet M. Kelly. 2000. "Performance Measurement: A Local Government Response." *Journal of Public Budgeting, Accounting, and Financial Management* 12 (1): 74–86.

Rønsholt, Frans, Richard Mushi, Bedason Shallanda, and Paschal Assey. 2003. "Results-Orientated Expenditure Management Country Study—Tanzania." Working Paper 204, Overseas Development Institute, London.

Rubin, Irene. 2000. *The Politics of Public Budgeting,* 4th ed. New York: Seven Bridges Press.

Scheers, Bram, Miekatrien Sterck, and Geert Bouckaert. 2005. "Lessons from Australian and British Reforms in Results-Oriented Financial Management." *OECD Journal of Budgeting* 5 (2): 133–62.

Shah, Anwar. 2005. "On Getting the Giant to Kneel: Approaches to a Change in the Bureaucratic Culture." In *Fiscal Management,* ed., Anwar Shah, 211–28. Washington, DC: World Bank.

Siddiquee, Noore Alam. 2005. "Public Accountability in Malaysia: Challenges and Critical Concerns." *Journal of Public Administration* 28 (1–2): 107–29.

Treasury Board of Canada. 2003. *Linking Resources to Results.* Ottawa: Treasury Board of Canada, Ottawa.

Wang, Xiao-Hu. 1999. "Conditions to Implement Outcome-Oriented Performance Budgeting: Some Empirical Evidence." *Journal of Public Budgeting, Accounting, and Financial Management* 11 (4): 533–52.

———. 2000. "Performance Measurement in Budgeting: A Study of County Governments." *Public Budgeting and Finance* 23 (3): 22–48.

Wildavsky, Aaron. 1979. *The Politics of the Budgetary Process.* Boston: Little, Brown.

———. 1986. *Budgeting: A Comparative Theory of Budgetary Processes.* New Brunswick, NJ: Transaction Books.

Xavier, John Antony. 1996. "Budget Reform—The Malaysian Experience." *Public Administration and Development* 16 (5): 485–501.

6

Accrual Accounting in the Public Sector: Lessons for Developing Countries

PAUL BOOTHE

One of the key developments in public sector governance over the past 15 years has been the strong encouragement by international agencies such as the Organisation for Economic Co-operation and Development (OECD), the International Monetary Fund (IMF), and the World Bank for countries to move from traditional public sector–based cash accounting to private sector–based accrual accounting. Some international accounting bodies, such as the International Federation of Accountants (IFAC), have also supported this direction.

Proponents of such a change point to a number of benefits. They believe that accrual accounting, because it recognizes expenses when they are deemed to have occurred rather than when they are paid, provides a more transparent picture of government operations. In addition, accrual accounting provides a clearer treatment of capital assets, explicitly recognizing the depreciation of physical capital over time and variations in the value of financial assets and liabilities, regardless of whether these events result in cash transactions.

In 2003, it was estimated that about 5 of 28 OECD member countries had adopted full accrual accounting, with a further 2 adopting a modified form of accrual. A small number of developing countries had also followed suit.

However, the support for adoption of accrual accounting in the public sector is by no means universal. Opponents express a number of concerns. Some commentators wonder whether private sector–based accrual accounting, in which the main focus is financial performance, is appropriate for the public sector, whose main focus is democratic accountability. Others question whether the sophisticated judgments regarding valuation that accrual accounting demands actually broaden the scope for political manipulation. Finally, some express doubt that the cost of moving to the more technically demanding accrual system is justified by the benefits it brings over traditional cash accounting.

One relatively new area of academic research is the study of fiscal institutions. Although a good deal of work has been done on the properties of fiscal rules, relatively little analysis has been done of the interaction of fiscal rules and accounting regimes. In particular, it is interesting to consider how the adoption of different accounting regimes changes the incentives faced by budget makers in different fiscal environments and how it results in different fiscal outcomes.

Beyond the debate over the benefits and costs of moving to accrual accounting in industrial countries like the OECD member states, a parallel debate is taking place in some developing countries over the adoption of accrual accounting. Developing countries face a number of unique challenges. Such challenges include the large number of competing priorities for public sector reform. Developing countries face serious constraints in the area of human resources and information technology (IT) capacity. They operate in environments where even traditional cash accounting may not be well established. Finally, they often struggle to overcome weak governance regimes and combat corruption.

The purpose of this chapter is to examine the debate over the adoption of accrual accounting in the public sector, with a particular focus on providing guidance to policy makers in developing countries. The first section presents a brief review of the workings of cash- and accrual-based accounting systems in the public sector. The second section reviews the arguments for and against adoption of accrual accounting in industrial countries. The third focuses on the interaction between fiscal rules and accounting regimes. The fourth section reviews the arguments for and against the adoption of accrual accounting in developing countries. The chapter concludes by drawing some lessons for policy makers.

Differences between Cash and Accrual Accounting in the Public Sector

What are the key differences between cash and accrual systems of accounting as applied to the public sector?[1] The cash system of accounting is one in which expenses and revenues are recorded in the period that payments are made or received. The accrual system of accounting is one in which revenues are recorded in the period in which they are earned (whether received or not) and expenses in the period in which they are incurred (whether paid or not).

The cash system of accounting has traditionally been used in the public sector. It matches well with the annual budgeting and revenue collection systems used by governments and legislatures in industrial countries. More recently, led primarily by the international agencies, such as the OECD, the IMF, and the World Bank, and by some international accounting bodies, such as IFAC, countries have been strongly encouraged to adopt the accounting system generally used by the private sector: accrual accounting.

The most profound difference between the two accounting systems relates to the time transactions are recorded. For example, under a cash accounting system, revenue is not recorded until it is actually received, whereas under an accrual system, revenue is recorded when it is earned, even if it is not received until far into the future. Likewise, under a cash system, expenses are not recorded until they are actually paid. In contrast, under the accrual system, expenses are recorded when they are incurred, even if they are not actually paid until far into the future.

The difference between the two systems can be made clear by considering a couple of examples. Consider first the accounting treatment of the purchase of a capital asset. Suppose a government purchases an office building. Under a cash system of accounting, the full cost of the building is recorded as an expense in the year it is purchased. Under an accrual system, the depreciation of the building is recorded as an expense in each year of the useful life of the building.

A second example relates to public sector pensions. Under a cash system, recorded pension expenses are measured by the payments made to beneficiaries during the relevant accounting period (usually a year). However, under an accrual system, recorded pension expenses are measured by the change in estimated pension liabilities. Thus, all other things equal, if the government changes a pension policy that will result in higher pension payments in the future, the estimated discounted sum of those additional payments is recorded as a pension expense in the period the policy change occurred.

Of course, both accounting systems have strengths and weaknesses when applied to the public sector. Table 6.1 highlights the key strengths and

TABLE 6.1 Cash Accounting versus Accrual Accounting

Characteristic	Cash accounting	Accrual accounting
Operational requirements	Relatively simple	Relatively complex
Links to traditional budget and revenue systems	Relatively strong	Relatively weak
Coverage	Records only transactions that result in cash payments or receipts	Records estimated noncash transactions as well
Timing	Records only transactions that occur within the accounting period	Records the estimated future effects of current transactions and policy changes
Audit and control	Relatively simple	Relatively demanding

Source: Adapted from Athukorala and Reid 2003: 26.

weaknesses of the two accounting systems. The cash system of accounting, because of its simplicity, is relatively easy to implement and operate. The relative ease of audit and control is also a positive characteristic. However, its coverage is limited only to transactions that result in cash payments or receipts, and it considers only transactions that occur within the relevant accounting period. Conversely, the accrual system of accounting is relatively complex to implement and operate and demanding in terms of audit and control. However, its strengths include coverage of noncash as well as cash transactions and recognition of the future effects of transactions and policy changes.

Finally, it is worth noting that relatively few governments actually use a pure cash or pure accrual system of accounting. Modified systems are often used. For example, governments may accrue revenues and expenses but account for capital purchases in the period that they occur. In addition, public sector accounting systems are often in a state of transition, continually being modified to reflect changes in practice or changes in the external environment in which they operate.

Accrual Accounting in OECD Countries

As noted above, there has been strong encouragement for OECD countries to adopt accrual accounting in the public sector: "Multilateral institutions, such as the International Monetary Fund (IMF) and the World Bank, are encouraging governments to introduce accrual accounting, and much work to facilitate this is being undertaken by the international accountancy profession, with the support of these multilateral institutions" (Hepworth 2003: 37).

International accounting bodies such as IFAC have been in the forefront of efforts to encourage the move of the public sector to accrual accounting:

> Over the last 20 years, there have been increasing calls for governments and public sector organisations to move to accrual based accounting and adopt private-sector-style financial statements. Thus, for example, the IFAC Public Sector Committee has set itself the task of developing a full set of international public sector accounting standards and ensuring that these are adopted as widely as possible. (Wynne 2004: 2)

The IMF, in particular, has been a champion of public sector accrual accounting. In 2001, the IMF argued, "Best practice is that the accounting system should have the capacity for accounting and reporting on an accrual basis, as well as for generating cash reports" (IMF 2001b: 51). The IMF now requires that countries' submissions to one of its key statistical publications, *Government Financial Statistics Manual*, present government revenue and spending statistics in accrual terms:

> Although a cash overall balance will continue to be used by many countries for some time, the revised *GFS Manual* will use accrual standards for fiscal reports, in line with other economic statistics standards. Moreover, the need to supplement cash basis financial reporting by at least some elements of accrual reporting is being increasingly recognized. Several countries are adopting an accrual or modified accrual accounting standard. (IMF 2001b: 50)

In his introduction to the 2001 *Government Financial Statistics Manual*, Horst Kohler, then managing director of the IMF, added his particular encouragement to move toward the standards of accrual accounting:

> Of particular note is that the *Manual* introduces accrual accounting, balance sheets, and complete coverage of government economic and financial activities. Although only a few countries are currently capable of meeting the standards promulgated in this *Manual*, the number is increasing steadily and I hope that the trend continues. I commend the *Manual* to compilers and users as an important instrument in their work and urge member countries to adopt the guidelines of the *Manual* as the basis for compiling government finance statistics and for reporting this information to the Fund. (IMF 2001a: vii)

One of the leading proponents of the move to accrual accounting has been the OECD. In 2002, the OECD *Journal of Budgeting* was launched, containing articles on budgeting and on reporting best practices. Accrual budgeting and accounting figure prominently in the OECD's review of best practices. An example is the best-practice advice dealing with accounting for capital assets:

> Non-financial assets will be recognised under full accrual-based accounting and budgeting. This will require the valuation of such assets and the selection of appropriate depreciation schedules. The valuation and depreciation methods should be fully disclosed. (OECD 2002: 13)

By 2003, Blöndal (2003) estimated that 5 of 28 OECD member countries had adopted full accrual accounting and 2 more had adopted modified accrual (that is, no capitalization or depreciation of assets). Moreover, 3 of 28 had adopted accrual budgeting, with an additional 3 using modified accrual.

Rationale for Adoption of Accrual Accounting

After reviewing the differences between cash and accrual accounting, it is useful to examine the rationale provided by the proponents of accrual accounting. Blöndal (2003: 45) outlines the case in favor of accrual accounting for the public sector:

> The objective of moving financial reporting to accruals is to make the true cost of government more transparent; for example, by attributing the pension costs of government employees to the time period when they are employed and accumulating their pension rights rather than having this as an unrelated expenditure once they have retired. Instead of spikes in expenditures when individual capital projects are undertaken, these are incorporated into the annual operating expenditures through an allowance for depreciation. Treating loans and guarantee programmes on an accrual basis fosters more attention to the risks of default by those who have been granted them, especially if there is a requirement for such default risks to be pre-funded. Outstanding government debts can be designed in such a way that all interest expenditure is paid in a lump sum at the end of the loan rather than being spread through the years when the loan was outstanding. All of these examples show how a focus on cash only can distort the true cost of government.

Thus, the key benefit of accrual accounting is to allocate the revenues and expenses of government correctly *over time*. All of the examples Blöndal cites are ones in which both cash and accrual accounting will recognize the relevant expenses and revenues, but at different points in time. In his view, accountability is better served by accrual accounting, which recognizes expenses when they are deemed to have been incurred, rather than when they were actually paid, as in cash accounting.

Athukorala and Reid (2003: 2) also review the arguments in favor of accrual accounting in the public sector: "At one extreme, supporters of accrual accounting in government argue that 'if it's good enough for the private sector, it's good enough for the public sector.'" Athukorala and Reid go on to list the main arguments in favor of accrual:

- It matches with national accounts economic statistics.
- It recognizes transactions when they occur rather than when cash is paid.
- It separates ongoing spending from capital spending.
- It gives better information on the sustainability of policies.
- It discloses liabilities such as public sector pensions.
- It promotes intergenerational fairness.
- It identifies payments arrears.

They argue that accrual accounting is the preferred approach for industrial countries:

> In summary, evidence suggests that at the aggregate level, accrual-based fiscal indicators provide better information about the sustainability of fiscal policies (for instance, the effects of pension policies on a government's balance sheet are disclosed) and provide a stronger basis for government accountability (accrual accounting information can not be manipulated as easily as cash-based information). Furthermore, accrual-based fiscal indicators arguably provide a better measure of the effects of government policies on aggregate demand; and, at the organization level, accrual-based financial statements provide better measures of organizational efficiency and effectiveness. Accrual-based financial information also reduces opportunities for fraud and corruption, particularly as regards stewardship of assets. (Athukorala and Reid 2003: 28)

Concerns Regarding Accrual Accounting in the Public Sector

Despite the enthusiasm of international institutions and some professional accounting organizations for accrual accounting in the public sector, there is a sizable body of opinion to the contrary. The criticisms range from concerns over technical issues such as the valuation of assets to broader questions regarding differences in the requirements of the public sector versus the private sector and democratic accountability.

A fundamental concern arises over the question of whether the accounting requirements of private and public sector organizations are comparable and are well served by a common basis of accounting. Andrew Wynne of the U.K. Association of Chartered Certified Accountants (ACCA) has been a forceful critic of the applicability of private sector accounting norms to the public sector:

> [A]ccrual accounting was specifically developed to measure the profit earned by an entity that should be attributed to a particular financial year. Accrual accounting also enables private sector businesses to match the cost of the provision of goods and services with the revenue gained from their sale. For private sector companies, this single performance measure neatly encapsulates their financial performance and the achievement of their prime objective, to make a profit. For public sector organisations, the same concept, profit, cannot be expected to be as effective. Despite the role and objectives of accounting being different in the public and private sectors (due to the different objectives of entities in these two sectors), these differences are frequently ignored. (Wynne 2003: 21)

As a result of these differences between private and public sector organizations, Wynne (2003: 21) is skeptical that they are likely to find the same financial statements appropriate:

> We should recognise that the aims and objectives of public sector organisations are fundamentally different from those of private sector companies. Consequently their financial statements are also likely to be fundamentally different.

A key element in the argument that private and public sectors need different financial statements stems from the different kinds of accountability they face. The accountability of the private sector is to individual investors and is based on firms' achievement of financial targets: profit and loss. In contrast, the public sector must be politically accountable. The most important financial aspect of that accountability is whether public funds are expended in the ways voted by the legislature. Wynne (2003: 6) focuses on the issue of accountability to the legislature:

> A fundamental objective of the financial statements for any public sector organisation should be to fulfill the stewardship function by providing an audited comparison of the actual use of recourses with the agreed budget. A government's financial accountability arises from the budget setting process during which it gains agreement to the levels of taxation which will be levied and to the funding which will be allocated to the various services which it intends to provide. Thus the budget out-turn report is the prime document by which governments are held to account for the regularity and probity of their financial management.

Even proponents of accrual accounting recognize the accountability problems inherent in mixing accrual accounting with the traditional cash budgets presented to legislatures that result in one-year appropriations being voted. Blöndal (2003) addresses the dilemma. He writes that accrual accounting seems more attractive than accrual budgeting for two reasons:

> First, an accrual budget is believed to risk budget discipline. The political decision to spend money should be matched with when it is reported in the budget. Only cash provides for that. If major capital projects, for example, could be voted on with only the commensurate depreciation expense being reported, there is fear that this would increase expenditures for such projects. Second, and somewhat contradictory to the first reason, legislatures have often shown resistance to the adoption of accrual budgeting. This resistance is often due to the sheer complexity of accruals. In this context, it is noteworthy that the legislatures in those countries that have adopted accrual budgeting generally have a relatively weak role in the budget process. (Blöndal 2003: 44)

One of the key differences between cash and accrual accounting is the need, under accrual, to form estimates of revenue and (especially) expense relevant to the period in question. In contrast, cash accounting is based on direct measurement. Both are susceptible to manipulation. In the case of cash accounting, financial statements can be manipulated by managing the timing of transactions. In the case of accrual accounting, the scope for manipulation is inherent in the formation of estimates of revenue and expense. Hepworth (2003: 38) has outlined concerns with manipulation of financial statements under accrual accounting:

> The main criticism of cash accounting is that cash accounts can be (and are) manipulated to ensure certain cash outcomes are achieved. Exactly the same criticism can be leveled at accrual accounting, which offers even greater scope for manipulation.

He goes on to caution that the adoption of accrual accounting may lead to greater financial control problems:

> Accrual accounting (which requires that income and expenditure are recognized as they are earned or incurred, not as with a cash basis of accounting, when they are received or paid) will not solve underlying financial control problems—it can only make them worse. This is because it leaves considerable scope for judgment, and if financial control is not effective under a cash accounting system, then it is likely to be even less effective under an accrual-based system. (Hepworth 2003: 37)

Accrual accounting poses some significant challenges to public sector managers because it requires estimation of the value of assets that have no market and of the current effect of programs that may make payments far into the future. Blöndal (2003) notes that the valuation of so-called heritage assets (museums, national monuments, and so forth); military assets; and public infrastructure (such as transportation and health care facilities) is likely to be contentious. Programs like public pensions that make uncertain payments far into the future are also difficult to value. The required judgment by public servants in these cases leaves them open to political pressure and more difficult to hold accountable.

As a result of these concerns, some experts have urged caution in the move to accrual accounting in the public sector. For example, in a recent piece in a respected accounting journal, Hepworth (2003: 37) writes, "One purpose of this article is to urge caution on those who are contemplating or encouraging the change to accrual accounting in central government, unless the conditions are absolutely right.

Wynne (2004: 3) focuses on the gap between the theoretical benefits claimed for accrual accounting and the experience to date:

> A wide range of benefits [is] often claimed to arise from making this fundamental change to financial accounting in the public sector. These include improved accountability, management of assets, and generally increased efficiency. These advantages have yet to be clearly demonstrated in practice, but the costs of such reforms are clear and significant.

Accounting Regimes and Incentives for Policy Makers

Over the past couple of decades, scholars have invested a good deal of effort in studying the economic, political, and institutional determinants of fiscal policy.[2] Part of that literature has focused on fiscal rules: commitments by political leaders to certain norms of fiscal behavior. The creation of the European Monetary Union and the related Stability and Growth Pact provided strong motivation to examine all aspects of fiscal rules and their effects on fiscal policy in Europe. However, this literature has focused on other OECD countries and developing countries as well.

With the economic effects of various fiscal rules now relatively well understood and the political determinants of fiscal policy extensively studied, attention has turned to the effect of budget institutions on fiscal policy outcomes (for example, see Poterba and von Hagen 1999). This section looks at this emerging literature to examine the interaction of accounting regimes and fiscal rules.[3] The particular focus is the incentives for policy makers that are created when governments change the way that they account for capital—a change that is currently under way in a number of countries.

A simple model of a government budget is sketched out to aid in analyzing the accounting regime–fiscal rule interaction. The model is first used to examine the effect of accounting regimes on some standard fiscal rules related to deficits, government debt, and accumulation of public sector capital. This section then turns to the incentives created by accounting regimes when governments have preferences regarding the mix of capital versus operating spending or find themselves in different fiscal circumstances regarding starting values for deficits, debts, or capital stock.

Fiscal Rules and Budget Institutions

According to Tanzi (2003), the virtues of a balanced budget have long been recognized. He cites as his authorities well-known historical figures such as Cicero, David Hume, and George Washington (Tanzi 2003: 4). Although it is unlikely that such individuals concerned themselves with public sector accounting, Wynne (2003) tells us that the cash basis of accounting has been used to measure fiscal balance for the past 150 years.[4] Of course, regardless of accounting regime, there are many methodological issues related to the measurement of fiscal balance (Blejer and Cheasty 1991). As well, fiscal rules are more or less effective depending on their design and a host of other, external factors (Kopits 2001).[5]

Research has shown that one of the key external factors affecting fiscal policy outcomes is budget institutions. For example, Poterba and von Hagen (1999) claim, "Higher levels of transparency are associated with lower budget deficits." Furthermore, they go on to argue that "institutions must themselves be regarded as endogenous. The questions when, and why, governments adopt institutional reforms remain important challenges for future research in the political economy of fiscal policy" (Poterba and von Hagen 1999: 4).

An important institutional reform currently under way in industrial countries is the move from cash to accrual accounting for capital. Analysts' views on this change are mixed. Proponents argue that such a change will correct an inherent bias against the accumulation of public sector capital inherent in a cash accounting regime.[6] For example, Balassone and Franco (2001) point to the double burden of transition to balanced budget and lower debt levels and to the effect of consolidated balance fiscal rules on public investment.

However, others are less supportive of the move to accrual accounting for capital. They cite the benefits flowing from the simplicity of cash accounting, including accountability and ease of administration.[7] For example, Tanzi (2003) quotes *Financial Times* columnist John Plender, who argues that "the further the budget discussion moves from cash, the greater the risk of becoming lost in the fiscal fog of war" (Plender 2003: 18). Indeed, Canada's Public Sector Accounting Board recommends that the cash accounting focus on the government deficit be replaced with five separate measures under accrual accounting (PSAB 2003).

The Model

To help analyze the interaction of fiscal rules and accounting regimes, a simple government budget under alternative accounting regime is sketched out. The model combines accounting identities with government behavior described by fiscal rules relating to deficits and capital accumulation. First, a cash accounting regime is described.

Assume that the revenue side of the government budget is exogenous. Then total revenue grows at the same rate as the nominal economy. Total expenditure is the sum of transfers to individuals and firms, gross public sector investment, services to individuals and firms, and debt-service payments. The budget surplus is simply the difference between total revenue and total expenditure. Assume that the government adopts a no-deficit fiscal rule. Then transfers are set in each period to ensure that the budget is in balance—that is, total expenditures are equal to (exogenous) total revenues.

Investment in the model is determined by the government's fiscal rule. To begin, assume that the government adopts a rule for capital accumulation whereby public capital grows at the same rate as the economy; that is, the ratio of capital to revenue is constant. This assumption means setting investment at the level required to get the appropriate level of public capital (that is, to offset depreciation and add enough capital in each period to increase the capital stock at the same rate as government revenue). Government services, which are produced using public capital, are set equal to a fixed proportion of last period's capital stock. The stock of government financial assets (or debt) is determined by adding the current period's surplus or deficit to last year's stock of assets (debt). Debt-service costs (or interest income) are determined by applying the interest rate to the government stock of debt and assets. The capital stock is assumed to the depreciate at a constant rate and to grow through gross investment.

To transform the basic cash accounting model of the budget into one that conforms to an accrual accounting regime, one must modify the definition of total expenditure and the way the accumulation of government financial assets and debt is measured. Under accrual accounting, spending on public sector capital is excluded from total expenditure, whereas the depreciation of public sector capital is included. Thus, the definition of total expenditure is changed by eliminating gross investment and adding depreciation.

An antideficit fiscal rule under an accrual accounting regime becomes an anti–operating deficit rule because spending on capital is no longer included in the definition of expenditure. As shown later, the change in the fiscal rule from no cash deficit to no operating deficit has important implications for budget outcomes.

Assume that the fiscal rule for the accumulation of capital is the same as before. Then also modify the way government financial assets and debt are measured. Under the accrual regime, set this period's financial assets (and debt) equal to the last period value, plus the difference between the surplus and net investment. In other words, any net investment that cannot be financed by the operating surplus must be financed by borrowing, with the attending impact on government financial assets.

Benchmark Fiscal Rules

To establish a benchmark for comparison, begin by looking at the behavior of a government that adopts the two fiscal rules referred to earlier. The first is a rule for the accumulation of public sector capital—that is, that a constant ratio of capital to revenue be maintained. The second is an antideficit rule. Under a cash accounting regime, the two rules imply that a portion of current revenue must be reserved to fund new capital. Under an accrual regime, capital accumulation can be financed by borrowing.

Assume that the overall government goal is to maximize total spending while respecting the two fiscal rules. Interestingly, the interaction of the different accounting regimes with the fiscal rules produces different incentives and government behavior. It does so because the variable on which one of the fiscal rules is based, the deficit, is measured differently under cash accounting than under accrual accounting. For example, under the cash accounting regime, the level of financial debt is constant—the direct consequence of the antideficit rule. Under accrual accounting, the level of financial debt grows because capital accumulation can be financed by borrowing. The mix of spending also differs across accounting regimes. Under the cash regime, capital spending is financed by current revenue, hence reducing the revenue available for other purposes. Under the accrual regime, capital spending is partially financed by borrowing, initially leaving more revenue available for other purposes. However, as debt accumulates, so do interest charges, which reduce the revenue available for other spending. Thus, as time goes on, spending on services and transfers may ultimately be lower under accrual accounting than under cash accounting.

These differences illustrate an important policy implication. Changes in accounting regimes may require corresponding changes to fiscal rules. Maintaining the same fiscal rules while changing accounting regimes may result in important changes in the trajectory of public debt and mix of expenditures over time.

Alternative Fiscal Rules

Advocates of accrual accounting for the public sector have recognized the need for new fiscal rules and corresponding indicators to accompany the change of accounting regime (see PSAB 2003). One such rule change is to focus attention on changes in government debt rather than on deficits. Next consider a case in which the antideficit rule is replaced with a debt rule—that is, a rule that requires that a constant ratio of debt to revenue be maintained.[8] However, retain the capital accumulation rule from the benchmark case.

To implement the new rule under the cash accounting regime, now set transfers so as to make room for enough capital spending to satisfy the capital accumulation rule without causing the ratio of government debt to revenue to rise. No changes are required to implement the rule under an accrual accounting regime because an antideficit rule and a constant debt ratio rule are equivalent under accrual accounting.

When comparing government behavior under the two regimes, note that levels of government spending, debt, and capital accumulation are equivalent even though deficits are incurred under cash accounting but not under accrual accounting. The results are the same because the variables on which the fiscal rules are based are measured in the same way under both accounting regimes. These findings lead to the policy implication that key fiscal trajectories under a debt rule are insensitive to the choice of accounting regimes.

Not many fiscal authorities actually constrain their actions by rules for both deficits or debts and capital accumulation. Much more common are situations in which governments specify rules for deficits or debt but are unconstrained with respect to public sector capital. Indeed, as discussed, one of the key reasons for advocating a move to accrual accounting has been the view that during periods of deficit reduction, governments using cash accounting simply replace fiscal deficits with infrastructure deficits by ignoring the depreciation of public capital.

Deficit Elimination Rules

What are the effects of different accounting regimes if fiscal authorities want to eliminate an existing deficit but are unconstrained with respect to the level of public capital? Assume that authorities begin with a deficit and commit to reduce it smoothly so that it is eliminated by a specified future date. Subject to the deficit elimination constraint, assume that authorities' objective is to maximize operating spending.

In any given period, authorities must choose between providing transfers or investing in additional capital. Whether they operate under a cash or an accrual accounting regime, authorities' optimal strategy is to concentrate incremental spending on transfers. The reason is that under both regimes their deficit target requires that they forgo transfers in the current period to create cash to finance investment. Although the capital stock declines in an equivalent manner under both regimes, the debt trajectories and mix of spending over time differ. Under accrual accounting, the cash generated by amortization is used to reduce debt, whereas under cash accounting all revenue not allocated to services and debt payments can be spent on transfers. Thus, under cash accounting, transfer spending is higher.

The policy implication of this analysis is that a fiscal consolidation program is less stringent under cash accounting than under accrual. The reason is that under cash accounting, authorities are able "finance" a portion of the adjustment through unrecorded depreciation of capital. Or put another way, a cash deficit is easier to eliminate than an accrual deficit. Whether such a strategy is desirable depends on one's perspective. For policy makers searching for the least politically costly way of eliminating a structural deficit, cash accounting may be preferable—especially if the period of adjustment is relatively short and the resulting decline in public sector capital is manageable.

Of course, it may be that fiscal authorities, especially those who have achieved fiscal balance, have objectives other than maximizing operating spending. For example, it may be that authorities wish to maximize capital accumulation because of the particular political benefits that flow from public investment. Next, consider how authorities with these alternative objectives behave under the cash and accrual accounting regimes.

Constrained only to avoid deficits, the investment-maximizing government would simply eliminate all transfer spending. To avoid this unrealistic outcome, impose the additional constraint that transfer spending cannot be reduced below its initial value. For the government facing these two constraints, the optimal strategy under both accounting regimes is to hold transfers constant and to devote all revenue in excess of that needed to fund the operation of existing capital and debt service to new investment.

Although the optimal strategy is common to both accounting regimes, the fiscal outcomes differ substantially. Under cash accounting, no deficit means no borrowing, so that capital accumulation must be financed out of current revenue. Under accrual accounting, the accumulation of debt-financed capital does not affect the no-deficit constraint in the current period but only in future periods through its impact on the level of services provided and on interest payments on government debt. Thus, capital accumulation is constrained only by its impact on the budget constraint in future periods. Under cash accounting, government debt remains constant, whereas under accrual it grows substantially. Not only is investment higher under accrual accounting, but spending on services from capital is substantially higher as well. The policy implication of this analysis is that in an environment where authorities are constrained to maintain budgetary balance, governments that favor capital accumulation will find an accrual accounting regime more attractive than a cash regime.

The results of this analysis of the effects of accounting regimes on the incentives facing fiscal authorities are easily summarized. Turning first to positive issues, note that because fiscal balance means different things under the two accounting regimes, rules that discourage or prohibit deficit financing are harder to satisfy under cash accounting and easier to satisfy under accrual accounting. However, fiscal rules that focus on net debt provide the same degree of fiscal discipline under both regimes.

Depending on (a) current fiscal circumstances (that is, is the government embarking on a program of fiscal consolidation or debt reduction?); (b) preferences with respect to spending on capital-based services versus transfers to individuals and organizations; and (c) the trajectory of revenues (that is, are revenues growing, shrinking, or static?), authorities will prefer some combinations of accounting regimes and fiscal rules over others. For example, in periods of fiscal consolidation, authorities seeking to satisfy an antideficit rule will prefer cash accounting because it allows some of the "deficit" to be eliminated through (unmeasured) depreciation of public sector capital. In periods of fiscal balance, authorities seeking to satisfy an antideficit rule will prefer accrual accounting because it allows the overall level of government spending to be higher while maintaining fiscal balance.

Turning next to normative issues, note that accountability is best served if changes in public sector accounting regimes are accompanied by corresponding changes to (or, at least, clarification of) fiscal rules. It is unrealistic to expect that legislators, the media, and the public will be able to change their fiscal policy focus from a single measure, the government balance under cash accounting, to the multiple measures under accrual accounting suggested by some professional accounting bodies. Accountability might be best maintained if government adopted net debt measures as the primary fiscal indicator when operating in an accrual accounting environment.

Accrual Accounting in Developing Countries

In previous sections, views are mixed on the value of accrual accounting in the public sectors of industrial countries. Furthermore, the interaction of accounting regime and fiscal rules can result in very different incentives facing budget makers. How relevant are these debates to developing countries?

In a study for the Asian Development Bank, Athukorala and Reid (2003: x) argue that developing countries face a fundamentally different public sector environment and challenges:

> DMCs [developing member countries] confront obstacles that developed countries do not face: (i) capacity constraints can be overwhelming; (ii) there may be more urgent priorities than improving accounting; (iii) corruption and vested interests can undermine efforts; (iv) donor activities may reduce coherence; (v) reform fatigue may impede efforts; (vi) limited technological infrastructure may reduce options and raise costs; and (vii) supreme audit institutions . . . may have limited capacity.

These different environmental factors lead Athukorala and Reid (2003: 54) to question whether the accounting changes advocated by some for industrial countries will have positive results in the context of developing countries:

> The challenges faced by DMCs are fundamentally different from those of developed countries—the prescriptions and processes that are appropriate for the latter may hold disappointing results in the former. DMCs generally have greater difficulty maintaining fiscal discipline and pursuing efficient budget outcomes. They have weaker control of their budgetary fate, and outcomes that appear to be the result of lax expenditure management often are byproducts of under-development.

Furthermore, transitional economies face additional challenges:

> Countries transiting from central planning to a market basis (e.g., Uzbekistan) are different too. Many DMCs have small public sectors, but transitional country governments tend to be very large relative to the overall economy. They do not have the option of allowing public management institutions to evolve as the public sector grows, but must replace subsidies with transfers, dismantle state enterprises, establish and administer new tax systems, and forge regulatory institutions that facilitate open, robust markets. The progress made by some

transitional countries has been remarkable, but the adjustment of others has been less rapid. However, even the most advanced of the transitional economies still have much unfinished business in managing their finances. (Athukorala and Reid 2003: 54)

Thus, it may be that because of the environment and challenges they face, the benefits promised by the advocates of accrual accounting are not available to developing countries.

One of the key questions developing countries must ask is whether they have the capacity to implement accrual accounting in the public sector. Capacity may be very constrained in two key areas: human resources and IT. As Allen and Tommasi (2001: 306) argue, the level of accounting sophistication needed to fully benefit from accrual accounts is quite high:

> Making accrual accounting effective requires a true and fair recognition of expenses. Applying only formal accounting rules does not increase transparency. Accrual accounting therefore requires the availability of many highly skilled accountants both inside and outside the government. Accrual accounting can improve transparency but only if decision-makers and the public are well informed about the nature of the information provided and its financial implications. This is not always the case, even in many OECD countries where reporting by the financial media is often inadequate.

Hepworth (2002: 9) focuses on the demanding IT requirements of accrual accounts:

> Without an information technology (IT) capability, it will be difficult to assemble the information required and provide the information necessary for or efficient management of operations. More complex IT systems will be required than those associated with a traditional cash system.

In addition to these capacity constraints, developing countries may face obstacles related to the underlying state of their revenue collection systems. In the view of Allen and Tommasi (2001: 298), transition economies in which tax collection is a problem and tax arrears accumulate may find cash accounting to be the better option.

The valuation of physical assets and estimation of the cost of long-term social programs are also problematic. On the issue of public sector pensions, Allen and Tommasi (2001: 299) suggest that estimation of pension liabilities is technically demanding and requires sophisticated judgments. These judgments may be open to manipulation. Such payments should be reported on a cash basis, with parallel attempts to estimate accrued costs.

In summary, developing countries face many barriers to adopting accrual accounting in the public sector. Some barriers stem from the challenging environment they face relative to industrial countries. Others stem from their lack of capacity in the areas of human resources and IT. Finally, all of the sophisticated judgments required to make accrual accounting work—whether they be the estimation of accrued revenues, the estimation of accrued social program costs, or the valuation of physical assets—test the institutional capacity of developing countries. Furthermore, because all such judgments are open to manipulation, they may create yet another obstacle to countries struggling to control corruption and improve governance.

Lessons for Policy Makers

A number of lessons for policy makers can be drawn from the analysis in this chapter. Despite strong encouragement from a number of international agencies and accounting organizations, it is clear that considerable controversy surrounds the adoption of accrual accounting for the public sector in industrial countries. At the most fundamental level, there is ongoing disagreement about whether the accounting needs of the public sector, which center around democratic accountability, are well served by private sector–based accounts that focus primarily on financial performance and profitability.

This concern is underscored by the difficulties encountered in valuing assets such as museums, hospitals, and military hardware, which produce no income stream and for which no market exists. The fundamental difference between the public and private sectors becomes obvious when one is attempting to estimate accrued costs of social programs such as public sector pensions that will result in uncertain payments far into the future and for which the value of such payments is itself under the control of the policy maker. A final area of disagreement is related to whether the benefits of moving to accrual accounting in the public sector outweigh the substantial costs of the transition from cash accounting.

The chapter also explored the interaction of accounting regimes and fiscal rules. The analysis showed that seemingly simple fiscal rules such as committing to budget balance have substantially different implications under cash and accrual accounting. Indeed, the initial fiscal environment and the nature of the fiscal rule could lead authorities to prefer one accounting regime over another. Finally, only one of the simple fiscal rules considered— a net debt rule—was neutral with respect to accounting regime. Thus, careful attention should be paid to the implications for fiscal rules when changes in accounting regimes are being considered.

The review of the literature on accrual accounting and the public sector in the developing world produced a number of lessons. The main thrust of the literature is to highlight the different policy environment faced by developing countries. Developing countries face a number of obstacles that are not found in the industrial world. For example, developing countries are generally greatly constrained in the area of human resources—in this case the large number of trained professionals required to implement and operate a public sector accrual accounting system. Another constraint is the lack of modern IT capacity, which forms the basis of most accrual accounting systems.

Accrual accounting requires a significant number of sophisticated judgments in areas such as revenue collection. In countries where revenue collection is a problem and substantial arrears are normal, estimates of accrued revenues may be significantly less informative than actual cash collections. Furthermore, in countries faced with significant issues related to governance, such judgments may, in fact, widen the scope for political manipulation or corrupt practices. As Hepworth (2002: 8) explains, "Governments are sovereign and therefore the temptation is to set in place accrual rules that allow the system to be manipulated."

In deciding whether to proceed with the adoption of accrual accounting in the public sector, policy makers in developing countries should ask a number of questions. The most fundamental is where such a change fits into its priority list of public sector reforms. Is a move to accrual accounting a pre-requisite to other important reforms, or are other public sector reforms more urgent or cost-effective? Allen and Tommasi (2001: 301) also underscore the need for a benefit-cost approach to the decision to adopt accrual accounting:

> A full accrual accounting system provides a framework for setting up asset and inventory registers. However, assessing the value of all assets and recording them correctly in the accounts need time, and many countries have more urgent priorities. Thus, to improve asset management, it can be more cost-effective to begin with registering physical assets, rather than refining the accounting system.

If the adoption of accrual accounting is set as a goal for public sector reform in a developing country, it is important to ensure that the proper groundwork is laid. The most important prerequisite is that a well-functioning system of cash accounting be in place. As Allen and Tommasi (2001: 306) put it, "A gradual approach to implementing accrual accounting can be considered once a country has a sound and robust cash accounting system in place." Hepworth (2002: 8) argues:

> Accrual accounting is far more complex than cash accounting and it requires the exercise of relatively sophisticated judgments. Therefore, the change should only be attempted if the cash accounting system is working effectively and has been doing so for some time.

Once an effective cash accounting system is in operation, an incremental approach to accrual accounting can be made, moving to modified cash, to modified accrual, and finally to full accrual as human resources and IT capacity permit (Athukorala and Reid 2003). Allen and Tommasi (2001: 306) lay out one possible transition path:

> It [the transition to accrual accounts] might start with those areas of government activity that require information on the value of physical assets, their uses, and full costs (e.g., agencies that charge users for services provided). Taking into account the need to strengthen fiscal management, transition countries should focus first on implementing methods to better recognize financial liabilities in their accounts.

In summary, in deciding whether to set accrual accounting as a goal of public sector reform, policy makers in developing countries need to make a hard-headed assessment of their institutional environment and capacities, as well as of the benefits and costs of such a reform. Accounting regimes are not an end in themselves. Rather, they are a tool to serve managers, elected officials, and ultimately citizens as these individuals work to improve the operation and governance of the public sector. It is on that basis that they should be judged.

Notes

1. This section draws heavily on Graham (2007, chapter 4), who provides an accessible review of the issues surrounding cash and accrual accounting in the public sector.
2. For a recent survey, see Alesina and Perotti (1999).
3. This section draws heavily on Boothe (2004).
4. It is useful at this point to define more precisely the terms *cash* and *accrual accounting*. Until recently, many governments in industrial countries have used what accountants call *modified accrual accounting*. Under this accounting regime, physical capital is treated as an expenditure in the year it is constructed, and no depreciation of the capital is charged as an expense in subsequent years. Because this chapter

focuses on the accounting treatment of capital, we call this regime *cash accounting*. We call the regime in which capital is not expensed and depreciation is charged *accrual accounting*. This regime corresponds to what accountants sometimes call *full accrual*.

5. For example, von Hagen, Hallett, and Strauch (2002) show that fiscal consolidations based on expenditure reductions are more likely to succeed than those based on revenue increases. This finding is confirmed for Canada in Boothe and Reid (2001).
6. Proponents include Blanchard and Giavazzi (2003); Brunila, Buti, and Franco (2001); Buti, Eijffinger, and Franco (2002); Dur, Peletier, and Swank (1997); Robinson (1999); and Salinas (2002).
7. Skeptics include Tanzi (2003) and Wynne (2003). Diamond (2002) is cautious in recommending the change to developing countries, which may not have the systems in place to support accrual accounting.
8. As before, this could be easily thought of as a debt-to-gross domestic product rule.

References

Alesina, Alberto, and Roberto Perotti. 1999. "Budget Deficits and Budget Institutions." In *Fiscal Institutions and Fiscal Performance*, ed. James Poterba and Jürgen von Hagen, 13–36. Chicago: University of Chicago Press.

Allen, Richard, and Daniel Tommasi, eds. 2001. *Managing Public Expenditure: A Reference Book for Transition Countries*. Paris: Organisation for Economic Co-operation and Development.

Athukorala, S. Lakhsman, and Barry Reid. 2003. *Accrual Budgeting and Accounting in Government and Its Relevance for Member Countries*. Manila: Asian Development Bank.

Balassone, Fabrizio, and Daniele Franco. 2001. "The SGP and the 'Golden Rule.'" In *The Stability and Growth Pact: The Architecture of Fiscal Policy in the EMU*, ed. Anne Brunila, Marco Buti, and Daniele Franco, 371–93. Basingstoke, U.K.: Palgrave.

Blanchard, Olivier, and Francesco Giavazzi. 2003. "Improving the SGP through a Proper Accounting of Public Investment." CEPR Discussion Paper 4220, Centre for Economic Policy Research, London.

Blejer, Mario, and Adrienne Cheasty. 1991. "The Measurement of Fiscal Deficits: Analytical and Methodological Issues." *Journal of Economic Literature* 29 (4): 1644–78.

Blöndal, Jón R. 2003. "Accrual Accounting and Budgeting: Key Issues and Recent Developments." *OECD Journal on Budgeting* 3 (1): 43–60.

Boothe, Paul. 2004. "Accounting Regimes and Fiscal Rules." In *Public Debt*, ed. Danielle Franco, 315–32. Rome: Banca d'Italia.

Boothe, Paul, and Bradford Reid, eds. 2001. *Deficit Reduction in the Far West*. Edmonton: University of Alberta Press.

Brunila, Anne, Marco Buti, and Daniele Franco, eds. 2001. *The Stability and Growth Pact: The Architecture of Fiscal Policy in the EMU*. Basingstoke, U.K.: Palgrave.

Buti, Marco, Sylvester Eijffinger, and Daniele Franco. 2002. "Revisiting the Stability and Growth Pact: Grand Design or Internal Adjustment?" CEPR Discussion Paper 3692, Centre for Economic Policy Research, London.

Diamond, Jack. 2002. "Performance Budgeting—Is Accrual Accounting Required?" IMF Working Paper 02/240, International Monetary Fund, Washington, DC.

Dur, Robert, Ben D. Peletier, and Otto H. Swank. 1997. "The Effect of Fiscal Rules on Public Investment If Budget Deficits Are Politically Motivated." Discussion Paper 97-125/1, Tinbergen Institute, Rotterdam, Netherlands.

Graham, Andrew. 2007. *Canadian Public Sector Financial Management*. Montreal: McGill-Queen's University Press.

Hepworth, Noel. 2002. "The European Experience of and Attitudes to the Development of International Accounting Standards." In *Innovations in Governmental Accounting*, ed. Vincente Montesinos and José Manuel Vela, 73–84. Dordrecht, Netherlands: Kluwer.

———. 2003. "Preconditions for Successful Implementation of Accrual Accounting in Central Government." *Public Money and Management* 23 (1): 37–44.

IMF (International Monetary Fund). 2001a. *Government Finance Statistics Manual*. Washington, DC: IMF Statistics Department. http://www.imf.org/external/pubs/ft/gfs/manual/pdf/all.pdf.

———. 2001b. *Manual on Fiscal Transparency*. Washington, DC: IMF. http://www.imf.org/external/np/fad/trans/manual/index.htm.

Kopits, George. 2001. "Fiscal Rules: Useful Policy Framework or Unnecessary Ornament?" IMF Working Paper 01/145, International Monetary Fund, Washington, DC.

OECD (Organisation for Economic Co-operation and Development). 2002. "OECD Best Practices for Budget Transparency." *OECD Journal of Budgeting* 1 (3): 7–14.

Plender, John. 2003. "Wheezing through the Fiscal Fog." *Financial Times*, April 4, 18.

Poterba, James, and Jürgen von Hagen, eds. 1999. *Fiscal Institutions and Fiscal Performance*. Chicago: University of Chicago Press.

PSAB (Public Sector Accounting Board). 2003. *20 Questions about Government Financial Reporting: Federal, Provincial, and Territorial Governments*. Toronto: Canadian Institute of Chartered Accountants.

Robinson, Marc. 1999. "Accrual Financial Reporting in the Australian Public Sector: An Economic Perspective." Faculty of Business Discussion Paper 65, Queensland University of Technology, Brisbane, Australia.

Salinas, F. Javier. 2002. "Accrual Budgeting and Fiscal Consolidation in the EMU." *Contemporary Economic Policy* 20 (2): 193–206.

Tanzi, Vito. 2003. "Role and Future of the Stability and Growth Pact." Paper presented at the Cato Institute's conference on "The Future of the Euro," Washington, DC, November 20.

von Hagen, Jürgen, Andrew Hughes Hallett, and Rolf Strauch. 2002. "Quality and Success of Budgetary Consolidations." In *The Behaviour of Fiscal Authorities*, ed. Marco Buti, Jürgen von Hagen, and Carlos Martinez-Mongay, 17–38. Basingstoke, U.K.: Palgrave.

Wynne, Andrew. 2003. "Do Private Sector Financial Statements Provide a Suitable Model for Public Sector Accounts?" Paper presented at the European Group of Public Administration conference "Public Law and Modernizing the State," Oeiras, Portugal, September 4–6.

———. 2004. "Is the Move to Accrual Based Accounting a Real Priority for Public Sector Accounting?" Association of Chartered Certified Accountants, London.

7

Activity-Based Cost Management in the Public Sector

GARY COKINS

There is a growing desire among organizations to understand their costs and the behavior of factors that drive their costs. However, there is also confusion over how to understand costs and how to distinguish competing cost measurement methodologies (such as activity-based costing, standard costing, and project accounting). The result is that managers and employees are confused by mixed messages about which costs are the correct costs. On closer inspection, various costing methods do not necessarily compete; they can coexist, be reconciled, and be blended.

To overcome the overgeneralizations of traditional costing systems, with their excessively simplified cost allocations and resulting hidden indirect costs, organizations have been adopting activity-based costing (ABC) systems. These systems are based on cost modeling, which traces an organization's expenses, both direct and indirect, to the products, services, channels, and customers that cause those expenses to be incurred.

Activity-Based Cost Management Supports Fact-Based Decision Making

In recent years, government organizations have begun to look to private industry for ideas about how to improve their business

203

practices and their efficiency in resource use. Activity-based cost management (ABC/M) is one of the most important tools being introduced in the effort to achieve these ends.

ABC/M provides fact-based data. In the absence of facts, anybody's opinion is a good one. And usually the most important opinion, which may be the opinion of a supervisor or the supervisor of a supervisor, wins. To the extent that decision makers are making decisions based on intuition, gut feel, or misleading data, an organization is at some risk.

Many senior managers have become used to making decisions without good information, so they think they do not need it. But the pressure to make better decisions and use resources more intelligently has increased. ABC/M provides valuable information that can be used to make a broad range of decisions on issues from outsourcing to operational planning and budgeting.

In its initial stages, ABC/M has often met with a mixed response, despite widespread discontent with traditional accounting mechanisms and despite its proven track record. This chapter describes what ABC/M is intended to do—and not do—in the hope that such enlightenment will help in applying ABC/M principles to the critical problems now facing much of the public sector.

Activity-based concepts are very powerful techniques for creating valid economic cost models of organizations. By using the lens of ABC/M, organizations of all sizes and types can develop the valid economic models required for executives and managers to be able to make value-creating decisions and take actions to improve their productivity and resource use—and ultimately to better serve their constituencies. This chapter describes the pressures for improved cost accounting in government, misapprehensions about and other sources of resistance to ABC/M, and successful applications of the system in the public sector.

Political Pressures to Hold Down Costs

Public sector organizations at all levels and of all types are facing intense pressure to do more with less. Federal, national, state, county, municipal, and local governments in almost all countries are feeling some sort of fiscal squeeze. This pressure affects departments, administrations, branches, foundations, and agencies of all kinds.

The pressure on spending has many sources. It can come indirectly from politicians aiming to win taxpayers' approval or directly from taxpayer special-interest groups. There is pressure from competition with other cities to attract homebuyers or with other counties, states, or nations to attract businesses. In the United States, not only do cities compete with other cities; each city also competes with its own suburbs. Those suburbs often have an advantage in attracting residents and businesses. They may offer lower taxes, better schools, and less crime. As residents and businesses relocate, the cities and towns they departed from lose a little more of their tax bases. Less spending is possible, unless tax rates are raised.

Additional pressure may come from declining demand, regardless of the reasons. An example is rural road maintenance. In such cases, economies of scale are less easily achieved, and fixed costs become less affordable.

In the United States, the federal government is shifting some responsibilities to state and local governments but is providing only limited funding to fulfill those obligations. Regardless of where the pressure is coming from, it sends the same message: better, faster, cheaper—hold the line on taxes but do not let service slip. Meeting this daunting challenge often requires the following:

- Determining the actual costs of services
- Implementing process improvements
- Evaluating outsourcing or privatization options (that is, is it better to deliver internally or to purchase from external organizations?)
- Aligning activities with the organization's mission and its strategic plan.

The solution for governments under pressure cannot be simply to uncover new sources of revenue or to raise tax rates again. Some have succumbed to these quick fixes, only to fall into a downward spiral as more businesses and families move to more economically attractive locations. Governments must get a handle on their problems. Holding the line on raising taxes must be more than a hollow campaign slogan; it may become an absolute requirement to retain the tax base. This restriction creates more reasons for understanding costs. Efficiency and performance, once reserved for the private sector, will increasingly be part of the language of the public sector.

ABC/M and its integration with strategy mapping and balanced scorecards (that is, performance measures) offer potential solutions to the problem. Providing meaningful, fact-based information to government officials, managers, and employee teams can be a cost-effective means of bringing about beneficial change and improved performance in government and not-for-profit environments. Intuition and political persuasion are becoming less effective means for decision making. The pressure on the public sector is undeniable. People want government to work better and to cost less. To do so, public sector managers will have to change their way of thinking about the true costs—and value—of the services they provide.

An Excessive Focus on Functions

When a newly elected mayor takes office in a city, he or she may be told by city managers that the finances are reasonably healthy. Expenditures and resources are in balance; there is no fiscal deficit. But can those same managers tell the new mayor how much it costs to fill a pothole, to process a construction permit, or to plow a snow-covered mile or kilometer of highway?

Reference to the cost of outputs will resonate throughout this chapter. It is inescapable. The need to consider outputs, not simply the level of human resources, equipment, and supplies, is what is forcing awareness and acceptance of ABC/M. At a very basic level ABC/M is simply a converter and translator of expenditures restated as outputs—more specifically, the costs of outputs.

ABC/M answers fundamental questions such as "What do things cost?" and "Why?" It answers "Why?" by displaying the drivers of activity costs. It also answers "Who receives them?" and "How much of the costs did they each receive?" Examples of output costs are the cost per type of processed tax statement or the cost per type of rubbish pickup. ABC/M serves as a calculation engine for converting employee salaries, contractor fees, and supplies into outputs. The work activities are simply the mechanisms that produce and deliver the outputs. The work is foundational; all organizations do work or purchase it. All work has an output. This topic of outputs will be revisited throughout this chapter; it is a critical aspect of ABC/M.

The dilemma for many not-for-profit and government agencies, branches, administrations, and departments is their fixation on determining budget levels for spending without having many facts to work from. From the budget requestor's perspective, an annual budget negotiation is usually an argument to retain or increase the level of resources relative to the existing level. Regardless of whether this behavior is due to an ego display by ambitious or fearful managers or a lack of any better means for determining resource requirements, it is the rare manager who accepts a reduction— except maybe a reduction in headaches caused by his or her daily problems.

An advanced application of ABC/M data is to apply calibrated consumption rates from past periods against the future volume and mix of expected outputs and services to determine the future level of resources required. In this way, ABC/M enables better budgeting.

A Fixation on Inputs

The actual or planned spending levels reported by the general ledger or fund balance accounting system eventually emerge as the primary financial view for each functional manager. They have become the typical way in which functional managers think about what level of spending can satisfy the needs of people relying on them for good service. Most managers are reasonably confident in the reported numbers underlying this view. They roughly know their employee salaries and benefits, have authorized most of the purchasing requests, and understand (but may despise) the allocation for support costs that they are internally charged with. That is, the managers understand the bookkeeping system, including its archaic cost-chargeback schemes. Figure 7.1 illustrates the limited view that many managers have of their fiscal condition.

The traditional accounting structure mirrors the hierarchical organizational structure. Each function is a cost center of sorts, and the accountants consolidate the functional expenses into totals with elegant rollup procedures. But is managing a cost structure all about focusing on the supply side of resources, which is basically the organization's capacity to serve? Or should the focus begin with reacting to the demands for work placed on the organization from service recipients and customers? ABC/M brings visibility and understanding to the service view—fulfilling the needs of the service recipients and customers who consume the organizational outputs. It focuses on the demand side for resources.

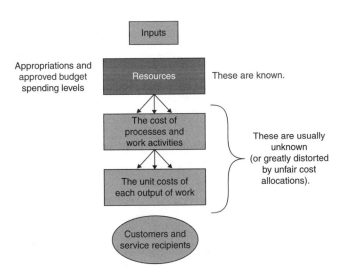

Source: Author's representation.

FIGURE 7.1 The Primary View of Most Managers

The ABC/M view is a radical departure from the norm for governments and defense organizations. Consider how politicians campaign for votes. They communicate in terms of inputs. Politicians who want to be viewed as tough on crime will propose spending more money on police forces and prisons. Those who want to be perceived as kind and generous will offer more money for social programs. This fixation with inputs, the supply side of resources, does not conclude with the election. Following the politician's campaign rhetoric, press releases applaud the funding of programs as if the act of putting money in automatically ensures that desired results will come out.

In the military services, newly assigned field commanders regularly arrive at their bases sharing a single interest: a bigger budget. They may be granted the money. But holding them accountable for the results or how they use the government's money is a separate matter.

Government employees and managers often view the annual fiscal budgeting process with cynicism. ABC/M practitioners have learned that it is better if buyers and consumers, including government buyers and procurement agents, purchase outputs instead of inputs. Fortunately, the focus within the public sector has begun to shift from budget management to performance-based results measurement.

Removing the Blindfold: Outputs, Not Just Resources and Expenditures

The traditional financial accounting system has evolved in such a way that all public sector managers reasonably know what expenditures they have made in past time periods. But none of them know what the costs were either in the aggregate or for the individual outputs. So what are the costs of outputs? What is the cost of each output? How does one accurately calculate these costs?

Expenses and costs are not synonymous. In simple terms, resources are used and expenses or expenditures are incurred when money is exchanged with third-party suppliers and with employees. In contrast, costs are always calculated costs that restate expenses as work activities or as outputs. Expenses and costs equate in total but are not the same things.

Figure 7.2 illustrates how management's limited view can be fruitfully extended beyond the resource and expenditure level. Traditional financial management systems focus on the expenses of labor, supplies, and the like, rather than on what work within processes is performed and what outputs result from using these resources. ABC/M makes visible what has been missing in financial reporting.

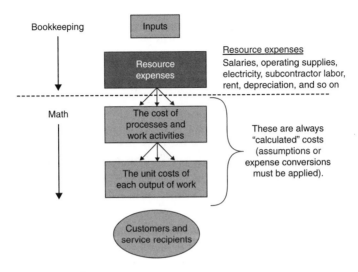

Source: Author's representation.

FIGURE 7.2 Expenses and Costs Are Not the Same Thing

Governments adhere to and comply with standard government accounting principles. For example, fund accounting is similar to the general-ledger bookkeeping that commercial businesses use, except that fund accounting adds an extra step. In the simplest terms, fund accounting first establishes a planned or budgeted spending ceiling for various funds and their accounts. (Funds are comparable to responsibility cost centers in general-ledger accounting.) Approved spending often comes in the form of appropriations.

The extra step in fund accounting involves requisitions. Managers basically use requisitions for spending; if the spending ceiling has been reached or if the requisition fails other tests, then the purchase is prohibited. In effect, government and not-for-profit accounting adds an extra level of spending control. However, although these extra controls deter government managers from committing fraud or stealing money, they do little to stop them from wasting money.

In many cases, the accounting system calculates overhead or support costs and arbitrarily allocates them to the final outputs of the organization on the basis of broad-brush averages (such as the number of units delivered). This basis for how the cost allocation is distributed is usually convenient for the accountants, but it does not reflect the unique and relative relationship between resource consumption and final outputs, much less the work processes involved. That is, different types of outputs uniquely consume work activities in varying ways, but the arbitrarily averaged cost allocation does not reflect it. Hence, costs of some outputs are overestimated and others must be underestimated—because it is a zero-sum error situation.

A Simple Way to Understand ABC/M

Here is a simple way to understand the basic principles of ABC/M. Imagine that four friends go to a restaurant. One orders a small salad, and the others each order the most expensive item on the menu—a prime rib steak. When the waiter or waitress brings the bill, the others say, "Let's split the check evenly." How would the first friend feel? He or she would find this suggestion unfair and inequitable. This is similar to the effect on many products and service lines in the cost-accounting system when accountants take a large amount of the indirect and shared support overhead expenses and allocate it as costs without any logic. There is minimal or no relationship to how the products or service lines actually consumed the expenses. This system is inequitable and unfair to each product's or service's cost. It is somewhat like taxation without representation. ABC/M gets it right. In the restaurant example, ABC/M is equivalent to the waiter or waitress providing four individual checks—each person is charged for what he or she consumed.

Allocating costs using broad averages is flawed, inaccurate, and misleading. In the end, many managers dismiss the calculated costs from their accounting system as a bunch of lies. They may accurately reconcile in total, but not in the pieces. Unfortunately, these same managers have little choice but to go along with the flawed costs. They have little influence or control over the accountants. The accountants count the beans, but they are not tasked to grow the beans. ABC resolves this problem by tracing activity costs to products using factors that reflect cause-and-effect relationships.

When managers and employee teams do not reliably know what the costs are for their current outputs, they have a difficult time knowing what the future costs may be for future levels of demand or for changes in requests for their outputs. Most managers consciously or subconsciously stick with the primary view of the costs they are familiar with—their spending. And the accounting system, which is structured to report spending this way, reinforces this view. As mentioned, no managers willingly volunteer to continue into a future year with fewer resources, so they fight for the same or (usually) more resources at budget-planning time.

From the Spending View to the Activity and Output View

When managers receive their monthly responsibility center report calculating the favorable or unfavorable variance between their actual spending and their budget, what does that information really tell them? When they look at their variances, they are either happy or sad, but they are rarely any smarter. ABC/M extends the minimal information in the departmental spending reports to make managers and employee teams smarter. This extended information is then used for making decisions—better decisions than are made without the ABC/M data. ABC/M's strength is that it gives insights based on understanding past costs, not just past spending, allowing managers to apply the same data to make better decisions.

Some more realities can be added to this description of government and defense organizations as service providers. Consider the key players—public sector workers, taxpayers, and users of the government services:

- The civil service worker or military member might simply prefer the status quo or whatever may be a little bit better for him or her.
- The taxpayer prefers to be taxed less.
- The user of government services desires more and higher-quality service.
- The functional manager defends the existing level of his or her resources and fiscal budget.

It is a no-win situation. Something has to give. The combination of these disparate interests creates tension and conflict. Untangling these knots is difficult when the primary financial view that is used by management shows only spending for resources. There must also be an equivalent financial view of the outputs. Questions and discovery begin when the costs of outputs can be made visible and compared. A more reasonable discussion about spending levels occurs when spending and what the service recipients get for the spending are equated with the costs of outputs and outcomes.

Even when two outputs, such as the unit cost per rubbish disposal for two neighboring houses per month, appear to be the same amount, each house may have consumed different work. One may have had fewer containers but more cumbersome items, such as wood blocks and metal rods, for the material handlers to deal with. The other may simply have more containers with standard contents. Alternatively, compare two municipal rubbish disposal services with the identical number of residential stops and work crew members at similar weekly wages. All things being equal, if one crew averages seven hours per day while the other averages eight hours, the cost per house for disposal is equal for each municipality, but the material-handling content (the actual work) is not. One has more unused capacity than the other. One has a higher disposal cost per home for the productive work.

By adding the financial view of the outputs to the financial view of the resources, managers and employee teams can much better understand the behavior of the cost structure. The visibility that comes from knowing the costs of outputs becomes the stimulant for understanding the cost structure. Outputs are the links to the external recipients, such as citizens, as well as to the internal work activities. The distribution of the workload adapts to changes in demand levels for outputs. Output costing can also benefit cross-functional processes. An ABC/M information system gives visibility into all these relationships (and even more with the additional capability to score or tag costs with ABC/M's attributes, such as value added versus non–value added costs, described later).

ABC/M Is a Cost Assignment Network

Why do some public sector managers shake their heads in disbelief when they think about their organization's cost-accounting system? A public official once complained, "You know what we think of our cost-accounting system? It is a bunch of fictitious lies—but we all agree to them." Of course, he was referring to misallocated costs based on the broad averages that result in flawed and misleading information. What a sad state it is when the users of accounting data simply resign themselves to a lack of hope. Unfortunately, many accountants are comfortable if the numbers all foot and tie (reconcile) in total; they care less if the parts making up the total are correct. The total is all that matters, and any arbitrary cost allocation can tie out to the total.

How can traditional accounting, which has been around for so many years, suddenly have become considered so bad? The answer is that the data are not bad so much as somewhat distorted, woefully incomplete, and partly unprocessed. Figure 7.3 provides the first hint of a problem. The left side shows the classic monthly report that responsibility center managers receive under the general-ledger system. Note that the example used is a back-office department of a license bureau, such as for driver or hunting licenses. It is a factory, too, only its outputs are not tangible products but documents. This example demonstrates that, despite misconceptions, indirect white-collar workers produce outputs just as factory workers do. Substitute any department, government or commercial, for the license bureau department in the example and the lessons will hold.

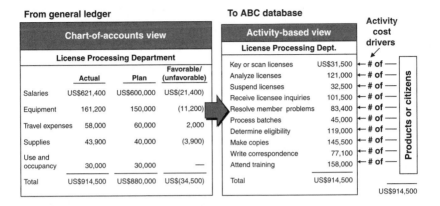

From general ledger

To ABC database

Activity cost drivers

Chart-of-accounts view				Activity-based view		
License Processing Department				**License Processing Dept.**		
	Actual	**Plan**	Favorable/ (unfavorable)	Key or scan licenses	US$31,500	← # of —
				Analyze licenses	121,000	← # of —
Salaries	US$621,400	US$600,000	US$(21,400)	Suspend licenses	32,500	← # of —
				Receive licensee inquiries	101,500	← # of —
Equipment	161,200	150,000	(11,200)	Resolve member problems	83,400	← # of —
				Process batches	45,000	← # of —
Travel expenses	58,000	60,000	2,000	Determine eligibility	119,000	← # of —
Supplies	43,900	40,000	(3,900)	Make copies	145,500	← # of —
Use and				Write correspondence	77,100	← # of —
occupancy	30,000	30,000	—	Attend training	158,000	← # of —
Total	US$914,500	US$880,000	US$(34,500)	Total	US$914,500	

Products or citizens

US$914,500

Source: Author's representation.
Note: In addition to showing the content of work, the activity-based view gives insights into what drives each activity's cost magnitude to fluctuate. When managers see a report with the chart-of-accounts view, they are either happy or sad, but they are rarely any smarter!

FIGURE 7.3 The Language of ABC/M

If one asks managers who routinely receive this report, "How much of these expenses can you control or influence? How much insight do you get from this report into the content of your employees' work?" they will likely answer both questions with "Not much!" This is because salaries and fringe benefits usually make up the most sizable portion of controllable costs, and all that the manager sees are those expenses reported as lump-sum amounts.

Translating the chart-of-account expenses shown under the general-ledger or fund-accounting system into the actual work activities that consume those expenses begins to increase a manager's insights. The right side of figure 7.3 is the ABC/M view that is used for analysis and as the starting point for calculating costs both for processes and for diverse outputs such as services. In effect, the ABC/M view begins to resolve the deficiencies of traditional financial accounting by focusing on work activities. ABC/M is very work-centric, whereas general-ledger and fund-accounting systems are transaction-centric.

Another key difference lies in the language used to depict cost allocations (that is, absorption costing). ABC/M describes activities using an "action verb–adjective–noun" grammar convention, such as "process building permits" or "open new taxpayer accounts." This language gives ABC/M its flexibility. Such wording is powerful because managers and employee teams can better relate to these phrases, and the wording implies that the work activities can be favorably affected through change, improvement, or elimination. General-ledger and fund-accounting systems use a chart of accounts as their language, whereas ABC/M uses a chart of activities. In translating the data from a general-ledger or fund-accounting system into activities and processes, ABC/M preserves the total reported budget funding and costs but allows the individual elements to be viewed differently.

Another criticism of the chart-of-accounts view: notice how inadequate those data are in reporting the costs of processes that run cross-functionally and penetrate the vertical boundaries of a government agency's organization chart. The general-ledger and the fund-accounting systems are organized around separate departments or cost centers. This arrangement presents a real reporting problem. For example, in a city's department of public works, what is the true total cost for processing equipment repair requisitions that travel through many hands? For a service organization, what is the true cost of opening a new account for a citizen or service recipient?

Many organizations have flattened their hierarchies so that employees from different departments or cost centers frequently perform similar activities and multitask in two or more core workflow processes. Only by reassembling and aligning the work-activity costs across the workflow processes, as in "process homebuyer permits" or "open new taxpayer accounts," can the end-to-end process costs be seen, measured, and eventually managed.

The structure of the general-ledger and fund-accounting systems is restricted by cost center mapping to the hierarchical organization chart. As a consequence, this type of reported information drives vertical and hierarchical behavior, not the much more desirable process behavior that customers consume. In effect, with traditional accounting systems, public sector managers are denied visibility of the costs that belong to their end-to-end workflow processes—and visibility of what is driving those costs.

How Do Cost Drivers Work?

Additional information about what drives costs can be gleaned from the right side of figure 7.3. Look at the second activity—"analyze licenses," at a total cost of US$121,000—and consider what would make that cost significantly increase or decrease. The overall answer is the number of licenses analyzed. That number is that work's activity driver. Figure 7.3 illustrates that each activity on a stand-alone basis has its own activity driver. At this stage, the costing no longer recognizes the organization chart and its artificial boundaries. All the employees' costs, regardless of their department, have been combined into the work performed. The focus is now on the cost of that work and on what influences and affects the level of that workload.

Yet more can be gained from this view. Assume that the department analyzed 1,000 licenses during that period. The unit cost for each license analyzed is US$121. If one specific group—senior citizens over the age of 60, for example—was responsible for half those claims, then more would be known about the sources of demand (that is, the workload). Senior citizens caused US$60,500 of that work (500 claims multiplied by US$121 per claim). Married couples with small children required another fraction, married couples with grown children a different fraction, and so on; ultimately, ABC/M will have traced all of the US$121,000. If all the other work activities were similarly traced using the unique activity driver for each activity, ABC/M would have allocated the entire US$914,500 among the groups of beneficiaries. This reassignment of the resource expenses would be much more accurate than any cost allocation applied with traditional accounting systems that use broad averages. As in the restaurant example, the cost is for what the individual alone consumed.

Note that the expense and costs are equal in the resource, activity, and cost-object views; they must reconcile. This reconciliation is comforting to accountants, who by nature desire some sense of control or at least the knowledge that they have not left something out or made a math error. But the more important message is that the general-ledger and fund-accounting chart-of-accounts view answers only What was spent? whereas transforming expenses into calculated costs in the next two views gives more valuable and useful answers to these questions: Why was it spent? What caused the rate at which it was to be spent? For whom or for what was it spent?

This cost-assignment network is one of the major reasons that ABC/M calculates costs of outputs more accurately. The assignment of the resource expenses also demonstrates that all costs actually originate with the ultimate end user, service recipient, or beneficiary of the work. That location or origin of costs could be a citizen, welfare recipient, new homebuyer seeking permits, or another government agency relying on those services. This is the opposite of how people who perform cost allocations think about costs.

Cost allocations are structured as a one-source-to-many-destinations redistribution of costs. They ignore that the destinations are actually the origin for the costs. The destinations (usually outputs or people) place demands on work, and the work draws on the resource capacity (the spending)—hence, the costs measure the effect by reflecting backward through the ABC/M cost-assignment network.

In sum, in one sense the report on the left side of figure 7.3 represents an "accounting police" or a "budget police" command-and-control tool. This tool is the most primitive form of control. Has a budgeted target been overspent? Who says that budgeted target amount was fair when it was imposed? As mentioned earlier, when managers receive the left-side report, they are either happy or sad but rarely any smarter. That is unacceptable in today's world, which expects much more out of organizations than in the past. Today is witnessing the emergence of learning organizations, not organizations that are strait-jacketed with spending restrictions. The right side of figure 7.3 restates the same expenses as appear on the left side, but the costs are reported in a much more useful format and structure for supporting decisions.

When expenses are expressed as activity costs, they are in a format that can be traced into outputs. Expenses are transformed into calculated costs. As a result, employees can never say, "We could care less about what anything costs." Employees care more when they know what things cost and believe in the accuracy of those costs. Cost accounting is outside their comfort zones. ABC/M makes costs understandable and logical.

The modern movement toward managing with a process view has created a growing need for better managerial and costing data. Managing processes and managing activities (that is, costs) go together. By current definition, a workflow process comprises two or more logically related work activities intended to serve end recipients and beneficiaries; thus, having a means of integrating processes, outputs, and measured costs has become an even more important requirement for managers and employee teams. ABC/M data provide a logical way to visualize and report on those links.

In sum, ABC/M resolves the structural problems inherent in the general-ledger and the fund-accounting systems by first converting account balances into activity costs. ABC/M then assigns the activity costs to cost objects or reassembles the activity costs across processes. These transformed cost data can be used to identify operating relationships that are key to making good decisions related to products, service lines, and customers.

Multiple-Stage ABC/M Approach

To trace costs adequately using the ABC/M method requires more stages than the two-stage assignments displayed in figure 7.3. Rather than simply tracing the cost of resources to activities and then to cost objects, the multiple-stage approach models cost flows in a manner that more closely reflects the actual flow of costs through an organization. Often there are support people who support other support people, who ultimately support the primary workers who make products for or deliver services to external parties such as citizens or other agencies. These cascading stages of indirect and shared costs should not use arbitrary, broad, averaged cost allocations but rather should follow ABC/M principles. The multistage cost-assignment approach includes an understanding of the relationships between indirect work activities and other activities, as well as between those activities and cost objects. Costs are traced from activity to activity in a series of stages, all based on cause-and-effect relationships.

Figure 7.4 disaggregates and expands the two-stage view of figure 7.3 and rotates it to a vertical view, to reveal a generic ABC/M structure that is a good representation of a universal costing model for any organization. To understand figure 7.4, imagine the cost-assignment paths (the arrows) as pipes and straws; the diameter of each path reflects the amount of cost flowing. The power of an ABC/M model lies in the fact that the cost-assignment paths and their destinations make it possible to trace segment costs from beginning to end, from resource expenditures to each type of (or each specific) customer—ultimately the origin for all costs and expenses. The cost-assignment network captures and reflects the diversity and variation in how cost objects uniquely consume the activities and

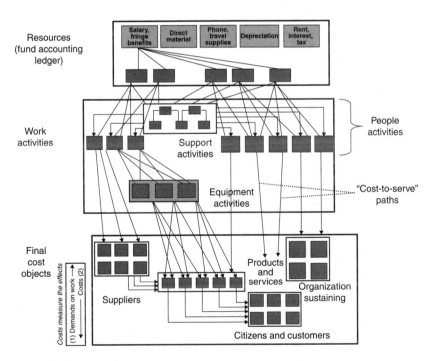

Source: Author's representation.

FIGURE 7.4 The Expanded ABC/M Cost-Assignment Network

resources they draw on. To understand costing, mentally reverse all the arrowheads in figure 7.4. This polar switch reveals that all expenses originate in a demand-pull from customers. The calculated costs simply measure the effect of that demand-pull. Costs are always a measure of effect; this is a basic principle in costing.

The bottom portion of figure 7.4 reveals multiple final cost objects—supplier-related activity outputs, products and services, and citizen-customers. It displays a nested consumption sequence of final cost objects. A metaphor for this consumption sequence is the predator food chain, in which mammals eat plants and large mammals eat small mammals. The final-final cost object in this figure is the citizen-customer, who ultimately consumes all the other costs of the final cost object, except for the organizational sustaining costs.

Organizational sustaining costs are activity costs not incurred by making products or delivering services to customers. The consumption of these costs cannot be traced logically to products, standard service lines, channels, or customers. (They can be allocated arbitrarily but not with causal relationships.) For example, when the accountants close the books each month, they can trace the costs of that activity to senior management as an example of organizational sustaining cost objects. Allocating them to products, services, or customers is misleading because neither products nor services nor customers caused these activities; allocating them thus would overstate those costs, sending the wrong signals to employees who use product cost information for making decisions.

The direct costing of indirect and shared costs is no longer an insurmountable problem, given the existence of commercial ABC software products. ABC allows intermediate direct costing to a local process, an internal customer, or a required component that is causing the demand for work. In short, ABC connects customers with the unique resources they consume—in proportion to their consumption—as if ABC were an optical fiber network. Visibility of costs is provided everywhere throughout the cost-assignment network.

One City's Benefits from ABC/M

Indianapolis, Indiana, was one of the first major cities to embrace ABC/M. In the mid-1990s, the municipal government joined forces with local business leaders to apply contemporary business improvement practices. Knowing what things cost was considered a prerequisite to focusing on what to change.

The city applied ABC/M in several areas. Some of the earliest results were remarkable—and in some ways amusing:

■ When managers in the Department of Public Works analyzed their costs of picking up trash, they discovered that, over four years, they had spent US$252,000 on repairs to a garbage truck that could be purchased new for US$90,000. The city garage where the repairs were made had no reason to care how much it spent to fix the same truck. When the managers accumulated all the costs associated with that truck, they discovered that it was costing the taxpayers US$39 per mile to operate, obviously an enormous amount when compared with other vehicle-use costs.

■ An employee of the Department of Parks and Recreation bought stacks of chalk to line softball fields. He made the purchase at year's end out of fear of having his annual budget reduced if he had any money left over. (The requisitioner had exhibited classic use-it-or-lose-it spending behavior at the end of the fiscal year.) As a result, the city owned enough chalk to line all the city's softball fields for five years. Ironically, another department had independently determined that it was more economical to spray paint the lines rather than chalk them. But it was too late to change. The chalk had already been purchased.

■ The Department of Public Works was spending US$2.9 million annually to collect sewer water bills that amounted to US$40 million. This equated to 7.25 cents on the dollar just to get paid. The city opened the process to competitive bidding. The local, privately owned water company that won the bid produced a 30 percent annual savings in expenses and recognized that it could identify previously unbilled or underbilled sewer users. The company proposed, if given the chance, to give the city the first US$500,000 in collections and then evenly split the collections beyond that. In the first two years, the city and the company split US$11 million.

■ Before the ABC/M analysis, the city was spending US$1.4 million annually to operate three printing and copying centers that had more than 200 copiers. Each print center operated independently, without any coordination. The operation was let out for competitive bid, and annual expenses were reduced by about 35 percent, to US$900,000. The private company generated additional unexpected savings when it offered its expertise in helping the city conduct a "red tape" initiative to reduce the number of forms used by city departments.

As the printing and copying center example reveals, governments may operate businesses when commercial companies perform comparable work.

Despite the similarities, both business leaders and public officials often have a misconception that the government and commercial services are in some way different. This is an artificial mental block. The differences are minor, and this mindset only gets in the way of improving productivity and service levels for all concerned.

One of the main messages to be gleaned from these examples is the long-known fact that competition creates innovation. By defining the problem and its scope, a new approach can lead to large magnitudes of savings and improvements, not just marginal increments.

A second message involves accountability. When government services are reviewed and measured, including the costs of the work activities, processes, and their outputs, accountability is likely to increase. The process of writing contracts, establishing performance measures, assessing costs, and measuring results creates a level of accountability to the public well beyond what existed before.

ABC/M is decision neutral here. ABC/M data do not take sides. They simply make visible some facts and some cost rates that can be used to estimate reliably what the cost consequences might be for future scenarios and options. Although government must ensure the provision of certain services, there is no reason government must also produce and deliver those services. ABC/M data are, however, very work-centric. Regardless of who does the work, ABC/M measures the costs. In the end, governments still set policy for the delivery of services to the citizenry, so important issues beyond the cost of providing services can always be addressed.

Operational ABC/M for Productivity

Managers and employee teams are seeking more transparency and visibility of their costs. Reliably knowing ABC/M's unit costs of their outputs of work is useful for benchmarking, in searching for best practices, or in reporting trends to measure performance improvement. ABC/M removes the illusion that support overhead (that is, indirect) expenses are necessary and therefore are free. They are not free. The costs of an output, product, or service (a final cost object) can be reduced by the following:

- Reducing the quantity, frequency, or intensity of the activity driver (for example, having fewer inspections reduces the cost of the "inspect product" activity)
- Lowering the activity driver cost rate through improvements in productivity (for example, shortening the time needed for each "inspect product" activity)

■ Understanding the sources and causes of waste leading to non–value adding activities, so as to reduce or eliminate them (for example, solving the problem that makes an "inspect product" activity necessary).

These three examples show how ABC/M data lead to managing costs so as to improve productivity. The idea is do more with less—that is, to produce more outputs with the same amount of resources or the same amount of outputs with fewer resources. Note how these actions support the continuous improvement principles of the Six Sigma quality and "lean management" initiatives that operations and quality communities embrace.

ABC has a bonus feature (available with commercial ABC software) referred to as ABC/M attributes. This feature can report another dimension of costs—the "color of money" spent. It applies cost attributes, usually to an activity, by tagging or scoring each activity with a code. This dimension of cost does not exist in general-ledger accounting systems because attributes are tagged to activities or to cost objects, not to resource expenses.

An example of an attribute would be deeming an activity to be value adding or not. Another example is the five sequential "cost of quality" categories of work, which increase in their severity: error free, prevention related, appraisal related, internal failure work, and external work. Attributes do not alter the cost of anything calculated by ABC/M. Costs remain unaffected. But attributes facilitate grouping activity costs into various categories (such as non–value added costs) that, in turn, help focus managers' attention and can suggest actions. Commercial ABC/M software can keep track of a work activity's attribute and trace it to cost objects. So, for example, one may discover that the unit cost of delivering two similar service lines is relatively the same, but that one consumes much more non–value added activity costs than the other. If the presumption is that operational improvements will reduce those non–value added costs, one service line has a greater likelihood of costing less in the future. This insight could never arise using general-ledger cost center reporting or traditional broadly averaged cost allocations.

But Our Department Does Not Have Outputs

Some departments believe, presumably because of the nature of their work, that they have no outputs. Managers and workers who think, plan, and give direction conclude that since their work deals with intangibles, there is no definable output from their work. But outputs can be intangible. Many are. What is the output of a university education? Is it the diploma? Is it each professor's course? Is it the learning by each student? All these may appear to be intangible. But the financial cost for each one is measurable. There is no dichotomy between workers who think and plan and workers who deliver services and tangible products.

Several years ago, one of the U.S. government laboratories, where well-paid physicists wrestle with theory and advances in their field, conducted a study of the effectiveness of business processes study. Debate surrounded how to map inputs, processes, and outputs. Some of the physicists believed their work was unmappable. The physicists argued that one could not rigorously define the brain's thinking process when it comes to innovation. However, that is not the point in ABC/M.

All work has outputs. For example, when one of this same government laboratory's experiments is conducted, the activity results in a completed experiment. When a research paper is written and submitted by a physicist, there is a completed research paper. Lots of thinking, preparation, tests, typing and copying support, and so on may have gone into finishing the research paper, but the costs of these activities can be appropriately assigned. When the report is done, the aggregate output can be described as a completed research paper—including the costly tests.

Moreover, all completed research papers are not equal in the time, effort, and support needed and used. There can be great diversity and variation. ABC/M measures that variation and links the costs back to how much the organization spent in paying for salaries and supplies. The focus is not on who funded that spending, although there is a clear audit trail back to the source. ABC/M focuses on the facts that spending occurred, that money was used somewhere, and that it went into something for somebody.

Seeing the true cost of outputs can produce some organizational shock. If a completed report, after all the time, effort, and support is traced into it, costs $325,000, that may be a surprise. If it is read by only three young advisers to a U.S. senator and they brief the senator in a quick hallway conversation but make no more use of that report, it is not clear whether the report was worth the cost. Yet a significant piece of information is now available—the true cost of producing that particular report. The $325,000 price tag would make some other government service provider—perhaps one that is very strapped on budget and whose mission is feeding and caring for children in need—really think about whether appropriations are fairly distributed. Employment by government is not an entitlement program for the workers. The value of the contribution of work must be understood and compared with the value of alternatives.

The purpose here is not to get emotional or political. ABC/M does not take sides. It simply reports the facts. People can then debate the value of it all. But ABC/M does provide the basis for determining cost-benefit tradeoffs and thus allows comparison with other services that are competing for tax dollars. This type of dialogue and discussion cannot easily occur when funding is simply stated in the form of salaries, supporting expenses, and supplies (for example, budgets). Dialogue is better stimulated when costs are stated in other terms, such as unit costs per output, permitting comparisons to be made.

A recognized need to shift emphasis from inputs to outputs is leading some civilian and defense organizations to adopt financial funding relationships that are based on pay for performance—rather than disbursing cash to service providers as if they were entitled to it. As an example, one city government had historically funded one of its social service agencies on the basis, essentially, of inputs. The mission of this particular social service organization was to prepare and place unemployed people into jobs as workers. Historically, the agency billed the city's central funding authority in accordance with the number of unemployed candidates interviewed and the number of hours of job training provided. Whether any of these candidates got a job was irrelevant to the agency. The bases for payment were the events involved in the process, rather than the relevant results—successful hirings—that the city had hired the agency to produce.

The city government altered the payment arrangement to one based on the number of jobs lasting for at least six months that were secured for the former welfare recipients. This output-based solution worked much better. The agency recognized that it needed to customize its training according to individual needs and shortcomings. In the end, the agency benefited as well—its revenues are now increasing at a 20 percent annual rate.

Annex 7A, which concludes this chapter, is an example of ABC calculations for a government road maintenance department. It illustrates the visibility and insights an organization can benefit from.

ABC/M Uses (and Some Pitfalls)

A significant lesson learned from previous implementations of ABC/M is the importance of working backward with the end in mind. That is, it is to management's benefit to know in advance what it might do with the ABC/M data before it launches the calculation effort. The end determines the level of effort required.

Although ABC/M is basically just data tracking, one of its shortcomings is the wide variety of ways the data can be used. Different uses require more or less detail or accuracy. Accordingly, the system should be built with a clear idea of the types of decisions or assessments that the ABC/M data will be asked to support. Some ABC/M implementations may miss the mark by being either overly detailed or not detailed enough.

Eventually, as the ABC/M data are applied as an enabler for multiple uses, the size of the system and the level of effort to maintain it stabilize at an appropriate level. Through using the data, the ABC/M system balances the tradeoff between the level of administrative effort to collect and report the data and the benefits of having the data, as the system meets various users' needs.

Here are examples of the more popular uses of ABC/M by governments and defense organizations:

- *Fees for service and cost-to-serve.* ABC/M is used to calculate the costs of specific outputs as a means of pricing services provided to customers and other functions or agencies.
- *Outsourcing and privatization studies.* ABC/M helps managers determine which specific costs would remain or disappear if a third party were to replace an existing part or all of an organization. Increasingly, commercial companies are positioning themselves to perform services once viewed as exclusively in the public sector's domain. Some government agencies are learning that it is better to proactively measure their costs to prevent the possibility of a poor decision by an evaluation team. For example, the team may mistakenly conclude that outsourcing makes the most sense and discover after the fact that more accurate data would have reversed that decision. ABC/M can also help a government organization bring its costs in line with those of a commercial provider; its governing authority may allow a grace period for doing so.
- *Competitive bidding.* Increasingly, commercial companies are positioning themselves to perform services, such as operating prisons, that were once exclusively the domain of the public sector. But the reverse is possible too. Some government departments, such as those that maintain roads or trim trees, may excel and compete with commercial companies.
- *Merging and diverging agencies or functions.* ABC/M is used to identify administrative services that could be shared or combined among multiple agencies or functions.
- *Performance measurement.* ABC/M can provide some of the inputs to weighted and balanced scorecards that are designed to improve performance and accountability to taxpayers.
- *Process improvement and operational efficiency.* ABC/M helps to optimize resource use and, at times, serves as a key to an agency's survival. Some

agencies are facing budget cuts (or taking on additional activities owing to consolidation) and are unclear about the costs of their internal outputs. What does it cost to process a new registrant versus a renewal? Why might these two costs be so different? Do both costs per event seem too high?

■ *Budgeting.* ABC/M helps managers routinely plan for future spending on the basis not of the current rate of spending but, more logically, of the demand volume and mix of services anticipated.

■ *Aligning activities to the strategic plan.* ABC/M corrects for substantial disconnects between the work and service levels that an organization is supplying and the activities required to meet the leadership's strategic goals. It can be shocking for organizations to discover that they are very, very good at things they do that are deemed very, very unimportant to the strategic plan.

Managerial accounting data have many uses. The idea is not to start an ABC/M implementation process just because it feels right or because an authority commands or dictates it. The idea is to know in advance what problems the better data will solve.

Multiple Views of Costs Are Empowering

When senior leaders, managers, and employee teams are provided reliable views of not only their resource spending but also the costs of their work activities, the costs of processes involved in these activities, and the total and unit costs of the various outputs deriving from the activities, they have a much better basis for making decisions. Compare all that with what they have today. They have the spending view, but no insight as to how much of that spending is or was really needed or why. Managers need to know the causal relationships. When employees have reliable and relevant information, managers can manage less and lead more.

An ABC/M system provides a good starting point for any nonprofit or government organization to model its cost behavior. It is a solution looking for problems—and all organizations have problems. ABC/M provides a top-down look at how an organization's resources get used, why, by whom, and how much.

Divide resource spending into two categories: resources used and resources unused (that is, idle capacity). For the first category, a cost can be incurred only if some person or piece of equipment does something. In other words, to understand cost behavior, one must understand which activities the organization performs, which other work activities or services these activities support, what outputs derive from these activities, and the characteristics of whoever is requesting and using these outputs. An ABC/M system models these links and reports the results. Managers gain multiple views of the costs plus an understanding of the relationships.

A major benefit from ABC/M is that data of varying detail and accuracy can be provided to managers and employee teams in a distributed fashion. These data allow each person to see, analyze, and manage the costs and activities that are within his or her control. It is at this level that real and meaningful changes in cost structure, performance measurement, and service delivery will occur. Today, this type of management data can be provided with commercially available software products that link to existing fund-accounting, cost, and metric systems. As a bonus, ABC/M software can flexibly deliver meaningful reports to an individual's workstation—whether through integrated systems or Web delivery. This approach is a cost-effective way of achieving performance improvement.

ABC/M can be applied in different ways to achieve different outcomes. It is a flexible and powerful methodology that has a unique ability to deliver true cost information from which critical decisions can confidently be made. As demand pressure mounts and budget funding is reduced, the public sector and not-for-profit organizations clearly need this kind of information to achieve effective results.

Realizing True Cost Savings or Future Cost Avoidance

Staff members in many organizations imagine that if they introduce productivity improvements and streamlining actions, they will automatically save costs. But being more efficient does not equate to realizing savings in expenses—as opposed to costs—unless resources are removed (or unless, when volume increases, extra resources do not have to be acquired).

Where do cost savings come from? All things being equal—and if there are no significant changes in revenues or funding following a change in services—the only positive effect on cash flow must come from reduced variable costs. If purchased materials and supplies are reduced a certain percentage, those costs are totally variable and are consumed as needed. The financial savings are real. That is, the cost savings are truly realized as savings in cash outlays for expenses.

But when an organization works more efficiently and staffing remains constant, then unused capacity in the workers is freed up. These workers become available to do other things. But as long as they continue to get paid their salary and wages, the organization realizes zero expense savings. Unlike the variable, "as needed" purchased materials, workers entail "just in case" fixed costs when their full capacity is, in effect, contracted in advance of the demand for their services. If they are not needed all the time, the government pays for their idle time as well.

As efficiencies are produced, managers can realize cost savings or avoid future costs in staffing in only two ways:

1. They can fill the freed-up worker's time with other meaningful work, ideally addressing new volumes of customer orders.
2. They can remove the capacity by removing the workers, realizing savings in staffing expense.

The issue is that of transferring employees, demoting them, or removing them. One of the most difficult political issues stemming from privatization is the loss of public sector jobs. This problem can be mitigated, however, if government and its private sector partners work together to ensure the least pain and the most gain for the individuals displaced. Similarly, kinder and gentler ways can be found to reduce staff when required by gains in efficiency or changes in demand level. But in the end, any organization requires a minimum of distractions from its core role of delivering products or services efficiently.

The loss of jobs must be dealt with openly, compassionately, and comprehensively. For example, in an outsourcing situation, the private sector company can rehire a number of the existing government employees, who are, after all, already experienced in the outsourced activities. Other ways to address the loss of jobs is through transfer and attrition. Some employees can be placed in growth areas of the organization or elsewhere in the government as opportunities arise. In the interim, some organizations set up a temporary job bank that uses the displaced workers in a meaningful way until attrition or new needs create job openings.

Why Change Now?

It is flip to say that change is the only constant, but it is so often true. The question for the public sector is whether it will drive change—or be driven by it. In the United States, large federal budget deficits and new regulations, such as the Government Performance and Results Act of 1993, have acted as catalysts for change in the way that government units perform their functions. Competition from the private sector will place additional pressures on governments, agencies, and the military to provide good service economically.

Without visible, relevant, and valid data, it is difficult for organizations to stimulate ideas and evaluate what options are available—and what their financial effect will be. ABC/M data provide fundamental information that is part of the solution. Applying ABC/M may well be critical to an organization's survival.

Government is moving past the initial stage of rethinking what government does and how it does it. Restrictive funding pressures have already jump-started that activity. Now government units are adopting a greater performance orientation and are replacing a detailed micromanagement style with a more practical approach, one in which the costs are justified by the benefits. ABC/M is now playing and will continue to play an important role in helping the government to manage its affairs.

As important as it is, however, ABC/M is not a panacea. As mentioned earlier, cost management should always be done in the broader context of performance management, integrating time, quality, service levels, capacity planning, and costs. But an organization's understanding of its cost-structure behavior is critical, so a managerial accounting system that supports managerial economic analysis, which ABC/M does, is critical for all stakeholders—employees, the community, loyal customers, and shareholders.

Annex 7A: Case Study

ABC/M in a State Road Maintenance Department

The "end of the road" final-final cost objects consume all the cost assignments that have occurred to that point. Some cost assignments are direct to the final-final objects, but in increasingly overhead-intensive organizations, most costs arrive as indirect and shared costs.

As an example, a government road maintenance and repair department does not directly service individual types of cars or trucks or individual types of drivers. The inherent diversity originates in the type of road. The characteristics of the road cause the work crews to do more or less work. The weight of trucks may cause more road damage than the weight of automobiles, but the type of vehicle is more of a higher-order cost driver than an activity driver. The causal force of trucks versus automobiles may certainly be discussed when seeking ways to improve costs. However, for the purposes of ABC/M, the roadbed itself serves as the best source (that is, the final-final cost object) for understanding the interdependencies of costs. The roadbed is the only practical way of connecting an output of the department's workload back to the used resources (types of trucks, garages, employees, and so on). Figure 7A.1 provides a simplified diagram of the ABC/M cost-assignment network

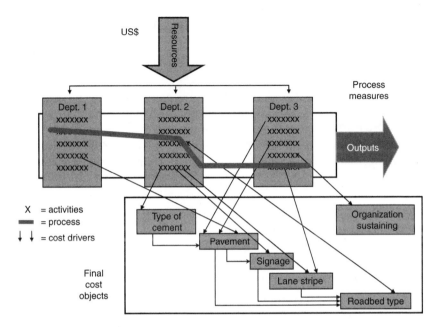

Source: Author's representation.

FIGURE 7A.1 Highway Road Maintenance ABC/M Cost Assignments

for a road maintenance function with an incomplete but representative example of final cost objects that are consumed in different proportions by various types of roadbed—the final-final cost object.

The inherent diversity of the road can be segmented into several dimensions with two or more classifications:

- Number of lanes: two-lane versus four-lane
- Road surface: cement versus asphalt
- Location: rural versus urban
- Designation: expressway, state highway, or city road.

Using only those four dimensions and choices produces 24 ABC/M final-final cost objects ($2 \times 2 \times 2 \times 3 = 24$). The organizational discovery and learning comes when the costs for each type of road are compared on a relative basis—for example, the average cost for each mile or kilometer of road. Many roadway organizations have already captured data describing the number of miles or kilometers for each of these 24 combinations. By dividing the annual cost (or any time range) for each unique type of road, the organization may be shocked to discover that the four-lane urban expressway costs 800 percent per mile (or per kilometer) more than the smallest, slowest-traveled type of road. But during the cost analysis, this comparable difference could be supported by the facts. For example:

- The four-lane road requires twice as many passes of a snowplow truck as a two-lane road.
- The snowplow trucks for expressways may be maintained in large garages with technical equipment and a complete organization of mechanics, whereas for rural roads drivers may get a hammer and a wrench and a good-luck wish.
- The expressway may receive more frequent line painting.
- The expressway may have more sewer culverts to maintain.
- The expressway may have more electronic road direction signs.

Dozens of other characteristics can result in the four-lane urban expressway being much more expensive relative to other types of roads, after the effect of distance has been removed. Regardless of whether one can articulate all these characteristics, the level of activity costs used to service the road is inherently governed by the type of roadbed.

Notice that each final cost object in figure 7A.1, such as the signage, has different types. For example, signage may consist of expensive electronic signs on main roads, metallic signs on all roads, and wooden signs on rural roads. ABC/M traces all the sign maintenance work activity costs to the signs as if they were the only purpose for costing. In fact, many organizations dedicate a local ABC/M model to such a final cost destination. But in this example, all the signage costs are further reassigned into the roadbed depending on the unique number and type of signs for each specific roadbed. This assignment relies on cost-object drivers; the activity drivers have already completed their mission to trace the workload costs to their cost object.

Also notice in figure 7A.1 how the type of cement is assigned to the pavement, not directly to the roadbed. In this case, there are enough costs and diversity in types of cement to dedicate a final cost object. Then these costs are mixed like a recipe's ingredients into various types of pavements. The pavements ultimately are reassigned to the types of roadbeds.

In the end, all the activity costs, excluding operational sustaining costs, must be traced to the final-final cost object—the types of roadbed—regardless of how the ABC/M design team chooses to configure the model. But those teams that follow the rules on defining drivers and add common sense—not getting too detailed beyond incremental benefits—will compute the most reasonable final-final cost-object costs.

ABC/M Model Analysis

Continuing with this highway maintenance and roadbed example, table 7A.1 illustrates fictitious costs that compare the unit cost of the output of work for each type of road's cost per mile. This type of report is very popular with ABC/M users. It not only provides the total unit costs of the output—now validly computed—but also subdivides that same total unit cost among the various work activities that are being consumed.

This deeper visibility of activity costs within a unit of output provides a form of internal benchmarking. It allows the employee teams and managers to ask much better and more focused questions. For example, why does this cost so much more than that? This is particularly relevant for large costs. Note that ABC/M does not automatically conclude that one observation is good and another is bad. ABC/M simply provides opportunities to ask much better questions. In this way, it becomes an excellent focusing tool for highlighting where to look for potential changes for improvement.

However, when the same information revealed in table 7A.1 is combined with ABC/M's powerful attributes, ABC/M becomes more suggestive about what to change. For example, if a relatively high cost per unit of work activity was also scored as a postponable or discretionary cost, rather than as a critical one, then employees could consider scaling back on their workload for that activity. At a minimum, employees could intelligently discuss what underlying factors are leading to the large relative costs compared with the other final cost objects. In this way the final cost-object module of the ABC/M cost-assignment network provides insights that stimulate teams to think and to discuss how their limited resources are being used and may be better used.

ABC/M versus Process Flowchart Analysis

The key message is that when employee teams and managers understand how the diversity and variation of their cost objects cause the levels of their cost structure, they can better consider ideas to change things. The quality management community occasionally proclaims that "variation is the enemy," because variation can lead to higher costs of nonconformance. But some variation is market generated, so diversity must be accepted—as must the indirect costs that come with it.

TABLE 7A.1 An Example of "Unitized Costs": Types of Roadbed Costs

Road surface	Lanes	Location	Total cost (US$)	Miles	Work activity	Unit cost per mile (US$)
Asphalt	4	Interstate	270,137,078.40	125,342	Total	2,155.20
					Cut grass	120.00
					Install electronic signs	334.25
					Fill potholes	150.00
					Plow roads	975.60
					Paint stripes	450.50
					Replace signs	124.85
Bituminous	2	Rural	29,783,384.10	43,578	Total	683.45
					Cut grass	220.00
					Install electronic signs	0.00
					Fill potholes	65.00
					Plow roads	250.00
					Paint stripes	112.20
					Replace signs	36.25
Asphalt	4	County	95,567,207.84	65,672	Total	1,455.22
					Cut grass	395.60
					Install electronic signs	101.57
					Fill potholes	153.80
					Plow roads	505.75
					Paint stripes	221.75
					Replace signs	76.75

Source: Author's representation.

Ironically, process flowcharts do not always stimulate the questions and thinking that ABC/M stimulates. The process view, which is time sequenced, does not give much visibility to the varying mix of outputs and different types of recipients that truly cause the need for additional activity costs. Process flowcharts are mix blind. They simply map steps without adequate insight into who or what uses the steps. Because greater differences and variation of outputs cause higher costs, seeing the cost relationship becomes valuable. Because process flowcharts do not shed much light on variation, ABC/M becomes the solution to provide that needed visibility.

Admittedly, if process flowcharts include only the constituent activity costs, employee teams may come up with some suggestions. After all, process-based thinking is a major leap over the hierarchical organizational (stove-pipe) thinking that is now recognized as old thinking. But the primary interest for any analytic exercise is to stimulate employee teams and managers to be innovative. ABC/M is stronger at accomplishing this than is the process view of costs.

Note

Gary Cokins can be reached at garyfarms@aol.com.

8

Budget Preparation and Approval

SALVATORE SCHIAVO-CAMPO

This chapter focuses on the core processes of budget preparation, mainly in light of the objectives of aggregate expenditure control and strategic allocation of resources. The third objective of public expenditure management—operational efficiency—underpins chapter 9 on budget execution, and performance monitoring issues are discussed in chapter 12 on budget reform priorities and sequencing. This chapter discusses first the most important requirements of good budget preparation as well as the most frequent bad practices in budgeting. The chapter then describes the various stages of a sound budget preparation process and concludes by discussing the division of labor within the executive and budget approval by the legislature.

Although this chapter focuses on the technical aspects of budget preparation, in every country the budget process is inherently political, requiring as it does choosing between different programs. No objective technical rules can really determine whether, for example, three additional rural health centers for one group of beneficiaries are "better" than one additional urban primary school for a different group of beneficiaries. One hears sometimes the wistful wish to "get the politics out of the budget." This wish is not only impossible but wrong, because the legitimate authority of public expenditure managers does not include making decisions about expenditure policy. Instead, the characteristic of good budget preparation is to confine the politics to the start, when the key policy decisions are made, and to the end of the process, when coherent technical proposals have been prepared and are then submitted to the political leadership for its consideration and disposition. In the middle, no political interference should occur, *precisely* to allow the administration to prepare a budget consistent with the policy choices. Paradoxically, such political interference in the midst of the budget preparation process would weaken the political relevance of the budget, not improve it.

Three Prerequisites for Budget Preparation

Three major conditions are needed for the desired outcome of a budget that is both technically sound and faithful to political directions: taking a medium-term perspective, making early decisions, and setting a hard constraint.

The Need for a Medium-Term Perspective

To be an effective instrument of financial management, the government budget must in the first place be credible. To be credible, the expenditure program must be affordable. Therefore, budget preparation must take as its starting point a good estimate of revenue—although the revenue estimate may change before the budget is finalized in order to produce a consistent revenue-expenditure package. Thus, *fiscal marksmanship*—that is, the accuracy of revenue forecasts as manifested in closeness of actual revenues to those estimated—is the linchpin of the budget preparation system.

To meet the government's objectives, the budgeting system must provide a strong link between government policies and the allocation of resources through the budget. (Chapter 2 listed the characteristics of good policy decisions.) Because most of these policies cannot be implemented in the short term, the process of preparing the annual budget should take place within a fiscal perspective several years into the future.[1] The future is inherently uncertain, and the more so the longer the future period considered: the general tradeoff is between policy relevance and certainty. At one extreme, budgeting for just next month would suffer the least uncertainty but also would be almost irrelevant as an instrument of policy. At the other extreme, budgeting for a period of 10 or more years would provide a broad context but carry much greater uncertainty as well.[2] In practice, *multiyear* means medium term—that is, a perspective covering no more than four years beyond the budget year. In Africa, given the more fluid situation of developing countries, a perspective covering two years beyond the coming budget year is probably most appropriate for framing the preparation of the coming budget.

Clearly, the feasibility of a multiyear perspective is greater when revenues are predictable and the mechanisms for controlling expenditure are well developed. These conditions are not fully met in many developing countries, precisely where a clear sense of policy direction is a must for sustainable development and where budget managers have a special need for predictability and flexibility. Nevertheless, some sort of medium-term forecast of revenues and expenditures remains essential to frame the annual budget preparation process.

Specifically, the annual budget must reflect three paramount multi-annual considerations:

1. The future recurrent costs of capital expenditures (which constitute the largest single category of public expenditure in most African countries).
2. The funding needs of entitlement programs (for example, pensions and transfer payments), where expenditure levels may change even though basic policy remains the same. This consideration is relevant for industrial countries, with large social security and public health obligations, but much less so in Africa.
3. Contingencies that may result in future spending requirements (for example, government loan guarantees; see chapter 2 by Schiavo-Campo for a discussion of contingent liabilities).

A medium-term outlook is especially necessary because the discretionary portion of the annual budget is small. At the time the budget is formulated, most of the expenditures are already committed. Salaries of civil servants, debt-service payments, pensions, and the like cannot be changed in the short term, and other costs can be adjusted only marginally. In developing countries, the available financial margin of maneuver is typically no more than 5 percent of total annual expenditure. As a result, any real adjustment of expenditure priorities, if it is to be successful, has to take place over a time span of several years. For instance, should the government wish to substantially expand access to technical education, the expenditure implications of such a policy are substantial and stretch over several years, and the policy can hardly be implemented through a blinkered focus on each annual budget.

Multiyear spending projections are also necessary to demonstrate to the administration and the public the direction of change and to allow the private sector time to adjust, in the interest of the economy as a whole. Moreover, in the absence of a medium-term framework, adjustments in expenditure to reflect changing circumstances will tend to be across the board and ad hoc, focused on inputs and activities that can be cut in the short term. But often, activities that can be cut more easily are also more important, such as major public investment expenditures. A typical outcome of isolated annual budgeting under constrained circumstances is defining public investment expenditure in effect as a mere residual. Finally, by illuminating the expenditure implications of current policy decisions on future budgets, a government can evaluate cost-effectiveness and determine whether it is attempting more than can be financed.

The multiyear framework must have, among other things, political involvement and a clear link to the budget preparation process. A good example is provided by South Africa's experience, after a false start in the mid-1990s (see box 8.1).

Four pitfalls should be avoided. First, a multiyear expenditure perspective can itself be an occasion to develop an evasion strategy, by pushing expenditure off to the future years. Second, a multiyear expenditure perspective could lead to claims for increased expenditures from line ministries, because new intentions are easily transformed into entitlements as soon as they are included in the projections. Third, as is the case for any good budgeting practice, a multiyear expenditure perspective should not be pushed

---

BOX 8.1 The Link between the MTEF and Budget Preparation in South Africa

The initial experience with a medium-term expenditure framework (MTEF) in South Africa, started in 1994, lacked political involvement, and had no clear link with the budget preparation process. Taking these shortcomings into account, beginning in 1997 the government merged the MTEF and budget processes, which now include the following coordinated activities:

■ *Initial policy review.* The review takes place from May to September (the fiscal year begins in March) and includes the following critical steps:
  —May: The cabinet considers spending priorities.
  —June–July: Technical committees of national, provincial, and local governments meet.
  —July–September: The macroeconomic and fiscal frameworks are revised.
  —September: A cabinet meeting considers and approves the macroeconomic and fiscal frameworks.

■ *Preparation of MTEF/budget proposals.* Line ministries' proposals must be submitted to the Ministry of Finance by August 2, structured to identify clearly the proposed policy changes and to include the following items:[a]
  —A baseline medium-term allocation. The resource envelope used to determine this baseline consists of the two MTEF forecast years prepared the previous year.
  —Identified savings and reprioritization, within the baseline allocation.
  —Program options that propose changes to the medium-term baseline allocation (for example, new programs, change in the level of output, change in implementation schedule of a program). These options should be related to the strategic priorities of the line ministry. For non-recurrent expenditures, estimates should cover five years (two years beyond the MTEF period).
  —Various relevant documents (for example, personnel, analysis of risks and contingent liabilities).
■ *Review of proposals.* During August and September, the provincial and national Medium Term Expenditure Committee, composed of senior officials from the Ministry of Finance and other ministries, evaluates the MTEF-budget submissions of line ministries and makes recommendations to the Ministry of Finance.
■ *Submission to Cabinet.* The Ministry of Finance submits to the cabinet the draft Medium Term Budget Policy Statement and adjustments estimates, which, after cabinet approval, are tabled in the Parliament of South Africa at end-October, to inform the policy debate, not as a binding document. The draft includes chapters on growth; economic policy and outlook; fiscal policy and budget framework, including a medium-term fiscal framework; taxation; sectoral priorities for the medium term; and provincial and local government finance.
■ *Finalization.* In early November, after cabinet approval, the MTEF allocations to ministries and for conditional grants to subnational government are communicated through allocation letters by the Ministry of Finance. On that basis, the line ministries prepare their draft MTEF-budget during November and December, which includes under the same format the estimates for the coming budget year and indicative projections for years two and three of the MTEF. The complete MTEF-budget is tabled in Parliament in February.

Source: Adapted from Fölscher and Cole 2004.
a. Line ministries are also required to prepare annual financial statements and an annual report, which must be submitted to the Ministry of Finance three and four months, respectively, after the end of the fiscal year. In addition, in 2005 line ministries were required to prepare a five-year strategic plan, which was tabled in Parliament after the budget.

past the point of diminishing returns. In some African and other developing countries, the medium-term expenditure framework (MTEF) has become a juggernaut of increasingly fine detail and geographic reach, imposing time and resource costs on the country's public administration far out of proportion to any benefit. A good reformer should know not only when to seize the opportunity to introduce an innovation, but also when to stop pushing it. Fourth, introducing MTEF is complicated enough without saddling it with major changes in the budgeting system itself. Ghana, where the MTEF introduction gave promising initial results that were negated shortly thereafter, provides an example (see box 8.2). As argued in chapter 12 on the reform process, budget reform is easy to introduce in Africa. The challenge is to make such reforms last and produce benefits that more than justify their costs.

To avoid these pitfalls, many industrial countries have limited the scope of their estimates of multiyear expenditures to the future cost of *existing* programs. Comparing this cost with the revenue forecast yields the aggregate financial margin available for new programs—which the government should begin to prepare but would not *budget* until they are ripe to be launched. Three variants of medium-term expenditure programming can be considered:

1. A mere technical projection of the future costs of ongoing programs (including, of course, the recurrent costs of investment projects).
2. A strict programming approach, which entails (a) programming savings in low-priority sectors over the period to leave room for new higher-priority programs, but (b) including in the multiyear framework ongoing programs and only those new programs that are to be included within the annual budget under preparation, or for which financing is certain (for example, the Public Investment Program prepared in Sri Lanka until 1998).
3. The "traditional planning" approach, which identifies explicitly all programs and their cost over the entire multiyear fixed period. Examples of this approach include the development plans of the 1960s and 1970s covering all expenditures or the kind of first-generation public investment programs still being prepared in several developing countries. Where the institutional mechanisms for realistic revenue projections, sound policy decision making, and budget discipline are not fully in place, this approach can lead to overloaded expenditure programs and can thus harm the credibility of both the plan and the annual budget.

The feasibility of implementing formal multiyear programming depends on the capacity and institutional context of the specific country. When multiyear programming is not feasible, two activities are still a must: (a) considering the

BOX 8.2 MTEF in Ghana: Promising, but Quickly Disappointing

In mid-1996, Ghana implemented an integrated public financial management reform program that included a medium-term expenditure framework component. The MTEF was fully implemented with the 1999 budget. The reviews by MTEF enthusiasts concluded in March 1999 that "so far what was achieved was extraordinary. The first year budget under the MTEF has produced a change, which has not been seen in any other country, in such a short period. The first clear message is that it has been an extraordinary process already, but success is not guaranteed" (*PURMARP News*, March 1999, as quoted in Short 2003; see also Holmes n.d.) This last reservation proved wise. Three years later, an Overseas Development Institute study concluded, "By 2002, the message was one of relative failure in the MTEF" (Short 2003). In 2004, the International Monetary Fund confirmed this diagnosis and noted that "the MTEF falls short of its potential as it tends towards being a form-filling exercise and is not yet getting established as a tool for rational allocation of resources, review of priorities, and decision making" (IMF 2004).

Various factors explain this failure, including the following:

■ The MTEF seems to have been implemented as a "project" rather than as a fundamental reform within the ministry and owned by it.
■ The MTEF was aimed at developing an output-oriented budget, which, aside from its utter unsuitability to a developing country, simply could not be implemented at short notice. The information requirements were extremely heavy, and the number of activities reported by each line ministry was very large (more than 2,500 cost centers in total).
■ From both weaknesses in macroeconomic programming and external shocks, the annual budgets turned out to be unrealistic on the expenditure side. Revenue was forecast fairly accurately, but in large part because of the impact of higher inflation. When the country faced a large trade adjustment, the annual budget was quickly overtaken, and so was the MTEF—with a very negative impact on the credibility of the MTEF for line ministries (Potter 2000).
■ The coverage of the budget and the MTEF remains incomplete.
■ Resources allocation is still based on what was allocated in previous years, rather than on policy reviews. Personnel and nonpersonnel administrative expenditures are outside the MTEF process. Personnel costs are overspent, while investment ends up being unfunded.

Source: Author's compilation.

estimated future costs of ongoing programs when reviewing the annual budget requests from line ministries and (b) defining aggregate expenditure estimates consistent with the medium-term macroeconomic framework (see the section discussing the stages of budget preparation). The objection is often raised that estimating future costs is difficult, especially for recurrent costs of new public investment projects. Although true, this factor is irrelevant: without such estimates, budgeting is reduced to a short-sighted and parochial exercise. In addition to including a multiyear perspective, good budgeting should meet some key conditions and avoid several common pitfalls, as discussed next.

The Need for Early Decisions

By definition, preparing the budget entails hard choices. These decisions can be made, at a cost, or avoided, at far greater cost. The ostrich that hides its head in the sand pays a heavy price. The necessary tradeoffs must be made explicit when formulating the budget. Doing so will permit a smooth implementation of priority programs and prevent disruption of program management during budget execution. Political interference, administrative weakness, and lack of needed information often lead to postponing these hard choices until budget execution. This postponement makes the choices harder, and the consequence is a less efficient budget process. As repeatedly noted, an unrealistic budget cannot be executed well.

When revenues are overestimated and expenditures underestimated, sharp expenditure cuts must be made later when executing the budget. On the revenue side, overestimation can come not only from technical factors, such as a bad appraisal of the impact of a change in tax policy or of increased tax expenditures (see chapter 2), but often also from the desire of politicians or ministries to keep in the budget an excessive number of programs while downplaying the difficulties of financing them. Similarly, on the expenditure side, while underestimation can come from unrealistic assessments of the cost of unfunded liabilities (for example, benefits granted outside the budget) or of permanent obligations, underestimation can also be a deliberate tactic to launch new programs, with the intention of requesting increased appropriations later, during budget execution. Unfortunately, governments are commonly reluctant to abandon an expenditure program after it has been started, forgetting that one should never throw good money after bad. When combined with bureaucratic and political momentum as well as vested interests, this natural reluctance leads to continuing an expenditure program even when a broad consensus exists that it is ineffective and wasteful. No technical improvement can by itself resolve institutional and political problems of this nature. It is that much more important, therefore, to put in place robust gatekeeping mechanisms to prevent bad projects and programs from getting started in the first place. By the time they are in the budget pipeline, it is usually too late to stop them.

An overoptimistic budget also leads to accumulation of government payment arrears, which create their own inefficiencies and destroy government credibility. Clear signals on the amount of expenditure compatible with financial constraints should be given to spending agencies at the start of the budget preparation process. During budget execution, no satisfactory way exists to correct the effects of an unrealistic budget. Thus, across-the-board appropriation sequestering leads to inefficient dispersal of scarce resources among an excessive number of activities. Selective appropriation sequestering combined with a mechanism to control commitments partly prevents these problems, but spending agencies still lack predictability and have no time to adjust their programs and their commitments. Finally, selective cash rationing politicizes budget execution, enables corruption, and often substitutes suppliers' priorities for program priorities. Such an approach has recently come to be known as *cash budgeting*. This term is highly misleading. First, it has nothing to do with the basis of budgetary appropriation, which is on a cash basis almost everywhere. Second, it is merely a tactic during budget execution to deal with the inevitable consequences of an unrealistic budget. Cash budgeting is, simply, cash rationing and not a budgeting system. The problem lies upstream, in an unrealistic budget. Accordingly, an initially higher but more realistic fiscal deficit target is far preferable to an optimistic target based on overestimated revenues or underestimated expenditure commitments, which can lead only to inefficiency, payment delays, arrears, and gamesmanship.

Isolating a core program within the budget and giving it higher priority during budget implementation are often suggested as a means of alleviating problems generated by overoptimistic budgets. In times of high uncertainty of available resources (for example, very high inflation or a postconflict situation), this approach could be considered as a second-best response to the situation. As general practice, however, it has little to recommend it and is vastly inferior to the obvious alternative of using a realistic budget to begin with, because, when applied to current expenditures, the core program typically includes personnel expenditures, whereas the noncore program includes a percentage of goods and services. Cuts in the noncore program during budget execution would tend to increase inefficiency and reduce further the already meager operations and maintenance expenditure in most African developing countries. The core-noncore approach is ineffective also when applied to investment expenditures because of the difficulty of halting a project that is already launched, even when it is noncore. Indeed, depending on the political interests involved, noncore projects may in practice chase out core projects. (The preparation of the investment budget is discussed later in this chapter.)

The Need for a Hard Constraint

Giving a hard expenditure constraint to line ministries from the beginning of budget preparation favors a shift away from a wish list mentality. As discussed in detail later in this chapter, annual budget preparation must be framed within a sound macroeconomic framework and should include a top-down stage, a bottom-up stage, and an iteration and negotiations stage. It is at the top-down stage that the hard expenditure constraint, or ceiling, should be communicated by the ministry of finance to all spending agencies; it is the most effective way of inducing them to confront the hard choices early in the process.

Bad Practices in Budget Preparation

The absence of a hard expenditure constraint at the start of the process, which forces early decisions, will invariably lead to one or more of a number of dysfunctional practices in budgeting.

Incremental Budgeting

Life itself is incremental. And so, in large part, is the budget process, which has to take into account the current context, continuing policies, and ongoing programs. Except when a major shock is required, most structural measures can be implemented only progressively. Carrying out every year a zero-based budgeting exercise covering all programs would be an expensive illusion. At the other extreme, instituting a mechanical set of changes to the previous year's detailed line-item budget leads to very poor results. In that scenario, the dialogue between the ministry of finance and line ministries is confined to reviewing the different items and to bargaining cuts or increases, item by item. Discussions focus solely on inputs, without any reference to results, between a ministry of finance typically uninformed about sectoral realities and a sector ministry in a negotiating mode. Worse, the negotiation is seen as a zero-sum game and is usually not approached by either party in good faith. Moreover, incremental budgeting of this sort is not even a good tool for expenditure control, although that was the initial aim of this approach. Line-item incremental budgeting generally focuses on goods and services expenditures, whereas the "budget busters" are normally entitlements, subsidies, hiring or wage policy, or—in many developing countries—expenditure financed with counterpart funds from foreign aid.

Nonetheless, recalling that credibility is a critical feature of a good budget, even the most mechanical and inefficient forms of incremental budgeting are not as bad as large and capricious swings in budget allocations in response to purely political whims or power shifts.

Open-Ended Processes

An open-ended budget preparation process starts from requests made by spending agencies without clear indications of financial constraints. Because these requests express only needs, in the aggregate they invariably exceed the available resources. Spending agencies have no incentive to propose savings, because they have no guarantee that any such savings will give them additional financial room to undertake new activities. New programs are included pell-mell in sectoral budget requests as bargaining chips. Lacking information on the relative merits of proposed expenditures, the ministry of finance is led into making arbitrary cuts across the board among sector budget proposals, usually at the last minute when finalizing the budget. At best, a few days before the deadline for presenting the draft budget to the cabinet, the ministry of finance gives firm directives to line ministries, which then redraft their requests hastily, themselves making cuts across the board in the programs of their subordinate agencies. Of course, these cuts are also arbitrary, because the ministries have not had enough time to reconsider their previous budget requests. Further bargaining then takes place during the review of the budget at the cabinet level or even during budget execution.

Open-ended processes are sometimes justified as a decentralized approach to budgeting. Actually, they are the very opposite. Because the total demand by the line ministries is inevitably in excess of available resources, the ministry of finance in fact has the last word in deciding where increments should be allocated and whether reallocations should be made. The less constrained the process, the greater is the excess of aggregate ministries' request over available resources, the stronger is the role of the central ministry of finance in deciding the composition of sectoral programs, and the more illusory is the ownership of the budget by line ministries.

Excessive Bargaining and Conflict Avoidance

An element of bargaining always exists in any budget preparation, because choices must be made among conflicting interests. An apolitical budget process is an oxymoron. However, when bargaining drives the process, the only predictable result is inefficiency of resource allocation. Choices are based more on the political power of the different actors than on facts, integrity, or results. Instead of transparent budget appropriations, false compromises are reached, such as increased tax expenditures, creation of earmarked funds, loans, or increased contingent liabilities. A budget preparation process dominated by bargaining can also favor the emergence of escape mechanisms and a shift of key programs outside the budget.

A variety of undesirable compromises are used to avoid internal bureaucratic conflicts—spreading scarce funds among an excessive number of programs in an effort to satisfy everybody, deliberately overestimating revenues, underestimating continuing commitments, postponing hard choices until budget execution, inflating expenditures in the second year of a multiyear expenditure program, and the like. These conflict-avoidance mechanisms are frequent in countries with weak cohesion within the government. Consequently, improved processes of policy formulation can benefit budget preparation as well, through the greater cohesion generated in the government.

Conflict avoidance may characterize not only the relationships between the ministry of finance and line ministries, but also those between line ministries and their subordinate agencies. Indeed, poor cohesion within line ministries is often used by the ministry of finance as a justification for its leading role in determining the composition of sectoral programs. Perversely, therefore, the all-around bad habits generated by open-ended budget preparation processes may reduce the incentive of the ministry of finance itself to push for real improvements in the system.

Dual Budgeting

Frequently, confusion exists between the issues of the *presentation* of separate current and investment budgets and the *process* by which those two budgets are prepared. The term *dual budgeting* is often misused to refer to either the first or the second issue. As discussed earlier, however, a separate presentation is always needed. Dual budgeting refers, therefore, only to a *dual process* of budget preparation, whereby the responsibility for preparing the investment or development budget is assigned to an entity different from the entity that prepares the current budget.

Dual budgeting was aimed initially at establishing appropriate mechanisms for giving higher priority to development activity. Alternatively, it was seen as the application of a golden rule that would require balancing the recurrent budget and borrowing only for investment. In many developing countries, the organizational arrangements that existed before the advent of the public investment programming approach in the 1980s typically included a separation of budget responsibilities between the key core ministries. The ministry of finance was responsible for preparing the recurrent budget; the ministry of planning was responsible for the annual development budget and for medium-term planning. The two entities carried out their responsibilities separately on the basis of different criteria, different staff, different bureaucratic dynamics, and (usually) different ideologies. In some cases, at the end of the budget preparation cycle, the ministry of finance would simply collate the two budgets into a single document that made up the "budget." Clearly, such a practice impedes the integrated review of current and investment expenditures that is necessary in any good budget process. (For example, the ministry of education would program its school construction program separately from its running costs budget and try to get the maximum amount of money for both, while not considering variants such as building fewer schools and buying more books.)

In many cases, coordination between the preparation of the recurrent budget and the development budget is poor not only between core ministries but also within the line ministries. Although the ministry of finance deals with the budget departments of line ministries, the ministry of planning deals with their investment departments. This duality may even be reproduced at subnational levels of government. Adequate coordination is particularly difficult because the spending units responsible for implementing the recurrent budget are administrative divisions, whereas the development budget is implemented through projects, which may or may not report systematically to their relevant administrative division. (In a few countries, whereas current expenditures are paid from the treasury, development expenditures are paid through a separate development fund.) The introduction of rolling public investment programs was motivated partly by a desire to correct these problems. That rolling public investment programs were introduced with World Bank support can be seen as an attempt to correct dual-budgeting problems that the World Bank itself, among other donors, was partly responsible for creating.[3]

Thus, the real dual-budgeting issue is the lack of integration of different expenditures contributing to the same policy objectives. This real issue has been clouded, however, by a superficial attribution of deep-seated problems to the "technical" practice of dual budgeting. For example, dual budgeting is sometimes held responsible for an expansionary bias in government expenditure. Certainly, as emphasized earlier, the initial dual-budgeting paradigm was related to a growth model (the Harrod-Domar model) based on a mechanistic relation between the level of investment and gross domestic product (GDP) growth. This paradigm itself, not dual budgeting, caused public finance overruns and the debt crises inherited in Africa or Latin America from bad-quality investment programs of the 1970s and early 1980s. In hindsight, the disregard of issues such as implementation capacity, efficiency of investment, mismanagement, corruption, and theft is difficult to understand. However, imputing to dual budgeting all problems of bad management or weak governance and corruption is equally simplistic and misleading. Given the same structural, capacity, and political conditions of those years (including the Cold War), the same wasteful and often corrupt expansion of government spending would have resulted in developing countries—with or without dual budgeting. If only the massive economic mismanagement in so many countries in the 1970s and early 1980s could be explained by a single and comforting "technical" problem of budgetary procedure! In point of fact, the fiscal overruns of the 1970s and early 1980s had nothing to do with the visible dual budgeting. They originated instead from a third invisible budget: "black boxes," uncontrolled external borrowing, military expenditures, casual guarantees to public enterprises, and so forth.

At this point, let us dispel the fallacy that public investment programming is inherently fiscally expansionary. First, a good public investment program strengthens the coherence between policy and the budget, and to the extent that policy is grounded on a macroeconomic framework that enhances price stability, the program bolsters that objective. Second, a good programming system raises the efficiency of investment and, by ensuring that the financing is available, its sustainability and the country's overall development. Third, the facts point in the opposite direction. In the 1990s, countries participating in structural adjustment programs, which among other things emphasized restraint in public expenditure, had slightly lower capital expenditure relative to total expenditure, and higher current expenditure, than countries not undergoing structural adjustment. (Participating countries also had much lower military spending and a much lower civilian wage bill.) Furthermore, during that period, these countries were in effect required by the donors to have a dedicated public investment programming process.

Indeed, the causality runs the opposite way: it is the absence of a good public investment programming process that results in inefficiencies and lower growth because the expenditures that are protected are, in practice, the ones that cannot be cut in the short term—namely, salaries and other current expenditures. Given the macroeconomic and fiscal forecasts and objectives, the resources allocated to public investment have typically been a residual, estimated by deducting recurrent expenditure needs from the expected amount of revenues (given the overall deficit target). The residual character of the domestic funding of development expenditures may even be aggravated during the process of budget execution, when urgent current spending preempts investment spending—which can be postponed more easily. In such a situation, dual budgeting yields the opposite problem: unmet domestic investment needs and insufficient counterpart funds for good projects financed on favorable external terms. Insufficient aggregate provision of local counterpart funds (which is itself a symptom of a bad investment budgeting process) is a major source of waste of resources.

Certainly, investment budgeting is submitted to strong pressures because of particular or regional interest (the so-called pork barrel projects) and because it gives more opportunities for corruption than current expenditures. In countries with poor governance, vested interests may favor keeping separate the process of preparing the investment budget, and thus a tendency exists to increase public investment spending. However, under those circumstances, to concentrate power and bribery opportunities in the hands of a powerful unified-budget baron would hardly improve expenditure management or reduce corruption. On the contrary, it is precisely in these countries that focusing first on improving the integrity of the separate investment programming process may be the only way to ensure that some resources are allocated to economically sound projects and to improve over time the budget process as a whole. The appropriate organizational decisions will come at a later stage.

Recall that the real issue is lack of integration between investment and current expenditure programming and not the separate processes in themselves. This fact is important, because to misidentify the issue would lead (and often has led) to considering the problem solved by a simple merger of two ministries—even while coordination remains just as weak. A former minister becomes a deputy minister, organizational "boxes" are reshuffled, a few people are promoted, and others are demoted. But dual budgeting remains alive and well within the bosom of the umbrella ministry. Instead, when coordination between two initially separate processes is close and iteration is effective, the two budgets end up consistent with each other and with government policies, and dual budgeting is no great problem. Thus, when the current and investment budget processes are separate, whether they should be brought under the same roof depends on the institutional characteristics of the country. In countries where the agency responsible for the investment budget is weak and the ministry of finance is not deeply involved in ex ante line-item control and day-to-day management, transferring responsibility for the investment budget to the ministry of finance would tend to improve budget preparation as a whole. (Whether this option is preferable to the alternative of strengthening the agency responsible for the investment budget can be decided only on a country-specific basis.) In other countries, one should first study carefully the existing processes and administrative capacities. For example, when the budgetary system is strongly oriented toward ex ante controls, the capacity of the ministry of finance to prepare and manage a development budget may be inadequate. A unified-budget process would in this case risk dismantling the existing network of civil servants who prepare the investment budget, without adequate replacement. Also, as noted, coordination problems may be as severe between separate departments of a single ministry as between separate ministries. Indeed, the lack of coordination *within* line ministries between the formulation of the current budget and the formulation of the capital budget is in many ways the more important dual-budgeting issue. Without integration or coordination of current and capital expenditure at the line-ministry level, integration or coordination at the core-ministry level is an illusion.

For African developing countries, however, on balance the assumption should be in favor of a single entity responsible for both the investment and the annual budget (although that entity must possess the different skills and data required for the two tasks). Where coherence is at a premium, skills are in limited supply, and a single budget is difficult enough to prepare, choosing two budgeting processes and two sets of officials over a single set may not be appropriate. The organizational keynote in poor countries should be simplicity. The more complicated the decision making, the less likely it is to work well. As already stated, however, this suggestion is only presumption; the organizational choice must be country specific.

Earmarking "High-Priority" Development Expenditures?

A peculiar form of dual budgeting has emerged with the requirement of the Heavily Indebted Poor Countries (HIPC) initiative's debt relief process to track pro-poor spending and raise the budgetary allocation of poverty-reducing expenditure. In its general form, this issue is framed as whether "high-priority" development expenditure should receive special consideration in the budget preparation process. The issue is politically and socially difficult. It requires a balance between the objectives of unity of the budget and an integrated budgeting process (discussed in chapter 2) and the legitimate requirement of aid creditors that the debt relief granted to poor African countries go to reducing poverty instead of financing low-priority expenditure or, of course, sheer waste. In other regions, too, an occasional suggestion has been made to identify high-priority development activities and make sure their funding is protected through the budget process. Given that in developing countries high-priority expenditures are those that are growth enhancing, poverty reducing, or both, the consensus among a group of experts in public expenditure management coalesces around the following four criteria (as summarized by Mountfield 2001):[4]

1. Ineffective expenditure management is neither pro-poor nor pro-growth. Only by strengthening public expenditure management can countries improve the pro-poor and pro-growth quality of expenditure in a lasting way. Particularly through a multiyear perspective, a pro-poor strategy can be articulated into a restructuring of expenditure over a number of years. Establishing and monitoring medium-term targets for broad categories of expenditure have valuable roles to play in indicating the longer-term direction.

2. Because strengthening expenditure management is a medium- and long-term institutional challenge, in special cases a need may exist for transitional targeting and monitoring of expenditure priorities within the budget.

3. Nevertheless, micromanagement must be avoided. The ministry of finance (and the donors) must resist the temptation of negotiating individual expenditures on specific budgetary line items. Doing so would further reduce the already very limited flexibility afforded to operational budget managers in African developing countries and prevent them from moving gradually in the direction of greater results orientation and thus greater effectiveness of expenditure in the interest of poverty reduction and growth.

4. Moreover, because money is fungible, such transitional targeting must be done on the basis of broad expenditure categories and avoid creating a "budget within a budget," which would do the following:
   - Undermine the budget as an instrument of government policy.
   - Lead to neglecting cuts in "bad" expenditure even though identifying the most wasteful programs is often as important as increasing spending on the good ones.
   - Make economic comparisons impossible, obscure the true distribution of resources, and create coordination problems for spending departments and local service providers.

- Generate an incentive to spend up to the target—regardless of whether the activities being financed are well designed—and even serve to create new corruption opportunities. "White elephant" projects are not necessarily confined to economic infrastructure and can emerge in social sectors generally associated with pro-poor activities. (Large and underutilized urban hospitals are a case in point.) Especially counterproductive is the donor practice to set given percentages of spending on specific categories as conditions for eligibility for debt relief or other special favorable treatment, thereby turning an expenditure target into a floor. Most appropriate, instead, is the requirement to conduct expenditure tracking to ascertain that the budgeted expenditure reaches the intended beneficiaries. Indeed, donors should insist on and governments should perform more robust tracking of expenditure.

Alternative approaches to pro-poor targeting within the HIPC process were identified in a comparative study of five African heavily indebted poor countries commissioned by the European Commission, as described in chapter 2 in box 2.4.

The Budget Preparation Process

In both logical and chronological sequence, the main stages in the budget preparation process proceed from the elaboration of the macroeconomic and fiscal framework to the issue of budget instructions, preparation of budget proposals, negotiations on those proposals, and finally presentation to and approval by the legislature.

The Macroeconomic Framework

The starting points for expenditure programming are (a) a realistic assessment of resources likely to be available to the government and (b) the establishment of fiscal objectives. (Iteration follows between the two until the desired relationship between resources and expenditures is reached.) Both starting points depend in large part on a sound and consistent macroeconomic framework in pursuit of economic growth, employment, poverty reduction, and low inflation, by means of fiscal policy, exchange rate and trade policy, external debt policy, and policies affecting the real economy. For example, the policy objective of low inflation is influenced by the level of the fiscal deficit, and the specific instruments can include tax measures and credit policy measures, among others.[5] Projections should cover the current year and a forward period of two to four years.

Preparing the macroeconomic framework

A macroeconomic framework typically includes four interlinked modules— on the balance of payments; the real economy (that is, production in the various sectors); the fiscal accounts; and the monetary sector. It is a tool for checking the consistency of assumptions or projections concerning economic growth, the fiscal deficit, the balance of payments, the exchange rate, inflation, credit growth, and the share of the private and public sectors on external borrowing policies. Preparing a macroeconomic framework is always an iterative exercise. A set of initial objectives must be defined to establish a preliminary baseline scenario, but the final framework requires a progressive reconciliation and convergence of all objectives and targets. Considering only one target (for example, the fiscal deficit) in this iterative exercise risks defining other important targets as de facto residuals instead of independent policy goals.

The preliminary baseline scenario gives the macroeconomic information needed for preparing sectoral and detailed projections, but these projections usually lead, in turn, to revisions of the baseline scenario. Such iterations should continue until overall consistency is achieved for the macroeconomic framework as a whole, and close dialogue is critical among all concerned government authorities. This iteration process not only is necessary for sound macroeconomic and expenditure programming but also is an invaluable capacity-building tool to improve the awareness and understanding of involved agencies—and therefore eventually to improve their cooperation in formulating a realistic budget and implementing it correctly.

The preparation of a macroeconomic framework should be a permanent activity. The framework needs to be prepared at the start of each budget cycle to give adequate guidelines to the line ministries. As noted, it must then be updated throughout the further stages of budget preparation, also to take into account intervening changes in the economic environment. During budget execution, too, macroeconomic projections require frequent updating to assess the impact of exogenous changes or of possible slippage in budget execution.

In addition to the baseline framework, formulating variants under different assumptions, such as changes in oil prices, is important. The risks related to unexpected changes in macroeconomic parameters must be assessed and policy responses identified in advance, albeit in very general terms, of course.

In this effort, the importance of good data cannot be underestimated. Without reliable information, the macroeconomic framework is literally not worth the paper it is written on. The task of obtaining reliable information includes collecting economic data and monitoring developments in economic conditions (both of which are generally undertaken by statistics bureaus), as well as monitoring and taking into consideration changes in laws and regulations that affect revenue, expenditure, financing, and other financial operations of the government. Cost-effectiveness remains, however, the central criterion for the collection and elaboration of statistics: only information that is essential to the preparation of a sound macroeconomic framework should be collected—the user needs always come first.

Making the macroeconomic projections public

Although the iterative process leading to a realistic and consistent macroeconomic framework must remain confidential in many of its key aspects, when the framework is completed it must be made public. The legislature and the population at large have a right to know clearly the government's policy objectives, expectations, and targets, not only to increase transparency and accountability, but also to reach a consensus. Although such a consensus may take additional time and require difficult debates, it will be an invaluable foundation for the robust and effective implementation of the policy and financial program.

Typically, a macroeconomic framework is at a very aggregate level on the expenditure side and shows total government wages, other goods and services, interest, total transfers, and capital expenditures (by source of financing). Assumptions and underlying policy objectives therefore concern the broad economic categories of expenditures, rather than the allocation of resources among sectors. Moreover, transfers or entitlements are not reviewed in sufficient detail, and assumptions on future developments are not compared with continuing commitments. Thus, the fiscal framework elaborated as part of the overall macroeconomic framework needs to be much more detailed on the expenditure side.

The Fiscal Framework

A key component of the macroeconomic framework is the fiscal framework of revenues and expenditures, broken down first in the respective major component categories. For revenue, the categories are direct taxes, indirect taxes, grants, other taxes, and nontax revenue; for expenditures, they are salaries, interest, goods and services, subsidies, and capital expenditures. The setting of explicit fiscal targets frames the preparation of the detailed annual budget, calls on government to define clearly its fiscal policy, and allows the legislature and the public to monitor the implementation of government policy, ultimately making the government politically as well as financially accountable. Fiscal targets and indicators should cover fiscal position (for example, fiscal deficit); fiscal sustainability (for example, debt-to-GDP ratio); and fiscal vulnerability (for example, future liabilities and fiscal risk).

Fiscal position and deficit measures

The summary indicator of a country's fiscal position used most commonly is the *overall balance on a cash basis*, defined as the difference between actual collected revenues plus grants (cash or in kind) and actual expenditure payments. The cash deficit is by definition equal to the government borrowing requirements (from domestic or foreign sources) and is thus integrally linked to the money supply and inflation targets and prospects. The overall deficit is obviously a major policy target and is used for international comparisons as well. How the deficit is financed also requires attention: the same level of fiscal deficit can be manageable or not, depending on whether it is financed in cost-effective and noninflationary ways.

The cash deficit does not take into account payment arrears and floating debt. In countries that face payment arrears problems, the cash deficit plus the net increase of arrears is also an important indicator; it is very similar (but not necessarily identical) to the deficit on a commitment basis—that is, the difference between annual expenditure commitments and accrued revenues and grants. When the fiscal accounts are on a cash basis, the International Monetary Fund's Code of Fiscal Transparency requires that countries report payment arrears as a memorandum item at least, to avoid mistaking a fragile situation for a healthy one when the government is simply pushing off payment obligations to subsequent years.

The *primary balance* is the overall balance excluding interest payments. Because interest must be paid in any event, the evolution of the primary deficit is a better measure of the government's efforts for fiscal adjustment. It is a better policy target also because it does not depend on the vagaries of interest rates and exchange rates.

The *current balance* is the difference between current revenue and current expenditure. By definition, it thus represents government saving and, in theory, the contribution of government to investable resources and economic growth. (A current deficit represents government *dis*-saving, and thus the subtraction of resources from resources available for investment.) Defining the fiscal position in this way would insulate investment expenditure from necessary cuts or other adjustment efforts. Because, however, in developing countries current expenditures may be as important for growth and poverty reduction as capital spending (for example, the teachers and the books needed to make the new school buildings productive), this indicator should be interpreted with care. Finally, when the investment program is in good shape, an additional useful indicator is the *primary current balance*, which focuses on streamlining and making more effective the noninterest portions of current expenditure (largely, salaries, subsidies, and goods and services).

Fiscal sustainability and vulnerability

It is essential to underline that the broad objective of fiscal policy is not a specific level of deficit by any definition, per se, but a fiscal position that is sustainable in light of policy goals and likely resource availability. A temporary budget surplus, for example, may mask structural fiscal problems when the tax base is shrinking, when expenditures are dominated by rigid entitlements, and when financing possibilities are limited to expensive foreign borrowing. By contrast, a significant budget deficit may not be a cause for any concern if it emerges from financing productive investment or—as in post-conflict African countries—is an essential corollary of a reconstruction and recovery program. Moreover, the terms of financing are especially relevant to African countries: if, as would be highly desirable, a high proportion of financing is on grant terms and not tied to specific aid project expenditures, a higher level of fiscal deficit may be perfectly acceptable. The issue is one of practical economic policy and not one of fiscal ideology.

Indicators of fiscal sustainability include the ratio of debt to GDP, the ratio of tax to GDP, and the net unfunded social security liabilities. The calculation of the deficit on an accrual basis would in principle allow a better assessment of liabilities and therefore their impact on sustainability. For developing countries, however, accrual budgeting is out of the question, owing to its high costs and small benefits, if any. In general, large movements in apparent net worth of the state can be caused by valuation changes in assets, such as land, that the government has no immediate intention of liquidating. Hence, Blejer and Cheasty (1993) argue that it is dangerous to use net worth measures as targets of fiscal policy in the short and medium terms.

An assessment of fiscal vulnerability is also needed, especially in countries that benefit from short-term capital inflows and those where loan guarantees have been given out too generously and without adequate scrutiny. The standard deficit measures may indicate a healthy fiscal situation that is in reality fragile. However, guidelines for assessing fiscal vulnerabilities are doubtful and unclear. At budget preparation time, a good judgment must be made of the government's fiscal exposure to future obligations and contingent liabilities.

Which level of government?

Ideally, "general government" (see chapter 2) should be considered when preparing the fiscal projections and defining the fiscal targets, but the targets should also be broken down between central and local governments. In some decentralized systems, a fiscal target cannot be directly imposed on subnational and local government. In those cases, the feasibility of achieving a fiscal target by means of the different instruments under the control of the central government (such as grants, control of borrowing) must be assessed. However, the constraints on running fiscal deficits are typically much tighter on subnational entities than they are on the central government. The main reason is the central government's capacity to regulate money supply. Therefore, in some federal systems (for example, the United States), many states have their own constitutionally mandated requirement of an annual balanced budget. In many African countries, reliable data on subnational government are not available. It is, on balance, better not to include suspect data or guesswork and to limit the fiscal framework to central government. In such cases, the limitations of the fiscal picture should be kept in mind, as well as the need to guard against the temptation to "download" the fiscal deficit onto local government entities by assigning to them expenditure responsibilities without the wherewithal to perform them. In any case, all the deconcentrated units of the central government must be fully included in the fiscal framework and the budget. Those who control the money and the activities should be accountable; accountability does not depend on where in the country the activities are carried out. (See chapter 2 for other considerations relevant to coverage of the budget.)

Consolidation of the Fiscal Commitments

Making the projections credible

As noted at the outset of this chapter, a key requirement of a good budget is to be credible. If the budget preparation is framed by medium-term macroeconomic and fiscal projections, these must be credible, too. In some countries, the government projections are submitted to a panel of independent and respected experts to ensure their reliability and to remove them from partisan politics, while preserving the confidentiality required on a few sensitive issues.

In other countries, such as the United Kingdom, the projections are validated by the independent auditor general. In most African developing countries, the macroeconomic and fiscal projections are developed with the support of external organizations, which gives them a measure of added credibility. In some countries, such as Tanzania, this cooperation has become close enough to make the formulation of these frameworks a virtual partnership (albeit without infringing on the country's sovereign authority to make its own decisions).

A major issue in this regard is whether to adopt binding rules on fiscal outcomes (for example, a prescribed level of deficit) or behavior (for example, prohibition against borrowing except for investment spending). This issue, often going under the name of fiscal responsibility, is briefly discussed below.

Whose "fiscal responsibility"?

Several countries have laws and rules that restrict the fiscal policy of government and prescribe fiscal outcomes.[6] For example, the so-called golden rule stipulates that public borrowing must not exceed investment (thus in fact prescribing a current budget balance or surplus, as in Germany). In many federal countries, the budget of subnational government entities must be balanced by law. In the European Union (EU), the Maastricht Treaty stipulated specific fiscal convergence criteria, concerning both the ratio of the fiscal deficit to GDP and the debt-to-GDP ratio. (The former criterion has been by far the more important.) EU member countries whose fiscal deficit is higher than the permitted 3 percent of GDP limit are, supposedly, liable for large penalties. Box 8.3 summarizes similar arrangements in countries of the West African Economic and Monetary Union.

A frequent criticism of such rules is that they favor creative accounting and encourage nontransparent fiscal practices by burying expenditures or listing as regular revenue one-off revenues. Also, when the rules are effectively enforced, the criticism is that they can prevent governments from adjusting their budgets to the economic cycle, thus making worse both recessions and inflationary pressures. The European experience has, unfortunately, also shown that the Maastricht rules are selectively enforced, with no penalties exacted for violation by the largest and most important EU members.

In contrast with an approach based on rigid targets, other countries (for example, New Zealand) do not mandate specific fiscal targets but refer to criteria such as prudent levels and reasonable degrees. The government is left to specify the targets in a budget policy statement, which presents

BOX 8.3 Fiscal Rules in the West African Economic and Monetary Union

The West African Economic and Monetary Union (WAEMU) consists of eight countries (Benin, Burkina Faso, Côte d'Ivoire, Guinea-Bissau, Mali, Niger, Senegal, and Togo), which have a common central bank (the Banque Centrale des États de l'Afrique de l'Ouest) and a common convertible currency pegged to the euro (the CFA franc). To coordinate macroeconomic policies, WAEMU countries have set up convergence criteria within the framework of the Convergence, Stability, Growth, and Solidarity Pact adopted by WAEMU governments in 1999. As in the Maastricht Treaty, the convergence criteria pay special attention to the fiscal deficit and to public debt sustainability, because these factors can undermine the viability of the common currency. In addition, the pact prohibits use of the exchange rate and interest rate as policy instruments by member states.

The convergence criteria include the following first-order criteria:

- Average annual inflation rate of no more than 3 percent, based on the objective of keeping a low inflation differential between the WAEMU and the euro area. All WAEMU countries met this criterion in 2003 and 2004, but only one of the eight countries managed to do so in 2005, owing to increases in oil prices and a decline in crop production.
- Zero or positive fiscal balance (defined as nongrant revenues minus expenditures excluding foreign-financed investment). In 2005, four WAEMU countries met this criterion.
- Overall debt-to-GDP ratio lower than 70 percent. In 2005, five WAEMU countries met this criterion.
- No change in the domestic and external stock of arrears. In 2005, four WAEMU countries met this criterion.

These first-order criteria are supplemented with the following second-order criteria:

- Government wage bill less than 35 percent of tax receipts. In 2005, three countries met this criterion.
- Ratio of domestically financed investment to tax receipts no lower than 20 percent. In 2005, five countries met this criterion.
- Tax-to-GDP ratio of at least 17 percent. Only one country met this criterion in 2005.
- External current account deficit, excluding grants, lower than 3 percent of GDP. Only one country met this criterion in 2005.

Each year the WAEMU member-states prepare a three-year convergence, stability, growth, solidarity program, and every six months the WAEMU commission publishes a report to assess progress in implementing these programs.

Sources: Convergence, Stability, Growth, and Solidarity Pact and WAEMU 2005.

total revenues and expenses and projections for the next three years. This statement is published at least three months before the budget is presented to the parliament and is reviewed by a parliamentary committee but not formally voted.

The problem with fiscal responsibility rules is they are usually a government's contract with itself. In a presidential system of government, the system has extreme difficulty enforcing on itself a fiscal discipline rule when the chief executive feels the need to violate it, as he or she can always claim reasons of state and unusual needs. In a parliamentary system, where the government is a creature of the legislature, for the legislature to enforce a fiscal rule is equivalent to declaring no confidence in its own government. The issue is thus the oldest issue in contract law: a contract, however freely entered into, has no legal or practical meaning unless it is enforceable, and no enforcement mechanism exists in a government's contract with itself to respect certain rules of fiscal behavior.

This reality still allows three situations in which binding fiscal rules may be useful. First, in countries with a vibrant civil society and an active political exchange, breaking a major and public commitment may entail a political price. Second, in countries with fragile coalition governments, fragmented decision making, and legislative committees acting as a focus for periodic bargaining, setting up legally binding targets may be effective to limit political bargaining. Third, and probably most relevant, fiscal responsibility rules may apply to states in a federal country, for in this case the contract enforcement authority does exist: the national government. In any case, binding fiscal rules must not be confused with the need to provide aggregate expenditure ceilings to all line ministries and agencies at the start of the budget preparation process, emphasized in the next section.

Stages of Budget Preparation

In the budget formulation process, close cooperation between the ministry of finance and the top leadership (president's office or prime minister's office) is required. The role of the leadership is to oversee that the budget is prepared along the policies defined, to arbitrate or smooth over conflicts between the ministry of finance and the line ministries, and to ensure that the relevant stakeholders are appropriately involved in the budget process. An interministerial committee is needed to tackle crosscutting issues and review especially sensitive issues. That being said, a sharp distinction exists between the three stages of budget preparation: the top-down, bottom-up, and negotiation stages.

The top-down stage

As previewed earlier, the starting points for budget preparation are a clear definition of fiscal targets and a strategic framework consisting of a comprehensive set of objectives and priorities. Thereafter, strong coordination of the budget preparation is required to achieve the necessary iteration and to prevent major departures from the initial framework.

Giving a hard constraint to line ministries from the start of budget preparation favors a shift from a "needs" mentality to an "availability" mentality. Moreover, to translate strategic choices and policies into programs, line ministries require clear indications of available resources. Finally, a hard constraint increases the de facto authority and autonomy of the line ministries, weakening the claim of the ministry of finance to a role in determining the internal composition of the line ministries' budgets. (The same is true of each line ministry vis-à-vis its subordinate agencies.)

This constraint calls for notifying spending agencies of the initial budget ceilings, preferably in absolute terms or at least through the provision of accurate and complete parameters. These ceilings may be defined either at the very beginning of the dialogue between the ministry of finance and the line ministries or after a first iteration when line ministries communicate their preliminary requests. In practice, two variants are found in countries that have good financial discipline. In some, line ministries are notified of the sectoral ceilings at the very start of the budget preparation process. Other countries, where budget preparation may last more than 10 months, establish ceilings in two steps. In the first step, some flexibility is left to line ministries to translate guidelines in terms of budget envelopes. Then, after a brief review and discussion of the preliminary requests, the ministry of finance notifies the line ministries of the binding ceilings. In countries with strong government cohesion and stable and well-organized arrangements for budget preparation, the two variants are equally workable, because financial constraints are more or less taken into account by line ministries when preparing their preliminary request. Moreover, when budget preparation lasts nearly one year, setting definite ceilings at the start of the process would be very difficult.

However, in most African developing countries, adopting a gradual approach to building financial constraints into the budget preparation process could mean simply defaulting to a fully open-ended process. Therefore, the notification of definite budgetary envelopes at the beginning of the budgetary process is highly desirable in these countries. The budget circular or budget instructions, which the ministry of finance sends to each ministry and spending agency to set in motion the process of budget preparation, must specify all relevant rules for preparing budget proposals, including the expenditure ceilings for current expenditure and capital spending, respectively.

Coordination and consistency of budget policy with overall economic and social policy are a central concern of the cabinet, although the ministry of finance must play the key role in analysis and formulating recommendations. Generally, the ministry of finance should be responsible for setting the sectoral ceilings, but it should, of course, coordinate with the center of government, which must also review the ceilings in detail and approve them. In some countries, the sectoral ceilings are discussed within interministerial committees; in other countries, proposed ceilings and guidelines for budget preparation are submitted to the cabinet. Where responsibilities for budgeting are split between a ministry of finance and a ministry of planning, the preparation of sectoral expenditure ceilings must be undertaken by a joint committee including representatives of at least the two ministries. The institution responsible for overall financial management should coordinate the setting of the sectoral ceilings to ensure that they fit the aggregate expenditure consistent with the macroeconomic framework.

The bottom-up stage

Line ministries are responsible for preparing their requests within the spending limits provided. Depending on the severity of the fiscal constraint and the organization of the budget preparation process, additional requests from line ministries could be allowed for new programs. However, the principal request should be consistent with the notified ceilings or guidelines, and costs of programs included in the additional requests should be clear and fully adequate for proper implementation, without any underestimation. Naturally, no request for new programs should be entertained without a clear demonstration of its purpose and, where appropriate, an estimate of the demand for the services to be provided.

Line ministries' budget requests should clearly distinguish (a) the amount necessary to continue current activities and programs and (b) proposals and costing for new programs. Before deciding to launch any new expenditure program, the line ministry must assess its forward budget impact. This step is particularly important for development projects and entitlement programs, which may generate recurrent costs or increased future expenditures. This assessment is required whether or not a formal exercise of multiyear expenditure programming is carried out. For this purpose, requests must show systematically the forward annual costs of multiyear or entitlement programs, and the ministry of finance should take into account the forward fiscal impact of these programs when scrutinizing the budgetary requests from line ministries. Estimates of future costs related to multiyear commitments could be annexed to the overall budget document. These estimates would facilitate the preparation of the initial ceilings for the next budget.

In addition to their budget requests, the submission from the line ministries should include the following materials:

- A brief policy statement spelling out the sector policies and expected outcomes
- Where applicable, realistic and relevant performance indicators, including results from the previous period and expected performance for the future
- A statement of how the objectives will be achieved
- Proposals for achieving savings and boosting efficiency
- Clear measures for implementing the proposals effectively.

Line ministries must coordinate the preparation of the budgets of their subordinate agencies and give them appropriate directives. The submission of budget requests from subordinate agencies, in general, should meet the same criteria as noted for line ministries' requests.

The review, negotiation, and iteration stage

When it receives the requests of line ministries, the ministry of finance reviews their conformity with overall government policy and their compliance with the spending limits. (Ideally, any submission that exceeds the spending limit by even the smallest amount should be returned to the originating ministry forthwith with an instruction to resubmit one within the ceiling.) The ministry of finance then reviews performance issues and takes into account changes in the macroeconomic environment since the start of budget preparation. Almost always, these reviews lead the ministry of finance to suggest modifications in the line ministries' budget requests. Negotiation follows.

Negotiation between the ministry of finance and line ministries can take the form of a budgetary conference. Professional staff members from the ministry of finance and line ministries should also hold informal meetings to avoid misunderstandings and minimize conflicts. Major differences of opinion will normally be referred to the center of government, depending largely on the relative balance of administrative and political power between the ministry of finance and the specific line ministry concerned.

Other Relevant Issues

Several other issues must be taken into account in preparing a budget, discussed below in no particular order of importance.

A suitable budget preparation calendar

A pragmatic compromise must be found to establish a calendar of budget preparation that fits the realities of developing countries and the requirements of good budgeting. If the calendar is not long enough, one or another phase of budget preparation would be unduly constrained, the legislature would not be given sufficient time to debate and approve the budget, or both. If the period is too long, changes are likely to intervene after the issuance of the budget circular that may invalidate some of the initial assumptions and targets and require revision of the draft budget proposals. In African developing countries, seven or eight months would be an appropriate budget preparation period, from issue of the budget circular to legislative approval. This period in fact corresponds to the budget calendar for Morocco, shown in table 8.1 (although delays of about a month have been frequent in that country).

Reaching out: the importance of listening

Consultations can strengthen legislative scrutiny of government strategy and the budget. Legislative hearings through committees and subcommittees, particularly outside the high-pressure environment of the annual budget, can provide an effective mechanism for consulting widely on the appropriateness of policies.

The government should try to get feedback on its policies and budget execution from the civil society. Consultative boards, grouping representatives from various sectors in society, could discuss government expenditure policy. On crucial policy issues, the government could set up ad hoc groups. Preparing evaluation studies, disseminating them, conducting surveys, and so forth provide information to stakeholders and the civil society and help the government receive reliable feedback. User surveys and meetings with stakeholders and customers when preparing agencies' strategic plans or preparing programs can enhance the effectiveness of such plans or programs. Finally, and most concretely, in countries with weak budget execution and monitoring mechanisms, only mechanisms for eliciting feedback from far-flung citizens can be effective in revealing such malpractices as "ghost schools," shoddy infrastructure, incomplete projects, theft, and waste. Such mechanisms are often resented by the executive branch, but governments (and external donors) should see them as remarkably cost-effective monitoring devices and encourage and support them as such.

Although these consultations must have an influence on budget decisions, a direct and mechanical link to the budget should be avoided. As

TABLE 8.1   Morocco: Annual Budget Preparation Calendar

Schedule	Activity	Legal basis
January 1	The fiscal year begins.	Organic budget law
January–April	The Ministry of Finance constructs a macroeconomic framework and prepares budget aggregates.	Administrative circulars
May 1	The minister of finance presents to the government council the outline for the draft budget law of the following year.	Decree of April 26, 1999
May	Line ministries receive written policy guidelines and the budget circular, signed by the prime minister, which describe the fiscal strategy (deficit, revenue, debt); establish the terms on which the ministries must prepare their budget proposals; and give the expenditure ceilings that are binding on each ministry.	Decree of April 26, 1999
May–July	Ministries prepare their budget proposals. The Ministry of Finance may revise the macroeconomic and budgetary framework.	
July 1	Line ministries submit their draft budgets to the Ministry of Finance.	Decree of April 26, 1999
July 1–October 21	Budget negotiations take place between the Ministry of Finance and line ministries. Arbitration by the prime minister takes place (if needed). The Ministry of Finance (budget directorate) prepares the draft budget law and its annexes. The council of ministers adopts the draft budget.	Administrative circulars
October 21 (70 days before the end of the year)	The draft budget law is deposited with one of the two chambers of the Morocco Parliament, together with its annexes. The first chamber has 30 days in which to issue its decision.	Organic budget law
November 21 (30 days after submission to the Parliament)	The draft budget law is deposited with the second chamber, which also has 30 days in which to issue a decision.	Organic budget law
Before December 31	Formal vote on and promulgation of the budget law take place. (Should the budget law not be be approved by December 31, the government issues a decree opening the appropriations needed to cover public service tasks, essentially based on the draft budget law.)	Organic budget law

Sources: IMF 2005; Morocco Ministry of Finance; http://www.finances.gov.ma/LoiDeFinances/Essentiel/ Elaboration/ Preparation.htm; and these legal texts: Loi organique no. 7-98 relative à la loi de finances (Bulletin officiel no. 4644 du 3 décembre 1998); Décret no. 2-98-401 du 26 avril 1999 relatif à l'élaboration et à l'exécution des lois de finances.

noted, the budget preparation process needs to be organized along strict rules so that the budget can be prepared in a timely manner while avoiding excessive pressure from particular interests and lobbies. Participation, like accountability, is a relative, not absolute, concept.

Preparing expenditure ceilings

In the preparation of sectoral expenditure ceilings, the following elements must be taken into account:

■ The macroeconomic objectives and fiscal targets
■ The results of the review of ongoing programs for the sector
■ The impact of ongoing expenditure programs on the next budget and their degree of rigidity (notably expenditures related to continuing commitments, such as entitlements)
■ The government's strategy concerning possible shifts in the intersectoral distribution of expenditure and the amount of resources that could be allocated to new policies as well as service demand projections, where appropriate.

Preparing these initial ceilings is largely an incremental-decremental exercise. Budgets are never prepared from scratch. Debt servicing; multiyear commitments for investment, pensions, and other entitlements; rigidities in civil service regulations; and the simple reality that government cannot stop at once all funding for its schools, health centers, or the army limit possible annual shifts to perhaps 5 to 10 percent of total expenditures. In theory, this percentage could be higher in developing countries than in industrial countries (where the share of entitlements is higher). But in practice, because of earlier overcommitments, the room to maneuver is often even lower in developing countries. If one excludes emergency or crisis situations, the government should, when preparing the budget, focus on new policies, savings on questionable programs, and means of increasing the efficiency of other ongoing programs. Clearly, any significant policy shift requires a perspective longer than one year and some advance programming, in whatever form that is appropriate and feasible in the specific country.

Efficiency dividends

In recent years, Australia demanded from each spending unit efficiency dividends—that is, required savings in their ongoing activities (about 1.5 percent annually). On the surface, this practice may look like the typical (and undesirable) across-the-board cuts made by the ministry of finance when finalizing the budget. However, two major differences exist:

1. Efficiency dividends are notified early in the process and within a coherent multiyear expenditure framework.
2. The allocation of savings among activities and expenditure items is entirely the responsibility of the spending agencies, which alleviates the arbitrary nature of the approach.

Naturally, savings measures are much more likely to be implemented when the ministry concerned is itself proposing them than when they are set by the ministry of finance.

This approach appears to have achieved effective results in Australia from the mid-1980s and in Sweden since the late 1990s. In other industrial countries, the potential for fiscal savings and efficiency improvements also exists—although the evidence is that savings are limited to the initial years, and common sense suggests that one cannot raise efficiency forever within the same production function.

In developing countries, before considering efficiency dividends, one must carefully review the country context. Efficiency dividends are different from inefficient across-the-board cuts only if adequate technical capacities are available in line ministries and the line ministries are willing to make their own hard choices. In those developing countries where the current budget is too inadequate to allow departments even to function normally (and the capital budget is determined largely by donor funding), the real question is not how to generate a gradual increase in efficiency, but how to restructure the public expenditure program by eliminating questionable programs altogether (and how to increase tax collection). Moreover, where evaluation capacity is weak, the risk that the efficiency dividends are achieved by diminishing service or program quality is very real. However, this practice may be an invaluable aid in introducing greater performance orientation to a complacent administrative system and in triggering more structural improvements. Spending agencies ought to be regularly asked during budget preparation whether they can provide the same level of services at lower cost without diluting quality and—more bluntly—whether some of the waste can be eliminated.

A subceiling for capital expenditure?

As discussed earlier, a separate budget preparation process for capital and current expenditure (dual budgeting) presents problems, but a separate presentation is desirable. Aside from that question, however, should separate ceilings for capital and current expenditures be set at the start of the budget preparation process? The answer depends on the sector concerned.

Obviously, if only a global ceiling is set, line ministries would be able to make tradeoffs between their current spending and their capital spending, and if separate ceilings are set, the distribution between current and capital spending would be fixed for each sector. In certain sectors, such as primary education, leaving the choice between current and capital spending partly to line ministries is generally preferable, because both current and capital expenditures are developmental, and line ministries presumably know better than the ministry of finance what would be the most efficient allocation of resources within their sector. In some cases, however, the sector budget depends largely on the decision whether to launch a large investment project. For example, the budget of a ministry of higher education would largely depend on the decision whether to construct a new university. Because such large investment projects are a government policy issue, not only a sectoral policy issue, separate ceilings would be appropriate in these cases. Depending on circumstances and fiscal policy issues, separate sub-ceilings may also be needed for other expenditure items, such as personnel expenditures and subsidies.

Division of Roles and Responsibilities: Finance and Planning

In the section discussing dual budgeting, the suggestion was made that, owing to a scarcity of skills and administrative capacity, African countries might do well to have a single ministry of finance and planning instead of two separate ministries. Recall, however, that this suggestion is simply a presumption, and such organizational issues must be decided mainly on the basis of the country's specific characteristics—including the political landscape. Also, however the division of labor is organized, the basic functions to be performed are the same. Moreover, recognizing and managing realistically financial constraints is as important as looking out for the long run and assisting the political leadership in formulating a vision for the country's equitable development. The organizational structure must therefore ensure that neither the long-run prospects nor those for the short term are neglected. It is critical to have a dedicated entity to handle financial issues and a separate one for long-term prospects. Financial stability is very different from stagnation, and a sound long-term development strategy is much more than a set of targets and wishes. Finally, because the short run and the long run are part of the same time continuum, the core institutional requirement is for close cooperation between the two entities, whether they are located in different ministries or under the same roof, as stressed earlier.

The Finance Function

The main roles of the entity responsible for finance are as follows:

- Advise the government on all domestic and international aspects of public finance.
- Propose a revenue, expenditure, and budgetary policy, consistent with the government's objectives, and manage the implementation of such a policy.
- Devise and manage an efficient system for government payments.
- Mobilize internal and external financial resources (in collaboration with the planning entity).
- Ensure an efficient financial regulatory framework to promote financial integrity and combat fraud and manipulation.
- Supervise all activities that entail an actual or contingent financial commitment for the state.
- Supervise the corporate governance of public enterprises and other nongovernmental public sector entities, and monitor their financial performance.
- Take all measures to protect state assets and encourage their best use.

In pursuit of these roles, the entity responsible for finance must do the following:

- Prepare the medium-term macroeconomic framework in consultation with the planning entity, consistent with broad government objectives, for government consideration and approval.
- Prepare the medium-term fiscal framework, consistent with the macro-economic framework and sectoral government policies, for government consideration and approval.
- Prepare the government budget, consistent with the medium-term fiscal framework, in consultation with the other government entities, but not sharing the responsibility.
- Ensure consistency between capital and current expenditures (in consultation with the planning entity).

■ Monitor the financial execution of the budget (in consultation with the planning entity).
■ Guide and coordinate activities in internal audit throughout the government.
■ Interact with the legislature and other concerned stakeholders on all these matters.

The Planning Function

The main roles of the entity responsible for planning (or economy) are as follows:

■ Prepare a medium- and long-term development strategy for government approval.
■ Prepare a poverty reduction strategy, consistent with the development strategy, for government approval.
■ Monitor implementation of these strategies and recommend adjustments.
■ Facilitate formation of a national policy on population and environment.
■ Coordinate foreign aid for development and poverty reduction (in collaboration with the ministry of finance).
■ Prepare the public investment program.
■ Coordinate and facilitate sectoral expenditure programs.
■ Monitor the physical execution of those programs (in collaboration with the ministry of finance).

A Simplified Organizational Structure

On the assumption of a single ministry of finance and planning, the appropriate organizational structure is shown in figure 8.1. If the country chooses separate ministries, the only required changes are to split the right side from the left side and to elevate each deputy minister to minister rank. In any case, the two need to have equal rank, even if one may carry seniority of one sort or another.

Budget Approval and the Role of the Legislature

The enactment of the budget should not merely be a formal exercise carried out to comply with the letter of the constitution. The legislature is the locus of overall political and financial accountability, and its role should go much beyond rubber-stamping decisions already taken.

Legal counsel -------------- MINISTER   ----------------- Secretariat

Deputy minister (finance)   Deputy minister (planning)

Macroeconomics   *Long-range planning*
  Policy analysis   Growth and trade
  Medium-term framework   Poverty reduction strategy
Aid management   Other crosscutting policies
Budget   *Public investment*
  Budget systems   Large projects evaluation
  Budget preparation   Sector coordination
  Budget execution   Public investment program
Treasury   Investment monitoring
  Debt management   *National economic database*
  Asset register   (joint with statistics bureau,
  Payments and cash management   which, however, must be
Revenue   totally autonomous)
  Customs
    Administration   *Regulation and facilitation*
    Investigation/inspections   Guidelines and manuals
  Domestic revenue   Technical assistance (on request)
    Policy, planning, statistics
    Operations (returns processing, collection, and so forth)
    Audit and taxpayer services
Financial regulation
Public enterprise monitoring
Accounting and reporting
Internal audit

Source: Author's representation.

FIGURE 8.1 Simplified Organizational Structure of a Combined
Ministry of Finance and Planning

Presentation of the Budget to the Legislature

To permit informed debate and approval, the budget should be presented to
the legislature in a timely manner—that is, two to four months before the
start of the fiscal year. In some countries, the budget is submitted to the legislature after the start of the fiscal year, owing to unavoidable delays in budget
preparation, change in the composition of the cabinet, or pending financial
negotiations with international financial institutions. In other countries,
however, delay is institutionalized, and the budget is systematically presented
to the legislature only days before the beginning of the fiscal year. This system puts the legislature in the impossible position of either preventing the

government from operating or giving formal approval to a budget of which it knows virtually nothing. In some extreme cases, the legislature does not meet to consider the budget until *after* the commencement of the fiscal year and is thus asked to give retroactive approval to a budget that is already being implemented. Systematic delays in presenting the proposed budget to the legislature are a symptom of grave governance problems.

Under special circumstances delays may be justified. The organic budget law (see chapter 2) should include provisions authorizing the executive to commit expenditures before the budget is approved, under explicit specified circumstances. These provisions should be based on the budget of the previous year, rather than on the new budget that has not yet been scrutinized. (An example is the continuing resolution used in the U.S. Congress, when the budget is not approved before the start of the fiscal year in October, to authorize the executive to commit each month up to one-twelfth of the appropriations of the previous year.) In all cases, in developing and industrial countries alike, care must be taken lest these special provisions be abused and become a systematic way to sidestep the normal budget process.

Individual members of the legislature have different preferences regarding the manner in which resources are allocated and are subject to a variety of pressures from their constituents. The sum of these various preferences and related claims can generate a systematic tendency to increase expenditure during budget debates (a phenomenon known as *logrolling*). Much worse is the practice of "pork," whereby certain expenditures are introduced in the budget by influential members of the legislature at the last minute, without any scrutiny of their economic and social viability and even without the knowledge of members of the legislature who vote on the final package. (In the United States, this practice has grown dramatically since 2000, reaching more than 13,000 different projects in 2005, accounting for a total of more than US$60 billion.)[7] Accordingly, many countries have adopted procedural rules to regulate and limit such practices. These rules cover the sequence of voting on the budget and the legislature's powers to amend the budget. In parliamentary systems with a clear majority of one party, the budget prepared by the executive is routinely approved by the legislature; in most parliamentary systems, legislative refusal to approve the budget is equivalent to a vote of no confidence and normally results in the resignation of the government.

To enforce ex ante fiscal discipline, in several countries, such as France, the budget is voted in two phases: the overall amount of the budget is voted first, and appropriations and allocation of resources among ministries are voted only in the second phase. This procedure is aimed at protecting the overall fiscal target and the aggregate expenditure limit. The real effect of this procedure is unclear because legislators can anticipate the incidence of the overall amount of the budget on their pet programs before the first vote and decide the overall amount accordingly (see Alesina and Perotti 1996). However, reviewing aggregate expenditures and revenues together has the advantage of allowing the legislature to discuss macroeconomic policy explicitly.

Legal powers of the legislature to amend the budget vary from one country to another. Three situations are possible:

1. *Unrestricted power* gives the legislature power to change both expenditure and revenue up or down, without the consent of the executive.[8] Some presidential systems (for example, in the United States and the Philippines) fit this model—although the "power of the purse" granted to the legislature is counterbalanced by a presidential veto. This situation implies substantial and direct legislative influence on the first two objectives of public expenditure management (fiscal discipline and expenditure allocation) as well as some indirect influence on the third (operational management).
2. *Restricted power* is the power to amend the budget but within set limits, often relating to a maximum increase in expenditures or decrease in revenues. The extent of these restricted powers varies from country to country. In France, the United Kingdom, and the British Commonwealth countries, parliaments are not allowed to propose amendments that increase expenditure and have very restricted powers to propose any other amendment. By contrast, Germany allows such amendments, but only with the consent of the executive. This situation implies very limited legislative influence on resource allocation and (indirectly) on operational management.
3. *Balanced power* is the ability to raise or lower expenditures or revenues as long as a counterbalancing measure maintains the budget balance. This intermediate arrangement, known in the United States as PAYGO, channels legislative influence to the sectoral allocation of resources, where it is more appropriate.

Limits on the power of the legislature to amend the budget are particularly needed where legislative debates lead systematically to increased expenditures, as was the case in a number of former Soviet republics in the 1990s. The organic budget law should stipulate that legislative actions that increase expenditures can take effect only if these expenditures themselves are authorized in the budget or its supplementary acts. However, these limits should never hamper legislative review of the budget. In some countries, the budgetary role of the legislature may need to be increased rather than limited.

Strong and capable committees enable the legislature to develop its expertise and play a greater role in budget decision making. Generally, different committees deal with different facets of public expenditure management. For example, the finance or budget committee reviews revenues and expenditures, a public accounts committee ensures legislative oversight (and the supreme audit institution normally reports to the public accounts committee), and sectoral or standing committees deal with sector policy and may review sector budgets. In countries where the role of the legislature in amending the budget is significant, amendments are usually prepared by committees rather than proposed on the floor by individual members.

The time allocated for the legislative budget process and, within this process, for committee reviews is important for a sound scrutiny of the budget and informed debate. The budget debate lasts up to 75 days in India's Lok Sabha; in the German Bundestag, it may last up to four months; in the U.S. Congress, it sometimes lasts even longer.

The legislature and its committees should have access to independent expertise for proper budget scrutiny. In India, for example, parliamentary committees are supported with secretarial functions, and legislators have access to the parliament library and associated research and reference services; the U.S. Congress benefits from the competent staff of the appropriations committees and the services of the large and well-equipped Congressional Budget Office, as well as assistance from the Government Accountability Office with audits and information on program compliance and performance.

Legislative committees should have access to administrative information. In Germany, the budget committee interacts quasi-permanently with government departments through regular departmental briefings and expenditure reports. In India, the Public Accounts Committee receives reports and departmental accounts and revenue receipts from the comptroller and the auditor general (although this interaction concerns the oversight function of the parliament, rather than budget preparation and approval). Regular consultations between the administration and the legislative committees on budget policies and their implementation strengthen the capacity of the legislature to review the budget and, after approval, increase the legitimacy of the budget and thus the authority of the executive to implement it rigorously.

Budget Amendments and Reallocations

The general principle is that any amendment of the budget during budget execution should receive legislative approval in the same way as the budget is originally approved. In practice, too many amendments during the year weaken the credibility of the budget; nonetheless, in the fluid conditions of most African developing countries, precluding any amendment would be quite impractical. In general, budget amendments should be limited to once or twice a year, which should be brought to the legislature as a package of proposed changes instead of the inefficient practice of requesting approval of each individual change.

On reallocations, procedures differ between parliamentary systems, where the executive is a creature of the legislature, and presidential systems. In general, however, any reallocation between ministries should be in the form of a budget amendment and require approval by the legislature— because the individual ministers are theoretically accountable for the use of the resources. (However, in the organic budget law or at the time of budget approval, it is possible to specify that legislative approval is not required if a change in appropriations between ministries does not exceed a specified percentage of the budgeted amount.)

Within the budgetary appropriation to a given ministry, the executive branch should be generally free to reallocate as it judges best. Naturally, pragmatic rules should define the level of authority required for different types of changes. Such rules, normally promulgated by executive decree or administrative instruction, should specify that certain minor reallocations required for operational reasons (for example, between different types of current supplies) can be effected on the sole authority of the department head concerned; more significant changes (for example, between current supplies and durable goods) can be effected by the line minister; and still more important ones (for example, from durable goods to fuel) will require ministry of finance approval if they exceed a specified percentage of authorized expenditure.

Reallocations between budget categories (for example, from salaries to operations and maintenance) may or may not require prior legislative approval, depending on the country, but the legislature should always be notified on a timely basis and have the opportunity to raise questions or objections. Simple disclosure after the fact is not sufficient. However, in many African countries, which are implementing a civil service reform program or have other understandings with international organizations on the level and composition of subsidies, reallocations between budget categories without prior consultation are normally precluded by the logic of the reform program or by the understandings with international institutions. Generally, in African developing countries such reallocations between major budget heads are highly undesirable without express approval by the legislature and, if and when appropriate, consultation with international partners.

The situation is different for investment projects, because their pluri-annual nature and uncertainties require giving the executive branch more flexibility in the timing of expenditure. In addition to projects, for a program (that is, a collection of complementary activities aimed at the same objective but with different individual allocations) the line ministry must have the authority to shift resources between activities—again with ministry of finance approval if the reallocation goes beyond a certain percentage of authorized expenditure. Instead, reallocations between large projects or between major programs would normally call for some form of consultation with the legislature, and reallocations between ministries should require a formal budget amendment.

In actual practice, much depends on the quality of overall governance. Aside from the appropriate procedures for approving and amending the budget and the rules for reallocations during the year, in a healthy governance system consultations between the executive and the various legislative committees are substantive, continuous, and not limited to one-off events such as the budget debate or the presentation of a supplementary budget. When this situation prevails, and external participation by civil society is provided for as well, a broad understanding of the reasons for budgetary decisions is generated, conflict and dissension are minimized, and a much higher probability exists that a good budget is executed well.

Notes

This chapter is based in part on material in Salvatore Schiavo-Campo and Daniel Tommasi's (1999) *Managing Government Expenditure*, Asian Development Bank, Manila, by permission. The views expressed in the publication are those of the authors and do not necessarily represent those of the Asian Development Bank or its Board of Directors or the governments the directors represent. For information related to development in Asia and the Pacific, see http://www.adb.org.

1. Such a perspective has been referred to at various times as indicative of multiyear programming, medium-term public expenditure programs, multiyear estimates, and a medium-term expenditure framework. The *medium-term expenditure framework* designation is currently used most frequently and is used in this chapter as well.

2. The reader familiar with statistical inference will recognize here the well-known tradeoff, for a given sample size, between the precision of a statistical estimate and its probability of containing the true value, with narrow-band estimates being more precise but less likely to include the true value for the population and wide-band estimates more likely to be correct but more vague as well.

3. Aside from the legacy of the planning practices of the past, other factors contributed to dual budgeting, such as pressure or recommendations from donors or international finance institutions. The desire of donors to "enclave" their projects, to minimize risks of mismanagement and maximize provision of counterpart funding, has

also increased the fragmentation of the budget system. For example, at the recommendation of international finance institutions, Romania attempted in 1993 to 1997 to implement an investment coordination unit outside the Ministry of Finance to prepare the capital budget and screen projects through its own investment department. "A frequently debated issue in the World Bank is the tendency to 'enclave' . . . inherent in any project-centered approach to lending. But they reduce the pressure on government to reform, and they may weaken domestic systems by replacing them with donor-mandated procedures" (World Bank 1997: 54).

4. Only the substance is provided here, leaving out various organizational recommendations and other purely internal considerations.

5. For a brief and readable summary, see the article on the subject by the main architect of the model, Jacques Polak (1997). For a fuller description of the technical aspects of a macroeconomic framework, see Davis (1992) and Martin and others (1996).

6. For an early definition of the issue, see Kopits and Symansky (1998).

7. In January 2007, the U.S. Congress approved new rules to require, among other things, identification of the members of Congress sponsoring each "earmark." If these rules come into effect and are enforced, they will make a major contribution to restraining this fiscally and economically wasteful practice.

8. The U.S. Congress attempts to restrict its own power through the annual budget resolution, which contains an overall spending cap as well as spending targets for congressional committees. Among other things, the pay-as-you-go (or PAYGO) rule prescribed that new expenditures or tax reductions could be made only to the extent that expenditures were cut or revenues raised elsewhere. (This budget rule should not be confused with the pay-as-you-go system of funding pensions or health funds, as contrasted to a fully funded system, whereby funds are set aside in advance to meet 100 percent of all foreseeable obligations.) These restrictions, however, are self-imposed and can be lifted at any time by legislative action; they are thus different from a restriction imposed from outside the legislature. Indeed, the PAYGO rule was not applied in the United States after 2001, a fact that was partly responsible for the historic levels of fiscal deficit in the country (see also the discussion of fiscal responsibility). As of early 2007, prospects are good for a restoration of the rule.

References

Alesina, Alberto, and Roberto Perotti. 1996. "Budget Deficits and Budget Institutions." NBER Working Paper 5556, National Bureau of Economic Research, Cambridge, MA.

Blejer, Mario, and Adrienne Cheasty. 1993. "The Deficit as an Indicator of Government Solvency: Changes in the Public Sector Net Worth." In *How to Measure the Fiscal Deficit: Analytical and Methodological Issues*, ed. Mario Blejer and Adrienne Cheasty, 279–96. Washington, DC: International Monetary Fund.

Davis, Jeffrey J., ed. 1992. *Macroeconomic Adjustment: Policy Instruments and Issues*. Washington, DC: International Monetary Fund.

Fölscher, Alta, and Neil Cole. 2004. "South Africa: Transition to Democracy Offers Opportunity for Whole System Reform." In *Budget Reform Seminar: Country Case Studies*, ed. Alta Fölscher, 109–46. Pretoria: National Treasury of South Africa.

Holmes, Malcolm. n.d. "Ghana, Issues in MTEF." World Bank, Washington, DC. http://www.worldbank.org/publicsector/pe/GH.doc.

IMF (International Monetary Fund). 2004. "Ghana: Report on the Observance of Standards and Codes—Fiscal Transparency Module." IMF Country Report 04/203. Washington, DC: IMF.

———. 2005. "Morocco: Report on Observance of Standards and Codes—Fiscal Transparency Module." IMF Country Report 05/298. Washington, DC: IMF.

Kopits, George, and Steven A. Symansky. 1998. "Fiscal Policy Rules." IMF Occasional Paper 162. Washington, DC: International Monetary Fund.

Martin, Michael, S. Rajcoomar, John R. Karlik, Michael W. Bell, and Charles A. Sisson. 1996. *Financial Programming and Policy: The Case of Sri Lanka.* Washington, DC: IMF.

Mountfield, Ed. 2001. "High Priority Development Expenditures." Internal memorandum, South Asia Region, World Bank, April 17.

Polak, Jacques. 1997. "The IMF Monetary Model: A Hardy Perennial." *Finance and Development* 34 (4): 16–19.

Potter, Barry. 2000. "Medium-Term Expenditure Framework Debate." Debate at Poverty Reduction and Economic Management (PREM) Week, University of Maryland Conference Center, College Park, MD, November 21. http://www1.worldbank.org/publicsector/pe/mtefpremweek.htm.

Schiavo-Campo, Salvatore, and Daniel Tommasi. 1999. *Managing Government Expenditure.* Manila: Asian Development Bank.

Short, John. 2003. "Country Case Study 4: Assessment of the MTEF in Ghana." Overseas Development Institute, London.

WAEMU (West African Economic and Monetary Union). 2005. *Rapport semestriel d'exécution de la surveillance multilatérale.* Ouagadougou: WAEMU.

World Bank. 1997. *Helping Countries Combat Corruption: The Role of the World Bank.* Washington, DC: World Bank.

9

Budget Execution

DANIEL TOMMASI

Budget execution is the phase when resources are used to implement policies incorporated in the budget. A well-formulated budget can be poorly implemented, but a badly formulated budget cannot be implemented well. Good budget preparation comes first. Budget execution procedures must ensure compliance with the initial programming, but they are not simply mechanisms for ensuring compliance. Successful budget execution depends on numerous other factors, such as the ability to deal with changes in the macroeconomic environment, the implementation capacities of the agencies concerned, and the problems met in program implementation. Hence, efficient budget execution calls for (a) ensuring that the budget will be implemented in conformity with the legislature's authorizations, (b) adapting the execution of the budget to changes in the economic environment, (c) resolving problems met in program implementation, (d) procuring goods and services and managing efficiently, and (e) preventing any risk of abuse and corruption.

This chapter reviews the following issues:

- Stages of the budget execution cycle
- Basic compliance controls
- Issues related to the management and monitoring of budget execution
- Conditions for efficiency in cash management
- How to address the current weaknesses in the existing systems in Africa.

279

The Budget Execution Cycle

The expenditure budget execution cycle includes the following stages:

- Authorization and apportionment of appropriations to spending units
- Commitment
- Acquisition and verification (at this stage, liabilities are recognized)
- Issuance of a payment order
- Payment.

The Authorization and Apportionment Stage

After the budget is approved by the legislative body, spending units are authorized to spend money through various mechanisms, such as ministry of finance warrants, decrees, and apportionment plans. This authorization is generally granted for the entire fiscal year, but in several British Commonwealth countries it is granted for shorter periods (for example, the authorization to spend may be granted quarterly for goods and services). In some countries, the authorization procedure may include two steps:

1. A warrant or a decree authorizes line ministries to use the appropriations or a part of the appropriations.
2. Line ministries (or main spending units) apportion the authorization to spend to their subordinate spending units.

Sometimes, the ministry of finance uses this authorization procedure to freeze a part of the approved appropriations. Such a procedure could indicate prudent budget management, but its implementation too often stems from the fact that hard choices have been brought forward from budget preparation to budget execution.

Funds should be allocated to spending units as soon as the budget is approved. However, in some countries, the apportionment procedure can take several weeks. In particular, in several francophone countries, funds allocated to remote spending units can be available only during the second quarter of the fiscal year. This practice is generally a major source of inefficiencies that should be addressed.

The Commitment Stage

The commitment stage is when a future obligation to pay is incurred. This stage is very important in budget management, because at this time expenditure decisions become effective. In practice, however, what constitutes a commitment in budget management varies from one country to another and depends on the nature of the expenditure.

Generally, for goods and services as well as for investment expenditures, the *commitment* in the budgetary sense should be defined as the legal commitment, which consists of placing an order or awarding a contract for delivery of specified goods, services, or physical assets. Such a commitment entails an obligation to pay (a liability) only when the supplier has complied with the provisions of the contract. If the goods are not delivered or the services not rendered, the commitment will not entail a liability, and it should be written off. This last situation is comparatively frequent in countries with a weak private sector and a poorly organized budget system. Also, committing expenditures does not mean that all related payments should be made within the same fiscal year. For investment expenditure in particular, the legal commitments may cover a multiyear period.

For debt service, personnel expenditures, transfers, and also some categories of expenditure on goods and services (such as consumption of electricity and telecommunication services), the obligation to pay comes from an event upstream or outside the expenditure budget execution cycle (staff recruitment, disbursement of a loan, office heating, and so forth). In such cases, the commitment in the budgetary sense corresponds generally to the stage at which a new liability is recognized (for example, the monthly wage bill, interest due, or electricity charges). Consequently, for those categories of expenditures, the commitment stage and the verification stage, described below, are combined in the budget execution cycle.

Sometimes, the commitment in the budgetary sense is only a reservation of appropriation, that is, a request from a spending unit to the budget authority to put aside an allotment for a future expenditure or to subordinate units.[1] In other countries, liabilities are termed commitments, and no distinction is made between the verification stage, discussed below, and the commitment stage.

For a multiyear expenditure project (for example, a road project), the term *commitment* refers in many countries to either the incurred liabilities[2] (for example, the invoices) or the annual tranche of the multiyear legal commitment (for example, the road-building work planned for the fiscal year), not to the legal commitment itself (for example, a multiyear contract for building the road). Monitoring the commitments is very important for cash planning and program management, to prevent any risk of budget overruns and arrears, but this oversight requires defining properly and clearly what is a commitment. For budget administration and expenditure control, commitment in the budgetary sense should correspond to the earliest stage within the expenditure cycle at which a claim against the appropriation can be recognized. The commitment should be defined as (a) the legal commitment, when it makes sense to define the commitment in the budgetary sense on this basis, and (b) expenditures at the verification stage for other items (personnel, debt servicing, utilities bills, and transfers). Therefore, the commitment in the budgetary sense preferably should be defined as follows:

- For personnel expenditures and social contributions, the commitment should correspond to the amount of the compensations, allowances, and contributions due.
- For goods and services, the commitment should generally correspond to the legal commitment, which consists of placing an order or awarding a contract. However, in some special cases, the commitment in the budgetary sense may correspond to the liability, and the commitment stage and the verification stage may be combined. These special cases may concern (a), by necessity, expenditures such as utilities consumption and some other expenditures arising from the execution of medium- and long-term rental contracts and (b), for convenience, petty expenditures and low-cost purchases.
- For debt service, the commitments over a period should correspond to the debt service due over the same period.
- For transfers, what is a commitment may depend on the nature of the transfer. For example, concerning scholarships, the commitments should correspond to the amounts due (as for personnel expenditures), but concerning transfers that are not related to a contract or a formal promise, the commitment may correspond to the stage at which a payment order is issued.
- For investment expenditures, the same definition as for goods and services should preferably be used. The commitment should correspond to the contract. For multiyear contracts, the definition of the commitment varies from one country to another, but, whatever the budgetary jargon, the following elements should be systematically monitored and accounted for: (a) the legal commitment (the contract), which can be of a multiyear nature; (b) the annual tranche of the legal commitment; and (c) the expenditures at the verification stage (the liabilities arising from the execution of the legal commitment).

Because what is a commitment may depend on the economic category of the expenditure, its definition should be precisely indicated in the financial regulations, expenditure category by expenditure category.

To monitor and control effectively commitments related to multiyear projects, the organic budget law of many francophone countries stipulates that the budget should include, for multiyear programs and projects, both *payment appropriations* and *commitment authorizations*,[3] although, in practice, this differentiated authorization system is implemented in only a few African countries. A commitment authorization gives the upper limit of the amount of the contracts that can be passed for a multiyear project during the fiscal year. It authorizes only passing the contracts. It does not authorize the payments. The payment appropriation gives the amount that can be paid during the fiscal year. Setting up in the budget or in an annexed document commitment authorization for multiyear projects will reinforce expenditure control and planning.

The Verification Stage

The verification stage immediately follows the deliveries. It consists of verifying the conformity of the delivered goods, or rendered services, and the bill with the contract or the order and recognizing the debt toward a third party (the supplier). As noted, for debt service, personnel expenditures, and a few other expenditure items, the verification stage and the commitment phase are combined.

At the verification stage, assets and liabilities of the government are increased and recorded in the books, if the country has an accrual—or a modified accrual—accounting system. Expenditures at the verification stage should be taken into account in the calculation of the net lending/borrowing balance, as defined in the International Monetary Fund (IMF) Statistics Department's *Government Finance Statistics Manual* (IMF 2001).[4]

Even though it represents an accrued liability, the verified expenditure may not yet represent a cash liability when a 30-day or 60-day grace period is included under the terms of the purchase order. Recording expenditures at the verification stage differs from accounting on the due-for-payment basis, which would consist of recognizing the expenditures at the latest times they can be paid without incurring additional charges or penalties or, if sooner, when the cash payment is made.[5]

Recognizing expenditures on a timely basis requires goods and services to be verified as soon as they are delivered. Actually, in some countries, physical deliveries can precede verification by some period of time. Such weaknesses should be identified and addressed.

The Payment Order Stage

When the goods and services are verified, the authorizing officer issues a payment order, which is forwarded to the officer responsible for making the payment. In the francophone budget systems, the budgetary expenditure is recognized and recorded at this stage, both in the books of the public accountant and in the books of the authorizing officer whether the payment order will be immediately paid or not.

The Payment Stage

The bill is paid by cash, check, or electronic funds transfer. Payments through checks are, in most countries, recorded when checks are issued. Comparisons with bank statements should be systematically carried out, at least monthly. Many countries do not make these comparisons and should address this issue. In many African anglophone countries, the budgetary expenditure is recognized and accounted for in the books only at this stage.

When the float of unpaid checks is significant, payments must also be reported on the basis of checks paid. In some African anglophone budget systems, in order to bypass the annual rule (described shortly), some accountants issue checks at the end of the year that cannot be immediately paid. Such a practice leads to high fiduciary risks.

The organization of the payment system and the related distribution of responsibilities are discussed later in this chapter.

Controlling Compliance in Budget Execution

The basic compliance controls during budget execution are the following:

- At the commitment stage (financial control), verify that (a) the proposal to spend money has been approved by an authorized person, (b) money has been appropriated for the purpose stated in the budget, (c) sufficient funds remain available in the appropriate category of expenditure, and (d) the expenditure is classified in the correct way.
- When goods and services are delivered (verification), the documentary evidence that the goods have been received or that the services were carried out as required must be verified.
- Before payment is made, confirm that (a) the expenditure has been properly committed; (b) a competent person has signified that the goods have been received or that the service has been carried out as expected; (c) the invoice and other documents requesting payment are complete, correct, and suitable for payment; and (d) the creditor is correctly identified.
- After final payment is made (audit), examine and scrutinize the expenditure concerned and report any irregularity.

The distribution of responsibilities in carrying out these regularity controls is discussed later, but whatever agency is responsible for carrying out these basic controls, they must always be carried out.

The commitment control is particularly important because it can prevent blatant cases of misuse of appropriations, overspending, and irregularities. In the African anglophone budget systems, commitments are, in principle, monitored by spending units, but data on commitments are not systematically available at the ministry of finance level. To address these weaknesses, some anglophone countries are implementing a commitment control system with the support of the IMF (see box 9.1). However, results are still uneven (see box 9.2). As discussed later, the issues related to commitment control are of a different nature in francophone budget systems.

BOX 9.1 The IMF-Proposed Approach to Commitment Controls in Anglophone Budget Systems

The key objective of commitment control is to require spending ministries to focus on controlling the initial incurrence of liabilities rather than the subsequent cash payments.

The key elements of a commitment control system are as follows:

■ Each line ministry sends to the ministry of finance a quarterly expenditure plan supported by projected monthly cash requirements. On the basis of annual and quarterly cash plans, the ministry of finance issues quarterly expenditure ceilings, along with the projected amounts of monthly cash release to line ministries, before the beginning of each quarter.

■ The line ministries must limit the commitments to the level of quarterly expenditure ceilings and keep planned payments within monthly cash release.

■ The line ministries prepare a monthly report on outstanding commitments and unpaid bills and submit it to the ministry of finance.

■ Each line ministry should have a commitment control officer (usually the controlling or accounting officer) who is responsible for managing the system.

■ Detailed procedures for approval of commitments, payment, and accounting are issued. The onus is on the commitment control officer to ensure that commitments entered into are consistent with the quarterly ceilings—without incurring any payment arrears.

Source: IMF 2006a.

BOX 9.2 Implementing Commitment Control Systems

Uganda

In Uganda, the package of measures included (a) implementing a commitment control system (CCS) for nonwage recurrent expenditures for all central ministries and departments in July 1999; (b) introducing the CCS for development expenditure effective October 2000; (c) maintaining quarterly expenditure ceilings, fully backed by monthly cash releases, on the basis of improved cash management; (d) providing adequate funds for priority and essential budget items and more realistic budget estimates; (e) creating public awareness through the media about the CCS and the responsibility of accounting officers to pay bills within 30 days; (f) strengthening internal audit and inspection to enforce compliance and improve the quality of commitment data; and (g) comprehensively auditing the stock of arrears by the auditor general and implementing a strategy for their liquidation. At the end of the first year of implementation of these measures, new nonwage arrears were reduced by nearly 70 percent compared with the previous financial year; in the subsequent years, the gains were maintained. Areas of concern still exist, however. New arrears have been generated in 2004/05, albeit moderately (by 0.2 percent of gross domestic product), if newly verified arrears from previous years are excluded (1.7 percent of gross domestic product).

The following table shows that stock of arrears. These arrears come mainly from items such as pensions, salaries, court awards, and rents, which must be reviewed or sufficiently funded at the budget preparation stage.

Verified Domestic Arrears, End-June 2005

Indicator	Pensions	Wages	Court awards	Other[a]	Total
U Sh billion	304	20	62	187	573
Percentage of gross domestic product	2.0	0.1	0.4	1.2	3.9

Source: Data from the Ugandan Ministry of Finance, Planning, and Economic Management.
a. Includes arrears on payments for utilities, rents, membership fees to international organizations, and other mainly nonstatutory payments.

Zambia and Malawi

Considerable difficulties arose in implementing a CCS in Zambia and Malawi.

In Zambia, the CCS was not effective because implementation was difficult beyond the recording and monitoring of outstanding commitments and unpaid bills, which were needed to control commitments, and the CCS was not combined with other supporting measures.

In Malawi, the CCS introduced was very similar to the one used in Uganda. Despite some initial progress in recording and reporting expenditure commitments and audit of arrears, the accumulation of new arrears was not affected. The system has not progressed further because of noncompliance by the spending agencies and lack of enforcement and penalties by the ministry of finance. Political neglect and lack of institutional capacity have also undermined reform efforts.

Sources: IMF 2006a, 2006b.

Notwithstanding those efforts, financial control of commitments is not sufficient to keep expenditures under control. As shown by figure 9.1, commitments may be made through different channels, which in a number of cases are upstream from the annual budget execution cycle. For example, controls on the consumption of utilities—such as electricity and telecommunications, which represent a significant part of the government's current expenditure—need to reinforce internal management systems, not necessarily the budgetary procedures. Control of overruns on the investment programs requires monitoring of multiyear commitments, which is not systematically done. Contingent liabilities and other fiscal risks may lead to budget overruns if they are not assessed and taken into account during budget preparation.

In a number of anglophone countries, for certain programs (for example, unemployment benefits), moneys are appropriated by specific acts of parliament called *special and standing appropriations*, not by the annual appropriation act. These appropriations do not lapse at the end of the fiscal year. *Standing appropriation* refers to open-ended appropriation, the amount spent depending on the demand for payments by claimants satisfying program eligibility criteria specified in the legislation. Similarly, in the francophone budget systems, besides *limited appropriations*, which give expenditure ceilings, the budget includes *open-ended estimated appropriations*, but this last category of appropriation is used only for debt service and a very few special expenditure items, such as legal costs. Controlling legal commitments authorized by standing appropriations or estimated appropriations requires decisions upstream from the annual budget execution cycle.

More generally, keeping expenditure under control requires, in addition to controlling the uses of annual appropriations, the following:

- Sound budget formulation and policy decision to ensure the conformity of permanent commitments with budget forecasts
- Control of multiyear commitments

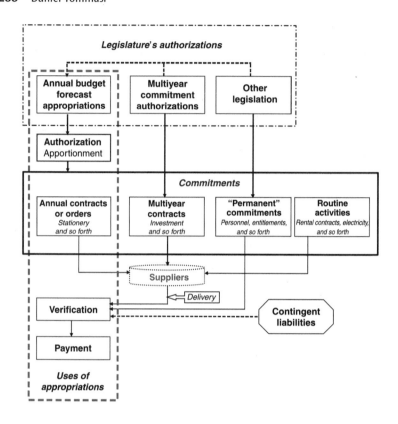

Source: Adapted from Allen and Tommasi 2001.

FIGURE 9.1 Implementation of Budgetary Expenditure

- Good administration, because many liabilities arise, in practice, from routine activities or informal procedures (for example, telephone calls) rather than from formal contracts or orders
- An effective and comprehensive internal control system, which should cover all key systems and procedures in government agencies (notably, besides financial controls, personnel controls and procurement procedures)
- Internal audit to ensure that the controls are in place and function effectively.

Managing and Monitoring Budget Execution

This section covers the distribution of responsibilities for budget execution, budget appropriation management rules and budget revisions, various special issues related to budget execution, and the monitoring of budget execution.

Distribution of Responsibilities

Budget execution covers both activities related to the implementation of policies and tasks related to the administration of the budget. Both the central agencies (the ministry of finance, the ministry of planning in a dual-budgeting system, and the prime minister's office) and the spending agencies are involved in these tasks. The distribution of responsibilities in budget management should be organized according to the agencies' respective areas of responsibility and accountability.

The responsibilities of the ministry of finance and line ministries

The ministry of finance should have the following responsibilities:

- Concerning the control of budget execution, administering the system of release of funds (warrants, budget implementation plan, and the like); preparing the in-year financial plan; monitoring expenditure flow; preparing in-year budget revisions; managing the central payment system (if any) or supervising government bank accounts; administering the central payroll system (if any); and preparing accounts and financial reports
- Concerning policy implementation, reviewing progress independently or jointly with spending agencies, identifying policy revisions as appropriate, and proposing to the council of ministers reallocations of resources, within the framework authorized by the legislative body.

The spending units should have the following responsibilities:

- Concerning budget administration, allocating funds among their subordinate units, making commitments, purchasing and procuring goods and services, verifying the goods and services acquired, preparing requests for payment (and making payments if the payment system is not centralized), preparing progress reports, monitoring performance indicators, and keeping accounts and financial records
- Concerning policy implementation, periodically reviewing the implementation of the relevant program, identifying problems and implementing appropriate solutions, and reallocating resources among sector activities within the policy framework of the budget.

When several departments in the ministry of finance and other central agencies are involved in the supervision of budget execution, close coordination of their activities is required, and their respective functions should be clearly delineated. In particular, in many countries, coordination between the budget department of the ministry of finance, which is responsible for budget preparation, and the treasury, which is primarily responsible for budget execution, is often insufficient. The budget department should be responsible not only for preparing the budget but also preparing budget revisions and reallocating resources among sectors. The treasury should provide the department with all the information it needs related to budget execution.

Problems may arise concerning the allocation of responsibilities between the central departments of the line ministries and their subordinate agencies. In some countries, continuous interference by the central departments in the management of projects and programs impedes the effective implementation of these programs. In other countries, powerful agencies implement programs without reporting to their parent ministries. The distribution of responsibilities within line ministries needs to be clarified to ensure that the central departments are fully responsible for coordinating sector policy and that subordinate agencies carry out their activities under the supervision of these departments but without unnecessary interference in day-to-day administration.

The principle of separation of duties

The principle of separation of duties is a powerful internal control device. It states that duties (roles) should be assigned to individuals in such a manner that no one individual can control a process from start to finish. Everyone occasionally makes mistakes. Separation of duties provides a complementary check by another individual. It allows an opportunity for someone to catch an error before a transaction is fully executed or before a decision is made on the basis of potentially erroneous data. In addition, having adequate separation of duties reduces the opportunity factor that might encourage an employee to commit fraud or to embezzle.

Thus, according to this principle, the implementation of the budget rests on the existence of three different functions, which must be performed separately by the authorizing officer, accountant,[6] and financial controller.

■ The authorizing officer *administers the appropriations.* He or she has the power to commit the expenditure and to authorize the payment. The authorizing officer is subject to disciplinary action and may be held financially liable if he or she fails to comply with financial regulations or neglects tasks relating to his or her function.
■ The accountant *makes the payments.* He or she is the only person empowered to handle moneys and other assets and is also responsible for their safekeeping. The accountant is subject to disciplinary action and may be held financially liable for payments in which a procedural error is detected.

■ The financial controller *checks the legality of operations.* He or she checks the commitment and authorization of all expenditure and ensures that revenue, if any, is properly collected. The financial controller checks whether all procedures were carried out, all authorizations obtained, and all necessary signatures obtained. To carry out this task, the financial controller has access to all the necessary documents and information. The financial controller is subject to disciplinary action and may be held financially liable if he or she approves expenditure in excess of the budget appropriations.

Comparison between African budget systems

Significant differences exist between the francophone and anglophone budget systems in the application of the principle of separation of duties and, more generally, in the distribution of responsibilities in budget execution management. These differences center particularly on the role and powers of the ministry of finance and the degree of delegation of financial management to spending units.

FRANCOPHONE SYSTEMS. The separation between the authorizing officer *(ordonnateur)* and the public accountant is a fundamental principle of the French system. It applies for both expenditure and revenue (revenue assessment is separated from revenue collection). This principle is an extension of the principle of separation of duties discussed earlier, which in many other budget systems is an internal control principle.

The public accountant, who makes the payments, does not report to the authorizing officer. He or she is a staff member of the ministry of finance's treasury (or public accounts) department. The public accountant is empowered to reject any irregular payment orders issued by the authorizing officer. He or she has special duties and is personally responsible, in his or her own money, for compliance and administrative errors. The payment orders are recorded both in the books of the public accountant and in the books of the authorizing officer. In principle, the authorizing officer and the public accountant should reconcile their books at the end of the accounting period. However, this reconciliation process is not always undertaken, as shown by the frequent discrepancies between those two sets of data on payment orders.

In France and in Maghreb countries, line-ministry managers are authorizing officers; however, in the majority of Sub-Saharan francophone countries, the payment orders are issued by a department of the ministry of finance, usually the budget department. The principle of the separation between the authorizing officer and the public accountant still applies, but between two departments of the ministry of finance, which concentrates the authorizing and paying functions, not between the line ministry and the treasury department of the ministry of finance.

In addition, ministry of finance or third-party controls are performed at different stages of the expenditure cycle:

- Commitments are controlled ex ante by the financial controller, who in many countries is a ministry of finance officer, posted within line ministries. In some countries (for example, Tunisia), the financial controller reports to the prime minister, not to the ministry of finance.
- Verification is generally made by line ministries, but in some countries, the financial controller is also involved in the verification.
- Payment orders are prepared by line ministries, but, as previously noted, in most Sub-Saharan francophone countries they are issued by the ministry of finance.
- Payment orders are controlled in a number of countries by the financial controller.
- Payment orders are systematically controlled by the treasury department.
- Payments of domestically funded expenditures are made by the treasury department of the ministry of finance.

Controls overlap. Thus, the request for payment prepared by line ministries can be controlled two or three times by ministry of finance departments (financial controller, budget department responsible for issuing the payment orders, and the treasury department). These numerous third-party ex ante controls lead to excessive interference of central agencies in the day-to-day management of line ministries. They may also cause delays in budget implementation and hinder efficient management. Despite this centralization of financial management powers within the ministry of finance, rejections of the issued payment orders are numerous. The treasury officials can reject for "irregularity" payment orders issued by the ministry of finance's budget department and sometimes also controlled by the ministry of finance's financial controller. In countries with poor systems of governance, multiplying controls has perverse effects and increases corruption, as unofficial tolls or levies are imposed at the different checkpoints. For example, centralization of payment decisions within the treasury in a period of cash shortages increases favoritism, with payments being prioritized in favor of well-connected suppliers instead of high-priority sectors.

Tight and cumbersome control rules have the perverse effect of generating special procedures for circumventing them. Various forms of special payment orders are used, which are generally not properly documented. In some cases, these special payment orders are controlled against the appropriations, and their issuance could be explained by the slowness of the normal procedure. In other cases, however, they are not controlled against the appropriations, but they may be issued at the request of the highest political levels. Special payment orders are paid by the treasury department, which centralizes all cash payments. They are registered in the treasury accounts, but in a credit or in a suspense account—not in the budgetary expenditure accounts. They are supposed to be "regularized" later as budgetary expenditures, but the regularization procedure is not systematically undertaken. In some countries, special payment orders, not accounted for in the appropriation accounts, can amount to a significant share of goods and services expenditure. As a result, budget execution is not monitored, and priorities stated in the budget are distorted in favor of sectors managed by powerful politicians and well-connected suppliers.

Although numerous and redundant, the ex ante ministry of finance controls do not prevent arrears generation not only because, as discussed earlier, expenditures are committed in different ways, but also because the control procedures are not systematically enforced. In addition, integration of in-year cash management systems with budget execution controls procedures is weak.

COMMONWEALTH SYSTEMS. In anglophone countries, financial control before the payment stage is largely assigned to line ministries. The accounting officer, who is generally the head of the line-ministry administration (the *permanent secretary*), has the authority to set up the arrangements for making expenditure commitments and issuing the payment order. He or she is accountable for budget management in his or her area of responsibilities.

Budget execution is often regulated through warrants issued by the ministry of finance or through cash releases to imprest accounts (imprest systems are discussed later). For example, annual warrants can be provided for salaries, and quarterly or monthly warrants can be provided for other current expenditures. In principle, expenditure commitments are recorded against the appropriations in the ministry or department books and should be reported to the ministry of finance. As previously noted, however, in several countries the ministries' reports on expenditure commitments are incomplete and received late by the ministry of finance; as a consequence, the ministry of finance is unable to exercise control over expenditure commitments.

With weak accounting and poor coordination between budget and accounting divisions of line ministries, expenditure commitments can be made without reference to cash availability and may even exceed voted appropriations. In the 1990s and 2000s, several countries implemented cash budget systems to ensure stability of the macroeconomic and fiscal systems, but in many cases, this procedure led to increased arrears (see box 9.3).

The anglophone systems provide managers with more flexibility in budget management, and the budget execution system is less cumbersome than the francophone system. Decentralization of powers is appropriate,

---

BOX 9.3 Cash Budgeting

In the 1990s and early 2000s, several countries adopted cash budgeting systems. Although the specifics of these arrangements differ from country to country, they have two general characteristics:

- First, monitoring of cash disbursements is the main expenditure control mechanism rather than monitoring of commitments entered into by line ministries.
- Second, provisions exist for planned cash disbursements to be reviewed at regular intervals to allow for swift fiscal policy adjustments in response to unexpected shortfalls in tax revenue or donor finance.

When strictly implemented, cash budgeting is a very effective method of eliminating a fiscal deficit and maintaining macroeconomic stability. However, when budget releases are not predictable, public sector managers cannot be held to account for the performance of their programs (Stasavage and Moyo 1999). This shortcoming undermines the budget-policy link.

A review of Zambia's experience during the past decade by Dinh, Adugna, and Myers (2002) concludes that after some initial success in reducing hyperinflation, the cash budget has largely failed to keep inflation at low levels, has created a false sense of fiscal security, and has distracted policy makers from addressing the fundamental issue of fiscal discipline. More important, it has had a deeply pernicious effect on the quality of service delivery to the poor. Features inherent in the cash budgeting system facilitated a substantial redirection of resources away from the intended targets, such as agencies and ministries that provide social and economic services. The cash budget also eliminated the predictability of cash releases, making effective planning by line ministries difficult.

Analyzing Uganda's budget management, Williamson (2003: 8) noted, "Budget discipline in Uganda has been relatively good . . . ; however disbursements against budget can vary significantly between sectors and agencies within those sectors. . . . Institutions that are neither within [the Poverty Action Fund] nor politically powerful are exposed to greater resource cuts and irregular disbursements." Williamson (2003: 32) continues, "This undermines the ability of and incentive for managers to plan for activities in advance, as they do not know when or whether they will actually be able to carry the activities out."

Source: Author's compilation.

provided that accountability is adequate; however, in many anglophone African countries, accountability at the level of the spending-ministries has been deficient. Nevertheless, anglophone countries have external audit arrangements that play a comparatively more important role in the budget process than is the case in francophone countries. In theory, supreme audit agencies in anglophone countries provide parliament and the public with information on budget execution and the integrity of annual accounts.

Budget Appropriation Management Rules and Budget Revisions

This section deals with budget appropriation management rules that cover the period of the budget, transfers between budget items, and sequestration and within-year budget revisions.

Period covered

ANNUAL RULE. A classic principle of budget management is the *annuality principle,* which means that the budget is adopted for one budget year at a time and that appropriations for the current budget year must, in principle, be used in the course of the year. Therefore, at the end of the year, unused appropriations are canceled. This principle is aimed both at ensuring fiscal discipline, by preventing implementation of several budgets at the same time, and at encouraging good expenditure planning.

However, the annual rule can create a rush for spending at the close of the fiscal year. This spending bulge at the end of the fiscal year can be the result of prudent purchasing procedures. Nevertheless, the potentially adverse effects of a strict annual rule are many. The annual rule may encourage line ministries to make unplanned and economically inefficient expenditures at the end of the year. To avoid such perverse effects, several countries of the Organisation for Economic Co-operation and Development (OECD) have recently authorized the carryover of a certain percentage of these unspent appropriations to the next fiscal year.

Systematically authorizing carryover for recurrent expenditures in developing countries would pose problems regarding expenditure control, however. If appropriate accounting procedures are not in place, altering the annual rule can lead to executing two budgets at the same time— and confusion. An eventual alteration of the annual rule for recurrent expenditures should be considered only in those countries where the budget preparation process is fully satisfactory. In any case, carryover for operating expenditures should be limited to a small percentage of appropriations and be submitted to the approval of the ministry of finance.

Because capital investment expenditures are difficult to manage within an annual budget framework, procedures for carrying over unused appropriations may be desirable for capital expenditures; however, caution is required. The budget should include sound estimates of investment project costs. Carryover of capital expenditures should involve only ongoing projects that are not sufficiently funded in the budget for the year in question (year t), because the appropriations of the year $t - 1$ budget—for which carryover is requested—were expected to be used. The request should be submitted to the approval of the ministry of finance. For externally financed expenditures, carryover should be authorized, but it is the common practice, even when it is not stipulated in the financial regulations.

COMPLEMENTARY PERIOD.   In many countries, books are closed immediately at the end of the fiscal year. Expenditures not paid must be paid from the following year's budget. This rule is simple and could encourage good cash planning. It has, however, some perverse effects: some checks are issued but kept in the drawer, and expenditures may be registered in nontransparent suspense accounts from which they will be paid later.

Some countries have adopted a modified cash-basis accounting system. During a complementary period of one or two months after the end of the fiscal year t, a pending payment order can still be paid from the appropriations of the year t budget.

In African francophone budget systems, the budget expenditure is the payment order, not the cash payment. Therefore, unpaid payment orders at the end of the year can be paid the following years.[7] In addition, there is often a complementary period to account for payment orders of the previous year.

Each of the previous procedures has both advantages and perverse effects. It is necessary to be aware of the perverse effects and analyze them to define corrective measures.

DELAYS IN ENACTING THE BUDGET.   When the legislature has not yet approved the budget before the fiscal year starts, the legal framework generally includes provisions that allow the executive to start spending on the basis of the previous year's budget appropriations, often restricted to one-twelfth of the previous year's appropriations per month.

Transfers between budget items

Rules for transfers between budget items (chapters, line items, and so forth) are generally stipulated in the financial regulations. (These transfers are termed *virements* in the budgetary jargon of some countries.)[8] Such rules should distinguish between (a) transfers that may be made freely by spending unit managers; (b) transfers that require the approval of the line ministry's headquarters; (c) transfers submitted for the approval of the ministry of finance; and (d) transfers that require legislative authorization, which should be defined in the organic budget law.

THE SCOPE OF LEGISLATIVE AUTHORIZATIONS TO SPEND. The scope and the purpose of the authorizations to spend that are granted by the legislature—that is, the *appropriation*—should be clearly defined. In British Commonwealth countries, the executive is authorized to spend through an appropriation act distinct from the budget. This act contains budget totals for each ministry or for each major subdivision of the line ministries' budget (for example, for each program). The budget provides background information to the appropriation act. In many other countries, there is no separate appropriation act. The scope of the legislature's authorization is defined implicitly through rules set out in the organic budget law that determine the degree of freedom of the executive in using budgeted resources. For example, the legislation will stipulate a level within the budget structure (a chapter or program) at which transfers are limited to a small percentage of the outlay. These two different approaches are equivalent as regards the legislature's role. However, in a number of countries that have adopted the latter approach, the scope of legislative authorization is either not clearly defined or not well understood.

The scope of the legislature's authorization to spend should be defined to ensure that the budget is implemented according to the government's policy objectives. However, an excessive number of appropriations tends to impede efficient implementation of the government's expenditure programs.[9]

TRANSFERS WITHIN THE APPROPRIATIONS. Regulations for transfers within the appropriations vary from one country to another. In many developing countries, the control of transfers between budget items is one of the major activities of the ministry of finance budget department during budget execution. The procedures involved are time consuming and absorb large amounts of administrative resources.

To implement policies and programs in the most efficient and cost-effective way, line ministries and agencies should have adequate flexibility to manage their resources within the policy framework of the budget. Determining the exact composition of the inputs of a program is difficult. Moreover, concerning investment programs, one investment project can be delayed because of bad weather, while the implementation of another project can be accelerated.

Granting a certain degree of flexibility to line ministries, however, should not alter the policies stated in the budget, hinder the achievement of macrofiscal policy, or lead to arrears generation. Depending on the internal capacities of line ministries to control their programs, the nature of problems met in budget implementation, and the fiduciary risks, restricting the ability of ministries to reallocate budgetary resources within their sectors will usually be necessary. A few OECD countries (for example, Australia) have implemented block appropriations for operating expenditures, including personnel expenditures. Line ministries are free to determine the best composition of inputs to implement their programs and achieve results. However, such a degree of freedom would have perverse effects in countries with a high degree of protection of civil service jobs and would increase difficulties in addressing overstaffing in most developing countries.

Typically, virements between personnel expenditures and other economic categories need to be regulated in most developing countries and should be submitted for ministry of finance approval. However, the effects of these regulations need to be carefully reviewed to ensure that they are designed properly. In some countries, switching from other economic categories to personnel expenditure is forbidden; in other countries, switching items from personnel expenditures to other economic categories is forbidden. In the first case, regulations for virements aim at capping personnel expenditures. In the latter case, the regulations aim at protecting personnel expenditures. Spending caps should always be preferred because they have the advantage of giving a clear signal to spending agencies.

Having rules either to protect some nonwage items for which arrears are frequently generated (such as electricity consumption) or to cap some categories of expenditures (such as missions abroad) may also be desirable. These rules should focus on what is necessary and should not apply forever. What can be a problem of compliance one year will not necessarily be a problem the following year.

Box 9.4 presents examples of regulations governing transfers between budget items in two countries: South Africa, where the budget is structured into programs, and Tunisia, which has a line-item budget. In South Africa, to ensure compliance with the policy objectives stated in the budget, transfers between programs are capped at 8 percent of the amount appropriated for the concerned programs.[10] In Tunisia, within a line ministry, for recurrent expenditure the transfer regulations focus on the economic nature of the expenditure. In both countries, transfers to personnel expenditures and transfers between recurrent and capital expenditure are controlled; in

BOX 9.4 Transfers between Budget Items: Virements

South Africa

According to South Africa's Public Finance Management Act of 1999 (PFMA) and Treasury Regulations of March 2005 (National Treasury of South Africa 2005), an accounting officer for a department may transfer a saving in the amount appropriated under a main division within a vote (that is, a program) toward another main division within the same vote, but only under certain conditions, notably the following:

- The amount transferred should not exceed 8 percent of the amount appropriated under the main division within the vote (PFMA, article 43).
- Virements are not authorized for (a) amounts appropriated for a purpose explicitly specified under a main division within a vote, (b) changes to the beneficiary institution of transfers to institutions, and (c) transfers of amounts appropriated for capital expenditure to current expenditure (PFMA, article 43).
- The accounting officer must within seven days submit a report containing the prescribed particulars concerning the transfer to the executive authority responsible for the department and to the relevant treasury (PFMA, article 43).
- Compensation of employees and transfers and subsidies to other institutions may not be increased without the Treasury's approval (Treasury Regulations, article 63).

Tunisia

According to the Tunisian Organic Budget Law of 2004, virements are authorized under the following conditions:

- They are authorized by governmental decree:
  —Within each chapter (that is, line-ministry or major institution budget), between the recurrent expenditures "part" and the capital expenditures "part," within a limit of 2 percent of each part. However, virements that would increase personnel expenditures are forbidden.
  —Within each part, between articles. An article corresponds either to a broad economic category or to a particular function. More than 100 articles exist.
- They are submitted for ministry approval if the virements are between paragraphs within the same article. For current expenditures, a paragraph corresponds to a detailed economic category (for example, buying radio and television programs).
- They are submitted for the approval of line-ministry management if the virements are between subparagraphs within the same paragraph (for example, buying radio programs is a subparagraph of the paragraph on buying radio and television programs).

Source: Author's compilation.

addition, the Tunisian organic budget law stipulates detailed ministry of finance controls for transfers between line items. The South African approach meets the recommendations made in this section on transfers between budget items.

Sequestrations

Sequestrations are the withdrawing or withholding by the ministry of finance of certain appropriations. Sequestrations are done under special circumstances when cuts to appropriations are needed—for example, to meet the deficit objectives in case of revenue shortfall. The legal framework should allow the ministry of finance to sequester appropriations under certain conditions, but such an instrument should not be used except under special circumstances. It should not become a substitute for making tradeoffs at the budget preparation stage. Before sequestering appropriations, the ministry of finance should review existing commitments to ensure that sequestration will not generate arrears.

In-year budget revisions

Accurate forecasts are often difficult to make for the implementation of certain programs or of key macroeconomic developments, such as changes in the world economy, inflation, interest rates, or exchange rates. Moreover, some spending needs that were not foreseen during budget preparation may appear during budget execution. Flexible rules for transfers are needed to limit the effects of such problems, and a contingency reserve should be included in the budget.

In the case of in-year changes that alter the purpose or the cash limit of the legislature's authorization to spend, the budget may have to be revised. Mechanisms for revising the budget vary from country to country and should be clearly stated in the organic budget law. Some broad principles are as follows:

- Because the budget has been passed by the legislature, revisions should generally be made by law.
- In general, changes in appropriations above a certain percentage of the initial appropriation, or changes that affect the total amount of expenditures, must be submitted to the legislature for approval.
- To allow the government to address urgent problems rapidly, the legislature can consider procedures authorizing exceptional expenditures before it approves them. However, such authority should be regulated and

time limited, and the executive should be required to present a revised budget to the legislature shortly thereafter.

■ The number of in-year revisions should be strictly limited (preferably to only one), and requests from line ministries should be reviewed together. Some countries present supplementary appropriations to parliament on a case-by-case basis each time the council of ministers approves a request from a line ministry, and numerous supplementary appropriations are thus voted every year. Such procedures should be avoided. Budget execution is difficult to control when the budget is continually being revised. Moreover, supplementary appropriations granted to one sector may all too soon seem better allocated to a higher-priority sector.

The budget revision should preferably be made within the context of a midyear review, which will assess budget implementation and identify possible implementation problems (midyear reviews are further discussed later).

Special Issues

Good fiscal control of personnel expenditures and administration of procurement are essential for efficient budget implementation.

Fiscal control of personnel expenditures

Issues of personnel management cover different areas. On the one hand, fiscal stress and the changing role of the government are focusing attention on procedures for controlling personnel expenditures. This problem is mainly a policy issue, but it also requires appropriate tools for budgeting personnel. On the other hand, systems for personnel management should aim at fostering efficiency in delivering public services. This section focuses on some key issues in the fiscal control of personnel expenditures.

CAPPING PERSONNEL EXPENDITURES. The budgets of many developing countries include ceilings for personnel expenditures. This approach may be insufficient for personnel expenditure control. Personnel expenditure ceilings are often more of a floor than a spending limit. In practice, the system has a certain degree of flexibility but tends toward an increase in personnel expenditures. It needs to be complemented by a system that allows the government to monitor and control these legal commitments (recruitment and any other decisions that affect personnel expenditures).

Several industrial and developing countries use staff ceilings, which are included in the budget documents. These staff ceilings generally give the permissible full-time staff equivalent and are subject to internal or external controls or both. When the size of the civil service must be significantly reduced, personnel plans must often be prepared to determine the specific staff sectors to be trimmed, to define an incentive policy, to estimate the amount of redundancy payments, and so forth. Staff ceilings would then be the annual implementation targets corresponding to these personnel plans.

Staff ceilings should either be aggregated or be broken down into a few broad categories. Some countries set very detailed staff ceilings by personnel category, grade, and so forth and manage budgetary posts on this basis. Such approaches can make personnel management rigid and should be avoided.

Staff ceilings serve as a tool for controlling the fiscal effect of the personnel policy of agencies and as an aid in personnel management. Line ministries should be made fully responsible for establishing staff ceilings for their subordinate agencies, within the line ministry's total staff ceiling. Appropriations for personnel expenditures and staff ceilings should be consistent.

In the few developing countries where the size of the civil service does not pose major problems and where methods for estimating personnel expenditures are satisfactory, compulsory staff ceilings may not be needed. In any case, however, information on personnel levels is required during budget preparation and should be made public (as an annex to the budget).

THE ROLE OF THE MINISTRY OF FINANCE. Personnel management is preferably performed by line ministries; however, certain central control and coordination mechanisms are needed. Schematically, two main types of control and coordination tasks are used in managing government personnel expenditures:

1. *Budgetary control*, which concerns financial aspects of the pay structure for macroeconomic and fiscal management purposes and the setting of policy priorities
2. *Managerial control*, which generally concerns technical aspects of the pay structure and, more broadly, issues regarding working relations between the government and its employees.

The managerial control measures are often coordinated and exercised by central personnel management offices, such as civil service commissions, civil service boards, and establishment boards, but any decision about personnel management issues that affects the budget needs to be prepared in consultation with the ministry of finance and must be subject to similar restrictions and controls as other items of public expenditure.

The areas in which the ministry of finance must be involved and that should be integrated into the budgeting process concern the determination of (a) personnel levels in line ministries, (b) long- and short-term financial implications of staff reductions and retrenchment policies, and (c) financial components of the pay structure for the civil service as a whole. The organizational dualism that consists of making establishment boards responsible for the creation of posts, while providing funding through the ministry of finance, should be avoided.

ADMINISTERING THE PAYROLL AND PERSONNEL DATABASES. The payroll is underpinned by a personnel database that provides a list of all staff members who should be paid every month. This list can be verified against the approved establishment list and the individual personnel records.

The link between the personnel database and the payroll is key for control of personnel expenditures. Therefore, the following actions should be taken:

- Required changes to the personnel records and payroll should be updated monthly, generally in time for the following month's payments.
- Where they are computerized, personnel and payroll databases should be electronically linked to ensure data consistency. Whatever the degree of computerization, a monthly reconciliation procedure should be in place.
- Any amendments required to the personnel database should be processed in a timely manner through a change report and should result in an audit trail. Authority to change records and payroll should be clearly defined.
- Payroll audits should be undertaken regularly to identify ghost workers, to fill data gaps, and to identify control weaknesses.

Value for money in procurement

The main objective of the government as a purchaser is to obtain goods and services of the required quality at a competitive price. Procurement procedures should provide fair opportunity to all bidders and should be designed to achieve good value for money and to minimize risks of corruption and patronage.[11]

The legal framework should be aimed at enforcing the key principles in procurement, which are open competition and transparent procedures.

Major multinational trade arrangements, such as the World Trade Organization's Government Procurement Agreement, also set legal obligations for national procurement systems and practices. For expenditures financed by external sources, procurement procedures must conform to the guidelines established by the external lender or donor. The legal framework or the government's code of ethics should include standards about procurement. A good procurement system uses the participation of the private sector as part of the control system by establishing a clear, regulated process; enabling the submission of complaints; and giving access to the process and information on complaints.

Therefore, for both efficiency and transparency, the following principles should be enforced:

- No conflict of interest should exist between the official duties and the private interests of civil servants. Appropriate levels of financial delegation and proper separation of duties must be established. Rotation of duties is generally needed to avoid the risk of collusion arising from the development of too close relationships between the buyer and the supplier.
- To implement the budget efficiently and avoid delays in its program implementation, each line ministry should prepare a procurement plan for the fiscal year in advance. This procurement plan should be consistent with the in-year financial plans (cash and commitment plans) and, if needed, be adjusted accordingly.
- The procurement procedure should be specified for each planned tender.[12]
- For transparency, the tendering process of procurement should be made open to public scrutiny. For competitive bids, a formal tender announcement is normally published, specifying the characteristics of the project or the goods and services to be supplied, the selection criteria, and the award arrangements. The results of the bidding must be made public. The list of suppliers submitting tenders, their bid prices, and the name of the successful bidder should be disclosed.
- Contract awards and the overall procurement process must be subject to the scrutiny of the national legislature and the supreme audit institution. There should be well-defined and widely understood procedures for the control and audit of procurement transactions, including antifraud and anticorruption measures.
- Written (or computerized) records must be maintained and be publicly accessible. These records should show which suppliers were approached,

which ones were selected, the reasons for the procurement decision, details of prices, reports on the acceptance of work done or the receipt of goods ordered, and comments on the performance of the supplier.
■ There should be methods of appealing decisions on awards of contracts or other complaints that arise during the procurement process. Such complaints can be handled through specific arbitration committees or through the courts.

Monitoring of Budget Execution

To keep budget execution under control, a comprehensive and timely system for monitoring budget transactions is required.

Budget execution reports

For domestically financed expenditures, a report should be produced each month on budget execution at each stage of the expenditure cycle, detailed by organization, function, program, and economic category, while aggregate in-month "flash reports" are needed for efficient cash management. At least every six months, and preferably quarterly, a comprehensive financial budget execution report, including both expenditures financed from domestic resources and expenditures financed from external sources, should be published.

The uses of appropriations need to be systematically registered and tracked. Budget monitoring (or appropriation accounting) should cover appropriations, apportionment, increases or decreases in appropriations, commitments and obligations (including special procedures to monitor forward commitments), expenditures at the verification and delivery stage, and payments. Such a system is only one element of the government's accounting system, but it is the most crucial one for both formulating policy and supervising budget implementation.

Accounting for expenditure at the different stages of the budget execution cycle is aimed at meeting the following purposes:

■ For budget preparation, the forward costs of multiyear investment projects and the expenditures that are already committed are important.
■ For fiscal analysis, the cost of outstanding invoices—that is, the difference between expenditures at the verification stage and payment—must be assessed.
■ For program management, information on both commitments and expenditures at the verification stage is needed. Spending agencies need

to follow up accurately the orders and contracts they have awarded. Accounting for expenditures at the verification stage gives the main elements for assessing costs, shows how far program and project implementation has progressed, and is required for managing payables and contracts.

■ For cash planning and funds release, monitoring the actual payment and knowing the obligations to pay that will occur over the period of the budget are important. Obtaining this information requires monitoring the commitments and, for procured items of large size and all multiyear projects, also estimating the expected dates of payment obligations (within the context of the preparation of an in-year financial plan, as discussed later).

Comprehensive budget monitoring generally requires an overhaul of the reporting and accounting systems. As noted, many African anglophone countries do not centralize data on commitments. Francophone budget systems centralize data on commitments and payment orders according to the budget classification, but with only a few exceptions, statements on payments according to the budget classification are not available.[13] This information gap poses problems when the time lag between the date on which the payment order is accounted for in the books and the date on which the payment is made reaches several months. In the francophone budget systems, payment orders could correspond to the expenditures at the verification stage if they are issued as soon as the expenditure is verified. In practice, they are rarely issued so quickly.

Expenditures financed from donors' project aid should be monitored regularly, which can require special arrangements and donors' surveys. Data available within the government also should be systematically compiled. Data on loan disbursements are available at the ministry of finance department responsible for debt management; the framework agreements with some donors stipulate that a "national authorizing officer" will centralize data on project financial execution, and project managers should forward financial statements for projects to their parent line ministry.

Investment programs are often beset by implementation problems because of insufficient implementation capacities and other factors, such as delays in mobilizing external financing, overoptimistic implementation schedules, climatic hazards, or difficulties in importing supplies. Mechanisms for reviewing the most significant or problematic projects are needed. These methods could consist of a regular monthly or quarterly review of projects within line ministries and a midyear review involving line ministries and central agencies (midyear reviews are discussed later).

Arrears issues

Unpaid liabilities arising from budget execution are the difference between the expenditures at the verification stage and the payments. They include (a) genuine arrears, which are liabilities unpaid at the payment due date, and (b) the float, which consists of invoices not immediately due for payment.

Monitoring unpaid liabilities is essential for cash planning and avoiding any risk of overruns in budget execution. If implemented, comprehensive budget monitoring will cover most unpaid liabilities, but perhaps not all. The exceptions could concern expenditures irregularly committed and unavoidable expenditures, such as electricity consumption.

As shown in box 9.5, unpaid liabilities may be found at different levels of the budget execution cycle. Therefore, special surveys may be needed to make a comprehensive assessment of the stock of unpaid liabilities and to identify the required measures to stop arrears generation.

Midyear review

A comprehensive midyear review of the implementation of the budget is needed to ensure that programs are implemented effectively and to identify any policy problems. This review of budget execution should cover financial, physical, and other performance indicators. Cost increases caused by inflation, unexpected difficulties, insufficient initial study of projects, and budget overruns must be identified so that appropriate countermeasures can be prepared.

Many countries have a formal midyear review by the cabinet of developments in the execution of the budget. This review encompasses the following:

- An update on any changes to projected macroeconomic variables and revenue forecasts or projections
- An analysis of budget execution by programs against budget, including reasons for any significant over- or underexpenditures
- Consideration of all requests from ministries for program or agency supplementation.

A midyear budget review is emphatically not, however, an opportunity to revisit or review all budget allocations. It should be seen more as

---

BOX 9.5   Where Are the Arrears?

An arrearage may be found at several stages of the budget execution cycle:

- *When the expenditure is not invoiced.* The supplier may agree with the spending unit not to submit the bill. For example, if the expenditure cannot be financed from an unused appropriation, the supplier and the spending unit may decide to await a budget revision or the next budget. In francophone systems, such expenditures are often not regularly committed (because the commitment must be submitted for the visa of the financial controller).
- *Before the payment order is issued at the line-ministry level.* The official at the spending unit who sanctioned the expenditure can put the bill in a drawer. In anglophone systems, this sometimes occurs because no money is available under a monthly cash limit. In both anglophone and francophone systems, it happens because the expenditure was not regularly committed (no appropriation available for the moment).
- *Before the payment order is issued at the ministry of finance level.* In several francophone systems, the ministry of finance department responsible for issuing payment orders may delay this issuance for various reasons.
- *Before the payment is made at the treasury or accountant level.* The payment order has been passed to the treasury or to the line ministry's accounting department responsible for payment, but it is not paid. In francophone budget systems, such unpaid payment orders are accounted for; however, they are not necessarily accounted for in other budget systems.
- *After the "payment" is said to be made.* In some countries, checks are issued and not sent to the bank. In the past, in some francophone budget systems, the supplier was "paid" with treasury checks or to an account with the treasury, but the cash was not available.

Source: Adapted in part from Potter and Diamond 1999.

---

a fine-tuning of the budget to accommodate any revisions in revenue forecasts and any urgent and unavoidable new or additional expenditure priorities. This midyear budget review, covering the enumerated issues, should be provided to the legislature, along with the supplementary budget for approval.

Cash Management

This section presents the treasury function and the objectives of cash management. It reviews the payment systems, including the treasury single account, which is a key instrument for efficient cash management, and discusses procedures for in-year financial planning.

The Treasury Function

The treasury function aims at ensuring both efficient implementation of the budget and good management of the financial resources. It covers some or all of the following activities:

- Cash management
- Management of government bank accounts
- Accounting and reporting
- Financial planning and forecasting of cash flows
- Management of government debt and guarantees
- Administration of foreign grants and counterpart funds from international aid
- Financial assets management.

The organizational arrangements and the distribution of responsibilities used to carry out these activities vary considerably according to country. Depending on the country, the scope of activities of the organization named the treasury can be wider or narrower than those covered by the treasury functions. In some countries, the ministry of finance itself is named the treasury. In other countries, the treasury department focuses only on cash and debt management functions.

Objectives of Cash Management

Cash management has the following purposes: controlling spending in the aggregate, implementing the budget efficiently, minimizing the cost of government borrowing, and maximizing return on excess operating cash balances. Control of cash is a key element in macroeconomic and budget management.

For efficient budget implementation, the government must ensure that claims will be paid according to the contract terms and that revenues will be collected on time, that transaction costs are minimized, and that borrowing is at the lowest available interest rate or that additional cash is generated by investing in revenue-yielding paper. Payments must be made on a timely basis, which is accomplished by tracking accurately the dates on which they are due.

Efficient cash management is having the right amount of money in the right place and at the right time to meet the government's obligations in the most cost-effective way (Storkey 2003). It does not mean trying to control the timing of government expenditures to match the timing of cash receipts.

Centralization of Cash Balances and the Treasury Single Account

So that borrowing costs can be minimized or interest-bearing deposits maximized, operating cash balances should be kept to a minimum and centralized daily where possible, and the payment system should be properly designed. Some key features of the payment system are reviewed below, including the treasury single account (TSA) systems, through which cash balances are centralized efficiently.

Treasury single account principles

A TSA is an account or set of linked accounts through which the government transacts all payments. The TSA can address weaknesses met in a number of developing countries, where spending units maintain their own bank accounts and the government may have hundreds or thousands of bank accounts, which are credited with self-raised revenues or transfers from the "consolidated fund" managed by the ministry of finance. Such arrangements can result in idle cash balances, which are inaccessible to the ministry of finance for cash management purposes. These idle balances increase the borrowing needs of the government, which must borrow to finance the payments of some agencies, while other agencies have excess cash in their bank accounts. Operating cash balances should be kept to a minimum in order to minimize borrowing costs or maximize interest-bearing deposits. Also, if the accounts of spending agencies are held at a commercial bank, the idle balances can help loosen constraints on credit, by giving the banking sector additional resources for credit.

Within the broad concept of a TSA, there are various methods of centralizing transactions and cash flows. The choice of method will depend on several factors, such as the quality of the country's technological and banking infrastructure, as well as the nature of the control functions that are assigned to the treasury department responsible for managing the TSA.

TSAs can be grouped very broadly into the following categories:

- *Centralization of payment transactions.* The TSA consists of only one central account. This type of TSA is illustrated by case 1 in figure 9.2. All payment transactions are made through this central account. Exceptions to this principle are limited to special cases (such as transactions of remote agencies or through letters of credit). Within this category of TSA, two methods of transactions control can be considered:
  —*Centralization of payment transactions and "active" treasury controls of individual transactions.* Requests for payment and documents justifying

Case 1. Payment through centralized treasury

Case 2. Payment through spending agencies' bank accounts

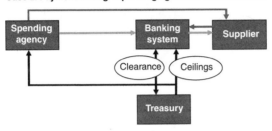

Case 3. Payment through imprest system

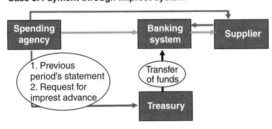

Source: Adapted from Allen and Tommasi 2001.

FIGURE 9.2 Three Payment Systems

them are sent to the treasury, which controls them and plans their payment. The treasury manages the float of outstanding invoices.[14]

—*Centralization of payment transactions and "passive" treasury single account.* Payments are made directly by spending agencies, but through a TSA. The treasury, through the budget implementation plan and a warrant system, sets periodic cash limits for the total amount of transactions but does not control individual transactions.[15]

■ *Centralization of cash balances only.*[16] This type of TSA is illustrated by case 2 in figure 9.2. In such cases, the TSA is organized along the following lines:

—Line ministries hold accounts at the central bank that are subsidiary accounts of the treasury's account, and spending agencies hold accounts either at the central bank or with commercial banks that must be authorized by the treasury.

—Spending units' accounts are zero-balance accounts: either their accounts are automatically swept at the end of each day (if the banking infrastructure allows daily clearing), and money is transferred to these accounts as specific approved payments are made, or the banks accept the payment orders sent by spending agencies up to a certain limit defined by the treasury.

—The central bank consolidates the government's position at the end of each day, including balances in all the government accounts.

This system of centralization of cash balances allows but does not require diversified banking arrangements. Payments can be made through banks selected on a competitive basis.

When the central bank does not have an adequate network of regional branches or lacks the capacity to handle the large volume of transactions that are associated with government payments and receipts, the retail banking operations are delegated to a fiscal agent (normally an authorized commercial bank). The fiscal agent makes payments on behalf of the treasury, the central bank recoups all payments made by the fiscal agent that relate to government operations, and the agent makes daily deposits of all government revenues to the TSA in the central bank. These arrangements can be set up both so the payments are channeled through the treasury and so government agencies are directly responsible for authorizing payments.

The imprest system

Many developing countries use an imprest system either for all transactions or for special cases. The principle of an imprest account is that the unspent balances, either cash on hand or in the bank, plus the value of money paid out, must always equal the value of the imprest. An initial imprest advance is provided by the treasury department. Thereafter, the expenditures made from the imprest account are reimbursed by the treasury department on receipt of an account verifying the use of the previous advance and including reconciliation with bank statements. This reimbursement process allocates expenditure against the budget. The imprest system is illustrated by case 3 in figure 9.2.

The imprest system is used in several African anglophone countries for processing line ministries' payment transactions. This system can lead to favoring generation of idle cash balances within government bank accounts. In the francophone systems, imprest accounts are used for petty expenditures and also in some countries for bypassing the ex ante commitment controls. The imprest accounts are often kept at the treasury in francophone systems, but the fact that they are considered a "special procedure" could explain why transactions from these accounts are poorly monitored.

Although, in principle, advances and imprests are used in the francophone system only for petty expenditures, in some countries imprest accounts are mushrooming. In some, but not all, countries the imprest accounts can be kept in the treasury. To a certain extent, these special procedures are not very different from the normal procedures in several anglophone budget systems. They could even lead to more efficient cash management, provided that the imprest account is kept in the treasury. However, the fact that these procedures are deemed exceptional and not subject to proper audit leads to increased fiduciary risks.

The imprest systems present many weaknesses. Reporting and controls are often weak, a significant amount of cash can be kept outside the treasury account at the central bank, and risks of mismanagement are high.

In countries with underdeveloped infrastructure, however, imprest accounts can be considered for remote agencies. Also, in some developing countries, they can be considered for petty expenditure transactions that facilitate routine management. In any case, whatever the coverage of the imprest system, proper control and audit procedures and reporting requirements must be set up to ensure that the system will be limited to special cases (for example, expenditures under a certain ceiling) and to ensure expenditures will be classified and reported in the same way as other expenditures. In countries with modern infrastructure that can use electronic transfers and automated teller machines, imprest accounts can be totally eliminated.

In developing countries, external aid is very often managed through special accounts that function under the same type of procedures as imprest accounts.

Design of the payment system

Figure 9.2 illustrates schematically the different variants for processing payment transactions. As noted, case 1 summarizes the TSA model in which payment transactions are centralized within the treasury single account, which can play either an active or passive role in expenditure control in the sense previously described; case 2 refers to a TSA that centralizes only the cash balances; and case 3 illustrates the imprest procedure.

Concerning the cash management objective of minimizing the costs of borrowing, the modes of centralizing cash balances of case 1 and case 2 give identical results. However, satisfactory implementation of the method described in case 2 can be difficult in many developing countries. In countries with an underdeveloped banking infrastructure, sweeping bank accounts daily or, to a lesser extent, managing a system of credit limit could pose problems. The existence of a large number of bank accounts can hinder the implementation of appropriate daily clearing and consolidation procedures.

If compliance is weak and commercial banks are subject to political pressure, the TSA model that centralizes only the cash balances (case 2) could present higher fiduciary risks than the TSA model that centralizes all payment transactions (case 1).

In the case of the TSA model that centralizes all payment transactions, different control systems can be considered, as noted earlier. At first glance, the variant that places controls on the processing and accounting of payment transactions under the full responsibility of the treasury department might seem more efficient from the viewpoint of both cash management and expenditure control. However, the experience of some francophone systems indicates that the centralization of accounting controls and the central management of floats can lead to inefficiencies—and even corruption—in countries with poor governance, particularly where the treasury is responsible for selecting the suppliers to be paid. Such a system should evolve toward making line ministries more responsible and accountable. Implementing a financial ledger system, in which all transactions are recorded, is generally seen as a good method for balancing properly the needs for control and the needs for giving line ministries full responsibility.

For remote agencies, the organization of the payment system must take into account the system of public administration and banking infrastructure in the country concerned. Using an imprest system can be considered for these agencies. Because most countries use the greater portion of their cash either for transactions at the central level (for example, debt payments and expenditures managed by the central departments of line ministries) or for payments that are due on a fixed date (for example, wage payments), such arrangements would allow most cash balances to be centralized. In many countries, streamlining cash management could consist of (a) daily centralization of transactions made at the central level, through a TSA, and (b) for remote agencies, a procedure based on imprest advances.

Whatever the institutional arrangements, the centralization of cash balances should cover all the government accounts used for payment transactions, including accounts managed by extrabudgetary funds.

Tax collection

The interval between the time when cash is received and the time it is available for carrying out expenditure programs should be minimized. Revenues need to be processed promptly and made available for use. By virtue of the banking sector infrastructure, commercial banks are often able to collect revenues more efficiently than tax offices can. Tax offices should therefore focus instead on tracking taxpayers, issuing tax assessments, monitoring payments, and reporting results. When revenues are collected by commercial banks, arrangements must be defined to foster competition and ensure prompt transfer of collected revenues to government accounts. Systems of bank remuneration through a float, which consist of authorizing the banks to keep the revenues collected for a few days, are inconvenient. Stringent rules to ensure prompt transfers should be established. Moreover, bank remuneration through fees is more transparent and promotes competitive bidding. An appropriate system of penalties for taxpayers is also an important element in avoiding delays in revenue collection.

Payment techniques

Payment methods affect the transaction costs of cash outflows. Depending on the banking infrastructure and the nature of expenditures, various payment methods may be considered (check, cash, electronic transfer, debit card, and so forth). Modern methods of payment—for example, payment through electronic transfer instead of by check or cash—allow the government to plan its cash flow more accurately, expedite payments, and simplify administrative and accounting procedures. However, whether one mode of payment is preferable to another depends on many factors, such as the degree of economic development of the country, the extent and maturity of the banking network, and the level of computerization.

For payments within the government sector (for example, when a ministry or government agency provides services to another agency), many countries use nonpayable checks, while others make accounting adjustments. Non-payable checks have the advantage of preventing delays in the preparation of accounts. In some developing countries, nonpayable checks are used to pay taxes related to imports financed with external aid, a practice that avoids loopholes in the tax system created by duty-free imports.

Banking arrangements

Whatever the organization of tax collection or expenditure payment, the treasury should be responsible for supervising all central government bank accounts. This procedure will enable the government to negotiate better arrangements and to ensure that requirements for cash and budget management are appropriately taken into account. In addition to using bank accounts for budget management, the treasury may have deposit accounts with commercial banks, which should be selected on a competitive basis to secure higher-yielding terms.

Accounts of counterpart funds generated by sales from commodity aid should be placed under the responsibility of the treasury.

In-Year Financial Planning and Cash-Flow Forecasts

In-year financial planning and cash-flow forecasts are needed both to ensure that cash outflows are compatible with cash inflows and to prepare borrowing plans. Except in an emergency situation or if the budget has been badly prepared, in-year financial planning should be driven by the budget.

In-year financial plans

An annual financial plan including cash inflows and cash outflows month by month should be prepared for the entire fiscal year before the start of the fiscal year. Borrowing plans are derived from the monthly forecasts of cash inflows and outflows. They should be regularly updated. In addition to the monthly cash-flows projection, the forecast should include quarterly commitment projections.

The financial plan must take into account the timing of payment obligations arising from commitments over the fiscal year. In particular, it must consider the schedule of disbursement for investment projects, which are not equally distributed by month. It should also take into account the seasonal distribution of revenues and the expected disbursement planning of external aid. Many countries merely slice the budget into quarterly parts or release one-twelfth of the budgeted amount every month. Of course, this method is not satisfactory. For example, the monthly schedule of disbursements for investment projects can be highly variable depending on various factors, such as contractual payment schedules or the physical advancement of works.

The procedure to update the financial plan could be the following:

- Each quarter at least, both the commitment plan (if it is prepared) and the cash plan should be updated for the entire year, which requires that the larger investment projects update the payment obligations planning for the entire year.
- Each month the cash plan for the quarter should be updated, taking into account revised revenue forecasts and expected outflows (derived from the commitment plan). The domestic borrowing program for the month is derived from this cash plan. If the cash plan indicates that cash inflows available over the quarter may be insufficient, action should be taken immediately, which may include identifying measures for increased tax collection, revising the borrowing policy, and delaying expenditure commitment. Therefore, the commitment and cash plans should be revised for the entire year.

Cash planning must be done in advance and communicated to spending agencies to allow them to implement their budgets efficiently. Moreover, reducing uncertainty about a borrower's debt management program is generally rewarded with lower borrowing charges. Even when a commitment plan is not formally prepared, the preparation of monthly cash outflow plans requires thorough monitoring of both payments and commitments. To ensure effective and efficient implementation of the budget, the government should adopt the following principles in preparing the budget implementation plans:

- To prepare the implementation of programs, agencies should know in advance the funds that will be allocated to them.
- Funds must be released in due time, without delay. In case of cash problems, the plan for releasing funds must be revised, but the revised plan should be communicated to the line ministries instead of making a nontransparent revision by delaying the release of funds.
- Particular attention should be given to agencies located in remote geographic areas. These agencies require adequate planning of the release of funds and good coordination between the central departments and the regional offices of the ministry of finance or the line ministry concerned.
- The financial needs of ongoing commitments should be included. Regulating cash flows without regulating commitments generates arrears. In many countries, when monthly cash limits are established, it is unclear whether spending units are allowed to make commitments up to the ceiling given in the budget appropriations or up to the monthly cash limits.
- Adjustment of commitments needs time. Imposing monthly limits is generally more of a regulation of cash payments through a float than a regulation of commitments, because even for nonpersonnel goods and services, one month may be too short a period to adjust commitments. So that arrears generation can be avoided, monthly cash limits should be consistent with quarterly cash and annual commitment limits. A period of at least three months is needed to regulate nonpermanent commitments, whereas issues related to permanent commitments should be addressed during budget preparation. In an emergency situation, strict monthly cash limits are needed and should be preferred to day-to-day rationing. However, regulating cash on a monthly basis is not sufficient to address problems related to overcommitment.
- The preparation of the cash plan and its updating require close coordination between the treasury, the budget department, and the tax

administration department. Preparing monthly cash outflow plans is more of a treasury task than a budgeting task. However, the treasury should coordinate with the budget department, in case any adjustments to the budget implementation plan appear necessary.

In-year financial planning should not be confused with the so-called cash budgeting procedure. Cash budgeting is described in box 9.3. It is aimed at ensuring macroeconomic and fiscal stabilization, even if the budget has been badly prepared. Such procedures should not be dismissed in emergency situations, but they should be used temporarily only, because they may lead to policy distortions in budget policy implementation and are insufficient to prevent arrears generation.

Revenue forecasts

Forecasts of the monthly distribution of revenues should be prepared. These forecasts should be updated regularly, preferably every month, because changes in the macroeconomic environment or in the tax administration system may affect revenue collection.

The preparation of monthly revenue forecasts requires economic analysis as well as management expertise, to take account of changes in the tax administration system. This exercise should be carried out by the tax and customs departments, in close cooperation with the treasury and the departments responsible for macroeconomic analysis. In some countries, monthly forecasts prepared by the tax administration departments are stronger on administrative detail than on economic analysis. They show the distribution of budgeted revenues over the fiscal year but do not take into account fiscal and economic developments after the budget has been adopted by the legislature. The government may therefore have to strengthen the forecasting capacities of tax administration departments.

A good monitoring system is a prerequisite for effective forecasting. Thus, revenue collections need to be monitored on the basis of the major tax categories and adjusted to reflect changes in the assumptions underlying the forecasts. In-year revenue forecasts should be based on revenue assessment and tax collection reports, the results of economic surveys, and the like. Short-term forecasting tools, such as short-term macroeconomic models and tax forecasting models, are also helpful.

The revenue forecasts must also include forecasts of nontax revenues prepared by the treasury in close coordination with the agencies responsible for the management and collection of these revenues.

Organizational arrangements

Cash planning is generally coordinated at a technical level by a division of the treasury department. This division should work closely with the tax administration department or the division of the treasury department that is responsible for debt management. A cash management committee chaired by the head of the treasury department and including officials from the budget department, tax administration, customs services, and the central bank should be set up.

Strengthening African Budget Execution Systems

Generally, the weaknesses in budget execution are caused not by the budget systems themselves, but by the way they operate. Actions should be directed toward enhancing budget discipline and improving accountability of all those responsible for budget execution and reporting.

Getting the basics right is particularly important. Both to ensure efficient program implementation and to keep expenditure under control, the most pressing needs are to strengthen the arrangements for reporting and accounting. Whatever the basis of accounting, improvements in bookkeeping and accounting procedures are generally required. Budget execution reports should be regularly produced. Budget execution monitoring systems need to cover all expenditures, whatever their economic nature or their financing source, and all special funds or procedures. Expenditures should be monitored at each stage of the expenditure cycle. Doing so will require setting up monitoring and control systems in many anglophone African countries. In the francophone countries that face arrears problems, reports according to the budget classification should be produced at the payment stage, not only at the payment order and commitment stages, as is currently done.

Clear definitions of tasks and responsibilities are required. For efficient program implementation, the ministry of finance should avoid excessive interference in line ministries' budget management. This issue is particularly important in the francophone budget systems, but it is important in other countries as well.

Internal control systems should be strengthened in most countries. This improvement includes setting up or reinforcing financial control procedures within spending units and more generally strengthening the different management systems, such as the personnel and the procurement management systems. Sanctions should be applied on those contravening regulations, and the results should be made public. In francophone budget systems, a two-pronged approach should be developed. First, internal control procedures should be implemented within spending units, and special budget execution procedures (such as the special payment order procedure discussed earlier) should be eliminated. Second, budget execution procedures and ministry of finance controls should be simplified.

Cash management and in-year financial planning should be strengthened in most countries. The policies stated in the budget should not be altered during budget implementation. Reliance on arbitrarily determined cash control systems, notably on cash budgeting systems, should be reduced, through preparing a more realistic budget and controlling commitments in a transparent manner.

To increase efficiency in cash management, governments in countries that still have fragmented banking arrangements for public expenditure management should consider implementing a TSA.

Strong political willingness to ensure that the budget is implemented according to the policies adopted by the legislature and to enforce the existing rules with rigor will be required to bring about lasting improvements in the public expenditure management system in Africa.

Notes

1. For example, allotments of appropriations to remote spending units (called *delegation of appropriations*) are reported as commitments in several francophone budget systems.
2. Some anglophone countries name the expenditure at the verification stage *commitment/liability,* while the forward tranches of the legal commitment are named *deferred commitment* or *forward commitment.*
3. Various terms, such as *program authorization, commitment appropriation,* and *commitment authorization,* are used. The European Commission uses the term *commitment appropriation* for its own budget.
4. In the IMF (2001) *Government Finance Statistics Manual,* the *net lending/borrowing* balance is defined as equal to the net acquisition of financial assets minus the net incurrence of liabilities. The incurred liabilities do not include the commitments related to undelivered goods and services.
5. See IMF (2001, chapter 3, paragraphs 3.44 to 3.53) for further discussion of this issue.
6. This office is not to be confused with the accounting officer of line ministries in British Commonwealth countries, who is the head of the line ministries' administration.
7. Some countries cancel the unpaid payment orders after a certain number of years.
8. This French term is frequently used in the financial regulations of British Commonwealth countries. In the majority of francophone budget systems, the term *virement* refers only to the transfers between budget items that change the economic nature of the expenditure.

9. Since the 1990s, most OECD countries have reduced the number of appropriations included in the budget. For example, in the United Kingdom, the number of appropriations is fewer than 100. In France, since 2006, the budget structure is based on only 150 programs, instead of the 800 chapters used previously, although within the programs, reallocation to personnel expenditure items from other items is not authorized.

10. The budget of the South African Ministry of Education includes six programs; the budget of the Ministry of Health has four programs.

11. A detailed discussion of procurement processes would be outside the scope of this chapter; only some broad principles are recalled in this section.

12. The procurement law may include a number of options, such as open competitive bidding, local competitive bidding, or restricted tendering. It may also provide for a prequalification procedure, depending on the tendering procedure.

13. They are not available because of the organization of the double-entry accounts of the treasury.

14. This type of TSA corresponds to the TSA implemented in all francophone countries.

15. This type of TSA corresponds to the majority of TSAs that have been recently implemented in transition countries and several TSAs implemented in British Commonwealth countries.

16. This kind of TSA is implemented in India and Sri Lanka (in Colombo only).

References and Other Resources

Allen, Richard, and Daniel Tommasi, eds. 2001. *Managing Public Expenditure: A Reference Book for Transition Countries.* Paris: Organisation for Economic Co-operation and Development.

Bouley, Dominique, J. Fournel, and Luc Leruth. 2002. "How Do Treasury Systems Operate in Sub-Saharan Francophone Africa?" Working Paper 02/58, International Monetary Fund, Washington, DC.

Dinh, Hinh T., Abebe Adugna, and Bernard Myers. 2002. "The Impact of Cash Budgets on Poverty Reduction in Zambia: A Case Study of the Conflict between Well-Intentioned Macroeconomic Policy and Service Delivery to the Poor." Policy Research Working Paper 2914, World Bank, Washington, DC.

IMF (International Monetary Fund). 2001. *Government Finance Statistics Manual.* Washington, DC: IMF Statistics Department. http://www.imf.org/external/pubs/ft/gfs/manual/pdf/all.pdf.

———. 2006a. *Selected African Countries: IMF Technical Assistance Evaluation—Public Expenditure Management Reform.* Washington, DC: IMF.

———. 2006b. *Uganda: Sixth Review under the Three-Year Arrangement under the Poverty Reduction and Growth Facility.* IMF Country Report 06/43. Washington, DC: IMF.

Lienert, Ian. 2003. "A Comparison between Two Public Expenditure Management Systems in Africa." Working Paper 03/2, International Monetary Fund, Washington, DC.

Lienert, Ian, and Feridoun Sarraf. 2001. "Systemic Weaknesses of Budget Management in Anglophone Africa." Working Paper 01/211, International Monetary Fund, Washington, DC.

National Treasury of South Africa. 2005. "Treasury Regulations for Departments, Trading Entities, Constitutional Institutions, and Public Entities." *Government Gazette* 477 (8189): 3–103.

Potter, Barry H., and Jack Diamond. 1999. *Guidelines for Public Expenditure Management.* Washington, DC: International Monetary Fund.

Schiavo-Campo, Salvatore, and Daniel Tommasi. 1999. *Managing Government Expenditure.* Manila: Asian Development Bank.

Stasavage, David, and Dambisa Moyo. 1999. "Are Cash Budgets a Cure for Excess Fiscal Deficits (and at What Cost)?" Working Paper 99-11, Centre for the Study of African Economies, Oxford, U.K.

Storkey, Ian. 2003. "Government Cash and Treasury Management Reform." *Governance Brief* 7: 1–4.

Williamson, Tim. 2003. "Targets and Results in Public Sector Management: Uganda Case Study." Working Paper 205, Centre for Aid and Public Expenditure, Overseas Development Institute, London.

10

Automating Public Financial Management in Developing Countries

STEPHEN B. PETERSON

In recent years, integrated financial management information systems (IFMISs) have become core components of financial reforms in developing countries. This chapter sets out the functions of those systems and how to manage them, with particular reference to the choices that developing countries face as they seek to introduce improved financial management. Because IFMISs require a relatively complex information technology (IT) platform, the chapter also discusses at some length the questions that surround the decisions that governments must make when procuring an IFMIS—above all, whether to purchase off-the-shelf (OTS) systems and customize them or to develop their own tailored systems. The subject is important because of the apparent general consensus that IFMISs have not met the high expectations that seem to have been attached to them.[1]

Moreover, a second dimension needs to be addressed: the same literature that analyzes the failure of IFMISs argues that IT systems not only should provide a technology platform to manage transactions and the budgetary process, but also should go further and *drive* budgetary reform. In the process, the demands of IFMISs (especially OTS) force governments to adapt their systems to meet those demands. Governments in this situation, therefore, make reforms that they would not otherwise make (Diamond and Khemani 2006).[2] Such situations are an important reason for IFMIS failure.

Two themes underlie this discussion about IT in public financial systems. First, IT should *support*, not drive, public financial management reform. Second, the introduction of IT systems comes with considerable risk, and the single most important factor in deciding on a strategy of automation is the management of the associated risks, both of failure and of wrong functionality.

Financial reform in developing countries should be driven by the design of financial procedures. After the financial system design is formulated, the automation strategy needs to be determined. That strategy must focus on what components should be automated, what components should be integrated, and what components should be both manual and automated.

Procedural reform can take two different forms: process change or process innovation (typically called *business process reengineering*) (Davenport 1993: 11–15). *Process change* evolves existing procedures and workflows using IT in a supportive role. Process change is a less risky strategy of reform because it works with existing requirements and with existing developed knowledge and user capacity, which is relatively low in developing countries. *Process innovation* involves a radical and comprehensive restructuring of procedures and workflows, and it uses IT as the driver of change. The limited success of reengineering efforts in both the private and public sectors in the 1980s, 1990s, and even now in industrial countries underscores the risks of a strategy of process innovation, particularly in developing countries (Varon 2004).

Therefore, IFMISs may fail or underperform in developing countries because they typically involve a high-risk strategy of process innovation. Public bureaucracies in those countries have limited capacity, and improvements are often best made through gradual strengthening of processes and skills. The presence of limited capacity does not necessarily imply the presence of dysfunctional financial procedures. In other words, process change is a strategy of improvement, whereas process innovation is a strategy of replacement, and the central question for financial reform, in the context of automation or simply basic design, is whether existing procedures should be improved or whether they should be replaced.

In his review of financial systems in anglophone and francophone African countries, Ian Lienert concludes,

> [T]he disappointing features observed are due not to the PEM [public expenditure management] systems themselves, but in the way they operate. . . . [I]n the absence of attitudinal changes by all players of the budget

process . . . it is unlikely that significant improvements will occur. Critical actions will be those directed towards enhancing budget discipline and improving accountability of all those responsible for budget preparation, execution, reporting and evaluation. Lienert (2002: 31)

Lienert's conclusion—that the basic designs of public finance systems in Africa (with exceptions) are reasonably sound while their execution is not—may not be universally accepted,[3] and clearly scope for improvement always exists. Nevertheless, his conclusion supports the contention of this chapter that in most African countries there is a reasonably strong base, existing or potential, from which to evolve financial systems—a process change approach.[4] A major reason for the success of the budget and accounts reforms in Ethiopia was that the existing system was evolved through a process of learning by doing—process change.

In summary, the current approaches to IFMIS development as set out in most of the existing literature (the same literature that testifies to widespread failure) often propose excessively sophisticated solutions to an ill-defined problem (the need for better information for management, control, and reporting) in an unsupportive and risky environment. Automation strategies thus should be driven by procedural improvements (process change) and should manage risk.

The rest of this chapter is in four sections. The first section outlines an automation strategy that supports process change. The second presents a framework for managing risk in financial information systems and examines several country examples. The third section illustrates an appropriate automation strategy of process change in a difficult environment using the example of the Ethiopian reform. The final section concludes with a summary of the issues that developing countries should consider when they embark on the automation of their financial systems.

An Automation Strategy for Process Change

A complex system that works is invariably found to have evolved from a simple system that worked.

—John Gall (1977)

Emerging experience from the public sectors in both industrial and developing countries suggests that the greater the complexity and scale of the IT platform to support financial systems, the greater the risk of failure or underperformance of that platform and, by extension, the system as a whole. IT systems that started small and are iteratively expanded are less likely to fail or underperform because the associated risks can be managed better (Heidenhof and others 2002: 13). According to the Organisation for Economic Co-operation and Development (OECD),

> Public sector budgeting systems can encourage the funding of large and highly visible IT projects [that] often fail. A radical approach, increasingly adopted in the private sector, is to avoid large projects altogether, opting for small projects instead. One expert has called this change a shift from "whales to dolphins." Adopting dolphins does not mean breaking big projects into small modules. Rather, it involves a shift to a different way of working and thinking, with total project time frames of no more than six months, technical simplicity, modest ambitions for business change, and teamwork driven by business goals. (OECD 2001: 2)

Process change does not require whales. Dolphins will do.[5]

The vision of an OTS IFMIS is appealing to many. It seems, all at the same time, to install international standards, instill discipline, improve efficiency, and strengthen control by connecting all the financial subsystems. The menu of features offered is attractive and seems to provide a one-stop shop for public financial sector reform. Indeed, it is not an exaggeration to say that, in the minds of many authorities, an IFMIS raises the bar of financial management and lifts it out of the reach of corruption. The apparent virtues of OTS IFMISs in aid-dependent countries are very attractive to donors and creditors concerned with fiduciary risk, as well as governments, that wish to fulfill conditions to gain access to foreign aid resources. The adoption of an OTS IFMIS is viewed as international best practice[6] and seems to have become a tangible indicator of a government's commitment to reform.

In his comparative study of information systems in developing countries, Richard Heeks (2002) found that systems with "design divisibility" that feature modularity and are incremental promoted "improvisation": that is, they fit information system design (imported from developed countries) to local conditions rather than change local conditions to fit system design. Improvisation approaches were more successful than standardized approaches that were rigidly integrated:[7]

> The design divisibility meant staff could learn from early, relatively small failures, and could address subsequent improvisations of both design and actuality [local context] to manageable project components. They were not overwhelmed as they would have been by a single, whole system design. Design divisibility is therefore a frequently cited prophylactic against failure that should be adopted more widely. However, many donor-funded IS [information

system] projects in developing countries take the opposite approach, partly because of short donor time scales and attention spans. Where design comes as this single whole, "big bang" implementation, opportunities for local improvisation are reduced and risks of failure correspondingly increase. (Heeks 2002: 110)

The conventional OTS IFMIS approach may be characterized as a "big bang" reform that usually imposes standardized procedures (from industrial countries and often from commercial—not public—applications). The rigidity, limited capacity, and high customization cost of such systems mean that public bureaucracies must adapt to the system rather than evolve the system to fit their needs. Indeed, some specialists are emphatic that a decision to procure an OTS application must be a decision not to customize. Customizing an OTS application, they contend, "is no cheaper and no less risky than building a system from scratch" (Dorsey 2000: 9).

What Is an IFMIS?

An IFMIS provides governments with a tool that can support financial control, management, and planning. By managing a core set of financial data and translating these data into information for management, these three financial functions are supported.

More narrowly defined, an IFMIS is a computer application that integrates key financial functions (for example, accounts or budgets) and promotes efficiency and security of data management and comprehensive financial reporting. An IFMIS is one way of addressing the problem of stovepiped financial systems that do not talk to each other and do not produce a timely and comprehensive picture of a country's financial position. Figure 10.1 presents what an IFMIS is, and figure 10.2 presents how it works. A detailed discussion of the IFMIS functions shown in figure 10.1 follows.

Financial function of an IFMIS

IFMISs are usually considered in terms of core and noncore financial functions.[8] Although public financial management is a broad field with multiple systems, the commonly cited specification of the core functions of an IFMIS is strikingly limited. The conventional specification of the IFMIS core is accounting and reporting functions, while noncore functions include budgeting, commitment control, cash management, and disbursement functions.[9] The common specification of the core functions does not include all of the components needed for effective financial control and, by definition,

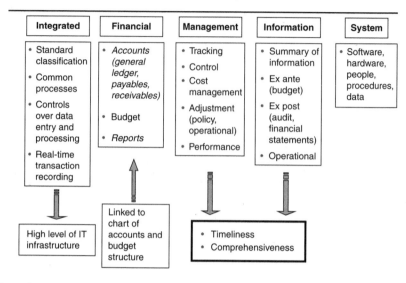

Source: Penrose 2005.
Note: Core IFMIS functions are in *italics*.

FIGURE 10.1 Features of a Typical IFMIS

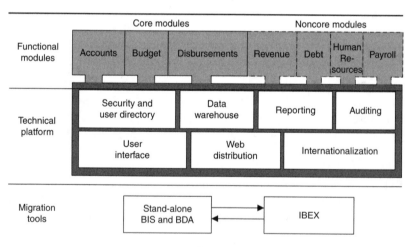

Source: Abate and Chijioke 2006.
Note: BIS (Budget Information System) and BDA (Budget Disbursement and Accounts) are the legacy financial systems. The IBEX (Integrated Budget and Expenditure) system is the Ethiopian custom IFMIS.

FIGURE 10.2 An Example of the Platforms of an IFMIS: Ethiopia's IBEX System

therefore will increase risk. The limited comprehensiveness of the conventional core functions of an IFMIS stems in large part from the private sector origins of IFMIS technology. In short, IFMISs do not get the basics right for public sector financial management. This failure raises the question of how they can constitute best practice.

At a minimum, in addition to accounting, a proper core of financial functions should include budget, commitments, cash management, and disbursement. Many IFMISs lack a core cash management function that ensures adequate cash to disburse against the commitment. The absence of a commitment module is a serious omission. Strong financial control requires a linked set of core modules, as follows:

- A budget module that sets ceilings. Budgetary control requires that an adjusted budget be maintained at all times and that it be available at the end of the fiscal year for the prompt closure of accounts. (Although the inclusion of a budget module is ideal, the commonly accepted definition of a core IFMIS does not include a budget module for preparation and adjustments.)
- A commitment control module that controls balances incurred but not disbursed. Commitment control is critical for avoiding arrears (again, not conventionally specified as a core module).
- A cash management module that shows cash available to pay commitments (again, not specified as a core module).
- A disbursement module that records disbursements.
- An accounts module that records expenditures when goods and services are received.[10]

Even if IFMISs do include the five listed financial components that are needed for effective control (budget, commitment, cash management, disbursements, accounts), that comprehensiveness would not prevent their disuse or misuse, nor would it make up for a lack of financial discipline. For example, weak commitment control is a problem in many anglophone African countries, resulting in the accumulation of arrears. Commitments could be controlled through manual procedures (warrant withdrawal), but this is "rarely done" and "reflects the generalized lack of financial discipline," according to Lienert (2002: 22).

Integrated function of an IFMIS

IFMISs are designed to manage financial data efficiently so that, once entered, data are securely stored and shared with different financial functions (for example, budgets and accounts). The management of data from the user's standpoint is standardized with common input screens and report formats. Integration is within the core modules but is also meant to include real-time (online) data sharing across administrative entities to promote financial control. One limitation is that the online requirements of a conventional IFMIS can be significantly constrained by the low bandwidth found in many developing countries.

IFMISs are integrated two ways: in terms of data management and in terms of modularity. Integration is both a virtue and weakness of IFMISs. When IFMISs are integrated in terms of data management but at the same time are not modular, this arrangement may impose a rigidity that limits customization. Modular systems by definition can be developed by adding independent modules as user requirements evolve, and modules can then be linked for sharing data.

Five virtues of modularity may be noted in particular:

1. Independent development of finance components as user requirements evolve
2. Flexible sequencing of a financial reform (budgets first; then accounts)
3. Appropriateness to the relatively unintegrated structure of public bureaucracies in developing countries
4. Operation of different scale systems at different levels of administration demanded by fiscal decentralization
5. Evolution of migration tools to consolidate data from different versions of the same financial subsystem (for example, old and new chart of accounts), thus managing a financial reform at different stages.

Modularity supports process change, which is uneven between financial components and administrative levels.

Understanding the concept of modularity in the context of the design and implementation of an IFMIS is important. A well-designed IFMIS will have discrete modules (for example, budget and accounts) that are integrated. One design issue is whether these modules are sufficiently independent to allow multiple versions. For example, can the system provide a single-entry and a double-entry version of accounts and consolidate both? Even for the same module (accounts), can different versions be developed for different administrative levels and then be consolidated? Furthermore, can the systems operate in different configurations: stand-alone configurations, local area network (LAN), and wide area network (WAN)? IFMISs have to be significantly customized to meet the varied demands of a financial reform, and some applications are simply unable to support certain configurations (stand-alone configurations) or different versions (single- or double-entry versions).

Modularity of design is essential in supporting a modular or sequential implementation of a financial reform, especially in the common case of countries that are at the same time implementing fiscal decentralization—because administrative levels will be at different stages in the decentralization and financial reform. A virtue of the custom IFMIS developed in Ethiopia, for example, is that it was extremely flexible and was able to run multiple versions of financial modules, which were customized to each major administrative level, and to consolidate the data. Similarly in Ghana, Heidenhof and others (2002) found,

> [Financial Management Systems] reforms should be divided up into self-contained modules. This is one of the key lessons from the Ghana experience where the high interdependency of the various components and sub-components has created significant implementation problems. A modular approach would allow a focus on changes that become necessary during project implementation on the specific module. The repercussions on the remaining project would be limited even in the case of delays or other difficulties with one module. (Heidenhof and others 2002: 14–15)

The conventional IFMIS almost invariably overlooks the issue of integration with manual systems. Prudent financial management, especially in developing countries, requires reliability more than efficiency.[11] Operating parallel manual and automated systems (at least until reliability has been established in the use and operation of the automated systems, which can be a very long time) provides redundancy, which increases control and reliability in financial management.[12] Moving financial management to lower and less capable levels of administration means that different financial systems are likely to coexist (manual at the lowest levels, with automation upstream). Should the infrastructure supporting the automated systems fail or come under strain, the manual systems allow governments to maintain their operations.

The manual system also provides a platform from which the user and the application developer can rapidly and cost-effectively evolve the system. It provides the user with a familiar and accessible prototype of new procedures and ways to adapt them.[13] This approach promotes government ownership and also provides technology developers with clear, workable, and user-accepted requirements. The failure of information systems to meet user requirements is arguably one of the principal sources of failure and underperformance of

IFMISs. A strategy of developing IT systems from robust manual systems does not need to take a long time, because application development is rapid and considerably less costly and because user acceptance is continuous and assured.[14] This approach promotes sustainability because the manual and computer application are developed incrementally and are embedded step by step. Because time is taken in the early stages of the financial reform, appropriate basics are established, user ownership is promoted, and costly and time-consuming application development is avoided.

It is not possible to automate everything.[15] Manual systems that complement computerized systems will always exist, and both systems require discipline in their execution. The continued role of manual systems reinforces the case for a modular process change approach to reform, because the manual systems will require improvements and these, in turn, will affect the automated systems, which also will have to be improved.

Management function of an IFMIS

The management function of an IFMIS applies the information function to execute the three roles of a financial system: control, management, and planning.

Information function of an IFMIS

This function translates financial data into information. IFMISs provide a wide range of reports.

System function of an IFMIS

Finally, an IFMIS is an information technology that embeds financial procedures in software applications, data stores, and communications infrastructure.

Figure 10.2 uses the example of the Ethiopian custom IFMIS (the Integrated Budget and Expenditure, or IBEX, system) to show how an IFMIS is constructed. The *functional modules* deliver the content of the application: in this case, budgeting, accounts, and disbursements. The *technical platform* is the capacity of the system, which includes the volume and speed of data processing, data security, connectivity (in this case to the Web), the front-end interfaces for the user, and the languages it presents the modules in. The third part of the application constitutes the *migration tools*, which allow data to be exchanged between the legacy financial systems—Budget Information System (BIS) and Budget Disbursement and Accounts (BDA)—and the new IBEX system. One limitation of an OTS IFMIS is the management of legacy systems and their data. Although in principle these data can be shared, building a custom migration capability is often necessary, thereby increasing costs.

In other words, an OTS is not necessarily synonymous with a turnkey system. A virtue of custom systems is their inclusion of custom migration tools.

A Risk Management Framework for Financial Information Systems

Risk management is at the center of any policy decision to introduce or upgrade a country's financial information systems. This chapter argues that because the financial procedures that are set out in most countries' public finance statutory and regulatory frameworks are generally likely to be sound, pursuing a strategy of process change, as contrasted with a strategy of process innovation, is both possible and desirable—improve what exists rather than institute a comprehensive replacement.

Automation projects (like all projects) are driven by three variables: scope, schedule, and budget. Scope is a function of resources and time (Chijioke 2004). *Scope* refers to the number of activities and objectives to be achieved: many IFMIS planning schedules are complex and require multiple tasks across weak institutions and complex management processes. *Schedule* refers to the development timelines. *Budget* determines the ex ante financial constraints within which the project has to be managed and how those constraints are staged over time.

This "iron triangle" represents the three critical (and interrelated) project design constraints, and the management of those constraints is a necessary and possibly sufficient condition for successful automation projects.[16] Tailoring the scope, schedule, and budget to local circumstances limits risk. The iterative ("dolphin") approach mitigates risk by limiting the scope; by sticking to short, frequently updated, and tight schedules; and by relying on modest incremental budgets. Scope is the key angle of this triangle: the project design objective should always be to reduce scope as much as possible at any given stage.

IFMISs in many developing countries have underperformed or failed because their scope has been excessive, their development schedules have been long and often indeterminate, and they have lacked hard budget constraints because they have been funded by overly generous and indeterminate concessionary foreign aid. There is no indication of a departure from this trend.

Instead of the iron triangle of effective project management, IFMISs have all too often been driven by a perverse triangle of incentives: government officials acquire rents, contractors milk a cash cow, and foreign aid agencies move money and impose unrealistic best practice as conditions of grants and loans.[17]

The perverse triangle explains why an inappropriate IFMIS strategy continues to be pursued in developing countries despite the consensus by information systems specialists and even foreign aid agencies of the poor performance of the conventional IFMIS approach and the need for iterative strategies. Indeed, why supposedly scarce resources are applied so lavishly to IFMIS projects rather than other, arguably more needed projects is often not clear. Few if any incentives to economize exist. The central question should be whether an IFMIS can improve the outcomes of public expenditure: aggregate fiscal discipline, allocative efficiency, and operational efficiency, leading to better lives for the population. If an IFMIS is principally justified for marginally improving reporting, is such a risky and costly investment justified? The cost-benefit calculus, both financial and social, of large public sector financial projects has generally been missing from most decisions to establish new systems: because costs and benefits in the form of net present financial or social values should guide marginal decisions, the tendency to inflate the scope of IFMIS projects discussed in this chapter is not surprising. I do not consider the economics of an IFMIS further, but they must be central decision criteria, along with the more technical criteria that are the subject of this chapter.

Risk is a function of scope, which in turn is a function of schedule and budget. Conventional OTS IFMISs are the highest risk because of their long schedules and cost overruns. A customized iterative solution, in contrast, has a lower risk because scope is better managed with tighter schedules and budgets.

Scope

The scope of a financial information system should be determined by four factors: the content to be automated (which functions—budget, accounts, and so forth); the quality of existing financial procedures (whether they can be evolved or must be replaced); the capacity of public bureaucracies to absorb and sustain IT; and a conservative and healthy skepticism about the capability of contractors.

In regard to content, a coherent core set of financial functions needs to be automated and linked. As argued earlier, the commonly accepted core for IFMISs is not comprehensive, because a coherent core should cover budget (formulation and management, as well as adjustments and commitments); accounts (general ledger, payables, receivables, and reporting); and disbursements (and cash balances if possible). The user requirements of these systems need to be relatively stable.

The second factor that affects scope refers to the quality of the existing procedures for these functions and how effectively they are integrated. For example, do commitment data from the budget module control the disbursement module? Effective integration of modules requires not only the sharing of data but also the existence and execution of procedures for management and control.

The scope of a system affects whether the public bureaucracies are able to absorb and sustain these systems. Public bureaucracies are typically weak in developing countries in the context of the management requirements of complex projects and have limited capacity to manage sophisticated IT systems.

The fourth factor of scope is the capability of contractors. A striking finding from the experience of African countries with IFMISs is the unreliability of contractors.[18] Turnover is frequent, and several systems have suffered starts and stops caused by repetitive procurement of contractors. Several internationally known contractors have failed in their efforts to implement IFMISs.[19]

Contractors do not have an incentive to reduce scope or to recommend lower-cost options to governments. Contractors often prefer packaged rather than customized solutions (often such solutions are based on current or recent engagements) so that they can leverage their experience and charge current clients for previous customization work. Contractors have little incentive to review the existing procedures and systems extensively enough and to work with the government to evolve the processes. A strategy of evolving financial systems has limited short-term profits, and the overall profitability of the project is lower than a replacement approach. Replacing existing processes with a computer application is more profitable because costs are substantial and are front loaded with the procurement of software, hardware, and staff (system integrators, or operating staff members and managers). An evolutionary strategy of systems reform is less attractive to contractors than a replacement strategy because total profits are lower and are spread out over time.

The modest objectives of the iterative approach reduce the scale of the project and lessen the risk of contractor failure. Frequent delivery of system updates allows government to assess periodically the performance of contractors and to detect early deficiencies. Demanding that each version be tested and well documented lessens the risk to government if the contractor fails or quits.

Schedule

Quite rarely, automation projects are completed on time. Conventional IFMIS solutions have very long time frames: five to seven years, on average, in developing countries and seven to nine years in Africa (Dorotinsky 2003). It is frequently claimed that OTS IFMISs can be rapidly introduced, especially if little or no customization is to be undertaken. However, these claims do not appear justified in most developing countries. Of the four major stages in an automation reform—procurement, design, implementation, and handover—the first and last seem to have the most risk for OTS IFMISs. An IFMIS, especially a high-end OTS solution, is a complex and costly project and involves a lengthy procurement process that can take several years.[20] If customization is limited, the design phase can be relatively rapid, but as a consequence, the implementation schedule is extended because procedures need to be rewritten and staff must be retrained. At the other end of the process, handover seems to have been neglected, and it takes considerably longer with an OTS IFMIS, if it occurs at all. Such systems are proprietary, and contractors are often unwilling to give up source code to the government. The complexity of the systems exceeds the capacity of most governments and local computer firms to manage.

The virtue of an iterative approach is that it continuously develops an operational system. Risk is lower because disruptions of daily operations are limited and continuous improvements can be verified.

Budget

When asked why his government did not procure an elaborate OTS IFMIS, a senior government official from a Mexican state recently remarked, "We could not afford one so we built a custom system."[21] Without concessionary foreign aid, most developing countries would also be faced with a hard budget constraint for their automation projects and would have to adopt a low-cost solution. The absence of a hard budget constraint means that the scope is excessive and that overruns in budget and schedule are tolerated. Effective project management is undermined, which leads to overly complex designs that fail or underperform.

Why are these systems typically so expensive, and why do they often overrun their generous budgets? Failure to contain scope leads to costly customization and long time frames. Information systems specialists command high salaries, and contractor management fees are based on multiples of these salaries. The applications are expensive, and vendors are moving to new pricing mechanisms that escalate costs (for example, license fee per user rather than blanket site licenses). Contractors often have links to application vendors, which means that low-cost options are not adopted (Parry 2005). Frequent upgrades of OTS IFMISs, which are marketed as a virtue in keeping financial systems up to date, are costly because they involve additional customization and training. Often overlooked is the annual cost of maintaining a system, which as a rule of thumb is 15 to 25 percent of the application development cost.

To be sustainable, the recurrent costs of government operations should not be funded by volatile foreign aid; yet these considerable and critical costs are either overlooked or assumed to be funded by continuing concessionary assistance. The systems are risky not just because they are complex or because governments lack the staff to operate them, but also because governments strapped for funds cannot afford the recurrent costs to support them.

In general, sophisticated OTS IFMISs also do not meet the necessary conditions of effective information system development from the standpoint of the user—governments in developing countries (although they would appear to meet the necessary conditions of most foreign aid agencies, given how strongly they recommend IFMISs). The necessary conditions are trust, need, help, and urgency (Peterson 1998a). It takes time for governments to trust the contractors and to entrust them with their financial systems. Except for external conditionalities and the availability of concessionary funding, the need for a new financial system is often not clear to government, nor do governments always see how the IFMIS solution helps (especially when compared with their legacy systems). Governments in developing countries often do not understand IT or manage it effectively. Finally, unlike firms in a market economy that embrace IT to obtain a competitive edge, no urgency exists for the public sector to reform (except to meet foreign aid conditionalities and use concessionary finance).

The Ethiopian Financial Reform: A Case Study

The Decentralization Support Activity (DSA) Project, which is implemented by the John F. Kennedy School of Government, Harvard University, was contracted to implement the budget, accounts, and expenditure planning reforms under the government of Ethiopia's Civil Service Reform Program. The project began in January 1997 and is scheduled to end November 2007. This case study is about the experience of the DSA Project in implementing these reforms.[22]

The Strategy of Ethiopia's Procedural Reform

The budget, accounts, and disbursement reforms in Ethiopia were a challenge because of the size of the country and its remoteness, poor infrastructure, limited capacity, changing government, and foreign aid policies, together with continuous political, economic, and environmental shocks.

The continuous evolution of the administrative structure has also posed a major challenge to financial management, especially second-stage devolution to *weredas* (districts) in 2001. Overnight, the number of reporting agencies that needed to be included in the financial reform increased by a factor of 15. During the reform, the country faced a series of serious shocks: two droughts (including a 50-year drought that threatened 13 million people), a 2-year war, and two elections (the fairness of the latest, in 2005, is still being questioned).

When the reform started, an accounts backlog of six years existed. The budget was formulated and consolidated by spreadsheet. The accounts system was a single-entry system, and the chart of accounts was loose, resulting in a large "other" category and misspecified expenditures. In short, most of the public finances were run manually, and even that system was not well managed.

The strategy of the DSA Project was to consolidate first and then reform. That strategy was justified by the low level of skill, the evolving fiscal decentralization, and the general degradation of the financial system that had taken place over the previous years. At the same time, Ethiopia managed its fiscal aggregates reasonably well, did not generally run a deficit, and maintained an exchange rate pegged to the U.S. dollar. In other words, the DSA strategy was to get the basics right.

The reform has for the most part been based on a (partially) sequential platform, which is summarized in figure 10.3. The logic of this strategy is the need to ensure that basic systems are in place before proceeding to more complex higher-order systems. The first task was to get the *transaction platform* (budgets, accounts, disbursements, and their automation) functioning smoothly and then develop key elements of a *policy and performance platform* (particularly focused on regions). In brief, the project's strategy for improving the transaction platform was to evolve the existing budget and accounts procedures and to drive the automation from the procedural requirements that were defined by the user. The approach has been very incremental and iterative, with the government staff extensively involved. This approach takes time but promotes an appropriate and sustainable reform that is accessible to devolved administrative levels that have little capacity. The platform approach of this strategy fits with the conventional wisdom of sequencing financial reform (Schick 1966).

Several principles of sequencing the reform had been established that had proven effective in piloting the reform. The key elements of those

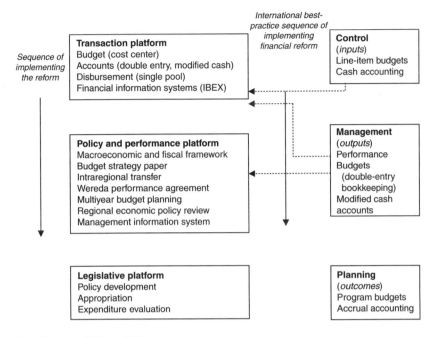

Source: Penrose and Peterson 2003.

FIGURE 10.3 The DSA Strategy of Public Financial Management Reform in Ethiopia

principles were simplification, elimination of backlogs, and sequential procedural change (budget first, followed a year later with accounts). Before a regional government implemented the budget and accounts reforms, it had to bring the existing systems up to date. Financial management was simplified (for example, limit the number of budget institutions, concentrate financial management into a single pool), and the budget reform was then initiated, to be followed by the reform of accounts procedures. Implementation was carefully designed and heavily resourced, and mass training programs in detailed procedures were launched using extensive training materials developed in local languages.

In summary, the approach involved bringing efficiency and closure to the existing system and partially introducing the new system (budget reform in the first year, followed by accounts reform in the second year). The existing system was first completed so that scarce finance staff could move on to managing the new system and not be burdened with managing two systems simultaneously. Limiting the burden on scarce staff members was a key consideration and was one reason the budget and accounts procedures were introduced separately over two financial years. Imposing a new and comprehensive system would have been inappropriate because it would have exceeded the capacity to absorb it.

The sequence of reform was characterized by its emphasis on completeness and selectivity, rather than on integration. Bringing existing systems up to date *before* introducing new systems was critical, because the necessary staff members were released to learn and operate the new systems. Although integration is held to be a centerpiece of best practice of financial reform as well as a dominant attribute of the recommended IFMISs (Schick 2002), the Ethiopian reform demonstrates that integration must be carefully defined in the context of the wider financial reform. The budget and accounts were procedurally integrated from the start through the budget classification and chart of accounts, but they were not operationally implemented in an integrated sequence (that is, the budget and accounting reforms were not made at the same time).[23]

The Ethiopian financial reform has been under way for more than 10 years and provides insights into the sequencing of financial procedures and information systems in a rapidly decentralizing developing country. The reform is an example of process change, not innovation. The DSA Project implemented a three-step approach to process change of financial procedures: comprehension, improvement, and then expansion (Peterson 2001). Comprehension meant documenting and training the staff on existing procedures. Improvement meant marginal changes (creating better forms and streamlining procedures), and expansion meant introducing new procedures (moving from single- to double-entry bookkeeping). This three-step approach to process change of procedures, in turn, necessitated an iterative, customized approach to automation.

The approach to process change focused on getting the existing system understood and operating efficiently. Improving efficiency of financial management was as much, if not more, a result of streamlining the organization of financial management (for example, how many budget entities) as improving financial procedures. This step was critical because the rapid second-stage devolution to weredas created an extensive number of reporting units at the wereda level (up to 81 in each wereda in Oromia, the largest region in the country). Simplifying the organization of financial management facilitated the absorption of the financial reform. The objective was to free up scarce finance staff members, who could work on further improvements and not be burdened with managing two systems simultaneously.

The alternative approach of process innovation, by contrast, requires a high level of government human resources to operate the new reform.

The capacity of those human resources determines the pace of a reform. A weakness of process innovation is that it does not always adequately take into consideration the need to clean up administrative backlogs (a six-year backlog in accounts in the case of Ethiopia). The iterative approach in Ethiopia started with this step. The government's decision to clear up the accounts backlog before implementing the double-entry bookkeeping reform was prudent but also meant that the accounts reform was delayed by two years. It also meant that the procedural improvements, training, and computer systems had to support the existing accounting system and not just a new system.

The Strategy of Automation of the Ethiopian Reform

The strategy for automating the budget, accounts, and disbursement reforms in Ethiopia has four attributes. First, it is a customized and iterative approach. Second, it is driven by procedures. Third, it simultaneously managed multiple versions of the system at different administrative levels. Fourth, the systems are developed in phases, which are based on user demand and resource availability.[24]

The baseline financial information systems at the start of the financial reform were rudimentary. Budgets were prepared on Microsoft Excel spreadsheets and a simple accounting system written in COBOL (common business-oriented language) operated on the mainframe.

Three distinct phases existed in the development of these systems (table 10.1):

- *Phase 1: Translating the requirements and operational testing.* The first phase of automation focused on replicating the new manual procedures by creating a seamless interface between the manual forms and the input screens of the application. Phase 1 system development went hand-in-hand with the procedural design; the manual formats were meticulously designed and brought a new standard of clarity to budget and accounts preparation. Phase 1 produced an operational prototype that was tailored to the needs of users who had never used customized computer applications. The risk of using an operational prototype for budgeting (the BIS) was limited because the new manual formats could have been processed using the previous rudimentary spreadsheets.[25] The risk of using an operational prototype for accounts (the BDA system) was reduced because an existing operational application was available. In summary, in this critical first stage of reform, risk was carefully managed by having redundant computer systems and by having the new system mirror the new manual formats. In phase 1, the distinctive contribution of the automation team was form design (translating the new manual procedures into the application's input screens). The technology platform of phase 1 was rudimentary (Visual Basic and a Microsoft Access

TABLE 10.1 Evolution of the Ethiopian Financial Information Systems

Item	Phase 1 (2000–02)	Phase 2 (2002–04)	Phase 3 (2004–present)
Features			
Functionality	Partial (IFMIS) core	Partial (IFMIS) core	Partial (IFMIS) core
Architecture	Stand-alone	LAN	WAN, LAN, and stand-alone
Level of integration	Limited	Limited	Comprehensive
Implementation	Weak but delivered	Adequate—just in time	Excellent—systematic
Data migration	Limited	Limited	Full
Complexity	Low	Medium	High
Visibility	Low	Medium	High
Expectations	Low	Low	High
Iterative development	High	High	Low
Factors of success			
Cost (development)	Low—under US$200,000	Modest—under US$1.5 million	Modest—under US$2 million
Quality	Barely acceptable	Acceptable	International standards
Speed	Slow	Slow	Fast
Risk	Low	Low	Low
Assessment			
Virtues			
Development	Requirements driven; clear forms	LAN capability; rapid new reports	WAN capability; international standards; functional review
Implementation	Operational on time	Rapid piloting in region	Rapid national rollout
Deficiencies	Documentation; expandability	Organizational risk related to subcontractors; technical proficiency of subcontractors	Sustainability; questions whether government can assume product development

Source: DSA Project staff: Stephen Peterson, Adam Abate, and Eric Chijioke.

database), and the costs were modest at under US$100,000 per year. The IT investment of this phase was modest because this activity was not part of the scope of work.

- *Phase 2: Expansion of the applications and implementation.* Phase 2 emerged with the government's introduction of second-stage devolution, when the automation reform had to cope with two requirements simultaneously: the introduction of double-entry bookkeeping and second-stage devolution by the government from zones to weredas. At a stroke, second-stage devolution expanded the administrative scope of the system by a factor of 15, and the challenge for the automation reform was to support the devolution and manage the dramatic increase in data processing. During this phase, the database of the accounts application (BDA) was upgraded and introduced (along with the budget application—the BIS) into LANs.[26] This outreach phase involved extensive training and support for the applications. To manage this expanded scope, the project subcontracted a local firm to assist in software development, training, and application support. Scaling up the support task was critical to meet the dramatically expanded scope of the operations. Because these applications were customized, relatively simple, and not proprietary, the capacity to develop and maintain them could be augmented locally. If the system had been an OTS IFMIS, it could not have been customized quickly, much less supported as broadly in a timely, cost-efficient manner. During phase 2, IT was budgeted and became an explicit part of the reform project's brief.

- *Phase 3: Upgrading to international standards.* In the third and current phase of development, the budget (BIS) and accounting (BDA) systems have been upgraded to meet and exceed international standards. The DSA Project made the argument that in this final phase it was prudent to leave the government with a system that would meet its needs (and international standards) long after the project had ended and before a potential OTS IFMIS would be operational.[27] The project began work on the IBEX system, which allowed data migration from the existing budget and accounts systems. Three other factors influenced the decision to upgrade the BIS and the BDA: the government's development of a nationwide voice, data, and video network called WeredaNET; the growing requirement to strengthen financial management at the wereda level; and the continued delays in the government's procurement of an OTS IFMIS. The IBEX system was meant to meet the current and future needs of government. From a functional perspective, the IBEX system replicates the manual procedures already automated in the existing BIS and BDA systems and supplements them as required to meet additional requirements from government. From a technical perspective, the IBEX system is a complete architectural redesign to meet the strategic requirements (international standards, WAN connectivity, and long-term sustainability). The IBEX demonstrates that a customized system can meet and exceed international standards. In this third phase of systems development, the project is implementing a two-track strategy of financial information systems. Track 1 is continuing to roll out and support the BIS and BDA legacy systems nationwide in regional and zone finance organizations (not weredas). Track 2 is the completion of the IBEX in a WAN, LAN, and stand-alone version and the replacement of the BIS and BDA applications. The flexibility of the customized IBEX to operate within a full range of connectivity using modest bandwidth makes it suitable to the varied and limited information and communication technology (ICT) conditions in Ethiopia. The two tracks ensure that operational needs are continually met while the country moves to a more robust solution.

A custom approach not only limits complexity and delivers the system to the user with the user's own specifications, but it also ensures the suitability of the system to the country's ICT capacity. An OTS IFMIS solution requires a WAN, whereas the broadband infrastructure that is to be found in developing countries is frequently inadequate. In some countries, for example, Oracle's forms and the interfaces, which are bulky and require "real" bandwidth, have thwarted implementation until the ICT is upgraded. Adam Abate, director of the DSA Project in the Ministry of Finance, has stated,

> [C]ustomization has its limits. Typically if we speak about customizing an OTS system, we are speaking of business processes, inputs, outputs (i.e., functional components). Oracle is not going to customize its fundamental platform (e.g., its interfaces). It might customize what you see, but not how you see it. (Adam Abate, personal communication, July 29, 2006, Addis Ababa)

In contrast, the customized IFMIS system developed to support Ethiopia's expenditure system (IBEX) has interfaces that were designed to operate with minimal bandwidth and can run even with 28.8 kilobits per second connections (that is, modem).[28] The ability of the IBEX to operate with minimal bandwidth means it is able to use the emerging nationwide WAN (WeredaNET), which uses VSATs (very small aperture terminals) to link all of its wereda finance offices.

The upgrade to IBEX addresses the following main concepts and demonstrates that a customized IFMIS can have the full capability of an OTS IFMIS (DSA Project 2005):

■ *Scalability.* The current BIS and BDA applications are desktop applications that must be installed separately on every workstation that needs them. The implication is no marginal decrease in both the rollout and support tasks of implementing these systems nationwide. IBEX is a browser-based application, hosted from a few centers, thus making it highly scalable in terms of implementation and support.

■ *Security.* IBEX improves data security by using a state-of-the-art security framework to ensure the integrity of national financial data.[29]

■ *Data integrity and manageability.* By unifying the data store for all application functions, IBEX eliminates the problems caused by multiple data stores. IBEX also upgrades to a full-scale database product that will handle the volumes of data present in the system for the foreseeable future.

■ *Extensibility.* Besides implementing the automation of the core financial management functions, IBEX exists as a framework for integration of financial functions in general. The application architecture means that the addition of integrated financial modules, or functions or reports within the existing modules, is greatly simplified.

■ *Functionality and usability.* The IBEX application brings with it a redesigned interface that is intended to replicate what users are accustomed to while improving interface controls where possible. In addition, the IBEX framework provides for dynamic internationalization, which allows users to change the language of the application on the fly, and it supports the addition of other language sets should they become necessary.

Institutional Issue: The Virtues of Benign Neglect

The Ethiopian experience presents an interesting counterhypothesis to the conventional wisdom that information system reform requires top management commitment (from either the government or foreign aid agencies): benign neglect can actually facilitate reform. Neglect by both the government and the donor-creditors meant that technical development could proceed unimpeded by external micromanagement or duplication.

On the government side, the two-year war between Ethiopia and Eritrea starting in 1998 was fortuitous for the financial reform because it insulated the reform from government and foreign aid agency micromanagement during the critical early development stage and allowed the iterative development of the foundations of a financial system—the budget classification and the chart of accounts.

Moreover, the senior official responsible for the reform faced a weak and fragmented Ministry of Finance that had to coordinate financial management with an equally weak and fragmented Ministry of Planning. As a political appointee, this senior official was unable to direct the work of the ministry's middle managers (department heads), who were permanent civil servants and could ignore the directions of senior officials. Ethiopia demonstrates that even a high level of commitment by senior officials does not ensure effective reform, because the middle-level bureaucrats have to implement the reform. In this case, the middle managers were indifferent to the reform until the project could demonstrate its value to their particular work. Even when such benefits were demonstrated, some individuals still resisted change (Peterson 1998b).

The power of the senior official responsible for the reform was highly circumscribed; his contributions to the reform included securing funding at critical phases of the project, accepting the recommendations of the chief technical assistance adviser, and closely monitoring the project's progress. Fortunately, he did not divert project resources, nor did he micromanage the project. In this environment of indifference—and at times hostility—managing the overall reform of these financial components as well as their automation fell to the project.

The donor-creditor community was another source of neglect. The initial design of the financial reform contractually separated the procedural reform from the automation reform. The DSA Project, which was responsible for the procedural development of the budget and accounts and disbursement systems, was eventually asked to automate those systems because of delays in procuring the separate automation project. Closely coordinating procedural and automation development within a project framework promoted a coherent reform driven by procedures. Because automation was not part of the contracted scope, the systems developed were rudimentary and very inexpensive. These systems have always been viewed as interim, awaiting the original automation procurement—the "final solution"—which is an OTS IFMIS. Ten years later, the procurement has still not been completed.

The institutional environment presented in Ethiopia determined the DSA strategy of financial reform and its automation. Benign neglect on the part of the government and foreign aid agencies, coupled with the limited and at times even hostile government management, meant that the reform was driven by a project and not by government or foreign aid agencies. The project faced a complex and rapidly evolving environment (Ethiopia introduced a massive second-stage devolution to weredas literally overnight just as the reform was being piloted in the first region). The need to bring the government along at all levels of administration and to support the rapid devolution meant the adoption of an evolutionary strategy or process change. The virtual lack of resources for the financial information systems meant a custom rather than a costly OTS system driven by a rapidly evolving procedural reform.

In summary, the custom automation strategy of the Ethiopian budget and accounts reform was an appropriate scale and sequenced to the pace of the procedural rollout and the limited financial resources available. It has managed risk well by keeping a focused scope and by adhering to a tight and frequent schedule of system updates. The very limited budget has reinforced a clear scope and schedule.

Lessons for Developing Countries

Automation of Ethiopia's financial procedures exemplifies a dolphin approach. The financial reform was focused on a limited core of functions (budget, accounts, disbursement, reporting) and was procedurally driven. Automation supported the procedural reform by matching the periodic improvements in procedures.

This case is an appropriate example for other developing countries for several reasons. First, it is based on firsthand experience over 10 years, unlike much of the literature, which is based on static second- and thirdhand descriptions and, in many cases, interpretations of outcomes at particular points in time. Second, it is an example of an effective financial reform that has been supported by an appropriate financial information systems strategy (customized and iterative) in a difficult and unsupportive task environment (ARD Inc. 2006). This task environment is similar to that faced by most developing countries. Third, the information systems have been successful. Their success, however, cannot be fully separated from the broader reform in which they were embedded.

Several criteria are used to argue that the systems were successful. They worked. They never failed. They were promptly delivered and never delayed the procedural rollout. They were rapidly expanded to meet new user needs. They were relatively inexpensive. They have been continuously upgraded and are now technically robust and sophisticated and meet international standards. They were inextricably linked to dramatic improvements in the performance of budgets and accounts.[30]

The example of the automation of the Ethiopian budget and accounts system provides five key lessons in automating financial reforms in developing countries:

1. Institutional factors are far more important than the technical choice in determining the outcome of automation.
2. Information technology should not be the driver of financial reform. Indeed, if it had been, the Ethiopian reform would probably not have been implemented.
3. There is no a priori technical reason to favor either an OTS or a custom solution: the choice depends on the circumstances. However, the opportunities offered by a custom solution for learning by doing and for creation of ownership provide strong arguments to balance the putative advantages of an OTS solution.
4. Effective project selection and management are major factors in the success of automation.
5. A financial and social cost-benefit analysis should be undertaken in reviewing a policy of introducing or continuing with a customized system or upgrading to an OTS solution.

Lesson 1: Important Institutional Factors in Determining the Outcome of Automation

The literature contends that success of an IFMIS depends on strong high-level commitment and support (Diamond and Khemani 2006). Such commitment is not always to be found in developing countries, where bureaucratic rivalry, limited technical competence at the top, and reluctance to change (which is often well founded) may all be factors. The example of Ethiopia demonstrates that even when "saints" (Peterson 1998b) and high-level commitment exist, they do not ensure effective reform, because the middle-level officials have to implement the change.

The DSA Project managing the Ethiopian reform of budgets, budget planning, and accounts faced benign neglect, and in many ways, as described earlier, this situation benefited the reform. Optimal obscurity can be a key factor in the success of development projects more broadly. Projects that are optimally obscure do not have the high expectations and scrutiny of highly visible and political projects, which spares them criticism and unrealistic time frames. Optimal obscurity allows projects to learn by doing, to make mistakes, and to progress incrementally.[31] Large-scale OTS IFMISs are not optimally obscure. They are hugely expensive, which alone makes them visible and prone to delays and corruption, and unrealistic expectations about functionality and schedule are commonplace.

In developing countries, high-level commitment to any reform will at best be modest and episodic. Financial reforms and the information systems that support them are by their nature long-term endeavors, so long-term support, however defined, is required. Equally if not more important to high-level commitment are acceptance and use by the middle echelons of the government. It is there that the systems are introduced, used, or ignored. Obtaining middle-management commitment involves four factors: trust, need, help, and urgency (Peterson 1998a). Government officials, especially middle-level managers, need to trust the contractors providing the solution; gaining that trust takes time. They have to see the need for the change and recognize that the solution will help them. Finally, urgency to implement the change has to exist.

The foreign aid community needs to have realistic expectations about the limits and time scale of financial reform and the computer systems that support them. Improving supporting manual systems is as important as introducing the automation of some of the modules. Although no quick hits exist in financial reform, ironically, relatively more rapid improvement is often possible in manual procedures than in the automation of procedures. Foreign aid agencies need to consider support for improvements in both manual and automated procedures. Foreign aid agencies tend to overstate the benefits of a process of innovation approach and underestimate the complexities and risks of this approach. Foreign aid agencies need to better understand the process change approach and its virtues. The experience of IFMISs, particularly in Africa, has shown that contractor failure or poor performance has been a major risk. In evaluating the selection of contractors, consideration should be given to their understanding of and experience with process change, not just process innovation. The critical task for any contractor is integration of the computer system with the organization and its staff. This process requires familiarity and experience with the local context.

Lesson 2: Information Technology Should Not Be the Driver of Financial Reform

Typical OTS IFMIS systems do not have all of the core modules necessary for good financial management. Good financial management requires both manual and automated procedures, and IT alone is not enough. IT systems should support sound financial procedures, not define them.

Because IT takes a long time to develop, procure, and implement, it allows time to start with changes in financial procedures that can be done quickly. Procedural reform gets the user requirements right, and user requirements are determining factors in the success of information systems.

A focus on IT as a driver means that more serious institutional issues are not addressed or can be finessed. Experience from Ethiopia clearly demonstrates that institutional issues are far more important and far harder to manage than technical issues.

One reason IT is a driver of reform in aid-dependent countries is that IT is a conditionality of foreign aid agencies because it is presumed to improve financial management. The high failure rate of IFMISs suggests that IT is not a route to improve financial management. It is a negative, harmful conditionality that imposes inappropriate levels of risk on weak financial systems. The appropriate strategy is to gradually strengthen weak financial systems through process change, not innovation.

Lesson 3: No Presumptive Reason Exists to Favor an OTS or a Custom Solution

The conventional wisdom is that an OTS solution is preferable to a custom solution. Research has not shown this presumption to be the case (see table 10.2). It is not clear whether the OTS characteristics are related to the high failure rate of IFMISs. As noted previously, large-scale, complex information systems (whales) are increasingly believed to be more prone to risk than small-scale, iteratively developed systems (dolphins). In the case of Ethiopia, the rapidly changing fiscal devolution combined with the adequacy of the baseline financial systems meant that a customized, iterative automation strategy was appropriate from the standpoint of user requirements and availability of financial resources.

All large-scale financial information systems involve risk, whether developed by a customized or an OTS solution. The central question for developing countries is which approach, in principle, best minimizes risk in a given context. The Ethiopian case suggests that a custom system was appropriate in that context. The institutional issues required a flexible approach, and custom systems, by definition, are more flexible. Moreover, a small-scale iterative approach on the technical side minimizes risk. All told, custom systems are better in many cases. Research has not related the approach (OTS versus custom) to the failure of IFMIS. It has been argued that institutional factors far outweigh technical factors, and institutional factors require a flexible approach to automation. A custom system by definition is small scale in this sense, and

TABLE 10.2 Pros and Cons of OTS versus Custom IFMISs

Type of system	Pros	Cons
OTS IT systems	Standardized Tested Continuity of vendor	User required to come to the system High customization costs Proprietary Long lead time for procurement Government locked into a technology Increasing costs Lack of local sustainability
Custom, iterative IT systems	System required to come to the user Lower cost Rapid delivery Meets exact user specifications System that can evolve with technology Development costs that are dramatically declining	System design not proven Lack of continuity of developer Perception that a brand name is needed

Source: DSA Project staff: Stephen Peterson, Adam Abate, Eric Chijioke, and Sally Houstoun.

the decision between an OTS and a custom solution, though important, is not critical. A flexible OTS solution or a custom solution could, in principle, be appropriate in a particular context.

The problem with OTS systems is not just lack of flexibility in meeting user requirements. OTS systems lock countries in for many years. Technology is rapidly improving and becoming more flexible, less expensive, and more accessible. Locking countries into OTS systems precludes developing countries from taking advantage of new technologies. One new technology, the new XBRL (extensible business reporting language) protocol, allows a custom financial application to share data across multiple systems.[32]

Lesson 4: Effective Project Selection and Management Are Major Factors in the Success of Automation

A central risk in implementing financial information systems is the project, not the package. Contractors are a major risk in the implementation of financial information systems regardless of whether an OTS or a custom solution is used. In Nigeria, for example, implementation of a high-end OTS IFMIS (SAP) failed because a reputable international consulting firm failed to properly integrate the solution to the business processes. The system integration process failed. As Dorsey (2000) notes, even for U.S. corporations, hiring reputable international firms or purchasing expensive OTS systems does not mitigate risk. Effective financial information systems are based on an integral strategy of financial reform. The broader strategy of financial reform; the breadth of its content (for example, budget, accounts, disbursement, commitments); and the IT solution must all be coherent. One reason financial reforms fail or underperform is the absence of this coherence. The Ethiopia case was unique in that these three factors were all under the same project, which permitted a coherent approach. A critical task for governments is to ensure this coherence.

A challenge for funders of aid-dependent countries is to understand the need for that coherence, as well as the long time lags required to implement financial reforms, including automation, and allow the government to take over the reform.

Lesson 5: Financial and Social Cost-Benefit Analysis

One of the main reasons that aid-dependent countries adopt OTS systems is the availability of concessionary aid for these systems, coupled with the belief by the providers of this aid that OTS systems are superior and the most cost-effective solution for improving public financial management (OTS systems reduce their fiduciary risk). This assertion is not substantiated.

As noted previously, budget is a key variable affecting the scope and thus the risk of a financial system. Without a hard budget constraint, the scope of information systems expands and their schedules extend—that is, their risk increases.

One benefit of a custom solution is the social benefit of the development of a local computer industry. For example, the state of Andhra Pradesh in India adopted a "middle-ware" solution to link its existing legacy systems together rather than procuring an expensive foreign OTS IFMIS. The government of Andhra Pradesh was able to do so because a robust computer industry existed in Andhra Pradesh. This custom solution was very inexpensive and effective. Similarly, in Ethiopia, members of the computer staff of the DSA Project are principally local Ethiopians or Ethiopians returning from the diaspora. The value of building such local capacity extends far beyond the particular financial application and supports the broader process of endogenous economic growth. Moreover, the risks associated with the introduction and sustainability of IFMISs are reduced if local contractors can do it.

A Concluding Word

Many years ago Goran Hyden (1983) concluded his study of rural development in Tanzania by observing that there are no shortcuts to development. This conclusion is true of financial reform and the development of financial information systems. The conventional wisdom of both needs to be reassessed. This chapter has argued for a more balanced view of the technical recommendations for IFMISs. The conventional wisdom is not working.

Notes

I am grateful to Adam Abate, Eric Chijioke, Sally Houstoun, and Perran Penrose for helpful comments, exchanges of ideas, or references, some of which influenced me quite a bit, although none of the three should be held responsible.

1. For example, many authorities have recently demonstrated the near universal failure of IFMISs to meet their objectives. I do not analyze those cases but take them as generally accepted (see Diamond and Khemani 2006). The International Monetary Fund has also found that IFMISs are disappointing and significantly divert its technical assistance staff in developing countries (see IMF 2006: 53). Large-scale information systems are risky, with estimated failure rates from 50 to 80 percent in the private sector in industrial countries (see Dorsey 2000). Dorsey is an authority on large-scale systems development and Oracle applications.
2. They do so on the advice of foreign aid agencies to adopt IFMISs. See Hashim and Allan (1999).
3. Whether one can extend Lienert's argument to other developing countries is an empirical question. Experience from selected Latin American countries highlights the virtues of existing procedures and the inappropriateness of new procedures imposed by a technology solution: "[A]n original design option for a new hospital [information system] in Guatemala was to reengineer administrative processes to make them more efficient. But in reality, hospital directors supported current procedures and wanted controls to remain in place to ensure corruption was held in check. The design was therefore amended to ensure that these current work processes were supported by the new system" (Heeks 2002: 108).
4. Lienert's research also points out the limits of introducing complicated procedural reforms in developing countries—which is what an IFMIS does. Francophone countries in Africa have elements of accrual accounting (for example, recording of financial assets and liabilities), but their systems do not function well because they are "either too complex and archaic to operate and/or the rules are flouted" (Lienert 2002: 29). Despite the relative sophistication of the accounting systems, they are unable to deliver the basics (prompt monthly and year-end reports) (see Lienert 2002).
5. The iterative "dolphin" approach to financial systems development is also supported by a recent World Bank study of financial systems in Africa, which found that a "well-focused, incremental approach is more likely to succeed" than a comprehensive approach (see Heidenhof and others 2002: 13). The dolphin approach accords with an extreme programming approach to systems development that is based on very rapid development of a system that allows the user and the developer to fine-tune requirements.

6. Best practice is a much misused concept, particularly when applied to systems that are not yet fully proven. After all, financial reforms in OECD countries have been under way for many years and are continually evolving: categorizing changing systems under the static rubric of best practice would be a mistake. IFMISs are considered best practice, but generally they do not work. Also, IFMISs are not common practice in most OECD countries (see Wynne 2005: 17).

7. For developing countries, Heeks (2002) stresses the virtue of improvisation rather than standardization: do not change the local conditions to fit the information system design; rather, change the design to fit the situation.

8. Deepak Bhatia (2003) of the World Bank provides the following specification (which is the accepted convention) of what the core of an IFMIS should be. The core functions are general ledger and accounts payable and receivable; they may also include financial reporting, fund management, and cost management. The noncore functions are human resources and payroll, budget formulation, revenue (tax and customs), procurement, inventory, property management, performance, and management information.

9. The Tanzanian reform had to customize at considerable expense the OTS IFMIS (Epicor) to include budgeting and commitment (Wynne 2005: 22). Although Bhatia (2003) includes fund (presumably funds) management in his definition of the core modules of an IFMIS, Diamond and Khemani (2006: 100, 102) exclude disbursement altogether.

10. In the Kenya reform, four of these modules (budget, commitments or votebook, cashbook, and accounts) were automated with a stand-alone system. Because the reform was in a sector ministry, the cash management component was not automated. It was assumed that the Treasury would fund the warrants—an assumption that was often not forthcoming in the fourth and even third quarters of the fiscal year. The accounting system was a stand-alone system (see Peterson and others1996).

11. Excessive reengineering or streamlining procedures that remove redundancy are inappropriate for systems needed to check rent-seeking and improve reliability in developing bureaucracies (see Peterson 1997).

12. One weakness of the Uganda IFMIS was the absence of a parallel manual system (see Heidenhof and others 2002).

13. A further virtue of developing a robust manual system is that it entails starting the not-so-insignificant translation of procedures into local languages and developing user guides and training manuals. The accounts manual for Oromia in Ethiopia took two years to translate. By proceeding early with this step, the computer application, which had internationalization capability, could be quickly modified to operate in the local language.

14. A virtue of having a manual system is that it puts a structure—an architecture—to the system.

15. Many industrial countries do not have comprehensive integrated financial systems, and even comparatively large and advanced transitional developing countries (China and India), which have the technological capability to develop and operate large-scale information systems, have opted for simpler customized systems. China currently uses a custom system, although it is reviewing OTS solutions. The Indian state of Andhra Pradesh adopted an innovative "middleware" solution that linked its legacy systems together (see Government of Andhra Pradesh 2001).

16. Getting the requirements of an information system, of course, is the most important factor determining its success.

17. According to the contractor, the government of Tanzania adopted a "risky" strategy of using an OTS IFMIS (Epicor) because the financial procedures were deemed to be "completely dysfunctional" (see Murphy and Bhatt 2000: 168).

18. This issue was a topic of discussion at the Joint ACBF/East Afritac Workshop, "IFMIS: The Challenges of Designing and Implementing Budget Preparation Modules," held in Nairobi in 2004. It was also discussed in the session on financial information systems at the Executive Program in Public Financial Management, held at the John F. Kennedy School of Government, Harvard University, Cambridge, Massachusetts, during the summer of 2006.

19. Even in the private sector of industrial countries, large-scale information systems projects have failed, and hiring large, established consulting firms or using brand-name applications is no guarantee of success (see Dorsey 2000).

20. Procurement of an IFMIS in Ethiopia has been under way for 11 years and still has not been done. For an explanation of the most recent two-year delay in this program, see the whimsical and self-exculpating handover report by the IFMIS adviser (Walsh 2006).

21. The remark was made by a participant of the Executive Program in Public Financial Management, held at the John F. Kennedy School of Government, Harvard University, Cambridge, Massachusetts, during the summer of 2006.

22. This section draws heavily upon a recent summary of the DSA Project (DSA Project 2006).

23. Amhara regional state attempted to implement both the budget and accounts reforms simultaneously and failed. Tigray regional state, a much smaller and homogeneous area, implemented both reforms simultaneously, but the process was extremely difficult.

24. The financial reform was piloted and rolled out sequentially, not comprehensively, so leads and lags arose in the overall system configuration. For example, some regions were operating the new chart of accounts with double-entry bookkeeping, some were operating the new chart of accounts with single-entry bookkeeping, and some were operating the old chart of accounts with single-entry booking. All three systems needed to operate simultaneously and be consolidated at the end of the fiscal year.

25. Several versions of the BDA system exist.

26. The migration was from Microsoft Access to Microsoft SQL Server.

27. Introducing the IBEX was a prudent strategy even if the government later decides to procure an OTS IFMIS, because full implementation will take several years.

28. These specifications are according to Adam Abate, director of the DSA Project in the Ministry of Finance, personal communication, July 29, 2006, Addis Ababa. IBEX requires only minimal bandwidth because only those parts of the interface that need to be refreshed are reloaded.

29. IBEX uses Siteminder security software by NetIntegrity.

30. For example, monthly reports from weredas are now processed within two months by the regions where the reform has been implemented. Previously, these reports took up to two years to produce. The backlog of accounts in Ethiopia has been reduced from six years, when the reform began in 1997, to less than one year in fiscal year 2001.

31. Albert Hirschman's (1995) theory of the "hiding hand" of development projects contains many of these attributes, which he considered essential for success. Hirschman argued that preplanned projects often failed. David Korten (1980) also argued for the value of a learning approach rather than a blueprint approach for successful development projects.

32. The XBRL standard is a free and open standard. Its development to date has been principally used to link business to government information in industrial countries, and most major accounting software companies are working to support this standard. The implications of the XBRL protocol are that it facilitates links across a variety of software, thereby allowing greater flexibility in applications (see Bishopp 2006).

References

Abate, Adam, and Eric Chijioke. 2006. "Integrated Budget and Expenditure System (IBEX) Technical Overview," Decentralization Support Activity Project, Report IT-IBEX-24. Cambridge, MA: John F. Kennedy School of Government, Harvard University.

ARD Inc. 2006. "Evaluation of the In-Service Training Project [the DSA Project]." ARD Inc., Burlington, VT.

Bhatia, Deepak. 2003. *IFMS Implementation: Aspects for Consideration*. Washington, DC: World Bank.

Bishopp, Richard. 2006. "Local Urban Computerisation of Income and Expenditures ('LUCIE'), Addis Ababa: Capacity Building for Decentralized Service Delivery Project." Ministry of Federal Affairs, Federal Democratic Republic of Ethiopia, Addis Ababa.

Chijioke, Eric. 2004. "Managing Large-Scale Information Systems Development: A Demystifying Approach." Paper presented to the Executive Program in Public Financial Management, John F. Kennedy School of Government, Harvard University, Cambridge, MA, July 17.

Davenport, Thomas. 1993. *Process Innovation: Reengineering Work through Information Technology*. Boston: Harvard Business School Press.

Diamond, Jack, and Pokar Khemani. 2006. "Introducing Financial Management Information Systems in Developing Countries." *OECD Journal on Budgeting* 5 (3): 97–132.

Dorotinsky, William. 2003. "Technology and Corruption: The Case of FMIS." PowerPoint presentation at the International Anti Corruption (IACC) Conference, Seoul, March 26.

Dorsey, Paul. 2000. "The Top 10 Reasons Why Systems Projects Fail." Dulcian Inc., New York. http://www.dulcian.com.

DSA (Decentralization Support Activity) Project. 2005. *IBEX: Executive Summary*. Project Report 026. Cambridge, MA: John F. Kennedy School of Government, Harvard University.

———. 2006. *Overview of the DSA Project: Reform Strategy, and Components of Reform (Budget, Budget Planning, Accounts, and Financial Information Systems)*. Project Report M-70. Cambridge, MA: John F. Kennedy School of Government, Harvard University.

Gall, John. 1977. *Systemantics: How Systems Work and Especially How They Fail*. New York: Quadrangle.

Government of Andhra Pradesh, India. 2001. "Request for Proposal: Integrated Finance Information System." Hyderabad, Government of Andhra Pradesh.

Hashim, Ali, and William Allan. 1999. "Information Systems for Fiscal Management." In *Managing Government Expenditure*, ed. Salvatore Schiavo-Campo and Daniel Tommasi, 451–76. Manila: Asian Development Bank.

Heeks, Richard. 2002. "Information Systems and Developing Countries: Failure, Success and Local Improvisations." *Information Society* 18 (2): 101–12.

Heidenhof, Guenter, Helene Grandvoinnet, Daryoush Kianpour, and Bobak Rezaian. 2002. "Design and Implementation of Financial Management Systems: An African Perspective." Africa Region Working Paper 25, World Bank, Washington, DC.

Hirschman, Albert O. 1995. *Development Projects Observed*. Washington, DC: The Brookings Institution.

Hyden, Goran. 1983. *No Shortcuts to Progress: African Development Management in Perspective*. London: Heinemann.

IMF (International Monetary Fund). 2006. *Selected African Countries: IMF Technical Assistance Evaluation—Public Expenditure Management Reform*. Washington, DC: IMF.

Korten, David. 1980. "A Learning Process Approach." *Public Administration Review* 40 (5): 480–511.

Lienert, Ian. 2002. "Comparison between Two Public Expenditure Management Systems in Africa." IMF Working Paper 03/2, International Monetary Fund, Washington, DC.

Murphy, Peter, and Harish Bhatt. 2000. "Integrated Financial Management in Tanzania." Paper presented at the International Consortium on Government Financial Management, Miami, FL, March 27–31.

OECD (Organisation for Economic Co-operation and Development). 2001. "The Hidden Threat to E-Government: Avoiding Large Government IT Failures." PUMA Policy Brief 8, OECD, Paris.

Parry, Michael. 2005. "Why Government IFMS Procurements So Often Get It Wrong." *ACCA International Public Sector Bulletin* 4: 4–7.

Penrose, Perran. 2005. "Financial Statements and Reporting." John F. Kennedy School of Government, Harvard University, Cambridge, MA.

Penrose, Perran, and Stephen Peterson. 2003. "DSA Project Brief." John F. Kennedy School of Government, Harvard University, Cambridge, MA.

Peterson, Stephen. 1997. "Hierarchy versus Networks: Alternative Strategies for Building Organizational Capacity in Public Bureaucracies in Africa." In *Getting Good Government: Capacity Building in the Public Sectors of Developing Countries*, ed. Merilee S. Grindle, 157–76. Cambridge, MA: Harvard University Press.

———. 1998a. "Making IT Work: Implementing Effective Financial Information Systems in Bureaucracies in Developing Countries." In *Information Technology and Innovation in Tax Administration*, ed. Glenn Jenkins, 177–94. The Hague: Kluwer Law International.

———. 1998b. "Saints, Demons, Wizards, and Systems: Why Information Technology Reforms Fail or Underperform in Public Bureaucracies in Africa." *Public Administration and Development* 18 (1): 37–60.

———. 2001. "Financial Reform in a Devolved African Country: Lessons from Ethiopia." *Public Administration and Development* 21 (2): 131–48.

Peterson, Stephen, Charles Kinyeki, Joseph Mutai, and Charles Ndungu. 1996. "Computerizing Accounting Systems in Developing Bureaucracies: Lessons from Kenya." *Public Budgeting and Finance* 16 (4): 45–58.

Schick, Allen. 1966. "The Road to PBB: The Stages of Budget Reform." *Public Administration Review* 26 (4): 243–55.

———. 2002. "Opportunity, Strategy and Tactics in Reforming Public Management." *OECD Journal of Budgeting* 2 (3): 7–34.

Varon, Elana. 2004. "For the IRS There Is No Easy Fix." CIO Government, Australia. http://www.cio.com.au/index.php/id;66216935;fp;4;fpid;21.

Walsh, Ray. 2006. "Completion Report: Integrated Financial Management System Pilot Phase." Ministry of Finance and Economic Planning, Government of Ethiopia, Addis Ababa.

Wynne, Andy. 2005. "Public Financial Management Reforms in Developing Countries: Lessons of Experience from Ghana, Tanzania, and Uganda." ACBF Working Paper 7, African Capacity Building Foundation, Harare.

11

What Would an Ideal Public Finance Management System Look Like?

MATTHEW ANDREWS

In their 2006 meetings, the finance ministers of the Group of Eight (G8) came out in support of elaborating a public finance management (PFM) code—a document described by the minister of the Russian Federation as one that "should make people understand how the financial policy priorities are chosen and how the finance management is arranged" (RosBusinessConsulting 2006). Such a code, the minister added, would provide a standardized approach to thinking about what PFM processes look like (or should look like), covering "public finance management spheres" including policy development and financing, "fiscal transparency, measures securing finance stability, and result-oriented budgeting" (RosBusinessConsulting 2006).

The donor community can certainly claim to have preempted this call, having already created a tool to standardize thinking about PFM process quality: the Public Expenditure and Financial Accountability (PEFA) indicators. The "PFM Performance Measurement Framework is an integrated monitoring framework that allows measurement of country PFM performance over time" (PEFA 2006: ii). Introduced to help "assess and develop essential PFM systems," it is meant to provide "a common pool of information for measurement and monitoring of PFM performance progress and a common platform for dialogue" (PEFA 2006: 1).[1]

This intention suggests that the PEFA model could provide an excellent basis for identifying a common and standardized PFM code. This suggestion is the starting point of this chapter.[2] The chapter does not stop at this point, however, because complexities inherent in all PFM systems suggest limits in using any single indicator set such as PEFA. An effort to identify a PFM code requires thinking about exactly how to use the PEFA indicators and, indeed, considering what is required beyond PEFA:

- PFM's systemic nature is a primary complexity. Systems derive their strength from the quality of individual process areas *and* from links between processes. PFM systems have multiple processes, which are often developed at different levels and poorly linked. Although PEFA indicators cover most process areas, some are not covered at all (including policy development), some are covered in very basic ways, and there is no real treatment of the dynamic links between processes.
- PFM's multiplicity of role players is another complexity. PFM outcomes result from the engagement of many role players across the system—from central ministries of finance to line ministries and agencies, procurement departments, and even civil society entities at various levels of government (central, regional and local). If the role-player population behaves in a fragmented and poorly coordinated manner, the system's results are compromised. PEFA's treatment of this issue is limited,[3] as indeed is the "stove-piped" approach many governments take to PFM (which seems to hold that individual process areas stand alone).[4]
- The appropriate "look" of a PFM system is contingent on the kind of goal the system is addressing—another complication in the effort to standardize thinking about what PFM systems should look like. There is a strong argument that systems focused on achieving fiscal discipline require different process elements than systems intended to foster efficient resource allocation—with the different process elements reflecting different levels of development and stimulating different kinds of accountability.[5] Single indicator sets such as PEFA are arguably too static to reflect on the ideal PFM look at different levels—PEFA's indicators do not extend beyond critical basics, for instance, thereby limiting the indicator set to assessments of only the foundational levels of PFM development.

The above complexities pose a significant challenge to all who want to develop a standardized approach to thinking about PFM—especially to the G8 finance ministers wanting to identify a PFM code. How do you standardize a way of thinking about systems that are obviously highly contingent on the kinds of role players engaged and the kinds of goals being addressed? Although systems should of necessity look different across different contexts, this article argues that it is certainly useful to think about a guiding code that can be used in all situations to assist governments in thinking about their own systems. This code needs to allow for a truly integrated approach to thinking about PFM systems, the complex engagements between role players in the PFM "population," and the contingency of PFM "look" on PFM goals.

This chapter provides some background thoughts intended to build on the PEFA indicator set and lay an even stronger foundation for full elaboration of a dynamic and useful PFM code (not to prescribe and fully standardize, but to guide thinking). The chapter begins by introducing the PEFA indicators in brief. It then discusses the three dimensions of complexity in analyzing PFM systems and in all areas notes what the elaboration of a PFM code will require beyond PEFA. Some specific ideas are presented for further study, though they are not provided as final solutions but rather as initial thoughts. The chapter concludes with a summary of the "PEFA and beyond" discussion.

Basics of the PEFA Indicator Set

In the first half of 2005, the multidonor PEFA group concluded a two-year initiative to identify basic indicators of a "critical" PFM system (PEFA 2006: 2). The PEFA framework is shown at its most basic in box 11.1, which identifies major areas that the donor group considered important in the PFM system.

The 28 indicators in PEFA's framework are structured into four categories: (a) PFM system outturns, such as the comparison of executed budget with the formulated budget and the level of arrears; (b) cross-cutting features of the system, such as basic transparency and comprehensiveness; (c) budget-cycle issues, which capture the "performance of the key systems, processes and institutions within the budget cycle of the central government" (PEFA 2006: 3); and (d) donor practices, which capture "elements of donor practices which impact the performance of country PFM system" (PEFA 2006: 3).

Figure 11.1 shows the framework in diagrammatic form. The framework links outturns (or goals) with process quality, implicitly arguing that PFM system performance can be assessed only by looking at both dimensions. This broad "effectiveness" approach to organizational assessment is increasingly embraced in initiatives like the Government Performance Project in the

BOX 11.1 PEFA's Broad Focal Points for Public
Financial Management

Shown below are the broad headings of the PEFA indicators, as they pertain
to public expenditure management issues (revenue management issues are
omitted).

- **Public Financial Management Outturns: Budget Credibility**
    —Aggregate expenditure outturn compared with original approved
    budget
    —Composition of expenditure outturn compared with original approved
    budget
    —Aggregate revenue outturn compared with original approved budget
    —Stock and monitoring of expenditure payment arrears

- **Key Cross-Cutting Issues: Comprehensiveness and Transparency**
    —Classification of the budget
    —Comprehensiveness of information included in budget documentation
    —Extent of unreported government operations
    —Transparency of intergovernmental fiscal relations
    —Oversight of aggregate fiscal risk from other public sector entities
    —Public access to key fiscal information

- **Budget Cycle: Policy-Based Budgeting**
    —Orderliness and participation in the annual budget process
    —Multiyear perspective in fiscal planning, expenditure policy making,
    and budgeting

- **Budget Cycle: Predictability and Control in Budget Execution**
    —Predictability in the availability of funds for commitment of expenditures
    —Recording and management of cash balances, debt, and guarantees
    —Effectiveness of payroll controls
    —Competition, value for money, and controls in procurement
    —Effectiveness of internal controls for nonsalary expenditure and assets
    management
    —Effectiveness of internal audit

- **Budget Cycle: Accounting, Recording, and Reporting**
    —Timeliness and regularity of accounts reconciliation
    —Availability of information on resources received by service delivery units
    —Quality and timeliness of in-year budget reports
    —Quality and timeliness of annual financial statements

- **Budget Cycle: External Scrutiny and Audit**
    —Scope, nature, and follow-up of external audit
    —Legislative scrutiny of the annual budget law
    —Legislative scrutiny of external audit reports

■ **Budget Cycle: Donor Practice**
  —Predictability of direct budget support
  —Financial information provided by donors for budgeting and reporting
   on project or program aid
  —Proportion of aid that is managed by use of national procedures

Source: PEFA 2006. See also http://www.pefa.org.

United States and even in undertakings such as the National Performance Review.[6] Figure 11.1 shows that PFM process areas (in the budget cycle, including policy-based budgeting, budget execution, accounting and reporting, and external scrutiny and audit) foster cross-cutting system qualities (for example, transparency) as well as PFM outturns (for example, budget credibility). PEFA's framework requires governments with strong outcomes to show exactly where these outcomes arise from—allowing the identification of potential process weaknesses even when outcomes are strong.

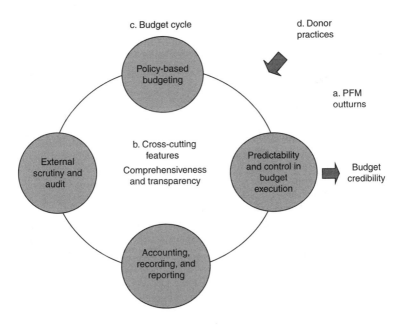

Source: PEFA 2006: 4.

FIGURE 11.1 A Simplified PEFA Framework

The 28 indicators used in the PEFA set are titled *high-level indicators.* This terminology means that they address quality issues at a fairly broad level, to allow for standardization at this level but country-specific variation in the detailed practices and processes. They routinely involve a number of dimensions. One of the two policy-based budgeting indicators, called *multiyear perspective in fiscal planning, expenditure policy, and budgeting,*[7] has four dimensions, for instance: (a) preparation of multiyear fiscal forecasts and functional allocations, (b) scope and frequency of debt sustainability analysis, (c) existence of sector strategies with multiyear costing or recurrent and investment expenditure, and (d) links between investment budgets and forward expenditure estimates.

Table 11.1 shows how the PEFA framework facilitates analysis of the individual process areas, with reference to the subindicator known as *existence of sector strategies.* Very simply, governments compare their current practices with the descriptions in the table, identifying whether they score an A, B, C, or D. The assessment has an obvious theoretical and comparative basis—in this case, the argument that strategies underlying the budget are important influences on budget quality, are better when fully costed, and are better when covering all spending types and when consistent with fiscal forecasts (costs are identified on the basis of such forecasts, for instance). The assessment

TABLE 11.1 Assessing Performance against the PEFA Indicator for Existence of Sector Strategies

Score	Type of strategy
A	Strategies for sectors representing at least 75% of primary expenditure exist with full costing of recurrent and investment expenditure, broadly consistent with fiscal forecasts.
B	Statements of sector strategies exist and are fully costed, broadly consistent with fiscal forecasts, for sectors representing 25% to 75% of primary expenditure.
C	Statements of sector strategies exist for several major sectors but are substantially costed only for sectors representing up to 25% of primary expenditure or costed strategies may cover more sectors but are inconsistent with aggregate fiscal forecasts.
D	Sector strategies may have been prepared for some sectors, but none of them have substantially complete costing of investments and recurrent expenditure.

Source: PEFA 2006: 27.

approach is meant to be evidence based (practices should be verifiable), although in practice this approach is always difficult.

PEFA's strengths are many—even obvious in this brief discussion:

- The framework treats the PFM area appropriately—as a system in which processes need to connect to produce outturns.
- The framework adopts an increasingly respected approach to thinking about system effectiveness—combining assessments of outturns and processes in the context of a theoretically disciplined model (suggesting argument as to why process 1 + process 2 can lead to outturn 3).
- The framework has fairly extensive coverage (of many process areas), in an elegant and concise set of indicators (only 28 in total).
- The indicators are at a high level, allowing standardization or general processes but also recognizing the need to accommodate variation in the details.
- The individual assessment approaches are simple, theoretically applied, and open to evidence-based analysis.
- The indicators are highly actionable—meaning that governments scoring themselves poorly can identify exactly what they need to do to improve.

Given those characteristics, the PEFA framework must be seen as an appropriate and strong foundation on which to build the kind of PFM code desired by the G8 finance ministers—outlining critical system components with some thought on how these components interrelate and with some detail on the ideal look in each process area. However, PEFA lacks the key qualities necessary to deal with common complexities in PFM systems—and because of this lack, a PFM code would need to draw from ideas beyond PEFA.

PFM Complexity: Process Multiplicity and Interaction

Figure 11.1 shows clearly that the PEFA framework presents PFM processes in a system. This characteristic is a strong point of the PEFA framework, but PEFA's treatment of the system can also be faulted for its simplicity, which—though elegant—can mask the complexity of the PFM system.[8]

In particular, PEFA does not integrate all relevant process areas into the framework, deals with some process areas at too broad a level, and neglects the importance of connections between process areas in complex systems. Dealing with these weaknesses requires introducing complexity that goes beyond PEFA, but such complexity is necessary. The argument here is simple:

■ There are a number of processes in a PFM system, and all of them are required to produce desired outturns (so they must be correctly identified).
■ System effectiveness derives from implementing appropriate mechanisms in all process areas and ensuring connections between the various process areas (so enough attention must be given to each area and—of great importance—to the connections between areas).
■ If some process areas look appropriate (as assessed in PEFA) but some areas do not exist at all (but are missed in PEFA), or if the appropriate mechanisms in place in different areas introduce different kinds of control or accountability, outturns will be compromised.

Figure 11.2 illustrates the multiple process complexity well and allows for an effective discussion of PEFA's weaknesses. First, it identifies at least seven key process areas in the PFM system, from national and sectoral policy review and development through strategic budgeting; budget preparation; resource management in budget execution (including cash management, procurement, and personnel and capital management); internal controls, internal audit, and monitoring; accounting and reporting; and external audit and accountability.[9] Second, it identifies the fact that all of these areas are necessarily connected—by one continuous line in the figure. Connections between the process areas are required to ensure consistency and operational integrity of the system.

PEFA's Framework Does Not Include All of the PFM Process Areas

In particular, PEFA lacks treatment of the policy review and development process, which is shown as connected to the core PFM system (though having some external standing as well). PEFA does not introduce the process by which policy goals and outcomes are identified into either the framework or indicator set, but "rather focuses on assessing the extent to which the PFM system is an enabling factor for achieving such outcomes" (PEFA 2006: 3). This omission reflects the complexity of the process area (variation between countries is particularly high in this area, and the donors could not agree on even high-level characteristics of strong systems), as well as obvious thoughts that PFM is not about policy making (but rather about policy implementation only).

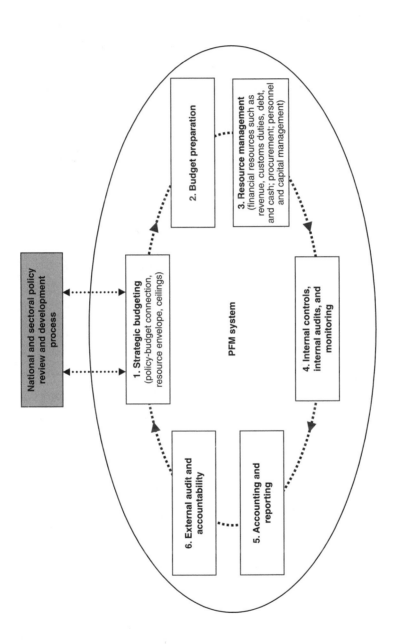

Source: Andrews 2005b.

FIGURE 11.2 The Various Processes within a PFM System

This dichotomous approach to the subject is arguably outdated, and it is hard to find scholars or practitioners who are unaware of the political nature of budgeting and public financial management structures and processes.[10] The G8 finance ministers explicitly note the importance of the policy orientation of spending as something they want reflected in their code, which "should make people understand how the financial policy priorities are chosen" (RosBusinessConsulting 2006). This characteristic will not be easy to reflect, but it certainly should be given some explicit treatment, especially for governments interested in the policy or performance orientation of their budgets. (Such interest explicitly requires that these governments think about their policy-making processes in a comparative sense.) Box 11.2 proposes a basic structure for incorporating this

---

BOX 11.2 Basic Characteristics of Effective Policy-Making Processes

Effective policy-making processes have the following basic characteristics:

- National policy-making and review process
  —A national policy-making process exists, producing a national policy product.
  —National policy is reviewed annually, and policy changes are transparent (fiscal and sectoral policy changes).
  —The national policy-making and review process has political and technical dimensions (hence ensuring that policy enjoys political support and is technically sound).
- National policy product
  —The national policy product details, concisely and clearly, multiyear fiscal strategy and clear sectoral priorities.
  —The national policy product provides clear and prioritized policy goals and measurable indicators of those goals.
- Connection between policy and PFM processes
  —Sectoral plans and multiyear budget frameworks explicitly show how allocations reflect national priorities.
  —Budget proposals show how spending requests contribute to meeting national goals.
  —The annual budget document shows how spending allocations contribute to meeting national goals.
  —A formal process ensures that national goal achievement is monitored and that there is (at least) annual reporting on progress in meeting national goals.
  —Ministers have to report to the cabinet on their ministries' progress in meeting national goals.

Source: Author's representation, accessible at http://ksghome.harvard.edu/~mandrew/.

process area into a full PFM assessment mechanism, identifying characteristics arguably important for effective PFM: the existence of a national policy-making process and some kind of national policy product, with connections to the PFM process.[11]

The PEFA Framework Does Not Consider Links between Process Areas

The PFM system in figure 11.2 shows the importance of links between process areas. These links come in at least two forms:

1. Processes build on each other and thus need to link to each other in an operational sense.
2. Processes introduce different kinds of rules and accountability-enhancing controls and mechanisms, which need to be similarly focused to ensure that a consistent set of incentives and accountability relationships exist in the system.

The links between process areas in a system are often considered as important as the individual processes themselves. It is no different in the PFM system. If a budget process has a state-of-the-art program budgeting classification approach, but the treasury can only allocate money by economic item (such as wages), the system is fragmented. Different kinds of languages are being spoken in the different process areas: one speaks of organizing money by strategic program, while the other speaks of controlling it by unstrategic economic item.

PEFA's indicators are relationally static—reflecting process qualities in individual areas only. They do not speak to the need for relational connection between processes. The strategic planning indicator in table 11.1 is not picked up in the budget preparation indicators, for example, through indicators checking if budget drafts are actually built on strategic plans. It is highly possible that governments could score an A on their multiyear planning activities but actually develop budget drafts with no reference to such activities. This kind of indicator entrenches a stove-piped approach to PFM—in which professionals in different process areas keep to themselves, adopt reforms in their narrow process areas, and speak very little to professionals in other process areas. This stove-piped approach is arguably a primary cause of PFM system weaknesses.

Examples of potential disconnection or fragmentation can be identified throughout the PEFA framework. A more complete PFM code that presents a picture of how PFM "should be" structured would remedy such deficiencies. In the spirit of box 11.2, such a code will incorporate questions about the links between one process area and another (in box 11.2, see the bullet "Connection between policy and PFM processes"). Box 11.3 presents potential "linkage characteristics" one could consider in regard to strategic planning in line ministries. (These characteristics could be used to go beyond PEFA's table 11.1 indicator and could be used to guide governments in developing plans that could, indeed, be integrated into budget and financial management processes.)[12]

PFM Complexity: Role-Player Multiplicity and Role-Player Interaction

Figure 11.2 shows a degree of process complexity that challenges PEFA's framework of how the PFM system works—in terms of both the number of processes included and the need for serious consideration of connections between processes. It should be noted that the model in figure 11.2 is itself simplified in two important respects:

1. It presents each process area in one block, seemingly inferring one role player in each domain.
2. It emphasizes horizontal aspects of PFM integration only (where each process area seems to have only one level of complexity).

BOX 11.3 Considering Strong "Linkage Characteristics" of Strategic Plans

Strategic plans that link to annual budgets have these characteristics:

- Strategic plans differentiate clearly between objectives, outputs, and activities that are already financed through existing budgets and those presented as new initiatives for new financing.
- Strategic plans provide a section reconciling prior plans and budgets and showing how annual budget allocations did or did not reflect prior plans.
- Strategic plans are classified in a manner that allows comparison with budget documents.
- Costing data in strategic plans are compared with expenditure and costing data emanating from annual budget execution reports.
- Strategic plans provide monitoring and reporting (financial and nonfinancial) information, including a report on prior-year results (derived from financial and nonfinancial reports).

Source: Author's representation, accessible at http://ksghome.harvard.edu/~mandrew/.

There are relational dimensions of the PFM system that should be noted and that introduce (necessarily) even more complexity into the discussion of developing a PFM code. These dimensions relate to the fact that PFM issues can be raised in regard to central entities in national governments (such as ministries of finance, treasuries, and supreme audit institutions), as well as in implementing agencies in national governments (ministries, departments, and agencies) and even in noncommercial organizations (quasi-governmental organizations, state-owned enterprises, and so forth) and civil society and multinational organizations that work in the PFM area to assist in budgetary planning, monitoring, and so on. PFM issues also matter in deconcentrated and decentralized governments, including regional and local governments (where PFM processes exist in parallel in different levels of government). This role-player multiplicity is shown in stylized form in figure 11.3, where the relational complexities across and within the system are apparent.

Figure 11.3 shows that PFM processes all involve role players from different domains and cut across different levels of government. Unfortunately, this role-player multiplicity is not typically acknowledged in PFM assessments, models, or reforms. These products are systematically biased to work in the core PFM entities such as the ministry of finance, supreme audit institution, or parliament. These entities create and administer the rules of the PFM system and thus attract significant attention. However, they are not the ones that actually spend money (spending entities such as line ministries) nor the ones that contribute the funds to be spent and that ultimately receive services (civil society, which pays taxes and fees and sits at the receiving end of the process by which institutions of basic governance and service provision are funded).

The PEFA measures are also biased toward analyzing processes relevant to the activities of core PFM entities and processes at the center of government. Some of the indicators reflect coverage across noncore spending entities (for example, the planning indicator shown in table 11.1), but these indicators are presented from a defined ministry of finance perspective (rather than a managerial perspective relevant to spending ministries).[13] Failing to acknowledge the fact that the population of PFM role players extends beyond core agencies leads to specific weaknesses in the PEFA framework. For example, the indicators ask whether the government completes its accounts and reports on the basis of international standards.[14] Many treasuries score highly on this indicator because they produce reports that suggest compliance with international accounting and reporting standards. But the accounting and reporting in line ministries in many governments are way below international standards. An approach is

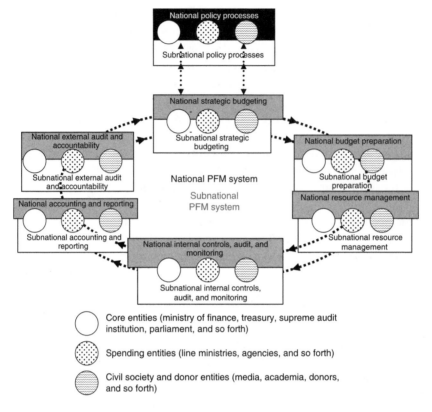

Core entities (ministry of finance, treasury, supreme audit institution, parliament, and so forth)

Spending entities (line ministries, agencies, and so forth)

Civil society and donor entities (media, academia, donors, and so forth)

Source: Author's representation.

FIGURE 11.3 The Multiplicity of PFM Role Players and Complexity of PFM Relationships

needed that probes practices at core and noncore organizational levels to truly show what processes look like.

Two of the indicators reflect on intergovernmental relationships, but again these reflections are from a core agency control perspective (asking about the coordination of budget preparation across levels of government and the quality of reporting from subnationals to central government). No indicators acknowledge the role of civil society in the PFM process, although internationally this role has been increasing and reflects a growing recognition of the "new governance" (in which civic voice in policy-making processes defines resource allocation over time, civic groups play a major role in monitoring governments, and so forth). Box 11.4 provides a brief description in the context of external audit.

BOX 11.4 Civil Society and the External Accountability Function

In many governments, external audits were generally conducted and appraised without public participation. Audit reports were made available only to the legislature or client agencies; most members of the public had no manner of accessing such reports, of knowing what was going on in government, or of helping to improve governance. People's rights to participate in the conduct of public affairs and to be informed were impeded by the lack of transparency of the auditing process and the absence of mechanisms to demand public accountability for expenditure use. This impediment, in turn, increased possibilities for corruption, fund mismanagement, and ineffective service provision.

Audit entities across the globe, in line with their governments' commitment to promote transparency and good governance, have developed reform strategies that include piloting civil society participation in the auditing process or in the scrutinizing of audits. Participatory audit using a value-for-money approach, for example, allows the determination of results and effects or of values and benefits actually derived through public expenditures by the community itself. This development, in turn, has had important consequences.

On the one hand, value-for-money reports are a form of performance audit that goes beyond merely stating rule compliance to assess actual "value" obtained from public spending. Thus, value-for-money reports can be used as planning and decision-making tools as well as audit documents. These audits are particularly valuable in settings where the supreme audit institution lacks its own capacity to do performance audits.

On the other hand, through strengthened citizen participation in the auditing process, government accountability, transparency, and credibility are effectively enhanced. The existence of mechanisms for public participation is in itself an important deterrent against corruption. It is expected to promote more prudence in the use of public resources for projects that would benefit local communities.

Last, by bringing the auditing process closer to the public, service providers are able to find out the adequacy of their target expenditures to the perceived civic demand. The community is able to assess government's performance in this regard and to advocate for specific improvements in expenditure targeting and use. Such public participation should ultimately lead to improved design and efficiency of public expenditures.

Source: Author's compilation.

The new governance literature argues explicitly that the quality of governance, strength of accountability relationships, and performance of government are highly dependent on the existence of strategic relationships between public and civic entities. The PEFA framework does not heed this vital issue. Any further elaboration of a PFM code should do so, firmly elaborating the principles that multiple role players are required for effective PFM and that a true picture of PFM system quality requires knowing the full population of role players and ensuring that they are relating to each other in constructive ways.

PFM Complexity: Goal Multiplicity and Implications for the "Look" of PFM Systems

The final area of complexity that potential authors of a PFM code should consider is the contingency of PFM systems on goals. This characteristic simply means a PFM system's main and immediate goal defines its ideal look. In one respect, it suggests that there is no ideal or standardized system on which to base a code. This may be true. However, it may be possible to identify different kinds of standardized systems relevant for different goal focuses and situations.

This perspective emerges from the general agreement that PFM goals come in three major shapes—establishing fiscal discipline and fiscal reliability, enhancing the policy-based quality of fiscal allocations, and improving the technical or cost efficiency of spending. The goals are often presented as PFM progress levels:

- *Fiscal discipline* concerns are often termed *level 1 outcomes* because they relate to the fundamental goals of budgetary stability and fiscal viability. The failure to achieve these goals threatens the entire health of the PFM system. The fiscal discipline goal is typically reflected in targets for expenditure control and deficit and debt reduction, with connections to inflation targets. These targets are increasingly introduced as budget rules—the rule that budget size is determined with regard to these issues—because the goals are so difficult to attain and maintain.
- *Resource allocation* concerns are often termed *level 2 outcomes*. They concentrate on ensuring that resource allocation matches strategic priorities in the budget, often shown in measures of allocations to specific policy goals and of deviation in expenditure composition (ensuring that budgeted money is allocated as planned). Allocative efficiency is perhaps the most difficult goal of government, attested to in the experience in many countries. Budgetary allocations are often disconnected from desired outcomes in key expenditure areas, sometimes across sectors (such as education and defense) and sometimes within sectors (where the allocation problem is an intrasectoral issue). There are good reasons governments may and do

have difficulty improving allocative efficiency. In its simplest form, allocative efficiency means a government spends money on the right things. But what is right depends on (a) the priorities of society and (b) the cost of programs and activities needed to meet those priorities. The first element, the setting of priorities, is largely a political process, and because the preferences of politicians and bureaucrats need not coincide with welfare-enhancing objectives, the outcomes—and as a consequence service delivery—may and often do fall short of what is desired.

■ *Technical efficiency* is commonly presented in the literature as the *level 3 outcome*. It relates to the efficient and effective use of resources in implementing strategic priorities. Common measures here include audit results of service provision costs. The degree of operational efficiency is predominantly influenced by the budget execution process. Implementation of programs, activities, and projects occurs as budgets are executed. But implementation is plagued by two fundamental problems: (a) principal-agent relations and (b) the government as monopoly provider of public services.

There is an argument that different kinds of PFM systems and processes are required to achieve the goals at the different levels. Although some implications of this argument are overly rigid,[15] it provides a useful framework for thinking about the way in which the ideal look of a PFM system is necessarily contingent on the challenges facing a government. Figure 11.4 shows this argument in simple form.

Figure 11.4 introduces the idea of four levels of PFM system development—as related to the three-level goals noted above:

■ Level 0 is that in which PFM systems are informal and weak. There is limited accountability, little transparency, weak discipline, and poor budget quality. Budgets are informal and unreliable, and there is an overall lack of fiscal discipline. The major concern is to control deficits and restore PFM system integrity.

■ Level 1 systems are characterized by a high degree of regulation and control, and they focus on entrenching fiscal discipline. Systems entrench control and a disciplined, reliable budget—what could be called "critical" PFM systems—but there is little attention to spending quality. There is an ex ante control focus, whereby rules are set in a detailed fashion at the start of a budget process and managers cannot depart from them. Compliance is the order of the day. The budget is formal and reliable, but it is not very strategic.

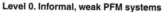

Level 0. Informal, weak PFM systems
System is characterized by limited accountability, little transparency, weak discipline, and poor budget quality. Budget is informal and unreliable.

Level 1. Regulation and control: PFM goal focus is fiscal discipline
Reforms entrench control, resulting in disciplined and reliable budget-critical PFM systems, but little attention is paid to spending quality, and there is an ex ante control focus. Budget is formal and reliable but not very strategic.

Level 2. Structured discretion: PFM goal focus is allocative efficiency
Reforms blend ex ante and ex post controls and move toward enhanced roles for central agencies and budget users. Some more strategic practices are in place. Budget is formal and some thought is given to allocations.

Level 3. High discretion, performance orientation: PFM goal focus is technical and operational efficiency
Emphasis is on ex post controls, with budget users held accountable for performance. More strategic practices are in place. Budget is formal and the focus is on strategy and efficiency.

Source: Andrews 2005b.
Note: See http://ksghome.harvard.edu/~mandrew/ for a full discussion of this approach and other materials.

FIGURE 11.4 Levels of PFM System Development

- Level 2 systems introduce a certain amount of structured discretion. The PFM goal focus is allocative efficiency. The system blends ex ante and ex post controls and moves toward enhanced roles for central agencies and budget users—allowing some practices that are more strategic and that foster strategic resource use.
- Level 3 systems are characterized by high levels of discretion and by a performance orientation. The PFM goal focus is on technical or operational efficiency. The emphasis is on having ex post controls, with budget users held accountable for performance. More strategic practices are in place. The budget is formal, and the focus is on strategy and efficient resource use (in an allocative and cost sense).

Figure 11.4 provides a graphic presentation of the argument that different goal focuses should yield different-looking PFM systems. The case is most regularly presented in a basics first argument that suggests governments move gradually from level to level (as the arrows in the figure suggest). Such a progression would imply that governments in industrial and developing contexts should have different-looking systems—and that it is possible to know what the differences should be (judging the achievement of goals will yield information about what stage the system should be reflecting).

The evidence of a linear pathway from one goal to another—and hence from one level to another—is actually quite ambiguous, however. It is not apparent, for example, that governments always need to progress through the steps without leapfrogging. Level 1 may not be required before level 2 can be attained—governments could move directly from level 0 to level 2.[16] Furthermore, attaining level 1 does not mean automatic movement to level 2.[17] Finally, because governments face uncertain environments, goals that were attained in the past (fiscal discipline, for instance) may pose challenges in the future—requiring some governments to adjust level 2 systems to combat level 1 problems in some instances.[18]

The central point of figure 11.4 still holds even if one does not buy the basics first argument of step-by-step progression: different goals are associated with different kinds of systems. Figure 11.5 shows the variations in different system dimensions more clearly, detailing how key processes might look at different levels.

It is important to note that processes at each level in figure 11.5 are related to different kinds of accountability and control. Obviously level 0 has no real accountability or control. Level 1 has accountability for compliance with the rules of budgeting and for the detailed use of inputs in the PFM system (whether these inputs are financial, personnel oriented, or other). Level 2 reflects a mixed accountability for compliance and input use and accountability for results (measured ex post). Level 3 has accountability for results where there are no ex ante controls (by which managers are held accountable for their use of inputs), but managers are rather held accountable for what they do with the money (the results they produce).

Any PFM code needs to recognize that differences between PFM systems are required in the face of differences in goals being addressed. Thus, there is not necessarily one right way of structuring a PFM system, and there is not one right set of technical tools or indicators for effective PFM. If a government is pursuing level 1 fiscal discipline as its primary objective, it should have a system that looks quite different from that of a government that has well-established discipline and is tackling level 2 and level 3 issues of budgetary efficiency.

This point has multiple implications. One is that the definition of *best practice* relevant to a specific government must be seen as contingent on the kind of goal being addressed in that government. Hence, there is a strong reason not to derive a PFM code using any best-practice approach. A second is that any kind of indicator set used to reflect on PFM system quality must show how the indicator dimensions relate to different levels and thus pertain to different kinds of goal achievement. This is not done in PEFA, which presents an indicator set that seemingly holds for all governments and at all

Level 0. Informal, weak PFM systems
1. Weak budget frameworks—unreliable resource forecasts, no policy foundation, no top-down budget limits
2. Poor structure and lack of respect in budget preparation process—budgets often late, unreliable
3. Weak resource management—no guidance or control of cash flow, debt, procurement, capital, or personnel and no monitoring of resource use—resource mismanagement, unreliable budgets, corruption, waste
4. Weak or nonexistent budget controls—budget adjustments frequent, uncontrolled, opaque
5. Fragmented accounting and reporting system
6. No (or ineffective) external audit—limited accountability, transparency, weak discipline, poor budget quality

Level 1. Regulation and control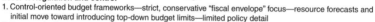
1. Control-oriented budget frameworks—strict, conservative "fiscal envelope" focus—resource forecasts and initial move toward introducing top-down budget limits—limited policy detail
2. Focus on budget comprehensiveness—strong annual cash budget prepared in accordance with strict timetable, driven by ministry of finance, with detailed economic classification—focus on operational spending
3. Highly controlled resource management—many centrally developed and implemented controls on cash disbursements (short-term control)—high level of central control over personnel, procurement, capital
4. Very strong budget controls and monitoring, but done centrally—very little budget adjustment, based on rigid rules—adjustments within and between economic items controlled
5. Cash-based central accounting and reporting system, with highly detailed controls based on economic item—still fragmented accounts
6. External audit emerging, but only looking at compliance—high level of discipline, reliable budget, but little attention given to spending quality—ex ante control focus

Level 2. Structured discretion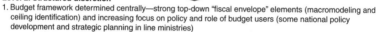
1. Budget framework determined centrally—strong top-down "fiscal envelope" elements (macromodeling and ceiling identification) and increasing focus on policy and role of budget users (some national policy development and strategic planning in line ministries)
2. Budget prepared according to timetable, with increasing role for budget users—budget still cash based with requests reflecting economic classification controls, but reduced in detail—information provided on strategic dimensions of spending (objectives, indicators of performance)—budget with some multiyear details and increasing focus on capital spending
3. Resource management being decentralized—rules and regulations set and overseen centrally, but actual resource management processes implemented by budget users, with some discretion—some commitment controls introduced
4. Internal controls and audit and monitoring mechanisms developed in line ministries for use in managing—internal controls and audit policies still centralized—budget adjustments still subject to rules, but with more discretion for budget users (reallocation of a percentage of funds or within programs permissible)
5. Accounting and reporting system still cash based, but with some commitment and accrual information—focus on developing strong accounting and reporting in line ministries, with central consolidation
6. External audit entity growing in influence and doing some financial and performance audits—blended ex ante and ex post controls and move toward roles for central agencies and budget users

Level 3. High discretion, performance orientation
1. Strong budget frameworks established—reliable "fiscal envelope" elements locating budget in macroeconomic context—national policy process yielding entrenched national expenditure priorities—line ministries developing strategic plans that tie directly to budgets and detail performance goals and so forth—budget ceilings reflecting both macro limits and policy direction
2. Multiyear budgets reflecting strategic plans that are classified predominantly by program, with performance indicators and some accrual elements—budget users playing dominant role in developing budget, with ministry of finance assisting and analyzing—parliament assessing strategic content of budget and appropriating significant funds over multiple years
3. Strong, largely decentralized resource management, with built-in discretion for budget users (in procurement, personnel, and so forth)—budget users entering into performance contracts and using resources to deliver—central agencies playing role overseeing and enforcing contracts (with individuals and budget users)
4. Internal controls and audit fully decentralized, serving managers in budget users—monitoring mechanisms in place providing in-year information on progress in meeting performance commitments—central oversight of control policy
5. Accounting and reporting modified accrual basis, with strong processes in budget users and strong, reliable reporting—significant focus on transparency—reporting also on performance
6. External audit entity strong, performing financial and performance audits—annual reports provided to parliament—emphasis on ex post reporting and controls, with budget users held accountable for performance

Source: Author's representation.

FIGURE 11.5   Key Processes at Different Levels

times. Close inspection of the PEFA measures, however, suggests that they relate to critical dimensions of PFM—level 1 with some level 2 elements—and have very little content relevant to a more strategic performance orientation in PFM. Thus, PEFA is useful to most governments (because most are still struggling with fiscal discipline), but it also has limited use in addressing the G8 request for a PFM code speaking to "results management" issues (RosBusinessConsulting 2006).

This observation calls for the need to introduce a complementary set of indicators to go beyond PEFA. These indicators could be called *more strategic practices* (MSP) and would relate to PEFA as follows:

- PEFA would provide the critical dimensions of PFM. This first set of criteria would represent the critical or basic dimensions of PFM, as reflected in the PEFA's PFM indicators. These indicators would show whether individual process areas have progressed to a point where they facilitate basic fiduciary control and accountability. Governments performing well against these indicators would tend to have strong fiscal discipline and to be in the early stages of addressing allocations quality and technical efficiency problems. (This stage equates roughly with having achieved a level 1 competence in the system.)
- The MSP indicators constitute the second set of criteria. They relate to the quality of PFM processes in the context of more strategic government. These criteria are derived from various sources and characterize the processes seen in more strategic PFM systems, in which level 2 and level 3 allocations of quality and operational efficiency are emphasized. The criteria center on some key principles: (a) there is a strong policy orientation (political and managerial) in the PFM system; (b) PFM accountability relationships are clear and are based on policy implementation and service delivery; (c) there is clear capability to manage money around policy goals; (d) there are clear incentives across the system for the compliant, efficient, and effective use of resources; (e) the system provides appropriate information to facilitate accountability relationships and decision-making processes; and (f) there are appropriate decision rights in the system (politicians can hold managers accountable, managers can decide how best to structure their organizations to deliver, and so forth).

The difference between criteria sets is apparent in an example of line ministry planning (building on the discussion arising in table 11.1). The highest PEFA score is given to governments where strategies for sectors reflecting at least 75 percent of primary expenditure exist with full costing of recurrent and investment expenditure, broadly consistent with fiscal forecasts.[19] The PEFA score does not ask about the quality of costing (only that there is full costing) or the quality of strategic plans (only that they cover recurrent and investment expenditure and are disciplined by a broad fiscal framework). In governments that are more strategic, one finds additional quality dimensions clearly addressed, to ensure that plans facilitate strategic decisions and introduce incentives for efficient management. The following quality criteria are important, for instance:[20]

- Strategic plans identify goals well.
- Strategic plans identify activities required to meet these goals through a full assessment of strengths, weaknesses, and so forth.
- Strategic plans provide measurable indicators of all outputs and objectives, including baseline data for each.
- All objectives, outputs, and activities are fully costed, with a clear description of costing methods and assumptions.
- Strategic plans differentiate clearly between goals and activities already financed through budgets and those presented as new initiatives for new financing.
- The annual strategic planning process is sufficiently long to allow sector ministries (and other entities) enough time to plan effectively.
- Both the budget and the policy staff are responsible for developing strategic plans, which may be developed with some external support (through consultants) but are largely internal products.

The more strategic indicators go into quality dimensions of the PEFA indicators as well as beyond these indicators—suggesting that progress from level 1 to level 2 to level 3 involves both steps to deepen technical processes and improve the substance within and steps to add new processes and concepts. A fuller set of more strategic practice indicators is proposed for discussion at http://ksghome.harvard.edu/~mandrew/. It should be noted that, when one is making the comparisons with practices in more strategic systems, there are no comparators in the world that would routinely be called more strategic in all process areas. However, some countries might be considered more strategic in individual process areas: for instance, New Zealand, South Africa, Sweden, and the United Kingdom in strategic planning and budget preparation; Australia in accounting and reporting; or Germany in internal and external audit. This is one of the interesting aspects of the work on establishing more strategic PFM systems—few governments have really established such processes across their entire PFM systems. This could be one of the main reasons that the results of strategic budgeting, with its performance orientation, are still muted in even the best cases.

Moving Ahead: Toward a Full Response for the G8

In working with countries that are trying to improve their PFM systems, many colleagues have been amazed at the number of officials who have asked if there is any one best way. Unfortunately, there is not: no silver bullet or magic potion. This fact makes the G8 call for a PFM "code" quite interesting. It seems to be a call for the identification of a one-best-way or a how-it-should-be-done model for PFM.

This chapter interprets the call a little differently. It sees the call coming at a time when there are many different approaches to PFM, lots of money being spent on PFM reform, and many governments facing PFM results that suggests suboptimality. Against that backdrop, the G8 finance ministers are asking for some clarity, some standardization, and some guidance as to how to look at PFM systems in a structured manner.

This chapter attempts to provide some ideas in this light. It introduces the PEFA framework as a potential foundation for a PFM code and then discusses the need to go beyond PEFA:

- To ensure full, integrated coverage of all PFM processes and of connections between such processes
- To ensure that all role players are given attention in the framework, especially spending agencies and civil society entities
- To ensure that the goal contingency of PFM processes is clearly presented, even to the point where different indicator sets are used to reflect the "appropriate" look for PFM systems at different levels of goal achievement.

The PEFA indicators have been useful to many governments and to many in the donor community by providing a guide for PFM reform and a mechanism for evaluating PFM system quality. Moving beyond PEFA in the ways discussed in this article could facilitate the development of an even more useful product in the future—a more complete code to meet the demand of the G8.

Notes

1. The framework draws on the Heavily Indebted Poor Country expenditure tracking benchmarks, the International Monetary Fund's Fiscal Transparency Code, and other international standards.

2. More than 20 countries have already found the framework useful in thinking about their PFM systems, further suggesting its value.

3. Apart from limited reference to intergovernmental financial interaction in budget preparation and reporting stages.

4. See http://ksghome.harvard.edu/~mandrew/ for a full discussion of fragmentation and integration. For an applied discussion in the context of Armenia, see Andrews (2005a).

5. There is generally an ex ante accountability focus in situations in which fiscal discipline is in focus, whereas a greater focus on efficiency and performance requires ex post accountability mechanisms.

6. This approach to understanding effectiveness is discussed in chapter 5 of Rainey's (2003) influential text *Understanding and Managing Public Organizations*.

7. PEFA Indicator 12.

8. The PEFA indicator set is purposefully simplistic to facilitate usefulness—and indeed many might find it too complex in its current form. However, if the indicator set is intended to show what a sound system looks like, it must do so effectively—and this chapter suggests that it may not do so.

9. See http://ksghome.harvard.edu/~mandrew/ for a full presentation of this model.

10. Wildavsky's (1964) *The Politics of the Budgetary Process* and other key works argue strongly that politics and policy making are vital elements in the PFM system.

11. See http://ksghome.harvard.edu/~mandrew/ for a fuller discussion.

12. A complete set of linkage indicators is provided in the text of the full mode and in the more strategic practice indicator set that is available for comment at http://ksghome.harvard.edu/~mandrew/.

13. The alternative approach would require asking if a line ministry developed plans and found these plans useful in budgeting and in managing funds. The approach would also ask whether the plans are actually the basis for budgetary implementation.

14. PEFA Indicator 25 (iii) gives an A if International Public Sector Accounting Standards or corresponding national standards are applied for all statements.

15. The basics first argument suggests this type of approach as the basis of a rigid sequencing model, but the evidence is unclear (a) that achieving level 1 in a rigidly sequenced model will lead to levels 2 and 3, (b) that governments cannot address levels 2 and 3 without fully achieving level 1, or (c) that governments cannot leapfrog a level altogether. Furthermore, it is unclear that progress through the levels is necessarily linear. It appears more likely that governments achieving level 1 in year t may face level 1 fiscal discipline problems again in level $t + n$ (often because of environmental factors such as economic slowdowns, which exert pressure on the revenue and expenditure sides of the budget, and so forth). A model prescribing linear sequencing of different types of PFM processes simply does not reflect such situations (see Andrews 2006; Schick 1998).

16. Andrews (2006) makes this argument with respect to South Africa and Tanzania, where governments introduced many basics simultaneously with reforms that introduced elements of performance management. The result was that the governments (especially Tanzania's) seemed to pass very quickly through level 1 to a level 2 standing.

17. Andrews (2006) makes this observation with respect to Thailand, where the control-oriented Bureau of the Budget held the government at level 1 and would not allow structured discretion into the system.

18. Andrews (2006) argues that this was the case in Florida in the late 1990s, when a government faced with fiscal austerity attempted to replace a fledgling program-performance budget system with a zero-based budget system that introduced a high level of ex ante economic item controls.
19. PEFA Indicator 12 (iii).
20. Plan quality is often compromised by (a) failure to define end states (objectives) correctly, (b) incomplete analysis with respect to the desired end states, (c) lack of creativity in identifying possible strategies, (d) strategies incapable of obtaining the desired objective, and (e) poor fit between the external environment and organizational resources infeasibility.

References

Andrews, Matthew. 2005a. "Background and Summary of an Integrated PFM Model." Background paper to a presentation at a Poverty Reduction Strategy Paper Learning Event, World Bank, Washington, DC, December 19, 2005. http://web. worldbank. org/WBSITE/EXTERNAL/TOPICS/EXTPUBLICSECTORANDGOVERNANCE/ EXTADMINISTRATIVEANDCIVILSERVICEREFORM/0,,contentMDK: 20762325~menuPK:51428063~pagePK:210082~piPK:210098~theSitePK: 286367,00.html.

———. 2005b. "Focusing and Integrating PFM Reforms to Ensure They Matter." Presentation at a Poverty Reduction Strategy Paper Learning Event, World Bank, Washington, DC, December 19, 2005. http://web.worldbank.org/WBSITE/ EXTERNAL/TOPICS/EXTPUBLICSECTORANDGOVERNANCE/EXTADMINIS-TRATIVEANDCIVILSERVICEREFORM/0,,contentMDK:20762325~menuPK:514 28063~pagePK:210082~piPK:210098~theSitePK:286367,00.html.

———. 2006. "Beyond 'Best Practice' and 'Basics First' in Adopting Performance Budgeting Reform." *Public Administration and Development* 26 (2): 147–61.

PEFA (Public Expenditure and Financial Accountability). 2006. *Public Financial Management Performance Measurement Framework.* Washington, DC: World Bank.

Rainey, Hal G. 2003. *Understanding and Managing Public Organizations.* San Francisco: Jossey-Bass.

RosBusinessConsulting. 2006. "St. Petersburg: Participants of G8 Meeting Supported Elaboration of the Public Finance Management Code." RosBusinessConsulting, Moscow. http://www.g8finance.ru/g8news7_100606.htm.

Schick, Allen. 1998. "Why Most Developing Countries Should Not Try New Zealand Reforms." *World Bank Research Observer* 13 (1): 123–31.

Wildavsky, Aaron. 1964. *The Politics of the Budgetary Process.* Boston: Little, Brown.

PART Two

Reforming Public Expenditure Management in Developing Countries: The African Case

12

Strengthening Public Expenditure Management in Africa: Criteria, Priorities, and Sequencing

SALVATORE SCHIAVO-CAMPO

Although a variety of international technical assistance activities have been undertaken for at least 30 years to improve public expenditure management (PEM) in developing countries, the incorporation of PEM reforms in African policy programs supported by adjustment assistance is comparatively recent. Most of it began at the end of the 1980s, when it was recognized that effective budget support requires an agreement on the government expenditure program as well as management systems adequate for its implementation.[1] Because of a lack of prior experience, however, guidance concerning the more urgent improvements and a realistic sequencing of reforms was rarely provided.

At about the same time as PEM reforms began to be incorporated into adjustment assistance in African countries, important changes in macroeconomic and fiscal management were being introduced in a few industrial countries—notably Australia, Iceland, New Zealand, and Sweden. Efforts were first made at restoring fiscal and macroeconomic sustainability, by providing full independence to the monetary authorities, reformulating entitlements programs, and disabling the expenditure ratcheting mechanisms that have largely underpinned Wagner's Law.[2] These policy efforts were successful, by and large, and were followed in short order by radical changes in the implementation mechanisms—the instruments themselves—both in expenditure management and in public administration in general. Some of these changes proved successful, some did not, and almost none were suitable candidates for export to Africa. However, their partial success in a few highly industrial countries led many in the World Bank and other organizations to view these management changes as a single set of universally desirable innovations— the "best practice" of the New Public Management (NPM). Enamored of the semantics, oblivious to the pitfalls of transplanting institutional models, and encouraged by the international consulting industry, a growing number of national and international officials attempted to push several developing countries to leapfrog all the way to the end point of institutional change in public expenditure and financial management. Inevitably, reality eventually won out. The innovations did not take root in the entirely different institutional and administrative climate, and the NPM bubble has been judged as comparable to the "new economy" bubble of the late 1990s. The differences between the two are, of course, vast, but the grandiose rhetoric, the weight of fashion, and the abdication from simple common sense are symptoms of the same technocratic delusion and unwillingness to do the hard work needed to tailor innovations to reality.

The reaction against the NPM was long overdue. However, at this stage, salvaging from among the PEM innovations those that are most likely to be suitable (with adaptation) to African developing countries is important. Thus, although the return to a focus on the basic plumbing of public financial management is welcome, it must be complemented by a road map of subsequent improvements and a reasonably clear view of the end point of reform. The purpose of this chapter is accordingly to try to sketch out for each of the different aspects of the PEM cycle both the basic initial reform priorities and the medium- and long-term introduction of advanced systems and practices. The underlying paradigm is a combination of the "two Ps" of traditional public administration—*probity* and *propriety*—with the "two P's" of the NPM—*policy* and *performance*.[3] The pitfalls of fashion can best be avoided by establishing and following a set of clear principles for budget reform, as in South Africa (box 12.1).

Protect the Money

If the government budget is to become the financial mirror of society's economic and social choices, as emphasized in chapter 2, the first obvious requirement is to protect the resources mobilized from society or provided

BOX 12.1 Principles of South African Budget Reform

The South African public expenditure management system has undergone substantial reform since the mid-1990s. Although the early reforms strengthened macroeconomic stability and expenditure control, the more recent emphasis has been on efficient resource allocation and effective service delivery. The highlights have been rollout of a new intergovernmental system that requires all three levels of government to formulate and approve their own budgets, introduction of three-year rolling spending plans for all national and provincial departments, new formats for budget documentation with a strong focus on service delivery information, and enactment of new financial legislation. In addition, changes to the budget process have allowed decision makers to deliberate on key policy choices and on the matching of available resources to plans, rather than on item-by-item cost estimates.

Underlying the reforms were the following principles:

- *Providing comprehensiveness and integration.* The main national budget framework coordinates, integrates, and disciplines policy and budget processes for the country at the national, provincial, and (increasingly) local levels.
- *Allowing political oversight and a focus on policy priorities.* Choices between priorities are inherently political. The South African system recognizes this fact and structures the integration of political and administrative practices to ensure that funding choices align with the priorities of government and that political oversight is reinforced.
- *Using of information strategically.* The reform process systematically sets out to improve the timeliness, reliability, and usefulness of information on the allocation and use of funds, internal and external, to improve policy and funding choices and enable accountability.
- *Changing behavior by changing incentives.* Responsibility was devolved to spending departments for spending choices and use of funds within approved ceilings and consistent with policy commitments.
- *Ensuring budget stability and predictability while facilitating change at the margin.* The budget process includes various mechanisms to manage uncertainty and maximize predictability of funding and policy over the medium term, while promoting alignment with policies at the margin, through the use of rolling baselines and a contingency reserve, among other measures.

Source: Adapted from material drafted by Daniel Tommasi, based on Fölscher and Cole 2004.

by donors to assist in the achievement of society's goals. Preventing public resources from being stolen or otherwise misappropriated is the paramount fiduciary duty of public financial managers. It is the basic PEM prerequisite from a technical viewpoint as well. If you cannot protect the money, you cannot control it; if you cannot control it, you cannot allocate it; and if you cannot allocate it, you obviously cannot manage it well.[4] Corruption is the greatest single impediment to effective management of public financial resources, and conversely, improvements in PEM are at the center of the struggle against corruption. Preventing corruption in financial management must therefore be the absolute priority in those African countries that, because of past civil conflict or other reasons, have extremely weak revenue forecasts and cash management systems. However, in those countries, it is also essential to (a) tighten financial accountability and expenditure control in ways that do not jeopardize the improvements in sectoral allocation and operational management that should eventually follow and (b) have a clear ex ante sense of how far to push improvements in expenditure control and cash management before strategic allocation and management issues become timely and necessary. The law of diminishing returns applies to institutional development even more strongly than to physical production.

Corruption in Public Financial Management

In Transparency International's Corruption Perceptions Index rankings for 2005, most African countries regrettably score very low.[5] On a scale of 1 (most corrupt) to 10 (least corrupt), the greatest government integrity is perceived to be in Iceland, with a score of 9.7, and the "distinction" of the most corrupt country in the world goes to Chad. Scores for other African countries range from a relatively favorable 5.9 for Botswana and 4.5 for South Africa, to a disappointing 2.1 for the Democratic Republic of Congo and Kenya, to just 1.9 for Nigeria, which is ranked as the sixth most corrupt country in the world. Other African countries' scores are clustered around 3.0 to 3.5—even African countries generally known as good performers in public financial management (for example, Rwanda was scored at 3.1 and Tanzania, at 2.9). The good news is that public integrity appears to have improved over the past decade for most African countries that do not suffer from severe internal security problems. Also, image tends to lag behind reality, and the positive changes in public expenditure management of recent years in many countries will soon be reflected in more favorable international perceptions—including the Transparency International ratings. By contrast, and understandably, countries in conflict or recently emerging from civil conflict have shown an increase in official corruption. For example, in Burundi, which was scored at 2.3, corruption was modest and predictable until the early 1990s; it has become pervasive, however, after the decade of civil war.[6] In Africa, as in most developing countries, the areas in which corruption problems are especially widespread are public procurement, direct taxation, and customs.

Procurement

In public procurement, problems are mainly in bulk purchases of goods, because corruption in large public works is limited (although not eliminated) by the direct oversight of the external donors who fund most large projects in African countries owing to the limited domestic resources of the government. In purchase of goods, the extent of the problem is illustrated by the frequency of sole-source contracting—notwithstanding legal provisions in most countries specifying in detail the circumstances in which sole-source procurement can be permitted. The direct result is gross overbilling of the government—with documented cases of goods and services for government use purchased for between 10 to 20 times the international price—and repeated purchase contracts given to the same individuals. The indirect result is the draining away of financial resources from operational and maintenance expenditure needed to perform the ordinary functions of government.

Even when procurement is formally on a competitive basis, the rules can be easily sidestepped. A typical mechanism works as follows. An "understanding" is reached between the public official and the private "partners" to supply a certain amount of a commodity or a service at the (inflated) price to be officially charged. The corresponding expenditure is then introduced by the public official into the government budget. After budget approval, the tender is subsequently tailored to make the private partner appear most qualified and is also launched with a timetable too short to give potential competitors enough time to submit their bids—except, of course, for the private partner, who had months of advance warning.

In a few countries, procurement laws and rules are inefficient or obsolete, and the reform priority is obviously to modernize and improve them. However, the attention given by donors to reducing fiduciary risk (see chapter 2) and the requirements of the Heavily Indebted Poor Countries (HIPC) initiative's process for debt relief have led most countries to introduce sound procurement legislation and standards. Where procurement laws and formal procedures are generally adequate, the main recommendation on how to fight corruption in procurement is self-evident: enforce the law. Equally evident is the locus of responsibility for doing so: the ministry of finance, which has the legal authority in all countries to approve all state expenditure. The ministry of finance is also the sole organ that can short-circuit, through improved scrutiny of expenditure proposals, the procurement corruption scenario previously described. Finally, the budget documentation should systematically include a report on questionable major bulk purchases made during the previous fiscal year. Naturally, uprooting corruption in the ministry of finance itself is fundamental.

Taxation

In domestic taxation, the problem of corruption may be masked by the apparently reasonably good "fiscal marksmanship" on the revenue side (that is, the close correspondence between revenue actually collected and revenue forecast at the beginning of the fiscal year). The forecasts of tax revenue may appear reliable both in relation to previous years' revenue and in relation to tax revenue actually collected. However, the right question when looking at public financial corruption is not whether actual revenue is close to the estimated amount, but whether it is reasonably close to the *potential* revenue that should be collected on the basis of the tax rates and the profile and number of taxpayers. Sometimes, even the number of taxpayers is not known with certainty. Such ignorance is convenient, because it precludes the estimation of potential tax revenue and hence permits avoiding the question of whether actual revenues are anywhere close to the potential—and, if not, why. In these cases, the first reform priority is to conduct a comprehensive census of all taxpayers and, on that basis, to reestimate potential tax revenue. The taxpayers' census and the results of the estimates of potential revenue should be made public and should include disaggregation of the potential-actual revenue gaps between the different forms of taxation and between different groups of taxpayers. The focus should first be on large taxpayers. A second necessary reform is to introduce a single identifying number for taxpayers, to combat tax evasion.

Customs

In customs, the main tried-and-true corruption techniques are falsification of certificates of origin, deliberate misclassification of the imported item into a lower-tariff category, abuse of exemptions and exonerations, outright manufacture of false documents, and underinvoicing of exports. Even a cursory look at the volume of imports and their composition will help reveal a large undershooting of customs revenue officially collected. This particular set of problems is very persistent, and corruption in customs is an especially hardy weed.

The single most effective anticorruption measure would be to drastically reduce the exemptions regime and make the tariff rate structure more uniform. Other avenues of improvement may include reducing individual discretion by greater use of electronic technology. However, the introduction of information technology without complementary changes in the incentives framework has proven to be ineffective, not only in customs,[7] but also in public sector management in general. The same is true of better training of customs officials, when the issue is not their insufficient skill but dishonesty combined with inadequate oversight. Changes in the incentive framework may include giving more authority to lower-level customs officers to make routine decisions, thus limiting the excessive involvement of higher-level officials. A bonus system linked to actual customs duties collected may perhaps also be considered. However, all of these measures have a spotty record of success and carry risks as well as potential benefits. In particular, bonuses to customs collectors (like all tax farming) generate abuses of power and destructive competition for the jobs to which they are attached, thus eroding government legitimacy. Cleaning up customs has proven a tough challenge in every country. In general, reducing the occasions of face-to-face contact between traders and customs officials serves to shrink the opportunities for bribery and extortion. However, careful consideration of all implications is needed before any action is taken, and a package of modest, mutually reinforcing measures has proven more effective than searching for a "magic bullet."

In the mid-1980s, much improvement was expected from the introduction of preshipment import inspection (PSI). Regrettably, although with occasional good results, PSI has not materially reduced corruption in customs, and the high fees to PSI firms were not always justified by higher customs proceeds. Generally, improving efficiency and integrity in the government customs agency is preferable to investing substantial hopes and resources in PSI. In postconflict African countries, however, outsourcing customs operations altogether for a transitional period may be advisable—following the "Crown Agents model" (whichever firm is actually contracted for this purpose)—provided that the contractor has, as a central responsibility, the training of local officials so that at the end of the transitional period the government has acquired its own efficient customs organization.

Local Government and Petty Corruption

One should not look for public financial irregularities only in central government. In most African and other countries, local governments and municipalities are also a source of the problem, with bribes required to obtain most services, permits, certifications, or licenses. The magnitude of corruption may be less, but its effect on the everyday life of citizens may be greater. The issue of corruption in local government is given added emphasis by the current efforts of donors to support decentralization initiatives.

One useful pointer, among others, is to look at the local government budgetary allocation for "travel," "information gathering," and "entertainment"—easy sources of illicit cash in conditions of inadequate expense recording and monitoring. But, in general, the issue of petty corruption cannot be tackled successfully by prosecuting a few small malefactors. When, as in many African countries, badly inadequate government salaries are a reason or an excuse for bribery, corruption must be addressed in the context of a comprehensive reform of the civil service—which would provide a living wage to lower-level employees and adequate market-related compensation to higher-level officials. However, doing so in isolation would simply produce better-paid crooks. Thus, a salary review and increase must be preceded— or at least accompanied—by credible strengthening of the performance monitoring and accountability mechanisms, with swift and certain penalties for malfeasance, especially for higher-level personnel.

The Entry Points

The two main avenues to begin strengthening accountability and improving public financial integrity are found at the very start of the budget process and at its end. Ex ante, to begin addressing corruption in procurement, the ministry of finance could exert closer scrutiny of expenditure proposals to determine the soundness of the proposed procurement, the need for and expected use of the goods, the unit price, the availability of budget funds, and the respect for legal requirements—before the inclusion of the expenditure item in the budget. This scrutiny could be accompanied by a procedure for spot-checking smaller proposed contracts to prevent contract splitting. Ex post, as Aristotle recommended 23 centuries ago, a strong and independent external audit function is critical: "Some officials handle large sums of money: it is therefore necessary to have other officials to receive and examine the accounts. These other officials must administer no funds themselves . . . we call them inspectors or auditors."

In the medium and long terms, a variety of additional reforms are needed, depending largely on the characteristics of the specific country. There is no magic remedy for corruption in public financial management, no guarantee that progress in any one area will be irreversible, and no approach that is exactly suitable to all countries. Nevertheless, the generally effective efforts in anticorruption follow the broad example of the Hong Kong, China, independent commission against corruption,[8] which emphasized three concurrent efforts—awareness raising, prevention, and enforcement. Like the three legs of a stool, each of the three efforts is necessary; none is sufficient alone in the long run. Prevention and enforcement cannot succeed if corruption is viewed as normal or inevitable, awareness and strict enforcement cannot be effective if the opportunities for corruption are too many and too easy, and limiting opportunities for corruption combined with greater awareness may be equally ineffective if enforcement is lax or nonexistent.[9]

In African countries, where reliable data are notable for their absence, the awareness-prevention-enforcement model needs to be adapted and expanded into five major avenues of reform and intervention:

1. Find the detailed facts about the loci and circuits of financial corruption, through surveys, targeted expenditure tracking, and other means.
2. Disseminate the facts, and enlist civil society to shed light on bribery problems and blow the whistle.
3. Prevent corruption through appropriate streamlining of the regulatory framework.
4. Strengthen enforcement.
5. Build the capacity of public financial accountability institutions.

Balance the Objectives

In the majority of African countries where expenditure control and cash management are already minimally acceptable, none of the three PEM objectives of expenditure control, resource allocation, and good operational management should be pursued in isolation from the others (just as the overall policy goals of growth, stability, and equity are interrelated). Improvements in one or another area can and should go forward as and when circumstances permit. But a coherent vision of the entire reform process is needed to prevent progress in any one objective from getting so far out of line as to compromise progress in the other two—and thus the PEM reform process in its entirety. Moreover, equity is an additional critical objective of PEM in poor developing countries, including most of Africa. Three important general criteria emerge from these considerations:

- A multiyear fiscal and expenditure perspective is essential to formulate a coherent vision of reform.
- A pro-poor expenditure composition should be deliberately encouraged. Moreover, a reorientation of the government budget toward the needs of the poor and most vulnerable is an explicit requirement of

eligibility for debt relief under the HIPC initiative. (The links between budget reform and the HIPC process are illustrated in box 12.2 for the case of Madagascar.)[10]

■ Advanced expenditure management systems should not be introduced until and unless the basic building blocks of financial management are in place, as in the approach to budget reform in Ethiopia summarized in box 12.3.

BOX 12.2 Selected Measures in the HIPC Action Plan for Madagascar

The list below presents selected measures in Madagascar's HIPC action plan. Note that most measures relate to the basics of public financial management and call for enforcement of existing regulations rather than new regulations. Indeed, effective pro-poor financial management reforms often consist of strengthening the fundamental systems and enforcing the rules in a uniform manner.

Budget Coverage and Preparation

Comprehensiveness
■ Integrate on an informational basis semiautonomous public agencies in the budgetary documents, and develop and implement regulations for their fiscal reporting.
■ Better integrate donor-funded projects into the budget and report project expenditures.

Classification
■ Include in the budgetary documents summary tables on the priority sectors expenditures, and establish a specific coding for poverty-reducing expenditures.

Forecasting
■ Improve forecasting and collection of revenue.

Process
■ Observe the budget preparation timetable.

Budget Execution

Arrears
■ Monitor utility arrears and ensure the payment of utility bills.
■ Take sanctions against line ministries responsible for unpaid and unrecorded bills.

Internal Control and Reconciliation
- Develop or strengthen internal audit. Establish a mechanism for followup actions by the Madagascar Ministry of Finance on reports of internal auditors.
- Issue and enforce Madagascar Treasury regulations on surcharge and penalties.
- Standardize methodology, and disseminate results of expenditure tracking and surveys, including the proportion of public funds that reach their final destination.
- Ensure that each office in the Treasury prepares a banking reconciliation statement.

Reporting
- Produce quarterly fiscal reports in a timelier manner (a maximum of four weeks following the reference period).
- Establish poverty-reducing tracking at the local level.
- Strictly observe the legal limit for the complementary period.
- Produce the final accounts according to the relevant regulations.
- Reduce the number of imprest accounts.
- Strengthen the supreme audit institution.
- Improve cash planning.

Source: Adapted from material drafted by Daniel Tommasi, based on Lazare, Hélis, and Nguenang 2004.

BOX 12.3 A Building-Block Approach to Budget Reform in Ethiopia

The *first objective* of the budget reform is to strengthen the line-item budget. Inputs must be well organized to promote effective external control. This improvement, in turn, makes possible the introduction of techniques such as cost centers that promote effective internal control. Improving the existing budget process is done through a number of activities: simplifying expenditure codes, improving the chart of accounts, and introducing a financial calendar. The *second objective* of the budget reform is aid management. The design of the budget formats identifies for the first time the specific external source of funding and the amount of that funding by line item of expenditure. The *third objective* of budget reform is to improve expenditure composition.

The budget structure must reflect the stage of evolution of the financial system. Control through a line-item structure is stressed because the process

(Box continues on the following page.)

of devolution is moving budgeting to new administrative levels that have had little or no experience in budgeting. Furthermore, because the accounting system does not provide prompt reporting, the budget performs a critical role in financial control through the system of monthly request and disbursement, which is based on the budget allocation and chart of accounts, and the line-item structure needs to be retained in the medium term.

The design of the accounts, budget, and expenditure planning in Ethiopia was challenged by some. The accounts design, which retains single-entry accounting, has been criticized for not adopting double-entry accounting. The budget design, which retains the line-item format, has been criticized for focusing on control and not adopting output-outcome budgeting. The expenditure planning design has been criticized for first adopting capital planning instead of an integrated capital and recurrent planning process. These criticisms were misplaced. The project design was developed through intensive consultation, was based on a correct appreciation of the state of Ethiopia's public financial system, and provided a realistic and systematic approach to improving public financial control and then management.

Source: Adapted from material drafted by Daniel Tommasi, based on Peterson 2000.

Reform Priorities and Sequencing in the Various Aspects of PEM

Specific reform priorities and sequencing considerations especially relevant to conditions prevalent in African countries are suggested below, following the classification of the major components of PEM elaborated by the Public Expenditure and Financial Accountability Secretariat (see Allen, Schiavo-Campo, and Garrity 2004).[11] All of these suggestions are grounded on public financial management principles as well as the lessons of international experience, but they are advanced here only as a menu of options and alternatives—some may apply to certain African countries and not to others. The design of a sound budget reform program must be based on the characteristics of the individual country, particularly its administrative and institutional capacity, as discussed in the section of this chapter on capacity. Note also that the distinction made in the following sections between "basic priorities" and "subsequently" is not identical to the distinction between short term and longer term. The implied sequence is a logical one, not necessarily a chronological one: certain reforms can be conducted, or at least initiated, in parallel with more basic reforms even though they cannot be expected to have positive results unless the basic reforms are actually implemented and in place.

Legal and Organizational Issues

Weaknesses in budgeting depend in large part on political factors and on the organization of the government. Lack of coordination within the cabinet, unclear lines of accountability, or overlaps in the distribution of responsibility lead to inefficient budgeting and perverse outcomes. As discussed in chapter 2, the legislative and regulatory framework for budgeting and policy formulation should be explicitly designed for three purposes:

1. Clarifying roles and accountabilities
2. Enabling coordination and cohesion in decision making
3. Keeping political decisions at the right political level and thereby avoiding both technical intrusions into policy choices and undue political interference into technical programming and budget execution.

The fundamental governance principle that no moneys can be taken from the citizens nor expended without express authorization of their representatives implies that the locus of overall public financial accountability resides in *both* the executive branch and the legislative branch of government. The basic priorities include the following:

- As the obvious first step—too often disregarded by outsiders—examine the country's constitution to assess whether actual PEM processes in the concerned country deviate from it, as well as to make sure that eventual recommendations for improvements are not inconsistent with the constitution.
- Next, ascertain the existence of an organic budget law or its equivalent— that is, the basic legislative framework defining the budgetary rules and the responsibilities of the executive and the legislature. The purpose is to ensure that proposed budgetary reforms are consistent with existing law or to flag the legal amendments they may require.
- Verify that the legal framework stipulates that laws that have a fiscal impact take effect only if the fiscal measures are authorized in the budget or amendments.
- Seek information on how expenditure *policy* decisions are made at the political level (see chapter 2).

Subsequently, attention can be given to the strength and effectiveness of the executive mechanisms for policy making and the legislative role in budgeting by the following measures:

■ Assess the political mechanisms for policy coordination and strategic decisions, and make appropriate recommendations that are based on experience elsewhere—with cabinet offices; government secretariats; and similar option-sifting, traffic-regulating bodies—and are consistent with the constitutional and political context of the country.
■ Give adequate information and means to the legislature to review policies and the budget.
■ Present the budget to the legislature on time, to allow for proper scrutiny and completion of the budgetary debates before the start of the fiscal year.
■ Review revenue forecasts, expenditures, and fiscal targets together.
■ Evaluate the appropriateness of limits on the powers of the legislature to amend the budget (for example, a pay-as-you-go provision, by which any amendment that increases expenditures or decreases revenues must be accompanied by a counterbalancing measure to maintain the initial deficit target).
■ When appropriate, consider fiscal responsibility provisions (see chapter 3), whether through formal legislation or other means.

Expenditure Programming and Budget Preparation

The reform directions and priorities in the various stages of budget preparation are suggested below, beginning, however, with certain recommendations concerning the improvement of revenue forecasting. Parts of this and subsequent sections recapitulate material presented in the earlier chapters in this book.

Revenue forecasting

Although tax administration is by definition outside the scope of PEM, good expenditure management always begins with realistic forecasts of revenue. Indeed, without a reliable idea of the resource constraint, all planning is an empty paper exercise—and budgeting is no exception. Accordingly, the basic priorities are as follows:

■ Examine on an annual basis the historical differences between actual revenue and budgeted revenue.
■ Recommend a "mechanical" adjustment for the next budget year corresponding to the average differences in a few prior years.

- Set in motion a ministry-by-ministry review of the historical accuracy of their revenue forecasts.
- Ensure that the database of taxpayers is accurate or, if not, conduct a census to establish an accurate database and, on that basis, estimate potential revenue and compare that estimate with actual revenue.
- Introduce a single identifying number for taxpayers.

Subsequently, systematic attention can be given to improving fiscal marksmanship:

- Improve the methodology of revenue forecasting, tax by tax and nontax revenue by nontax revenue.
- Examine realistic possibilities for automation and more timely communications through information and communication technology.
- Establish appropriate institutional rewards for greater accuracy in revenue forecasting.

Budget coverage and budget systems

As repeatedly noted, covering revenue and expenditure proposals in the budget presented to the legislature is fundamental. In budget coverage, basic priorities are as follows:

- A reasonably comprehensive coverage of the budget
- Inclusion in the budget documentation of all revenues and expenditures of extrabudgetary funds, in gross terms
- An expenditure classification system that fits the needs of both policy analysis and management and covers *all* government expenditures, including those of extrabudgetary funds
- Assessment and disclosure of all policy decisions that have an immediate fiscal effect, such as tax expenditures and quasi-fiscal expenditures, and of those entailing fiscal risk, such as loan guarantees and other contingent liabilities.

Subsequently, key reforms can include the following:

- Put in place instruments for better assessment of actual liabilities, contingent liabilities, and policy commitments with major expenditure implications—in the context of some form of multiyear expenditure programming (discussed in the next subsection).
- Review options for the gradual elimination of unjustified extrabudgetary funds and incorporation of their activities into the normal budgetary

allocation process and for improved transparency and governance of extrabudgetary funds that will continue to exist.

■ Develop special management arrangements for some expenditure programs (for example, user chargers and service delivery agencies) that can improve their operational efficiency without weakening expenditure control and accountability to the legislature.

■ Strengthen line-item cash budgeting and expenditure control while improving flexibility by (a) reducing an excessive number of line items, (b) providing greater discretion for transfers between items, or (c) both.

■ Set up a classification of expenditure by activity and program, to allow the definition of the right performance indicators at an appropriate level, although without introducing formal program or performance budgeting systems. This classification can and should be selective, by focusing on the definition of programs of major economic and social significance, and should complement—rather than replace—the line-item classification.

■ Examine the various possibilities of strengthening the performance orientation of the budget system short of abandoning cash-based line-item budgeting—for example, by identifying expenditure programs of key economic or social interest and systematically reviewing results in the context of annual budget discussions.

Multiyear expenditure frameworks

To strengthen the essential link between policy and the budget, and because the discretionary expenditure margin on a year-to-year basis is typically very small, the annual budget preparation should systematically be framed by a multiyear perspective. This perspective requires, as basic priorities, the following:

■ A set of medium-term macroeconomic projections, even if at a highly aggregated level, showing the interrelationships among the balance of payments, the fiscal accounts, real sector developments, and the monetary accounts

■ Within the above, a medium-term fiscal framework consistent with fiscal sustainability (that is, stabilizing the ratio of debt to gross domestic product while providing adequate resources for priority economic and social expenditures) and with realistic revenue forecasts

■ Aggregate expenditure estimates, based on realistic estimates by functional category and broad economic costs of major programs.

Subsequently, the expenditure projections can be gradually replaced by genuine multiyear expenditure programs consistent with the macroeconomic framework, linked with the annual budget preparation, and including only programs or projects for which financing is certain. The aim is to eventually prepare annually a formal rolling medium-term expenditure framework (MTEF) with the same coverage and in the same degree of detail as the annual budget. This framework should be composed of bottom-up programs—formulated by each ministry and consistent with government policy for the sector—focusing only on the estimated future cost of existing activities (ongoing policies), with expenditures for new policies decided only during the preparation of the annual budget. (To do otherwise would risk turning medium-term expenditure programming into medium-term expenditure entitlements.) This ambitious objective, which requires substantial capacity building in line ministries, should be approached gradually:

- At first, the overall multiyear programs would include bottom-up programs by only one or two major ministries and still rely on aggregate estimates for the remainder of expenditures.
- The bottom-up expenditure programs would gradually be expanded to more and more ministries.
- Eventually, some vertical deepening of the MTEF mechanism to subnational levels of government may be realistic and desirable. However, here again, the realities of opportunity cost and diminishing returns must be confronted. To push an ill-equipped and overstretched local government to formulate detailed MTEFs with full costing of specific activities linked to various outputs would raise transaction costs way beyond the benefits and—worse—would absorb very scarce local capacity needed to meet urgent poverty reduction and service priorities. The right cost-benefit balance must be struck, in terms relevant to the local context.
- Concurrently, aid-dependent African countries should move to preparing a strong public investment program (PIP) on a rolling basis and estimate the forward local costs of projects financed by external sources. (This process is discussed at greater length in the next section.)
- A country can gain experience toward an MTEF by preparing a full-sector expenditure program for one or two key sectors—provided that the program is framed by sound aggregate projections of expenditures, by function and broad economic category.

The right question, therefore, is not the elementary one of whether a comprehensive MTEF is preferable to medium-term programming of investment alone—obviously, it is. The right question is *how* to arrive at a comprehensive MTEF. The clear first step is to have good medium-term programming of the largest single category of expenditure. In industrial economies, the largest public expenditures are in pensions and health insurance. In almost all African countries, the largest category of government expenditure is public investment.

Investment programming

Investment is a source of growth and at the same time of future debt service and recurrent expenditure commitments—and thus potential fiscal risk. The quality and efficiency of investment determine whether its growth impact is greater than the fiscal costs. In turn, investment quality and efficiency demand realistic programming. Without good programming of investments, including sound preparation of investment projects, neither the growth potential nor fiscal discipline can materialize. In the 1980s and early 1990s, PIPs in most African developing countries were "first-generation PIPs," largely consisting of wish lists and project-pushing devices to attract foreign aid. By contrast, in a "second-generation PIP," the strategic decisions and the good project choices come first, and only then is the right financing sought. This inversion of priorities puts the recipient government back in the driver's seat and ensures that the growth and social effect of public investment will far outweigh the resulting debt service and justify the future recurrent costs. Thus, a second-generation PIP (a) raises investment efficiency by improving project quality; (b) brings investment allocation in line with country policies and sectoral priorities; (c) ensures consistency between investment programs and available financing at favorable terms; and, as noted, (d) leads, in time, to a more comprehensive MTEF.

The following are PIP priorities:

- First, design ironclad procedures against the birth of "white elephant" projects. Once a project of large size is on the drawing board, the bureaucratic dynamics from both donor and recipient sides make the project very difficult to stop. Among these procedures, the involvement of high-level policy makers (and, for very large projects, the cabinet) must be built in at a very early stage.
- Also basic is the need for reasonably sound economic appraisal of projects. Because of the need to economize on scarce capacity (and to minimize reliance on expatriate expertise), in developing countries simple appraisal methods are preferable to sophisticated ones. Also, selectivity is needed: only projects of significant size should be analyzed in detail, with smaller projects bundled and the bundles evaluated only for their general correspondence with sectoral policies and common sense.

▣ No project should be included in the PIP, even for the out-years, unless financing is reasonably assured.

▣ An agile procurement process that permits managerial efficiency while minimizing the opportunities for corruption is needed.

▣ Also needed is effective physical monitoring of project implementation and completion. Obtaining systematic feedback from local entities can be extremely useful to strengthen monitoring of project progress and completion.

▣ A realistic procedure and a minimum capacity for estimating the total cost of investment projects and their recurrent costs are a must. This priority is always preached but rarely done. The absence of these estimates, however, is sufficient in itself to cast a cloud on the usefulness and integrity of the public investment programming process and of the broader medium-term expenditure framework. Conversely, the experience gained through these forward estimates of recurrent costs of investment projects can be invaluable for the eventual move to a comprehensive multiyear program.

▣ Finally, setting up a technical "kick-the-tires" group, responsible to the core ministry of finance or planning but with full operational autonomy, can be useful to ascertain that line ministries have followed the required procedures in preparing and appraising large projects and to give clearance for the inclusion of such projects in the investment budget. One contemporary example of such a technical group, in Algeria, is described in box 12.4. Although the country's income level and other characteristics differ from those of most Sub-Saharan African countries, some features of the Algerian technical group are likely to be generally applicable.

Budget preparation process

In this area, as discussed in chapter 8, the basic priorities are as follows:

▣ Set and announce spending ceilings for each spending agency, at first on an incremental basis but strictly consistent with the overall availability of resources (see the previous discussion of revenue forecasting), and refuse to receive ministerial budget requests in excess of the specified ceiling. (The ceilings should be included in the budget circular that sets the process in motion.)

▣ Assess coordination problems in the preparation of the different components of the budget (revenue, current and capital expenditures, expenditures from extrabudgetary funds, and so forth).

BOX 12.4 Providing Technical Contestability for Investment Proposals in Algeria

To help address the weaknesses in investment project preparation and execution, Algeria launched in 2005 the National Center for Infrastructure for Development (Caisse Nationale pour l'Équipement et le Développement, or CNED), which is expected to be fully operational in 2007. The CNED's essential functions are (a) technical oversight of the preparation, execution, and evaluation of major projects and (b) guidance and facilitation of capacity building in the line ministries. It is governed by a board chaired by the minister of finance and including four other ministers (in addition to the minister directly concerned with an agenda item), and its management is entrusted to a director general with the autonomy and responsibility appropriate to a professionally run enterprise.

The CNED has the responsibility and authority to do the following, in sequence:

- Advise on the general viability of the ideas of major projects before the launching of the detailed feasibility studies.
- Confirm that the project preparation procedures were respected in form and substance before a project can be included in the investment budget.
- Follow up project execution.
- Lead the preparation of relevant manuals for the line ministries.
- Initiate the postcompletion evaluation of projects and programs and facilitate the creation of an evaluation capacity in the line ministries.

The authority of the CNED is limited to "major projects." The criteria for defining such projects are (a) the total cost, including both initial investment and estimated future recurrent costs, with a uniform threshold as well as higher ones established sector by sector, and (b) qualitative criteria, such as the special innovative nature or special risks of a project or program.

In its review of project preparation, the CNED is expected to ascertain, among other things, the consistency of the proposed project with the sector strategy. It may comment on the strategy, but only to the extent that weaknesses impede the preparation of economically sound projects. As a technical body, the CNED has no authority to review the sectoral strategies themselves— let alone contribute to their formulation, which is the core responsibility of the ministries concerned, in consultation with the Ministry of Finance, and approved by the highest levels of government.

The CNED is expected to by lightly structured, with short lines of command and a small but highly competent staff. It will operate mainly by commissioning and supervising studies by external consultants. Its overhead costs will be covered by a regular budget allocation, with the Ministry of Finance's allocating additional amounts as needed to cover the costs of studies and other project scrutiny activities. This mode of financing will permit the CNED activities to expand and contract easily as and when required. Accountability will be provided through the same external audit court and general state inspectorate of Algeria as for any other public enterprise. However, in the particular case of the CNED, a special "review of the reviewers" should be provided, in the form of a substantive audit of the technical quality of CNED activities, to be conducted periodically by an independent and external entity.

Even though the CNED is expected to be active for a number of years, the logic of its creation is inherently as a temporary structure, to transition from a system without effective quality controls to a system in which such effective controls do exist and are exercised primarily where they should belong—in the line ministries themselves.

Source: Extracted and adapted from World Bank forthcoming.

- In countries where responsibilities for capital budgeting are separate from those for the current budget, as an initial priority require joint reviews of the two components of the budget at each stage of budget preparation and at each administrative level.
- Pay some attention to budgeting capacity in at least one or two line ministries rather than only in the core ministries of finance and planning, and begin selected budgeting capacity-building activities in those ministries.

Subsequently, strengthening budget preparation requires the following:

- Derive the sectoral spending ceilings from the preparation of a macro-economic framework and the appropriate multiyear expenditure programming (as previously described).
- Devise positive budgetary incentives for ministries that submit more timely multiyear cost estimates of ongoing policies and programs better linked to sectoral government policies.
- Establish and enforce rules for better cooperation between the core ministries of finance and planning (or the different departments in a unified ministry) and for vertical coordination between the core ministries and the line ministries.
- Seek appropriate participation of civil society in budget preparation, beyond customary legislative hearings.
- Review the distribution of responsibilities in budget preparation and the structure of controls with a view to giving the line ministries sufficient authority to formulate their programs and making them accountable for implementation.

■ In aid-dependent countries, pay more attention to the programming of expenditures financed with external aid, and review the budget as a whole, regardless of the source of financing (even though the project approach adopted by donors creates a tendency toward fragmentation in budgeting).

Budget Execution

Chapter 9 began with the proposition that it is impossible to execute an unrealistic budget well. Thus, improving budget preparation is in many ways a prerequisite for improving budget execution. Focusing attention on the symptoms of the problem rather than its genesis is not likely to produce significant improvements. As concluded by the International Monetary Fund (IMF), for example, "technical advice about compiling and controlling commitments [is] not likely to be successful" if the root cause of unrealistic budget preparation is not addressed (Diamond and others 2006: 12). However, it is entirely possible to execute badly a well-prepared budget; good execution is not an automatic consequence of good preparation. Given a realistic budget to begin with, improving budget execution calls mainly for strengthening expenditure control to ensure conformity with the budget and for creating the conditions for increased operational efficiency and effectiveness. These objectives are sometimes in conflict—stronger expenditure control would lead to closer supervision, while better management would require greater freedom of action—and an adequate balance should be found. In general, however, as repeatedly noted in this chapter, protecting the public funds and ensuring expenditure control should be the first priority.

In order to ensure conformity with the budget and basic expenditure control, the basic priorities are as follows:

■ Formulate a cash plan, in conformity with the budget authorization and taking into account ongoing commitments, that is based on seasonality of *actual* revenues and expenditures and is progressively more detailed on the basis of experience.
■ Release funds on a timely basis consistent with the cash plan.
■ Put in place adequate cash management, providing, first, for centralization of cash balances (not necessarily of payments) to prevent large idle balances and, eventually, for a more sophisticated system to maximize the returns from government cash and minimize borrowing costs.
■ For payments, in African countries where the payment system is in disrepair—mainly postconflict countries—a centralized treasury system

may need to be built from scratch. (Such a system is already in place in almost all francophone countries and almost half of anglophone countries.) In other countries, centralized or decentralized payments may be appropriate, depending on the geographic distribution of the payments offices, the telecommunications infrastructure, and the possibilities offered by information technology. (However payments are organized, the cash balances always need to be centralized.)

■ Introduce effective controls at each stage of expenditure (commitment, verification, and payment), progressively relying on internal controls in the spending ministries.

■ Set clearly defined procedures for registering transactions, notably for commitments. (These procedures can be simple and do not require extensive computerization or changes in the basis of accounting.)

■ Centralize monitoring of financial transactions.

■ Establish transparent and efficient procedures for procurement and, where they already exist, ensure their enforcement.

■ Strengthen debt management, at first by ensuring timely tracking of borrowings and repayments (on accrual basis) and eventually on a more sophisticated basis to minimize debt service costs and reduce fiscal risk. (For African countries that received large debt relief through the extended HIPC process and expect future assistance largely in the form of grants, the debt management capacity need not be large.)

Subsequently, after expenditure control is in reasonably good shape, operational efficiency and effectiveness in budget execution can be improved:

■ Introduce flexible rules for *virement* (transfers between line items) and regulated carryover provisions, especially for capital expenditure.

■ Progressively decentralize controls (*after* a reinforcement of procedures for auditing and reporting).

■ Gradually introduce clear, simple performance indicators for major expenditure programs that are capable of being monitored, with maximum feasible participation by front-line civil servants and service users and feedback into the budget preparation dialogue, not a mechanistic link between results and funding. (The critical issue of performance measurement and monitoring is discussed in some detail later in this chapter.)

■ Consider (very cautiously) possibilities for contracting out.

■ Most important, create new opportunities for participation and systematic public feedback on the integrity and quality of expenditure.

Accounting, Reporting, and Audit

Financial accountability requires independent scrutiny, which, in turn, depends on timely and reliable accounting and financial reporting. The emphasis should be on strengthening cash accounting, ensuring simple and regular financial reports, building reliable management controls, and ensuring the effectiveness of the external audit function—in all cases, improving as much as possible the existing procedures before jumping to more complex systems.

Accounting and reporting

In a majority of developing countries, the basic priorities include the following:

- The cash-based accounts must be clear and prepared on a timely basis.
- In countries that monitor only payments, a commitment register and an ancillary book for outstanding payments should be implemented.
- A debt-accrual accounting system should be developed if none exists, and reports on debt should be prepared regularly.
- Operations of extrabudgetary funds should be consolidated, and all government entities should be made to follow the same classification in their reporting.
- Contingent liabilities, especially loan guarantees, should be individually recorded, and statements should be prepared and published, including amounts and beneficiaries.
- Basic financial statements should be published, in a form accessible to the public or at least the media. (In most countries, substantial assistance to the media is likely to be needed to raise their capacity, integrity, and professionalism.)

Subsequently, the following measures can be considered:

- Recognition of all liabilities (including pensions and other entitlements)
- Systematic registration and publication of contingent liabilities
- Introduction of modified accrual accounting by also recognizing all financial assets (but not all physical assets)
- Construction of selective physical asset registers, focusing on categories of assets that are both valuable and at risk of wastage or theft, and thereafter monitoring of their use, including in the context of the dialogue on preparation of the next budget.

When (and only when) the enumerated reforms have been implemented and tested and are on a solid basis can a move toward full accrual accounting and the accompanying financial reporting be considered. For several industrial countries, most middle-income countries, and all African countries, a possible net benefit of such a move lies in the very distant future, owing to the very high costs and implementation requirements and questionable benefits in terms of the essential objectives of PEM. Even at that time, accrual accounting should be implemented very gradually, beginning with agencies in which the need to assess full costs is more urgent.

Audit

EXTERNAL AUDIT.   As noted, the fundamental criterion of financial accountability is that the resources must be spent by the executive branch of government in conformity with the budget approved by the legislative branch. External audit closes the legitimacy loop in PEM, by providing the legislature with information concerning the uses of the money that it had authorized. Therefore, the key requirements of effective external audit (whether through a court of audit as in francophone African countries or an auditor general's office as in anglophone African countries) are as follows:

- Independence from the executive branch
- Reporting to the legislature
- Total freedom of access to public financial information
- Predictable source of funding
- Full management and operational autonomy
- Adequate internal capacity.

Accordingly, strengthening the supreme audit institution is a critical component of PEM reform. In many African countries, some of these requirements are met but not others—in some cases for acceptable reasons of gradual progress and maintenance of due process. However, countries must continue to make persistent progress toward meeting all of the requirements for robust external audit. Technical assistance can usually be obtained from the International Organization of Supreme Audit Institutions (INTOSAI) or by "twinning" the external audit entity with that of an industrial country.

The external audit entity, too, bears a responsibility—not only to function with integrity and courage, but also to focus its limited capacity on the priority public financial problems in the country. Thus, as a general rule, considering the state of affairs in public financial management in many African countries, external audit should focus on financial integrity and compliance. Value-for-money issues should be addressed only if and after financial and compliance audits are on a solid basis and corruption ceases to be a major concern. However, efficiency audits of specific programs of major economic or social importance can take place—preferably subcontracted to specialized firms, although under the guidance and leadership of the country's supreme audit institution.

INTERNAL AUDIT.   Internal audit is frequently misunderstood as an additional layer of financial control by the ministry of finance over the line ministries. Indeed, most francophone African countries follow the practice of placing financial controllers from the ministry of finance in each line ministry. In those cases, the appropriate role of the financial controller should be limited to ensuring the conformity of the expenditure with the budget and its regularity before the payment can be authorized—and must not extend to questioning the reasons for the transaction or its probable effectiveness. Properly understood, instead, internal audit is a *management support* function, aimed at reporting to and advising the head of the agency (who is the accountable official) on the soundness of the internal accountability mechanisms in the ministry or agency and the incentive frameworks for ensuring service efficiency. Therefore, internal audit capacity can most usefully be developed only in countries with an already reasonably solid system of financial control and external audit. Once again, this general rule does not preclude initiating internal audit in ministries that administer specific programs of major importance; indeed, in those cases, development of internal audit and of selected value-for-money audits by the external audit entity becomes strongly complementary.

Capacity: The Missing Link

Without sufficient institutional, administrative, and technical capacity to implement them, the best reform programs and carefully designed measures are hardly worth the paper they are written on. A budget reform strategy paper—indeed, *any* strategy paper—is a paper, not a strategy, unless it addresses convincingly and realistically the questions of *how* the reforms are to be implemented, by *whom* they are to be implemented, *with what* resources they are to be implemented, and *when* they are to be implemented. In all developing countries, including African countries, the issue of capacity building stands left, right, and center of the budget reform agenda. Yet budget reform programs have been too often designed and pushed onto African countries' governments with no attention to implementation capacity, no consideration of all the other commitments the civil servants concerned have to meet, and obliviousness of the red tape and transaction costs imposed on the local public administration. The previous recommendations of priority reforms and their sequencing, stemming from the international experience in developing countries, are partly grounded on the imperative to consider local institutional and administrative realities.

What Is *Capacity*?

Capacity building is among the most misused and least understood terms in the economic development literature and is too often narrowly constructed as simply training.[12] Undertaken in isolation, however, training has been a recipe for waste of resources on a vast scale. A clarification is needed.

To begin with, *capacity* is inherently relative—mainly in terms of the complexity of the tasks the system is asked to perform. Regrettably, experience over the past 50 years shows a troublesome supply-driven dynamic at work, whereby external technical assistance and international consultants have often pushed complex new budgeting practices onto a reasonably well-functioning system and thus created capacity constraints where none may have existed. In turn, these "capacity limitations" are then used to justify the need for continuing assistance. The perverse outcome is that the creation of local capacity is preempted by the expatriate assistance, rather than facilitated by it. For this reason, the IMF recommends an agreement with the government on an exit strategy for external technical assistance (Diamond and others 2006: 12).[13] Although institutional innovation and progress must stretch local capacity to some extent, they cannot get too far ahead of it, on penalty of failure. Also, as and when budgetary innovations do require additional capacity, assistance to help build it must be a core ingredient of the innovation design itself.

The components of an entity's capacity go well beyond employee skills and include the institutions—that is, the rules and incentives (both formal and informal) governing the behavior of individuals in that entity; the organization that enforces or implements those rules (institutions and organizations are often confused, and often with confusing results); the information needed within and without the organization; and finally, the stock and quality of resources in the organization, including human capital. Thus, capacity building should comprise activities to support, in sequence, the following:

- *Institutional development.* Improvements in the mandate, incentives, and the other basic rules of the game will translate into a decrease in transaction costs. In African countries, where habits of interministerial cooperation are not well rooted, a top institutional development priority is to establish and enforce rules requiring systematic dialogue and cooperation between the core ministries of finance and planning and between the line ministries and the core ministries.

■ *Organizational development.* The organizational architecture must adapt to fit the evolving institutional framework. After the appropriate institutional changes have been decided, a fresh look at the organizational structure of the core ministries of finance and planning is normally needed to make sure they are consistent with the new rules. The structures of the line ministries, too, would benefit from a light-handed review to ensure that they are conducive to good horizontal coordination within the ministry and with the improved vertical coordination that is required for stronger budgeting.

■ *Information development.* Improving the flow of relevant information decreases the cost of acquiring it. This activity is usually identified with information and communication technology (ICT) innovations, but should not be strictly limited to ICT.

■ *Resource development.* After the institutional and organizational review and decisions on appropriate information development, sufficient financial resources must be provided to each line ministry to prepare its budget proposals and monitor budget execution. Finally, of course, guidance and support are also required for human capital development, through training and other forms of knowledge transfer. Although generic training in budgeting is appropriate in some circumstances, training should otherwis center on specific skills, determined by comparing a staff member's actual skills with those required for better performance in a current or prospective job. If the skills provided through the training are germane to the institutional and organizational context of the individual employee, they will actually be used and reinforced after they are imparted. For this reason, training programs should be designed as a corollary of the institutional, organizational, and information changes and initiated only after those changes have been put in place, or at least on a coordinated basis with those changes.[14]

Among these four components of capacity, ICT deserves special attention because of its high potential relevance to budget preparation, execution, and monitoring.

How and How Not to Introduce Financial Management Information Systems

The monumental change wrought in every field by ICT is still only in its initial phase in African developing countries. The subject of ICT is too vast to be adequately discussed in this volume, but certain considerations are generally applicable.

Potential and risks

First, ICT is a tool, immensely powerful yet essentially no different from a photocopier or a bulldozer in the sense that the needs and requirements of the users must dictate whether and how the ICT tool should be used. For certain functions, a pencil, a telephone, a face-to-face meeting, or a visit to the document center is far more effective than computers or the Internet. This obvious point must be stressed, because governments, consultants, or donor agencies frequently encourage computerizing anything in sight. Indeed, some observers have argued that ICT innovation is now largely supply and marketing driven rather than dictated by the needs and requirements of the users. Therefore, assessing realistically the costs of a given ICT change and comparing it with the benefits expected are essential.

Second, neither the ICT "techie" nor the budget manager should work in isolation from each other. As noted, improvements in effectiveness stem largely from better rules and organization in the entity concerned. On the one hand, to apply advanced ICT to obsolete or inefficient rules and processes means in effect to computerize inefficiency. Doing the wrong thing faster is not progress. On the other hand, the absence of technical ICT competence risks either costly mistakes or missed opportunities for dramatic service improvements.

Third, ICT cannot substitute for good management and internal controls. Indeed, the introduction of computers can give a false illusion of tighter expenditure control in cases where a large part of the expenditure cycle occurs in parallel outside the computerized system.

Fourth, faster and integrated public financial management information systems carry correspondingly greater potential risks for the integrity of the data and can even jeopardize the financial management system in its entirety if developed carelessly and without sufficient checks, controls, security, and virus protection. Indeed, the first advice to an African government moving from a partly manual public accounting and recording system to a fully computerized one should be to keep the manual ledgers going alongside the new system until the new system is working well and is secure and free of risk.

Fifth, ICT can substantially reduce corruption. Nevertheless, although computer technology does eliminate almost all opportunities for corruption for those who do not understand fully the new technology, it also opens up new corruption vistas for those who understand the new systems well enough to manipulate them—particularly when their hierarchical superiors are unfamiliar with the new systems.

In sum, the adoption of more advanced ICT should meet the following criteria:

- Always fit the user requirements and the real objectives of the activity.
- Ensure that the more advanced ICT goes hand in hand with improved rules and processes.
- Protect data and systems integrity.
- Aim at an integrated strategy, and avoid a piecemeal approach (which can fit specific needs but adds up in time to a ramshackle and even dangerous system).

If these criteria are met, ICT offers a wonderful potential in Africa for increasing government accountability, transparency, and participation; improving the efficiency and effectiveness of public sector operations; widening access to public services; and disseminating information to the public and getting feedback from relevant stakeholders and service users.

Do it slowly and do it well—or don't do it at all

An integrated financial management information system (IFMIS) is a computerized system covering the entire PEM cycle, from budget preparation through budget execution, accounting, and reporting. It links line ministries and spending agencies in a fully integrated way and provides information in real time. Although an IFMIS must interface with other information systems on other government activities, it need not encompass all those activities. (Indeed, to attempt to do so would be an exercise in costly futility, given the variety of government functions and attendant information requirements.) Box 12.5 lists the features of a well-designed financial management information system, as identified by Jack Diamond and Pokar Khemani (2005) in a recent IMF study on the subject.

The payoff from a well-functioning IFMIS includes greater fiscal transparency for the executive branch, the legislature, and the citizenry at large; the associated potential for stronger public financial accountability; the capability of tracking expenditure at its various stages and in its different categories; the shrinking of the space for corruption; and, in general, the provision of financial information that enables better achievement of all three objectives of expenditure management—expenditure control, linking of policy with the budget, and operational efficiency. Regrettably, the heavy costs and requirements of an IFMIS have not been highlighted with the same

BOX 12.5 Features of a Financial Management
Information System

A well-designed financial management information system should yield consistent and reliable information on government financial operations and their interaction, in real time and on a continuous basis, to allow policy makers and budget managers to reach informed decisions, keep track of actual expenditures, make required adjustments on a timely basis, and stay on top of emerging fiscal trends so that they can anticipate probable fiscal outcomes. For these purposes, the system should meet the following criteria:

- Be developed on a modular basis to permit progressive upgrading, and include dedicated modules to handle short- and medium-term forecasts of revenues and expenditures by each spending agency
- Offer a common platform and user interface to the different agencies responsible for financial management, to preclude the temptation for the agencies to develop their own information systems, incompatible with one another
- Maintain a historical base of budget data and transactions at the highest level of details
- Incorporate tools to analyze fiscal trends and permit a forward-oriented perspective on fiscal outcomes
- Compile the needed government accounts from its database of budgetary appropriations and cash allocations
- Enable real-time reconciliation of transactions, checks issued, bank statements, and so forth
- Provide all information defined by budget managers and other users, in the desired level of aggregation or detail.

Each of the listed characteristics entails specific prerequisites in terms of prior definition of user needs, data availability, informatics, administrative capacity, and targeted training—which illustrates the vastness and difficulty of the challenge of building a good financial management information system in any developing country, including in Africa.

Source: Adapted from Diamond and Khemani 2005: 5.

enthusiasm as the potential benefits, and the time required for effective introduction of an IFMIS and its reliable operation has been consistently and badly underestimated. In light of the severely limited statistical and administrative capacity in developing countries, the generally very poor record of success of attempts to introduce IFMISs should not be surprising.

Diamond and Khemani (2005) found the same poor record of success in Africa as well (the interested reader is encouraged to refer to their study). In brief, of the African countries examined in the study, only Tanzania and, to a lesser extent, Uganda have handled the introduction of financial management information systems properly and have thus been comparatively successful. The many reasons for the failures in other countries are identified as follows:

- Lack of clarity in ownership of the system and unclear authority to implement it
- Failure to specify the user needs and functional requirements
- Too little time spent on the design phase
- Failure to improve the underlying budgetary procedures (the "computer-ization of inefficiency" mentioned earlier) and neglect of the required complementary reforms
- Neglect to "sell" the system to spending agencies
- Overly ambitious scope and inclusion of too much information (related to the failure to specify clearly the user needs and distinguish the important from the unimportant)
- Unrealistically short timetables, often leading to damaging shortcuts
- Lack of incentives for the individuals involved
- Failure to provide funds for the requisite operations and maintenance
- Absence of many prerequisites, such as computer literacy and adequate information.

This daunting list of failures is not a reason to reject out of hand initiatives to introduce informatics into the financial management apparatus of African countries. It is abundant reason, however, to be extremely careful and to do so at the right moment and in the right manner; to allow for all required preliminary studies, design, implementation time, and resources; to take full cognizance of the mistakes of other countries; and, above all, to tailor the scope and pace of computerization to the realities and limitations of the specific country. This point leads to the next section.

Fit Capacity Building to Local Realities

In general, *simplicity* is a guiding criterion for capacity building. As well stated in a recent World Bank Institute publication (Levy and Kpundeh 2004: 3): "Instead of dwelling on politically unrealistic 'best practice' reforms, the focus shifts to a 'good fit' approach using modest, viable initiatives, with observable results." The technical assistance provider should particularly be on the look-out for evidence of a supply-side dynamic at work, because, as noted earlier, many international consultants assure themselves of a continuing market for their expertise mainly by advocating the introduction of inappropriately complex budgeting methods. The World Bank and other donors have not always followed their own prescription in this respect. On the contrary, donors' interventions have sometimes become part of the problem, rather than the solution, and have made a bad situation worse—as illustrated by the experience of Chad (box 12.6). This outcome is especially regrettable for the World Bank, which, with its credibility and lack of vested interest, has a unique role to play as debunker of fashionable nonsense.

BOX 12.6 The Price of Disregarding Country Realities in Budget Reform: The Case of Chad

Beginning in 2000, donors introduced budget reforms in Chad, including a new chart of accounts, rationalized budget execution controls, improved financial reporting, and a financial management information system. Except for the financial management information system, these measures were not overly ambitious in and of themselves. However, they turned out to be inappropriate in relation to country realities, particularly the weak human resources capacity, lack of political buy-in, and widespread corruption.

In 2001, the Chad Treasury Department's chart of accounts was slightly improved. However, because of lack of information technology specialists, the Treasury's accounting software was not adapted to the new chart of accounts, and some financial statements previously available are no longer being produced. Later, in 2003 and 2004, the budget preparation and execution information system used in Burkina Faso was transplanted into Chad, but without preliminary studies. As a result, the information system does not fit all of Chad's budget management procedures, and data have to be partly reprocessed manually, raising new doubts about their reliability. (The financial management information system covers only commitments and payment orders for the current budget, which may be acceptable in Burkina Faso, but not in Chad, where many payment transactions are made either from non-budgetary accounts or from the accounts of the previous budgets.)

Weak capacity made satisfactory results difficult to get from even basic changes. For example, the format of the budget was improved in 2000, but because of many calculation errors and last-minute changes, the budget documents have not become any more reliable. Similarly, COFOG (Classification of the Functions of Government) codes have been introduced, but most officials responsible for budget management do not understand their meaning.

The larger part of Chad's oil revenue has been earmarked for infrastructure, agriculture, and the social sectors, and rightly so. Unfortunately, instead of

(Box continues on the following page.)

using a virtual fund approach to present these earmarked expenditures in the budget and monitor them closely, the budget itself has been fragmented into several special accounts: "The multiplicity of parallel budgets creates an opaque budget management system, which seriously jeopardizes the quality of budget management" (Tandberg, Hélis, and Hovland 2004). In Chad, a number of experienced public accountants work in the Treasury Department, but the multiplicity of special procedures has contributed to scatter inefficiently their efforts.

Corruption, too, was not taken sufficiently into account in budget reform. Rationalizing the highly centralized and duplicative control procedures proved difficult because of the "tolls" levied by financial controllers from the Ministry of Finance at each stage of the expenditure cycle. Indeed, despite the ex ante financial controls along the lines of French practice, control is extremely weak. To address this crucial issue would go far beyond the technical aspects. Here are some examples. Many payment orders issued by the Ministry of Finance's Payment Order Department face excessive delays before being registered by the Treasury Department. The Ministry of Finance's financial controllers participate in the verification of the deliveries, but nobody checks whether the "delivered" goods actually reach the end users. For the general budget, the payment system is centralized, but the payments are prioritized by the Treasury's paymaster in a nontransparent manner. And management in even the priority sectors has been hampered by the fact that badly paid military officers have been authorized to be intermediaries between line ministries and suppliers.

Source: Adapted from material drafted by Daniel Tommasi, based on World Bank data and information from government officials.

One final observation: when introducing "more advanced" systems, one should make absolutely certain to protect the existing systems and continue them until such time as the new systems are fully established, owned, and debugged. Although progress should be encouraged and opportunities for more efficient practices seized, the risk of losing the good while reaching for the best is a reality of budget reform as of the human experience in general. Box 12.7 illustrates the damaging effect on Malawi's PEM of abandoning its reasonably informative investment programming system and replacing it with a comprehensive MTEF.

Fostering Performance Orientation in Budgeting

From the simplistic assumptions of about a decade ago, understanding of the complexity and pitfalls of the measurement of performance in the public sector has grown. This chapter is not the place for a review of the extensive

BOX 12.7 One Step Forward, One Step Back: Budget Reform in Malawi

Malawi's experience in reforming its public management system highlights the necessity of placing individual technical reforms within the larger context of budget management and taking into account local realities, ownership of reforms and political will, capacity, and sensible sequencing.

Phase I of the MTEF reform program began in 1995. The main components of this reform program were the reallocation of expenditures to priority activities, the preparation of activity-based budgets, and the integration of the development and recurrent budget. A bottom-up approach in expenditure programming was developed.

These reforms had some benefits—for example, improved capacity at line-ministry level to link policies and budgets. However, as an unintended result of the bottom-up approach developed in expenditure programming, detailed activity costing did not take into account the overall resource envelope, and unpredictable funding undermined the credibility of the exercise—thus undermining overall expenditure control. Sector development of detailed activity-based budgets and efforts to prioritize activities happened in a vacuum and largely amounted to empty annual compliance with procedural requirements—with only a limited effect on spending outcomes—rather than robust engagement with problems. The Public Sector Investment Programme (PSIP) was discontinued in 1997, under the assumption that it would be replaced by the MTEF. As a result, for several years the Ministry of Finance had little information about ongoing investment projects, and few of them were included in the development budget.

An MTEF II program was prepared in 2003 and 2004. The second phase of the MTEF reforms is aimed at strengthening the basis for reviving the MTEF. The objectives of the MTEF II program include improving macroeconomic and revenue forecasting capacity; improving cash management; strengthening financial control and accountability; streamlining the budget preparation process to provide timely hard budget constraints; and improving institutions for economic governance, including mechanisms for political involvement, transparency, and accountability. A few improvements have already been achieved. For example, cash planning has been streamlined to provide line ministries with a modicum of predictability. The legal framework has been streamlined. The PSIP was revived in 2004, to prioritize projects according to the objectives of the poverty reduction strategy. However, the initial objectives of the MTEF reform are far from being achieved. In the meantime, important information has been lost, and substantial transaction costs have been incurred.

Source: Adapted from material drafted by Daniel Tommasi, based on Durevall and Erlandsson 2005 and Simwakai 2004.

literature on the subject (see Schiavo-Campo 1999 and Smith 1996 for an introduction), but the key requirements for a good performance indicator can be summarized in the "CREAM" rule: a good performance indicator must be clear, relevant, economical, adequate, and monitorable. Also essential are the following criteria:

■ Never use either one single performance indicator to measure performance or too many. Usually, three or four well-chosen indicators are appropriate.
■ Because precise weights cannot be assigned to different indicators, and they cannot therefore be aggregated into a single quantitative measure of performance, the indicators should serve as the basis for a dialogue on performance and not be used to assign mechanical "points."
■ The *process* of choosing the performance indicators is critical. Because both front-line staff and the service users possess relevant information on the public activity in question, they must both be brought into the definition of the appropriate performance indicators, from the start of the process, as well as provide feedback after the fact.

Recently, an operational guide has been produced to measure and monitor performance in PEM (Collange, Demangel, and Poinsard 2006). Although developed for Morocco, and thus more directly applicable to francophone African countries, this guide is an excellent example of how to approach the important issue of introducing better orientation to results, in a pragmatic and sensible way that takes into account the lessons of international experience.

Lessons of International Experience

Among those lessons of experience, the fundamental one is that injecting new formal performance-related elements into the budget process requires extreme caution—both because better performance orientation is critical for improving PEM and because there are many wrong ways of pushing it and only a few ways of doing it right. In particular, international experience suggests the following:

■ Never confuse the end of better performance orientation with any one of the specific means for achieving it. In particular, there are many ways to foster attention to results, short of making formal changes in the budgeting system.
■ If the PEM system is performing reasonably well, be particularly mindful of the risk that changes may actually make the situation worse. Conversely,

if the budget process is extremely weak and corrupt, radical changes may be the only way to improve it.

■ Consider carefully the probable effect on individuals' behavior, especially in multiethnic societies or very small economies. For example, performance bonuses for public employees (which have a negative record in general) can lead in African countries to patronage, discrimination, internal resentments and conflict, and a generic loss of productivity.

■ Understand clearly the different uses and limitations of input, output, outcome, and process indicators, and tailor the use of each to the specific sector and issue in question.

■ If performance systems are introduced, ensure robust monitoring, with swift and predictable consequences. Nothing causes reforms to fail faster than the realization that no rewards will be given for good performance and no penalties will be given for underperformance.

■ Ensure systematic feedback from front-line staff, service users, and the public.

Moving Toward Results

The following sequence can be sketched of the desirable steps in introducing performance- and results-orientation into the budget system (which, to reiterate, does not at all require a wholesale transformation of the system into program or performance budgeting):

■ Pick two or three major expenditure programs in government departments that provide important services directly to the public.

■ Introduce performance indicators for these programs that are few, simple, clear, and hard to manipulate; that can be monitored; and that do not carry high data collection costs. To the fullest extent possible, these indicators ought to be developed with the participation of front-line personnel and the service users themselves (though the final decisions and the monitoring require involvement by the central core ministries).

■ Monitor closely the functioning and effect of the measures, again with reference to the views of front-line personnel and service users, and modify or adjust as needed, mindful of the risk of creating perverse incentives as the agents modify their behavior to adapt to the performance system.

■ Build in provisions for the systematic assessment of the performance of the performance measurement system itself.

■ Use the performance indicators systematically in the dialogue during budget preparation, but postpone to a much later stage any direct link to budgetary appropriations, and avoid in all cases purely mechanical links between results and future allocations.

■ Gradually expand the application of performance measures to other governmental areas as and when appropriate.

■ Perhaps most difficult, but critical, when the point of diminishing returns has been reached, *stop*.

The Link to the Budget Process

There is not much point to monitoring budget performance unless it is systematically linked to the subsequent budget preparation process. As noted, it is important to avoid the temptation to adopt a mechanistic system whereby various performance measures are given "points" that are then aggregated and used to adjust budget allocations. Not only would this process be antithetical to good budgeting sense, but any experienced bureaucrat would be able to manipulate such a system to produce favorable results. Instead, much more reliable information on performance can be obtained through a robust dialogue on the results of the previous year's expenditure. What is essential, therefore, is to build into the budget preparation process a requirement for such a dialogue—between budget managers and their minister within the line ministries, and between the line ministries and the ministry of finance. Ideally, this dialogue on performance would be continuous. In most African countries, however, a good and practical start would be to require such a dialogue at least at the very start of the budget preparation cycle and, if possible, also during the negotiations phase (see chapter 8).

One serious risk emerges from the coexistence of a general planning strategy for the country and a detailed MTEF. The two may not be fully consistent, because the planning strategy articulates the broad vision of the political leadership, whereas an MTEF is a technical financial programming instrument.[15] In such cases, the definition of *program*, and hence the choice of performance indicators, will differ between the strategy and the MTEF. This disconnect may make it difficult to identify each budget manager's relative contribution to the outcome and thus make it hard to allocate rewards, penalties, and resources on the basis of this identification. This problem could then lead to duplicate budgeting for overlapping functions located in different organizations, as well as provide openings for abuse and waste of resources. If so, tailoring the performance monitoring system to minimize such duplication may be important. Also important would be a strong mechanism of spot-checks, with appropriate penalties for those who abuse the system.

Finally, a word of caution about formal, detailed "contracts" within the budget process (or, indeed, the public sector as a whole): in brief, while an explicit (therefore written) understanding of the key results expected for the money provided is useful for accountability, such understanding must not be allowed to expand into a detailed fine-print contract. Experience shows that if the budget system gets straitjacketed into such detailed contracts—cascading from the ministry of finance to the line ministries to the directorates to the division chiefs to the office managers to the district chiefs to the heads of deconcentrated services, and so on—the chance for genuine accountability is gone, and all that is left is a monumental and time-consuming paper chase. The exercise of judgment is essential, and the guiding rule for performance monitoring in the budget system remains the "KISS" principle: keep it simple, sir.

Introducing Monitoring and Evaluation

As external audit closes the legitimacy loop, so good evaluation closes the programming loop—by feeding into the preparation of the next budget relevant information concerning the execution of the previous budget.[16]

Timing

The timing of monitoring and evaluation (M&E) introduction should be carefully tailored to the scope and time frame of the systemic institutional improvements under way in the public sector. In African developing countries, where processes are generally more fluid, M&E should be brought to bear at an early stage—even if in a partial manner and only focusing on some of the key issues. Although no substitute exists for allowing sufficient time for the evaluation of long-ripening outcomes, the habits of M&E should be built as soon as possible in the reform process—and preferably as an integral part of the reforms themselves (as, for example, in Uganda and, to a lesser extent, Ghana and Mozambique). Evaluation of effectiveness (that is, of the ultimate outcomes) can come only long after the completion of the activities themselves, but evaluation of process and outputs can take place at a very early stage. Early M&E are most applicable at both ends of the public service continuum. At the bottom end—the interface with the citizens—the connection between physical outputs and accountability is clearest and most immediate (for example, trash collection, pest control, water purification). But at the top end of policy review and program formulation, process indicators are most relevant—and performance can be assessed by judicious assessment of the views of the main participants in the process.[17]

By Objectives or by Results?

The classic approach to evaluation (assess the degree of achievement of the objectives stated at inception of the task) and the pragmatic approach (assess the results actually achieved, whether or not they match the initial objectives) do not necessarily produce the same verdict. The classic approach has been criticized for lending itself to excessive formalism and enabling a mutation of simple and useful ideas into monsters of red tape.[18] But because M&E capacity takes time to build, the pragmatic approach can degrade into an alibi for perennial postponement of reckoning and accountability. On balance, it is probably preferable to adopt the classic approach of evaluation by objectives but complement it with some form of midcourse assessments. Thus, evaluation shades into supervision.

In-house or External M&E Capacity?

The standard assumption is that M&E capacity should be created within the government itself. Regardless of whether this assumption is correct, it is surely fallacious to assume that because evaluation *of* government activities is important it must be conducted *by* government. In-house evaluation has the obvious advantage of inside expertise, savvy, and intimate operational knowledge of the programs being evaluated (as in Australia). The other side of the coin is a natural tendency to overstate results, and, where accountability systems are weak or nonexistent, even to provide a coat of whitewash to failed programs.[19] The advantages of external evaluation are, first, its presumptively stronger independence and, second, the greater probability that the evaluators are familiar with similar programs in other sectors or other countries.[20]

These advantages are not exclusive, however. In-house government evaluation organs can also be assured of a degree of independence close to that enjoyed by external entities. Conversely, if external evaluators contribute on a regular basis, they will develop the intimate understanding of operations that is needed for an informed assessment. The disadvantages, too, are not exclusive: in particular, if the governance climate is not conducive to candid evaluations, most probably even the best external evaluations will be suppressed or distorted to produce the desired results. The choice is entirely pragmatic. Thorough evaluations require a substantial input by economists, researchers, and auditors—skills that are in limited supply in African developing countries and are best used in designing and running sound programs, not in evaluating them. Thus, evaluation in developing countries inevitably should be conducted largely on the basis of expertise and inputs external to the government and, in many cases, external to the country. At the same time, an organic link to the regular administrative apparatus must be created. The approach to creating M&E capacity in African developing countries should therefore rest on two complementary efforts: (a) relying on external evaluations, especially for major expenditure programs, but (b) working to create a small but strong in-house capacity to design, guide, contract, *and monitor* the external evaluators. Such in-house capacity must not be confined to a separate small "evaluation ghetto" but requires systematic connections to the public finance function and to the line ministries, in whatever modality is effective in the specific country.

One more observation: the capacity to monitor and evaluate government action is too important to be left entirely to government, and one should also consider possibilities for using the service users themselves to provide feedback and contestability. Appropriate participation by civil society can augment limited governmental capacity for M&E. The role of nongovernmental organizations (NGOs) is especially relevant here. The Uganda experience, among others, has shown the potential contribution of NGOs to effective M&E as well as the NGOs' concern with the risk of being co-opted. The issue is delicate, but a balance between cooperation and independence can be struck.

Other lessons of experience in introducing M&E capacity in developing countries are summarized in box 12.8.

The Role of Donors

Issues of aid effectiveness are longstanding and too complex to be approached here. In aid for PEM, however, a major problem and a key opportunity may be mentioned. In general, donors themselves have sometimes caused or aggravated expenditure management problems in the aid-recipient countries. Most often, the sins of donors have been sins of omission—failing to exercise due diligence when introducing complex new systems, neglecting to consider capacity and implementation realities, and allowing the other problems frequently mentioned in the previous sections. The most critical role of donors in budget reforms is thus to make sure that, at a minimum, they do not themselves contribute to destroying workable systems and aggravate local capacity limitations through the design and implementation of their programs. One of the worst sins of commission has been payment of salary top-ups and bonuses for civil servants working on aid-assisted budget "reform" projects—despite the lip service paid to the need to avoid

BOX 12.8 Some Lessons from the Experience of Introducing Monitoring and Evaluation in Africa

Experience with M&E programs in Africa has yielded several important lessons:

- Simply placing M&E on the government agenda is itself a significant accomplishment (as in Sri Lanka and Malawi).
- Also a significant accomplishment is helping to build a common monitoring and evaluation language and conceptual understanding (as in Egypt).
- Cross-fertilization of ideas and country comparisons can be helpful, as in the effective use of the Chilean experience for other countries.
- An excessive focus on "macro" public sector management issues detracts from robust M&E "at the coal face." Better links of evaluation activities with specific line-ministry staff and service providers are important.
- Similarly, focusing M&E on the provision of services of specific sectors can be a highly promising entry point, which is often neglected.
- The mere availability of dedicated funding is insufficient to advance the M&E agenda if it is not targeted clearly on capacity building.
- Excessive monitoring, through a large number of indicators, produces little effective monitoring (as in Uganda).
- Inattention to bureaucratic realities produces delays or weak ownership.
- Overreliance on one-off workshops or similar events is not advisable. Although these events can be important to put M&E on the map, sustained capacity-building efforts are required to improve the performance of the public sector on a lasting basis.

Source: Adapted from OED 2004 (particularly the Uganda and Egypt case studies prepared by the author).

such practices. This practice makes de facto bribery a respectable alternative for civil servants not fortunate enough to be engaged in those projects and eventually destroys the integrity of the government budget as a whole.

On the positive side, donors can support a variety of activities that will improve PEM. To do so, the donor agency itself must have adequate competence in PEM (or make sure to obtain competent advice) and be knowledgeable about good and bad experiences in other countries. Institutions do not provide advice, individuals do—And if the understanding of the individual donor staff members of complex PEM issues is superficial or, worse, imprisoned by fashionable buzzwords, their advice is far more likely to cause damage than to be useful. In the same vein, if consultants are used, (a) preclude from the start their participation in downstream implementation activities, (b) build in strong and independent quality review provisions, and (c) demand that a genuine transfer of knowledge be at the core of the consultant's work. That being said, the foremost priority in external assistance to budget reform is to insist on, and to support, stronger public financial accountability, including through opening the door to user feedback and some appropriate form of civil society participation in budget preparation and a reality check in budget execution.

As public financial management systems improve, donors will more and more be able to move from project aid to budget support. The issue is usually presented as a binary choice: either assistance is strictly tied to a specific, narrowly defined project or general budget support is provided in exchange for appropriate policy understandings. However, the fungibility of money is conceptually and practically a continuum—ranging from the extreme of earmarking funds for individual items of expenditure to the other extreme of unconditional (and convertible) transfers. This perspective suggests a scenario of progressive increases in fungibility of assistance, including untied financing of selected groupings of activities smaller than the overall expenditure program. For example, short of financing the budget as a whole, donors could readily support "basket" financing for, say, malaria eradication or child immunization or rural road maintenance. (A current example is the untied assistance provided by some donors for Tanzania's Public Financial Management Reform Program.)

Once again, the operational issue is not *whether* general budget support is more likely to be effective than narrow project aid. It is, or it is not, depending on circumstances. The operational issue is *how* to improve the circumstances to permit a move to budget support—at either the sector or the general level, or both. Given the vested interests in project aid from both donor agency and recipient sides, and the economic, institutional, and political obstacles to moving away from project aid, strengthening of budgetary management, reductions of fiduciary risk, and improvements in service delivery acquire even greater importance.

A Concluding Word

The various pragmatic lessons of international experience in budget reform have often been referred to, with particular reference to the experience of developing countries. One general lesson, the world over, is that long-term sustainability of institutional reform always demands local ownership, political buy-in, and a degree of comfort among those responsible for implementing the reform. Without the active cooperation of budget managers and key staff members in both the core ministries and the line ministries, and without support from the top political leadership, budget reforms have generally remained largely a paper exercise to satisfy donor demands. Pushing on a string is not an option. Thus, the sequencing and time period of the reform process should be very carefully considered to make sure that it will fit the absorptive capacity of the system over time and not cause reform fatigue. Moreover, just as ex post evaluation is necessary for good budgeting, periodic reassessments of the actual costs and benefits of specific budget reforms and midcourse adjustments are necessary for sustainable reform.

This discussion leads to the advisability of occasional "digestion and consolidation" periods to make sure that the people in the system have understood, internalized, and learned how to use those changes and to give them a temporary respite from further change and the concomitant uncertainty. Accordingly, it appears wise to call a *reform timeout* from time to time. Without in any way halting the reform momentum and progress already under way, such timeouts will permit adjusting the course or speed of specific reforms, giving a fresh look at the marginal opportunity cost (including the transaction cost on the public administrators) of expanding certain activities as opposed to others, and carrying out reality checks on the various claims of reform success or, conversely, on the alibis for nonperformance. Introducing budget reforms is not difficult. But merely introducing the reforms, of course, is not the goal. The goal is to help achieve *permanent* improvements in expenditure control, strategic resource allocation, operational effectiveness, and public financial integrity in Africa.

Notes

1. The World Bank's (1989) public expenditure review for Madagascar (*Madagascar: Public Expenditure, Adjustment, and Growth*) was the first to include a major institutional component.
2. Wagner's Law states that the relative role of government in the economy tends to expand along with economic growth. Convincing evidence indicates that the "law," whatever its dynamics, has been operative through at least the latter part of the 20th century, as shown by the greater ratio of government expenditure to gross domestic product (or of government employment to population) in rich as compared with middle-income countries, and in the latter as compared with developing countries. From the late 1980s, Wagner's Law seems to no longer be operative in industrial countries—with government expenditure (or employment) essentially steady or, in some cases, declining.
3. The terminology originates with Stewart and Ranson (1988) and has been developed in Schiavo-Campo and McFerson (forthcoming).
4. A recent International Monetary Fund study (Diamond and others 2006: 8) lists among the major weaknesses in governance that have caused problems in PEM in Africa the failure to "restrain politicians and senior bureaucrats from benefiting

personally from lax fiscal controls." That study, covering in some detail 10 anglophone African countries, concluded that the record of budget reform had been comparatively good in Tanzania and Uganda, disappointing in Kenya and Zambia, and mixed in the other six countries (Ethiopia, The Gambia, Ghana, Malawi, Nigeria, and Rwanda).

5. See the Transparency International Web site, http://www.transparency.org. Transparency International's Corruption Perceptions Index measures the degree to which corruption is perceived to exist among a country's public officials and politicians. It draws on several surveys of opinions of business people and analysts, and it covers 159 countries (no reliable data are available for the other countries).

6. A survey of local business people revealed that, until the early 1990s, "informal commissions" averaged between 3 and 5 percent of the contract price or value of works and were stable. The same business people agree that today corruption in Burundi has become pervasive, acute, and less predictable—with the "bribe tax" varying between 25 and 60 percent and increasing.

7. Even the United Nations Development Programme's Automated System Customs Data Administration, widely praised as good practice and now used in 80 countries, has been highly effective in only one-third of the countries that use it. It has been wholly or partly ineffective in the remainder.

8. The commission was highly successful and, over a few years in the 1990s, turned Hong Kong, China, from one of the most corrupt administrations to one of the most honest in Asia—second only to Singapore.

9. Major exceptions exist. "Stroke-of-the-pen" reforms abolishing key controls (for example, on prices and exchange rates) can instantly eliminate a major opportunity for corruption. Unifying dual exchange rates to the market rate, for example, removes all possibilities of obtaining foreign exchange at the official rate only to sell it on the black market at a higher rate—the single quickest and most effective form of corruption. Or, as argued later in this chapter, sometimes enforcement is clearly the urgent priority. Beyond the immediate effect, however, concerted action on all three fronts is necessary if official corruption is to be reduced across the board in a sustainable manner.

10. Little difference in PEM performance appears to exist between anglophone and francophone African countries in an HIPC context, with good and bad examples in both groups (see IMF and World Bank 2002).

11. The Public Expenditure and Financial Accountability program is a partnership established in December 2001, involving the World Bank, International Monetary Fund, European Commission, Strategic Partnership with Africa, and several bilateral donors—France, Norway, Switzerland, and the United Kingdom. Subsequent to the formulation of the new approach, detailed indicators were developed that are currently used for assessing expenditure management systems, including those in most African countries. Although the assessments are useful, the need to minimize transaction costs on the recipient government and its personnel must be kept in mind.

12. Observations similar to those in this section are made in Schiavo-Campo and McFerson (forthcoming).

13. In Diamond and others (2006), the exit strategy recommendation is made in connection with accounting computerization, but it is generally valid for all external assistance to PEM. Although in most African countries, short-term targeted technical assistance will continue to be useful in the foreseeable future, a clear end point for resident expatriate assistance is especially necessary.

14. The literature on education and training shows that new skills that are not used are lost quickly. At best, unfocused training is a waste of time and resources. At worst, it corrodes staff morale or facilitates staffers' departure from government for pursuits where they can use their new skills.

15. Examples are, among others, the National Strategy for Growth and Reduction of Poverty in Tanzania and the detailed MTEF that has been developed and, in Morocco, the disconnect between the MTEF and the country's Strategic Results Framework.

16. This section is based in part on Schiavo-Campo (2005).

17. This dichotomy has been named the *accountability tradeoff*, whereby accountability can be either narrow and tight (when the manager is held strictly accountable for specific outputs) or broad and loose (when accountability is concerned with outcomes that, albeit more relevant, are also influenced by factors outside the manager's control), but never both broad *and* tight (see Schiavo-Campo 2005).

18. The typical abuse of the logical framework concept into lengthy, overly detailed matrices is a case in point.

19. The United States has created a framework to address this problem. Line agencies are required to rate the performance of all their programs. These self-ratings are reviewed—and often overridden—by the Office of Management and Budget (OMB), which manages the budget process in the federal government. OMB's reviews of the agencies' self-ratings include an assessment of the reliability of the agencies' M&E findings and constitute, de facto, a critique of agencies' M&E methods. However, these approaches are much too demanding in terms of data and resources to be of value in an African context.

20. Chile is one of a small number of countries that rely largely on commissioning independent evaluations, although the process is managed by a government ministry. In contrast with the U.S. approach, the cost-effectiveness of the Chilean approach may be a useful example for African developing countries.

References

Allen, Richard, Salvatore Schiavo-Campo, and Thomas Columkill Garrity. 2004. *Assessing and Reforming Public Financial Management: A New Approach.* Washington, DC: World Bank.

Aristotle. 350 BCE. *Politics.* Trans. Benjamin Jowett. Boston: Massachusetts Institute of Technology. http://classics.mit.edu//Aristotle/politics.html.

Collange, Gérald, Pierre Demangel, and Robert Poinsard. 2006. *Guide Méthodologique du Suivi de la Performance.* Rabat: Programme de Réforme de l'Administration Publique, Royaume du Maroc.

Diamond, Jack, Matt Davies, Pokar Khemani, Theo Thomas, and Feridoun Sarraf. 2006. *IMF Technical Assistance Evaluation: Public Expenditure Management Reform in Selected African Countries.* IMF Country Report 06/67, Washington, DC: International Monetary Fund.

Diamond, Jack, and Pokar Khemani. 2005. "Introducing Financial Management Information Systems in Developing Countries." IMF Working Paper 05/196, International Monetary Fund, Washington, DC.

Durevall, Dick, and Mathias Erlandsson. 2005. *Public Finance Management Reform in Malawi.* Stockholm: Swedish International Development Cooperation Authority.

Fölscher, Alta, and Neil Cole. 2004. "South Africa: Transition to Democracy Offers Opportunity for Whole System Reform." In *Budget Reform Seminar: Country Case Studies,* ed. Alta Fölscher, 109–46. Pretoria: National Treasury of South Africa.

IMF (International Monetary Fund) and World Bank. 2002. "Actions to Strengthen the Tracking of Poverty-Reducing Public Spending in Heavily Indebted Poor Countries (HIPCs)." IMF and World Bank, Washington, DC. http://www.imf.org/External/np/hipc/2002/track/032202.htm.

Lazare, Michel, Jean-Luc Hélis, and Jean-Pierre Nguenang. 2004. *Madagascar: Heavily Indebted Poor Countries Assessment and Action Plan.* Washington, DC: International Monetary Fund.

Levy, Brian, and Sahr Kpundeh, eds. 2004. *Building State Capacity in Africa: New Approaches, Emerging Lessons.* Washington, DC: World Bank Institute.

OED (Operations Evaluation Department, World Bank). 2004. *Evaluation Capacity Development: OED Self-Evaluation.* Washington, DC: World Bank.

Peterson, Stephen B. 2000. "Financial Reform in a Devolved African Country: Lessons from Ethiopia." Development Discussion Paper, Harvard University, Cambridge, MA.

Schiavo-Campo, Salvatore. 1999. "'Performance' in the Public Sector." *Asian Journal of Political Science* 7 (2): 75–87.

———. 2005. "Building Country Capacity for Monitoring and Evaluation in the Public Sector." Evaluation Capacity Development Working Paper 13, Operations Evaluation Department, World Bank, Washington, DC.

Schiavo-Campo, Salvatore, and Hazel M. McFerson. Forthcoming. *Public Management in Global Perspective.* Armonk, NY: M. E. Sharpe.

Simwakai, Chauncy. 2004. "Malawi." In *Budget Reform Seminar: Country Case Studies,* ed. Expenditure Planning Unit, Budget Office, 35–56. Pretoria: National Treasury.

Smith, Peter, ed. 1996. *Measuring Outcome in the Public Sector.* London: Taylor and Francis.

Stewart, John, and Stewart Ranson. 1988. "Management in the Public Domain." *Public Policy and Management* 8 (1–2): 13–19.

Tandberg, Eivind, Jean-Luc Hélis, and Ole Hovland. 2004. "Chad: Consolidation of Budget Management." Fiscal Affairs Department, International Monetary Fund, Washington, DC.

World Bank. 1989. *Madagascar: Public Expenditure, Adjustment, and Growth.* Washington, DC: World Bank.

———. Forthcoming. *Algeria—2006 Public Expenditure Review.* Washington, DC: World Bank.

Budgeting in Postconflict Countries

SALVATORE SCHIAVO-CAMPO

The focus of this chapter is on how to approach public expenditure management challenges in the special, and especially difficult, circumstances of a postconflict country. The sad realities of frequent conflict in Sub-Saharan Africa, especially over the past decade, have produced a substantial understanding of how to deal with postconflict reconstruction and recovery. First is a recognition that severe conflict, especially in its most virulent ethnic form, destroys more than physical facilities and, of course, human lives. Protracted conflict also short-circuits the rules that keep human interaction constructive and predictable, targets primarily the organizations and individuals who administer those rules, and wipes out most positive forms of social capital. Postconflict reconstruction is first and foremost an institutional challenge. The second imperative is balancing the immediate reconstruction priorities with sound long-term policy and institutional development. Accordingly, the experience in budgeting in Africa, reviewed in the previous chapters, and the recommendations flowing from that experience cannot be applied in their ordinary form to the special circumstances of a country emerging from protracted civil conflict.

Combining that experience with the understanding of the special challenges of postconflict countries, however, does permit elaborating a practical approach to budgeting in the early postconflict period. Although the principles of good budgeting are the same, the core requirements of budgeting in a postconflict situation are *simplicity* and *adaptation* to whatever limited capacity exists in the new transitional government. Postconflict budgeting must, in the first place, be fully cognizant of the realities of depleted resources, scarce information, and weak administrative capacity. Budgeting must be deliberately selective, tailored to the basic needs of the economy, and oriented in part toward the quick wins that are necessary to reestablish government credibility and to restore hope.

This chapter deals first with how to view the budget and approach the choices of investment for postconflict reconstruction, then discusses the experience with the management of external financial resources for reconstruction, and finally provides some practical rules of thumb on how to assemble rudimentary government budgets in the initial postconflict period. Although generally applicable recommendations do emerge from the international postconflict experience, including in Africa, the most important general advice is to tailor the design and sequencing of reconstruction investments and financing modalities to the circumstances of the case, each with its own core features.

Nothing in this chapter should be allowed to obscure the paramount priority of postconflict reconstruction—namely, to reestablish and maintain public order and security. The best policy framework, budgeting procedures, reconstruction investments, staffing, financing arrangements, and capacity-building efforts are worth little if the country suffers a general lack of physical security.

No Aid without a Program, No Program without a Budget

Among the lessons of international experience with assistance to postconflict reconstruction and recovery, none ranks higher than the need for an agreed program between recipient government and donors. This apparently obvious requirement must be underlined because it has often been violated in practice by uncoordinated donor actions to help with a variety of different urgent problems—all well-intentioned efforts but leading to fragmentation of activities, gaps and duplications, and dilution of government ownership.

In addition to an agreed program of reconstruction activities, the other key strategic criteria for postconflict reconstruction are as follows:

■ Commitment by donors to channel their aid in accordance with the agreed program

■ A good interface between donors and the government agency responsible for aid management
■ Fullest possible transparency
■ Widest consultation permitted by the security situation.

The main necessary condition to meet all of these criteria is a reasonably comprehensive government budget—realistic and public. It is through a unified budget that the coherent program of reconstruction activities can be reflected; it is through discussions on the draft budget that donors and the government can interact; it is through the budget that basic economic policies can be reflected; it is through the budget that the allocation of resources to different activities and regions can become clear to all concerned parties; it is through the budget that implementation and monitoring of the agreed activities can take place, in accordance with uniform rules, practices, and financial controls; finally, and most important, it is through the budget *process* that the practice of public consultation, open debate, and habits of compromise can be rebuilt.

In a postconflict setting, transparency and participation are especially important. The climate of reciprocal suspicion generated by the conflict means that every shadow is seen as a threat and every closed door as a conspiracy. In such a setting, no other public management practice can dispel those shadows and suspicions as effectively as a wide-open budgeting process—as consultative and participatory as possible.

Selecting Reconstruction Expenditure Priorities

This section discusses the issue of whether certain well-known strategic investment considerations apply in a postconflict situation, as well as a number of critical issues concerning the choice of investments and the need for managing the foreign aid to finance them.

Do "Strategic Projects" Exist? The Conceptual Foundation of Investment Choices

Aside from addressing the emergency priority needs that are evident in any postconflict situation, a major question is whether the agreed program of reconstruction activities—previously mentioned as the first condition for successful reconstruction—can be anchored by a number of strategic projects that can enable, facilitate, or even drive further investment and economic reconstruction and recovery down the line. This question has a long pedigree, going back to the debate of the early days of development economics between balanced and unbalanced growth. To place the following discussion in context, let us recapitulate briefly the basic terms of that debate.

Almost 50 years ago, Albert O. Hirschman (1958) made "unbalanced growth" the central theme of his approach to economic development. He started from the consideration that the scarcest factor of production in a developing country is not capital, or natural resources, or technology, or skilled labor—but the country's ability to invest. He concluded that a development strategy needed most of all to economize on the ability to invest, which could be achieved by focusing public investment on maximizing total links—both forward and backward—by investing in the intermediate sectors (those in the middle of the input-output table). The reason is that public investment in such large projects creates a demand for inputs—and thus facilitates subsequent decisions to invest in lower-level projects that produce such inputs—as well as produces inputs for higher-level activities, thus raising their potential profitability and facilitating decisions to invest in those activities. Hence, Hirschman advocated sequential and progressive investments—with public investment in strategic projects (strategic in the sense of economizing on the economy's ability to invest) as the initial motor. This approach contrasted sharply with the "big push" program of across-the-board simultaneous investments advocated by the balanced-growth strategy of Paul Rosenstein-Rodan (1943) and others in earlier years.

An important aspect of Hirschman's argument was that the role of different physical input constraints changes at different stages of development, with different conditions, and in different countries. Clearly, this viewpoint is far more relevant for the circumstances of postconflict economies than the orderly and linear view of the balanced-growth approach that implicitly takes as constant most of the factors that are by definition variable. The search for a *primum mobile* of development is a fruitless one, and the only realistic approach is to intervene opportunistically and on a timely basis. Moreover, Hirschman was one of the first development economists to understand that institutional factors are more important in development than the availability of the standard physical factors of production. This insight is particularly applicable to postconflict countries—in the midst of rapidly changing realities on the ground—than to countries in a "cruising-speed" development mode.

However, Hirschman did not take into account (any more than other development economists did until the late1980s) that the ability to invest, in the sense of making investment decisions, is very different from the ability to implement. Good investment decisions are the start, not the end, of good investments. In turn, the issue of implementation capacity cannot be intelligently debated without explicit consideration of the quality of governance. In the absence of strong public accountability, government decision makers can channel public resources and aid to projects that maximize their private gain. These projects, in fact, do tend to be the large projects that often cluster around the middle of an input-output matrix. The objective of good project implementation for development then becomes wholly secondary to the exploitation of the rent-producing potential of the project. As a former minister of planning of an African country—now "under new management"—once frankly told the author: "We don't care about the quality of implementation or the future recurrent costs; for us, the project has served its purpose when all the contracts have been privately negotiated." This attitude is one more reason that rebuilding stable and accountable governance is next only to restoring security as the primary challenge in postconflict countries.

The Need for Investment Programming

Connecting the previously mentioned conceptual perspective to the budget process helps explain why the need for programming public investment is, if anything, even stronger in postconflict settings than in stable developing countries. Without integrity and realism in investment programming, the difference between balanced- and unbalanced-growth strategies reduces to the distinction between facilitating a lot of corruption within a brief period of time or allowing the same amount of corruption spread out over a period of years. Thus, particularly in the fluid postconflict situations, public investment programming is needed not only on grounds of fiscal responsibility or efficiency, but even more as a way to shed light on the investment decisions of the postconflict government. In the absence of robust procedures for investment choices, "strategic" projects risk becoming those with the largest rent-seeking potential.

Naturally, as discussed in chapter 8, the need is for an affordable and rigorous programming process, not the wish list public investment "programs" all too common in Africa and elsewhere in the 1980s. Also, given the data and capacity limitations typical of postconflict situations, the investment program should be as simple, selective, and realistic as possible. Indeed, investment programming in postconflict countries can be robust and effective only if it is focused and simple. In answer to the question posed at the start of this section, in a postconflict setting, robust investment criteria and accountable governance give validity to the otherwise weak notion of strategic project—with proto-programs formulated around a few key priority investments chosen to shake the economy out of the tangle of despair and disrepair generated by the conflict.

The Importance of a Medium-Term Perspective

The subject of medium-term expenditure frameworks (MTEFs) was discussed in chapter 8 and need not be recapitulated here. MTEFs are often considered an unnecessary luxury in a postconflict situation. This view is certainly true insofar as detailed, technical MTEFs are concerned, but postconflict countries nevertheless have a special need for a broad medium-term fiscal perspective. This need arises from a perverse pattern in postconflict reconstruction financing, identified long ago but first analyzed in detail by Paul Collier (personal communication, 2001).

Collier noted that international interest in assisting the country is at its highest in the immediate postconflict period. This interest generates large financial support for the country, but precisely at a time when its capacity to absorb those resources effectively is at a minimum, because the country has barely come out of the conflict. As time passes, the country's capacity to invest in and implement good expenditure programs rises, but in the meantime international interest has waned and moved on to some other crisis situation, and external financial support falls off along with it. A credible medium-term expenditure perspective can help considerably to resolve this dilemma by providing the economic and political justification for firm donor commitments of external financial resources for a period of years, but to be disbursed over the medium term as and when the increase in the country's absorptive capacity permits. (Again, as in the case of investment programming, the medium-term expenditure perspective need only be realistic and credible—it need not be detailed and complex.)

Budgeting and Managing External Assistance

Although aid for postconflict reconstruction can come from a variety of donors and in different forms, the bulk of the financial assistance for the agreed program of reconstruction has often been channeled through an umbrella multidonor trust fund (MDTF) administered by the World Bank. Substantial experience has been gained with these devices during the past 15 years, resulting in a number of conclusions and recommendations (see especially OED 1998; Schiavo-Campo 2003; Schiavo-Campo and Judd 2005).

Structural and Design Issues

The main design issues of an MDTF are as follows:

- An MDTF must fulfill both a fiduciary and an executive function. The legal, accounting, disbursement, and reporting provisions required for the fiduciary function have been well defined through prior experience. The effective exercise of the executive function requires, in addition, meeting the key strategic criteria previously listed.
- Incentives must exist for individual donors to join an MDTF, including an MDTF design that gives them comfort that their aid goes for priority purposes while precluding earmarking of the aid, which would defeat the purpose of a budget support mechanism. Although all donor contributions must be commingled in a common pool, donors' preferences can be explicitly acknowledged, and expenditures in the broad categories can be regularly reported. This procedure permits each donor to claim that its money has gone to finance its preferred uses.
- MDTF governance arrangements must provide for systematic consultation with and reporting to the contributing donors.
- Large strategic projects, humanitarian aid, or security-related programs, such as demining, need not be—and usually are not—financed through an MDTF. Large projects will normally carry their own implementation arrangements, and to finance humanitarian and security programs, separate dedicated trust funds can be created.
- All other reconstruction and recovery activities—including recurrent costs—should be financed under the MDTF. The main advantage of an umbrella fund is the closer link with the recipient country's budget and, hence, the possibility of a robust dialogue on fiscal and development policy. In any case, as noted earlier, what is to be avoided is fragmentation of funding vehicles, especially between financing of recurrent costs and financing of investments.

Organizational and Procedural Issues

Among the organizational and procedural issues, the main ones are as follows:

- Time is of the essence for aid interventions in postconflict situations, and a practical compromise is needed between the two extremes of waiting until all contributions are deposited and starting MDTF operations as soon as the first pledges are made.

- No compromise can be made, however, with the need to put in place measures to minimize corruption and leakages before the MDTF enters into any financing commitment.
- Nonproject technical assistance (TA) for institutional development and capacity building can be financed either as a component of an umbrella MDTF or by a separate trust fund. In either case, the key requirements are an agreed framework of priorities, the closest possible involvement of the local counterparts, and tight monitoring and quality control. Nonproject TA activities should be linked with a host-government capacity-building program, and every single TA contract should include a training element. At a minimum, TA should take special care not to aggravate local capacity problems by introducing overly complex systems or methods unsuited to local conditions.
- Although, as noted earlier, an MDTF should be dedicated to financing the agreed reconstruction program and national budget, a financial cushion should be kept for urgent expenditure needs as they arise.
- Recurrent costs are well suited for financing through an MDTF, but monitoring of the broad expenditure categories (on the basis of clear budgetary understandings) is essential, especially for salaries. Also, the payments mechanism must function well—even if it must be initially subcontracted. On balance, in postconflict situations, hiring an international firm is advisable. The firm can act as an agent to verify the eligibility and correctness of withdrawal applications and can carry out spot-checks of the validity of transactions.
- The MDTF's managing institution should be prepared to halt disbursements in the event of serious and uncorrected deviation from the agreed policies and expenditure composition or of substantial corruption.

Government Aid Management Agency

By any name, the aid management agency (AMA) of the recipient government is the main bridge from donors to government and the primary source of initial government ownership. As noted, the fundamental strategic challenge of postconflict reconstruction is the reconciliation between immediate urgencies and sustainability over the longer term. In most cases, the government is extremely weak during the immediate postconflict period. Thus, the AMA must not only interface with donors and regulate aid traffic, as in steady-state situations, but also help formulate the reconstruction program, serve as proto-government, and implement directly a number of activities.

Aid management is too complex a subject to be recapitulated here. In postconflict situations, however, a special and serious issue is the "sunset dilemma." An AMA is necessary in the immediate postconflict period because the formal government structures do not yet exist or have extremely limited capacity and also because donors require transparent and reasonably corruption-free financial management. Over time, as the regular government institutions grow, competition emerges between the governmental structures and the parallel AMA. Instead of a smooth handover of responsibility, the parallel tracks tend to persist, partly because the AMA has built up greater implementation capacity and contacts with donors, and partly because accountability and financial transparency remain a must for donors. Thus, the AMA acquires a technocratic monopoly and stays active longer than envisaged, competing with regular government ministries for resources and authority and, in some cases, preventing their strengthening and improvement.

The key lesson of this experience is that the government and donors should agree from the outset on a clear sunset clause, by which the special AMA will be absorbed into the regular structure of government at an appropriate specific time. An exit strategy for the AMA is necessary. In turn, that strategy should be linked to appropriate conditionality vis-à-vis the emerging government structures. Finally, during the same period, concerted assistance is required to build institutional capacity in the regular organs of government—because proliferation of weak or corrupt government ministries is not a sound alternative to a technocratic monopoly of decision making by the AMA.

Assembling a Government Budget in Postconflict Situations

As noted earlier, simplicity and adaptation are the watchwords for postconflict reconstruction and recovery. Nowhere is this truer than in public expenditure management and financial accountability. The priorities discussed in this section are as basic as the budgeting systems are dilapidated.

Priority Number One: Protect the Money

In the circumstances typical of the immediate postconflict period, the first budgeting "reform" priority is to try to ensure that public financial resources, external or domestic, do not actually disappear. Protecting the public's money is the fundamental fiduciary duty of both the government and the donors. Thus, in postconflict countries, where almost by definition the revenue forecasts are uncertain and cash management systems extremely weak, the first and foremost objective is putting in place expenditure control. Without expenditure control, any effort at addressing the other two objectives of public expenditure management—resource allocation and operational effectiveness—in the immediate postconflict period would be futile. Protecting the money and expenditure tracking of the most down-to-earth sort are essential.

However, the imperative to balance the immediate reconstruction priorities with sound long-term policy and institutional development was also noted. Therefore, (a) systems for expenditure control must be designed and implemented in ways that do not jeopardize the eventual improvements in sectoral allocation and resource management, and (b) a clear ex ante sense is needed of how far to push improvements in expenditure and cash control before the time comes for addressing strategic resource allocation and operational management issues. The finer points of intra- and interprogram reallocation can perhaps follow in a second stage (while nevertheless keeping in mind that overbroad allocation rules and loose enforcement can themselves be a mechanism for waste, fraud, and abuse).

Following are a suggested set of simple but workable criteria and procedures for screening the different types of expenditure requests, prior to inclusion in the government budget. The discussion comprises the scrutiny of proposals for sectorwide programs, for the different categories of current expenditure, and for investment projects. The bottom-up budget thus assembled should correspond both to the more pressing needs of reconstruction and to the revenue and capacity constraints of the country.

For budgeting in postconflict situations, however, the iteration between needs and resources is different and much more important than in a steady-state system. It will be recalled from the discussion in chapter 8 that the obligatory starting point for good budget preparation is a firm forecast of revenue, which—together with clear government policies for each sector—permits formulating a hard expenditure constraint on each sector and thus serves to encourage both discipline and ownership in each ministry's budget proposals. In postconflict countries, the situation is very different. With domestic revenue wholly uncertain, the starting point of the process is an assessment of needs, conducted by a joint assessment mission (JAM) of donors and the government and normally led by the World Bank, the United Nations, or both in some form of cooperation. The results of the needs assessment are then presented to a donor conference for the purpose of mobilizing enough resources to finance the reconstruction program. Only after the outcome of the donor conference and a determination of the pledges from different donors and the probable timing of their contributions can some sense of available resources be obtained. The needs identified in the JAM are then articulated into more concrete projects and programs, and a rudimentary budget eventually emerges, hopefully consistent with the financial resources available. (The bulk of the financing is likely to come from donors, because in the immediate postconflict period, domestic resources and taxation capabilities are extremely limited.)

Thus, in postconflict countries, the forecast of (mostly foreign) revenue is only an initial point of reference for the construction of a budget, for which additional aid may well become available if the expenditure proposals are well justified and the system is ready to implement them. However, even if only as initial reference, a revenue forecast should still be used to frame budget preparation so that the country can gradually move toward a realistic, resource-constrained budgeting system when the immediate postconflict urgencies have been surmounted, and also so that it can begin creating good budgeting habits grounded on realism rather than wishful thinking. The other major requirement is to screen carefully the various expenditure proposals—whether included in the JAM or generated separately—with the help of the guidelines and tests suggested below.

Screening Sector Expenditure Program Proposals

Next to expenditure control, the second objective of public expenditure management—allocative efficiency—calls for distributing financial resources across different sectors to maximize the aggregate efficiency of resources. This criterion is good in theory but a practical chimera, especially in postconflict situations. One cannot decide on a technical basis whether refurbishing a destroyed primary school in district A is more efficient than rebuilding a rural road in district B. This conundrum does not imply, however, that sector allocation decisions necessarily have to be made only on political and discretionary grounds, and certain guidelines can be formulated. In practice, as stressed repeatedly, in postconflict countries all budgeting criteria must be applied with a great deal of flexibility, simplicity, pragmatism, and common sense. The following basic decision tests, however, are substantively the same, and their sequence is mandatory—that is, one does not query program costing before having determined that the program is more or less consistent with the policy for the sector. In a postconflict setting, of course, these criteria must be applied very flexibly.

1. Is the overall sector expenditure request within the sectoral expenditure ceiling? If *No*, return for downward adjustment *without* comment; if *Yes* →

2. Is the proposed program consistent with government policy for the sector? If *No*, return *with* comment; if *Yes* →

3. Is the amount requested consistent with a program that is (a) well designed, (b) realistically costed, and (c) well sequenced? If *No*, return with suggestion for redesign and reestimate of costs; if *Yes* →

4. Are implementation capacity and complementary resources adequate? If *No*, recommend adjustments in pace of implementation; if *Yes*, →

5. Approve the expenditure request, help the line agency concerned to implement it, and monitor program implementation.

Screening Current Expenditure Requests

Different criteria apply to the different budget categories of salaries, services, transfers, and operations and maintenance. Each is discussed in turn in the following sections.

Screening requests for wages, salaries, and pensions

The general criterion is that the expenditure requests must be fully consistent with government policy on wages, employment, and pensions. The basic checks to help meet that criterion are as follows:

■ Is the proposed number of employees in the ministry or agency consistent with the number of authorized posts?

■ Are ministry or agency procedures and records sufficient to prevent "ghost" employees, illicit payments, and other irregularities?

■ Have labor items been misclassified in the budget as part of capital expenditures? (Note, however, that a labor cost component in investment projects is normal and necessary.)

Because of the uncertainties of postconflict situations, the preceding criteria may have to be qualified or complemented by certain pragmatic guidelines and policy advice:

■ Undershoot on employment, by demanding convincing proof of staff needs. It is easier to correct insufficient staffing than to let employees go after they are hired.

■ Neither under- nor overshoot on wages. Agreeing to wage levels higher than necessary sets a problematic precedent for fiscal sustainability, but compressing wages below adequate levels makes it difficult to attract personnel and allow the new government to function.

- Discourage nonmonetary allowances, except as clearly required by conditions on the ground.
- Prohibit topping up of civil service wages by donors, and discourage employee moonlighting.
- Reward the special risks of certain jobs in postconflict countries (for example, road-building crews in rural areas that are exposed to attacks), but with transparent and temporary salary supplements—not unwarranted promotion to higher grades.
- Over time, encourage the monitoring of developments in the supply and demand for labor.

Screening requests for expenditure on services

INTEREST PAYMENTS. No screening is needed for interest payments because they are government obligations, but a careful and verified calculation of amounts, creditors, terms, and schedules is mandatory. (If a minimum capacity for debt-recording and debt management no longer exists, it should be put in place as a matter of priority.)

NONPROJECT TECHNICAL ASSISTANCE. Project-related TA is included in each project cost and should be screened as part of the review and appraisal of the project. This item concerns freestanding TA—normally for institutional development, capacity building, and so forth. Freestanding TA is a source of both potential benefits and significant problems, and these budget requests need to be scrutinized with special care, in accordance with, among other things, the following criteria:

- For expatriates, assess whether the proposed compensation is in line with international organization norms.
- For local experts, assess whether the proposed compensation is in line with national fees. (If data on national fees are not available or are obsolete because of the intervening conflict, fees in neighboring countries may be used as a reference point.)
- For diaspora experts—that is, nationals residing and working abroad—a reasonable compromise is needed between the "two inequities." The first inequity consists of paying returning nationals less than expatriates doing the same job. This practice creates justified resentment among the returning national experts and weakens their willingness to return as well as their motivation on the job. The second inequity consists of paying returning nationals more than local experts in the same profession. This practice creates generalized local hostility toward returnees, which is a frequent and

serious impediment to capacity building. Because the underlying inequity is inherent in the difference in incomes and salary scales between the postconflict developing country and the foreign country (typically an industrial country), it is a regrettable necessity to establish an intermediate compensation level that will limit both types of entirely understandable resentment at being paid less than others doing the same job.

- Insist that the terms of reference of expatriate experts include a compulsory and central component of knowledge transfer to the local staff. If possible, explore twinning local staff members to expatriate experts.
- Ascertain that the line ministry or government agency has given explicit consideration to whether consulting firms or individual consultants would be more cost-effective for the assignment.
- Most important, inquire whether a strategy exists for reducing dependence on expatriate services in the medium term, and, if it does not, encourage its early formulation—in light of the need to combine short-term needs with longer-term institutional development and, hence, achieve an eventual reduction in dependence on expatriate consultants.

Screening requests for transfer payments

Subsidies should generally be provided on the basis of affordability and in accordance with social and political criteria, but five technical tests may be suggested. These tests are the same as would apply in nonconflict settings, but in a postconflict country, the answers must rely far more on quick application of common sense than on extensive analysis, especially because some of these subsidies may be critical to reestablishing a measure of confidence and popular support:

- Is the proposed subsidy grounded on law, regulation, or policy? If not, can transitional but explicit criteria be elaborated?
- Is the expenditure request for the particular subsidy reasonably likely to achieve the stated objective?
- Do methods other than budgetary subsidies exist to achieve the same objective?
- Is the administration of the subsidy cost-effective (for example, is better targeting a realistic possibility)?
- Most important, do the administrative modalities provide reasonable assurance that the subsidy will reach the intended beneficiaries, including reality spot-checks with the intended beneficiaries themselves?

Several other transfers are needed in postconflict transition—for internally displaced persons, former combatants, and the like. No general decision rule or screening advice is possible in these respects. The programs themselves are normally negotiated with—and funded by—international donors, usually in the context of disarmament, demobilization, and reintegration initiatives and on the basis of substantial experience gained with the compensation schemes for transitional assistance, particularly in Africa. The following suggestions, however, may be relevant:

- Require bottom-up estimates of expenditures that are based on actual programs.
- View the transfer either as compensation for past merit or past suffering or as a means to facilitate the individual's reintegration and transition— or both—but do not meet these legitimate needs by giving a permanent government job.
- Budget the cost of these special programs as a separate item, without attempting to disaggregate them by economic function—recalling that they are inherently transitional programs, even if they are expected to continue for several years, and that they are normally negotiated and funded separately from regular government expenditure programs.

Screening requests for operations and maintenance expenditure

In screening requests for operations and maintenance (O&M) expenditure, both commonsense questioning and technical norms appropriate to the sector should be used. Although O&M expenditure needs are likely to be lighter in the initial postconflict period because many of the government physical assets have been destroyed, they should not be neglected. Three general considerations may be useful in assessing requests for O&M expenditure in a postconflict setting:

- Give the benefit of the doubt to O&M budget requests during the first postconflict year. In general, during a postconflict transition, underfunding O&M expenditure is much worse than overfunding. Provided that financial management and control mechanisms are adequate, overfunding is more likely to lead to underspending than to waste and abuse— leaving the unused resources available for reallocation to other uses during the same or the subsequent fiscal year. Underfunding, in contrast, is likely to lead to malfunctioning of government from lack of necessary funds, precisely at the time when it must regain some credibility by achieving demonstrable improvements on the ground.
- Require each government unit, as part of the process of approval of the O&M expenditure request, to start a selective inventory of its physical

assets, but limited to assets that are (a) very valuable, (b) at risk, and (c) in an economically usable state.

■ Related to the last point, do not assume that just because a physical asset exists it automatically deserves to be maintained. On the contrary, as part of the selective inventory mentioned, some assessment must be requested of whether the asset remains sufficiently valuable to warrant maintenance expenditure or has been so degraded by the conflict and prolonged deferred maintenance as to be best written off. Above all, do not rely on a preconflict asset inventory as a basis on which to decide the allocation of new O&M expenditure.

Screening Investment Project Proposals

It is in investment that most of the "technical" screening is needed, especially in postconflict situations—where investment is both the largest category of public spending and the mechanism for recovery and reconstruction.

Criteria and rules of thumb

The following two main criteria apply to investment project choices:

■ The project must fit within a sound overall public investment program (as defined, at the start, through the JAM).
■ The economic and social quality of the project itself must be demonstrated by both its consistency with government policy and its rate of return (in national economic terms)—the latter being measured in approximate terms.

Certain rules of thumb can be suggested:

■ Use the "double-sense" rule in assessing a project proposal—both economic sense and common sense.
■ Provide in the budget for sufficient counterpart funding in the aggregate. Adequate local funding does not guarantee good investment execution, but insufficient budgetary provision guarantees bad execution—forcing the shift of needed funds from one project to another or curtailing them across the board.
■ Beware of "free" money from aid. Focus first on project quality, and *then* look for the best financing terms. (However, as mentioned, the process of iteration between resources and needs is articulated differently in postconflict situations, and the project and funding choices

may well be made jointly during the same process of postconflict needs assessment.)

- A good "no" is better than several bad "yeses." Missed opportunities can be recouped, but major mistakes are hard to undo.
- Open the expenditure "black boxes"—for example, for military expenditure or resettlement or demobilization—or at least put them on the table so that the total amount of funding is known.

A zoological taxonomy of investment projects

To tailor the degree of scrutiny to different types of investment projects and decide on the appropriate policy response, decision makers may find the following analogy helpful:

- "Black Cows" are large, sound, well-financed projects with a major potential effect on economic activity and productivity. Black Cows are the strategic projects discussed at the beginning of this chapter and are to be encouraged and supported as the backbone of recovery and reconstruction. The key issue in examining Black Cows is optimal project design for maximum impact.
- "Pink Piglets" are smaller projects, usually undertaken for patronage; systems maintenance; or political, security, and regional reasons. They can be important for the political economy of reconstruction but should be individually programmed. Pink Piglets are normally unsuited to cost-benefit analysis, because the political or security benefits are largely intangible, but they should still be subject to the test of common sense, through a contestable dialogue between the central ministry and the project proponents.
- "Gray Rabbits" are small investments that are intended for geographically dispersed activities in pursuit of social and humanitarian objectives or to spur local production in certain areas. Their implementation is usually subcontracted to nongovernmental organizations (NGOs) or local communities. These projects can make a worthwhile contribution to the country's recovery and produce some important visible "quick wins." Gray Rabbits are too small to warrant cost-benefit analysis, but the overall total expenditure on them must be limited, and their implementation must be monitored—because these activities, like their zoological namesake, tend to reproduce very fast and cause unexpected accountability and integrity problems.
- Finally, "White Elephants" are extremely costly ideological or "prestige" projects, which also entail large future current expenditure requirements but have little impact on production and economic growth. Just one or two White Elephant projects can jeopardize the entire investment program

and place a dead weight on the public finances for years to come. The only appropriate policy response to the risk of White Elephants is to prevent their entry into the investment pipeline. Thus, contraception is the only effective strategy: once White Elephants are conceived, it is usually too late to stop them, because a variety of powerful vested interests will have been created. The main implication is the need to set up an early gatekeeping mechanism, to screen out bad ideas for large and uneconomical projects before any detailed feasibility studies are conducted.

Who Does the Screening?

The last point leads to the critical question of who screens expenditure requests. The general objective of the screening mechanism is to provide contestability, give informed challenges, and serve as an independent reality check. Thus, a good screening mechanism fosters stronger individual accountability, both within the public administration and vis-à-vis the service users and the public at large. The entity in charge should be the same in a postconflict situation as in stable developing countries—that is, the ministry of finance and planning (when the functions are combined in a single ministry) or the ministry of planning for investment decisions and the ministry of finance for other expenditures (and to assemble a unified budget). Also the same is the core principle that each line ministry is responsible for its own programs and expenditure requests.

In certain situations in the immediate postconflict period, however, the competent ministries may exist on paper only—without any capacity to perform the necessary scrutiny of expenditure proposals or the programming of investments. In these situations, the aid management agency can temporarily exercise those functions—subject to the caveats mentioned earlier—or other transitional mechanisms may be created. One such mechanism could be a technical group, contracted by the ministry of finance or planning, to provide the contestability, reality checks, and validation of the expenditure proposals. Such a group can help fill the capacity gap during the transitional period, while sustained efforts are made to build capacity in the regular organs of government, provided that the group

- has a clear mandate and specific terms of reference;
- is small, competent, and has full operational autonomy;
- enjoys the support of both the government and the donor community; and
- includes both outside experts and the core local staff of the ministries—who can learn through the experience and then serve as the nucleus of efficiency for building capacity.

Burundi: An Encouraging Case

Since its independence in 1962, Burundi has been in almost continuous conflict—repressed for some periods only to flare up periodically. Burundi's population consists of a Hutu majority, a large Tutsi minority, and a smaller Twa group. Until recently, Burundi's governments have been led by Tutsis. Coups and spasms of mass violence, with the victims mainly Hutus, have punctuated the history of the country. In 1963, and then again in 1972, 1988, and 1993, large-scale massacres preceded or followed military coups. The last such event, ensuing from the assassination in 1993 of Melchior Ndadaye, the first Hutu elected president of the country, led to widespread civil war for a decade. The total number of victims of internal conflict is always difficult to estimate with reasonable confidence, but over the entire period from 1962 to 2003, credible estimates for Burundi are of at least 500,000 people killed, 1 million people internally displaced, and another million refugees in neighboring countries, mainly Rwanda and Tanzania—in a country with a total population of barely 7 million.

Tragically, Burundi's history could have been entirely different from the beginning, were it not for the 1961 assassination of Prince Louis Rwagasore, a Tutsi slated to become prime minister as leader of an ethnically mixed party that advocated tolerance and interethnic amity. Thus, viewing the conflict in Burundi as exclusively ethnic—between the minority Tutsis in power and the majority Hutus—is an oversimplification. First, the ruling elite was only a segment of the Tutsi population, and many Tutsis were excluded from power. Second, economic causes—primarily conflict over land—were a major contributing factor. Nevertheless, however fostered, magnified, and exploited for the benefit of the ruling elite, ethnic fear and hostility have indeed become the major causes of the conflict.

The first step toward a resolution of the conflict was the Arusha Agreement of 2000, signed by the government and the main rebel groups, which set in motion a phased peace process. Although armed conflict continued, its intensity lessened, and the process gradually led to a new constitution, which was approved overwhelmingly by referendum in February 2005. This success was followed by rounds of free elections, culminating in the election of a new president, Pierre Nkurunziza (the leader of the former main Hutu rebel group), and the installation of a new government in August 2005. In mid-2006, the last holdout rebel group signed the peace agreement, and the political and security situation appeared stable—buttressed by the keen desire on the part of most Burundians to put their country's violent history behind them.

Owing to the years of conflict, the new government has inherited an economy characterized by endemic poverty, overwhelming debt, widespread corruption, diminished soil productivity and other severe environmental problems, and degraded public sector institutions. It has also inherited, however, a strong consensus—for the first time in postindependence Burundi—in favor of peace, ethnic reconciliation, good governance, and restoration of security throughout the country.

Rebuilding the Budgeting System

A gradual improvement in Burundi's economy is evident. After a dip in 2003, annual GDP growth recovered and is projected at about 6 percent in the next few years, with inflation dropping to single digits. The balance of payments was about in equilibrium (aided by external assistance) in 2005 to 2006, although a small deficit is projected for 2007 and 2008. The exchange rate has stabilized, with exports recovering to some extent. And the fiscal deficit has been kept under control. Many of the ingredients for sustained recovery and development are now in place. Progress has been made, too, in the public expenditure area, and some initial improvements in the dilapidated budgeting process have occurred.

Before the onset of overt civil war in 1993, and despite the periodic eruptions of violence, Burundi was deservedly known as one of the best-managed economies in Africa. Corruption, though present, was limited and predictable; budgeting was fairly well organized and transparent; civil servants were competent and disciplined; and basic public services were delivered in a reasonably efficient manner. This still-recent experience offers the country the memory of better times, the confidence of knowing that it did have the capability to manage the public finances, and a vision of how public management can be improved by a return to the good standards of the country's own past. This intangible asset, not present in many other postconflict situations, is very important for rebuilding the public expenditure management system in Burundi.

Functional priorities in reconstructing public expenditure management

Although the existence and reference point of good past management is an unusual asset, the functional priorities in budgeting and public expenditure management in Burundi are similar to those in other postconflict situations:

- Pending an eventual upswing in private investment, growth and poverty reduction depend on an improvement in public investment efficiency, which, in turn, will be critical for the effectiveness of aid. Better project selection and closer monitoring will be necessary in this regard, as will the formulation of a public investment program consistent with macroeconomic objectives and administrative capacity.

■ The initial progress in budgeting must be consolidated, including better preparation of budget proposals and tightening of their ex ante scrutiny by Burundi's Ministry of Finance.

■ Stronger mechanisms for public financial accountability are essential for both the efficient use of resources and the fight against corruption. The focus in this respect should be to provide all necessary assistance to the external audit court of Burundi, while fostering its independence from the executive and strengthening its autonomy in both management and audit operations.

■ Also important will be assistance to raise legislative assembly members' level of understanding about the budget process. A beginning must be made in outward accountability as well, by enlisting the cooperation of NGOs and civil society in monitoring public expenditure and, eventually, in participating in budget preparation.

A number of other budgeting innovations are being introduced or contemplated in Burundi, including a detailed MTEF, elements of program budgeting, and integrated financial management systems. Although these are all perhaps worthwhile long-term directions, the current institutional realities of the country mandate a resolute focus on the basics. As noted, the expenditure management priorities in Burundi, as in other postconflict countries, must be to ensure that basic budgeting is functioning, expenditure control is consolidated, budget execution is relatively free of fraud and misallocations, and external financial accountability becomes strong enough to change the current culture of impunity. This already vast and ambitious agenda would be jeopardized by pushing unnecessary and complex budgeting practices.

Institutional and capacity-building priorities

If the agenda is to be implemented, budgeting capacity and responsibility need to be gradually rebuilt in the line ministries, under the guidance of the Ministry of Finance and the Ministry of Development Planning. In turn, however, these core ministries should refocus on their core competencies. Currently, the Ministry of Development Planning in Burundi carries statutory responsibility for both investment programming and aid management. However, as a result of the long conflict, it has lost the capacity to perform either function. At the same time, the Ministry of Finance, where the function of aid management should normally be located, does not have the authority to manage foreign aid.

The main priority is therefore to review the division of labor between the two ministries—allowing the Ministry of Development Planning to concentrate on its core competence of investment programming by relieving it of responsibility for aid management, which should be moved to the Ministry of Finance, which is responsible for budgeting all resources, foreign and domestic. Such a move should be accompanied and supported by major external assistance to the Ministry of Development Planning for investment programming and to the Ministry of Finance to build aid management capability. However, coordination between the ministries is weak. Therefore, the two ministries should jointly constitute an aid and investment policy group, chaired by the vice president in charge of economic and social matters, to provide guidance and the highest-level political support for coherent investment choices and financing decisions.

The other major priorities are as follows:

■ Establish an ad hoc interministerial task force, chaired by the vice president, to identify the main problems in line ministries' budgeting capacity and define an action plan to address them, including incentives for better coordination.
■ Assess training needs with a view to formulating and delivering a targeted training program focused on the key functions.
■ Conduct a series of workshops on public financial management for members of the legislative assembly, starting with the basics and progressing to more in-depth treatment of certain topics (for example, external audit).
■ Establish a small cell in the Ministry of Finance to give special scrutiny to all purchasing proposals with a cost higher than a certain threshold and to give formal clearance for their inclusion in the budget, beginning with the budget for 2007.
■ Initiate the preparation of a medium-term rolling program of all sizable investment projects, which should include only projects of demonstrated economic viability and be fully consistent with resource availability in the macroeconomic framework.

Implementing these measures will require sustained technical and material assistance from donors. Unfortunately, local donor coordination is inadequate in Burundi, mainly because of insufficient World Bank efforts to facilitate it. In public expenditure management, the vacuum has been filled by European Commission, which has taken the lead to formulate and agree with the government on an assistance partnership framework, which also includes Belgium, France, the African Development Bank, and the World Bank, with the full association of the International Monetary Fund. The government welcomes new partners in this framework, which promises to provide a measure of coherence and to prevent duplication in external assistance to rebuild Burundi's public expenditure management apparatus.

Will It Last?

Burundi has made remarkable progress in national and interethnic reconciliation and in political governance. There are grounds to hope that the same will be true of a gradual return to the reasonably good public management standards of the late 1980s. Fiscal management improvements are an investment for the future and will take time to be implemented. But the needed budgeting systems, procedures, and personnel must be in place by the time political and financial circumstances are right for a more strategic allocation of resources and for increased efficiency and effectiveness in public service provision. Thus, the process of institutional reconstruction needs to accelerate now lest the degraded state of financial management become the operative constraint to growth in two or three years.

Fortunately, Burundi still has assets on which to build. At its center, the public financial management apparatus retains a degree of discipline and service ethos. Staff members are at their posts, documents can be found, fairly reliable statistics exist, requests for information are met, and the new government leadership is committed to a process of institutional improvement with neither illusion nor defeatism. Perhaps most important, although intangible and impossible to demonstrate, is a new sense of the possible among the key actors. Thus, by contrast to many other postconflict countries in Sub-Saharan Africa, the Middle East, and Southeast Asia, the public financial management situation in postconflict Burundi engenders serious concerns but not cynicism.

A Concluding Word

The objective of expenditure screening mechanisms is not only to reject bad expenditure proposals but also to foster the beginning of lasting expenditure management improvements. Hence, as the budget proposals are assessed, constructive feedback should be provided to the ministry and agency concerned, and the experience gained through the assessment of the first round of proposals should be incorporated into the parallel capacity-building activities.

Moreover, as mentioned earlier, transparency, consultation, and participation are even more important in a postconflict environment than in a stable situation. External feedback and civil society involvement, in some appropriate form and as permitted by the security realities on the ground, are an essential part of rebuilding a national consensus and creating positive forms of social capital, as well as a requirement for the effective implementation of reconstruction activities. The form of civil society involvement will depend on the sector and the region, but some mechanism to systematically obtain external participation and reality checks is essential. Because postconflict reconstruction is inherently a top-down affair, caution must be exercised lest existing NGO activities and local structures be inadvertently suffocated by the reconstruction assistance. Beyond protecting what exists, government and donors should make efforts to incorporate into the reconstruction program the contribution of local communities and of the local and international NGOs that have been laboring in the conflict vineyards for years. The potential contribution of NGOs and civil society goes much beyond assisting in implementation or even acting directly as implementing agencies. Some of the most effective components of postconflict reconstruction programs in the past have relied on empowerment of local communities and their partnership with NGOs. Moreover, capacity building at the local level is a necessary condition for the evolution of the rule of law, accountability, and transparency, and local structures can be essential to underpin the gradual rebuilding of the social capital destroyed by the conflict.

In conclusion, however well the urgent needs of the postconflict transition are handled through the budget process, the need for quick and visible achievements must not be allowed to short-circuit long-term institutional development. Even the simplest and most pragmatic approach to budgeting must facilitate moving in the direction of developing a robust institutional infrastructure for public expenditure management. Thus, although the starting point of budgeting in a postconflict situation must be to meet the immediate postconflict needs and limitations, the good budgeting practices described in the previous chapters do provide a vision of the end point toward which all interventions ought to move.

Notes

This chapter is based partly on the analysis and conclusions of the following documents and articles: Eriksson (2001); Sørbø and others (1998); Woodward (1995); and various governmental and World Bank studies, particularly Operations Evaluation Department

(OED) case studies on postconflict reconstruction, in Bosnia and Herzegovina (Kreimer, Muscat, and others 2000); El Salvador (Eriksson, Kreimer, and Arnold 2000); and Uganda (Kreimer, Collier, and others 2000). See also the OED country assistance evaluations on Cambodia (OED 2000), Guatemala (OED 2002a), Haiti (OED 2002b), Mozambique (OED 1997), and Sri Lanka (OED 2001). The section on Burundi is based mainly on Schiavo-Campo (2006), as well as on material from the Public Expenditure Review for Burundi (World Bank 1992) and the Interim Poverty Reduction Strategy Paper (Republic of Burundi 2003). For a more general analysis of the genesis of conflict, from among the now extensive literature on conflict and reconstruction, see Collier and Hoeffler (1998).

References

Collier, Paul, and Anke Hoeffler. 1998. "On Economic Causes of Civil War." *Oxford Economic Papers* 50 (4): 563–73.

Eriksson, John. 2001. *The Drive to Partnership: Aid Coordination and the World Bank.* Washington, DC: World Bank.

Eriksson, John, Alcira Kreimer, and Margaret Arnold. 2000. *El Salvador: Post-Conflict Reconstruction.* Washington, DC: World Bank.

Hirschman, Albert O. 1958. *The Strategy of Economic Development.* New Haven, CT: Yale University Press.

Kreimer, Alcira, Paul Collier, Colin S. Scott, and Margaret Arnold. 2000. *Uganda: Post-Conflict Reconstruction.* Washington, DC: World Bank.

Kreimer, Alcira, Robert Muscat, Ann Elwan, and Margaret Arnold. 2000. *Bosnia and Herzegovina: Post-Conflict Reconstruction.* Washington, DC: World Bank.

OED (Operations Evaluation Department, World Bank). 1997. *Mozambique Country Assistance Evaluation.* Report 17209. Washington, DC: World Bank.

———. 1998. *The World Bank's Experience with Post-Conflict Reconstruction.* Washington, DC: World Bank.

———. 2000. *Cambodia Country Assistance Evaluation.* Report SecM2000-708. Washington, DC: World Bank.

———. 2001. *Sri Lanka Country Assistance Evaluation.* Report 21771. Washington, DC: World Bank.

———. 2002a. *Guatemala Country Assistance Evaluation.* Report 25212-GT. Washington, DC: World Bank.

———. 2002b. *Haiti Country Assistance Evaluation.* Report 23637. Washington, DC: World Bank.

Republic of Burundi. 2003. *Boosting Interim Economic Growth and Poverty Reduction Strategy Paper.* Bujumbura: Republic of Burundi.

Rosenstein-Rodan, Paul. 1943. "Problems of Industrialization of Eastern and Southeastern Europe." *Economic Journal* 53: 202–11.

Schiavo-Campo, Salvatore. 2003. "Financing and Aid Management Arrangements in Post-Conflict Situations." Conflict Prevention and Reduction Paper 6, World Bank, Washington, DC.

———. 2006. "Managing Public Finance in Burundi: Control, Transparency, Effectiveness." Nathan Associates Inc, for U.S. Agency for International Development, Arlington, VA.

Schiavo-Campo, Salvatore, and Mary Judd. 2005. "The Mindanao Conflict in the Philippines: Roots, Costs and Potential Peace Dividend." Conflict Prevention and Reconstruction Paper 24, World Bank, Washington, DC.

Sørbø, Gunnar, Wenche Hauge, Bente Hybertsen, and Dan Smith. 1998. *Norwegian Assistance to Countries in Conflict: Lessons of Experience from Guatemala, Mali, Mozambique, Sudan, Rwanda, and Burundi.* Evaluation Report 11.98. Oslo: Ministry of Foreign Affairs.

Woodward, Susan. 1995. *Balkan Tragedy: Chaos and Dissolution after the Cold War.* Washington, DC: Brookings Institution.

World Bank. 1992. *Burundi Public Expenditure Review.* Report 8590-BU. Washington, DC: World Bank.

14

Country Case Study: Kenya

ALTA FÖLSCHER

Reforming systems of public finance management in Kenya has long been a priority for the Kenyan government. Improvements in planning, budgeting and budget execution, and oversight were recognized to be fundamental in achieving key development objectives. The first reforms to make the budget an instrument of prioritized policy implementation were introduced as early as the 1970s. The latest wave of reforms commenced in the late 1990s and early 2000s as deteriorating budget outcomes exacted a toll on macroeconomic growth, fiscal management, and service delivery. The reforms drew on experience in the region and introduced various instruments of expenditure review, budget formulation, and execution control to improve Kenyan outcomes. This case study reviews earlier reforms but focuses its discussion on the current system of budget management, including reforms. It highlights the challenges of reforming complex systems when human resource capacity is limited, accountability is insufficient, and the reforms do not address quickly the nuts and bolts of underlying budgeting systems.

A History of Budget Reforms

The Kenyan budget system functioned reasonably well during the economic boom of the 1960s and early 1970s, with five-year development plans funded selectively through projects in an annual

461

development budget and the recurrent budget recording government's ongoing costs. Together these two budgets formed the legal instrument that controlled public expenditure. The annual recurrent budget was the outcome of adjusting existing funding for administrative units incrementally by line item every year. The development budget consisted of the first year's funding for active projects from the five-year plan.

As the economy experienced a downtown in the 1970s, however, the resulting fiscal pressure started exposing the weaknesses in the budgeting system. Weak and short-term macroeconomic and fiscal planning processes exacerbated soft constraints on in-year spending, leading to increasing levels of debt. At the same time, shifts in the composition of expenditures marred the ability of state institutions to deliver quality services. In the absence of planning and budgeting tools to prioritize within existing recurrent spending, new recurrent costs, plus the increased cost of ongoing activities, squeezed out spending on public infrastructure. Within the recurrent budget, spending on interest and on wages and salaries crowded out spending on operations and maintenance, resulting in deteriorating public infrastructure and weakened public services.

The Kenyan government responded over the next two decades with several initiatives aimed at improving fiscal management, the link between planning and budgeting, and the link between budgeting and service delivery. In 1973, the country introduced the Programme Review and Forward Budgeting Procedure, a reform not unlike the medium-term expenditure frameworks that became popular more than two decades later. The procedure provided tools that brought policy analysis into the budget process through the review of ongoing programs, and it extended the planning horizon to three years. It gave spending ministries indicative three-year rolling ceilings. In return, ministries were allowed to identify the priorities on which the resources would be spent, but they were required to take the forward cost of their choices into account. However, as Byaruhanga (2004) argues, the new system did not pay sufficient attention to the process through which the allocations were made, with the result that instead of ensuring competition between spending proposals, the new system merely extended incremental budgeting over the medium term. It also did not succeed in providing realistic resource frameworks, because resource framework estimations were not based on credible macroeconomic forecasts. Spending ministries, therefore, still operated under conditions of resource uncertainty during the spending year.

As the government's ongoing expenditure obligations increased without commensurate macroeconomic growth, chronic fiscal imbalance threatened macroeconomic stability. At one point in the early 1980s, the deficit stood at just under 10 percent of gross domestic product (GDP). Investment expenditure and other, more discretionary spending items—such as spending on goods and services and on maintenance—came under increasing pressure. The development budget contained many incomplete and underfunded projects. An attempt to revitalize the Programme Review and Forward Budgeting Procedure in the early 1980s did not significantly change outcomes. However, it created new institutions that, in some form, persist today: a project appraisal and monitoring division in the Ministry of Finance, the estimates working groups, and the sectoral planning groups. Despite these interventions, the forward budget still remained, in essence, delinked from the annual budget because the ceilings used for annual budget preparation were not derived from the forward budget (Kiringai and West 2002).

In 1985, Kenya made another attempt at expenditure prioritization: the Budget Rationalisation Programme. The program was aimed at instilling fiscal discipline while ensuring adequate funding for infrastructure investment, operations, and maintenance through concentrating resources on priority programs and projects. It was introduced in response to concerns about persistent fiscal imbalances and their compounded effect on both the private sector and public budgets (by the mid-1980s debt service constituted 25 percent of expenditure). The program still saw the existing Programme Review and Forward Budgeting Procedure as the vehicle for change but insisted on a systematic review of all ongoing projects and programs. Rigorous appraisal procedures were introduced before new projects could be approved. Only those projects that contributed to increased production, created employment, generated income, targeted the poor, conserved foreign exchange, and minimized the requirement for recurrent resources were supposed to be funded (Kiringai and West 2002).

Although the program promised a smaller, more effective budget on paper, in practice it did not achieve the shifting of funds from lesser- to higher-priority spending items. The response to smaller resource envelopes was to cut expenditure items across the board without taking into account whether the spending was on the explicit priorities. At the same time, the number of ongoing projects could not be reduced in practice. The sectoral planning groups still did not operate well, failing in their mandate to ensure effective links between policy, project planning, and budgeting. The budget structure and classification system made their effective functioning virtually impossible. The recurrent cost of development projects still was not assessed properly for project appraisal or budgeting processes.

As the development budget became increasingly unmanageable and the need for renewed investment in public infrastructure grew, the early 1990s saw the introduction of a rolling public investment plan as a tool to improve the quality of investment spending. The plan profiled all government investment projects over the medium term and detailed financing arrangements and disbursements. It categorized projects into a ranking of core, high priority, and other. The first year of the plan was the development budget. The assumption was that a rolling public investment plan would help translate long-term development plans into annual investment activities (Byaruhanga 2004; Kiringai and West 2002).

Nevertheless, the plan faced similar problems as previous reform efforts. Although it was supposed to bring greater attention to priorities, it lacked a strong enough review mechanism and had inadequate links to the rest of the budget process. Agencies used the public investment plan to introduce new projects without completing existing ones. At the same time, projects were not justified in the context of overall sector strategies. The links between the public investment plan and resource planning were also inadequate: not even all the core projects were financed.

By the end of the 1990s, despite three major reform initiatives, fiscal management in Kenya still faced a number of core problems, including unaffordable levels of spending, insufficient attention to stated policy priorities, and skewed composition of expenditure, with spending on wages and interest crowding out necessary complementary spending on operations and maintenance. A key deficiency remained a failure to establish realistic resource envelopes. Not one of the three initiatives achieved in any fundamental way improved forward estimates of revenue. Although development plans contained longer-term estimates and the resource allocations in the forward budget added up to an expenditure total, these estimates were not the result of rigorous forecasting technologies and were unrealistic.

In addition, the introduction of new planning instruments was not accompanied by sufficient changes to the budget process to ensure rigorous implementation of new planning modalities. None of the initiatives paid much attention to the shortcomings of in-year internal control processes; all three initiatives were still bound by the inadequacies of the budget classification system and still focused on planning inputs without paying sufficient attention to measuring performance against policy objectives.

In 1997, the government undertook a critical joint public expenditure review. The review found that budgeting in Kenya was held back by continuing deficiencies in macroeconomic management, that the budget process had very low credibility, and that public sector productivity was very low (Kiringai and West 2002: 36). Although the reform initiatives were to some extent institutionalized, the preparation process was in practice still incremental line-item budgeting. Program reviews, including the evaluation of

There's a lot of weaknesses here.

current activities, were largely ignored. Critical weaknesses included poor forecasting ability, an ineffective medium-term perspective, the failure to cost future resource requirements properly, cash rationing and late release of funds, repetitive budgeting during the spending year, fragmentation of spending between budgets and revenue sources, dysfunctional political interference in budgeting, a limited classification structure, weak expenditure controls, and weak accounting and reporting systems (Byaruhanga 2004; Khasiani and Makau 2005; Kiringai and West 2002).

By 1997, Kenya was faced with consistently low economic growth (on average 1.3 percent over the six years since 1990), large public expenditure outlays (nearly 32 percent of GDP in 1997/98), and high debt stock and interest payments at 6.1 percent of GDP (Republic of Kenya 2003b). Against this macrofiscal background, the quality of spending was low. Wages and salaries to 228,000 public servants absorbed a high percentage of the budget. Transfers and subsidies demanded an increasing budget share as more activities moved off budget and outside routine budget scrutiny. Development expenditure was low (at 5.5 percent of GDP) and declining. Within the recurrent budget, actual expenditure and revenue were routinely lower than budgeted because resource estimates remained overly optimistic. Budget implementation remained weak. Although some ministries routinely underspent, others—particularly the National Assembly, State House, and the Office of the President—routinely overspent (Byaruhanga 2004; Kiringai and West 2002; Republic of Kenya 2003b, 2004a, 2005). Significant in-year shifts between items of expenditure took place within ministerial budgets, with the first requests for virement or additional funds arriving as soon as the budget was tabled in the country's legislature. Overall, the credibility of the budget process and the credibility of the budget were extremely low.

Concerns about the quality of public spending, rising poverty, and the long-term economic outlook caused the Kenyan government to again review its fiscal and budget management system. The result was a new wave of reforms, spearheaded by a medium-term expenditure framework (MTEF) approach to budgeting.

The New Reforms: Introduction of an MTEF

The 2000/01 budget was the first in Kenya to be prepared using an MTEF system of budgeting. The aim was to match a top-down, medium-term macrofiscal and policy perspective with bottom-up, medium-term sector and ministry policy priorities and expenditure estimates. The introduction of an MTEF spearheaded a series of reforms that recognized that poor links between policy and planning are not only a result of problems in budget preparation, but also a result of deficiencies in budget execution, monitoring, and audit.

The reforms included the following:

- Strengthening the legal framework for finance management, including new financial management and procurement legislation
- Developing macroeconomic forecasting capacity in the Ministry of Finance
- Developing a participatory MTEF-budget process, with various structures aimed at improving coordination between agencies and cooperation toward better budget outcomes
- Introducing review and evaluation instruments, particularly institution-alized ministerial public expenditure reviews, an overall public expenditure review, and public expenditure tracking methodologies
- Constituting central and ministerial MTEF structures to improve the link between planning and budgeting
- Reforming economic budget classification categories to comply with international standards
- Developing an integrated financial management information system
- Introducing automated payroll controls
- Creating a revamped cash management and expenditure commitment control system
- Improving systems to track and monitor external resources
- Improving debt management capacity.

The reforms are applied in the relevant phases of the budget process. This chapter focuses on the institutional arrangements of the budget preparation and implementation processes, discussing each reform instrument within the context of the budget process.

Improving the Macrofiscal Budget Link

A key finding of analytical work done on the Kenyan system in the early 2000s was that although previous reform initiatives emphasized the need for realistic projections of revenue, overly optimistic forecasts of macro-economic and revenue performance still regularly led to budget planning based on unrealistic resource envelopes. The result has been in-year cash-flow shortfalls, leading to (a) repetitive budgeting during the year as both the Ministry of Finance and spending agencies continuously assess funding priorities and make allocations and (b) additional ad hoc borrowing on the domestic market to cover unavoidable spending.

Underlying this disconnect were the lack of functional modeling capacity in the Ministry of Finance, lack of coordination between different stakeholders in fiscal policy, and poor sequencing of processes toward a macrofiscal framework. Fiscal framework decisions also had low legitimacy in the budget process: even if the numbers were based on reasonably accurate technical work in the first place, expenditure demands still edged budget forecasts upward toward overoptimism.

Problems with estimation of the domestic resource envelope were exacerbated by low predictability of donor funding. In the decade before the early 2000s, Kenya was faced twice with suspension of International Monetary Fund and World Bank operations. Although these events severely affected the country's macrofiscal management, they were isolated occurrences. Ongoing unpredictability of project and programmatic support funds affects planning and management more subtly but still has a negative effect on the budget. Although some of the blame rests with development partners for being unable to provide medium-term funding certainty, funding unpredictability was exacerbated by the lack of institutionalized central coordination and reporting mechanisms for development partner funds. The government of Kenya has therefore introduced a number of institutions to improve the quality of macroeconomic and revenue forecasts and to improve cooperation and coordination between the different actors involved in determining a macrofiscal framework.

The MTEF reforms introduced several changes to the Kenyan budgeting system to ensure that expenditure plans are prepared on the basis of a good estimate of available resources, given macroeconomic and fiscal policy objectives. The link between macroeconomic policy and the government's fiscal operations is established in Kenya through key institutions in the macrofiscal phase of the annual MTEF-budget process.

First, the budget process starts with a top-down consideration of macroeconomic outcomes and policy, fiscal outcomes and policy, and the preparation of revenue projections. These processes generate an indicative budget framework within which sectors compete for resources (see the section titled "Allocating Scarce Resources Strategically").

Building technical forecasting capacity

The Ministry of Finance invested in forecasting capacity with the development of a macrofiscal model. The first macrofiscal forecast is prepared in the September preceding the applicable fiscal year, using the Kenya Institute for

Public Policy Research and Analysis–Treasury Macro Model. The model analyzes the main components of aggregate supply and demand, assuming no change in fiscal policy, to generate a consistent macroeconomic and fiscal framework that shows the implications for public revenue and expenditure. Over the subsequent months, the budget process includes several iterations between drafting a fiscal strategy and the model.

The Macroeconomic Working Group

The Macroeconomic Working Group (MEWG) is the central institution in the macrofiscal phase of the MTEF-budget process. Its members include representatives from the Ministry of Finance (the Economic Affairs Department, the Budget Supply Department, the Debt Management Department, the External Resources Department, and the Investment and Public Enterprises Department); the Ministry of Planning and National Development (the Macro Planning Department and the Central Bureau of Statistics); the Kenya Revenue Authority; and the Central Bank of Kenya. It is responsible for coordinating the roles of these institutions in producing the forecasts required for the macrofiscal framework and in producing analysis toward macrofiscal policy. The MEWG, through its component members, produces the medium-term macroeconomic and revenue forecasts and discusses policy options. The group is also primarily responsible for producing the Budget Outlook Paper (BOPA), the first in a series of two Kenyan prebudget statements, and updating macrofiscal forecasts and the resulting framework as the budget preparation process unfolds.

The Budget Outlook Paper

The main instrument driving the annual consideration of fiscal policy and fiscal targets and the preparation of the macrofiscal framework is the BOPA. The BOPA is published six months before the minister of finance tables the budget in the legislature. In it, the government elaborates the medium-term fiscal framework and provides the background and parameters forming the basis for the allocative process and the detailed budget. The BOPA is intended to signal the government's policy intent to external stakeholders and discipline the internal budget preparation process by firming up the aggregate expenditure ceiling through publication. It also acts as an effective demand for quality information on analysis in the macrofiscal process. The document formally links annual fiscal and budget policy to long-term national strategic objectives by reviewing recent performance against the objectives and proposing a forward fiscal strategy. It discusses recent macroeconomic developments and provides the government's assessment for the forward economic outlook. It provides a projection of expected fiscal outturns for the current fiscal year, including revenue outturns, realization of grants, expenditure performance, debt management, and progress in major public sector structural reforms (Republic of Kenya 2006a).

The BOPA then provides a framework for budget decision making by discussing the medium-term fiscal strategy, including policy objectives and targets, strategies for financing the proposed deficit, and medium-term structural reforms. It projects domestic revenue, grants, and expenditure forecasts against the main economic categories of expenditure. It sets resource ceilings for the recurrent and development budgets. Finally, the BOPA provides a platform for the forward preparation process by publishing the MTEF guidelines for the planning period, including the technical submission requirements and guidelines regarding the criteria that will be used to allocate funds. The BOPA affirms the medium-term sector ceilings for the forward period (rolled over from the previous year) and provides an indicative ceiling for the new outer year (see the following discussion on the evolution of ceilings).

Political affirmation of resource ceilings

The BOPA is also the instrument through which the cabinet and the legislature endorse the macrofiscal framework. The BOPA and the decisions contained in it are at the heart of the Kenyan government's policy agenda; therefore, cabinet consideration and approval of the proposals are important. This action—together with the multiagency involvement in the MEWG—serves to legitimize the decisions, making them government decisions and not those of the Ministry of Finance.

Kenya has achieved relative success in improving fiscal discipline through an MTEF approach to budgeting. Over the first few years of the MTEF, public spending and the deficit contracted as a share of GDP. Interest payments as a share of public spending decreased as the debt stock declined.

However, the MTEF approach has been less successful in forcing more strategic allocations. Although spending on operations and maintenance increased in comparison with personnel spending in the early years of the MTEF, the link between actual spending and stated spending priorities is still weak. Some of the blame for this failure has to do with persistent weaknesses in expenditure control, but weak MTEF-budget institutions in spending ministries and weak links centrally between the MTEF and the annual budget phases of budget preparation mean that the valuable analytical work undertaken during the MTEF phase does not consistently translate into prioritized annual budget allocations.

Allocating Scarce Resources Strategically

A second key objective of introducing an MTEF was to ensure that public resources were used effectively and efficiently to support high growth of income and employment. The aim was to reduce the share of public expenditure in GDP so that the government's activities would be focused on a much narrower range of activities: protecting essential social services and providing essential infrastructure to support economic growth (Republic of Kenya 2005).

At the time the MTEF was introduced, improving allocative efficiency in Kenya had been long thwarted by a persistent disconnect between the different instruments used for planning and budgeting purposes. In fact, planning and budgeting processes were fragmented in several ways. The previous section highlights the separation of macrofiscal and allocative budget processes and details efforts under the new MTEF-budget process to remedy the situation.

In addition, Kenyan long-term planning—embodied in the five-year development plans—was disconnected from shorter-term planning and budgeting. This problem occurred largely because the long-term plans were not always constrained by a realistic assessment of available resources. Hence, the plans were allowed to propose policies and targets that would turn out to be unaffordable. In contrast, budgeting processes were far more focused on controlling inputs than on achieving objectives and targets against priority policies. New policies were introduced to government outside the budget process, often without an assessment of their budget implications or opportunity costs, and the budget process itself provided neither tools nor incentives for spending agencies to discontinue existing lower-priority spending in favor of new higher-priority policies (Byaruhanga 2004: 15–16).

The institutional separation of planning and budgeting at both the central and ministerial levels underlay the disconnect between planning and budgeting. At the central level, planning and budgeting functions were separately allocated to a Ministry of Planning and a Ministry of Finance: the former was responsible for long-term plans and worked with central planning units in ministries, and the latter was responsible for budgets and provided guidelines to finance and budget officers in ministries. The structure of the two ministries as separate or joined has changed over time. Even when they were joined, however, their integration was not necessarily the result of a thorough consideration of functions; instead, the two structures were combined, but the overlaps and gaps remained. Within ministries, policies were prepared without involving finance and budget officers, and budgets were done without substantive consultation with either the planning units or program managers.

A further disconnect occurred between development expenditure, which was budgeted in the development budget by the Ministry of Planning and National Development, and recurrent expenditure, which was budgeted in the recurrent budget under the direction of the Ministry of Finance. The development budget, as in many other countries, had lost its function as an exclusive vehicle for the financing of capital projects. Instead, its purpose had become blurred because it also served to record development-partner projects, although not comprehensively. The projects that did end up in the development budget were mostly those that required co-financing by the government. Thus, it contained a mix of recurrent and capital expenditure (not classified consistently with recurrent budget categories), whereas the recurrent budget funded exclusively Kenyan government capital projects. The development budget largely functioned outside the annual budget process besides being an input into the process. In other words, insufficient attention was paid to integrating financing under the development budget with financing through the recurrent budget. The development budget as a whole became a budget bid, rather than capital spending being considered as a strategic outlay at the sector level. The recurrent costs of funded projects were not budgeted on the recurrent side, and the budget process in practice did not offer sufficient opportunity for spending ministries to plan their expenditure holistically, taking both development and recurrent spending into account when considering tradeoffs within spending ceilings. In practice, the development budget functioned as a source of recurrent funding for spending agencies: in-year shortfalls on the recurrent budget were often covered by transferring funds from the development budget. Over time, this failure to consider the recurrent costs of funded projects resulted in a large stock of incomplete projects.

Despite the institutionalization of joint estimates working groups and sector planning groups, the recurrent budget remained, in practice, under the control of the Budget Supplies Department in the Ministry of Finance, offering little opportunity for spending ministries to make policy-driven tradeoffs jointly between the development budget and the recurrent budget.

In-year budget management also detracted from strong links between planning and budgeting. As control over fiscal aggregates became a priority, Kenya moved from predictable monthly releases of cash to spending ministries against budget to a cash-rationing system in which cash releases depended on revenue inflows. In this system, the budget at best became a guide to the menu of options for funding. At worst, it was mostly ignored as new policies and projects were parachuted into the budget during the spending year. These statements are true both at the central and ministerial levels. At the center, priorities between competing spending obligations were decided at the technical level against available cash. At the ministerial level, ministries soon became adept at playing the games that would maximize a ministry's share in available cash (for example, by first funding lower-priority avoidable activities and then applying for additional funds for high-priority unavoidable expenditures).

Ironically, although budget preparation was highly centralized, the cash-rationing system passed responsibility for making decisions about funding priorities at the ministerial level largely to ministries. In effect, responsibility for real budgeting—namely, budgeting in line with actual available resources—thus ended up with the spending agencies. But this responsibility came too late in the process. Instead of being able to plan comprehensively and make tradeoffs while time to implement the tradeoffs was still available, spending agencies were in constant crisis management. In addition to transferring funds from the development budget—where projects could be postponed or suspended more easily—spending agencies built up huge stocks of pending bills. Kenya ran a cash accounting system with authorities to incur expenditure issued at the ministry level against the votebook. This system allowed ministries to keep incurring expenditures—particularly on running credit arrangements, such as for utility bills—without having cash available to cover the obligation.

This disconnect between planning and budgeting was exacerbated further because the subsequent year's budget planning did not start from actual expenditure (including an assessment of arrears). Rather, it took as a starting point the previous year's budgeted expenditure, partly because the financial results were not ready in time for the next year's budgeting cycle.

The proposed MTEF budget cycle comprised several instruments to address these disconnects. Over the seven years of implementation, the process has evolved to include increasingly effective instruments of expenditure review and planning, an assessment of arrears, sector-based negotiation and tradeoffs, joint work by the Ministry of Finance and line ministries, and a new system of cash management and commitment control that attempts to balance macrofiscal management imperatives with the need for predictable cash releases.

The next section considers the current Kenyan allocative budget process, and the subsequent section examines reforms to budget execution processes.

Key institutions in the allocative budget process

As the MEWG enters the process to prepare the macrofiscal process and the BOPA, ministries are issued MTEF guidelines that start the bottom-up process of preparing detailed, costed expenditure plans. The circular includes the following:

- Guidelines and terms of reference for undertaking ministerial public expenditure reviews (MPERs)
- Guidelines and terms of reference for the sector working groups (SWGs) and the SWG reports (the document that details the sectors' MTEF expenditure strategies against policy priorities)
- An MTEF timetable and guidelines regarding key criteria for decision making in the MTEF-budget cycle.

The MPERs, SWGs, and SWG reports are key instruments of the MTEF-budget process, together with the Budget Steering Committee, the Budget Strategy Paper, and the core poverty programs. After providing a brief description of the whole process, the chapter discusses each of the main instruments in detail, including their evolution, where they fit into the process, and their strengths and weaknesses.

The Kenyan budget process

The budget process starts in August and September prior to the budget year, when the MEWG starts meeting to prepare a macrofiscal framework and the first budget circular goes out with the timetable and key terms of reference.

As the MEWG and its component organizations prepare macro-economic and revenue forecasts, make fiscal policy proposals, and prepare a macrofiscal framework for cabinet approval, ministries work on their MPERs. At the same time, ministries are supposed to request from their district offices inputs regarding spending pressures, needs, and proposed projects. At the district level, MTEF committees are supposed to be active during this period to coordinate inputs into ministerial review and planning. The district-level MTEF preparation, however, is still underdeveloped and largely inactive.

The MPERs (see later discussion) are critical inputs to the budget process. They are supposed to provide the necessary review of existing expenditure to facilitate greater realism in forward budgeting. They are also an instrument through which ministries can make clear bids for additional funds and motivate requests in the context of their circumstances and policy priorities.

The MPERs are targeted for completion in December, when the initial macrofiscal process draws to a close with the approval, publication, and submission to the legislature of the BOPA. The BOPA contains a budget framework in which indicative sector ceilings are proposed. These ceilings are in the future expected to be the rolled-over forward ceilings of the previous year's final MTEF, with an indicative ceiling for the third year.

Although the SWGs continue the bottom-up expenditure planning process, the public expenditure review (PER) secretariat in the Ministry of Planning and National Development undertakes an analysis of the MPERs, as well as of aggregate macroeconomic and fiscal outcomes to prepare the PER. The PER provides a cross-sector, cross-ministry, and cross-budget analysis of public expenditure and public expenditure management. It contains a detailed analysis of the fiscal aggregates and the composition across ministries in terms of economic classification.

Armed with the guidelines of the first circular and the BOPA regarding macro- and microfiscal strategy and informed by the MPERs—and in some cases ministerial SWG submissions—the SWGs craft sector expenditure strategies that link policy and budgeting and ensure intrasectoral linkages and tradeoffs within sectors. Toward the end of the SWG process, a series of sector hearings is held. Before the sector hearings, first drafts of the SWG reports are published on the Internet. The sector hearings are open, but the Ministry of Finance also invites key commentators in each sector. After the sector hearings, the SWGs finalize their reports, taking into account the discussions at the sector hearings.

The SWG reports are the main instrument through which sectors and their component ministries bid for additional resources and justify their current spending. After the finalization of the sector reports, a series of sector-based meetings is held with the Ministry of Finance and the Budget Steering Committee to discuss sector proposals.

Work on the Budget Strategy Paper (BSP) starts after the sector bid meetings. This paper details the allocation to sectors and ministries and draws on the SWG reports, the PER, and the MPERs to provide a detailed narrative on ministerial programs against allocations. The BSP is published approximately three months before the detailed budget is submitted to the legislature and is also approved by the cabinet and provided to the legislature (from 2007/08 onward). The BSP does not break down the expenditure allocations to the same level as the annual budget, but it provides aggregate allocations, a programmatic narrative, and targets for outputs and outcomes.

When the BSP is complete, ministries prepare their detailed annual budget submissions. These submissions are discussed in great detail with the

Budget Supply Department in the Ministry of Finance, which is responsible for compiling the annual budget estimates, the legal budget control instrument that is submitted to the legislature for approval. At the same time, the development budget is compiled. The annual recurrent estimates and the development estimates are laid before the legislature in June each year, starting the legislative budget process.

Instruments of the budget process

THE MINISTERIAL PUBLIC EXPENDITURE REVIEWS. MPERs have been a feature of the MTEF-budget process since the early years of the MTEF. The reviews are aimed at institutionalizing a review of the performance of existing expenditure against policy priorities within the budget preparation process. The reviews were first introduced under a joint Ministry of Finance and Planning. However, when the new government came to power in 2002, two separate ministries were created. The PERs—together with the MTEF Secretariat initially—were located in the Ministry of Planning and National Development. This institutional separation of the MPERs from the rest of the budget processes has underpinned ongoing overlap in functions and a disconnect in sequencing between the MPER and other budget process instruments, such as the SWG reports.

The MPERs involve reviewing ministerial programs and activities in line with core functions of the ministry and identifying the bottlenecks in expenditure management. The MPERs do not merely look backward; they also have a forward-looking component. Ministries are required to cost their baseline and new programs and prioritize the programs in line with their core functions. An example of a typical MPER is provided in box 14.1.

When the 2005/06 budget was prepared, the MPERs were integrated into the MTEF process. However, problems of coordination of timetables between the MPER and MTEF process remained. Some SWGs (see later discussion) reverted to asking ministries to prepare input papers for the SWG process because the MPERs were not completed in time to be used.

Coordination between the Ministry of Finance and the Ministry of Planning and National Development is insufficient regarding the function of different documents. Ministries find themselves having to use scarce capacity to prepare multiple and duplicative documents for the two ministries. In addition to the MPER, which is in essence a review document, ministries are required to prepare a monitoring and evaluation report on their progress toward the Investment Programme for the Economic Recovery Strategy for Wealth and Employment Creation (IP-ERS) targets (see box 14.2), a function that the Ministry of Planning and National Development

BOX 14.1 Kenyan MPER Contents

Introductory Section

The introductory section has three subsections:

- *Objectives of the MPER.* A brief section discussing the objectives of the year's MPER and how it relates to the previous MPER.
- *The ministry's mission statement.* A section stating the specific elements of the ministry and its programs. The section also must name all parastatals reporting to the ministry and describe how they relate to the ministry's mission and core functions. The mission statement should also provide a discussion of the relationship between the ministry's programs and the IP-ERS.
- *Situation analysis and recent reforms.* This section does a brief environment scan, listing the key factors that will affect the ministry's policy development or spending. It should also include a section on recent reforms and changes in the ministry's portfolio or modalities of service delivery.

Expenditure Analysis of Three Years prior to Budget Year

This section does basic budget analysis of the ministry's spending. It usually comprises three components:

- Trends in level and composition of expenditure (as budgeted, actual, and budgeted compared with actual). Here the ministry discusses the distribution of funding between development and recurrent costs by economic classification of expenditure and by functions of the ministry.
- Extrabudgetary resources and appropriations in aid (own revenue). This section should indicate sources, trends, and share in total budget (budgeted and actual) of charges, fees, and levies imposed by the ministry.
- A third section analyzes factors underlying divergence between budgeted and actual expenditure.

Review of Core Poverty Programs Related to Ministry

This section analyzes changes in the list of core poverty programs, trends in budgets, disbursement and spending against programs, and performance (in terms of outputs) against these programs.

Review of the Ministry Project Portfolio

This section provides a list of active projects and a discussion of their implementation status, in terms of both cost and nonfinancial progress. An analysis of stalled projects is required, including which ones should be completed and at what cost. The next step is for the ministry to detail what new projects it wants to initiate and how these relate to its core functions. Finally, the section includes a discussion of strengths and weaknesses in project management and implementation in the ministry.

Analysis of Outputs and Performance Indicators

This section identifies core outputs, given functions of ministry and related performance indicators, and discusses trends in outputs for the period under review. It also provides recommendations for forward indicators and targets.

Pending Bills

In this section, the ministry is required to provide an analysis of arrears by budget (development and recurrent) and budget head. It also must provide an analysis of the trends regarding pending bills over time and show how it intends to pay the bills, indicating sources.

Discussion of Public Expenditure Management Institutions in Ministry

This section reviews the institutions in the ministry for public expenditure management. It describes processes and structures used in the ministry for budget preparation, expenditure controls and budget execution, accounting, monitoring and reporting, and internal audit and provides a discussion of strengths and weaknesses together with proposals for reform.

Human Resources Development and Capacity Building

This section looks at human resource use and cost in the ministry. It provides a summary of trends over five years and a discussion of the constraints on service delivery on account of human resources. It also discusses training needs.

Recommendations and Implementation Plans

Finally, the concluding section is required to look at recommendations in light of the MPER analysis and provide an action plan for implementing recommendations with clear timeframes and targets.

Source: Republic of Kenya 2003a.

itself wants the MPERs to fulfill. The MPERs currently straddle the two ministries, used by both in their processes but with complete ownership resting with neither. The result is that both ministries demand additional documentation from line ministries (the monitoring and evaluation report, SWG

BOX 14.2   The IP-ERS, MPERs, and the MTEF

In 2003, the government of Kenya published the IP-ERS, the Investment Programme for the Economic Recovery Strategy for Wealth and Employment Creation. The IP-ERS identified a set of development priorities and strategies for short- and medium-term implementation toward achieving the three key pillars of (a) restoring economic growth, (b) promoting equity and poverty reduction, and (c) ensuring good governance. The IP-ERS, therefore, defines the government spending priorities in the medium term to be implemented through the MTEF.

In 2005, the government published a monitoring and evaluation framework for the IP-ERS that suggests 31 indicators and targets. In future years, the MPERs will play an important role in tracking the achievement of these targets. Following are examples of indicators and targets:

- Reducing the portion of the road network that is in poor condition by 23 percent by 2007 (Ministry of Roads and Public Works)
- Increasing power coverage in rural areas by 1 percent per year (Ministry of Energy)
- Increasing the growth of volume of exports to 5.7 percent through an export development strategy and improved business environment (Ministry of Trade and Industry)
- Reducing the infant mortality rate and under-five mortality, reducing HIV/AIDS prevalence to 8 percent in 2008, reducing maternal mortality, and reducing the burden of disease—for example, in-patient malaria morbidity to 7 percent in 2007 (Ministry of Health)
- Achieving 100 percent net primary enrollment, reducing primary dropout rates, reducing primary repetition, and increasing the transition rate to secondary school (Ministry of Education)
- Raising incomes in the agricultural sector and increasing the sectoral growth by 5 percent in 2007 (Ministry of Agriculture).

The introduction of an IP-ERS monitoring and evaluation framework and of priority programs holds potential for bringing a vital missing part to Kenya's public expenditure management processes. Despite improvements since 1999 in budget preparation and execution, the disconnect between (a) priority setting and (b) planning and budgeting is still a concern. Significant reallocations to higher-priority sectors and programs are not occurring, and even where they do, they do not necessarily filter through to actual expenditure patterns. The introduction of a monitoring and evaluation framework linked to budgeting may provide the motivation to shift resources, but only if the political will exists to hold ministries—both at the political and official levels—accountable for delivering the specific outcomes.

Source: Republic of Kenya 2005.

inputs), over which the Ministry of Planning and National Development or Ministry of Finance has complete control but which duplicate the function of the MPER.

At the ministry level, these requirements mean that thin analysis capacity is spread even thinner and that none of the documents receive proper attention, partly because of capacity constraints, but also because they are not perceived as the *one* instrument through which the ministry can justify its programs and spending, put its case forward for additional funding, and report on its achievements. The result is that the MPERs become compliance documents, detracting hugely from their value as ministerial decision-making tools. Ministerial capacity to undertake thorough PERs is varied. In most cases, the MPER does not succeed in being a budget document that drives a thorough ministerial MTEF process. The review is mainly undertaken by the central planning units, with little involvement from the budget and finance officers or from program managers. In some cases, ministries have hired consultants to produce the document. Although the quality of the resulting document is usually good, ministerial ownership of the analysis is not always certain.

This problem is symptomatic of the slow progress in Kenya of deepening the MTEF process to the ministerial and district levels: currently only at the central level—and to a lesser extent at the sector level—is the MTEF process starting to take on the characteristics of an MTEF approach. Only at that level are top-down resource ceilings used and forums established at which claims on available resources can compete on an equal footing. Moreover, the progress even here is not complete: despite the improvements in analysis and the layered discussion that happens in the SWGs and various sector hearings and forums, in the final instance the budget still is often prepared behind closed bureaucratic doors in an incremental fashion (see the following discussion of the annual budget phase).

Arguably, until ministries take on the task of running thorough MTEF processes involving all stakeholders, thereby bringing ministrywide commitment to decisions made, the link between policies, budgeting, and budget implementation will remain weak.

PUBLIC EXPENDITURE REVIEW. After ministries have completed the MPERs, the Ministry of Planning and National Development compiles a national PER. The review provides a critical analysis and assessment of government expenditure in terms of size, allocation, and management. In 2005, the PER analyzed whether the allocation and use of resources were in line with the IP-ERS objectives and priorities. The PER document consists of a review of the macroeconomic and fiscal framework and performance, an analysis of key public expenditure trends against both an economic and functional classification of government, a review of public expenditure management institutions, and a review of the MPERs to track implementation of the IP-ERS through the MPERs.

The PER is potentially a powerful document to inform budget allocations. Its analysis is based on the best information that government has, and it is robust and honest. However, so far its completion has come too late to inform the allocative process. The intention is to remedy this problem in the next budget cycle (2007/08 to 2009/10).

SECTOR WORKING GROUPS AND THEIR REPORTS. The SWGs were set up along similar lines to the earlier sector planning groups. The SWGs fulfill a core function in the budget process: at this point bottom-up expenditure planning and demands are reconciled with top-down resource constraints.

Currently nine SWGs exist (table 14.1). Each group is chaired by a permanent secretary from the sector. The sector convener is a senior officer from the Budget Supply Department in the Ministry of Finance, and the membership consists of representatives from the Budget Supply Department (one to five members), the sector ministries, the sector donors, and the sector nongovernmental organizations (NGOs), in addition to private sector delegates. Although in principle the membership is open to stakeholders outside the central government, in practice such members are co-opted when needed.

The SWGs channel ministerial expenditure proposals. In doing so they must take the following actions:

- Identify gaps and constraints, and conduct an assessment of sector performance for the previous fiscal year and an assessment of budget outputs against budget allocations.
- Define and articulate the sector clearly, and establish spending needs, including the definition of objectives and the identification of sector priorities and strategies.
- Analyze the cost implications of policies and strategies in the sector.
- Identify sector priority programs (those that would result in priority outcomes being achieved).
- Identify possible sources of funds in addition to allocations from the central revenue fund, including development partner resources.

TABLE 14.1   Sector Working Groups

SWG	Member institutions
Agriculture and Rural Development	Agriculture and Rural Development, Environment and Natural Resources, Lands and Settlement
Physical Infrastructure	Roads and Public Works, Energy, Transport and Communication, Environment and Natural Resources, Local Government
Health	Health
Education	Education
General Economic Services	Trade and Industry, Office of the President, Labor and Human Resource Development, Environment and Natural Resources
Public Administration	Office of the President, Finance, Planning and National Development, Directorate of Personnel Management, Foreign Affairs and International Cooperation, Public Service Commission, Office of the Controller and Auditor General, National Assembly
Public Safety, Law, and Order	Judicial Department, Office of the Attorney General, Office of the President, State House, Office of the Vice President, Ministry of Home Affairs, Heritage, Sports
National Security	Defense, National Security Intelligence Service
Communication and Technology	Ministry of Finance, Ministry of Planning and National Development, Tourism, Information

Source: Republic of Kenya 2003a.

- Identify outputs and outcomes given the level of resources allocated to the sector.
- Identify performance indicators and targets and modalities to monitor them.
- Identify key cross-sectoral issues and priorities and the activities in each of the component ministries' budgets that support the achievement of priorities.
- List and justify all the projects proposed for inclusion in the sector investment program.
- Coordinate a process to produce a sectorwide plan and produce a sector report.

The SWGs are most active in budget preparation, but they are also responsible for monitoring budget implementation and undertaking a midterm review for each sector.

SWGs operated within indicative ceilings issued by the government (on recommendation of the MEWG) in the BOPA. For the first few years of the

MTEF, these ceilings were derived by taking into account policy priorities and their relation to the functions of ministries (particularly objectives of enhanced economic growth for poverty reduction), historical sector resource allocations, proposed sector priorities, donor commitments, and projected realization of revenues.

The decision to roll over the MTEF sector ceilings from the previous years as the starting point for sector and ministry planning is a recent one. Over the seven years of budget preparation in an MTEF process, Kenya has varied the form and base of expenditure ceilings considerably.

At first, the Fiscal Strategy Paper, the precursor of the BOPA, provided input-denominated sector ceilings. All personnel expenditure was allocated to the public administration sector (under the argument that ministries in this sector control salaries and wages), and all capital infrastructure spending was allocated to the infrastructure sector. Other sectors, such as the social spending sector, worked with the remainder of spending items only. Although this method did allocate budgeting responsibility to the sectors that had the most control over the line items for which budgets were prepared, it hindered proper expenditure review, policy analysis, and consideration of the full cost of new policy proposals. Instead of improving the link between planning and budgeting, it weakened that link by a continued emphasis on line-item budgeting.

For the 2004/05 budget, the BOPA (which introduced a two-phased budget process preceding formation of the annual budget, as described in the next section) for the first time provided sector ceilings that included all expenditure lines. However, these ceilings also already included indications from the Ministry of Finance, working through the MEWG, of what sector shares in additional resources should be. This system worked reasonably well: even though sectors perceived that the bidding process would not change final ceilings significantly, the component ministries in each sector still had to compete for their share of the additional resources allocated to the sector. The sector as a whole also had an opportunity to bid for additional resources, on the basis of its analysis of policy and expenditure.

For 2006/07, after a review of the MTEF in 2004, the Ministry of Finance decided to issue indicative ministry ceilings in the BOPA. These ceilings already included an assessment of how projected additional resources should be allocated among ministries.

Allocating additional available resources to ministries so early in the MTEF-budget process had two drawbacks. First, it provided little incentive for ministries to undertake thorough policy and expenditure reviews because they perceived that allocations were as good as finalized. Ministries were also not interested in participating in the SWGs: they perceived the process to be of little value. Second, early resource allocation also meant that the MTEF did not operate as a rolling budget: issuing new ceilings at the start of the budget preparation process created the impression that each budget cycle started afresh, disconnected from what went previously.

For the 2007/08 budget, however, the budget framework presented in the BOPA will use the final sector ceilings of the previous year for years 1 and 2 and will add a third year. The framework will show the total pool of projected "new" money separately as unallocated funds. This new system will provide an incentive for spending agencies to improve the quality of their forward estimates (which will form the base of future budgets) and for new spending to maximize ministry shares in the indicated additional resources.

The Kenyan emphasis on the role of sectors in the budget process has brought significant benefits. Reports on the 2004/05 budget process—when the BOPA was first launched and sectors worked internally on intrasectoral allocations before the BSP—show that in some SWGs a real process of negotiation occurred. Ministries were prepared to concede that fellow sector ministries' priorities might be more pressing than their own, given the interests of the sector as a whole. They were prepared to relinquish funding in the short term—in favor of a priority ministry—in exchange for additional funding down the line. In effect, the cooperative nature of the SWG process forced individual spending ministries to better understand the opportunity cost of their own spending proposals, to provide better information on their own spending, and to be prepared to look for greater efficiencies in their own spending.

The SWGs' work culminates in the production of an SWG report. These reports document SWG analysis and decisions in accordance with the SWG functions listed previously. The report is a key document for ministries: it is the primary instrument through which their proposals for additional funding will be heard at the central level. The draft SWG reports are published before the sector hearings.

SECTOR HEARINGS. The sector hearings take place in February and March and provide an opportunity for government to consult with stakeholders on its spending proposals. The hearings are open to any member of the public. They are attended mostly by sector NGOs, research organizations, and sector donors.

THE BUDGET STRATEGY PAPER. The BSP is the second and final prebudget statement and marks the end of the MTEF phase of the MTEF-budget process. The paper updates the BOPA in terms of the macroeconomic outlook and the macrofiscal framework and provides a sector-by-sector discussion of recent fiscal performance, priorities, constraints, expenditure allocations, and performance indicators and targets. The paper is prepared by the Ministry of Finance and provides the final ministry ceilings for the preparation of the annual estimates. As such, it is discussed and approved by the cabinet.

The BOPA and the BSP are important fiscal transparency instruments in Kenya. Currently, the budget estimates themselves are still published in the detailed administrative and line-item format only. The only narrative information provided with the documentation package of the annual budget is the budget speech. The BSP, therefore, provides the only reference for external stakeholders to track how the allocations are related to spending priorities. Also, both the BOPA and the BSP impose discipline on the budget preparation process. The BOPA firms up the macrofiscal decisions, placing a firm ceiling on spending aggregates. The BSP provides the next decision-making platform: firm ministerial ceilings on which the annual budget preparation is based. Currently, however, the budget classification format makes tracking allocations at the subministerial level between the BSP and the annual budget very difficult.

PREPARING THE ANNUAL BUDGET. The preparation of detailed estimates commences when ministerial ceilings have been fixed through the SWG and BSP process. At this point, budget preparation still slips far too easily back into incremental line-item budgeting. The process revolves through several phases, with increasing involvement of more senior officials in the Ministry of Finance, and with involvement of the line ministries in the first two phases only. At the line-ministry level, proposals for the detailed estimates are prepared by budget and finance officers, often with insufficient consultation with planning officers and program managers. Because the budget and finance officials were not necessarily involved in the earlier phases of the MTEF process, the default process focuses on inputs and on existing spending pressures. It does not necessarily carry through any of the strategic prioritization that had been done in the preceding MTEF phase of budget preparation. The archaic and, at times, arbitrary ministry-specific budget classification does not facilitate easily tracking BSP commitments through to the annual estimates, leaving budget officers little option but to revert to more narrow, line-item-oriented allocation methodologies. As the annual estimates are taken through the Ministry of Finance review process, further decisions are made that relate to more traditional input-driven budgeting concerns than to the outcome- and output-driven policy concerns that guide the MTEF phase.

In the Ministry of Finance review process, ministerial estimates are first reviewed by the estimates working groups, which consist of officers from the line ministry, the Budget Supply Department, and the Ministry of Planning and National Development. The next review of the estimates is by the Budget Procedure Group, which is chaired by the director of the Budget Supply Department. The line ministry is not represented in this review, which culminates in ministerial budget statements. These statements are, in turn, reviewed by the Budget Steering Committee, which is chaired by the permanent secretary of the Ministry of Finance. A final step before finalizing the documentation and laying it before the legislature is seeking cabinet approval.

When the annual budget arrives in the legislature, it therefore contains decisions on intravote allocations that do not derive fully from the earlier MTEF processes and that have had insufficient input from line-ministry officials. This situation causes line ministries to question whether their inputs have been taken into account adequately. They thus will argue that they are underfunded by the Ministry of Finance and will therefore find it difficult to deliver on their mandates. The situation also prompts immediate requests for reallocations and additional funds. At the political level, the negotiation of final allocations at the ministerial level is done without sufficient participation from the cabinet, resulting in low political commitment to the tradeoffs made. This disconnect between the commitments made by ministries in the SWG and BSP process and their final detailed allocations is exacerbated by the tabling in the legislature of the recurrent and development expenditure estimates without narrative text to clarify how the detailed intraministerial allocations relate to ministry objectives, priorities, and activities. The MTEF phase's emphasis on line ministries being explicit about what they can deliver, given funding, thus is largely negated by the annual budget phase.

CLASSIFICATION REFORM. Up to the 2005/06 budget, all budget reforms in Kenya were undertaken using the same underlying budget structure and budget classification system. The budget was classified by vote, by budget head and subhead, and subsequently by line item. In 2005, the first phase of reforms to the budget structure and classifications was undertaken with the replacement of the line-item classifications with a *Government Finance Statistics Manual 2001*–compatible economic classification system (IMF 2001). However, this one-dimensional reform was grafted onto the existing head and subhead structure.

Across and within ministries, therefore, no consistency prevails as to how budget heads and subheads relate. They can be either administrative units or quasi-programmatic classifications (such as primary education in the Ministry of Education). It is therefore difficult to see what money is being spent on. When reallocations are made, they are usually by line item, making it difficult to see how adjustments relate to policy priorities.

The government aims to introduce a program-based classification for the 2007/08 budget. This reform would replace the head and subhead system of budget classification with a program and subprogram classification structure, clearly relating to ministerial objectives and identifying key indicators for each program. For the reform to be successful, however, it would need to be reflected in a redrafted chart of accounts and implemented in budget execution through a working integrated financial management information system (IFMIS). Although the design of programs and performance indicators and targets is a challenging task in itself, it can be done in a relatively short time. However, experience elsewhere suggests that implementing program budgeting without the ability to link it directly in a multidimensional classification and accounts system to expenditure can be a waste of limited reform capacity in a government. Kenya still faces significant challenges in implementing a working IFMIS (see later discussion).

CORE POVERTY PROGRAMS. The concept of core poverty programs was introduced into the MTEF-budget cycle in 2000/01. The expenditures are identified within the existing budget classification system using a set of predetermined criteria. These expenditures are prioritized during budget preparation and are supposed to be protected from budget cuts during budget execution. The core poverty list excludes wage expenditure.

Since the introduction of the concept, the core poverty expenditures have constituted a significant and increasing share of ministerial expenditure. In 2000/01, the recurrent core poverty program was estimated at 7 percent of nonwage and noninterest expenditure and the development component at 14 percent of the development budget. By 2003, the recurrent program accounted for 17 percent of nonwage and noninterest spending and 25 percent of the development estimates (Republic of Kenya 2003b).

The growth comes from two sources. First, a small portion of it is attributable to the growth in the original component spending activities on the program list. Second and more significant, the growth in the program is a reflection of changes in the original criteria. Transfers to the Local Authority Transfer Fund and the Road Maintenance Levy Fund—as well as donor funding for qualifying projects—have increased the program size significantly.

The original criteria for including spending in the core poverty program were agreed with development partners. Programs that directly created employment; provided access to basic education; increased agricultural productivity; ensured access to health services; reduced gender disparity; provided decent shelter, clean water, and sanitation; and rehabilitated criminals—as well as programs aimed at managing disasters and emergencies and protecting the environment—qualified for inclusion in the core poverty program. In 2003/04, these criteria were revised to take into account new programs that were identified in the IP-ERS. Specifically, the new criteria sought to cover pro-poor programs that would increase incomes of the poor and improve their quality of life, security, and social equality.

Although the core poverty programs are supposed to be ring-fenced from expenditure cuts, full disbursement rates have not been achieved. In many cases, the amounts disbursed are not used fully, and in some cases the disbursed moneys are used for other programs (Republic of Kenya 2004a). Since 2004, some effort has been made to improve the reporting on core poverty programs, including the development of a monitoring format. They are also covered in the quarterly in-year review of spending (Republic of Kenya 2004/05).

Most recently, the 2005 PER (Republic of Kenya 2005) recommended that the core poverty programs take an even more central role in budgeting, prioritizing expenditures at the ministerial level around the core poverty programs and linking them to the core performance indicators identified in the annual progress review of the IP-ERS (see box 14.2). The targets set for these indicators should be implemented by specific programs, forming a set of core *priority* programs. The identified core priority programs should replace the core poverty programs, receive priority in resource allocation and disbursement, and be monitored and evaluated regularly. At the time of writing, these recommendations were still under discussion.

Remaining challenges in the budget preparation process

Over decades, Kenya has carried out various reforms to its allocative budget process in an effort to focus scarce public resources on critical development activities. Yet, despite having many of the institutions required for a sound process—such as use of top-down ceilings, thorough review instruments, cooperative forums, and budget transparency mechanisms—government PERs and other analytical work have consistently found that key problems persist, such as poor links between policy and budget allocations, low budget credibility, pending bills, and stalled projects. A need exists to sequence the allocative process better and reduce duplication between phases and instruments, as well as to cure significant gaps and deficiencies that remain in the process.

CLASSIFICATION REFORMS. Although the reforms changed the structures and processes of the budget preparation process, only recently has the underlying budget structure and classification system been addressed. Insofar as core incentives for budget management are tied up with budget structure and classification—for example, if the budget is structured by administrative unit, allocations are more likely to be driven by the input cost of organizations than by the outputs required to meet policy objectives— this situation would tend to force budgeting back to line-item incremental budgeting. A programmatic classification that enables better links between policy priorities, ministerial objectives, and funding programs would help bring the final stage of detailed budgeting in line with earlier sector and ministerial allocation processes. Fully reforming the classification system and linking the new budget classifications to budget controls and the chart of accounts for implementation and reporting should be a priority on the reform agenda.

Ministerial-level budget processes have not been reformed at the same pace as central processes. Although ministries comply with the central demand for more and different types of information for budgetary decision making at the center, the production of this information within ministries is not the result of a thorough process that replicates central MTEF principles within ministries. This situation compromises ownership of the information that is passed on to the central level in most cases and the quality of the information in some cases. In addition to the political will to run thorough processes at the ministerial level, ministries also require the necessary capacity.

COSTING AND REPRIORITIZATION. The costing of spending proposals is not robust. In the MPERs, baseline spending projections are not robust. Ministries have little experience in costing, and although the Ministry of Finance has some capacity and has developed an internal generic approach to assist in budget preparation, there is a critical need to improve the quality of forward financial information. The MPERs and sector reports have not yet linked existing spending clearly enough to objectives. Partly, the quality of financial and nonfinancial information is at the root of weak information about the cost of government. But the guidelines within the budget process do not require a clear enough distinction between (a) existing spending and the adjustments to existing spending that ministries desire and (b) new spending that they may be proposing. In practice, key input budget documentation pays attention to these issues in the narratives but tends to jumble the financial information together in aggregate spending tables. This practice makes minimizing incrementalism and optimizing reprioritization very difficult.

Institutional barriers to integrating planning and budgeting

Issues between the Ministry of Finance and the Ministry of Planning and National Development about who does what in linking planning and budgeting at the central level interfere with the establishment of a stream-lined, coordinated central process. Both ministries are developing modalities to link policy making, financing, and monitoring and evaluation of performance—but separately. Although they do consult, it is often only after modalities have been developed.

The continued separation of planning and budgeting for investment and recurrent spending between the development budget and the recurrent budget, respectively, holds back the effectiveness with which ministries can plan for the best possible use of available resources in implementing policy priorities. Although the MTEF process does attempt to integrate the two budgets, even in the MTEF phase ministries are required to plan for the two budgets separately. Sector ceilings are broken down into component development recurrent parts, limiting ministries' ability to make tradeoffs between the two in the budget preparation phase. However, they do make the tradeoffs during the spending year, when money is shifted between the budgets.

Although some evidence indicates the SWGs function well when they perceive their tasks to have a meaningful effect on allocations, in some sectors they remain ineffective. The current SWG setup is problematic insofar as some ministries are represented in a number of sectors and some important line items, such as salaries and transfers, are outside of SWGs' sphere of influence. These items are still treated incrementally at the central level.

Although the SWGs can be successful as sector-level forums that ensure policy contestability, the central process through which tradeoffs are made between sectors (and their component ministries) is too diffuse, and the rules that govern allocations are not stated clearly enough. Even though the sector reports are the instrument for proposing new policies, it is not clear what instrument ministries should use to bring proposals to the sector and what the formats and criteria should be. The transition from the SWG phase to the annual budgeting phase is not clean enough, and it is not clear whether ministries have opportunities earlier and later in the process to influence their allocations. Finally, the involvement of the cabinet is not frequent enough in the process to ensure that decisions are perceived as government of Kenya decisions, rather than those of the Budget Supply Department in the Ministry of Finance. All these factors undermine the legitimacy and governmentwide ownership and acceptance of ministerial ceilings.

Comprehensiveness of the budget

The effectiveness of the budget preparation process is marred further by significant amounts of resources being planned for and spent outside the scrutiny of the central budget process. More than 20 percent of the budget is spent in transfers to public agencies (Khasiani and Makau 2006) in addition to funds such as the Constituency Development Fund (see box 14.3). Despite efforts by government to curb the growth in transfers to public agencies, they are still being created. Public agencies are either autonomous bodies that produce goods and services and are not necessarily dependent on the exchequer or semiautonomous bodies established through government legislation or decree to deliver specific services. Another set of organizations includes various funds that either charge fees or are funded by earmarked revenues.

Khasiani and Makau (2006) list several reasons governments choose to set up agencies to provide services. These reasons vary from improving effectiveness and efficiency, to offering incentives to raise more revenues (as in the case of the Health Fund and the Veterinary Fund), to attracting and retaining skilled personnel, to securing funding through earmarked revenues and protecting certain functions from undue political influence (as in the case of the Anticorruption Commission). Such funds, however, present particular budget management problems, including the following:

■ They create a burden on the exchequer without being subject to the same prioritization processes as the central civil service.
■ They are a source of contingent liabilities.
■ They duplicate activities undertaken by central ministries. (In some cases, specific mandates have long since lapsed and duplicate capacity has been set up inside the central government to deliver similar services.)
■ They have limited accountability because the agencies operate outside the budget process with revenues that do not pass through the exchequer and are not subject to the standard controls and procedures applicable to other public resources.
■ They are a source of budget inflexibility, requiring that some agencies receive a set percentage of available resources.
■ Exit plans to close down agencies when they are no longer relevant are lacking.

BOX 14.3   Budget Comprehensiveness and the Constituency Development Fund

The Constituency Development Fund was established by an act of the legislature to take development projects to the citizens at the grassroots level. The strategy was conceptualized as complementary to the government's other development activities, funded through the recurrent and development budgets. The act, drafted by the legislature when the new government came into power, stipulates that 2.5 percent of ordinary revenue must be set aside for the fund. The act stipulates that members of the legislature are responsible for establishing constituency development committees that will prioritize project proposals from each constituency. Allocations per constituency are based on a population poverty index, with each constituency receiving a base allocation plus a variable portion in line with constituencies' index scores.

Although allocation of some funds by constituencies to constituency priorities can have benefits in terms of local participation, accountability, and effectiveness, the fund's link to the legislators may trigger some of the governance problems associated with poorly managed participatory processes. Reports have circulated of legislators using the funds as an instrument of local patronage and of local elites capturing decision making regarding use of funds. Monitoring and reporting mechanisms that have been set up centrally are not functioning well enough to counter these types of problems.

As discussed in the 2005 public expenditure review (Republic of Kenya 2005), the establishment of various special funds by members of the legislature poses a number of public finance management problems. These funds are not subject to the same control, reporting, and accountability procedures as spending under the main budget. More significantly, this process fragments public spending, thereby hindering a comprehensive consideration of all claims on spending against the complete pool of available funds. In practice, the projects undertaken are not accounted for in recurrent budget allocations: when a constituency uses its funds to build a secondary school, no mechanism exists to ensure that the school is adequately staffed on completion. Of course, the fund also affects the efficiency of public resource use: the location of roads, schools, and other public infrastructure funded by the Constituency Development Fund—with a forward effect on the recurrent budget—is not determined by a consideration of cost and benefits across localities and of economies of scale. Although 2.5 percent of ordinary revenue is not a huge proportion on its face, it grows in significance when taken as a proportion of spending after interest and short-term rigid spending, such as salaries. In addition, the legislature has called to increase the proportion of ordinary revenue earmarked for the fund.

Source: Republic of Kenya 2005.

Realizing the costs and complexities of these agencies, the government of Kenya embarked on a reform program aimed at reducing the burden on the exchequer. The program would wind down some of the agencies and privatize their functions (Khasiani and Makau 2006). Ministries are now responsible for ensuring that they include agencies under their control and oversight in MTEF planning. From the 2005/06 budget, ministries are also required to fund any additional requests from agencies from within their own budget ceilings.

Implementing a stronger link between planning and budgeting is a function not only of the budget allocation process, but also of how well the institutions of budget implementation link the intentions expressed through the budget to activities that take place on the ground. The next section briefly discusses key reforms in budget execution.

Reforms in Budget Execution

Budget implementation in Kenya comes with a long history of deviation from the planned budget. The 2005 PER (Republic of Kenya 2005) found that underspending on the development budget has been substantial (42 percent underspending in 2003/04) and rising, making it very difficult for the government to achieve the IP-ERS objectives. Recurrent budget deviation varies but is still significant. Historically, some ministries overspend while others absorb that cost and underspend. In cash terms, spending is often understated, because arrears that are built up are not captured. Pending bills are a significant problem affecting financial management and control. Deviation and rising pending bills reflect poor budgeting and planning, undisciplined budget execution, lack of compliance with regulations, lack of accountability, poor recordkeeping and management, weak procurement and contracting systems, and low project completion rates. Often, incomplete projects and pending bills attract large penalties and interest, which diverts resources from identified priorities.

In contrast to the pre-MTEF years, the public finance reform program in Kenya extended its scope to include budget execution issues to address such deficiencies. The chapter now discusses a number of reforms that belong particularly to systems of cash release management, expenditure control, accounting, reporting, and monitoring.

Controlling cash management and commitment

The Ministry of Finance introduced a new system of cash-flow management and zero-balance drawing accounts to synchronize cash inflows with budget requirements and to reduce liquidity in the system, thereby reducing the demand for debt.

The new system revolves around improved cash-flow planning, at both the central and ministerial levels. Ministries are required to submit an annual cash plan from which a monthly breakdown can be derived. Cash management units were to be set up in ministries to prepare the plans and manage the ministries' zero-balance accounts. Different line items are treated differently. Salaries are estimated at one-twelfth of total spending, contractual obligations are derived from contract terms and summed, while capital goods, construction, and other procurement are forecast by ministry, taking into account timetables for procurement and delivery. Working from their annual plans and work and procurement plans, ministries are required to provide on a monthly basis a three-month rolling cash-flow forecast, which provides a weekly breakdown for the first month and aggregate data for the subsequent two months.

At the central level, the cash management unit in the Accountant General's Department receives and consolidates the cash-flow plans to develop an overall governmentwide cash-flow plan that synchronizes inflows, outflows, and debt issuance.

Zero-balance drawing accounts have been established at the Central Bank of Kenya, against which ministries make payments that are underwritten by the Treasury up to a ministry's credit limit. The limits are set on a monthly basis and are based on a ministry's approved cash-flow plans. At the end of each business day, a standing order payment settles all debits and credits on ministries' accounts against the Treasury funding account, restoring the balance to zero. The credit limit is immediately adjusted by the debits, thus determining the next day's credit limit. Any debit that exceeds the credit limit is rejected by the system. Memorandum accounts are also set up for each ministry to record the cumulative transactions. Daily statements on zero-balance and memorandum accounts are provided to ministries by the Central Bank.

Making clear budget implications of new policies

In the past, the cabinet often approved outside the budget process ministries' policy proposals with financial implications without reference to the Ministry of Finance. When the cabinet approved the proposals after the budget had been presented to parliament, the budget framework was undermined. For the 2005/06 budget, the Ministry of Finance issued a Treasury circular which stated that all policy proposals to the cabinet had to be accompanied by an assessment of the policy against IP-ERS objectives, an assessment of the proposal against priorities captured in the BSP, and an assessment of the likely financial implications on the ministry's published budget. Ministries are required to indicate how they intend to fund the new proposals from within their existing ceilings, and all submissions to the cabinet are now required to have Treasury signoff.

Using information technology better

Kenya initiated an IFMIS in 2003. In principle, this reform should be a cornerstone of a working financial management platform for fiscal discipline, spending effectiveness, and efficiency. Despite the original deadline of 2006, as yet the system is not being used in any ministry. One reason for the delay has been the introduction of the new *Government Finance Statistics Manual 2001*–compliant classification system (IMF 2001), which had to be integrated into a new chart of accounts and loaded into the IFMIS system. However, although the general-ledger, accounts payable, and purchase-order modules of the system were installed in the Ministry of Finance and the Ministry of Planning and National Development for the 2005/06 budget year, the ministries' staffs have not used the system fully but prefer to use the legacy systems. Although hardware, software, and training have been provided to an additional 21 ministries, the same pattern is repeated elsewhere. Having a working and used IFMIS is critical for improving implementation discipline: the envisaged system provides significant functionality to manage Kenya's particular public finance setup. For example:

- District and ministry spending can be reconciled, providing ministries with better up-to-date management information on implementation of activities and remaining resources.
- A separate classification code is provided to identify district spending, allowing transactions at this level to be distinguished from central transactions.
- Although the new cash management system reduces liquidity in the system, it does not provide robust commitment controls, which are required at an earlier point in the budget execution cycle. In principle, ministries can still issue authority to incur expenditure without the necessary funds being available in the required budget category. This problem is addressed in a functioning IFMIS that would not allow purchase orders to be issued.
- Expenditure control can be exercised on annual votebook data. However, given that the cash release system reconfirms authority to spend, the system can control on the basis of periodic cash releases. This function will assist in reducing arrears.

Like Kenya, governments face similar challenges in implementing reforms such as an IFMIS, program budgeting, and new charts of accounts. Reforms like these that are systemwide and require the participation of a range of officials in getting details right rarely succeed unless managed as a change-management process, with consistent training and implementation backup. Institutionalizing IFMIS at the core of the government's financial management is a huge outstanding challenge for the Ministry of Finance and an urgent one. Significant problems in budget execution can be addressed through the systematic, supported implementation of an IFMIS.

Publishing quarterly reports

The Ministry of Finance publishes a quarterly progress report that provides comprehensive information on budget implementation. Although the accuracy of these reports is not always guaranteed because of late reporting and nonreporting by spending ministries, difficulties in sourcing information from donors on the development budget, and doubts about the accuracy of information, their institutionalization as an important public source of information in the Kenyan system significantly improves the transparency of the public finances. The reports provide information on the overall fiscal balance; revenue collection; government expenditure (broken down by significant categories of spending, including spending on core poverty programs); the stock of pending bills; contingent liabilities; and debt.

Using public expenditure tracking surveys

Kenya has only recently started to institutionalize public expenditure tracking surveys (PETSs). As in many other developing countries, social outcomes do not correspond with rising spending on social services. Kenya has made considerable progress in introducing reforms to planning and budget preparation to improve the allocation of resources to priorities. It has also more recently started to look at reforms in budget execution, accounting, reporting, and monitoring systems to ensure a better link between the budget and implementation. However, increases in funding will not necessarily translate into improvements in the delivery of basic services, even if the funds are disbursed. A PETS is a useful instrument for tracking how funds are transferred and used right down to the location of service delivery. The first Kenyan PETS was undertaken in 2003/04, by the Kenya Institute for Public Policy Research and Analysis, an arm's length research institution. This first study looked at the core social service ministries of education, health, and agriculture and sourced information from ministry headquarters to the districts, divisions, and facilities on the ground. Random samples were selected across the country, using sampling methods that were statistically suited to the area and the sector being investigated. Data were collected for 1997 to 2002 on inputs, outputs, quality and quantity of service, financing and institutional mechanisms, and the accountability systems used (Nafula and others 2004). The results of the study were diverse but showed critical shortcomings in policy and in institutions for delivery. The study quantified and highlighted leakage of resources in the health sector, particularly drugs, and the presence of ghost workers in the education sector. Poor record-keeping and accountability, as well as inadequacies in the deployment of resources in the sectors, were uncovered (Nafula and others 2004: 63).

In 2004, the Ministry of Finance, together with the planning ministry, the health ministry, and the education ministry, undertook a joint PETS of two core poverty programs: rural health services and the secondary school bursary program. Similar to the initial survey, the findings showed the present budgeting process and financial administration of funds are weak and prone to fraud. In the education program, the report pointed to weaknesses in the reporting system that undermined accountability for funds received. The report also revealed weaknesses in targeting (Republic of Kenya 2004b).

Currently, the government has made no clear commitment to institutionalize PETSs. However, the first surveys have brought valuable information to light.

Looking for solutions for the remaining challenges

Overall, the public finance reform program (see the discussion in the concluding section) recognizes that, despite these reforms, key weaknesses in budget execution persist and further reforms in budget preparation will have very little benefit unless budget execution reforms provide a stable platform of in-year budget management. In addition to the issues previously discussed, several problems persist (Republic of Kenya 2006b):

■ The quality, accuracy, and timeliness of financial reports and accounting are still poor. The financial records do not provide sufficient information for decision makers and are limited in scope by one-dimensional accounting structures.
■ The quality of the information in financial reports is still low.
■ Compliance with Treasury instructions remains problematic. For example, the fiscal reporting system depends on the reconciliation of records of exchequer releases and expenditure returns from ministries. It is not

unusual for returns to reach the Ministry of Finance up to three weeks late (the deadline being the 15th of every month), and in some instances, returns have been two months late. Partly, accountability is weak because sanctions—although provided for in legislation, regulations, and circulars—are rarely enforced. Although the government has given the Exchequer Committee a mandate to hold back the release of funds to spending ministries until they submit their returns, this procedure has not been implemented.

- Payroll control and integration between the new payroll and IFMIS systems are poor.
- Although the government recently introduced a new legislative framework for procurement, including new structures and institutions, the system is weakened by the lack of further regulations.
- Audit reports continue to be late. The scope of the audit office's mandate is still too narrow, and its independence needs to be strengthened. A positive development is the program to change the scope of internal audit away from preaudit and verification to risk-based and systems audit. New audit committees have been set up, but guidelines and manuals still need to be completed.

Milestones and Remaining Challenges

Since 2000, Kenya has embarked on a comprehensive budget reform program aimed at addressing critical weaknesses in budget formulation, budget execution, accounting, monitoring, and reporting institutions. The introduction of MTEF budgeting in 2000/01 was a major reform in budget planning and formulation. Since then, the budget preparation process has been strengthened by the introduction of specific instruments within the MTEF-budget process. A major benefit of the reforms has been a significant increase in fiscal transparency: stakeholders within and outside of government have year-on-year access to much more information on policies, allocations, and spending effectiveness.

However, the process is still plagued by a critical disconnect between the MTEF phase and the annual budget preparation and by the shortcomings of the underlying budget structure and classification system. In addition, despite initial reforms on the budget execution side, budget implementation discipline is still very weak. These factors underpin difficulties in realizing political priorities in the budget.

In response, the government of Kenya—together with development partners—designed a comprehensive approach to further reforms that aims to be sequenced and prioritized to secure progress and build on existing successes. Key to the reform program is building professional capacity for public finance management, clarifying roles and reconfiguring structures at the central level to reduce overlap and improve coordination, and reviewing the legal framework to consolidate different existing legal instruments in comprehensive framework legislation.

The reform program will include components to improve the credibility of the budget, comprehensiveness and transparency, policy-based budgeting, predictability and control in budget execution, accounting and reporting, external scrutiny, and audit. Interventions in these categories have been sequenced through a series of enabling platforms, each with its own deliverables. The reform program is scheduled over a period of 7 to 10 years. The sequencing is structured as shown in table 14.2.

Although the design of a comprehensive reform program that recognizes the links between public finance management institutions represents important progress, the greatest challenge in Kenya is to harness sufficient

TABLE 14.2   Reform Program Sequencing

Platform	Deliverables
Short-term perspective	Improved quality of financial records and credibility in budget execution for central ministries Competitive and open procurement Improved payroll management and improved collection of revenue
Medium-term perspective	Improved quality of financial records and budget execution for remaining entities at central, regional, and local levels Improved budget preparation and allocations
Long-term perspective	Introduction of accountability and result-based management Improved control of payroll, fixed assets, and pensions Improved accuracy of forecast and projections Reduced tax evasion and increases in revenue Reduced costs of debt financing
Over 10 years	Substantial improvements in service delivery, with increases in allocation in accordance with political priorities Improved effectiveness and efficiency in public service

Source: Republic of Kenya 2006b.

political will at all levels of government to make the reforms count. This political will needs to be backed up by a core of motivated implementers who can manage changes, demonstrate benefits, and pass on skills. Over years of reforms, institutions and individuals in the system have learned that although budget reforms may introduce new ways of doing things at a surface level, they do not necessarily require fundamental changes in how actors in the system behave. Changing the behavior of institutions and individuals on the ground requires them to be accountable for the results of planning, budgeting, and spending. Accountability, in turn, requires political will to enforce sanctions and make clear where responsibility lies.

References

Byaruhanga, Charles V. 2004. *Review of the Medium Term Expenditure Framework.* Nairobi: Republic of Kenya.

IMF (International Monetary Fund). 2001. *Government Finance Statistics Manual.* Washington, DC: IMF Statistics Department. http://www.imf.org/external/pubs/ft/gfs /manual/pdf/all.pdf.

Khasiani, Kubai, and Phyllis Makau. 2005. "Kenya: Integrating Expenditure towards Policy Priorities." In *Budget Reform Seminar: Country Case Studies*, ed. Alta Fölscher, 21–34. Pretoria: Expenditure Planning Unit, Budget Office, National Treasury.

———. 2006. "Decentralising Public Functions to Public Entities." In *Managing Complexity: From Fragmentation to Co-ordination,* ed. Alta Fölscher, 109–28. Pretoria: CABRI Secretariat.

Kiringai, Jane, and Geoffrey West. 2002. "Budget Reforms and the Medium-Term Expenditure Framework in Kenya." KIPPRA Working Paper 7, Kenya Institute for Public Policy Research and Analysis, Nairobi.

Nafula, Nancy N., Paul K. Kimalu, Jane Kiringai, Raphael Owino, Damiano K. Manda, and Stephen Karingi. 2004. "Budget Mechanisms and Public Expenditure Tracking in Kenya." KIPPRA Discussion Paper 37, Kenya Institute for Public Policy Research and Analysis, Nairobi.

Republic of Kenya. 2003a. "MTEF Budget Preparation Guidelines for the Period 2004/5–2006/7." Treasury Circular 26/2003, Ministry of Finance, Nairobi.

———. 2003b. *Public Expenditure Review 2003.* Nairobi: Republic of Kenya.

———. 2004a. *Public Expenditure Review 2004.* Nairobi: Republic of Kenya.

———. 2004b. *Public Expenditure Tracking Survey Preliminary Report.* Nairobi: Republic of Kenya.

———. 2004/05. *Quarterly Budget Review, Fourth Quarter 2004/5.* Nairobi: Republic of Kenya.

———. 2005. *Public Expenditure Review 2005.* Nairobi: Republic of Kenya.

———. 2006a. "Budget Outlook Paper 2006/7–2008/9." Republic of Kenya, Nairobi.

———. 2006b. "Strategy for the Reform of Public Finance Management." Republic of Kenya, Nairobi.

15

Country Case Study: South Africa

ALTA FÖLSCHER

The 1994 transition to a democratic state brought many challenges for managing public finances in South Africa. Not only did the new constitutional dispensation determine a changed structure and distribution of power in the state, with implications for the way public funds were allocated and used, but the new government also had a critical political commitment to improving the coverage and quality of public service delivery to redress the racially based distortions of the past. The transition to a new system of budget management occurred, therefore, not in a context of policy stability but simultaneously with a major overhaul of government policies. In practice, the results have been uneven.

Although on the surface the government succeeded in introducing a medium-term expenditure framework (MTEF) approach to budget management, overhauled the legal framework for financial management, reformed the classification system, and put in place a functioning system of intergovernmental transfers, these changes have not consistently resulted in improved service delivery. Many gaps remain between public policy commitments and functional implementation.

This chapter describes the reform approach and milestones, noting where reforms fell short of their intent and where gaps remain.

Background to Reforms

The constitution provides the institutional framework for budget reforms in South Africa. It details the structure of the new state; provides a framework for expenditure and revenue assignment; sets out key institutions, roles, and responsibilities; and establishes the principle of cooperative governance, which sets the tone for a consensus-seeking budget process. However, the constitution largely leaves further national legislation and practice to sort out how these principles are given effect.

At the time of the democratic transition in 1994, the new government did not start with a clean fiscal slate. In fiscal year 1992/93, the main budget's net borrowing requirement had reached 8.7 percent of gross domestic product (GDP), and in fiscal year 1994/95, public debt rose to almost 47 percent of GDP (from a level of approximately 30 percent 10 years earlier), leaving very little fiscal room for the state to improve the equity of public services. The annual budgeting system that the new government inherited provided inadequate tools with which to stabilize fiscal balances and manage the required policy shifts. The system was highly fragmented, not only in terms of a delinking of policy, budgeting, and implementation, but also institutionally, increasing budgeting uncertainty, lack of clarity, and the scope for budget games. It planned and controlled for inputs and cash, with limited opportunity for systematically assessing the effectiveness and efficiency of spending or for relating allocations directly to policy. It was not transparent, with poor underlying information systems, hidden spending, and inadequate mechanisms to extract good information for use in the budget process and for accountability purposes. The budget process itself was largely incremental, offering insufficient opportunity for the new government to identify ongoing nonpriority activities and create fiscal room for higher priorities. Accountability was procedural, and the system was plagued by deeply entrenched inefficiencies.

The new structure of state also required a system rethink. Compared with a complex state with parallel structures of government serving different population groups, the new South Africa was a unitary state with three interdependent but distinct spheres of government: national, provincial, and local. The constitution assigns to each of the three spheres of government certain functions, which may be concurrent (shared responsibility between spheres) or exclusive (sole responsibility of the unit of government). The national government's main role is policy making, regulation, and oversight. It also administers exclusive functions (for example, justice, defense, and foreign affairs). Provinces are mainly responsible for social delivery, either concurrently with national government (for example, primary and secondary education, health, social services, and housing) or exclusively (for example, provincial culture matters and provincial sport, recreation, and amenities), while municipalities have localized functions (for example, stormwater management and firefighting) and deliver basic services (for example, water, sanitation, electricity, and refuse removal).

The expenditure mandates of provinces and municipalities are not matched by their assigned revenue-raising abilities, although less so for local government, which has access to property taxes and user charges for services. The lion's share of revenue is collected nationally. Provinces (and to a lesser extent municipalities) therefore depend on transfers from national government to fulfill their expenditure responsibilities. The constitution states that provinces and municipalities are entitled to an equitable share of nationally collected revenue and that they may borrow under certain conditions. A key additional intergovernmental-relations feature of the constitutional framework is cooperative governance. This feature requires that the spheres of government coordinate their actions and legislation and that they exercise their powers in a manner that does not encroach on the geographic, functional, or institutional integrity of government in another sphere.

The provisions of the constitution regarding intergovernmental relations and the intergovernmental fiscal system are supported by various pieces of legislation enacted in the first years after transition, providing the legal framework for ongoing intergovernmental relations supported by the evolution of practice. Neither the constitution nor supporting legislation spells out quantitative parameters for revenue sharing or explores the minutiae of cooperative governance. The constitution sets out the principles and requires subsequent acts of Parliament to determine how these principles are to be applied and their requirements met. The supportive legislation enacted in the first years after the 1994 transition also does not primarily legislate policy specifics but puts in place sets of institutional arrangements to facilitate the best possible substantive outcome to be found in any given year or circumstance. These institutions, together with procedural reforms, compose the new South African budget system.

Reform Outcomes

South Africa's reform process has had mixed results. Although better management of public finances has contributed significantly to the country's recent improved growth record (growth has accelerated since 2001 from about 3 percent a year to just below 5 percent) and international credit standing, success at the level of policy implementation has been more qualified.

On the positive side, the reforms facilitated the disciplined implementation of fiscal policy aimed at setting the economy on a renewed growth path. The first few years after transition were still marked by relatively high deficits and a steady increase in public debt (to almost 50 percent in fiscal year 1996/97). The period from 1997 to 2000 saw fiscal consolidation (in tandem with other macroeconomic reforms), which stabilized the level of debt and reduced the budget deficit to contribute to lower interest rates; improve fiscal sustainability; and free resources for social, developmental, and infrastructure expenditure. Simultaneously, the overall burden of tax was reduced, lowering the costs of investment and job creation while releasing household spending power. Since 2001, a more expansionary fiscal stance has been adopted, which reaps the benefits of the consolidation period. These gains would not have been possible without the establishment of a functional intergovernmental system, introduction of medium-term expenditure planning, and improvements in public financial management.

Despite these macrofiscal successes, the improvements in public service delivery envisioned when the MTEF was introduced in the late 1990s have not materialized consistently. Although significant inroads into service backlogs were made in some sectors (see box 15.1), other areas, such as the integrated justice sector, administrative services to citizens, land reform, education, and health service delivery, have been the subject of much public debate and criticism.

Also, although overall budget credibility improved markedly after the implementation of a medium-term budget framework and public financial management improvements, recent years have seen increasing underspending as the implementation capacity of government departments has not grown in tandem with growth in funding. In both fiscal years 1995/96 and 1996/97, fiscal outputs for consolidated national and provincial spending showed up to 20 percent underexpenditure. In fiscal year 1997/98, the first year of a block unconditional transfer to provinces, this output swung to over 10 percent overexpenditure. This shift, however, was reversed and stabilized at less than 2 percent in fiscal year 1998/99, the first year of the MTEF. At the end of fiscal year 2005/06, expenditure ran at 99.5 percent of budget (while revenue was at 100.2 percent). However, the aggregate spending number masks significant underspending in some sectors.

By and large, the reforms that have occurred since 1997 put in place the foundations for modern public finance management in South Africa. With improved basic budget and financial management, a better base is in place from which to investigate improved ways of financing certain public services, such as social security payments. Frameworks for public-private partnerships

BOX 15.1   Improving the Quality of Public Spending

In the first few years after the new constitution was enacted, rapid change in the structure and management of the budget was accompanied by equally rapid changes in economic and fiscal policies. The quality of public spending has improved in several dimensions since 1996.

Improvement in the Aggregates

The conventional deficit has declined from 9 percent of GDP in 1995 to a balanced position in fiscal year 2005/06, and interest on debt will fall over the medium term to a projected 9.7 percent of consolidated expenditure (national and provincial general government expenditure and the social security funds) in fiscal year 2008/09 from 15 percent in fiscal year 2002/03. Between 2002/03 and 2005/06, noninterest expenditure grew at an annual average of 13.5 percent.

Shifts in Distribution of Expenditure

Over the first 12 years of democratic government, the functional distribution of expenditure has shifted significantly, with social and developmental expenditure increasing at the cost of defense and business subsidies. At the same time, distribution of expenditure shifted between households, with the government spending relatively more on poorer and marginalized communities than in the past.

Between 2002/03 and 2005/06, social expenditure continued to grow faster than consolidated expenditure overall (at 15 percent compared to 12 percent per year). In fiscal year 2006/07, social services accounted for 60 percent of noninterest expenditure. Although social security spending fueled the growth with the expansion of the social security system (average annual growth of 21 percent per year) between 2002/03 and 2005/06, more additional funds will be allocated to housing and community development programs over the medium term. The education sector still absorbs a higher proportion of funds than any other sector, accounting for 20 percent of noninterest expenditure in 2006/07, although it grew at a slightly slower rate than did the rest of the social services sector.

In the later years, the government has also shifted the economic distribution of expenditure, turning around negative real growth in gross fixed capital formation of general government. In the consolidation period, spending on the acquisition of capital assets and capital transfers was reduced. More recently, however, it has recovered. Gross fixed capital formation by general government grew by 10 percent per year between 2004 and 2008, compared to 3 percent growth in employee compensation and 8.4 percent growth in nonwage expenditure.

(Box continues on the following page.)

Better Access to Services

The growth in social service expenditure was driven by an expansion of the social security system, with approximately a quarter of the population receiving support grants from the state. This increase has had a direct effect on alleviating poverty in the country and mitigating the effects of HIV/AIDS. One of the fastest-growing grants has been the disability grant, which benefits people living with HIV/AIDS. Beneficiaries of the grant doubled between fiscal years 2001/02 and 2004/05 (to 1.3 million), and spending almost tripled.

The first 10 years of democracy have also seen investment in social infrastructure to improve access to basic services. The drive included building 1.6 million houses, improving access to schooling for the poor, constructing and upgrading primary health clinics, and extending and improving potable water supplies to 9 million people and sanitation facilities to more than 6 million people. This activity has affected the quality of life of millions, as demonstrated by improved access to water, shelter, sanitation, and energy as measured in the general household survey.

Source: National Treasury of South Africa 2004a, 2006a, 2006b.

for the financing of large infrastructure projects have already been developed and are being implemented. Examples are toll roads, hospitals, prisons, government buildings, and tourism initiatives that attracted significant amounts of private sector investment. South Africa has also gained good experience with the use of specialist agencies to deliver discrete services. Examples of successful reforms include the Roads Agency, the Legal Services Board, and the National Water Resource Infrastructure Agency.

Reform of the Budget System

Management of South African public finances has undergone many reforms over the past decade. These reforms can be bundled into sets of interconnected concerns: integrating the intergovernmental system and the annual budget process, establishing a credible budget process, establishing credible budgetary rules for decision making, establishing credible budgeting institutions, reforming the classification system and chart of accounts, and reforming the institutions of public financial management.

Integration of the Intergovernmental System and Annual Budget Process

The annual budget process provides the vehicle for the practical fulfillment of the constitutional and legislative requirements. The share of available revenue for provinces and municipalities is determined finally by the cabinet, but only after a process of intergovernmental consultation. In addition to their equitable share, which is a block grant, provinces and municipalities receive specific-purpose grants and other transfers that are intended to fulfill national policy imperatives in the subnational spheres.

The allocation of the equitable shares is determined in the same sequence annually. The first call on available revenue in the main budget framework is a provision for debt service cost and the contingency reserve, on the rationale that both support the financing of government functions in all three spheres. The remaining available revenue is then first divided between the three spheres of government before being divided between the provinces and municipalities by a transparent formula in the horizontal division of revenue process (and between national government departments in the national budget process).

The division of revenue process lasts from early May, when the national cabinet and provincial executive councils consider policy priorities, through October, when the government signals the likely division of revenue in the pre-budget policy statement known as the *Medium-Term Budget Policy Statement* (MTBPS). The division of revenue process should not be seen as a separate process from the national and provincial processes; instead, it is an integrated process both informed by and providing the respective expenditure envelopes to these processes.

The division of revenue between spheres of government (vertical division) follows the principle that funds should follow function and is informed by the responsibilities of each sphere and its capacity to generate revenue to meet its obligations, among other considerations. It is managed primarily as a political decision, however, because it derives from the relative priority given to different functions of government and how these functions are shared between the spheres of government. As such, it is discussed in the administrative and political spheres through the work of intergovernmental forums and is underpinned by technical work undertaken jointly by national and provincial treasury task teams. However, it is finally determined by a meeting of the extended national cabinet (the national cabinet plus the premiers of the nine provinces).

Intergovernmental forums to improve allocations

The main intergovernmental forums are the Budget Council and the Budget Forum, both of which are constituted under the terms of the Intergovernmental Fiscal Relations Act of 1997. The Budget Council is a consultative body, comprising the minister of finance and the nine provincial members of the Executive Council for Finance, assisted by the heads of treasury and treasury advisers. In the council, consensus is reached on fiscal and financial matters affecting the provincial government, and recommendations are made to the cabinet. The Budget Forum comprises the Budget Council plus local government representatives and discusses local government matters.

Discussions take place (from June to September each year) between the three spheres of government on the overall budget framework and the division of revenue between the spheres of government, primarily through the Budget Forums. These political-technical forums are supported by committees of officials preparing and discussing technical background work for use in the budget process. They include national and provincial treasury and sector department officials.

Use of formulas to maximize transparency and predictability

Only after the share of each sphere has been established is the horizontal division of revenue between the provinces determined, using transparent formulas that take into account national priorities, relative demand for services between provinces, and particular provincial circumstances. The practice is to phase in any drastic shifts in allocations on account of changes in formula structure or key determinant data so as not to upset the stability of provincial budgets. Similarly, the redistribution of resources from previously advantaged to disadvantaged provinces, which resulted from the formula structure and weighting, was phased in over the first few years of the formula.

The formula was recently reviewed to take account of the shifting of responsibility for social security payments. These used to be a provincial expenditure and were included in the block grant. However, provinces experienced difficulty budgeting for these payments as they grew on account of extended coverage. Often, other social expenditure was squeezed out. In addition, the weaker provinces had difficulty administering the grants. From 2006, social security payments are funded through the national budget and are administered by a national social security agency.

In South Africa, therefore, the sequencing of annual decision making on the allocation of available revenue to competing policies is inextricably bound up with the intergovernmental system. The institutions created within the system are key structures in the annual budget process. Aligning the intergovernmental and budgeting system through the budget process strikes a balance between the need to reduce the fiscal risk associated with decentralized systems and to coordinate national policy objectives, on the one hand, and the constitutional requirements of provincial autonomy, on the other.

A Credible Budget Process

One view of the MTEF is that it is the end result of explicit and implicit policy decisions and policy tradeoffs that were made by bureaucrats following the broad policy commitment of the executive and were finally decided on by the political principals. So, although the MTEF is usually presented as a broad conceptual framework with certain desirable features, it is the outcome of many layers of smaller decisions made by program and project managers in different spheres and at different levels of government. A signal achievement of the MTEF process in South Africa is the degree of coordination of these decisions toward policy priorities. This section provides a brief overview of how these decisions are sequenced.

The budget process allows the government to involve various role players that provide political and technical advice when faced with tradeoffs between competing spending priorities. It starts with the national cabinet determining the policy priorities and with high-level consultation between the minister of finance and other members of the cabinet, including provincial finance ministers. In the months that follow, from April to September, the two parallel dimensions of budget preparation take place: the determination of available resources and the preparation of information about the competing claims on those resources.

Top-down macroeconomic forecasts and fiscal policy targets are updated to prepare the national budget framework, followed by the vertical and horizontal divisions of revenue. Bottom-up national and provincial spending departments prepare their budget submissions, including reviewing and adjusting their strategic plans, costing, and preparing financial and nonfinancial proposals. In the middle, the national and provincial treasuries engage departments in discussions of pertinent policy issues, and joint research teams work on specific expenditure issues. The division of revenue process interacts with both these dimensions, all culminating in a prebudget statement (the MTBPS) tabled in the South African Parliament in late October. The MTBPS discusses macroeconomic and fiscal issues and sets out the vertical and horizontal division of revenue and the macrofiscal and expenditure frameworks. National departments and provincial governments are subsequently informed of their allocations. At the national level, spending departments then prepare their budget documentation. At the provincial level, clarity on final allocations allows the provincial budget process to enter its final rounds. The national and provincial budgets are tabled in February and March, respectively, for the year beginning April 1 (figure 15.1).

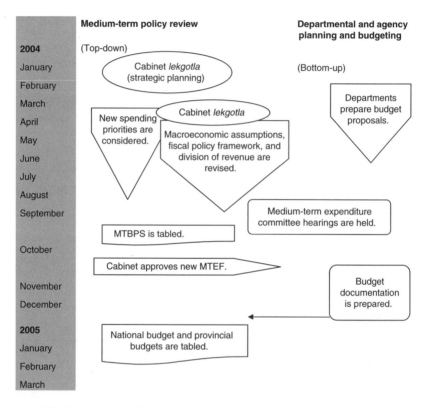

Source: National Treasury of South Africa 2004b.

FIGURE 15.1   The Budget Process, Fiscal Year 2004/05

Although a sequenced budget process has been a necessary part of reforms, the establishment of budgetary rules and improvements in transparency and accountability has made as important a contribution to creating a credible budget system.

Key Budgetary Institutions

Institutionalizing of an MTEF

The MTEF operates at the center of the South African budget reforms and frames, in the final instance, all policy discussions in the country. In the case of South Africa, the benefits of the MTEF have been realized, in part, through the application of clear objectives. The first of these objectives has been to ensure affordable program budgets through the preparation of spending plans within the context of existing macroeconomic and fiscal policies. The annual revision of these policies determines the extent of additional money that gets allocated for new priorities. The second objective of the MTEF is to strengthen the link between policy priorities and public expenditure, by ensuring early policy prioritization, rigorous evaluation of competing policies and programs, and matching of current and medium-term plans with available resources. Through this process, and over time, a higher proportion of public funds is spent on core programs that have the highest returns in terms of poverty alleviation, job creation, or whatever the government has put at the top of its agenda. In this way, the focus of public expenditure has gradually shifted with the changing needs of government and its main stakeholders. In recent years, for example, having a medium-term planning and budgeting perspective has assisted in facilitating a balance between spending on poverty alleviation, spending on economic services programs, and spending on physical infrastructure (see box 15.1).

Understanding how the MTEF operates to realize these objectives has two important dimensions. The first is that the MTEF system revolves around integrated sets of rolling national and provincial three-year forecasts, targets, and plans—from macroeconomic forecasts and fiscal targets, through revenue forecasts, to the forward projection of what public goods and services will be delivered by spending departments at what cost. These plans are the end product of the annual process by which the expenditure needs are matched to available resources. The second dimension is that the MTEF system is as much about the structures, institutions, and rules of the budget process as it is about the sets of three-year plans that result.

Differing from many other countries that have introduced multiyear budget frameworks, the South African system makes no differentiation between an MTEF and the annual budget process. Thus, the budget proposals that are voted by Parliament are prepared and considered in the MTEF process, coherently with the forward estimates, and are not revised separately from the forward estimates in a subsequent process. All budget estimates, down to subprogram level, are compiled for the full three-year period. This process strengthens the link between policy and planning. Instead of having two separated phases affecting budget allocations (with the first being of a more strategic policy nature and the second dealing with annual budgeting), the process in South Africa facilitates making strategic policy decisions in the context of budgeting decisions and vice versa. The sequencing, instead, is from larger aggregations of funding (and policy) to vote, program, and subprogram level, but keeping a medium-term perspective throughout.

The MTEF process is also the only avenue that spending ministries have for funding. Unless spending is unforeseen and unavoidable or caused by an emergency (in which case it is covered by a separate vote or the adjustment estimates), all spending is decided within the formal budget process and voted by Parliament (or the provincial legislatures) in one parliamentary budget process. Strict virement rules are applied in-year (discussed later). In addition, the budget process runs to a firm timetable with transparent rules and allocation norms.

A similarly disciplined process is followed for the adjustment estimates, which can be tabled legally at any time during the year. In practice, however, all claims on the additional available resources (from the drawdown of the contingency reserve, additional borrowing, or additional revenue collected) are brought together in one process, thereby improving contestability of policy.

Legislation that is tabled in cabinet (and eventually in Parliament) with spending and revenue implications is required to be accompanied by a memorandum that sets out what the financing implications are.

Fiscal policy to drive expenditure envelopes

As is common practice in most MTEFs, the top-down process starts with updating the forecasts for key macroeconomic variables over the medium term, including GDP and inflation. Fiscal policy targets are subsequently revised. Since the inception of the MTEF, these targets have included reducing the tax burden, reducing general government dissaving (use of domestic savings to fund recurrent rather than capital spending), reducing public debt as a percentage of GDP, and increasing public fixed-investment spending. The important point about budgeting systems is that fiscal policy targets are generally determined separately from any detailed expenditure bids. The overall available expenditure in the main budget framework is a function of what is fiscally affordable, which constrains and disciplines the subsequent spending choices. What is fiscally affordable is driven first by the targeted tax-to-GDP ratio and then by what level of borrowing is affordable.

The fiscal policy objectives translate into the budget framework, which in its various forms (depending on which component parts are included or excluded—see figure 15.2) presents a comprehensive and transparent aggregate picture of all revenue and all expenditure in general government at the national and provincial levels. All allocations at the national level are made from the available expenditure envelope in the budget framework, including funds for the national departments and unconditional and conditional grants to the provincial and local spheres of government. The nine provincial budget frameworks, therefore, reflect the national framework, with any differences being a function of a province's own revenue.

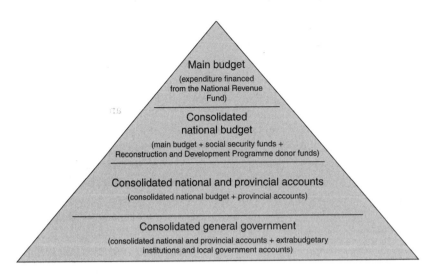

Source: National Treasury of South Africa 2006a.

FIGURE 15.2   Structure of Government Accounts

The annual budget documentation also includes an assessment of the wider public finances, including the public sector borrowing requirement and a discussion of contingent liabilities. This information provides transparency regarding all government's financial operations and its role in the economy.

In South Africa, implementation of the MTEF has not been hindered by overestimation of revenue, as is often the case. Three factors contribute to this result: the credibility of the macroeconomic assumptions, which are published in the prebudget statement and debated in public forums; the tax administration reforms, which buoyed revenue collection in the first few years, enabling the Treasury to provide predictability of funding to spending departments; and the use of the contingency reserve to absorb macroeconomic uncertainty.

Use of budget ceilings and forward (baseline) projections

All bids competing for the same envelope of available funds are considered in the budget process together within an overall hard budget constraint, forcing hard choices. This process may result in certain programs receiving additional funding, while others will be required to accelerate delivery within baseline budgets. In certain cases, the budget allocation process may result in programs having to release funding that can be used for new priorities.

At the same time as the top-down processes are completed to determine the available expenditure envelope, individual spending departments revise their forward plans, in accordance with their baseline funding envelopes of the previous year, and prepare spending bids advocating for additional funding. No adjustments are made to departmental ceilings at the beginning of the process. Departments can fund new policies only if they are able to convince the cabinet (or the provincial executive councils, in the case of provinces) to allocate a share of nationally (or provincially) available additional funds resulting from adjustments to the macroeconomic forecasts and fiscal targets or if they can find savings within their existing spending baselines. This practice of spending departments' starting their budget preparation from their existing funding baseline has the merits of imposing planning discipline and providing a stable medium-term funding and policy horizon. Forcing spending departments to live within their baselines, while holding them accountable for delivering on policy priorities, creates incentives to improve the quality of the forward projections.

In the system, flexibility around available additional funds and policy changes is least in the budget year, given existing policy and spending commitments, but increases toward the outer years because of a larger contingency reserve that can be allocated and because spending that is nondiscretionary in the short term, such as personnel costs, can be shifted over the medium term (for example, by restructuring a program or phasing in new priorities). In this way, South Africa has been able to reduce personnel spending as a percentage of revenue since the introduction of the MTEF, thus creating critical fiscal space for complementary inputs and investment spending.

For each budget round, baseline funding decisions have already been discussed for the bulk of spending in the first two years of any medium-term framework (those having rolled over from the previous year) and, particularly for the first year, the rule is to allow only minor changes. These factors shift the focus of discussions in the budget process to the use of funds in the outer year. Parliament is also increasingly centering its discussions on the outer years, when it can influence funding decisions more than in the year on which it is actually voting.

Evidence indicates, however, that the system of forcing tradeoffs against policy objectives over the medium term grows less robust lower down the allocation chain. For example, a weakness in the South African system is that in most cases at the departmental level, the available medium-term financing information is not consistently used to improve planning and implementation performance. At the end of the day, in managing programs and implementing projects on the ground, officials still very much operate in annual budgeting mode. For example, where schools choose their mix of textbooks and other support materials, they are provided neither with a ceiling nor a forward view on funding in future years. Hence, budgeting for textbooks still follows the traditional game of overrequesting followed by blanket cuts in a short-term planning horizon. And the budget request for textbooks that goes into the MTEF—one of the largest single items of expenditure after personnel cost—is the result of an incremental increase over the previous year's allocation.

However, in some cases, departments have switched internally to an MTEF approach to budgeting. The Western Cape Department of Health, for example, used the medium-term planning horizon of the MTEF to shift the mix of outputs that it provides to be more in line with a pro-poor policy stance (from secondary and tertiary care to primary care, for example) and to seek greater efficiency in the use of funds within the projected forward funding envelopes. A contributing factor to the department's adopting budget discipline and forward-planning norms was that the Western Cape Provincial Treasury treated expenditure overruns as borrowing from departments' own subsequent budgets.

The budget submission format encourages departments to focus on maximizing the alignment of policy and budgets over time by making changes at the margin. Reprioritization is pushed as an important budgeting principle that identifies savings that can be reallocated to priority programs. Departments are requested to provide information on their baseline spending (see box 15.2), changes within the baseline, and new proposals.

Changes to the baseline are either structural changes or policy options. *Structural changes* to the baseline are typically moderate adjustments for service delivery trends (such as higher than expected increases in demand for a service), higher salary increases, or the acquisition of specific scarce skills. These changes are considered by the medium-term expenditure committees (MTECs). *Policy options* involve changes within and in addition to the baseline to reflect changed priorities. Departments need to request additional resources. Requests involving new spending activities (policy options), as well as requests for additional funding given existing spending activities, need to be accompanied by a detailed costing of the proposals, spending plans over the MTEF period, legislative and administrative plans (such as personnel resource requirements), and implementation plans. Large new policy proposals or new services or activities that require careful examination to determine long-term affordability and alignment with government's priorities are also deliberated on and decided finally by the cabinet.

> **BOX 15.2** Examining Quality of Spending in Baselines
>
> The format and instructions for budget submissions require spending depart-
> ments to illustrate how spending within the baseline has been reviewed and
> how it will be reprioritized better to reflect departmental and government
> spending objectives. Departments are required to illustrate the following:
>
> - How they will revise their baseline spending in line with revised strategic
>   priorities and programs
> - What significant trends can be identified in recurrent expenditure
> - How savings can be realized for reallocation to higher-priority depart-
>   mental activities
> - How actual spending compares with allocations
> - How spending programs have performed from a nonfinancial perspective
> - How additional allocations (new money to the department) over the pre-
>   vious two years' baselines have been used and whether the outputs and
>   objectives for which they were awarded have been achieved.
>
> Departments are also required to detail their nonrecurrent expenditure,
> indicating when projects will draw to a close and when funding will be
> removed from their baseline.
>
> Finally, departments are required to demonstrate how they will address
> programs in which performance information is showing slow, inefficient, and
> ineffective implementation.
>
> *Source:* National Treasury of South Africa 2006c.

When evaluating policy options in order to advise the cabinet, the
National Treasury–led MTECs assess whether a clear link exists between
the department's budget proposals and the government's broad policy priorities and key sector challenges, whether new funding is required and the
proposal can be accommodated in the baseline through reprioritization,
whether the department is able to implement the plan over the MTEF
period, and whether the expected outputs are clearly defined. Departments
are also required to illustrate how they will generate savings within their
baseline to fund new policy options.

Use of the contingency reserve

The contingency reserve is taken out of the funds available for other budget
spending before available revenue is divided between and within the spheres
of government. It is not a separate bank account accumulating funds over
years but a budgeting device that entails reserving a percentage of the available
funds in the budget as a cover against uncertainty and a pool from which to

allocate funding to new spending priorities. This percentage is small for the budget year (the first year of the three-year medium-term period) but increases in the outer years, when policy and macroeconomic uncertainty is larger. In the budget year, the contingency reserve is allocated in the adjustment budget, is tabled six months after the start of the fiscal year, and is used to cover the balance of revenue shortfalls or expenditure overruns on the fiscal framework. During budget planning, the contingency reserve plays a key role in making available additional resources for new expenditure, which come from the drawdown of the contingency reserve and changes to the macroeconomic forecast. Thus, the contingency reserve has an important function in providing flexibility and stability and in protecting against uncertainty in the MTEF (and thereby protecting its credibility).

Political oversight of the budget process

Deciding and agreeing on the best allocation of scarce resources to fund government's many social, economic, and political goals is the main purpose of the budget process. The setting of these goals is a political matter. Tradeoffs between these goals within the resource ceiling are equally political, although technical work can identify policy options and make clear what the consequences of tradeoffs are likely to be. The South African budget process applies this principle through several mechanisms, thereby ensuring appropriate political oversight of the budget process and ensuring that policies are made within the context of budget constraints.

The budget policy process begins with the identification of national policy priorities by the national cabinet. These priorities are expressed in a spending priorities memorandum, which provides a basis for departmental planning and budgeting. Ministerial letters are also exchanged between the minister of finance and spending ministers on major policy drives, signaling the direction of sectoral policy early in the budget process. (Spending departments are required to get information to their ministers in time for this letter.) This procedure creates the opportunity for the National Treasury to engage in bilateral discussions with departments at an early stage, when critical spending pressures and major policy considerations exist, to undertake a more rigorous examination of the economic and fiscal implications over the medium- to long-term period. This procedure is formalized in the joint discussion of expenditure estimates between National Treasury teams and departments.

The Ministers' Committee on the Budget is another critical vehicle through which overall political oversight of the MTEF process is realized. It is a formal subcommittee of the cabinet that considers policy changes with budgetary implications, as well as all main budgetary decisions, before making recommendations to the cabinet. After the cabinet has approved the new MTEF allocations, allocation letters are sent to all departments informing them of their ceilings and triggering the final part of the budget process, when departments prepare their budget documentation for submission to the National Treasury and the National Treasury prepares the Budget Review, Estimates of National Expenditure, and other components for tabling on budget day.

Other structures through which political involvement in the budget process is secured are the Budget Council, the Budget Forum, and intergovernmental committees of sectoral ministers. Where the program is known to affect provincial or local expenditure (or expenditure pressures are known to arise at these levels), the fiscal implications will also be discussed in the Budget Council and the Budget Forum, and consensus on key tradeoffs will be sought. At a sectoral level, committees of national sector ministers and their provincial counterparts discuss sector achievements, policy priorities, and funding decisions that have provincial implications.

The national cabinet makes all the final decisions on consolidated medium-term policy priorities and spending; these decisions include the macro and fiscal framework, the division of revenue, the approval of the MTBPS, and changes to the medium-term allocations to national votes and provincial governments. An important event in supporting this decision-making process is the cabinet's periodic strategic planning *lekgotla*, at which budget policy and planning uses are discussed. At the provincial level, discussion on provincial policy priorities and the finalization of allocations to provincial departments take place in the provincial executive councils.

Good budget documentation

The MTEF system in South Africa uses key sets of budget documentation to extract strategic information for decision making, to ensure commitment to decisions made, and to enable accountability. Changing the format of budget documentation to achieve these objectives has been an important aspect of the budget reform process.

The first public document in the budget process is the MTBPS, which is tabled in Parliament at the end of October, approximately four months before budget day. The MTBPS was also the first "new" document to emerge (in 1997) from the budget reform process. This public document serves to conclude the broad prioritization phase of the budget process and consolidates the main budgeting ceilings. Thus, it signals the government's fiscal and budget policy intentions by providing information on the macroeconomic assumptions and policy priorities driving the budget, the fiscal policy framework, the vertical and horizontal division of revenue, and the expected functional and economic spending allocations.

The main budget documentation includes the Budget Review, the Estimates of National Expenditure, the Estimates of Revenue, and the Division of Revenue Bill. This documentation imparts a comprehensive and transparent review of the government's current and planned future fiscal and budget directions and of the consequences of past decisions.

The Budget Review provides information on national policy priorities and how they are to be realized through the budget. The budget framework, in its various forms, represents a comprehensive picture of all revenue—including off-budget revenue—and expenditure of general government and the main fiscal balances, framed within information on the macroeconomic outlook and the key macroeconomic assumptions. Information on the broader public finances (including, for example, the borrowing requirement and investment performance of state-owned enterprises) is provided with a discussion on its implications for fiscal policy. The Budget Review also discusses revenue issues in detail and the management of public assets and liabilities, including an assessment of contingent liabilities.

In the South African budget structure, expenditure information is first broken down by government unit (national or provincial), then by vote (usually coinciding with a main spending department at the national and provincial levels), and then by programs and subprograms within a vote. The programs relate to the objectives of spending departments. A view of the economic distribution of expenditure is also provided at each level. Updated financial information is provided for the current fiscal year (that is, the year in which the budget preparation is taking place), backed by actual spending information on the three previous years and by forward estimates for the budget year and two outer years.

On the expenditure side, the Budget Review provides aggregate information on the distribution of expenditure in the MTEF among spheres and functions of government and among the economic purposes of expenditure. It does so, however, in the context of a discussion on past policy and expenditure performance, current national expenditure policy priorities, and future policy and service delivery objectives.

Detailed financial and nonfinancial revenue and expenditure information is provided by vote in the Estimates of National Expenditure, a document that was developed and added to the stable of budget documents in 2001. The estimates provide seven years of financial and performance information aggregated by national vote and are aimed at providing parliamentary committees and other stakeholders with comprehensive information on departmental performance and plans. An important reform in 2002 was the publication of measurable objectives for each program in the Estimates of National Expenditure. Therefore, the document effectively serves to coordinate coherent planning (and information) from departments, because they are called to account in Parliament for their chapters. Departments are required to set out what their main objectives are, what strategies they will be deploying to achieve them, and how they intend to finance these strategies within their budget allocations. They also review their past performance, both financially and in terms of achieving objectives.

The Division of Revenue Bill details the respective shares of the three spheres of government in nationally raised revenue and, together with the Intergovernmental Fiscal Review, is the key public document in the intergovernmental system. It sets out how the provincial and municipal shares are to be divided horizontally; details conditional grants to the two subnational spheres; and provides for various procedural matters regarding the management of intergovernmental finances and the responsibilities of treasuries, accounting officers (individuals responsible for financial management in government departments and public entities), and the auditor general. It also legislates a number of rules of cooperative governance, including what must happen if actual revenue falls short of anticipated revenue, under which circumstances allocations to subnational governments may be withheld or delayed or a payment schedule changed, and how funds may be reallocated from one horizontal unit of government to another. Finally, it determines sanctions and consequences for individuals if the provisions of the bill are not met. The annexes to the bill include a framework analysis of each conditional grant, detailing its conditions, rationale, criteria for allocation, monitoring mechanisms, past performance, allocations, projected life, and payment schedule. This framework is published to provide clarity and certainty regarding the complex system of conditional grants to stakeholders, as well as for budget implementation and monitoring purposes.

Departments are expected to report in terms of the Division of Revenue Bill and its schedules, covering both financial and nonfinancial performance. The auditor general audits compliance with the bill in both the transferring national departments and the receiving provincial departments and municipalities.

In the intergovernmental system, the Division of Revenue Bill is supported by the annual Intergovernmental Fiscal Review, first published in 1999, which is a compilation of expenditure and service delivery trends and financial issues in the nine provincial governments and local government. The review is annual and provides invaluable overall information on provincial service delivery achievements and obstacles. Similar to other public documents in the budget cycle, the review has become an annual feature in the cycle, thereby contributing to a high and continuing level of transparency in a very complex system.

Finally, in addition to the spending information in the documents described above, actual spending information is published in-year on a monthly basis for all national departments and on a quarterly basis across national and provincial governments. Published by the National Treasury, this information provides vital information to Parliament and other stakeholders with which to monitor budget implementation. The information is submitted to the National Treasury under the statutory reporting requirements of spending departments and forms part of the early warning system whereby deviation from spending plans can be detected early and addressed by the treasuries.

A New Framework for Public Financial Management and Reporting

The introduction of an MTEF for fiscal year 1998/99 was followed by the introduction of a program of financial management improvement. A cornerstone of this program is the Public Financial Management Act of 1999 (PFMA), which came into effect in April 2000. The PFMA repealed the 10 exchequer acts that previously governed public financial management. It was developed to transform an environment in which financial administration was rule bound and management exclusively input focused, policy and financial responsibilities in departments were separated, capital resources and liabilities were not properly managed, and reliable and timely information was greatly lacking. The resources of the national and provincial treasuries were devoted excessively to exercising microcontrol (even mundane matters were referred to them for approval), while too little attention was paid to strategic management of public finances in line with policy and efficiency objectives. In short, practice of functional financial management of public resources in government as a whole was insufficient.

The PFMA put in place a legal framework for modern public financial management, shifting the onus of managing the use of resources from central control to the managers of spending departments and agencies. This change mirrors the shift in budget preparation practices from central decision making to discretion resting with spending departments for program choices within spending ceilings.

To engineer this shift, the PFMA does not prescribe specifics (for example, what payment approval procedures should be). Instead, the act specifies who is responsible for putting in place such procedures, what the procedures should achieve, what the information and reporting requirements are, how this work is to be overseen and monitored, and how compliance will be ensured. This section discusses the main public finance management institutions established under the PFMA.

The PFMA applies to national and provincial governments. It was followed by a municipal finance management act that fulfills a similar function for all local government structures.

Responsibility of individuals and ensuring checks and balances

Throughout the PFMA and the accompanying treasury regulations (as they appear in the official gazette), individuals are made responsible for ensuring the flow of funds and for establishing systems. In tandem, checks and balances have been instituted to ensure that individuals undertake their responsibilities.

The act designates heads of departments, heads of constitutional institutions, and boards of public entities as accounting officers or accounting authorities and gives them responsibility for the effective, efficient, economical, and transparent use of resources in accordance with the appropriation act (the annual act of Parliament that authorizes the executive to spend against its allocations). In doing so, the PFMA requires the accounting officers or authorities to produce monthly and annual financial reports and to ensure effective, efficient, and transparent systems of financial and risk management, internal control, and procurement. If they do not comply with these requirements, they are guilty of financial misconduct, and disciplinary or criminal proceedings can be instituted against them, depending on the nature of the offense. The act, therefore, provides the legal framework for devolving responsibility for the use of public funds to spending departments and for ensuring transparency and accountability.

The PFMA compels ministers to fulfill their statutory responsibilities within the limits of their vote amount in the appropriation act and requires them to consider the monthly reports submitted to them by their accounting officers. It also sets out a framework to clarify accountability when a political directive could result in unauthorized expenditure.

Legal underpinning for the role of treasuries in the budget process

In addition to regulating accounting officers and executive authorities, the PFMA provides a legal framework for the role of the national and provincial treasuries in the budget process, including coordinating the national and provincial budget processes; managing budget implementation; and enforcing revenue, asset, and liability management. In addition, it provides the legal framework for the National Treasury to develop the macroeconomic and fiscal framework, coordinate intergovernmental relations, and determine the banking and cash management framework. It also puts the national and provincial treasuries in charge of the revenue funds.

The PFMA makes its implementation the responsibility of the National Treasury. To this end, the National Treasury is required to gazette treasury regulations, giving practical effect to the framework provisions of the act.

In-year monitoring, management, and reporting

The provisions for in-year monitoring, management, and reporting of the PFMA, the Division of Revenue Act (DORA), the treasury regulations, and other best-practice frameworks prepared by the National Treasury are aimed at achieving balance between providing enough information at appropriate levels and information overload at the center.

The PFMA specifies a variety of financial budget progress reports— monthly, quarterly, and at year-end—with different responsibilities for executive authorities and accounting officers (figure 15.3). These are supplemented in the intergovernmental system by the reporting requirements of the DORA. Accounting officers are required to compile monthly financial reports (including information on conditional grants) for their executive officers and relevant treasuries, which publish monthly reports on the status of national budget implementation in accordance with the PFMA. Accounting officers are also required to prepare quarterly financial reports. These are consolidated for the national and provincial governments by the National Treasury and are published.

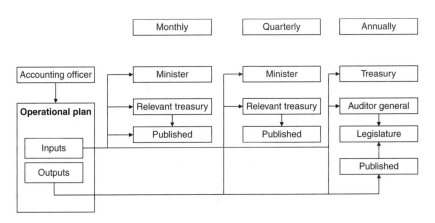

Source: Data from the National Treasury of South Africa.

FIGURE 15.3   PFMA Reporting Requirements

Shortening of the budget cycle

The PFMA shortens the budget cycle to bring audited actual spending information to Parliament seven months after the end of the financial year. This timing means that public accounts committees can deal with much more recent matters, thereby enabling improved oversight and allowing audited information to be used more effectively in the assessment of departmental spending plans. The shortening of in-year time horizons for capturing transactions assists in bringing early, accurate financial information to be used as a management tool. Whereas previous regulations and accounting systems allowed transactions to be written to a specific financial month up to three months after month-end, this period has been shortened to 10 days. Given that departments are required to provide cash-flow projections, that their cash use is made transparent through the monthly reporting system, and that the limits on virement and rollovers (see the next section) are by and large enforced, the new system has sharpened incentives for effective and efficient accounting practices considerably.

Provision of limited in-year flexibility

Given the uncertainty of revenue requirements and policy needs, the PFMA allows flexibility, within a framework, to make adjustments to budgets. The act, supported by the treasury regulations, provides several rules to manage this flexibility, to support incentives for sound planning, and to control for behavior that, in aggregate, could compromise fiscal policy. Managers are allowed to vire (that is, shift) funds between subdivisions of a vote (up to 8 percent of any subdivision total). However, further limits hold; for example, funds may not be vired from capital to recurrent spending, and personnel compensation may not be increased without prior approval by the National Treasury. Accounting officers are required to report to the National Treasury and to their minister within a week on any virement within the 8 percent limit.

Certain funds may be rolled over from one year to the next. Unspent funds on payments for capital assets may be rolled over only to finalize projects still in progress. Savings on transfers may not be rolled over for purposes other than those originally voted for, and savings on employee compensation may not be rolled over. Although there is no restriction on what types of other recurrent expenditure may be rolled over, a limit of 5 percent of a department's nonpersonnel recurrent expenditure applies.

Emergency expenditure must be authorized by the minister of finance. Moreover, it may not exceed 2 percent of the total national budget, must be reported to Parliament and the auditor general within 14 days, must be made public, and must be attributed to a vote.

The PFMA allows for a committee within the National Treasury to approve additional expenditure and deviations from expenditure, but only if the expenditure is recommended as "unforeseeable and unavoidable" by the cabinet. The treasury regulations further define "unforeseeable and unavoidable" as excluding (a) an expenditure that was submitted and not approved in the budget preparation process, (b) an increase in a tariff or price, and (c) an extension of existing—or initiation of new—services. The adjustment estimates approve rollovers, virements, allocations for unforeseeable and unavoidable expenditures, and savings.

Checks on the checks and balances

Accounting officers can be subjected to disciplinary proceedings if they permit unauthorized, irregular, fruitless, or wasteful expenditure or if they fail to comply with any of the requirements regarding implementing the budget, setting up the financial management systems, and reporting. If they are found to be grossly negligent, criminal proceedings can be instituted. In addition, any loss accruing to the state on account of negligent or willful action by an official must be recouped from the individual.

The treasury regulations require all departments to appoint chief financial officers, to whom accounting officers can delegate some of their functions under the act. As part of risk management, all departments must also set up internal audit committees and formulate three-year rolling internal audit plans that assess and address key areas of risk, as well as fraud prevention plans.

Provision for effective cash management

The South African budget is implemented in an environment of relative revenue certainty. In practice, departments can expect to receive their full budget allocation in a fiscal year. Any shortfalls in revenue are absorbed by the National Treasury. One of the key challenges in the system is to extract relatively accurate predictions of cash-flow requirements from spending departments so that these predictions can be matched with expected fluctuations in revenue collection and so that unnecessary borrowing or the unnecessary and inefficient practice of locking up cash in departmental accounts can be avoided. The regulations require departments and provincial treasuries to submit predictions of monthly cash-flow requirements at the start of the financial year. These estimates are updated monthly, throughout the year, but departments need to justify any changes to the approved cash flow to the National Treasury.

The PFMA made provision for its phased implementation over five years. Similar to the development of the MTEF, the approach was to put in place the scaffolding of a holistic system and then allow quality improvements to develop over time, driven by the changed incentives in the system itself. Thus, the PFMA was made immediately applicable to all government departments and entities and to all constitutional institutions. Specific areas were delayed, however, particularly if the necessary systems were not yet in place to enforce or support the PFMA. For example, the legal requirement of measurable objectives for all programs was delayed, as were some of the provisions relating to financial statements and public entities.

The National Treasury required all departments to submit implementation plans within six months after the act came into effect and provided best-practice guides, training, and capacity development support. The plans were structured to assess the financial management and accounting capacity in departments, the financial skills of line managers, and the quality of internal control systems. They were required to propose an implementation plan for each department, particularly the strategy for risk and performance management. In the first year of PFMA implementation, the appointment of chief financial officers was prioritized, as were the establishment of internal audit committees and the implementation of monthly reporting requirements.

Improvement of the Classification System

Before recent reforms, the South African budget was classified on functional, economic, line-item, administrative, and programmatic lines. However, the quality of information was suspect, with many inconsistencies in the application of the standards. The line-item classification was also archaic and a holdover from an earlier incremental, input-based budgeting system. The relations between budgeting, accounting for funds spent, and reporting by the auditor general and in the national statistics were not clear cut, disabling the link between policy and actual spending and ultimately affecting the quality of oversight and undermining accountability. Since 1997, the underlying classification structure has been modernized and the chart of accounts reviewed. This section briefly reviews the main features of the reforms.

The new economic reporting format

The old economic and line-item classification of inputs has been replaced by the new economic reporting format, which is aimed at providing better-quality information to legislatures on the economic nature of financial outlays toward policy objectives. The new format is in line with the 2001 *Government Finance Statistics Manual* standard of the International Monetary Fund, also enabling improved international reporting (IMF 2001).

However, to take into account the specific nature of the South African environment, certain modifications to the structure of the accounts and the labeling of receipt and payment items have been made. Most significantly, South Africa still operates a cash-based accounting system, although it is a modified cash base with entries for national budget data made in the time period in which transactions are captured on the financial systems, rather than when the actual cash flow occurs. The intention is to eventually move to accrual-based accounting.

The new format, which is used consistently for making budget estimates and for recording and classifying the economic nature of transactions in the revised chart of accounts, organizes the multitude of government transactions into three broad categories: receipts, payments, and financing. The budget deficit or surplus is calculated as receipts less payments; by definition, it is equal to net financing, but with the opposite sign. Payments are also divided into three broad categories: current payments (for example, employee compensation, goods and services, interest, and rent); transfers and subsidies (funds that are transferred to other institutions, businesses, and individuals and are not final expenditure by the spending unit); and payments for capital assets (buildings and fixed structures, machinery, cultivated assets, intangible assets, and land and subsoil assets).

Improved functional classification

The functional classification is complementary to the economic classification. It serves to distinguish transactions by policy purpose or expense by output. Its main purpose is to clarify how government spending contributes to social, economic, and other objectives. In the budget structure, four broad categories of functional classification are used: general government services, protection services, social services, and economic services.

Improved programmatic classification

In cooperation with spending departments, the National Treasury has been systematically improving the programmatic classification of the budget, to strengthen the link between policy objectives and financial information. One intervention has been to standardize vote structures across provinces to enable coordination of policy implementation and monitoring.

Mindful implementation

Although the careful redesign of the budget structure and chart-of-accounts framework is a necessary input to improving the quality of budget and financial information, it does not guarantee that spending departments, which are responsible for recording transactions in the South African system, will apply the frameworks well. A key feature of the South African reforms has been implementation support for spending departments, including working with departments to recode their transaction base correctly and providing training programs to financial management personnel (see table 15.1).

The new South African classification system is aimed at improving financial information for budget management and accountability purposes. The structure and presentation are fully compatible with, and can be converted easily to, the *Government Finance Statistics Manual* (IMF 2001) format (because the same classification base is used at a high level of detail). However, the South African system avoids the use of unclear terms such as *other* and *miscellaneous*, includes more detail on various transfer categories, and labels items more clearly.

Improvement of Budget Management for Service Delivery

The earlier phases of the South African reforms emphasized planning better for the financing of new policies and priorities and, ultimately, improved service delivery. The reform vision recognized from the start, however, that planning and budgeting need to be integrated with monitoring service delivery performance to strengthen the link between the services that departments provide and the benefits and costs of those services. Performance measures were to give effect to the emphasis on improved transparency and

TABLE 15.1   Implementation of Classification Reforms

Sequence	Reform
1998	Reclassification of existing expenditure items in line with the *Government Finance Statistics Manual* for compliance and International Monetary Fund data dissemination standards; capacity building
1999	Modernization of accounts to align with international best practices; capacity building
1999–2000	New economic classification based on the *Government Finance Statistics Manual* and rollout from national budget to provincial budgets; capacity building
2000–04	Development and implementation of the standard chart of accounts to support the effectiveness of the new economic format; capacity building
2005–present	Rationalization and refinement; capacity building

Source: Schoch and others 2006.

accountability for the management and use of public resources. As in many other countries, the development of effective and appropriate performance measures has been a difficult process and is still ongoing as lessons are learned and capacities built. This section reviews developments and discusses the main characteristics of the current system.

From a position of meager information on departmental policy and budget performance in 1997, several initiatives have slightly shifted the South African system from an input-focused one to an output-focused one. The National Expenditure Survey (NES) took the brief discussion of sector policies out of the Budget Review and expanded it at vote level in 1999. The PFMA requires that "measurable objectives" be formulated for each main division (that is, program) within a vote. In 2001, the Estimates of National Expenditure replaced the NES, bringing financial and narrative performance information together and making a first effort at formulating measurable objectives and indicators. The Intergovernmental Fiscal Review provides more information on the context of budget implementation.

Nevertheless, the introduction of service delivery and performance information into the budget documentation has meant that public service managers have had to grapple with new concepts and tools for monitoring and measuring performance. Experiences since 2001 have highlighted difficulties in developing appropriate output performance measures and service delivery indicators. Many of the indicators specified were not related to clearly measurable objectives of programs and did not actually relate to the outputs. These indicators have failed to show whether services contribute toward meeting the government's outcomes. They are, therefore, of little value to the public, Parliament, the executive, and even the department itself.

The project at the level of the National Treasury to develop a system for monitoring performance against policy intentions has taken on new momentum by an initiative to develop a governmentwide system that integrates performance information required for better budgeting with information required for political and administrative oversight. The development of the system is still in its infancy. In outline, each government institution at all levels of government will be required to provide to the governmentwide system strategic plans, comprising programs with the institution's commensurate input, process, and output measures and outcome indicators. The indicators need to be broken down into targets. This framework, developed by the presidency, is similar to the MTEF framework—set out in departments' budget documentation—of measurable objectives, indicators, and targets attached to programs and subprograms in votes.

Conclusion

South Africa has succeeded in radically altering the way it budgets for public services and how it accounts for public expenditure and commitments. It did so in a relatively short time and has already started reaping the benefits, with more realistic policy debates and increased funds available for much-needed investment and poverty-alleviating expenditure. Many other countries that have embarked on similar processes struggle to anchor changes and make them count. South Africa has several advantages over many developing countries: it has a modern economy that generates predictable resources for public spending, it has a functioning tax administration, donor financing is a minor proportion of its budget, and it started off from a base where cash was relatively well accounted for and with comparatively good capacity in the public sector. Despite these advantages, the reform process is far from complete. Some areas that were targeted for reform in the initial vision of a results-oriented, accountable budgeting environment have not yet been reached, such as a fully fledged accrual accounting system. Other issues, such as performance management and the planning, budgeting, and reporting links, have been tackled, but progress has been slow.

All in all, the South African system has reformed quickly up to a point, but it has struggled to deepen the reforms to further enhance service delivery. Arguably, whereas fiscal discipline has, by and large, been achieved and allocation of scarce resources to spending priorities has been improved, addressing efficiency issues is the greatest challenge remaining. Perhaps in those areas not only the public financial management systems are at fault, but further reforms need to be coordinated with improvements in parallel systems, such as human resource management. The improvements in the quality of information that were envisaged take time to materialize because they are a function of capacity developments, particularly in management.

Although the improvement in information availability is one of the achievements of the budget reform process, the information that is provided is not always used sufficiently. A lot of work remains to be done on developing and providing appropriate performance information in effective formats. Information sharing could improve; many departments are still not able to provide adequate information on policy priorities, budget allocations, and links between them. Moving further toward an output orientation and improving the outputs of the reporting system are current reform focuses. However, this focus needs to be supported by a reassessment of how well the information is being used—not only by program managers and their head of department, but also by ministers and Parliament. Within the current framework, considerably more leeway exists for action in cases of poor performance than is being taken.

Effective medium-term planning at the departmental level cannot be taken for granted. A lot of work needs to be done to realize the benefits of a medium-term planning horizon. The medium-term allocations stop at the program level, with financial planning lower down still being done largely on an annual basis. Deepening the reforms in this direction would require working with individual departments at the national and provincial levels to develop managerial capacities. The South African process allowed for that approach, and major reforms were implemented over a number of years. Table 15.1 shows the pace at which the reclassification of the budget and redevelopment of the chart of accounts were implemented.

Donaldson (2006: 4) notes that recent South African budget and policy reform history is marked by some successful reforms. However, many cases of ineffective or delayed reforms and persistent service delivery failures have also occurred. Although there "may have been cases of policy error, poor advice, or poorly planned reforms [and] cases in which the resource requirements for successful reform have been too steep, or where key personnel have not been equal to the task," these instances are not fundamental barriers to progress. Donaldson discusses two more fundamental problems, namely, that the South African reform case is plagued by institutional overload and that the assignment of powers and some objectives of reforms may have been incompatible with incentives.

In the case of the first problem, the argument is that in many areas of public service delivery, significant policy changes have preceded institutional capacity building, leading to delays and ineffective implementation. An overload of policy obligations has been a significant impediment to successful transformation of the South African state. This is true for sectoral reforms as well as for the underlying systemic reforms. However, as is illustrated in the following discussion on reform of the classification system and the chart of accounts, success is more likely when care is taken to systematically build human resource capacity together with systems capacity.

Donaldson's second argument touches on a key shortcoming of the South African reforms: the lack of a credible budget performance management system and lack of alignment between the accountability chain, institutional governance, managerial incentives, and public policy objectives. In South Africa, efforts to put in place performance management systems were not well located in a sensible existing framework of accountability, objectives, and performance indicators. Although pockets of sectoral reform progress exist across the government, the functional devolution of responsibilities and managerial autonomy within national and provincial structures is ambiguous, reported service delivery statistics are patchy and unreliable, governance structures are too hierarchical, performance assessment is haphazard, and remuneration remains largely unconnected to performance (Donaldson 2006: 5). A key factor contributing to the failure to get this component of the policy and budget management system in place has been overlapping policy space between the central finance and public administration ministries as well as the presidency.

However, these problems should not distract from the achievements of the past 12 years. Given the overlay of new and complex constitutional requirements and radical shifts in the structure of state institutions with far-reaching budget reforms and significant policy shifts, the institutionalization of a stable intergovernmental system and a largely credible budget process is positive.

Several lessons can be taken from South Africa's reform experience. First, the starting point for the reform was not to put in place a technical and sophisticated MTEF system (although an earlier version of the MTEF comprised an integrated set of forward projections of sector spending). The reforms were driven by an orientation toward changing behaviors—a political commitment to realistic macroeconomic projections, sensible budgeting norms, good accounting practices, and regular reporting through transparent budget documents—objectives for which medium-term budgeting and the public financial management reforms were tools.

All actors in the budget process need to grasp the framework approach behind the reforms so that they will be able to fulfill their adjusted responsibilities in a manner that allows the reforms to achieve their objectives. In the case of South Africa, reforms centered on putting in place credible three-year plans, focusing the budget process on changes to baselines, and devolving accountability to spending departments. These reforms were achieved through simple frameworks that were easy to communicate and easier to implement than systems with high levels of complexity. However, the complexity of the system has been growing as capacity and understanding develop, both in the center and in service departments. At the same time, the budget process was changed from being a "black box" to one with a degree of transparency, in which the criteria for decisions were communicated early and policy objectives publicly articulated. The rules that governed this process were made explicit and enforced.

Major reforms in South Africa, such as the MTEF and the PFMA, were implemented throughout government and replaced the existing frameworks. This method made sense. Because the MTEF is a framework approach and because ceilings are determined in a top-down manner within the framework, establishing credible forward funding projections would have been very difficult at any level if they were not connected to the fiscal framework and other projections. Anchoring reforms by linking them with other processes has also contributed to their implementation and was necessary for their effectiveness. For example, linking the MTEF to financial management through the PFMA (which makes it a legal requirement) and other reforms, such as those at the Office of the Auditor General, helped consolidate the MTEF as the only system for budget planning. Arguably, if the MTEF had been implemented in isolation, without links to improved fiscal and financial management, its benefits would have been fewer.

The implementation of the MTEF and PFMA was strengthened greatly by the amalgamation of the former Department of Finance (responsible for macroeconomic, fiscal, and budget policy planning) and the Department of State Expenditure (responsible for departmental budgeting and implementation) into the National Treasury. Institutionally, this change has brought expenditure planning and monitoring together and has located the full budget process, from macroeconomic forecasting and fiscal planning through to managing expenditure in-year and compiling reports on the state of the budget, under one executive authority and one accounting officer. Better integration in the budget process between budgeting and implementation has resulted. For example, one desk is now responsible for monitoring a spending department or sector, assessing budget plans, and monitoring in-year performance.

Any reform process is likely to meet with resistance from vested interests and to experience setbacks. Therefore, building support for the reform process is important at all levels of government by making sure that benefits show up. In the case of South Africa, the benefit of working within a multi-year budgeting framework was demonstrated early, when the fiscal framework for the 1999 budget had to contend with fewer resources than expected. Instead of having to institute budget cuts, as would have been required under a one-year framework to meet deficit targets, the government used the medium-term framework to keep spending stable in the short term, absorbing the shortfall by drawing down the contingency reserve and shifting the effect to the outer years. So whereas an annual budget cycle would have forced immediate expenditure cuts, the medium-term framework allowed the shock to public finances to be smoothed over the economic cycle. This outcome demonstrated the usefulness of medium-term planning, helped overcome resistance at the political and institutional levels, and contributed to making the MTEF a functional strategic budgeting tool.

The South African case illustrates the importance of being clear about objectives, getting the principles right when designing reforms to fulfill those objectives, and letting realism guide the reform process and the speed with which it is implemented. The South African experience also shows that although approaching budget reforms in terms of frameworks makes sense, time is needed for the reforms to take effect. Quality improvements in terms of expenditure estimates, actual spending information, performance information, and service delivery materialize slowly. Reforming the budgeting system is never the full answer to economic governance challenges; however, when backed by robust political support and decision systems and sound human resources management, it plays a significant part in improving public sector management.

Note

This chapter draws on Fölscher and Cole (2004).

References

Donaldson, Andrew. 2006. "Agency, Information, and Organisation in the Public Sector." Paper presented at a seminar on October 5, 2006, hosted by the Department of Economics, University of Stellenbosch, Stellenbosch, South Africa.

Fölscher, Alta, and Neil Cole. 2004. "South Africa: Transition to Democracy Offers Opportunity for Whole System Reform." In *Budget Reform Seminar: Country Case Studies*, ed. Alta Fölscher, 109–46. Pretoria: National Treasury of South Africa.

IMF (International Monetary Fund). 2001. *Government Finance Statistics Manual*. Washington, DC: IMF Statistics Department. http://www.imf.org/external/pubs/ft/gfs/manual/pdf/all.pdf.

National Treasury of South Africa. 2004a. "Budget Review." National Treasury of South Africa, Pretoria.

———. 2004b. *MTEF Guidelines 2004*. Pretoria: National Treasury of South Africa.

———. 2006a. "Budget Review." National Treasury of South Africa, Pretoria.

———. 2006b. *Estimates of National Expenditure 2006*. Pretoria: National Treasury of South Africa.

———. 2006c. *MTEF Guidelines 2006*. Pretoria: National Treasury of South Africa.

Schoch, Mickie, Alta Fölscher, Hennie Swanepoel, and Annelize Adendorff. 2006. "Achieving Objectives through the Classification System: Objectives, Principles, and Experiences." In *Managing Complexity: From Fragmentation to Co-ordination*, ed. Alta Fölscher, 46–65. Pretoria: CABRI Secretariat.

Index

Boxes, figures, notes, and tables are indicated by b, f, n, and t, respectively.